# WONDERS
## OF THE
## INDIAN
## WILDERNESS

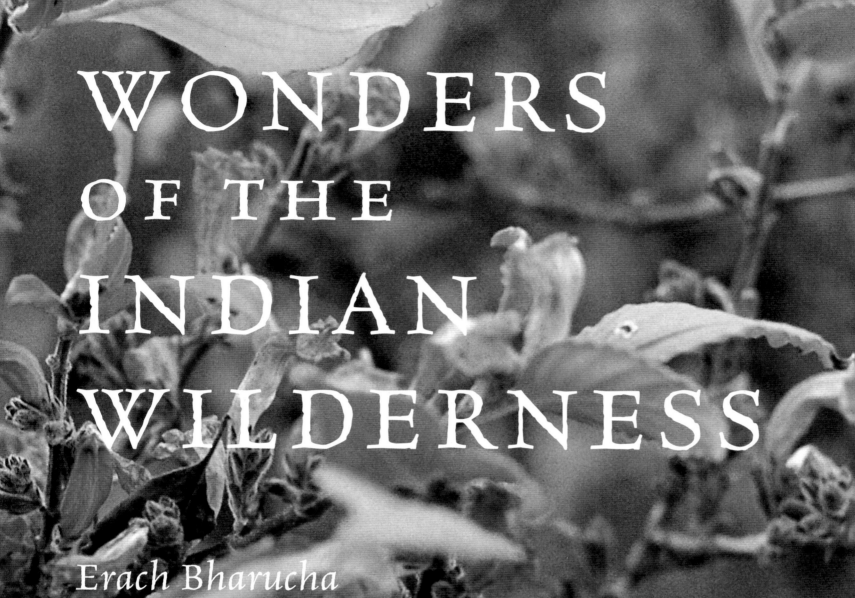

# WONDERS
## OF THE
## INDIAN
## WILDERNESS

*Erach Bharucha*

Abbeville Press Publishers

NEW YORK   LONDON

First published as a three-volume boxed edition in India in 2006 for Reliance Industries Pvt. Ltd, Maker Chambers IV, Nariman Point, Mumbai 400 021, India, by Mapin Publishing Pvt. Ltd., Usmanpura, Ahmedabad 380 014, India.

First published in the United States of America in 2008 by Abbeville Press Publishers, 137 Varick Street, New York, NY 10013. The Abbeville Press edition includes the first two volumes of the original edition, Volume I: *The Nature of Biodiversity in India* and Volume II: *National Parks and Wildlife Sanctuaries in India*.

*For the original edition*
Designed by Amit Kharsani / Mapin Design Studio
Assistant Designers: Gopal Limbad,
Revanta Sarabhai
Edited by Suguna Ramanathan
Editorial Coordinator: Diana Romany
Editorial/Design Assistance:
Behafrid Lord
Prasanna Kolte
Ernavaz Bharucha
Catrinel Dunca

*For the Abbeville Press edition*
Production editor: Austin Allen
Production manager: Louise Kurtz
Cover designer: Misha Beletsky

First edition
10 9 8 7 6 5 4 3 2 1
Library of Congress Cataloging-in-Publication Data

Bharucha, Erach.
  Wonders of the Indian wilderness / Erach Bharucha.—1st ed.
     p. cm.
  ISBN 978-0-7892-0999-3 (hardcover : alk. paper)  1.  Biodiversity—India. 2.  Habitat (Ecology)—India. 3.  Biodiversity conservation—India.  I. Title.

  QH77.I4B43 2008
  333.95'160954—dc22

  2008019346

Cover: Tiger in the Sal Forests of central India.
Page 1: A bright green, shiny jewel beetle uses its color to ward off predators.
Pages 2–3: An uncommon *Strobilanthus* shrub, which flowers only once every thirteen years.
Pages 4–5: The web signifies the fragile nature of the complex interrelationship of species that constitute life on earth. Every species lost through extinction weakens the web.
Pages 6–7: The Asiatic lion is restricted to the Gir Sanctuary in India.

For bulk and premium sales and for text adoption procedures, write to Customer Service Manager, Abbeville Press, 137 Varick Street, New York, NY 10013, or call 1-800-Artbook.

Visit Abbeville Press online at www.abbeville.com.

## PREFACE

The Indian wilderness conjures up different images for various people. There are those who nostalgically recall its past glory in the days of shikar and the jungles that were teeming with wildlife. And those who recall the excitement or exhaustion of long hours of trekking under the hot sun, of getting drenched in torrents of rain, or feeling the biting cold of the high snows. Some are perturbed that the wilderness is rapidly shrinking, and are concerned about the changes modern development has wrought on its integrity. Others see it as something to be 'conquered' and used for economic gain. For the local wilderness dweller it forms his common property village land from which he gets all his resources. For me, the wilderness with its many different faces has always been a place of wonder and mystery.

My initial interest in Nature and a growing curiosity in all things wild were triggered by the wonderful wilderness around Pune where I grew up in the 1940s and 1950s. My father loved being out in the wild. A small-time shikari, he once shot a leopard, but this was still at a time when it was legally permitted. He killed a few deer, an antelope or two, and several wild boar and hare that were ever present in the grasslands and agricultural lands on the outskirts of Pune. These last two were considered by local farmers to be vermin and terrible pests. He also went on duck shoots and on one occasion brought home a big mahseer that he had shot with a .22 rifle! But I was not really interested in the shikar or in the guns. What if the thing went off? It was more fun to drive the 1951 Chevrolet that took us everywhere, on rough cart tracks, and even through fallow farmland! I was driving, illegally of course, by age ten or twelve, when I could barely reach the accelerator. However, I soon found out that I had become the official shikar driver. By the time I was 15, in 1958, I could take the lumbering car almost everywhere. I didn't shoot until I went to Wadia College. My Zoology teacher, Professor Nadkarni, to whom I addressed a variety of questions on wildlife and taxonomy, began to appreciate my deepening interest and lent me rather boring books that were used by Third Year BSc and MSc Zoology students. In return I was to get him 'specimens' for his small museum. I believe those unfortunate victims are still standing dead in the Zoology Department. I can only hope that the generations of students after me at least got to know what a jungle cat, a civet, a jackal and a hyena look like in the field. That's where my brief shikar exploits ended.

Around 1961 I became increasingly interested in nature photography. Unfortunately, I owned highly inadequate hardware; initially a box camera, then a twin lens Yashika, later a small Zeiss rangefinder 35 mm, an Exacta with a small 100 mm telelens, an early Pentax, and finally my first Nikon with a second-hand 300 mm lens.

When I was in class IX or X, I realized that I could get birds only as tiny specks and mammals as microscopic hazy artifacts on the slow black and white films that were available in those days. I turned inevitably to landscapes. My father's friend Sangappa Kadapatti became my mentor. He was a brilliant black and white photographer and had a German degree of some sort in photography. His English was inadequate and my Marathi in those days was miserable, but his non-verbal ability to communicate visual aspects of the subjects I photographed have left indelible impressions on my mind, as when he made me use a camera in nature and his enlarger in the darkroom, where, while ostensibly making me feel I was doing the work, he was subtly dodging away unwanted parts of my negative! I remember

once trying to take a picture of a tree with a monster climber. He asked me, 'Baba, what do you want your picture to say?' I said that I wished to show the roughness of the bark and the shininess of the leaves. "Then you have the light all wrong—think of using the natural light from one side and the bark will become rough and the leaves will look smooth.' And then he left me to my own devices. I treasured that picture for many years.

The realization that several of the wilderness areas of my childhood were now vanishing rapidly made me wander around India for over three decades looking at areas that have been left relatively undisturbed. As I documented in pictures the diversity of life in the varied relict natural ecosystems, I began to feel the need to share this experience with those not fortunate enough to have had the opportunity to experience it themselves. I thus began to give slide-shows that could excite people into conservation action.

The majority of photographs I have taken are from more than eighty National Parks and Wildlife Sanctuaries that I have visited over a span of 30 years. They depict the wilderness tracts of India and its many threatened ecosystems. The pictures are different frozen moments of living

memories that I have experienced in the wilderness. This book is not exhaustive or complete, as a book on Nature can only be as comprehensive as the amount of time one can spend documenting its astounding variety. To achieve even a reasonable degree of completeness would take several lifetimes! Most wildlife photographers have concentrated their efforts on taking pictures of glamour species such as tigers and elephants, or our spectacular birds or highly colourful flowering plants. By contrast, this book focuses on the variety of less glamorous forms of life, and their habitats.

Wildlife enthusiasts and nature photographers, both professional and amateur, are always curious about how other photographers took their pictures. I have had my share of some lucky trips, many less productive experiences, and a large number of downright unlucky sojourns with my camera in the wilderness. All the pictures in this book are from the wild places I have visited. I have used a bare minimum of equipment, all of it within the reach of an average amateur photographer. The photographs have not been taken from specially made hides. No elaborate arrangements were made in these National Parks and Sanctuaries, beyond those that are made available to the average wildlife tourist.

I took pictures of whatever I saw—there are pictures of incredible insects, amphibia and reptiles, along with the more striking birds and mammals that draw the attention of most other photographers. Waterfalls have always fascinated me and I am thrilled by sunrises and sunsets. The pictures that satisfy my curiosity the most show what the creatures of the wilderness do in this incredible web of life. But above all, I began to love the forest folk whom I have met. I have always hesitated to intrude on their privacy with my camera and felt acutely uncomfortable at turning my camera towards them unless I had asked their permission. This has happened rather rarely and the results are all too posed in most instances.

It has been many years since I started putting words to my photographs. I always wanted to write a book, and in fact did write up a few chapters way back in the early 80s. I soon abandoned this for lack of time. What I did write, after I was literally forced into this by Dr Salim Ali, were short notes for the BNHS Journal. Later, it was Bittu Sahgal who encouraged me to write for the early editions of *Sanctuary Magazine*.

At a slideshow on biodiversity at the Tata Management Training Centre (TMTC) in Pune, a participant asked me why I hadn't 'done' a book. I said that I hadn't found the right

publisher. Much later, Kamal Nanavaty of Reliance, who had asked me this question, told Bipin Shah about my slide-show, and suggested that I should be asked to make an illustrated book on wildlife. My meeting Bipin Shah of Mapin was a chance encounter nearly a decade later, when his son, Revanta, introduced us to each other at Pune airport. We were going out on different flights. We met again and went through my pictures and decided to make a book. Kamal promised to provide the funds. When I met Kamal again, the first thing he said to me was, 'Do you know that your slide-show was instrumental in making me a wildlife enthusiast?' After I had written a large part of the book, I met Kamal and Bipin together in Mumbai. I realized then that what they wanted from me was a personal statement of my sojourns in the wilderness of India over the last three decades. While I could always talk about my experiences in the wilderness during my slide-shows, I could not get myself to write down these personal experiences. I reluctantly agreed to rewrite much of the book from scratch. It took several years while Kamal and Bipin waited impatiently.

I also wanted to write about the lives of the people who live in the wilderness and their much-neglected demands due to conflicts with the objectives of nature conservation. It is they who, in fact, pay the price for the preservation of India's wildlife. And I have described events that led to conservation of habitats and species and the researchers and policy makers who made this happen.

While this book is primarily about India's wilderness, which I know and love, it also describes the small fragments of wild places that are left in this country and their diverse forms of life. It focuses attention on many of Nature's fragile ecosystems that are being rapidly destroyed by the many development projects in our country. The changes I have witnessed kindled a desire to see that the residual wilderness, with all its intricate and wondrous ways, remains as untouched as possible. My encounters with all things wild have instilled in me a deep feeling of respect for Nature and of being in some way 'one' with the wilderness. This all-consuming feeling of wonder grows each time I am exposed to it. These memories have all gone towards creating in me a deep appreciation of Nature's magnificence, and it is those moments that I have attempted to capture in this book either through pictures or written text.

The desire to document the diversity of life in the wilderness has taken me to the lofty Himalayas; down through its foothills into Terai swamps and forests; to the wide plains along the banks of the great River Ganga; into the many varied forest types of the Indian peninsula, which include the last great patches of sal and teak forests; into the thorn forests of Rajasthan and the remote areas of the arid desert in the west; through the scrublands of the Deccan; along the rapidly disappearing evergreen forests of the Western Ghats; to the fascinating banks of rivers and lakes; on to the magnificent beaches and rocky coves along our long western and eastern seashore; into superb mangrove deltas and to the emerald green islands of the Andamans. It has been a series of unforgettable travels.

Nature in her wisdom has endowed this country with a profusion of exquisite habitats. Each region differs widely from the other. Their characteristics differ so greatly that they create highly specialized 'niches' for India's diverse wildlife. This natural mosaic of landforms, which together create an ecological jigsaw puzzle, itself makes the natural wilderness of India more vulnerable to human interference. Today much of this shrinking Indian wilderness is at death's doorstep. Is this book to become a statement of its twilight? Or, can we hope that humankind will realize that its survival is dependent upon the well-being of Nature and ensure the breaking of a new dawn upon what is left of the wilderness of India? If this book stimulates some of its readers into a concern for preserving the natural landscapes that form our threatened wildlife habitats, it will have achieved its purpose.

**Erach Bharucha**
Pune, 2006

# Reliance
Industries Limited

Human civilization has in its course of development left a serious casualty—the environment. The relentless pursuit of industrialization and the pleasures of good life have taken a serious toll on the flora and fauna of nations. India is no exception. While the days of grand shikar are over, the booming guns of the maharajas of yesteryears have taken their toll. The forests of India are no more the preserve of the majestic tiger, the unique one-horned rhinoceros or the gorgeous lions of Gir.

It is time we stood up and took notice. Laws have been enacted and conservationists have shouted themselves hoarse. Yet, poachers still make merry and even a tiger reserve like Corbett is not spared. It is time that we speak up in unison; it is time to let our conscience speak.

The irony of wildlife conservation today is that while millions visit the forests and zoos to admire these wonderful species, most of them remain indifferent to legislation that is enacted to prevent the decimation of these majestic animals. Our concern is often lip service, our admiration confined to an awestruck gaze at the Royal Bengal tiger.

Nations round the world have, however, taken notice. South Africa is a wonderful example. Tough legislation backed with public resolve has brought the flourishing ivory trade to a halt. The game reserves are immaculately maintained and poaching is punished with utmost severity. There is a lesson in it for us. We must understand and take pride in the fact that we are blessed with some of the most gorgeous species of animals ever to have roamed the earth—

from the tiger to the rhino, the Asian elephant to the Asian lion, the majestic peacock to the flaming flamingoes, India has it all. It is our duty to protect them.

Human enterprise and commitment can truly achieve wonders and we want to share our experience with you. When we set about building a green field refinery in a remote village of Motikhawdi near Jamnagar, Gujarat, all around was just arid land with a little touch of green. Inspired by the vision of our Founder Chairman, Shri Dhirubhai Ambani, and powered by the effort and imagination of Team Reliance, a sprawling green belt of 1,800 acres housing Asia's largest mango plantation came up in what used to be an inhospitable piece of land. In return, we have received a bounty—there has been a significant rise in rainfall and today the parks of Reliance Greens echo with the sounds of more than hundred species of birds, including the resplendent peacock, warbling terns and fidgety pelicans. All this because Shri Dhirubhai Ambani believed in an India that is as proud of its natural heritage as its entrepreneurial genius.

This book is a call to our conscience. It brings alive the mystery of the forests, captures the ethereal beauty of the wild and unveils a panorama that is coloured with the myriad hues of nature. It is a celebration of a unique treasure that belongs to our country. It is also a reminder to protect and preserve this treasure. The earth will be poorer without these wonderful creatures and the time has come for us to stand up and be counted to save and protect nature.

Mukesh D Ambani
Chairman & Managing Director
Reliance Industries Limited

Nita M Ambani
President
Dhirubhai Ambani Foundation

## ACKNOWLEDGEMENTS

This book was made possible by the generosity of Mr Mukesh Ambani of Reliance. I extend my sincere thanks to him for his support and genuine interest in wildlife conservation which was obvious during my meeting with him. I hope this leads to greater commitments from the Reliance Group to protect the threatened biodiversity of our nation.

Many people have fought for preserving the residual wilderness of India during the last three or four decades. I make references to only a few of the many individuals whom I have met or worked with. To them all, too many to thank individually, I can only say how much I appreciate their help and deep commitment to the environment. If this book has some good features, it is surely a reflection of their success as conservation people.

When I was barely ten years old, I met a small, wiry, tough man who was a great human being and India's foremost ornithologist. Dr Salim Ali, in his quest for *baya* nests, used to stay at my neighbour's house in Pune. Our house had a big unkempt garden with large trees and a bajra field next door on what is now a very busy Bund Garden Road. In the middle of the field there was a *baya* nesting colony in a well, and there I sat with him on several early Sunday mornings. Later, on the swing in our compound, under a large gulmohur tree next to a cage full of snow-white, smelly rabbits, Salimbhai, sitting in an old-fashioned cane chair would fascinate me with stories of his visits to exotic wild places. These initial interactions with a great scientist and human being led to several exchanges through letters. His response to my reporting that I had observed a sunbird raise the chick of a plaintive cuckoo was acknowledged in his book as being reported by a 'reliable observer from Poona!' Surely, a great compliment for a young schoolboy!

Dr Salim Ali always made one feel good. But that was the incredible humility of this wonderful man, who has done so much for the conservation of India's wildlife and wild places. To him I owe a great debt for furthering my interest in all things wild.

Then there was my encouraging teacher of Zoology, Professor Nadkarni of Wadia College, always ready to answer my queries, which were way outside the curriculum. And Maharajasaheb of Bansda, with whom I spent many days and nights travelling through the Dang Forests during my school days, who made me sensitive to the fact that these forests were rapidly disappearing. In the 1970s I had a chance meeting with the Pune WWF-I Committee soon after it was formed. I am grateful that they asked me to join them and I soon found myself deeply involved in the WWF's conservation awareness and research activities. Pradyumna Gogate worked with me on Bhigwan, a newly created wetland that had begun to attract flamingoes but was rapidly getting polluted. Kiran Asher worked with me on blackbuck in Rehekuri, where crop damage was a serious problem. Their deep commitment to field research was the basis for initiating an ecologically appropriate management strategy for these areas, through meagerly sponsored WWF research projects.

In March 1986, I got a telephone call from Dr Salim Ali requesting me to become a member of the Executive Committee of the Bombay Natural History Society (BNHS). I felt I was too young to join this august body. Besides I was clueless about the ways of committees! He persisted however, virtually cajoling me into agreeing, and thus began many years of association with this organization that is over a hundred years old. I was fortunate enough to become close to a large number of conservation people in the BNHS, among them JC Daniel, VS Vijayan, Robert Grubh, SA Hussain and Asad Rahmani, who shared with me their wide-ranging knowledge. Many of the younger scientists also enthusiastically discussed their fieldwork with me and willingly accompanied me in the field whenever I could find the time to be with them. In 1984, Bittu Sahgal encouraged me to write for *Sanctuary Magazine* and several of my articles appeared in the early editions of this excellent publication. Writing these often helped me clear my own concepts on conservation issues and I began to understand the urgent need for enhancing public awareness if conservation was to become a reality in India.

At a WWF-I workshop in Delhi a large jovial bearded man, with a sharp twinkle in his eye and a broad smile, came over to shake my hand and told me that he had enjoyed my slide presentation. Within a short time he became one of my very dear friends. WA Rodgers, known to everyone as Alan, worked at the Wildlife Institute of India. Quite apart from becoming a close friend, he became my readily accessible, walking talking

conservation encyclopaedia! As my concern for solving conflict issues in conservation deepened, his interest in eco-development grew to influence my thoughts and ideas. Alan helped me develop a project to evaluate the fragmented forests in the Dangs through an aerial survey that led to the first GIS work in India for ecological assessment. Sejal Worah, who was my field scientist, made this her PhD thesis and produced a much publicized work on the rare rusty spotted cat.

In 1993, Dr Patangrao Kadam learnt of my interest in conservation and encouraged me to set up an institute at Bharati Vidyapeeth to train young people in environmental sciences. To begin with, I had only two young people, Shamita Kumar and Dnyaneshwar Ghorpade, to help me. Today we have a band of young project staff, and conservation of biodiversity has become a key concern at the Institute. It has been a wild, exciting and long journey with many people, who helped me develop the concepts that have gone into the writing of this book.

In 1992, a chance event brought me in contact with the Tata Power Company (then Tata Electric Company). Dr Homi Sethna provided funds to document the effects of deforestation on the biodiversity of the incredible patches of forests around their hydel lakes. Many young people did the fieldwork for me, documenting the changes in the plant life, and birds and insects in this part of the Ghats; among them are Sujoy Chaudhuri, Aparna Watve and Sanjay Kadapatti. SN Ogale of the Tata Power Company, implemented many of the suggestions made and an Eco-restoration Programme that evolved over time. Much of this influenced what has gone into this book.

After several years of wandering in the wilderness I have come to the conclusion that a variety of other issues frequently influence conservation. My interactions with Professor Ron Herring from Cornell in the late 1990s led me to appreciate that conservation of a remote area is often linked to national and international events. Ron and I worked together to understand how India implements International Environmental Accords and Treaties, but more importantly he made me see the wider implications of conservation and development debates.

The large number of discussions I have had with Shekhar Singh of IIPA over the years led me to think deeply about methods of solving conflict issues that arise between the needs of conservation and development. Shekhar has the ability to enthuse everyone around him. This is even more evident once he is put on a dais—like the philosophers of old, he enthralls his audience.

As a young lecturer in surgery, living on a small salary, I spent all my spare money to buy rolls of film and all my spare time travelling around the country with my camera. I was welcomed at every place I visited by local forest officials, and am deeply appreciative of the help I received. For many years I gave slide-shows on conservation to a variety of audiences, ranging from school students to executives from industries and administrators from government agencies, and their numerous questions made me want to take a closer look at the biodiversity of India. Without that impetus this book could not have been written.

My colleagues at BVIEER—Shamita Kumar, Dynaneshwar Ghorpade, Shambhavi Joshi, Prasanna Kolte, Sanjay Kadapatti, Anand Shinde and Ajit Erawa—have persistently supported this long, tedious venture. I cannot thank them enough for their patience.

My friend Chinmaya Dunster did weeks of work on his laptop smoothing out all the rough edges. Aparna Watve's expertise in botany was a great help. Arundhati Pawar, Statira Wadia, Sheela Navlakha and Shilpi Daniel commented on numerous confused drafts through the last four or five years. Lyla Patel, Megha Yedati and Radhika Shah helped on the history of Indian forestry.

My search for old photographs took me to a box that belonged to Dr Salim Ali. JC Daniel and Rachel Reuben kindly gave me permission to use them. Surprisingly, I discovered pictures of Salim Ali at my own house in Pune in the 1950s. Another chance event led me to see Sharda Dwivedi, who gave me her pictures of shikar cars and pictures from old newspapers. But most incredible was how a conversation with my cousin, Aloo Reporter, made me travel back in time to when my naturalist uncle, Farokh Bharucha, collected rare and antique books on nature. His collections of botanical and zoological illustrated books have made my current book into a historical journey through India's wild places and its species of plants and animals. To Burjor and Aloo Reporter, I cannot express my thanks in any appropriate words. They have contributed greatly to this book. Piloo Kumarmangalam provided valuable pictures from her library that are included in this book. I thank her for this magnanimous gesture. There is also my anonymous friend who has let me use his beautiful Mughal miniatures. My very special thanks to all these people.

It has been a wild and exciting journey with many people who helped me to develop the concepts that have gone into the writing of this book. The patient confidence shown by Kamal Nanavaty and Bipin Shah, that I would finish it someday has been remarkable.

I thank my family for their patience with my obsession with wildlife photography. My sister, Ernavaz, Prasanna Kolte and Behafrid Lord have worked ceaselessly during the last few months to put together the text, captions and visuals. I am deeply indebted to them for the painstaking task of tying up the loose ends.

During the last few months I have had great support from Maya Mahale and Megha Yedaty at Jehangir Hospital, Dr Vivek Saoji, Vice Principal at Bharati Vidyapeeth Medical College and Shamita Kumar, Vice Principal at BVIEER. They shouldered much of my work leaving me the time I needed for the final stages of this book.

I am very grateful to my friends Pankaj, Ashwin and Ketan Mehta and their team at Reproscan, Mumbai, who have done more than their routine work to see that the visuals have retained their naturalness.

I appreciate Bipin Shah's personal input and thank him and his team, Diana Romany, Amit Kharsani with his designers and Paulomi Shah who have put this volume together. They have done more than most authours could dream of.

Finally, I thank the wild creatures that graciously allowed themselves to be photographed for this book.

# CONTENTS

## I. The Nature of Biodiversity in India

## India's Floral Heritage

88

## India's Rich Faunal Heritage

194

# II.  National Parks and Wildlife Sanctuaries of India

CATREUS WALL

# The Nature of Biodiversity in India

## Part I

*Catreus wallichi,* or chir pheasant; from Gould, 1850.

# Humankind and the Web of Life

In the dawn of Indian history, a man came upon a pair of cranes dancing ecstatically in the wilderness. As he watched in fascination, a hunter crept upon them with his bow and arrow, and killed one of the beautiful birds. Horrified and struck by this event, the man burst out in reproach at the shikari,

'Oh Hunter,
why hast thou killed this crane,
For thou art indeed accursed forever
for thy heinous crime.'

His great disgust at this act of cruelty induced him to write this as the first couplet of the *Ramayana*, one of the world's greatest epic poems. This first couplet appears to have been influenced by Valmiki's knowledge of the fact that cranes pair for life and the bereaved partner dies in loneliness. Though this understanding of the behaviour of cranes and the values ascribed to life has been passed down from one generation to the other in India, the population of our beautiful cranes, once seen in thousands, is rapidly shrinking. Today their wetland habitat continues to disappear at an ever-increasing pace. There seems to be little concern for their imminent extermination, or any understanding that this is closely related to the thoughtless degradation of their extensive wetland habitat that once dotted our countryside.

Valmiki begins the *Ramayana* with the story of the killing of a sarus crane. The hunter is admonished for having killed a crane, leaving its partner to pine to death. In spite of this, the species is under serious threat. The crane population has declined due to loss of its wetland habitat and the effects of pesticides and chemicals on the water quality of its residual habitat.

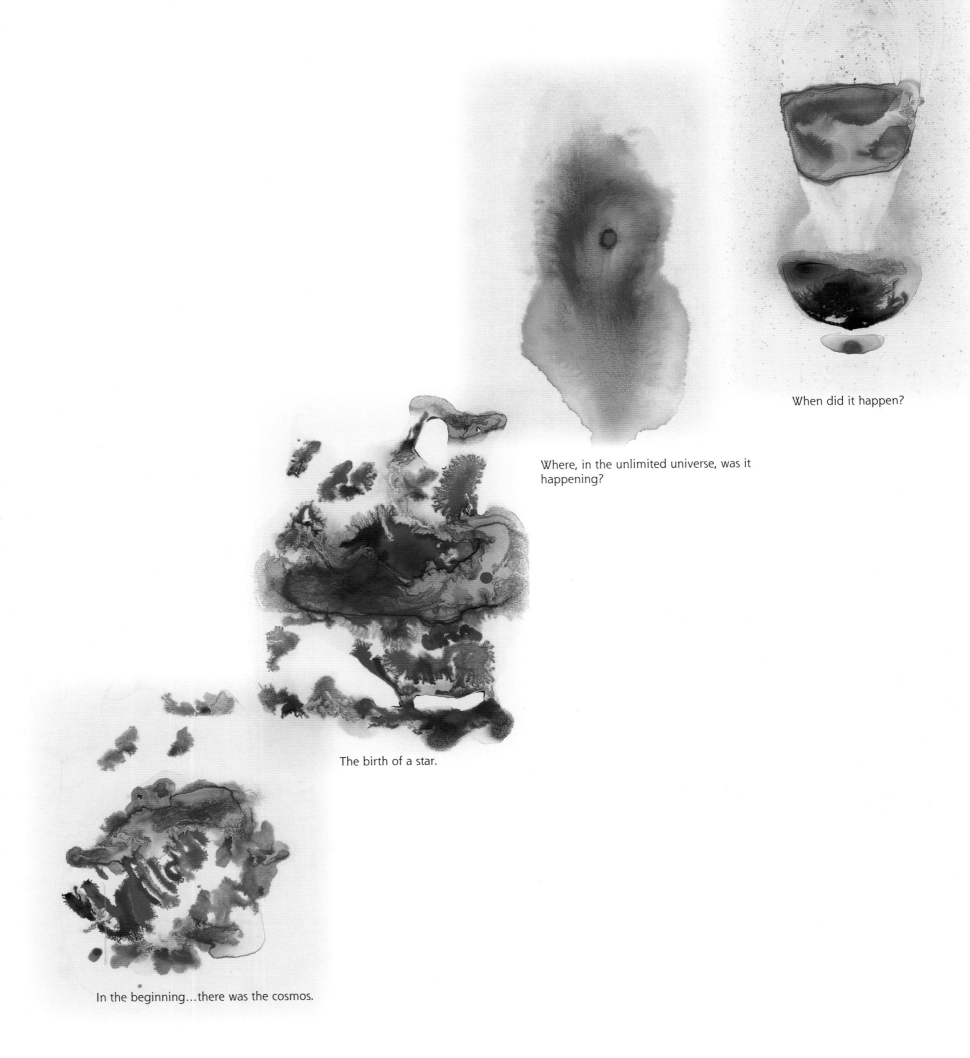

When did it happen?

Where, in the unlimited universe, was it happening?

The birth of a star.

In the beginning…there was the cosmos.

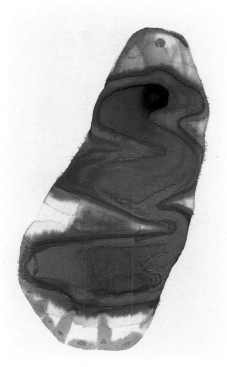

Why did it happen?

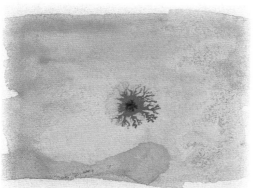

Was it just one small explosion
converting energy into matter?

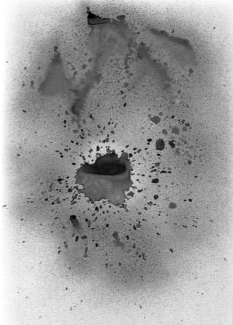

Or was there a Big Bang?

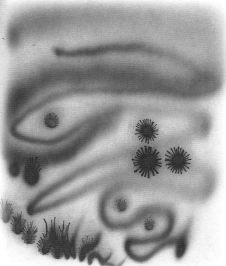

Or were there many little explosions?

We may never know.

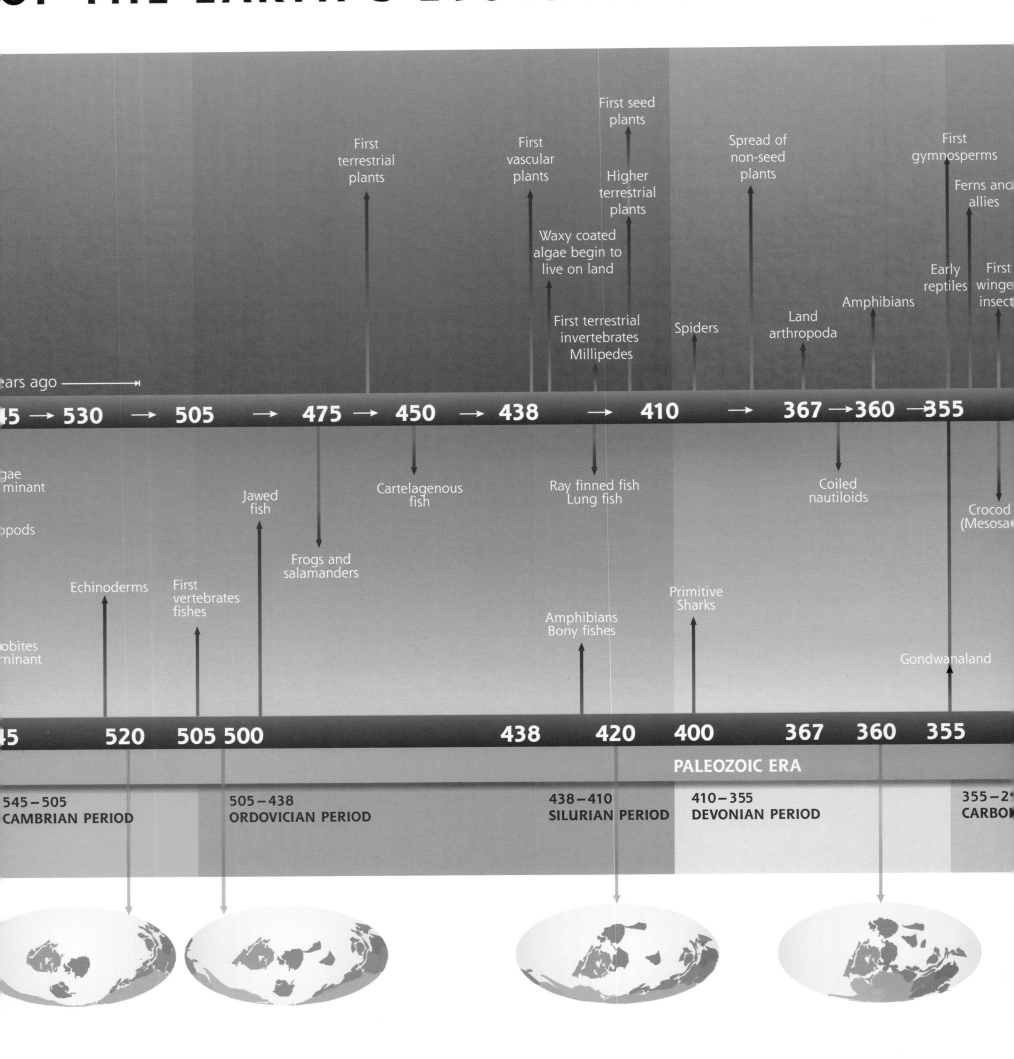

First seed
plants

First
terrestrial
plants

First
vascular
plants

Higher
terrestrial
plants

Spread of
non-seed
plants

First
gymnosperms

Ferns and
allies

Waxy coated
algae begin to
live on land

Early
reptiles

First
winge
insect

First terrestrial
invertebrates
Millipedes

Amphibians

Spiders

Land
arthropoda

ars ago ———→

45 → 530 → 505 → 475 → 450 → 438 → 410 → 367 → 360 → 355

Cartelagenous
fish

Ray finned fish
Lung fish

Coiled
nautiloids

Crocod
(Mesosa

gae
minant

Jawed
fish

opods

Frogs and
salamanders

Echinoderms

First
vertebrates
fishes

Primitive
Sharks

obites
minant

Amphibians
Bony fishes

Gondwanaland

45    520    505 500    438    420    400    367    360    355

**PALEOZOIC ERA**

545–505
CAMBRIAN PERIOD

505–438
ORDOVICIAN PERIOD

438–410
SILURIAN PERIOD

410–355
DEVONIAN PERIOD

355–2
CARBO

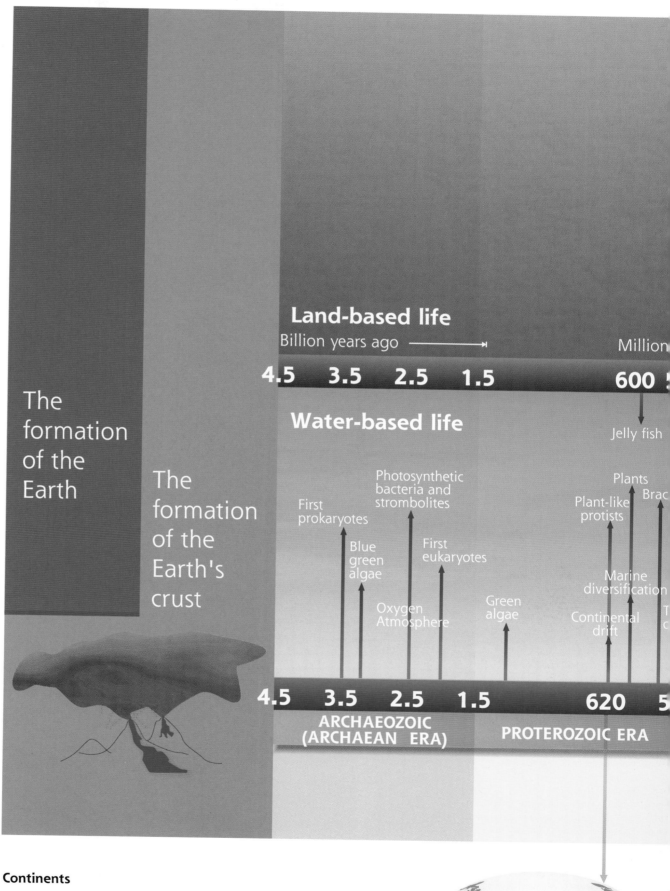

**Land-based life**

Billion years ago ⟶ ⊢                    Million

| 4.5 | 3.5 | 2.5 | 1.5 |       | 600 5 |

**Water-based life**

Jelly fish

Photosynthetic
bacteria and
strombolites                          Plants

First                                Plant-like              Brac
prokaryotes                          protists

Blue          First
green         eukaryotes                     Marine
algae                                        diversification

Oxygen            Green              Continental         T
Atmosphere        algae              drift               c

| 4.5 | 3.5 | 2.5 | 1.5 |       | 620 | 5 |

ARCHAEOZOIC                PROTEROZOIC ERA
(ARCHAEAN ERA)

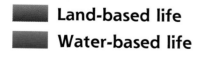

Land-based life
Water-based life

Numbers denote billions and millions of years

**Continents**

 North America    Africa    Australia

South America    Eurasia    Antarctica

Plant fossils from Madhya Pradesh show the ancient plant life of the region.

Fossil forms that are linked with aquatic environments prove that the Thar Desert was once a productive aquatic ecosystem. Time has moulded environments, favouring some species while decreasing the range of others. The shell in the desert is evidence of gradual changes that have taken place over thousands of years of geological timescales.

Looking around the landscape in the wilderness kindles a heightened sense of awareness of nature's magnificence. Nature herself teaches us what the diversity of life means, displaying the great variety of life that evolutionary processes have designed to inhabit our Earth. The mind-boggling magnitude of life's diversity is as difficult to account for as the stars that dot the night sky! Life is all the more fascinating because we do not know if anything even remotely similar exists anywhere else in the wide unfathomable Universe. It becomes evident that our own species (Homo sapiens) does not own the earth. We are just one of its millions of species. Humans are just one of the innumerable cogs in the wheel of life.

The great variety of species on earth has provided for human needs over thousands of years. Plants and animals form one of our most vital life-support systems and have been used by every culture as the basis for their growth and the development of their civilizations. Those who used this "bounty of nature" carefully and sustainably survived. Those who overused or misused it disintegrated.

## THE FUTURE

Mankind is now writing the history of the future. As we change our world through short-sighted development strategies, we lead different species on earth to extinction. Can the earth continue to support human civilization in isolation? When one thinks of how dependent each

one of us is on a host of other species, it goes without saying that the human species cannot survive without all the other life forms that inhabit the earth. Ancient Indian traditions supported the concept of Earth as the Mother of human civilization. Modern science has now come full circle and it also supports this view. If one thinks of the earth as a single living individual, each species can be thought of as a specialized group of cells making up one of its functioning organs. If all its different organs are healthy, the earth will remain a living organism throbbing with life. If any of its component species is destroyed, the earth must die. Every species is thus an important part of our living planet.

### The Gaia Hypothesis

James Lovelock, an English atmospheric scientist, proposed the Gaia Hypothesis in the 1960s, which was formally published in 1979. He hypothesized that the living matter of the planet functioned like a single organism. He named it after Gaia, the Greek goddess of the Planet Earth. Lovelock defined Gaia as: 'a complex entity involving the Earth's biosphere, atmosphere, oceans, and soil; the totality constituting a feedback or cybernetic system which seeks an optimal physical and chemical environment for life on this planet'.

## THE MYSTERY OF THE UNIVERSE

### IN THE BEGINNING

From the unknown cosmos, energy and matter came about. Was there a Big Bang that initiated the formation of the universe? Or did it happen through an inexplicable phenomenon we still don't understand?

The earth was formed out of a cloud of stellar dust between 4500 and 5000 million years ago. Its early history is shrouded in mystery. It remained an inhospitable, lifeless environment for millions of years.

### THE GENESIS OF LIFE

The origins of life on Earth are obscure. Its beginnings as a product of organic reactions in the primordial seas, so long accepted as an explanation, is now being questioned. Alternative possibilities, such as life beginning in hot springs, or in muddy ooze or below the seabed, are being considered instead. An even more dramatic theory is that life may have been seeded onto our planet from outer space! Though the origin itself is unclear, once the organic reactions essential to life were established on earth, about 3800 million years ago, it began to gradually diversify into different species. The capacity in early unicellular bacteria and single-celled plants and animals to duplicate themselves and change through mutations and natural selection, gave them the ability to

# From Pre-historic to Recent Era

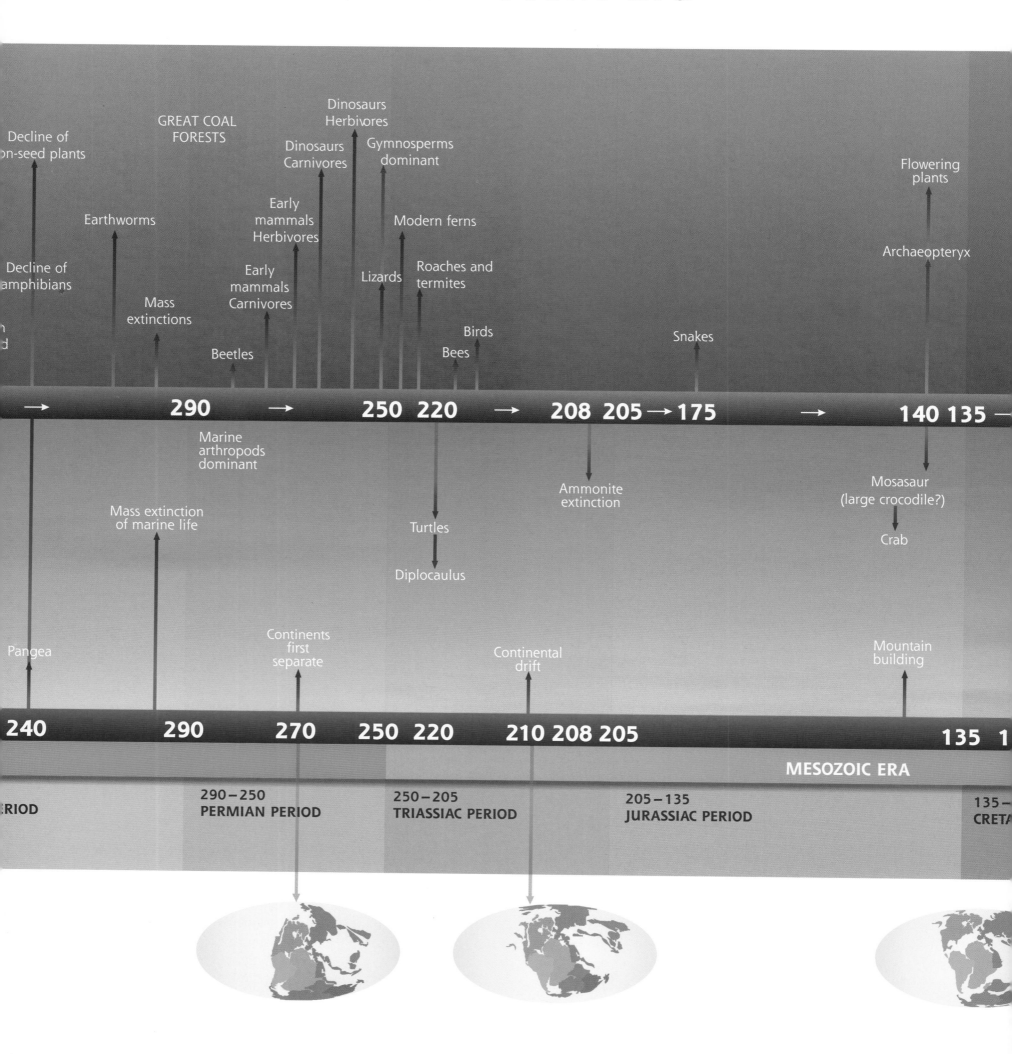

Decline of
on-seed plants

GREAT COAL
FORESTS

Dinosaurs
Herbivores

Dinosaurs
Carnivores

Gymnosperms
dominant

Flowering
plants

Earthworms

Early
mammals
Herbivores

Modern ferns

Archaeopteryx

Decline of
amphibians

Early
mammals
Carnivores

Lizards

Roaches and
termites

Mass
extinctions

Birds

Snakes

Beetles

Bees

→     **290**     →     **250 220**     →     **208 205** → **175**     →     **140 135** →

Marine
arthropods
dominant

Mass extinction
of marine life

Ammonite
extinction

Mosasaur
(large crocodile?)

Turtles

Crab

Diplocaulus

Pangea

Continents
first
separate

Continental
drift

Mountain
building

**240**     **290**     **270**     **250 220**     **210 208 205**     **135  1**

**MESOZOIC ERA**

ERIOD

290–250
**PERMIAN PERIOD**

250–205
**TRIASSIAC PERIOD**

205–135
**JURASSIAC PERIOD**

135–
CRETA

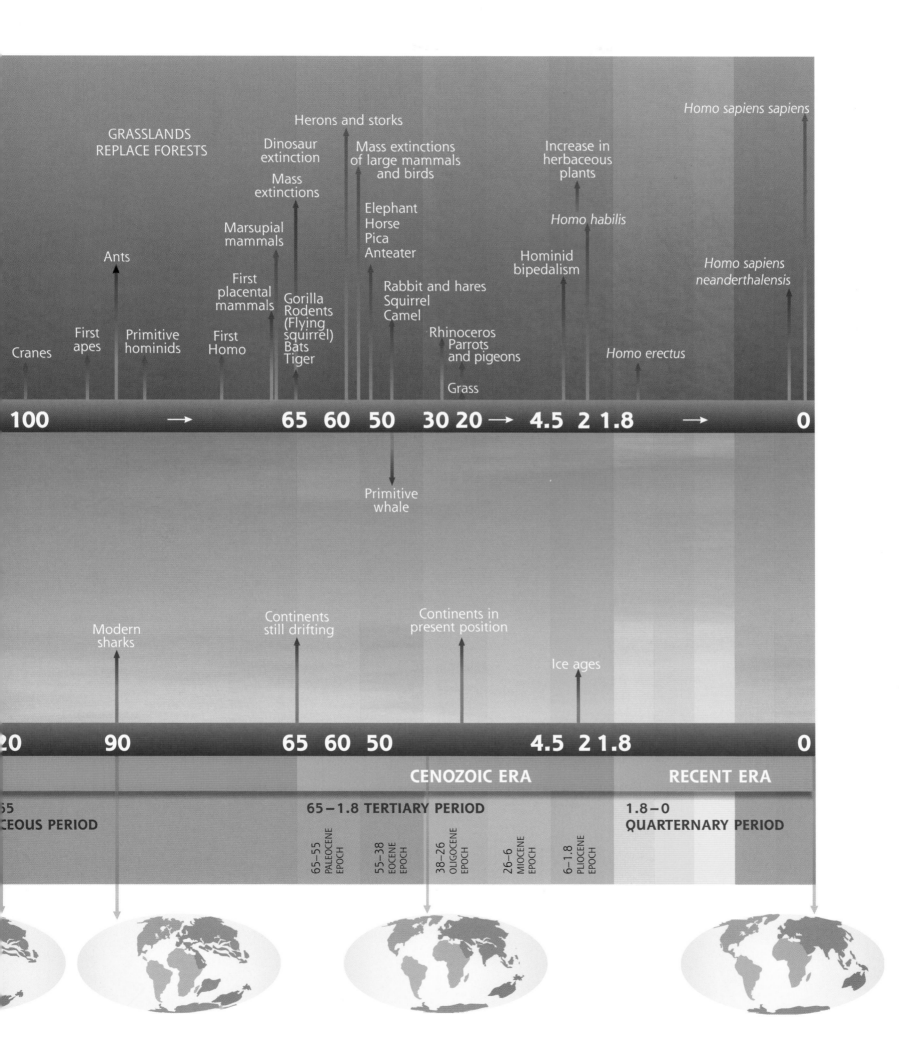

GRASSLANDS
REPLACE FORESTS

Herons and storks

Dinosaur
extinction

Mass extinctions
of large mammals
and birds

*Homo sapiens sapiens*

Increase in
herbaceous
plants

Mass
extinctions

Elephant
Horse
Pica
Anteater

*Homo habilis*

Marsupial
mammals

Ants

Hominid
bipedalism

*Homo sapiens
neanderthalensis*

First
placental
mammals

Rabbit and hares
Squirrel
Camel

First
apes

First
Homo

Gorilla
Rodents
(Flying
squirrel)
Bats
Tiger

Rhinoceros
Parrots
and pigeons

Primitive
hominids

*Homo erectus*

Cranes

Grass

| 100 | → | | 65 | 60 | 50 | 30 | 20 | → | 4.5 | 2 | 1.8 | → | 0 |

Primitive
whale

Modern
sharks

Continents
still drifting

Continents in
present position

Ice ages

| 20 | 90 | | 65 | 60 | 50 | | 4.5 | 2 | 1.8 | 0 |

**CENOZOIC ERA**  **RECENT ERA**

| 65 | 65–1.8 TERTIARY PERIOD | 1.8–0 |
| CEOUS PERIOD | | QUARTERNARY PERIOD |

65–55
PALEOCENE
EPOCH

55–38
EOCENE
EPOCH

38–26
OLIGOCENE
EPOCH

26–6
MIOCENE
EPOCH

6–1.8
PLIOCENE
EPOCH

## THE PAST

India's folklore and mythology are replete with stories of her beautiful mountains, lakes, rivers and forests. Our ancient philosophers, writers and rulers studied and documented the great diversity of our flora and fauna. They had identified and named those species that could be used, those that endangered their lives and those that had linkages with ancient rituals or religious beliefs. Numerous myths that have traditionally strengthened our ties with nature and have become a part of our traditions, are based on the value placed on life. Five hundred years before Christ, Buddha preached in this country about the sanctity of all forms of life. Three hundred years later, his teachings led to Emperor Ashoka's edict, asking his people to protect several species of animals and their forest homes. This need to venerate nature has always been an integral part of the Indian culture and religion.

## THE PRESENT

For hundreds of years and through various dynasties and invasions, these traditions persisted until recent times. A change has, however, come about; the wilderness is now rapidly disappearing and only small fragments remain. The growing human population and the rapid increase of agriculture and industry share the responsibility for the destruction of what is left of the wilderness. Modern society has modified the landscape at an unprecedented rate to suit its immediate needs, leaving forests degraded, water bodies polluted, and deserts and arid lands over-exploited. Many of the highly fragile natural areas have already been destroyed and will perhaps never be restored to their pristine glory. Our network of Wildlife Sanctuaries and National Parks provides only a small ray of hope for conserving what is left of the wilderness.

The foothills of the Himalayas in the foreground with the lofty ranges in the background, form the roof of the world. The Himalayas were considered sacred and meant to be left undisturbed. Modern science supports protecting this ecologically fragile region as it supplies life-giving water to the plains.

gradually adapt to different environmental conditions. Over long periods of time, this led to the formation of new and better adapted multi-cellular species. Changes in nature, such as climatic conditions, atmospheric upheavals, repeated glaciations, continental drift, the formation of geographical barrierssuch as mountain ranges, and separation by oceans, provided a milieu for the evolution of new species in each of the major continents. Changes in the Earth's crust through plate tectonics, resulting in the shifting and spreading of continents, led to geographical barriers that segregated plant and animal species into different communities across the planet. This in turn led to the formation of the six bio-geographical realms that

are to be found even today. Variations in the composition of species in different geographic regions are thus related to barriers that prevented the dispersal of their species from one realm to theothers. Oceans, deserts and mountain ranges formed major divides, segregating plant and animal communities from each other. Similar or allied species of floraand fauna found on different continents, which are now separated into isolated bio-geographic realms, can be explained on the basis of prehistoric connections or bridges of land between these landmasses, which are now separated by oceans or mountains.

## THE VARIETY OF LIFE

The primordial sea, the muddy organic ooze on its shores, the fresh water of rivers, all provided an ideal range of habitats for the first single-celled forms of life such as bacteria and protoctista, the forerunners of early plants, fungi and animals, to diversify into new species. Living organisms also began to support each other's needs for their mutual benefit. Indeed, it is now believed that several early forms of life evolved from their association with free-living bacteria. It took 2000 million years for these early life forms to evolve into multi-cellular plants and animals. As more animals evolved to fit into the same habitat, highly complex relationships were formed. A vast number of prey-predator relationships, for example, resulted in countless food chains that transferred energy through the evolving ecosystems. In order to escape from their predators, prey species developed camouflage mechanisms to blend into their surroundings, or became faster and more elusive. In response, predators evolved characteristics to merge

with the landscape so that they couldn't be seen approaching, they increased their speed, or improved their sensing abilities.

These resulted in long-standing linkages that have lasted for aeons. In a few instances, these paired relationships have been so strong that if one of the partners were to be eliminated, the other would also soon become extinct. These highly specialized partnerships fit into very specific 'twin' niches. Certain insect caterpillars, for example, can feed on the leaves of only one type of plant, while the plant in turn requires pollination by the moths of that species of caterpillars. Thus the pollinator and the pollinated plant have become totally dependent on each other for their survival.

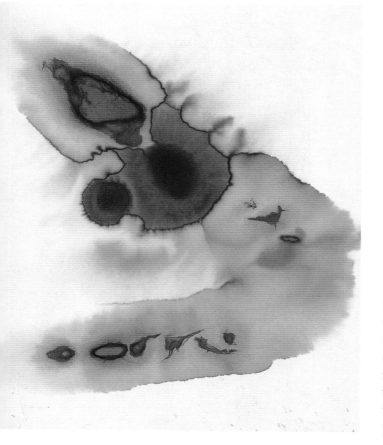

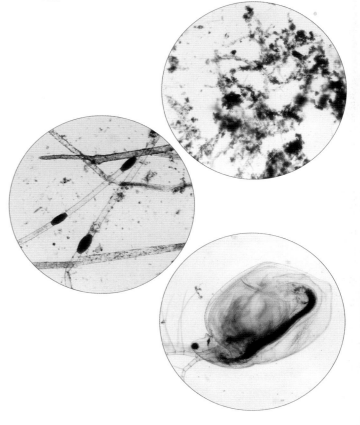

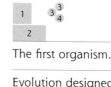

The first organism.

Evolution designed tiny microbes and great creatures like the whales.

Algae are among the earliest forms of life on earth and still inhabit aquatic ecosystems.

The zooplankton began to graze on microscopic plant and animal life, forming some of the earliest food chains on earth.

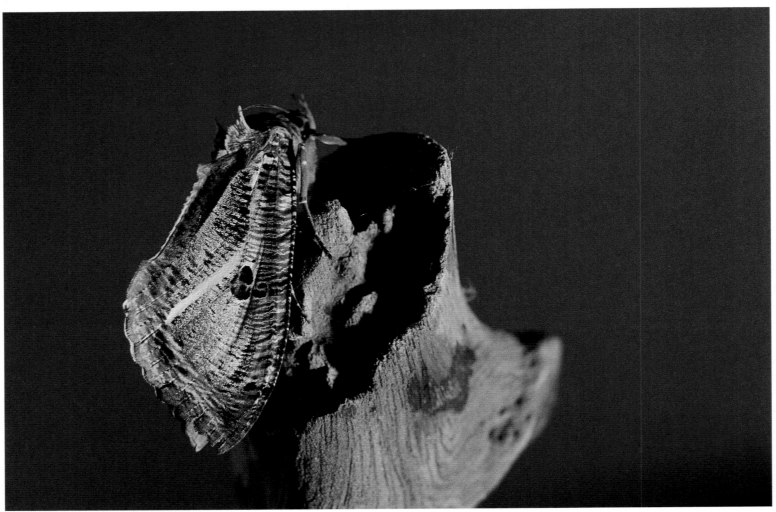

A moth with its closed wings camouflages itself superbly.

The camouflaged moth opens its wings to flash pseudo-eyes that scare away predators.

Little is known about ecological adaptations of insects in India. In some countries, it has been observed that moths have changed their camouflage colour to adapt to the bark of trees discoloured by air pollution.

Linkages between species are important aspects of distinctive ecosystems. The behavioural patterns of the component species, such as their breeding needs, feeding patterns, and migrations, have together influenced the formation of new species. As older species, unable to adapt to change, became extinct, they left behind empty niches in the habitat, which stimulated the formation of new species to fill them. Time has seen several periods of mega-extinction, like the one 65 million years ago, when the dinosaurs vanished from the surface of the earth forever. These periods of extinction were followed by periods of speciation in which new and better-adapted species evolved. The history of life on Earth shows that these changes took several million years to complete, and while periods of mega-extinction led to drastic reductions in the number of species, the earth as a whole was able to eventually recuperate through an increase in the number of species. Thus, there are probably more species existing on earth today than during any single period in the past.

About 1.8 million species of plants and animals on earth have already been identified and named by scientists. There is obviously a much larger number yet to be identified. Scientists discover new species of plants, insects and other forms of life all the time. Perhaps there are 30 to 100 times more species to discover, that have not even been collected by botanists, zoologists and microbiologists. Most of these would be in the tropical evergreen forests and in the seas among coral reefs, the two most species-rich habitats on earth.

The possible presence of some 30 to 60 million undiscovered species on our planet today is thus the end product of a long evolutionary process, and the present

community of organisms was preceded by several billion species that are now extinct. Our own species—*Homo sapiens*—arose at a point when the number of species had reached an all-time high.

All species of microscopic life and large plants and animals live in several distinctive, intact 'natural' habitats. The areas most rich in species are the tropical evergreen rain forests, which form regional concentrations of high species-diversity referred to as 'hot spots' of diversity. Other habitats with exceptionally high species-richness exist in the coral reefs in warm, shallow tropical seas. Species are thus not evenly distributed over the earth's surface, but concentrated in regions such as South America, South-east Asia, and in our own country and neighbouring countries in South Asia.

## THE GROWTH OF THE SCIENCE OF NATURAL HISTORY

The origin of the phases of growth in the science of life was when humans began to use plants and animals in more ways than other animals do. The human brain, a highly developed sense of speech and an opposable thumb all led to the development of a species with a higher level of intelligence. The members of this species have a super-sensitive grasping hand that could do things that even other primates could manage only at a basic level. This made the human of the past leapfrog into a civilizational process culminating in several complex societies. The humans' highly evolved brain led them to a new level of understanding nature. They began to develop communication skills using speech that evolved into multiple languages. And they began to use tools. The stage from hunter-gatherer to

agro-pastoralist, however, took thousands of years. Civilization accounts for some two million years of human history, starting from the Stone Age to the modern times.

Early Indian civilizations knew a large number of species, both from their utilitarian aspects as well as objects of veneration. Greek and Roman influences transferred knowledge to and fro when these militarized nations spread eastward to India.

In the West, the understanding of nature become a specialized subject of study, much later than in India. The modern science of Biology was thus reintroduced in India, which already had its own traditional science. The Western colonial expansion in the 1600s led to the domination, and in some ways to the annihilation, of Indian traditional thinking, taking us away from the way in which nature had been regarded in the past.

The word 'genus' in Biology dates back to 1608 and was coined from the Greek term meaning 'offspring' and the Latin term meaning 'race', 'stock' or 'kind'. The seeds of Western thinking on taxonomical classification had already been sown in European thought when colonization brought to India newly emerging scientific concepts. Surprisingly, the sciences of biology were witnessing an exponential growth in the 1600s—a time when the strength of the European naval powers was growing, bringing about the colonial empires that controlled the East from their distant country of origin. Their initial interest in establishing spice trade with the East began to change when they saw the richness of other raw material located in the East. It was thus essential for them to begin to study the Natural History of the countries that they dominated.

In the 1600s, scientists in the West had begun to look at the classification of plants and animals. Later they began to study their habitats as well. But their main concern was how this knowledge could be exploited for the economic benefit of the West. Trade in natural products from the East translated into a need to control and rule over the country where these commodities had their origin. The Western colonization process spread throughout the next 200 years.

The early work on species of plants and animals during the 1600s was based on a classification linked with the appearance of plants and animals. It enabled Botany and Zoology to be put to use in practical, economic development. Trade related to plants and animals found in the colonized countries led to the exploitation of species beyond nature's ability to sustain this expanding level of utilization. Man was endangering species and driving several of them to the brink of extinction. The term 'endangered species', however, came into use only in 1964. It required 400 years of exploitation!

## THE THEORY OF EVOLUTION

The understanding that species could evolve over time and that they adapted to changes in their environment brought about a rapid and radical change in biological sciences. In the early 1800s, Jean Batiste Lamarck, a French naturalist, was one of the earliest workers to use the term 'Biology' in scientific literature. Lamarck had brought up the possibility of evolution within the context of science, but had no evidence to prove what he was proposing. In 1859, Charles Darwin and Alfred Russel Wallace shook the world by challenging concepts that had been propounded for centuries in different religions across the globe. The discovery of fossils of ancient animals that were now extinct was strong evidence for their new theory of evolution. The world now understood how species were so diverse in nature.

Between 1856 and 1863, Gregor Mendel, an Austrian monk, cultivated 28,000 pea plants and showed that the plants' offspring retained their parents' traits and were not influenced by their environment. This was the beginning of our understanding of the concept of heredity.

## EVOLUTIONARY SCIENCE TODAY

In the recent past, experts working on species have developed new ways of classifying life by using modern techniques linked to molecular biology and the understanding of DNA. It is now believed that organisms like bacteria form a single

**Carolus Linnaeus** (1707–1778) is considered the father of the modern taxonomy of species. He was a Swedish doctor who was better known as a botanist. He also produced one of the earliest works on ecology. Linnaeus realized very early that stamens and pistils of flowers could act as a good basis for classifying plants. Although the system of binomial nomenclature had been developed some 200 hundred years earlier, it was Linnaeus who established it as a basis of all taxonomic work in the future. His work goes beyond taxonomy and the naming of a large number of the world's plants and animals, to a greater understanding of biological sciences. His grouping of species was based on shared physical characteristics, and though many of these have been modified in later years, his method of classification laid the foundation of a new approach to Botany and Zoology.

### Charles Darwin and the Origin of Species

Charles Robert Darwin (1809–1882) developed an interest in Natural History while he was studying medicine. He also studied theology to become a clergyman, but later turned to geology. He was evidently a highly versatile scientist and an exceptionally keen field observer. Darwin travelled through the coast of South America on HMS *Beagle* on a voyage that took five years, from 1831 to 1836. He studied seashores and coral atolls and found fossils that he linked to existing species. He developed an enormous collection of animals and birds, which he gave to taxonomists when he returned to England. Darwin appears to have been worried that the church would find his work offensive. He thus maintained a 'B' notebook called *Zoonomia* which he shared for several years only with his close scientific associates. He worked extremely hard and was frequently ill. Eventually his description of the 'Voyage of the Beagle' was published and he became a popular author. Darwin often bounced his ideas off his friend Joseph Dalton Hooker who had spent much of his time studying plant life in India. In 1856 Darwin's friend Charles Lyell came across a paper on the *Introduction of Species* by Alfred Wallace, who was working as a naturalist in Borneo. Lyell told Darwin that it was now imperative to publish his work on natural selection before Wallace did so. Darwin began to feverishly write up the ideas he had been working on for several years. In 1858, Wallace sent a paper to Darwin on the work he was doing. Curiously, it summarized Darwin's own findings on which he had been laboriously working for decades! Darwin was obviously greatly perturbed and asked Lyell and Hooker to arrange for a joint presentation at the Linnean Society. Once this was done he went on with the writing of his voluminous findings in *The Origin of Species* published in 1859. The controversy it raised in Victorian Society rocked the modern world. It became the most controversial book ever written. Darwin had revolutionized the science of Biology forever.

stream that has evolved through the early evolutionary period. Another stream has been called Protoctista, and includes organisms such as algae and protozoa (microscopic animals), which eventually diversified into modern multi-cellular plants, fungi and animals. Thus species such as bacteria, algal forms and protozoa appear to be the most primitive forms of life on earth. Another stream of living creatures has also recently been identified. These are highly specialized forms, living in extremely inhospitable environments of extremes of temperature and salinity where no other organism—except for a few types of bacteria—can survive. This evolutionary pattern of classification, linked to modern methods of separating organisms into groups of species, is still in its infancy and thus it constantly changes the organization of life into groups. Experts continue to provide new evidence on how species are to be scientifically classified on the basis of their evolutionary history.

Bacteria, as we know them today, were formed about 3500 million years ago. The earliest fossil evidence of life consists of filaments and spheroids seen in rocks near the sea, dating back some 3200 million years. Terrestrial forms of life were developed 2600 million years ago. Bryophyte-like forms evolved some 400 million years ago, followed by the earliest seed-bearing plants. The diversity of plant life was low till about 300 million years ago when, during the carboniferous period, the plant diversity increased enormously. Finally, the radiation of angiosperms replaced the gymnosperms as dominant species in most existing ecosystems around 170 million years ago.

The most ancient multi-cellular animal fossils, such as species of arthropods and echinoderms are 350 million years old. Most of them don't reflect the characteristics of existing animals (Groombridge and Jenkins, 2002).

## THE NATURE OF BIODIVERSITY

The great variety of life on earth includes the richness of species of plants and animals, the genetic variability within each of the species, as well as the organization of living creatures into communities belonging to distinctive ecosystems. These variations in nature are now referred to as biodiversity. Biological diversity is thus observed at three distinct levels.

Genetic diversity is the variability observed in different individuals of a species due to the large number of combinations possible in the genes that give each individual specific characteristics.

A diagrammatic representation of a chromosome which contains the basic units of heredity, the genes.

Genetic variability is essential for a healthy breeding population of plant and animal species. If the number of breeding individuals is reduced, inbreeding occurs; this concentrates unwanted genetic patterns in a population, eventually leading to the extinction of the species. Modern intensive agricultural systems have a relatively lower diversity of genes in the crop than there was in traditional farming systems, which used a large number of local varieties. We are thus losing genetic diversity, which is of great value to mankind.

**EO Wilson** (1929–) is a biologist with a special interest in entomology, ecology, evolution and socio-biology. He is thought to have coined the term 'biodiversity'. His work on the 'selfish gene' argues that evolution preserved genes rather than individuals. Wilson's work is of great importance, as he pointed out that in cutting an ancient forest one is not only removing a number of big trees, but also endangering the life of a large number of species that are closely linked to forests. He stresses upon the fact that many of these species are still unknown to science and could play a key role in maintaining an ecosystem. They would include micro-organisms, fungi, and insect life. In 1992 he published his book on the diversity of life which stressed upon the dangers faced by the planet due to the rapid rate of extermination of species. Wilson has previously worked on the theory of island biogeography, insect society and the complex issues related to socio-biology and genetics.

### Wallace's Line that Supported the Theory of Evolution

Alfred Russell Wallace (1823–1913) was a British naturalist, geographer, anthropologist and biologist. From 1854 to 1862, Wallace travelled through Malaysia and Indonesia, collecting specimens of animals. His observations led to his hypothesis of the zoogeographical boundary that separated species on the phases of evolution, now known as the Wallace Line. His studies were eventually published in 1869 as *The Malay Archipelago*.

In 1855 he proposed that 'every species has come into existence coincident both in space and time with a closely allied species.' His 1858 essay, which he sent to Darwin for a review, proposed the theory that explained the diversity of life. This was similar to Darwin's own observations and research which he had been carrying out for the past 20 years, but was yet to publish. This essay prompted Darwin to hurriedly publish his research on natural selection as we know it today.

In 1864, Wallace was the first to apply the theory of natural selection to the origin and evolution of mankind.

Diversity of species refers to the number of species of wild plants and animals present in a region. By 1990, conservation scientists claimed that the number of named species on earth was 1.4 million (Mc Neely et al, 1990).

By 2003, the number of species of wild plants, animals, fungi and unicellular forms of life accounted for over 1.75 million (Groombridge and Jenkins, 2002). Thus, between 1990 and 2002, scientists had added 0.35 million new species to the earth's biodiversity. Scientists now believe that diversity of species is crucial to the existence of life on earth. They are distributed both in terrestrial and aquatic habitats. The most species-rich groups are the flowering plants and the

The great species diversity of life on Earth.

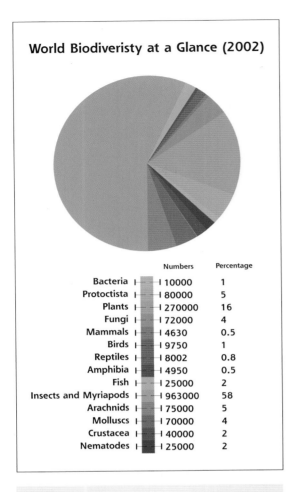

## World Biodiveristy at a Glance (2002)

| | Numbers | Percentage |
|---|---|---|
| Bacteria | 10000 | 1 |
| Protoctista | 80000 | 5 |
| Plants | 270000 | 16 |
| Fungi | 72000 | 4 |
| Mammals | 4630 | 0.5 |
| Birds | 9750 | 1 |
| Reptiles | 8002 | 0.8 |
| Amphibia | 4950 | 0.5 |
| Fish | 25000 | 2 |
| Insects and Myriapods | 963000 | 58 |
| Arachnids | 75000 | 5 |
| Molluscs | 70000 | 4 |
| Crustacea | 40000 | 2 |
| Nematodes | 25000 | 2 |

Adapted from Groombridge and Jenkins (2002), p. 18. Prepared by the UNEP World Conservation Monitoring Center.

insects. Insects are also the most abundant animals in nature. The diversity of species is seen both in the large numbers of wild species existent in Nature, as well as in the different types of crop plants and animals used in traditional agricultural systems. Natural, undisturbed tropical evergreen forests have much greater species' diversity than other types of forests, and all natural forests have higher species diversity than typical monoculture timber plantations. Natural ecosystems provide a large number of non-wood products that people depend on, such as fruit, fuel-wood, fodder, fibre, gum, resin and medicines. Intensive agriculture usually depends on developing a single crop, and though it provides rapid economic returns in the short term, such a practice makes the crop vulnerable to disease, which can destroy it all. In a traditional multi-crop system, if one crop is destroyed, the large range of other successful crops helps the farmer make ends meet.

**The familiar forest, grassland and marine habitats form only a very small part of the wide spectrum of ecosystem diversity found in india.**

The web signifies the fragile nature of the complex interrelationship of species that constitute life on earth. Every species lost through extinction weakens the web.

Species are classified into Kingdom, Phylum, Class, Order, Family, Genus, and Species. Each species is given a name that consists of its genus and species. There are five major kingdoms—bacteria, protoctista (algae and protozoa), fungi (mushrooms, moulds and lichens), plants (angiosperms and gymnosperms) and animals (vertebrates and invertebrates).

Ecosystem diversity refers to the variety of distinctive landforms and aquatic habitats observed in each geographical region. Different climatic and geographical features referred to as 'abiotic' or non-living conditions have created a large variety of natural ecosystems on earth, including forests, grasslands, deserts, mountains, wetlands, rivers, lakes, coasts, marine and island habitats. Topographic variations such as mountains, hills, plateaus, valleys and plains create a varied pattern of ecosystems in a region. Each of these abiotic features creates a habitat for specific plants and animals. Distinctive vegetation types are based on

the nature of the local temperature, the availability of water and variations in the soil characteristics. The ecosystem in an area is referred to as natural when it is relatively undisturbed by human activities, or 'modified' when it is adapted to other types of uses. Wilderness areas with their own wild plants and animals are of great economic value. If they are overused or misused, their productivity decreases and the ecosystem is eventually degraded.

EO Wilson is considered one of the pioneers of the modern science of Conservation Biology. In his first book, *Biodiversity I,* in 1989, he wrote extensively on the need to conserve tropical evergreen forest ecosystems, on the grounds that this ecosystem is extremely rich in species and should thus be considered a 'hot spot' of global importance. When he wrote *Biodiversity II,* in 1997, his approach had begun to change. He now stresses on the need to protect other ecosystems such as wetlands as, though they may be less species-rich, their total extent on earth is

much less than that of tropical forests and they are thus more severely threatened by conversion and pollution.

Ecosystems turned by humans into agricultural and pastoral landscapes, supply our ever-increasing need for food. They vary from traditional farming to intensively-used agricultural areas under modern irrigation systems. The latter require high levels of energy inputs and economic support, irrigation, fertilizers, pesticides, mechanization and biotechnological advances to maintain their productivity. This can have several drawbacks. Intensive irrigation may lead to water-logging, salinization of the soil due to evaporation of excess water, and pollution of water bodies in the area due to over-fertilization with chemicals. This, in turn, leads to an overgrowth of weeds or algae, and the use of pesticides leads to serious health hazards. All these effects are responsible for a loss of biodiversity as well as productivity in the long term.

## THE BIOSPHERE

The variability in nature at the levels of genes, species and ecosystems, is part of the living component of our planet—the 'biosphere'. Relative to its great size, the biosphere forms only a thin skin in the superficial layers of the earth's crust, where life can survive on land, in water and in the adjacent atmosphere. Thus, only a small portion of the earth houses all its living forms. The possibility of our actions seriously disrupting this thin, sensitive layer hardly ever comes to our minds. But this is what is happening as a result of many of our day-to-day activities. Earth's natural resources are usually sub-divided into non-renewable resources, such as air, water, minerals, oil; and renewable resources, mostly the products formed by life processes and species found within forests, grasslands, wetlands, agriculture and pastoral landscapes, all of which are capable of regenerating and reproducing themselves. However, there are limits to the extent to which these 'renewable' resources can recoup if they are overused. If a natural forest, with all its diverse forms of life, is severely disturbed, its species of interlinked plants and animals are unable to survive. Once the number of individuals of a species begins to fall below a critical level, the species can no longer make a comeback on its own. Other species, dependent on it in the complex web of life, are the next to go and the ecosystem may eventually break down catastrophically. It is not usually appreciated that a so-called 'renewable' resource can behave like a 'non-renewable' one. The extinction phenomenon is as permanent and irreversible as completely using up a non-renewable resource, such as oil.

## THREATS TO BIODIVERSITY

The major threats to biodiversity today include habitat loss, poaching and people-wildlife conflict. Human beings have been using natural ecosystems since forever. More recently, we have begun to overuse or misuse these ecosystems. While the exploding populations of the developing world require more resources to sustain the basic needs of a growing number of individuals, the people of the developed world use more and more consumer products, utilize ever greater quantities of energy and create enormous amounts of waste. This unsustainable resource use has led to the desertification of productive forests and grasslands and an increase in the wasteland. Mangroves are cleared for fuel-wood under the pretext of 'economic development' such as prawn farming. Intact mangroves must be preserved, since they act as a breeding ground for marine fish. Wetlands are drained to serve as agricultural land. Natural forest ecosystems are changed into monoculture plantations, destroying their complex community of plants and animals. The present rate of destruction of the remainder of our wilderness habitats, especially tropical forests and coral reefs that harbour high levels of diversity, is a major threat to biodiversity worldwide.

It is estimated that approximately 10 million species are likely to undergo extinction due to human activity by the year 2050. At the present rate of extinction, about 25 per cent of the world's species will become extinct within the next 20 to 30 years. Many species will disappear in the next few decades, even before being identified by science. Much of this mega-extinction episode can be attributed to human population growth, industrialization and changes in land-use patterns. Loss of wild habitats due to rapid human population growth and short term economic development is a major contributor to the rapid destruction of global biodiversity. Species are lost when natural ecosystems are destroyed, either by conversion to agriculture or industry, by over-extraction of resources, or due to pollution of air, water and soil. Habitat loss also results from human interference by introduction of species from one area into another, disturbing the balance in the existing communities. Some of these introduced species have become highly invasive 'weeds' (e.g. *Lantana*, *Eupatorium*, Hyacinth, Congress Grass are just a few common invasive exotic species). This leads to the extinction of a number of local species.

Certain species are under greater threat due to poaching, which involves large economic benefits. Skin and bones from tigers, ivory from elephants, horns from rhinos and perfume from the musk deer are in great demand worldwide. Bears

Over-fishing has led to a depletion of the population of marine fish—a serious threat to biodiversity.

The extraction of sand changes the ecology of riverbeds and threatens biodiversity.

Biodiversity is threatened by herds of cattle that graze in the forest.

are killed for their gall bladders. Coral is collected and sold for export. A variety of plants with medicinal value are over-harvested and plants such as orchids, that are valued for gardens, are collected extensively for export.

We know so little about the threat to the diversity of the species of our country. Most of us are only aware of the plight of a few glamour species, which mostly include the large mammals and a few well-known birds. But we also need to appreciate the greater threat to less known plant and animal species. Several little known species are now endangered. According to the level of threat, they can be categorized as vulnerable, rare, intermediate and threatened. The well-known endangered Indian species include the tiger, elephant, rhino, Indian wild ass, hangul, golden langur, Siberian crane, great Indian bustard, the Bengal florican etc. Equally threatened are several species of reptiles, amphibia, invertebrates, and a very large number of plant species.

Some species are found only in India and are thus considered to be endemic to the country. Species which are found in a limited range in very specific ecosystems or locales are considered highly endemic. As these are also frequently rare, they are under a greater degree of threat.

## CONSERVING BIODIVERSITY

In a developing nation such as India, where a burgeoning population, intense agriculture and urbanization expand at a great rate, the task of preserving creatures that represent the diversity of life in wild places presents a variety of challenges. How can a strategy be evolved for supporting the conservation of the wilderness at the policy level; how can it be implemented within various sectors of the administration; and how is conservation to be included in the mindset of the public at large? Questions such as: 'Why should biodiversity be conserved?' 'Who should use its benefits?' 'What is it worth?' 'How can it be preserved?' need to be addressed. These are complex questions. Unless we develop a new pattern of sustainable lifestyles the earth's finite bio-resources must inevitably be exhausted. The extinction of species is a symptom of such

unsustainable growth, and destroys the possibility of their use for the betterment of humankind in the future. If our own nation's long-term goals of economic development are to be fulfilled, the preservation of its unique biodiversity must take its place in programmes of sound environment management. As much land as possible must be set aside as wilderness to protect this invaluable living wealth.

All three levels of biodiversity—of genes, species and ecosystems—are thus important for the welfare of mankind, both as components of wilderness ecosystems and in the modified environment of rural and urban spheres.

**Maintaining genetic diversity** enables scientists to develop better crops and domestic animals through selectively breeding more desirable traits in plants and animals. This is further enhanced by modern biotechnology. For the long-term viability of wild species there should be enough individuals for the species to breed successfully. This can only be done by protecting their natural habitat.

**Protecting the diversity of species** is essential to provide many valuable products that are based on biodiversity, for example, medicines and new food products that are constantly being discovered from wild plant and animal life. The depletion of species is thus a great economic loss to humankind. As wilderness is increasingly converted to agricultural, pastoral and finally industrial and urban land, the number of extinctions rapidly increases. The loss due to the extinction of species is estimated to be in the range of several billions of dollars annually. Most species of plants and animals can only survive in fairly intact 'natural' ecosystems. Thus species can only be preserved in situ. 'Gene banks' that preserve tissue are expensive and do not support evolutionary processes. Botanical gardens and zoos can only protect species to a limited extent. Thus, demarcating enough land in wilderness areas to be kept aside in an Integrated Protected Area System of National Parks and Wildlife Sanctuaries is vital to maintain the world's diversity of species.

**Preserving ecosystem diversity** that is present on land and in water across the earth's surface must be implemented as

plants and animals can only survive in nature as closely-knit communities of life. As well as being highly productive, natural landscapes also perform several services for humankind. Forests, for example, complete the water cycle through transpiration from leaves; trees bind the soil and prevent its erosion on hill slopes; vegetation increases the percolation of water into the soil, while at the same time slowing down the run-off of rainfall over the land, and preventing floods. Some of these landscapes are ecologically robust and can withstand a fair amount of disturbance without a serious loss of biological diversity; others, like the tropical rain forests, with their thin soils, are now designated as Ecologically Sensitive Areas (ESA) and are extremely prone to rapid destruction by human activities.

## THE NON-UTILITARIAN VALUES FOR PROTECTING BIODIVERSITY

Quite apart from the economic dimension of conserving biodiversity, there are cultural, moral and ethical values associated with the sanctity of all forms of life. Over many generations, people have preserved nature through local traditions. Take for instance the large number of sacred groves in our country. These forests around ancient shrines or temples act as gene banks of wild plants. The sacred tulsi is planted at the entrance of our homes, and traditional Ayurvedic medicine is based on wild plants and animal products. Yet this biological diversity on which so much depends is now being destroyed for short-term gains.

We also need to conserve biodiversity because we do not know today which species may prove to be of value in the future. This is known as its 'option value'. Future generations have the right to the use of biodiversity, and our generation has no right to destroy this invaluable resource. We are trustees, protecting the rights of unborn generations who would need these biologically valuable resources.

The earlier concern with preserving species focused on the large mammals and birds that were prized by hunters. This changed to protecting habitats. As tropical evergreen forests were known to

The elephant is venerated in Buddhism—the Sun Temple at Konark, Orissa.

The lion is a symbol of Hinduism—the Sun Temple at Konark, Orissa.

At the entrance to Konark, the lion of Hinduism is shown dominating over the elephant of Buddhism. Both species are threatened by extinction today.

be extremely rich in species, this became a major cause of concern in the 1970s and 1980s. However, newer concepts began to emerge. While tropical forests still had fairly extensive tracts, the wetlands of the last century were vanishing even more rapidly. The inclusion of these disappearing habitats was now emphasized as a major issue in preventing the extinction of species. Other tiny microhabitats began to be seen as important. For example, rocky outcrops and lateritic plateau tops that have highly-specialized small populations of plant life began to be appreciated as a new focus of attention for conservationists. Perceptions on conserving biodiversity are constantly evolving and new management issues continue to emerge as more and more species are lost and ecosystems are disrupted by human civilizations.

## GLOBAL BIODIVERSITY CONCERNS

Though there are over 1.8 million species in the world which are known to science, the estimated total number is likely to be between 30 to 50 million! New plants, insects and other forms of life are continually being identified. Most of these are being 'discovered' in the world's biologically species-rich areas, in tropical evergreen forests and in the coral reefs of shallow warm seas. It has been estimated that the extinction of species may be occurring at the rate of 10 to 20 thousand per year! This is said to be a thousand or even ten thousand times faster than the expected natural rate would have been if humankind had not made serious ecological changes on earth.

The loss of wild habitats due to rapid human population growth and short-sighted economic development are major contributors to the escalating pace at which global destruction of biodiversity

is occurring. Industrial pollution, over-utilization and illegal capture and trade in a variety of products are further major contributory factors. Areas rich in biodiversity and which are being seriously affected by human activity are considered 'hot spots' of biodiversity. It has been estimated that 50,000 plant species (20 per cent of the global plant life), probably occur in only 18 hot spots in the world. The three major hot spots are in South America, South-east Asia, and South Asia. Countries such as India, that have a relatively large proportion of these hot spots of diversity are referred to as mega-diversity nations. India's Western Ghats and north-eastern states are classified as globally important hot spots. To these may be added the Andaman and Nicobar Islands, as new pressures of development are likely to damage their fragile island ecosystems in the near future.

Apart from the implications for preserving genetic resources, the world now acknowledges that the loss of forest cover is a contributory factor to global climatic change. Forests are also an important mechanism for the conversion of carbon dioxide into carbon and oxygen. The loss of forest cover, coupled with the increasing release of carbon dioxide and other gases through industrialization both contribute to the greenhouse effect. Global warming is now melting icecaps, resulting in a rise in the sea level, and threatening to submerge the low-lying coastal areas in the world. There is a further danger of a runaway 'positive feedback' effect, because increased levels of atmospheric carbon dioxide could lead to increased acidity of seawater, which affects the production of marine zooplankton. These tiny creatures are, in turn, an important source of removal of carbon dioxide from the atmosphere as they use up carbon. Major disruptions in the world's weather patterns are already occurring because of global warming and are likely to increase in severity over the coming years.

Biologically-rich natural areas are now being increasingly valued. International agreements such as the World Heritage Convention attempt to protect and support bio-rich areas. India is a signatory to this convention and has included several

Protected Areas such as Manas, on the border between Bhutan and India, Kaziranga in Assam, Bharatpur in Uttar Pradesh, Nandadevi in the Himalayas, and the Sunderbans in the Ganges delta in West Bengal, as globally important World Heritage Sites. India has also signed the Convention in the Trade in Endangered Species (CITES), which is intended to reduce the utilization of endangered plants and animals by controlling trade of these species and their products. The Convention on Biological Diversity (CBD) was negotiated and signed by nations at the United Nations Conference on Environment and Development (UNCED), the Earth Summit at Rio de Janeiro, in Brazil in June 1992. In 1994, India became a party to the convention which commits the country to conserve and protect our species and natural ecosystems. However, none of these mechanisms can be implemented without the desire and will of the people to bring about an ethic of conservation.

Globally, biodiversity is now looked upon as an immensely valuable economic resource. A North-South divide on the 'ownership' of biodiversity has become a major bone of contention at the international level. Most of the world's bio-rich areas are located in the developing countries of the south. In contrast, most of the countries capable of exploiting biodiversity through biotechnological processes are the economically and technologically advanced nations in the north, with low levels of biodiversity. India's geography and economics places it in the 'South'. Its bio-resources have been developed and used by people for generations and are clearly their physical and intellectual property. Biodiversity products should thus be equated with other resources such as oil and mineral wealth. If new products are generated out of India's bio-resources, the people of India must be given their fair share of the profits.

Think globally and act locally to protect our environment.

# The Biodiversity of India

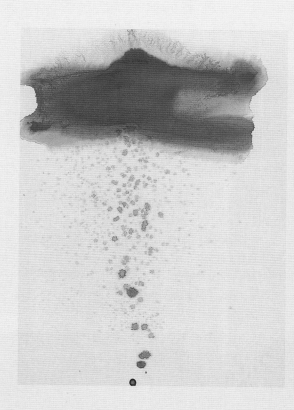

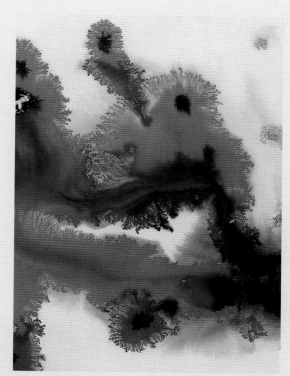

physical forces within the earth continued to fragment these two landmasses further and moved its component continents in different directions. In relation to India, Antarctica moved away southwards and Australia eastwards.

The early plants and animals of this Proto-India were common to those of Africa. But as India split away from the coast of Africa and began moving northwards, evolution on this new island of Pre-India now began to progress along divergent lines. During this movement of the subcontinent across the equator, long arid periods modified the life forms into

## EARTH'S HISTORY AND THE FORMATION OF INDIA

One hundred and eighty million years ago, India was a small part of the centre of Pangaea, earth's single super-continent. This giant continent was gradually split into two parts by the widening Tethys Sea, which separated the two large landmasses, isolating their plants and animals. From then onwards, these plants and animals evolved independently. Proto-India lay in the southern half, called Gondwanaland, sandwiched between the landmasses that now constitute Africa, Australia and the Antarctic. Immense

**Angry volcanic upheavals, splitting of continents and glaciations were formative events in the early history of the Earth. Glaciations were events that lead to many extinctions followed by the evolution of new species.**

ones rather similar to the present times. Eventually Pre-India collided against the southern coast of Asia, closing down the Tethys sea and resulting in the uplifting of the Himalayan ranges. During the period when the Himalayas had not been raised high enough to constitute a barrier between the Asian and Indian landmasses, an intermingling of plant and animal species occurred between Eurasia and India. A great period of adaptation and extinction followed, resulting in changes in the ecology of both the regions. Migration of plant and animal life from Europe and Malaysia to India occurred at this time. Since these species had evolved for climatic conditions already existing in the region, they were probably better suited to survive in the new location of India than those evolved in the Pre-Indian island, which had moved northwards into a new climatic region. The result was a gradual substitution of various native species by a new set of species. Fossils provide evidence of this great dispersal of species, with animals similar to the deer migrating into India from the West, and predators like the tiger moving southwards into the warmer climates of the Indian subcontinent, from the cold regions of central Asia. The last migration was from the Ethiopian realm, from where the lion and other forms of life adapted to arid scrublands arrived. Continued migration of animal and plant life was eventually checked by the gradual uplift of the Himalayan massif.

During the Pleistocene glacial periods, Indian plants and animals experienced several extinction spasms. The more mobile bird-life underwent changes in distribution. Due to the northerly drift of Eurasia after the breakup of Pangaea, some birds from its northern regions were forced to seasonally migrate south, to warmer climes. When India became attached to the Eurasian continent these birds probably extended their migration further southwards. As the Himalayas were formed, this pattern of migration was maintained and birds began to use corridors through the mountains to fly to their winter destinations. Within the subcontinent local

birds also had to respond to the climate change. To explain the similarity between non-migratory forest birds found now in the hill ranges of the Eastern Himalayas and the Western Ghats, separated today by several hundred kilometres of flat lands, one can only conclude that there must have once been a continuous belt of hill forests that linked them. Eventually, climatic stabilization and the development of the monsoon pattern produced ecosystems with their typical present-day fauna and flora. The large number of species of plants and animals in modern India can thus be attributed to this great mix of species, which migrated to India from the different regions in which they had evolved.

## INDIA—A MEGA-DIVERSITY NATION

A major factor that influences the high diversity of India's species of plants and animals is related to the monsoon climate, which helps create a mosaic of landscape types. The varied moisture levels, both in terms of the amount of rainfall and the length of the monsoon in different parts of the country, play a major role in producing varied patterns of diversity of species. Great physical variations, from the lofty mountainous regions in the Himalayas, to the hill ranges in the peninsula and low-lying plains, form multiple watersheds that are responsible for local variations in species diversity.

Hot spots of biodiversity which are rich in species are located in the evergreen forests of north-east India, the Western Ghats and the Andaman and Nicobar Islands. Although the many ecosystems appear structurally and functionally similar in these three regions, they are markedly different in their composition of plant and animal species. Many of their species are endemic to each of these regions.

This high ecosystem diversity is a special feature of India. In fact, some plants and animals are endemic to extremely restricted areas, or have very sparse populations distributed across large areas, and are thus rare. The bio-geographic zones in India include: the Trans-Himalayan zone in Ladakh, the Himalayas, the Thar Desert and the semi-arid lands of Rajasthan and Gujarat, the Gangetic Plains, the Western Ghats, the Deccan Plateau, the north-east of India, the coastal belts and the islands. Within each of these terrestrial zones there are diverse aquatic ecosystems, which include ponds, lakes, wetlands, streams, rivers and deltas, each with its own distinctive web of life.

India is rated as one of the 12 mega-diversity nations of the world (the others being Brazil, Colombia, Ecuador, Peru, Mexico, Zaire, Madagascar, Indonesia, Malaysia, China and Australia) (MoEF, 2002). With only 2.4 per cent of the world's land area, India accounts for 7 to 8 per cent of its recorded species. Over 46,000

The North-east—terai sal forest with its tangle of undergrowth, rich in plants.

species of plants and 81,000 species of animals have been documented in the country so far by BSI and ZSI respectively. India is an acknowledged centre of crop diversity, and harbours many wild relatives of crops and various indigenous breeds of domesticated animals. Of India's 46,000 species of plants, constituting 6.4 per cent of global plant species, about 18 per cent are endemic to the country and are found nowhere else in the world. Among the plant species, the flowering plants have a much higher degree of endemism—a third of these are not present elsewhere in the world. The Andaman and Nicobar Islands alone have 2200 flowering plants and 125 species of ferns.

India's animals include 375 species of wild mammals, a figure that ranks it eighth in the world. Out of 135 genera of land mammals in India, 85 (63 per cent) are found in the north-east. India's birdlife is also remarkably rich. Its 1200 bird species accounts for 14 per cent of the world's avifauna, and again ranks it eighth in the world, while its 453 reptile species places it fifth. Among lizards, of the 153 species, 50 per cent are endemic. A major proportion of amphibian and reptile species, especially snakes, are concentrated in the Western Ghats. Out of the total species of amphibians found in India, 62 per cent are endemic to this country. There are some 50,000 insect species in India of which 13,000 are butterflies and moths. It is estimated that the number of unknown invertebrate species could be several times higher than the one known at present. High endemism has also been recorded for various groups of insects. Several marine worms, centipedes, mayflies and fresh water sponges are also known to be endemic to India.

Countries with species' diversity rated higher than India are located in South America and South-east Asia. However, the species found in these countries are different from ours. This makes it imperative to preserve our own biodiversity as a major economic resource. Whereas few of the other developing countries that have been identified as mega-diversity nations have developed the technology to effectively utilize their own species for

The Western Ghats: The residual fragmented forests are considered to be one of the world's hot spots of biodiversity.

## Total Estimated Number of Species of Fauna in India

| Well-known taxonomic groups | No. of species in India | Share of India in the World (per cent) |
| --- | --- | --- |
| Protista | 2577 | 8.24 |
| Molluscs | 5070 | 7.62 |
| Crustacea | 2934 | 8.26 |
| Insects | 59353 | 6.83 |
| Arachnida | 5818 | 7.9 |
| Pisces | 2546 | 11.72 |
| Amphibia | 216 | 5.07 |
| Reptilian | 495 | 8.5 |
| Aves | 1225 | 13.66 |
| Mammalia | 390 | 8.42 |

Adapted from MoEF, 2002; Alfred et al, 1998; Das, 2001; BNHS, 2002; Silbley and Monroe, 1993.

The Andamans: One of the hundreds of tiny islands that are rich in endemic species.

genetic engineering; India has the same capability. Another major mega-diversity country with a similar technological capability is Brazil, which is extremely species-rich. It is not surprising that these two countries took strong and similar stands at the UNCED in Rio, impressing upon the world that biodiversity could not be freely exploited by technologically advanced nations for their own economic growth, at the cost of economically poor nations that are rich in biodiversity.

## Animal Endemism in India

- Hot spots: of 135 genera, 85 (63 per cent) are found in northeastern India (WCMC 1988).
- Mammals have a relatively low level of endemism in India.
- Birds have a relatively high level of endemism.
- Reptiles include 50 per cent of the endemic lizards.
- Amphibia have a very high level of endemism, as 62 per cent are endemic, mostly to the Western Ghats.
- Marine sediment worms, freshwater sponges, mayflies and centipedes have high levels of endemism.

## Plant Endemism in India

| Hot spots | North-eastern India, Western Ghats, Andaman and Nicobar Islands (WCMC 1988). |
|---|---|
| Plant endemism | 18 per cent of all plants are endemic to India (BSI). 33 per cent of Indian endemic species are flowering plants. |
| Western Ghats | 1500 plant species of the Western Ghats are endemic to India (WCMC 1988). |
| North-eastern Himalayas | 2000 plant species of the north-east are endemic to India (WCMC 1988). |

## THE THREAT OF EXTINCTION

India's explosive population growth, the concomitant need to convert wildlands to other uses and the rapid increase in the utilization levels of natural resources—forests, grasslands, wetlands and marine ecosystems—are rapidly eroding the biodiversity. The result is a loss of this great source of potential wealth. A lack of awareness regarding the value of biodiversity is responsible for policies that support short-term gains, but lead to long-term ecological and economic losses at every level. The policy-maker seldom has any knowledge of the potential wealth found in our biodiversity, and administrators who may be aware of its value often do not know of the existing legal instruments available to protect it.

The real rate at which the extinction of species is occurring at a national level remains obscure. With our wilderness areas shrinking as they are, it is likely to be extremely high. The rate of deforestation and fragmentation, as well as the degradation of other natural ecosystems, far exceed our capability to identify economically valuable species; they will forever remain unknown to science. Over the next decade, many of these unidentified species will become extinct unnoticed and will remain unnamed and unutilized.

India's forestland is said to cover 75 million hectares or 23 per cent of the total landmass. Only half of this, however, has a canopy covering more than 40 per cent of the ground. A large proportion is covered by plantations or secondary forests that have re-grown after the felling of the

Monoculture sal plantation forests threaten biodiversity.

original, natural forests. A major threat is conversion of natural forests to other forms of land-use such as agriculture, timber plantations and tea and coffee plantations. Collecting wood for fuel, burning hill-slopes for grass production and overgrazing by cattle degrade our forests. Even more significantly, development projects like mining and irrigation make things worse. Urbanization and industrialization are major factors responsible for the loss of our forest wealth. Grasslands—converted from grazing lands to intensive agricultural areas—are beginning to vanish. Current development by draining wetlands followed by industrialization is rapidly destroying the biodiversity of the neighbouring, terrestrial and aquatic ecosystems. Their species are rapidly disappearing through human interventions.

While the threat to both wild flora and fauna is primarily due to the high levels of human pressure on the habitat of these species, threats to some of our animals and plants arise from illegal trade. Tiger skin and bones for Chinese medicines, ivory from elephants for artefacts and jewellery, horns from rhinos, believed to have medicinal value and the perfume-base from the musk deer, are all extensively used abroad. Coral and shells are widely collected for export from the Andaman and Nicobar Islands. A variety of wild plants with real or dubious medicinal value are being over-harvested, mainly from the Himalayas. Many of these species are likely to become extinct in the near future due to these unprecedented human impacts.

We still do not fully appreciate the consequences of the extinction of species. Its effects on the world could be far worse than anticipated at present. As our lifestyles lead to climatic changes through global warming, many species are threatened. Coral reefs are already affected. Many species must move northwards due to the increase in the global warming. But with their natural habitats fragmented by human activities, many species will have no option but to slowly disappear from the face of the earth. Are we justified in standing by while this happens?

Human beings have modified extensively the natural ecosystems in their effort to set up systems that will make life more comfortable. The depletion of

Industrialization threatens both terrestrial and aquatic ecosystems by pollution.

The Biodiversity of India **47**

Large areas of natural forests have been replaced with tea plantations.

Urbanization has led to an enormous loss of forest wealth.

biodiversity in forests has resulted from the extensive clearing of natural forests for timber production. Cleared areas have been reforested using a single timber-yielding species, and more recently, by introducing monocultures of exotic species imported from other countries. Such plantations do not support the same biological diversity as a multistoried natural forest, which has a closed canopy and a rich under-storey of several layers of vegetation. Many insects, amphibia, reptiles, birds and mammals of natural forests cannot survive in such plantations. Here, only the more adaptable species survive, and they too cannot survive without an appreciable number of the linked species. The collection of firewood opens up the forest canopy, changing its ecological characteristics, and foraging herds of cattle and goats trample seedlings underfoot, with a consequent fall in the diversity of the species of plants.

Another factor that disrupts forest biodiversity is the accidental introduction of exotic weeds that are not a part of the natural vegetation. Common examples in India are the *Lantana* bushes, *Eupatorium* shrubs and *Parthenium* or congress grass. These have been imported into the country and have invaded several large tracts of our natural forests, spreading at the expense of the diverse range of local undergrowth species. The impact on the species of insects, birds and other wildlife dependent on the natural vegetation is likely to be serious.

## IMPORTANCE OF BIODIVERSITY IN MAN-MODIFIED SYSTEMS

Natural ecosystems have been modified by human beings for intensive use to set up agricultural, urban and industrial areas. Traditional agricultural systems permitted a wide variety of crops to be grown and used by the farmer, and also increased his ability to market products throughout the year. Planting mixed crops was an insurance against the failure of one of the crops. As farmers began to gain added economic incentives by growing cash crops for national or international markets rather than by supplying the local needs of the area, the trend shifted towards the cultivation of a single cash crop such as sugarcane. This has resulted in a reduction in the diversity of crops. Many of our traditionally grown crop varieties have disappeared in the course of the last few decades. A few survive in areas where development and modern agricultural strategies have not yet penetrated remote areas. New varieties are being produced from the germplasm of these original varieties. If the traditional varieties vanish, it will be difficult to continue to develop new crops with better yield or disease resistance. The preservation of adequate levels of natural and domestic biodiversity is important because it is a source of genetic material that can be used for biological control of pests in agriculture. Biological control reduces the need for large amounts of chemical pesticides injurious to human health.

In the past, domestic animals were selected and bred for their ability to adapt to local conditions. These traditional breeds must be maintained for their genetic variability as it is impossible to predict which of these will be of use in the future for the improvement of the domestic livestock. The overall preservation of biodiversity must include varieties already existing in crops as well as domestic animals developed over several centuries.

## LOSS OF DIVERSITY OF CULTIVARS AND DOMESTIC LIVESTOCK

While modern agriculture has dramatically improved crop yields and farm produce, it has drastically changed the economic scenario in rural areas, affecting the very foundations of agriculture. The loss of genetic diversity has reduced the ability of the farmer to develop his own varieties that are specially suited to the local climatic and soil conditions. Some understanding of ethno-botany as well as of the importance of domestic breeds of animals is necessary if our native varieties are not to vanish entirely. The traditional cultivars, which included for instance

A powerful Bhutia sheepdog is one example of the many indigenous Indian breeds.

30,000 to 50,000 varieties of rice and a very large number of cereals, vegetables and fruit, are now under threat. The highest diversity of cultivars is concentrated in the high rainfall areas of the Western and Eastern Ghats, Northern Himalayas and the north-eastern hills. Though gene-banks have collected over 34,000 cereals and 22,000 pulses, this cannot be expected to cover all the existing varieties. Several are likely to disappear in the near future.

One of the many varieties of wild rice found in India, from which 30 to 50,000 cultivated varieties have been derived.

The Nandi bull is one of 27 indigenous breeds of Indian cattle.

Several varieties of wild fruits, seeds and other products are used in traditional medicine, but have yet to be fully researched by science.

The diversity of fruit collected from wild sources is an important but unexplored aspect of genetic resources for horticulture.

India has 27 indigenous breeds of cattle, 40 breeds of sheep, 22 breeds of goats and 8 breeds of buffaloes. We also had breeds of horses for special purposes, many of which have disappeared. Hybridization for larger yields of milk has led to the loss of certain domestic varieties of cattle.

## LINKAGES OF CULTURAL DIVERSITY AND BIODIVERSITY

In India people have, over many generations, preserved nature through local traditions. We have in our country a large number of sacred groves. These forests around ancient shrines or temples act as gene banks of wild plants. Symbols based on our wildlife like the lion of Hinduism, the elephant of Buddhism and deities such as Ganesh have been venerated for thousands of years. The sacred tulsi has been placed at out doorstep for centuries. Traditional Ayurvedic medicine is based on wild plants and animal products. Yet

this biological diversity on which all our resources are dependent is now being destroyed for short-term gains, by a society which is mulitplying beyong the carrying capacity of Nature. The sustainable utilzation of biodiversity must become an important part of human development to secure our future. Biological resources though considered 'renewable' cannot be expected to support human utilization beyond a critical limit. There cannot be . a better reason to protect biodivoersity.

A decrease in genetic diversity occures when individuals of a species are reduced below a minimum viable number. Reducing the population of a species below a critical level affects breeding, which can eventually result in extinction. There is a minimum viable population of breeding pairs that is essential to maintain the genetic differences between individuals. Below this level inbreeding occurs creating a situation in which breeding success is lowered.

Loss of species diversity occurs due to the destruction of natural habitats that are essential for the survival of species

in an area. Human impacts on natural environments are related to changes in land-use patterns. The rapid rise of human numbers and the growth of industry have led to a dramatic fall in biological diversity during the last few decades which continues unchecked.

Natural forests are being increasingly converted to agriculture, urban and industrial tracts. These changes in land-use have perhaps led to the most serious losses of biological diversity. Natural wetland systems have been established croplands, resulting in loss of this incredible habitat and its aquatic species. Grasslands that were once sutainable used by a relatively smaller number of livestock have either been changed to other forms of land use or degraded by overgrazing.

A variety of factors have led to a depletion of biodiversity in forests. A major factor that culminates in loss of biodiversity is clearing of natural forests for timber production. During forestry activities, cleared areas have been reforested using a simple timber yielding species and, more recently, by introducing monocultures of exotic species. Such plantations do not support the same biological diversity as a multistoried natural forest that has a closed canopy and a rich understorey of vegetation. Many insects, amphibians, reptiles, birds and mammals of natural forests are specialists. In plantations only the more adaptable generalist species survive. Certain mammals, especially carnivores such as tigers and birds of prey are at the apex of the food pyramid in the forest and cannot survive without an adequate abundance of prey.

Human impact due to the collection of firewood opens up the forest canopy and foraging cattle retard the regeneration of seedlings that are trampled. This prevents the regeneration of the less robust plant species with the consequent fall in the species diversity of plants.

## PRESERVING INDIA'S BIODIVERSITY

A high level of naturalness for a particular area is an indicator of a healthy ecosystem. The three levels of biodiversity—of genes, species and ecosystems—are closely linked to each other. Genetic diversity is necessary to maintain the diversity of the species, because a reduction in genetic differences among individuals eventually leads to the extinction of the species, and thus reduces their diversity. The diversity of species is in turn responsible for an intact ecosystem. Changes caused in an ecosystem by human activities can degrade landscapes to a level in which the more sensitive species cannot survive. Thus the disturbed ecosystem develops widening ripples in its population structure, leading to a loss of naturalness, and finally to the extinction of its closely interlinked species. The loss of keystone species, which are linked to many other species of the food chain, affects an ecosystem most drastically. Species such as ficus trees are linked to a number of insects, like wasps which pollinate them, and frugivorous birds and animals, such as rodents, monkeys and bats that feed extensively on them. As the ficus trees fruit all year round, they are linked with food chains in all seasons, quite unlike most trees that fruit only during a brief season. When such keystone

species are destroyed, a major breakdown of the web of life is the end result. Unlike the spider that can rebuild its web, humankind does not know how to repair the shattered web of life of an ecosystem or how to recreate its extinct species.

Biodiversity can only be preserved as a valuable resource if wilderness areas having a high level of naturalness are identified and protected. Although there are now nearly 600 National Parks and Wildlife Sanctuaries in India, this amounts to only 4 or 5 per cent of its total landmass classified as Protected Areas (MoEF, 2002). The amount of land that has been set aside is far below the norms established in the rest of the world to preserve this great economic asset. The International Union for the Conservation of Nature and Natural Resources (IUCN) had stipulated that at least 5 per cent of every ecosystem must be protected. For Ecologically Sensitive Areas it was expected that this should be at least 10 per cent. In the recent past, discussions among experts suggest that this is insufficient to protect all biodiversity. Additional strategies to protect biodiversity must go beyond creating patches of National Parks or Wildlife Sanctuaries. We thus need to look for new, people-centred ways of supporting biodiversity conservation. This can be done by identifying community conservation areas. Some of these could be located in ancient sacred groves which have been protected through religious sentiment.

We thus require more Protected Areas to be established as an Integrated Protected Area System (IPAS) to represent all the ecologically different landscapes found in the country. These areas are not to be protected merely for their aesthetic value or their tourist potential, but as a resource for our economic development. Wild gene pools, preserved for purposes of genetic engineering, will produce better food crops and industrial raw material. However, the need to provide more land for agricultural and industrial development clashes with the interests of the wilderness. Under these circumstances, it is necessary to identify the remaining residual patches of unprotected wilderness for the creation of new Protected Areas, especially those areas with high levels of species-richness, a high portion of endemic species not found elsewhere, or

endangered plants and animals. The north-east and the Andamans are key areas in this respect. To achieve this, an inventory of the species in wilderness ecosystems must be made and studied. Without a database of the diversity of living organisms, sustainable development and the maintenance of biologically rich areas cannot be planned on a rational basis.

While National Parks and Sanctuaries in India were formerly meant to save major wildlife species such as tigers, lions, elephants and deer, the objective is now also linked to the preservation of relatively intact natural ecosystems, where biological diversity—ranging from microscopic unicellular species and the lesser known plants and animals, to giant trees and large animals—can all be preserved. Much of the natural wilderness has already undergone extensive changes. The land in our Protected Areas includes plantations of sal, teak, or other timber species, which are often relatively poor in diversity, and have a low level of naturalness. Man-made water bodies in the backwaters of hydel or irrigation dams have been included in sanctuaries, and these frequently have little significance for conserving an undisturbed aquatic ecosystem. Overgrazed wasteland in areas that were once flourishing grasslands have also been notified as Protected Areas. Most of these areas have low biological value and need careful management to help revert them to a more natural state.

The majority of India's Protected Areas have a number of settlements both on their fringes and within their boundaries, which provide local people with wood as fuel for cooking and fodder for cattle. This represents a clash between resource-use and biodiversity conservation. Good planning and management of these Protected Areas can reduce this conflict, but this requires more funds, more expertise and more manpower. Eco-development schemes provide a sustainable source of resources for local people living in and around Protected Areas. If a National Park curtails its traditional grazing land and fuel-wood sources, these must be provided by developing the lands in surrounding buffer areas. A carefully designed plan for each Protected Area must incorporate an eco-development component aimed at providing alternative sources of fuel-wood, fodder and income generation, which is an important aspect of the management of these Protected Areas.

The Integrated Protected Area System in India, as well as development of state-level networks of Protected Areas, need to be strengthened so as to ensure adequate representation of all bio-geographic zones. These must further include a network of other Multiple-Use Areas that constitute a second line of reserves to protect all natural ecosystems within them. Each state must develop its own Integrated Protected Area System, which gives a relatively greater importance to those ecosystems found only within the state. They must emphasize the protection of areas that have high levels of biodiversity, those with a large number of distinctive endemic or endangered species, and those ecosystems that are highly fragile or sensitive to human interference.

While biodiversity conservation is an important aspect of land-use planning and management, the management of ecosystems is still a concept rather than a set of well-defined techniques. The success stories, such as the preservation of the Silent Valley or public support for Project Tiger, have been initiated by a handful of amateur naturalists, even fewer scientists and very few sensitive bureaucrats. Historically, it has been done through the 'elitist' naturalists lobbying with the Government at the policy level and putting pressure on officials to initiate actions on crucial environmental issues. Perhaps the largest number of conservation gains was made when Indira Gandhi was Prime Minister. She was influenced by individuals such as Dr Salim Ali, MS Swaminathan, Anil Agarwal, Madhav Gadgil and others, and a number of conservation success stories were due to her direct intervention. In India, conservation as ethics has not had a broad foundation based on an educated and sensitive public, nor has it grown out of a grassroots movement. Recent developments have shown that an elitist approach cannot lead to sustained action in the long term. In the West the conservation movement has grown over several decades and is linked to high levels of literacy, increasing leisure, the growth of outdoor activities at school level and an integration of conservation awareness within school and college curricula. The battles between the diverse interests of farmers, livestock owners and land developers on the one hand and conservation groups on the other in the western world have not been fought by a small number of individuals, but supported by an increasingly aware public. This is lacking in India. Unless there is a general awareness at a local level, vested interests will continue to erode our biological wealth.

The principles and goals of ecosystem management include ecologically and socially defined aims and resource-management objectives. This can only be achieved through local support. Management must use a holistic approach that stresses the conservation of genes, species and ecosystems and initiates a dialogue between users, scientists, conservationists, bureaucrats and policy-makers. Only then can we ensure that the poor farmer or fisherman is not made to pay the price of conservation.

While conservation has international and national and regional concerns, it will fail without the support of local people. Where the larger interests of humanity are in opposition to those of local communities, the latter must be compensated if they are deprived of access to their local resource base. Ecosystem management and restoration techniques at the ground level are still experimental. The difference in management strategy for eco-restoration, which is based on the conservation needs of biodiversity, and eco-development, which aims at supporting people's resources, is still not clearly defined. Though they are based on the science and principles of ecology, their management has to be done in a social context. Society as a whole, once aware of such polarized issues, must dictate how ecosystem resources should be managed to protect and preserve biological diversity.

# The Nature of the Indian Wilderness

Wetlands are one of the world's most threatened ecosystems.

A giant liana twisting through the forest floor.

The Indian wilderness conjures up different images for different kinds of people. There are those who nostalgically recall its past glory in the days of shikar and describe the jungles that were teeming with wildlife. And those who recall the excitement or exhaustion of long hours of trekking under the hot sun, or drenched in torrents of rain, or the biting cold of the high snows. Some are perturbed that the wilderness is rapidly shrinking, and are concerned about the changes modern development has wrought on its integrity. Others see it as something to be used for economic development.

While most of us can appreciate the obvious differences in the nature of its various landscapes, a deep realization of its ecological complexity and uniqueness takes years of exposure to many different types of landforms. Information alone is insufficient to appreciate its variety. It is only when scientific facts are coupled with real-life experiences in nature that it leads to a deeper appreciation of nature's immensity and grandeur. And with this growing sense of its great value to humankind, comes an increasing concern for its integrity.

Classifying landscapes can be made at several levels. A bio-geographic zone has an overall homogenous ecology such as the Himalayan zone or the Thar Desert. This is divided into smaller biotic provinces. Within these there are landforms, specific hill ranges or water bodies. There are many distinctive ecological units that form an ecosystem.

All living organisms interact with each other and with their non-living environment at different points in time and at different places in an ecosystem. At the global level, this forms the earth's biosphere. At the sub-global level, this is divided into bio-geographical realms. These include Eurasia—the Palaearctic realm; South and South-east Asia (of which India forms a major part)—the Oriental realm; North America—the Neotropical realm; Africa—the Ethiopian realm; and Australia—the Australian realm.

## ECOSYSTEMS

An ecosystem is an area with a distinctive topography, soil and climate which forms the habitat for a variety of plants and animals which together forms a typical community of species that are specific to the area.

Ecosystems are divided into terrestrial land based ecosystems and aquatic, or ecosystems in water. These form the two major habitat conditions for the living organisms on earth.

Natural terrestrial ecosystems include landforms such as the forests, grasslands, semi-arid areas, deserts, coastal areas and aquatic ecosystems such as ponds, rivers, lakes in freshwater and the sea. Man-modified ecosystems include agricultural land and urban or industrial land-use categories. Thus, any landscape can have a single ecosystem or several different types forming a mosaic.

The nature of an ecosystem is based on its geographical features such as hills, mountains, plains, rivers, lakes, coastal areas or islands. It is also influenced by climatic conditions like the amount of sunlight, temperature and rainfall. A third factor is the characteristics of its soil. These geographical, climatic and soil characteristics form its non-living or abiotic component. The living part of an ecosystem which includes all its organisms, microbes, plants and animals is referred to as its biotic component.

India includes several distinctive, easily recognizable regions. The Himalayas, the Gangetic Plains, the highlands of central India, the Western and Eastern Ghats, the semi-arid desert in the west, the Deccan Plateau, the coastal belts and the Andaman and Nicobar Islands are examples of its major distinctive regions.

At an even more local level, each area has several structurally and functionally identifiable ecosystems such as forests, grasslands, river catchments, mangrove swamps, seashores, islands, etc. There

The word 'ecosystem' was derived from the term 'ecology' used in 1866 by a German zoologist, Ernst Haeckel. He derived the word, 'Okologie' from the Greek term, 'oikos', which means a 'house or a dwelling' and 'logia', thus meaning a study of habitation. Hackel worked on evolution and life processes. The term 'ecosystem' however, began to be used more extensively only around 1935 when it was first introduced by the ecologist Tansley. It now finds its place even in newsprint and the common people's language. Tansley used the word to refer to communities of plants, animals, other organisms and the physical environment of any given place. The term is now widely used, particularly in the context of environmental planning, to refer to broad biological communities of similar appearance, usually defined by physical, climatic, structural or phenological features. Ecosystem diversity is generally understood to refer to the range of different kinds of ecosystems, within a defined area.

are also microhabitats with their own components of species like a patch of a few trees, a pond or a *nala* course. Even a log of dead wood or a fig of a ficus tree has many different insects within it that can be thought of as a distinctive microhabitat. As each species of plant or animal has specific habitat needs its place in the environment has been referred to as its niche.

Each ecosystem consists of communities of living organisms that are closely linked with each other through multiple food chains that form a complex web of life.

The number of species known to science in the world that form these complex communities of life is now estimated to include around 1.8 million species. The enormous diversity of life on earth, of which a great proportion is yet to be discovered, is essential for humankind's own survival. Man is but a single cog in the wheel of nature. If he continues to disturb nature, the wheel will eventually grind to a halt.

Niche: In 1917, Joseph Grinnell created a concept that was revolutionary in ecology. He coined the use of the word 'niche'. He adopted it from the word used to depict a 'shallow recess on a wall' used in French. It began to be used commonly in a specific biological sense after 1927.

## THE STRUCTURE OF AN ECOSYSTEM

The structure of an ecosystem is related to its type. Forest, grassland, wetland, agricultural areas, industrial areas, etc. which have their own distinctive components, are formed by a combination of abiotic and biotic aspects of nature. Some ecosystems are fairly robust and are less affected by a moderate level of human disturbance. Others are highly fragile and are quickly and completely destroyed by human activities. Mountain ecosystems are extremely fragile, as the degradation of the forest cover leads to severe erosion of the soil and landslides, resulting in changes in river courses in the valleys. This can devastate villages through mounds of debris and flooding when the eroded material gives way. Island ecosystems are easily affected by different forms of human activity which can lead to the rapid extinction of several of their unique species of plants and animals.

River and wetland ecosystems can be seriously affected by pollution and by changes in surrounding land-use.

Evergreen forests and coral reefs, which are exceptionally rich in species, are highly fragile ecosystems. All these ecosystems must be protected against a variety of human activities that could

| The Components of an Ecosystem | | |
|---|---|---|
| **Abiotic components** | | |
| Climatic regime—latitude, altitude, temperature, moisture, light and topography. | | |
| Geological patterns—soil structure and composition. | | |
| Organic compounds—proteins, carbohydrates, and lipids. | | |
| **Biotic components** | | |
| Producers—plants. | | |
| Macro consumers—phagotrophs: animals. | | |
| Micro consumers—saprotrophs (absorbers), fungi, soil animals. | | |

lead to their degradation, by creating a network of Protected Areas that are located in either National Parks or Sanctuaries.

The living organisms of an ecosystem are inseparable from their habitat. The non-living components include the inorganic substances, organic compounds and the local climatic conditions, which depend on the geographical location, the amount of sunlight and the amount of rainfall, as well as the local geological nature of the soil.

The species that constitute the living component range from microscopic bacteria, which live in air, water and soil; the algae which live in fresh and salt water; to large terrestrial plants like grasses and herbs that grow after the monsoon every year; or the giant long-lived trees of the forest. Plants directly convert energy from sunlight into tissues for their growth and use this for the functions that support their lives. The plants act as the producers in the ecosystem which provides food for herbivorous animals in the ecosystem. The process by which plants produce their own tissues for growth and living processes is known as photosynthesis. This involves the conversion of sunlight into plant carbohydrates. Photosynthesis thus forms the bases of all the food chains in every ecosystem.

The animal life in the living or biotic component of the ecosystem ranges from micro-fauna, to small insects and the larger taxa such as fish, amphibia, reptiles, birds and mammals.

Human beings that developed early civilizations have been part of our living planet for only 2 or 3 million years, a short time-span in the earth's history which stretches over 4.5 billion years.

And yet this single species has learned not only to dominate the earth but to misuse and over-utilize all its resources. It is strange that evolution has produced only one animal species that has created great changes in the earth's biosphere by its actions. No other animal has been as unkind to the earth as mankind!

The **herbivorous animals**, which depend on plant life for their survival, are called **primary consumers**. They include insects, birds and mammals such as hare, deer and elephants in the forest. In grasslands there are antelopes like the blackbuck which feed on grass. In semi-arid areas, the *chinkara* or Indian gazelle is adapted to this ecosystem. In the seas, there are molluscs, fish and other forms of life that feed on algae and plants. Human beings and their domestic life forms are primary consumers of man-modified ecosystems such as agriculture, pastoral and even urban centers.

**Secondary consumers** or predators live on other animals. These carnivores include species such as tigers and leopards, jackals and jungle cats in the forest, wolves and foxes in grasslands, and predatory fish like sharks in the oceans. Non-vegetarian people are also secondary consumers along with their pet dogs and cats.

All the component organisms of an ecosystem are dependent on other organisms. This forms different groups of species that form **trophic levels** that are based on their food and feeding behaviour within the ecosystem. The trophic levels are related to the food chains which determine the dependence of a species that live by feeding on plant life or on other animals.

Some organisms live only on dead organic material and inorganic matter and

are known as **decomposers or detrivores**. These include bacteria, fungi as well as several species of insects and worms. Decomposition is a vital component of nature, as without this process, nutrients would be tied up in dead matter and would not be recycled into nutrition that plant life can absorb for their growth.

All organisms are classified into two trophic levels. **Autotrophic**, or those which convert simple inorganic substances into complex substances with the help of sunlight as in plants, and **heterotrophic**, or those which utilize and breakdown complex substances into simpler substances, as in animals. These form the two great '**Kingdoms**' of plants and animals that constitute life on earth.

Attributed to

**Chief Seattle
Chief of the Ogwamish**

Whatever befalls the earth,
Befalls the sons of the earth.
If men spit upon the ground,
They spit upon themselves.
This we know.
The earth does not belong to man,
Man belongs to the earth.
This we know.
All things are connected.
Man did not weave the web of life
He is merely a strand in it.
Whatever he does to the web,
He does to himself.

## THE FUNCTIONS OF AN ECOSYSTEM

An ecosystem functions through several cycles in nature, through its complex energy-transfer mechanisms in its food chains and its food web. The web of life is a complex system which is unique to different regions on which man is completely dependent. If its component species are disrupted, the fragile web of life begins to collapse, destroying man's ability to continue to live on earth in the long-term.

The energy from the sun is taken up by plants and moves through a series of three or four organisms in a food chain. At each transfer of energy, a large proportion is lost in the form of heat. These food chains are not isolated sequences, but have multiple interconnections with each other. This interlocking pattern forms a typical food web. Hence green plants occupy the first trophic or food chain level, herbivores the second, carnivores the third and secondary carnivores the fourth level. Thus each food chain can only have three or four direct linkages. But each species can form a link in innumerable food chains. The three trophic levels together form a food pyramid with a wide base of plants, less herbivores and only a few carnivores. At each level an organism spends energy derived from its food for its day-to-day activities. This includes moving about to find food, looking after their young and finding mates. Even breathing and digesting food needs energy.

**Food chains:** In nature, energy must pass from the sun and then from one living organism to another. When herbivorous animals feed on plants, the sun's energy is transferred from plants to animals. This is done by plants through photosynthesis, a chemical process that converts light energy into matter. As this matter has life, it is called biomass. In an ecosystem, carnivorous animals feed on herbivores. The herbivores feed on plant life. Some animals, however, feed on dead organic matter. The latter form the detritus in a food chain. At each linkage in the chain, a major part of the energy from the food is lost for daily activities. Humankind depends on these intact food chains.

**Food webs:** In an ecosystem there are a very large number of interlinked chains. This forms a food web. If the linkages in the chains that make up the web of life are disrupted due to human activities this eventually results in extinction of species, the web breaks down. Thus our daily activities and livelihood is jeopardized.

**Food pyramids:** In an ecosystem, green plants are called producers, as they utilize energy directly from sunlight and convert it into matter. A large number of these organisms form the most basic, or the first trophic level of a food pyramid. The herbivorous animals that eat plants are on the second trophic level and are called primary consumers. The biomass of herbivores is less than the producer level as much of the energy they derive from plants they feed on is lost during the daily activities of the herbivores. This includes energy used for moving about from place to place, during respiration, for digesting food, for breeding and bringing up the young and in fact all activities performed during their lives. The predators that feed on them form the third trophic level and are known as secondary consumers. Only a few animals can form the third trophic level consisting of carnivores at the apex of the food pyramid. They also use up energy for their daily activities. Thus energy, which is used by all living creatures, flows through the ecosystem from the base of the food pyramid to the apex. Much of the energy which is used up in activities of each living organism goes back into the non-living part of the ecosystem from faeces that animals defecate, or is returned to the soil when plants and animals die.

Only a part of this energy thus passes upwards to support the food pyramid.

## TYPES OF ECOSYSTEMS

Ecosystems are broadly divided into terrestrial or land based ecosystems and aquatic ecosystems in water. These two form the major habitat conditions for all living organisms on earth.

**Terrestrial Ecosystems**
Forest
Grassland
Semi-arid areas
Deserts
Mountains
Islands

**Aquatic Ecosystems**
Pond
Lake
Wetland
River
Delta
Marine

### TERRESTRIAL ECOSYSTEMS

These ecosystems include different types of habitats such as forests, grasslands, semi-arid areas, deserts and seacoasts. Man-modified terrestrial ecosystems include agricultural and pastoral land-use categories and more intensively modified urban and industrial centres. Although these man-modified land-use types have increased the production of food and provide the raw material

for consumer goods that we use more and more today, this unsustainable use of environmental resources such as soil, water, fuel-wood, timber, fodder, medicinal plants, etc. has led to a serious degradation of our environment. Overuse and misuse of resources through a variety of human activities destroys the services and processes of nature such as photosynthesis, disrupts local climate control and increases soil erosion. As human population grows, what was once a sustainable use of resources has now become increasingly unsustainable. Industrial development has led to a great increase in the consumption of resources resulting in unsustainable resource-use through deforestation water shortages; air, water and soil pollution; problems due to waste material disposal, all of which seriously affect human well being.

### FOREST ECOSYSTEMS

There have been several classifications developed to categorize forest patterns in India. The most frequently used classification is based on a combination of the temperature and humidity levels that give rise to a specific forest type. Some of the more recent classifications have a botanical basis related to the dominant tree species. Others have stressed on the need to classify forests on an ecological basis, which takes into consideration its dominant species as well as the nature of the habitat. Even more recent classifications take into account the plants, animals, the geographical situation, climatic conditions and human-induced biotic factors, which together constitute a bio-geographical basis for their differentiation. Other classifications are focused on the physiognomy or structure of the forest, which is based on its appearance. This includes terms such as 'broad-leaved evergreen' forest, 'deciduous' forest, 'thorn' forest, etc.

Forests are formed by a community of plants that grow in a particular region. Their character is predominantly defined by its trees, shrubs, climbers and ground cover. The most natural, undisturbed forests are located mainly in our National Parks and Wildlife Sanctuaries. Each forest type is distinct from the others and its typical plant species form the habitat for a specific community of animals that are adapted to live there. The type of forest depends on the abiotic characteristics of the site. For example, forests on higher elevations of a mountainous region differ in their species' composition from those along the lower river valleys. In a particular region, the higher slopes may have coniferous forests while lower foothills could be covered with sal forests.

The amount of rainfall, temperature and soil characteristics determines the forest type. The plant and animal species thus form communities specific to a forest type. Mangrove vegetation, for example, occurs in river deltas where the water is brackish and thorn forest trees grow in arid areas. The snow leopard is endemic to the Himalayas while mammals like the tiger and leopard are found in forests all over the rest of India. Many bird species in the Himalayas are unique to the mountains and do not occur in the rest of India.

The forest ecosystems are structurally organized into several levels, from the ground to the canopy. There are animals that use the canopy, some use the branches, and others live mainly at the trunk level. A different group of animals are found in the shrub layer. Still others use the undergrowth or live in the ground cover, among the grasses and herbs on the forest floor. The ground is covered with leaf litter in which there are millions of insects and masses of fungi and bacteria. These form an important part of the nutrient cycle of the forest. Insects, beetles and worms break down the dead material in the detritus into small fragments and the fungi and bacteria act on this humus to convert it into simple compounds that plants can absorb through their root systems.

Processes such as pollination link plant species with specific insect or bird species. Fruit-bearing trees are linked in the ecosystem to frugivorous birds and animals, which disperse their seeds. Several tree species are dependent on species of fungi that live on their roots for mutual benefit. Forest ecosystems thus consist of thousands of interlinked species that are found in the web of life of the forest and constitute its biological diversity.

Complex interactions that constantly occur between the plant and animal species in any natural forest system are responsible for the integrity of its food chains and food pyramid. The energy cycle drives the ecosystem through physical, chemical and biological processes. The sun provides energy for the growth of plants, that are consumed by herbivorous animals, which in turn become a source of food for carnivores at the apex of the food pyramid. The nature of these complex processes

of life is specific to each forest type. The processes of nature that maintain the cycles of life are as diverse as the ecosystems themselves. For example evergreen forest trees shed a few of their leaves throughout the year to form a thick moist layer of humus, while in a deciduous forest all the dry leaves are shed at the same time. The detritus cycle thus varies and is linked to the periods when the leaves form nutrients.

## FOREST TYPES BASED ON TREE SPECIES

There are 16 major forest types in India, according to studies by Champion and Seth (1968) and they are classified on the basis of their dominant tree species. This gives importance to the three or four most common tree species within them. Broadly it can be said that the most common tree species in several forest types of north-east India is sal, whereas in the south-western peninsula the most frequently encountered tree is teak. In the north, the Himalayas have coniferous forests with pine and fir, or broad-leaved trees such as rhododendron and oak. The forests of Western India and the Deccan are thorn forests, which have *Acacia* as a major dominant species. The forest of the Western Ghats, north-eastern India and the Andaman and Nicobar Islands are areas in which most of the trees are evergreen.

The forest structure consists of groundcover, the shrub layer, epiphytes and climbers at trunk level, and the canopy cover.

The belt of mixed forest, between sal and teak, near Panchmari is a unique forest type.

## Major Forest Types of India

The first rays of the sun over a coniferous forest in a Himalayan valley.

Tall stately conifers of the Himalayan forests hold the fragile soil on its steep slopes.

Oak trees in the broad-leaved forests of the Himalayan foothills.

Sal forest in Madhya Pradesh.

| 1 |
| 2 |
| 3 |

Dry deciduous forests change seasonally, from leafless to thick canopy cover, creating cyclic changes in the ecosystem.

A thorn forest in Rajasthan which has been heavily browsed by wildlife and cattle.

Evergreen forests of the Western Ghats form one of the most species-rich forests in the world.

Rhododendron forests in the Himalayan foothills.

Coniferous forests of the Himalayas.

In India, forests can be broadly classified into coniferous and broad-leaved forests. They can also be classified according to the nature of the tree species found there, viz. evergreen, deciduous, xerophytic or thorn trees, and mangrove plants that live in saline environments. Another classification method is according to the most abundant tree species such as sal or teak forests, where these species are said to be dominants.

A forest classification that is based on ecological considerations and the dominant common or distinctive species has been developed by GS Puri (Puri et al, 1983). This holistic classification describes about 29 distinctive types that range from the most arid thorn forests, to the high rainfall evergreen forms.

While these different forest types are based on important tree species, several of them also have characteristic types of open grass covered areas or degraded vegetation depending on the level of human pressure. Such open areas are frequently of biological value as they form a different habitat type for several plant and animal species.

**The Himalayas** have two major types of forests, coniferous and the broad-leaved types. The coniferous trees, such as pine and deodar, have needle-shaped leaves and are usually located at a high altitude. Some forests in which species such as oak (*Quercus*), or rhododendron are dominant are referred to as broad-leaved forests. The foothill forests form the Bhabhar region. In the zone between the foothills and the plains of the Ganges, lie the great Terai forests in which sal is a very common species. The Terai ecosystem has a mosaic of patches of forests, tall grasslands and wetland tracts.

**In the Thar Desert and in the surrounding arid regions** the vegetation is based on xerophytic plants such as the *Calligonium* series. In Kachchh, the common series is *Prosopis spicigera* (*khejdi*)—*Salvadora sp.—Capparis sp.—Ziziphus* (*ber*) which occurs in tracts where the rainfall is sporadic and has an average of 150 to 450 mm which may last less than a month. This pattern is seen in areas such as the Desert National Park and sanctuaries for blackbuck around Jodhpur. *Prosopis juliflora*, which was introduced in these regions to control sand dunes, has however spread rapidly at the expense of local vegetation. Overgrazing in these arid areas produces a *Euphorbia* scrubland.

**Thorn and dry deciduous forest types** consist of trees such as *Acacia senegal* (*khor*)— *Anogeissus pendula* series, or an *Acacia catechu* (*kath*)—*Anogeissus pendula* series. These forests are typically found in the Aravalli Ranges such as those of the forests in Sariska National Park. The trees are of a small stature and there are straggly climbers and shrubs with a ground cover of herbs and grasses. *Anogeissus* often forms isolated pure stands in this forest type. In some areas there is a low *Ziziphus* scrubland.

*Anogeissus pendula—Anogeissus latifolia* frequently occur with *Terminalia sp.* in other arid areas. This series is found where the rainfall is below 800 mm.

*Acacia—Anogeissus latifolia* are dominants in the Deccan trap, for instance in parts of the Purna Valley in Gujarat.

The *Anogeissus latifolia—Hardwickia binata* series is found in the Deccan Plateau. *Hardwickia* is patchily distributed in discontinuous areas where the rainfall is between 500 to 1200 mm.

*Anogeissus latifolia—Terminalia* forests occur in Western India and form a common type in areas with a rainfall of 700 to 900 mm.

*Terminalia—Anogeissus latifolia—Cleistanthus* series is found in forests that lie between the large teak and sal tracts. The rainfall ranges between 1000 and 1500 mm. The height of the trees is between 20 to 25 metres.

The most frequently encountered **dry-deciduous teak forests** include *Terminalia—Anogeissus latifolia—Tectona grandis* series. These forests cover the Peninsula from Madhya Pradesh to the southernmost tip of India. They occur in areas where the annual rainfall ranges between 800 to 1800 mm with a long dry season of 6 to 8 months. These are the deciduous, teak forests that are intermediate between very dry and very moist evergreen forms, in which the species along with teak are *Terminalia—Anogeissus* or with *Dillenia—Lagerstroemia*.

**Dry-deciduous sal forest types** including the *Shorea—Buchanania—Cleistanthus* series, occur in the eastern region as sal seeds remain viable for only 10 days. Thus their regeneration needs rain during this brief and highly specific period. These conditions are not seen in the western region of India. The annual rainfall for sal forests ranges between 1400 to 2000 mm.

Other forms include *Shorea—Cleistanthus—Croton* series in Bihar, West Bengal and Orissa. A form with *Shorea—Terminalia—Adina* series occurs in Palamau.

**The moist-deciduous sal forest types** are the *Shorea—Dillenia—Pterospermum* series. These are mixed with evergreen species. Sal itself has a very brief deciduous period.

A *Shorea—Syzygium operculatum—Toona—Symplocos* series is found in Bihar and Orissa on hill-slopes as in Similipal.

**The moist-deciduous teak type** has a series with *Tectona—Dillenia—Lagerstroemia lanceolata—Terminalia paniculata*. This occurs on the western slopes of the Western Ghats, in the north of Goa and again in Kerala. In Karnataka, these forests occur on the eastern side of the Ghats. The forest occurs at a height of 600 to 1000 metres.

**Semi-evergreen types** have a *Toona—Garuga* series. The canopy itself is semi-deciduous in nature, which makes the forest an intermediate type between more wet evergreen communities and the moist-deciduous types.

**The evergreen types** of forests have several forms that have a large variety of species. These areas are not only richer in their tree species, but have a relatively high diversity of species of undergrowth plants. At higher altitudes, the true montane type of vegetation is observed in the Annamalai and Nilgiri ranges. These are frequently referred to as Shola forests. The rainfall ranges between 1000 to 1500 mm with a very brief dry season of about a month. These forests are found to alternate with grasslands. A luxuriant tree growth occurs where the moisture content in the soil remains higher throughout the year, such as in depressions and along watercourses. True Sholas may have trees of a medium height of about 25 metres, with several short stunted trees. Others have gigantic trees with great buttress roots. The trees are covered with moss, lichens, ferns and orchids. A few of the species are similar to those of the wetter eastern-Himalayan region, while others are specific to these hills. These are some of the most ecologically sensitive forests in the country and once a rare species disappears from these hot spots of plant species' diversity, their richness in species is lost forever.

The Western Ghats in Karnataka have a *Gardenia—Schefflera—Meliosma* series as in Chikmangalur in the Badra Sanctuary. True sholas do not occur north of this region.

The *Memecylon—Actinodaphne—Syzygium* series of the Western Ghats north of Goa is a typical forest type that has been extensively fragmented. This typical form has as many as six

ficus species. These forests are seen in Mulshi, Mawal, Mahabaleshwar and Bhimashankar. This is a three-tiered, low, but extremely dense vegetation type, of mostly evergreen species. It rarely grows taller than 15 metres, especially in the exposed windy areas. It is usually located 700 metres above sea level.

Between 600 to 700 metres, the common series on western slopes and above 800 metres on eastern slopes of the Western Ghats is the *Bridelia—Ficus racemosa—Syzygium* series. This is a transitional form between the moist teak and the evergreen *Memecylon—Actinodaphne—Syzygium* series.

In the rainfall belt between 2500 and 3000 mm south of Goa are the *Persea—Diospyros—Holigarna* series. It forms the luxuriant tree cover of the Ghats in this region.

The *Dipterocarpus—Mesua—Palaquium* series in the western Ghats has a rainfall of over 2000mm. This moist evergreen form has towering trees where the canopy is at 35 metres and the emergent giants may reach a height of 50 metres. The number of plant species is remarkably high. The forest has climbers, lichen, moss, and ferns in a great profusion of vegetation.

The *Cullenia—Mesua—Palaquium* series is found only on the western slopes of the Western Ghats in extremely wet areas. The rainfall of over 3000 mm, in which there is a very brief dry season, produces this typical forest type. The canopy is over 35 metres high. In several areas these are used as plantations of cardamom, which have been developed around the large number of small human settlements. The *Acacia—Albizia amara* series is found below 600 metres in the eastern coastal belt. This is an uncommon forest form.

The *Manilkar—Chloroxylon* series and an *Allbizia amara—Chloroxylon—Anogeissus latifolia* series is seen in areas where there is rainfall at specific times of the year, and is related to the amount of rainfall during the summer and winter months.

GRASSLAND ECOSYSTEMS
Landscapes in which vegetation is mainly formed by grasses and small annual plants, form a variety of grassland ecosystems with their specific plants

and animals adapted to India's varied climatic conditions. Grasslands are usually formed in areas of low rainfall where there is poor soil depth or quality. These conditions inhibit the growth of trees and shrubs but are sufficient to support the growth of grasses and herbs, that spring from the ground during the monsoon. These grasses and herbs dry off during the summer months, only to grow back in the next monsoon. This changes the appearance of the grasslands according to the season, with a growth phase followed by a dormant phase. A variety of grasses, herbs, insects, birds and mammals have evolved to live in these grassland areas. Grasslands have been used by man as pastures for their livestock ever since he became a pastoralist in ancient times.

Grasslands form a variety of ecosystems according to the different climatic conditions ranging from near desert habitats, to patches of Shola grasslands among the moist evergreen forests on the hill slopes in south India. There are the high altitude, cold Himalayan pastures in the north above the tree line. The Terai belt just south of the Himalayan foothills has tracts of tall elephant grass. Western

India and parts of central India and the Deccan Plateau have extensive semi-arid grasslands most of which have been over-grazed or turned into agricultural lands through irrigation. Grasslands also occur when clearings are made in a forest, or when repeated fires are lit that do not allow the forest to regrow.

Each grassland type has its own community of grasses and herbs. They also form habitats for specialized animals. The mountain pastures of the Himalayas have several species of wild sheep and goats and the snow leopard. The Terai is home to elephants and swamp deer. Semi-arid grasslands have blackbuck, antelope and the *chinkara*.

Human beings began to use these as pastures to feed their livestock when they changed from being hunter-gatherers to pastoralists. In the past, such grassy areas were considered to be the common pastures of a village community, and were appropriately managed. Grasslands owned by powerful rulers or by the Government were relatively better protected till recent times. Changes in land-management have led to grasslands becoming degraded and unproductive. Our growing livestock population, however still depends mainly on these degraded grassland ecosystems. The grassland cover in the country in terms of permanent pastures is now only 3.7 per cent. A major threat is the conversion of lowland grasslands into irrigated farmlands. As pressures on land increased, these village commons were the first to be degraded.

Herbs are an important aspect of every grassland ecosystems.

The semi-arid grasslands of the Deccan, a rapidly vanishing landscape, was once home to large herds of blackbuck.

The Terai's tall grasslands with the sal covered hills beyond, form a mosaic of habitats for wildlife.

Residual snows on a grassy slope of the Himalayas.

## DESERT AND SEMI-ARID ECOSYSTEM

Arid ecosystems have their own important characteristics of great value to humankind, as their species are adapted to long dry periods. These xerophytic plants, which include grasses, bushes and trees, may well be used in the future to develop new agricultural crops as global warming modifies the earth's climatic conditions. These global climatic changes are being brought about by an increase in the concentration of carbon dioxide and other gases which accumulate in the atmosphere; by our industrial growth; by the burning of fossil fuels; the growing traffic; the burning of crop residue; and deforestation.

Desert ecosystems are characterized by their dry climate and a very limited amount of water. These vast tracts are either extremely hot and dry, or cold and dry. The typical desert landscape seen in the Thar Desert in Rajasthan forms a highly specialized habitat for species that are adapted to live only under these harsh conditions. It is characterized by sand dunes, and areas with sparse grasses and shrubs which grow if and when it rains. Most plant species found here are xerophytic, as the rain is scanty and sporadic. In the adjoining semi-arid areas, shrubs and thorny trees like kher and babul are found.

The cold deserts of Ladakh are located in the high plateaus of the Himalayas. They form sheer rock-covered mountains alternating with flat sandy areas which look just like the sands in a hot desert. For several months of the year they are covered in snow.

The Great and Little Rann of Kachchh are highly specialized arid ecosystems. Although representing a desert landscape in the summer months, they get converted to salt marshes during the monsoons due to their low-lying nature and proximity to the sea. At these times, an enormous number of aquatic birds such as ducks, geese, cranes, storks, etc. flock to these areas. The Great Rann is the only known breeding area for flamingoes in India, while the wild ass is endemic to the Little Rann of Kachchh.

The rare animals of the semi-arid and desert habitats include the Indian wolf, the desert cat, the desert fox and birds such as the Great Indian Bustard. Commoner birds include partridges, quails and sand-grouse, while a number of insects and reptiles are highly specialized to live in these areas.

The desert abounds in insect life that has been adapted to these harsh conditions. But this unique complement of plants and animals, that have evolved to live in arid conditions, begins to disappear as deserts and semi-arid lands are turned into irrigated agricultural land. This has already happened to much of the dry and semi-arid ecosystems of

Semi-arid ecosystem with grass and xerophytic trees.

the western region of India, where the spread of irrigation is threatening the desert species of plants and animals. As the arid area shrinks in response to irrigation, the pressure of livestock on residual arid areas is thus intensified. As their population is concentrated into a relatively smaller area of arid grassland, this unique ecosystem is all but vanishing.

The Thar Desert of western India is unlike the typical desert landscape that we visualize as an inhospitable, hot expanse of sand dunes devoid of any plant and animal life. The Thar receives sporadic showers of rain in different areas once every few years. When it rains, the bare ground turns into grassland. The common trees which are species of *Acacia* and *Ziziphus* begin to grow. The landscape can look quite different for a few months and it can attract great concentrations of wildlife.

In the flat expanse of semi-arid land of the Deccan there are mostly xerophytic species such as *Acacia nelotica* (*babul*). In some areas only Euphorbia occurs. Small patches of forest can be dominated by species such as *Tectona grandis* (teak), *Pterocarpus santalinus* (red sandalwood), *Hardwickia binata* and *Santalum album* (sandalwood). In teak forests, the other subdominants are *Anogeissus latifolia* (*dhura*), *Boswellia serrata*, *Garuga pinnata* (*kharpat*) and *Diospyros melanoxylon* (*tendu*).

Grass, a key component of many ecosystems.

Himalayan River.

Himalayan foothills.

Coasts.

Coasts.

Trans-Himalayan mountains.

Desert.

Semi-Arid.

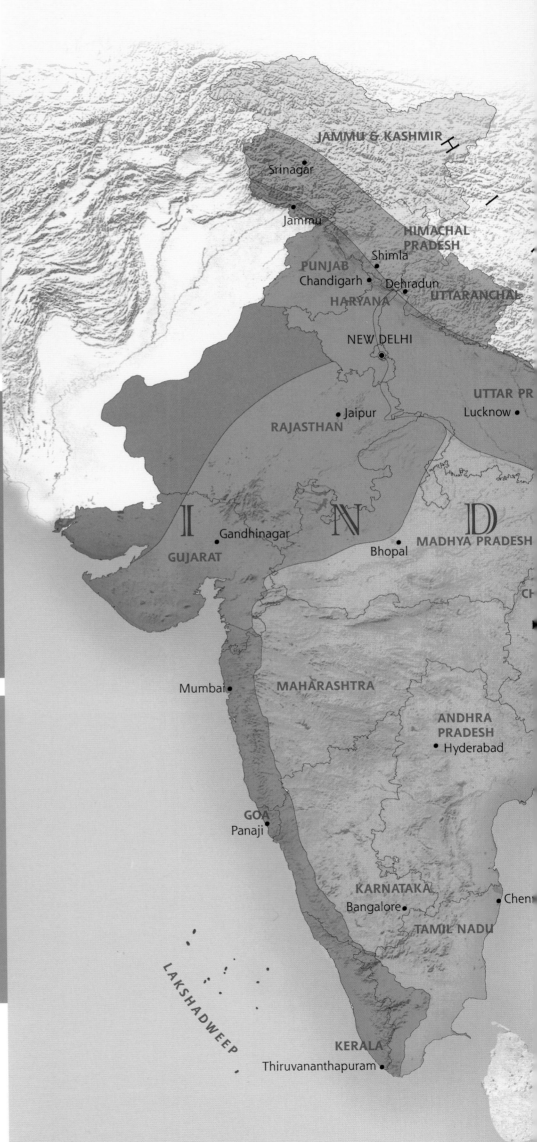

JAMMU & KASHMIR

Srinagar

Jammu

HIMACHAL
PRADESH

PUNJAB
Chandigarh
Shimla
Dehradun
UTTARANCHAL

HARYANA

NEW DELHI

UTTAR PR
Lucknow

Jaipur

RAJASTHAN

I N D

Gandhinagar
Bhopal
MADHYA PRADESH

GUJARAT

CH

Mumbai
MAHARASHTRA

ANDHRA
PRADESH
Hyderabad

GOA
Panaji

KARNATAKA
Bangalore
Chen

TAMIL NADU

LAKSHADWEEP

KERALA
Thiruvananthapuram

### COASTAL AREAS

Terrestrial ecosystems also include coastal areas that comprise sandy beaches and rocky or muddy coasts, which have specialized species adapted to living in this habitat. This not only consists of crustacea, molluscs, and other invertebrates that live in what is known as the splash zone where the tide moves in and out each day, but vast numbers of sea-shore estuarine birds such as gulls and terns.

```
1
2
  3
```

Semi-arid, overgrazed grasslands of the Deccan.

Scrubland in the Thar Desert.

Islands constitute some of India's most fragile ecosystems with a large number of endemic species not found on the mainland.

### MOUNTAIN RANGES

These constitute ecologically fragile regions where deforestation can lead to rapid erosion of soil. They are the regions from which many of our rivers are born. The Himalayan snows that melt in summer provide the water that the people of the Ganges and Bhramaputra valleys use throughout the year.

### ISLAND ECOSYSTEMS

Islands form the most unique and fragile ecosystems on earth. The forests of the Andaman and Nicobar Islands are varied and rich in plant species. There are mangroves at the edge of the sea; typical beach forests; tall evergreen, semi-evergreen and deciduous forests on the hillocks of the small islands, many of which have remained still relatively undisturbed. These great ancient forests have survived due to the extremely wet and inhospitable climate. Among some of these, live small tribal groups who have not been exposed to modern development and have maintained their traditional hunter-gatherer lifestyles. The vegetation of the Andamans is related to that of north-east India, while Nicobar's is similar to that of the Indonesian islands. The islands have a great number of endemic plants and animals not found in the forests of the mainland. These include mangrove and offshore coral reefs that together comprise of a very wide range of habitats in a relatively small area. The islands, one of India's most biologically rich regions, are now threatened by a growing tourist industry.

Western Ghats.

Trans-Himalayas: Wetlands.

Deccan Peninsula.

Islands.

Deccan Peninsula.

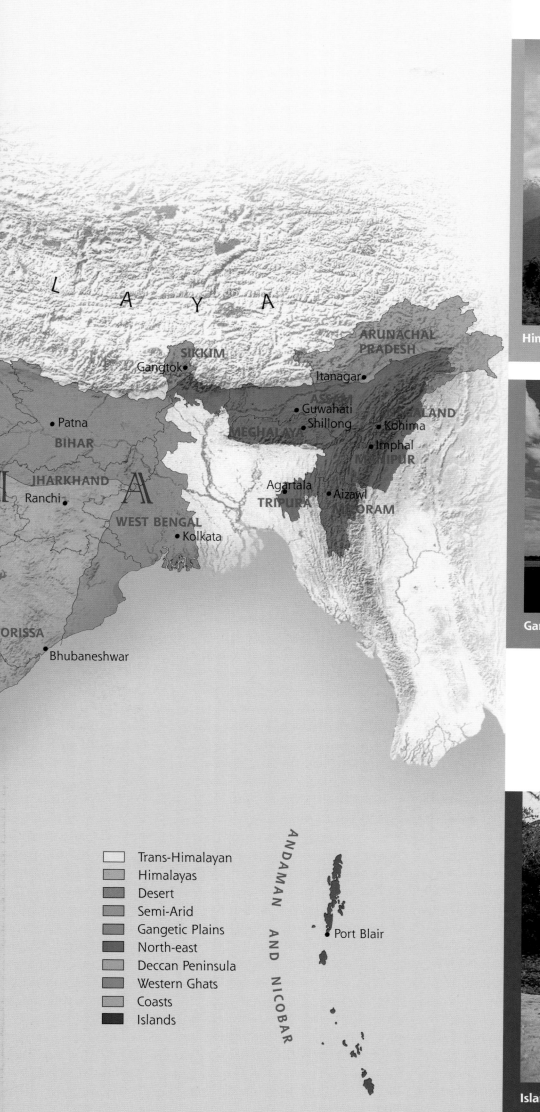

L A Y A

SIKKIM

Gangtok•

ARUNACHAL
PRADESH

•Itanagar

• Patna

BIHAR

ASSAM

•Guwahati

MEGHALAYA  •Shillong

NAGALAND

•Kohima

JHARKHAND

A

•Imphal

MANIPUR

Ranchi•

Agartala•

•Aizawl

WEST BENGAL

TRIPURA

MIZORAM

•Kolkata

ORISSA

Bhubaneshwar•

Trans-Himalayan
Himalayas
Desert
Semi-Arid
Gangetic Plains
North-east
Deccan Peninsula
Western Ghats
Coasts
Islands

A N D A M A N   A N D   N I C O B A R

•Port Blair

Himalayan mountains.

Gangetic Plain.

North-ea

Islands.

Turbulent Himalayan streams become slow moving rivers as they reach the plains.

Specialized forms of life are adapted to living in cold, fast-flowing Himalayan torrents.

## AQUATIC ECOSYSTEMS

These ecosystems include the marine habitats of the seas and oceans, and freshwater ecosystems like lakes, rivers, ponds and wetlands. These ecosystems are rich in their diversity and provide humans with a wealth of natural resources and services. Water, an essential ingredient for life, is provided by these ecosystems. Aquatic ecosystems include specialized plant and animal species that are adapted to live in water, ranging from microscopic plant life—phytoplankton and microscopic zooplankton, to the larger seaweed, fish and crustacea.

These aquatic ecosystems are characterized by their abiotic features or physical aspects such as quality of water, including salinity, rate of flow, clarity and oxygen content. In freshwater they are classified as being either still-water ecosystems such as ponds and lakes, or running-water ecosystems like streams and rivers. They are also classified according to their salinity into freshwater, brackish and marine ecosystems. The bed of the aquatic ecosystem, i.e. the mud, gravel or rocks at the bottom, alters its characteristics and influences its species composition.

Shallow bays and coastal marshes support high levels of locale-specific biodiversity of both flora and fauna, including a high diversity of fish, crustacea and waterfowl and the coastal belt has residual patches of mangroves in which a large number of marine fish spawn. Other less evident but important forms of life include a great variety of aquatic microscopic organisms, while offshore coral reefs constitute highly specialized ecosystems in which a great diversity of life is concentrated. Over-fishing due to mechanized trawling and industrial pollution from the shore constitutes a serious threat to these valuable ecosystems.

## FRESHWATER ECOSYSTEMS

Freshwater ecosystems with running water include streams, waterfalls and rivers. Ponds, wetlands, tanks and lakes are fresh water bodies that have still water.

1

2

3

A dry riverbed in the Himalayan foothills.

Pebble- and shell-covered beaches form a specialized microhabitat of the coastal region.

In a lake ecosystem, the water and its terrestrial surrounds are equally important for conserving biodiversity.

1. The ancient wetland ecosystems that man has drained away are now substituted by the backwaters of irrigation projects.

2. Very few lakes are now unpolluted.

3. The Dal Lake has become increasingly polluted over the last two decades.

4. Riverine ecosystem—The marble rocks sculpted by the river on the banks of the Narmada.

5. A Himalayan waterfall and the pool below constitute specific microhabitats for aquatic fauna.

6. Emergent vegetation at the periphery of a wetland is home to a myriad of habitat-specific species.

### The Pond Ecosystem

There are differences in a pond that is temporary and has water only in the monsoon, and a larger tank or lake that is an aquatic ecosystem throughout the year. Most of the small ponds become dry after the rains and are covered by terrestrial plants for the rest of the year.

When a pond begins to fill during the rains, its life forms such as the algae and microscopic zooplankton, aquatic insects, snails, and worms come out of the floor of the pond where they have remained dormant in the dry phase. Gradually, more complex animals such as crabs, frogs and fish return to the pond. The vegetation in the water consists of floating weeds and rooted vegetation on the periphery, which grows on the muddy floor underwater and emerges out of the surface of the water. As the pond fills in the monsoon, a large number of food chains are formed. Algae are eaten by microscopic zooplankton, which are in turn eaten by small fish on which larger carnivorous fish depend. These are in turn eaten by birds such as kingfishers, herons and birds of prey. Aquatic insects, worms and snails feed on the waste material excreted by animals and the dead or decaying plant and animal matter. They act on the detritus, which is broken down into nutrients which aquatic plants can absorb, thus completing the nutrient cycle in the pond. The temporary ponds begin to dry after the rains and the surrounding grasses and terrestrial plants spread into the moist mud that is exposed. Animals such as frogs, snails and worms remain dormant in the mud, awaiting the next monsoon.

### WETLANDS

Wetlands have a complex assemblage of living creatures with both terrestrial and aquatic components. These ecosystems have a variety of functions, acting as breeding areas for fish and crustaceans, as flood-control buffers, and as grazing areas for domestic animals. They are the home of a variety of aquatic birds such as ducks, geese, cranes, storks, flamingoes, pelicans, egrets and fish-dependent birds of prey such as the fishing eagle, terns and kingfishers.

### The Lake Ecosystem

A lake ecosystem functions like a giant permanent pond. A large amount of its plant material is formed by the algae, which derive energy from the sun. This is transferred to the microscopic animals, which feed on algae. There are fish that are herbivorous and are dependent on algae and aquatic weeds. The small animals such as snails are used as food by small carnivorous fish, which in turn are eaten by larger carnivorous fish. Some specialized fish, such as catfish, feed on the detritus on the muddy bed of the lake.

Energy cycles through the lake ecosystem, from the sunlight that penetrates the water surface to the algae and the aquatic plants. From aquatic plants, energy is transferred to herbivorous animals and carnivores. Aquatic animals and birds excrete waste products, which settle on the bottom of the lake. This is broken down by small animals that live in the mud on the floor of the lake. This acts as the nutrient material that is used by aquatic plants for their growth. During this process, plants use carbon from carbon dioxide for their growth and in the process release oxygen. This oxygen is then used by aquatic animals, which filter water through their respiratory system.

### Stream and River Ecosystems

Streams and rivers are flowing-water ecosystems in which all the living forms are specially adapted to different rates of flow. Some plants and animals such as the snails and other burrowing animals can withstand the rapid flow of the hill streams. Other species of plants and animals like the water beetles and skaters can live only in slower moving water. Some species of fish, such as the *mahseer*, go upstream from rivers to hill streams for breeding. They need crystal-clear water to be able to breed. They lay eggs only in clear water so that their young can grow successfully.

As deforestation occurs in the hills the water in the streams that once flowed throughout the year becomes seasonal. This leads to flash floods in the rains and a shortage of water once the streams dry up after the monsoon.

The community of flora and fauna of streams and rivers depends on the clarity, the rate of flow and oxygen content as well as the nature of their beds. The stream or river can have a sandy, rocky or muddy bed, each type having its own species of plants and animals.

River ecosystems have been cradles of human civilization, and in India, as elsewhere in the world, ancient settlements were established on river banks. As these settlements grew, people attempted to retain water, the most precious of resources, for longer periods by constructing dams. However, changing the flow patterns of rivers beyond a certain limit has in fact led to serious problems and a loss of productivity in the aquatic ecosystem and in the surrounding land.

Rocky outcrops on the seashore—the habitat of thousands of marine creatures.

## MARINE ECOSYSTEMS

The water of the marine ecosystems has a high salt content. They include large expanses of deep oceans and shallow seas. Coral reefs are found in a few shallow tropical seas and are extremely rich in species. In India these are found mainly around the Andaman and Nicobar Islands, in the Gulf of Kachchh, and off the coast of Tamil Nadu.

### Brackish Water Ecosystems

Brackish water ecosystems, such as river deltas and lagoons, have lower salinity than marine ecosystems. These include mangrove forests that are the most productive ecosystems in terms of biomass production. The largest mangrove swamps in India are found in the Sunderbans, in the delta of the Ganges.

## CORAL REEFS

Coral reefs have millions of living creatures of a diversity comparable with the tropical evergreen forests. Several species of fish breed in these protected reefs. India's reefs around the islands and along the coast are patchily distributed. Several have been destroyed by trawling for fish. Coral is also affected in areas where mangrove forests are being destroyed as mangroves stabilize the mud-banks in the river deltas. Once the mangrove is destroyed, the mud-banks disintegrate, with the result that the silt is washed away by the tide and deposited on coral reefs, which then die. The habitat of fish and other life forms changes rapidly, leading to a great loss of biological wealth.

Pollution can destroy the sensitive web of life found in marine ecosystems.

## THE DISTRIBUTION OF INDIA'S BIOGEOGRAPHICAL ZONES

In the Indian subcontinent, nature has produced a variety of landscapes. Each area is a highly specialized entity containing species that are bound together in the habitat by ancient bonds linked to food supply, commensals, parasites, pollinators, and ecological processes. Each species has

a defined abundance in the community of living creatures. Some of these biogeographic zones are fairly large tracts, while others are extremely small. In the recent past, the majority of these regions have been intensively modified by man, forming modified habitats. Vast tracts of forests have turned into scrub or arid grassland, while the overgrazed grasslands are gradually turning into deserts. River systems have been converted into lake ecosystems by thousands of dams, while wetlands have become agricultural land. A great proportion of agricultural land has been converted into towns and cities with industrial complexes. At the present rapid rate of land-use change in India it takes only a few years to watch the wilderness landscapes that Nature has devised over thousands of years being eroded beyond recognition. It is only the more spectacular glamour species in them that receive some degree of publicity when they disappear. Most threatened species pass off into the permanent oblivion of extinction without a whisper.

Habitats are highly dependent upon the vegetation on which herbivorous animals live and, in turn, carnivorous animals depend. The distribution of specific vegetation types in India is closely linked to the geographical configuration and the soil characteristics, rather than to a straightforward latitudinal variation as seen in many other parts of the world.

The vegetation patterns can be divided into clearly defined landscape-forms, which function as interdependent ecosystems. There is the Himalayan or alpine vegetation, found high up in the mountains and its oak and coniferous forests at lower levels. The Bhabar foothill forests and the low lying Terai and sal forests form a belt to the south of the Himalayan ranges. The flood plains of the Ganga, which were once covered with great tracts of forests of many different types, are now a major agricultural belt with only fragments of forests. These natural forests were cleared, and replaced either by agriculture or by sal and teak plantations. The arid and semiarid belts of Rajasthan, Saurashtra and the Deccan, consist of *Acacia* (babul) and *Ziziphus* (ber) thorn forests and scrubland. The hill ranges of the Deccan have residual patches of deciduous forests. The Western and Eastern Ghats are covered with several different types of forests, in which the species composition is dependent on altitude and rainfall.

The coast sports a vegetation pattern based on a variety of ecological conditions which, however, have been grossly altered by human activity. The river deltas support a highly specialized ecosystem based on mangrove swamps. The coastal lands include spectacular beaches and rocky cliffs. The semi-arid grasslands are found in the desert regions of Rajasthan and the Deccan Plateau. Other grasslands include short savannah-like patches that are found intermixed with deciduous forests. Tall elephant grass ecosystems form marshy areas, distributed patchily throughout the Terai region. Alpine meadows are found in the upper reaches of the Himalayas. In addition, several types of grasslands have arisen through a modification of dry thorn forests due to human interference. The Shola forests of the Nilgiri and Annamalai hills have large expanses of grassy areas maintained by complex factors such as topography, local hydrology and repeated fires. Unlike many other regions in the world, India's grasslands are interspersed with a variety of forest forms. This produces typical mixed landscape forms with their dependent fauna.

The monsoon winds that blow over the peninsula and into the Gangetic plains lead to a complex pattern of rainfall to which certain plants are specifically adapted. The variations seen in the vegetation are dependent not only on the amount of annual rainfall, but on its duration and seasonality. Forest trees have evolved to cycle their flowering according to the time when their seeds can germinate easily.

Vegetation patterns are greatly influenced by altitude and topography. The Himalayas form a great belt of mountains covered by high pastures and steep slopes that are clothed in both coniferous and broad-leaved forest. Other hilly tracts like the Western and Eastern Ghats have developed their own specific vegetation patterns, ranging from evergreen to dry deciduous formations. A small valley in these bio-rich hills where the rainfall is high can contain over 100 tree species and the shrubs, climbers and ground flora can amount to as many as 800 species. Extreme variations in temperature, from the freezing cold of the upper Himalayas, to the torrid summers of the western desert and the central plains of India, grossly modify vegetation. The distribution of many forest types is affected by the type of soil and geological conditions. In the hilly areas of the Western Ghats, millions of years have brought about the formation of small lateritic plateau tops of an acidic nature. This is suitable only for certain plants. These ancient plateaus formed along the crests of the Western Ghats have developed due to a severe degree of leaching related to the combined effects of heavy rainfall and high temperatures. The forests on the slopes of these hills are specific to this region, which is located in one of India's hot-spots of biodiversity. While it is commonly known that these evergreen forests are rich in species, it is only in the recent past that we have begun to appreciate that the ground flora of grasses and herbs that grow in the monsoon for a few weeks have a large proportion of endangered and endemic plant species.

## THE BIOGEOGRAPHIC CLASSIFICATION OF INDIA

India can be classified based on vegetation and animal life found in different geographical regions. Each of these are fairly distinctive in nature. On this basis, there are 10 distinctive forms that are typical of different regions, which are related to their climate, altitude and soil.

### THE TRANS-HIMALAYAS

This is the cold desert mountainous region in Ladakh. It is covered in many parts in perennial snows that feed the Indus and other rivers. Desolate though it is, great living wetlands spread across its lower flat valley. It has alpine shrubs and a large diversity of grasses and herbs. The snow leopard and wild goats and sheep are its important species. The rare black-necked crane breeds here. The amphibia in this region are now threatened by global warming and habitat changes.

### THE HIMALAYAS

The western and eastern Himalayas vary widely in their plant species. In the lower tropical and subtropical vegetation, up to about 1500 metres, the western Himalayas contain species such as *Juglans regia* (walnut), *Ulmus uvallichiana* (elm), and *Aesculus indica* (horse chestnut). In the east, at this low elevation there is mainly a *Shorea robusta* (sal) forest, which is moister in nature. In the eastern

The Himalayan region is divided at the snowline, above which the vegetation is sparse and consists of Himalayan pastures. Below the snow line lie the broad-leaved and coniferous forests.

The Trans-Himalayan region is a cold desert.

## BHABAR

Bhabar forest habitats cover the foothills of the Himalayan ranges along their southern extent, where the hills have steep, crumbly, boulder-strewn slopes. The average altitude is between 250 and 350 metres above sea level. The width of the tract of hills can range from a few kilometres to 20 kilometres in width. The common trees are *Terminalia sp.*, *Anogeisus latifolia* (ghatti tree), *Emblica officinalis* (amla) and *Adina cordifolia* (haldu). Some of these forests have sal as the dominant tree.

## TERAI

The Terai is the flat swampy and gradually low-lying area in which the Himalayan rivers first flow into the plains of the Gangetic valley. The altitude ranges from 200 to 250 metres. The undulating topography gives the area a dual ecosystem with patches of forest and tall, swampy grasslands. Most of this region has *Shorea robusta* (sal) dominated forests. The low lying boggy areas once had extensive wetlands, most of which have been drained for agriculture. This is the home of the wild elephant and the rhino, which are its flagship species.

Himalayas at a higher elevation there are mixed forests, frequently evergreen in nature, as there is a much heavier rainfall.

Between 1500 and 3000 metres, the western Himalayas have relatively few broad-leaved tree species and these are located in patches of mainly oak forests. At a higher level *Pinus sp.* (pine) forests predominantly cover the mountain slopes. At the same altitude the eastern Himalayas have more broad-leaved than coniferous trees. Here there are several species of *Quercus sp.* (oak), *Castanea* (chestnut) and *Acer sp.* (maple). Above 3600 metres in both the western and eastern Himalayas there are forests of *Rhododendron sp.* and *Juniperus sp.* (juniper). *Betula sp.* (birch) however is restricted to the Western region.

Coniferous forests of the Himalayan range.

A dry riverbed in summer in the Bhabar forests at the Himalayan foothills.

Terai grasslands constitute a rich ecosystem, especially for large mammals.

The Terai grasslands of Assam are home to the endangered rhino.

The Gangetic plains were originally covered with sal forests in the north-east and teak in the south-west.

## THE NORTHEAST

The rainfall is in the range of 2,000 to 10,000 mm per year in this area. This results in a luxuriant vegetation with *Artocarpus chaplasha, Michelia champaca* (champa), *Ficus elastica* (Indian rubber) and *Mesua ferrea* (ironwood of Assam). The thick ground-cover is formed of cane, climbers and evergreen shrubs. In the hilly areas the species are similar to the eastern part of the Himalayas, with *Rhododendron sp., Magnolia sp., Prunus sp.* (plum), *Acer sp.* (maple), etc. The northeastern zone is very rich in orchid species and is considered to be a globally important hot spot of biological diversity.

## THE GANGETIC PLAINS

This zone, covering the vast alluvial plain of the Ganga and Bramhaputra rivers, was once the home of ancient civilizations.

In this region the great sal and teak belts meet. The sal forests are located in the northeastern part of the plains. South of the Vindhya and Satpura ranges are the great teak forests. The transition from one type to another occurs within a few kilometres, where the forest has patches of both forms intermixed with *Tamarindicus* (tamarind) and other species. The Vindhya Range has distinctive vegetation in which *Tectona grandis* (teak) and *Madhuca indica* (mahua) are dominant species. The subdominant species found are *Terminalia tomentosa* (crocodile bark tree), *Bauhinia sp., Mangifera indica* (mango) and *Emblica officinalis* (amla). This extensive region in the plains now has large tracts of agriculture where once there were continuous tracts of extensive forests teeming with wildlife.

## THE WESTERN GHATS —MOIST TROPICAL FORESTS

The forests of the Sahyadharis in the Western Ghats of Maharashtra are known as tropical evergreen forests and cover the steep hill slopes. The plant community varies significantly in the different topographic features. There are open plateaus with a large diversity of herbs, many of which are rare, and steep precipices with specially adapted plants. The vegetation along *nala* courses differs from the rest of the forest. This feature leads to the formation of several microhabitats with their own plant communities. Those forests that are located in the southern part of the Ghats in Karnataka, Tamil Nadu and Kerala, are known as the Sholas. Typically they occur in depressions and along *nala* courses with the dome-shaped hilltops covered by open grasslands. The Nilgiris and Annamalais, which are offshoots of the Western Ghats, have some of the most incredible forests in India. The giant trees of the valley forests contrast sharply with the grassy slopes and crags that form vertical rock faces nearly devoid of vegetation.

These Shola forests are extremely dense. In most situations the trees grow to a height of about 45 metres. About 75 per cent of the trees are of species that may individually contribute only 1 per cent of the tree community. The height of the trees below the canopy is occasionally structured into well-defined layers with a specific canopy tree and a composition of different under-storey trees. At times the vegetation forms a tangle of thick foliage. The numerous climbers range from small vines to giant lianas, the latter standing on their own even after the supporting tree dies. In areas where the canopy is exceptionally dense, the floor of the forest has very little vegetation. The ground is covered with decaying leaves, fungi and rocky exposures. *Nala* courses and sloping soil from which subsoil water finds its way out in minute trickles have banks of ferns and bryophytes. These forests are extremely rich in orchids. The undergrowth has cane and bamboo in patches. *Strobilanthus* (*karvi* and *wayti*) shrubs frequently occur as ground cover especially along the edges of a forest patch or in forest openings. This group of plants occur gregariously covering large open

The crestline of the Western Ghats emerging through the cloud cover, which is home to habitat-specific species that need high levels of moisture.

areas with their dense impenetrable stalks. Each of these species flowers cyclically after several years of dormancy. The *Carvia callosa* flowers once every seven years; the *wayti* blooms occur every three or four years, while other species of *Strobilanthus* flower take as long as 11 years. The *karvi* in flower gives a profusion of large violet-blue blossoms that supposedly give to the Nilgiri hills their name, which means blue mountains. The *wayti* covers the hill slopes with small white flowers like snowflakes.

The northern part of the distribution of these evergreen patches between Mumbai and Goa are probably the worst affected by biotic pressures. Above 900 metres, the red lateritic soils support small relict patches of a special form of forest consisting of *Syzygium cumini* (*jamun*),

*Actinodaphnae sp.* (*pisa*), *Mangifera indica* (mango) with an under-story of *Memecylon sp.* (*anjan*) trees and an undergrowth of *Carvia callosa* (*karvi*). This is typical of patches in the northern part of the Western Ghats, where the rainfall is over 5000 mm. These forests are rich in forest birds, amphibia and insect life.

### THE SHOLAS

The Nilgiris and Annamalais have shola forests. They occur above 1800 metres. The trees are *Eurya japonica*, *Gardenia sp.*, *Michelia champaca* (*champa*), and *Syzygium sp.* The forests alternate with a typical open, short-grassland ecosystem. These are some of the most bio-rich areas of the hill forests and constitute an important hot-spot of biological diversity.

The Sholas of the Annamalai and Nilgiri hills are a typical ecosystem in which forests and grasslands form a mosaic.

## THE DESERT

The Thar Desert of western India is unlike the typical desert of our imagination. Far from being a hot expanse of sand dunes devoid of any plant and animal life, the Thar receives sporadic showers of rain once every few years in different locations, and when it rains, the bare ground changes into grassland. The common trees are species of *Acacia* and *Ziziphus*.

In the flat expanse of semi-arid land there are mostly xerophytic species such as *Acacia nelotica* (babul). In some areas only *Euphorbia* occurs. Small patches of forest can be dominated by species such as *Tectona grandis* (teak), *Pterocarpus Santalinus* (red sandalwood), *Hardwickia binata* and *Santalum album* (sandalwood). In teak forests, the other subdominants are *Anogeissus latifolia* (dhura), *Boswellia serrata*, *Garuga pinnata* (kharpat) and *Diospyros melanoxylon* (tendu).

It has a high variety of highly specialized fauna adapted to this region, such as the great Indian bustard, the sand grouse, reptiles and rodents.

## THE SEMI-ARID ZONE

The semi-arid tracts of Rajasthan include patches of rich grassland with species of xerophytic trees and shrubs. It has a high population of blackbuck, *chinkara*, wolf and birdlife.

| 1 | 2 |
|---|---|
| 3 | |
| 4 | |

Xerophytic vegetation in the Thar Desert ecosystem.

A shimmering mirage in the Thar Desert simulates a water-body in a bone-dry habitat.

Rock fields over the Deccan are home to reptiles and insects that use this dry microhabitat.

The Thar Desert.

## THE DECCAN PLATEAU

A large part of the Deccan Peninsula is covered by a semi-arid grassland ecosystem. It is also dotted with wetlands and crossed by several great rivers that flow from west to east.

In the northern part of the Deccan Plateau, the Satpura Ranges have forests of *Hardwickia binata* (anjan), *Boswellia serrata* (Indian frankincense—*salai*), and *Tectona grandis*. The plateau has a low rainfall mostly below 1000 mm.

The eastern slopes of the Ghats and their spurs have a much drier mixed deciduous forest with *Tectona grandis*, *Terminalia tomentosa* (crocodile bark tree), *Terminalia paniculata* (kinjal), *Dalbergia latifolia* (rosewood) and *Lagerstroemia sp.*

South of Goa, the forests extend from Shimoga down to Mangalore and Cochin. They reach the offshoots of the Ghats around Coorg, the Nilgiris, Annamalais and Agasthamalais.

The most peculiar group of species in these evergreen forests are the *Dipterocarpes*, which grow in abundance in the southern hills and along the coast. *Dipterocarpus hopea* is frequently a dominant species. Large bamboo breaks are less common as compared to drier forests. Cane frequently occurs in the undergrowth. The evergreen forests can be divided into low-level and high-level forms. In the flat coastal belt, most of these areas have been converted extensively into paddy fields. At higher altitudes the composition of species gradually changes, as one ascends into the hills. The demarcation on steeper slopes is more evident than at lower elevations.

The hill ranges at a higher elevation have a temperate climate with a completely different plant community. Typically in the southern part of the Western Ghats the hill forests have *Toona sp.*, *Dipterocarpus indicus*, *Hopea parviflora* (ironwood of Malabar), *Artocarpus heterophyllus* (jackfruit) and *Vitex altissima*. Ferns and tall herbs abound on the forest floor especially in moist pockets and in places where the soil depth is greater. These forests have a continuity with those of the more typical sholas of the Nilgiris and Annamalais.

The forests of the Deccan include evergreen, deciduous and thorn forests.

1

2

3

The jackfruit tree is an economically important species in the Deccan forests; from Forbes, 1813.

Many of the forests of the Deccan plateau and its hill ranges are now degraded.

Teak forests were extensively planted during the British period.

*Vitex heterophylla*

1 | 2
3

Vitex is a common species found in the Deccan; from Wallich, 1832.

A teak seedling in the Deccan can take several decades to grow into a mature tree.

Bamboo groves in a deciduous forest form a favourite habitat of the great cats.

## THE COASTAL AREAS

The coastal tracts on the western and eastern seacoasts form a variety of habitat types ranging from forests and grasslands to saltpans, marshes and lagoon-like brackish water lakes.

### THE EASTERN COAST

The coastline has a variety of sandy beaches, rocky outcroppings and coastal grasslands. The marshy areas and river deltas are covered with mangrove swamps, and there are small residual areas of coastal grasslands that are now highly threatened.

### THE WESTERN COAST

This is a region of highly diverse and luxuriant tropical vegetation, with areas that have been extensively converted into paddy crops and coconut plantations. The few residual forests have several distinctive strata at different altitudes. The coastal belt of rain forests is evergreen, and has massive trees covered with orchids, ferns and a thick tangle of vegetation in forest openings.

## THE ISLANDS

Islands form some of the most unique and fragile ecosystems on earth. The Andaman and Nicobar Islands are a great storehouse of biological diversity in terms of their plant-life. There are mangroves at the edge of the sea, typical beach forests, evergreen, semi-evergreen and deciduous forests on the hillocks of the small islands several of which are relatively undisturbed. The *Dipterocarpus* species are found in the undisturbed evergreen areas that dominate several of the uninhabited islands. These are great ancient forests that have survived due to the extremely wet and inhospitable climate. Among them live small tribal groups which, relatively untouched by modern development, have remained traditional hunter-gatherers.

Coastal forests have high levels of biological diversity.

The mosaic of sand and rocks creates a habitat for marine life dependent on the tide.

In the coastal region, mangroves form a highly productive ecosystem.

The evergreen forests of the Andaman islands are extremely rich in endemic species.

*a.* The Areca or Betele nut. *b,* the f[...]
ing of it. *c,* the same grown bigge[r]
at length the tree, *d.d,* whose und[er]
fallen leave the joynts bare, whi[le]
ones still sprout at the top *e e* ; ea[ch]
hath a sheath, *f,* incompaſſing a jo[ynt]
trunk. *g,* is a purse or husk conta[ining]
branches of flowers, which falle[n]
young nutts, *h.h,*
w.ᶜʰ increaſe as, *i.i,*
and ripen to ẏ form
of, *k,* whoſe tomen-
toſe husk taken off,
leaves the Areca nut, *a,* covered with a thin
shell. *ll,* shews the nut cut asunder.

*m.m,* the Bamboos as growing together
*n.n,* part of one drawn larger. *oo,* One
joynt yet much larger, to shew the leaf *p,*
and how the branches grow out of ẏ joynt.

*qq,* a branch of the Mango tree. shewing
the leaf *rr.* the flower *ss.* the fruit *tt,*
and the inside of it, *uu,* when slit.

*z,* the marking nutt yielding a black oyle.

*Pag. 40.*

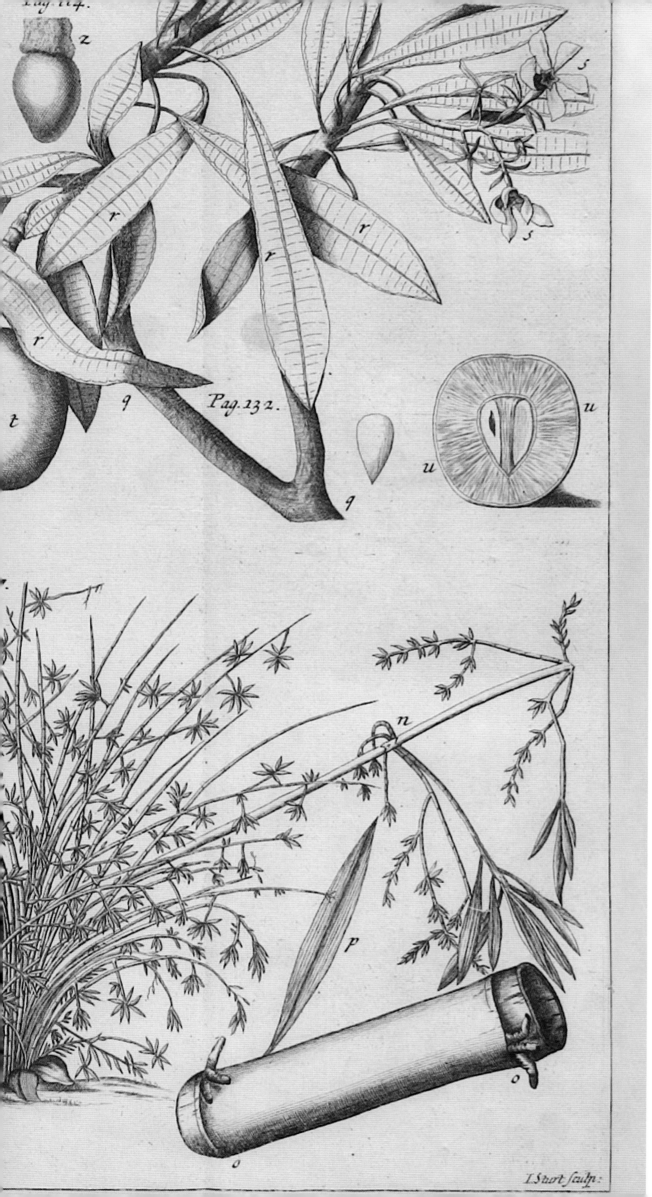

The early Europeans who came to look for spices also began looking for plants that could be used for other purposes. Thus began a study of India's flora that extended over the next 300 years.

# INDIA'S FLORAL HERITAGE

f one begins to explore wilderness ecosystems, one cannot help but come under the spell of this incredible world of plant life. It is as exciting as the glamorous world of animals. The world of plants consists of an enormous variety of species, ranging from minute, single-celled algae, to gigantic forest trees. In India we have over 45,000 plant species (MoEF, 2002). Plants have so many intricate life processes that I began to explore them with as much excitement as I would feel while watching birds or animals. Their fascinating lives appear in unexpected situations—forest trees that support epiphytes on their branches, flowers that form a ground layer in the forests and aquatic plants, are all equally intriguing.

Questions unravel only if one begins to carefully look into this wondrous world of plant life. We know that some coniferous trees have branches sloping gradually downwards so that snow falls off them. But why do some deciduous trees have branches at acute angles while others are at right angles? Leaves of conifers are pointed and needle-like, but why have some deciduous species evolved tiny leaves, while others have developed huge ones? One has to experience this diversity to appreciate the science of Botany.

Tree species can be identified by their typical shapes and branching patterns.

Dry leaves on the forest floor recycle nutrients for new life to grow on.

abound in the plant world, waiting to be seen, heard, smelt, felt and discovered. They are the stuff of life itself.

Most of all, I find plants exciting in their diversity and their adaptations to the environment, and even more fascinating simply for their indescribable beauty. The green, gold and red of a Himalayan autumn, the lush emerald green of an evergreen tangle of vegetation in the Western Ghats, the rolling green-yellow of the open semi-arid grassland as it transits from its monsoon growing season to the yellow-brown of winter—these are the colours of life on earth. There are thousands of variations of green shades and textures in the forest. And we have not even begun appreciating the great variability of structure that makes one plant so different from the next. It is mind-boggling in its diversity.

The world of plants consists of an enormous variety of species. In every forest, there are trees, shrubs, climbers, small flora of the ground layer, and epiphytes which are supported on the branches of trees. In each forest type these layers differ and create a variety of microhabitats for the animals that live there. While algae were regarded till recently as plants, modern taxonomists now classify them as a separate primitive group of microscopic protoctista, that were the forerunners of plants and animals.

We know that plant life varies significantly in each ecosystem. Each forest type has its own community of plant life. A great variety of grasses and herbs make up the grasslands. Wetlands have plants ranging from microscopic plant life such as algae, emergent reeds such as *Typha*, to floating plants such as the lotus, that form the producer system of the ecosystem. Plants that live in arid areas make even the desert a lively place.

Quite distinct from these 'green' plants with their magical chlorophyll that uses the sun's energy to build living matter, are the fungi, which are no longer considered to be a part of plant life. They are vital to nature's living processes of breaking down organic to inorganic matter, so important to the detritus cycle in various ecosystems.

Green plants synthesize their own food material through the process of

Sit in a dry deciduous forest at night and hear its living sounds. A dry large teak leaf has completed its life span and snaps off with a loud click. Softer clicks follow as it brushes past other leaves and branches and floats downwards before the final click that marks its landing on the forest floor. It has turned, from a producing machine in the photosynthesis factory of the forest canopy, into the raw material of the detritus cycle on the forest floor. Here the thousands of insects and worms will fragment it into tiny pieces, while fungi and bacteria will work on it to create new nutrient material for plant life to grow on. Those sounds of a single leaf fall are nature's audio signals of the many processes of life in the forest. Similar signs photosynthesis in which light energy from the sun is converted into chemical energy in the form of carbohydrates, for plant growth, development and reproduction. They are thus the 'producers' in nature's machinery. In this process, the plants release oxygen, a by-product of the chemical reaction between water and carbon dioxide. Leaves of green plants take in the carbon dioxide from the air. The water is absorbed through the roots. Plants thus maintain the oxygen levels of the atmosphere so essential for the respiration of animals. They play a vital role in the complex world of every ecosystem. They are the source of oxygen as well as food for herbivorous animals, which are, in turn, food for the carnivores.

We frequently think of plants as static forms of life, without realizing that they grow, flower, fruit and develop seeds which spread them from one location to another. They respond in intricate ways to varying conditions in their environment just as

| 2 | 4 |
| 3 | |
| 1 | |

Mangrove seedlings take root on sea shores and grow into a highly productive ecosystem.

Coniferous forest at the Himalayan foothills.

Riverine broad-leaved vegetation at the Himalayan foothills.

The moist deciduous forests in Madhya Pradesh.

animals do, but through a very different set of stimuli and responses. We rarely realize that some plants grow extremely rapidly, until we watch a climber that can grow by several centimetres every day! Or a spike of an orchid that grows to a length of 100 centimetres in a couple of days. Climbers even seem to know by some strange sensory system where they can find support that will take them towards sunlight. What an amazing sight-like sensory system must be located at the tip of a climber's tendril! How does a plant 'see'? Other plants can move so rapidly that they can catch insects on which they feed! A *Drosera* plant can catch and digest an insect's hard covering. And we rarely appreciate a plant's special linkages to specific animals. Caterpillars of different butterfly and moth species live on a specific host plant. Some plant species can be pollinated by only a single animal species! Plants are incredible, astonishing enigmas of evolution and have an intriguing role to play in every ecological process.

## A HISTORICAL BACKGROUND OF THE SCIENCE OF BOTANY

When botanists first began looking for plants in India, they were primarily concerned with documenting regional flora and naming new plants. They documented the districts where they first located a plant and occasionally identified a few of the local conditions in which they grew. They rarely documented exact locations, however, or the microhabitat needs of different plants, a lacuna that makes it almost impossible to relocate a small rare species unless searched for intensively. Until the 1900s, while the list of known species expanded, their ecological aspects remained neglected. Experts then woke up to the knowledge of plant species' habitat needs; in many cases too late to ensure that rare species were protected. Several species have been driven close to extinction, or may have already disappeared.

Information on the complex biogeography of plants has emerged relatively recently. Botanists such as FR Bharucha and VM Meherhomji worked on this growing field of interest around the 1950s, and Gadgil and Vartak brought sacred groves maintained by tradition (known as *devrais*, or forests dedicated to local deities) to the centre stage in botanical writing. Still others began to look at the traditional knowledge about medicinal plants in ancient India.

Terrestrial and aquatic ecosystems are usually named on the basis of the plant communities that characterize them—forests, grasslands, deserts, wetlands. While several plants can live in diverse habitats,

A Tickell's flowerpecker, with a sticky *Loranthus* seed in its beak which it will rub onto a neighbouring tree, to form a new parasitic plant.

These parasitic plants which take their nutrition from host plants are pollinated by birds.

## Selected Milestones in Botany Across the World

Indian sciences linked plants to food and medicine and ascribed spiritual value to aspects of plant life, predating what was known in Western countries.

The earliest cultivated plants were foodgrains. Ancient Egypt used the papyrus plant to make paper.

The earliest recorded documents of plants are found in the Old Testament and in Homer's works during the ancient Greek period. Aristotle wrote that plants were intermediate. forms between inanimate objects and animal life. About 1300 to 1400 plants were known to the Romans.

Scientific thought including that related to Botany, stagnated through the Dark Ages.

In the 1200s, Saint Albert, who lived in Laningen on the Danube, re-described plants known to the ancients.

In the 13th century, the Venetian Marco Polo travelled eastwards and documented the knowledge of useful plants in the East.

In the 16th century, Botany was closely allied to Medicine and the 'floras' of different countries begin to emerge.

At the same time, several workers began studying plant species in Germany and had documented about 6000 plants by the 1600s.

The era of Portuguese and other Europeans who voyaged eastward in the quest of spices, led to a race for acquiring plants.

By the 17th and 18th centuries, Botanical Science had been initiated and Carolus Linnaeus formally intiated the binary nomenclature of species. This remains the basis of naming species even today.

Darwin's theory of evolution strengthened the science of Botany.

## Selected Milestones in Botany in India

Garcia da Orta wrote *Medicinal Plants of Goa* in 1565.

Van Rheede, Dutch Governor of Malabar, put together *Hortus Malabaricus* from 1678 to 1693.

William Roxburgh's *Plants of the Coast of Coromandal* with illustrations was published between 1795 and 1820.

William Roxburgh wrote *Flora Indica* in 1832.

Robert Wight and Arnott wrote their *Prodromus Florae Peninsulae Indiae* in 1834.

Wight published *Icones Plantanum Indiae Orientalis* between 1840 and 1853, and *Illustrations of Indian Botany* between 1840 and 1850.

*Flora of British India* (1875 to 1897) containing 14,500 species, was written from the Kew Gardens by Sir Joseph Hooker.

In 1887 Sir George King wrote *Annals of the Royal Botanic Gardens and Botanic Species in India*, 12 volumes of plates in full colour with botanical notes.

Kirtikar and Basu published *Indian Medicinal Plants*, in 4 volumes, in 1935.

SK Jain wrote on *Medicinal Plants* in 1968.

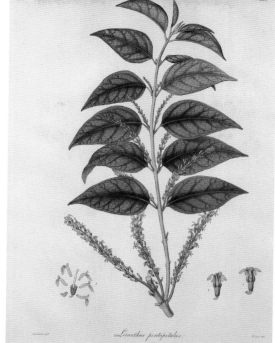

LORANTHUS OBTUSATUS (WALL.)

others are found only in very distinctive habitat conditions, such as rocky outcrops, precipices, plateau tops, and seacoasts. Some grow only on the edges of terrestrial and freshwater ecosystems. These habitat-specific species can easily disappear due to human activities, as their specialized habitats are extremely limited in size and distribution.

Ecosystems and their community of plants and animals can be rapidly destroyed if plants are used faster than they can reproduce and spread. But more sinister influences are now becoming apparent. For instance, as global warming progresses, several species will have to colonize new areas, to the north of their present range. Nature may not be capable of responding rapidly enough to this new change and many of these species are likely to be seriously threatened with extinction over the next few decades.

Loranthus; from Roxburgh, 1795.

Loranthus; from Wallich, 1832.

Loranthus; from Wight, 1838.

During the 1800s, botanists documented the great diversity of India's plant life. In the 1900s, the botanists began to see the complex linkages between plants and animals. For example, the link between the parasitic *Loranthus* and birds that pollinate and spread it through the forest was documented by both botanists and ornithologists.

**Carolus Linnaeus** was a Professor of Anatomy and Medicine and later Professor of Botany at Uppasala University. He knew zoology, botany and geology, all equally well. His major work, *Systema Naturae* was published in 1735. His work led to the concept of 'species'.

The plants in the forest are the basis of all its life processes. Trees and shrubs with small fruit and seeds are eaten and dispersed by birds, while large fruit and seeds are frequently dispersed by mammals. These interactions form millions of linkages between the animal and the plant world. Unless we respond quickly to the changes we have introduced in our race for development, many species will have passed into the darkness of extinction—

never to be seen again on the surface of the earth as a result of human actions. Life's intricate web, woven out of thousands of food chains, will lie in one great tangle of broken links.

Over 10 years ago, the Tata Power Company began to involve me in an afforestation programme for their catchments in the Western Ghats. I began to seriously explore methods for the ecorestoration of these degraded hills. I hoped that somehow we could re-grow the type of vegetation that once grew in these beautiful hills reduced to tiny islands of forests. I had a group of young botanists document the wide range of species of trees and shrubs of the least disturbed patches of forest, and also document the loss of species in degraded forests and scrublands around Andhra, Valvan, Shirowta and Mulshi lakes in the catchments of these dams. It was for this unique ecorestoration effort, which I planned for Tata, that SN Ogale of Tata Power Company developed a nursery of

over 40 species of indigenous trees and climbers. While wandering through the forest patches in the catchment areas of the dams in the Western Ghats, I began to realize that several rare and endangered plants were in fact located in the ground flora of scrublands, a habitat that we rarely consider as being of great conservation significance. This aspect had to be explored to implement an ecorestoration programme for these catchment areas. Apart from the more recent interest in grasslands, there has been very little appreciation of the value of conserving flora that lies outside forest tracts. For instance, in the Western Ghats, there are open plateau tops, with barely a centimetre of soil, on which there are more endemic and rare plants—among the hundreds of grasses and herbs—than in the adjacent evergreen forests! Many of these small but beautiful plant species may be found only in a few locations. And there are many plants specific to microhabitats such as streams and waterfalls. There are several

Pollination is a vital process in every ecosystem. This insect pollinating begonia flowers is just one example of thousands of vital associations in nature that link plants to animals.

other findings that show how difficult it would be to recreate a 'natural' forest.

Looking at the plants in a forest is as exciting as watching a tiger or an elephant. One only needs to know what to look for and the plant world begins to open up, providing a new and delightful experience.

## PLANT & ANIMAL LINKAGES

The linkage between animals and plants is usually seen as a dependence of herbivorous animals on plant life—a key aspect of the interlinked food chains in the web of life. What is frequently less appreciated is the dependency in the opposite direction. Several plants are pollinated and dispersed by animals. In the ecosystem, insects, birds and mammals play a major role, important for the survival and spread of several plants.

## POLLINATION & DISPERSAL

Plants are pollinated in a variety of ways. The flowers may self-pollinate or use external mechanisms to transfer pollen from one flower to another. The pollen of grass and other plants with very light pollen is dispersed by the wind. Pollination occurs only if the pollen falls on the stigma of another plant in flower. This means that enormous quantities of pollen need to be produced, as most pollen grains will never

reach another flower. During the tertiary period—when there was intense speciation of insect life—flowering plants evolved so that insects could help in cross-pollination. New adaptations in plants thus went hand in hand with the evolution of newer forms of insects.

Insects in search of flower nectar are attracted by the flower's bright colours or by its smell. These associations in some cases are highly specific and a specialized relationship has evolved between a plant species and a specific insect species. Incredibly, orchid flowers have evolved so as to look like a female insect, thus attracting male insects. In the attempted 'mating' with the flower, it is the plant which multiplies due to its pollination, with no benefit to the insect's population!

Plants pollinated by birds have very little fragrance, as birds have a poor sense of smell, but they are invariably brightly coloured and rich in nectar. Compared with insect-pollinated flowers, which require a large rim for the insect to settle on, bird-pollinated flowers have a narrow rim, which allows easy access. Prominent among bird-pollinated trees are *Bombax*, *Sterculia*, *Erythrina*, *Butea* and *Bauhinia*.

Night-flowering plants have white flowers that attract nocturnal pollinators like moths and bats, whereas brightly

coloured reds and blues attract butterflies and birds during the day. The diversity in the process of pollination is an incredible feature of nature.

Visits to grasslands are unforgettable inasmuch as the clothes worn retain the spike grass that pokes one even after the clothes have been washed! This is a result of the way the grass evolved to ensure that it is taken to a new location by various animals, spreading its seeds far and wide; the spike grass stays on the animal's skin as it journeys onward. Animals of several species thus aid in this mode of spread among grasses.

Fruits of several plants are also spread by animals. When a fruit is unripe it is not palatable, a stage that gives the seed the required time to mature. Once the seed is mature, its fruit becomes pulpy and juicy and takes on an attractive colour, to entice birds and mammals to feed on it. While the pulp is digested as food, the small seeds are ingested and finally defecated in distant places. This means that all the seedlings do not have to compete for growth at the same location. In fact, some seeds germinate better if they have been passed through the intestinal tract of birds or mammals.

### Charles Darwin—Plant and Animal Linkages

During his voyage on *The Beagle*, Darwin began to look at the distribution of species. He wrote 'one might really fancy that from an original paucity of birds in this archipelago, one species had been taken and modified for different ends.' Darwin presented his bird collection to the ornithologist John Gould. It was a collection of what he thought were wrens, blackbirds and slightly different finches. Gould found they were all different finches from different islands in the Galapagos. Their beak structure was linked to their feeding behaviour and the availability of food on different islands. The early evolutionary aspects of the linkage between plants and animals had begun to take shape.

## Plant and Animal Linkages

Recently GS Rawat of the Wildlife Institute of India has shown that the flowering and fruiting periods of wind-dispersed and bird-dispersed tree species are different. Large fruits ripen from March to May. Berries ripen between July and December. The peak of fruit abundance for trees where birds disperse seeds is between May and July, which is the breeding season of fruit-dependent birds such as hornbills, barbets, mynas, etc. For several large seeds, hornbills may be solely responsible for dispersal. Seeds regurgitated by hornbills have higher regeneration than those planted directly. Hornbills also move a considerable distance from a fruiting tree after foraging, thus dispersing the seeds widely. However, many seeds end up near their nest, thus leading to an aggregation of seedlings under the nest-hole. Birds that use broad-leaved forests have a more distinctive feeding pattern, while there are more generalized ones in coniferous forests. Bird composition also varies with altitude. Thus there are many complex linkages between plants, mammals, birds and insects which have an evolutionary basis.

| 1 | 2 |
|---|---|
|   | 3 |
| 4 |   |

Orchids attract pollinators by their colour, shape or scent.

There is a strange adaptation of feathers on the beak of the jungle myna which pollinates nectar-forming flowers of *Erythrina*.

Insect pollination—a butterfly pollinating the exotic *Lantana*.

Beetles in the process of pollinating a flower have eaten through it.

Animals such as rodents and ants store seeds when they are in season to be used as food during lean months when food is in short supply. This also aids dispersal.

Human beings have indeed been the most prominent plant-dispersal agents in the world. They have both deliberately and inadvertently dispersed plants, not only locally, but also from one country to another, and even from one continent to another. A plant thus moved to a different environment either cannot compete with the natural plants and dies out, or is so successful in its new habitat that it becomes a weed and overruns the other local species. This erodes the abundance of plants of a natural balanced ecosystem. *Lantana,* which was brought to what was then known as Ceylon as a garden plant in 1824, has now spread all over India because of the birds that have learnt to feed on its pulpy fruit. One can only imagine the great loss that resulted in the range of diverse species of local plants that once covered many different forest types with their varied species of indigenous shrubs. A single unthinking introduction and much of the diversity of shrubs was lost. When one thinks of all the animal

In 1932, Salim Ali and Priya Davidar documented the differences in pollinators in the seven species of *Loranthus* and identified how different nectar-dependent bird species used different types of specialized beaks and special behaviour patterns that lead to pollination.

species, insects, birds, mammals—linked to this diversity of plants in the shrub layer—that lost their natural habitat and diversity of foods, one begins to appreciate the damage to an ecosystem that can result from the introduction of an exotic species.

Wind-dispersal transports lightweight seeds that are often structured to sail for a long distance through the air. Other species have fine hair that acts like a parachute wafting the seed to a distant site even in the slightest wind. Silk cotton (*Bombax*) trees have a pod tightly filled with flimsy silken material containing a mass of seeds awaiting a strong breeze. The small white cloud of silk drops seeds along the way till none remain. Some plants have seeds with wings like the blades of a fan that help them to spin through the air, retarding the rate at which the seed falls and thereby helping it to be dispersed further by the wind. In many plants, wind or rain acts as a trigger for a seed capsule to burst and disperse its seeds. *Strobilanthes* (*karvi*) pods burst with a loud sound once it begins to rain, casting their seeds away from the parent plant.

Water dispersal of many kinds is seen in several groups of plants. The coconut floats for long distances, even across the sea, and it is probable that it is not a native species of India, but brought to Indian shores perhaps in this manner. Mangrove seeds form a seedling while still attached to the tree, and some fall during low tide and root at the same spot, while others fall during high tide, to be washed to other locations. Dispersal of plants in nature is an aspect of plant communities that is one more mystery among the innumerable phenomena that are a part of every ecological system.

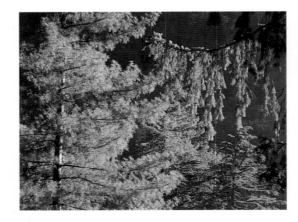

## THE STRUCTURE AND HABITS OF PLANTS
### TREES

Most tree species have a typical structure. The height, girth, branching pattern, leaves and flowers, all give a species its own character. The structure is highly modified by external environmental factors. Shallow soil stunts the trees. Windy areas twist them out of shape. The canopy of a tree species has different shapes, depending on whether a tree stands alone—and then it has a large spreading crown—or it grows tall and straight when packed closely together in a plantation. As trees age, they develop snags, break or fall, leaving behind their mass of woody tissue to be recycled into nutrients in the soil.

The banded button orchid (*Acampe sp.*) is an epiphyte which mimics an insect.

*Bombax* pod releasing its wind-dispersed seeds.

Broad-leaved trees can be either evergreen or deciduous.

Evergreen conifers have a tall conical structure with sloping branches.

A deciduous tree with its typical spreading branches.

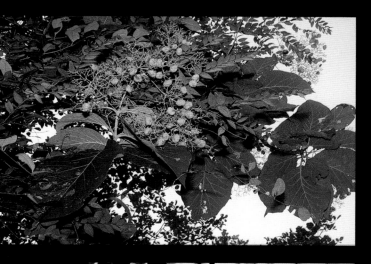

| 1 | 3 |  |
|---|---|---|
| 2 | 4 |  |
|  | 5 | 6 |
|  | 7 |  |

*Tectona grandis*—teak.

*Terminalia arjuna.*

*Terminalia* seeds.

*Lagerstroemia.*

*Ficus racemosa.*

Teak seedling.

*Michelia champaca.*

This tree has become highly contorted due to human influence.

| 1 | 2 |
|---|---|
| 3 | 4 |

| 5 |
|---|

*Emblica sp.—amla.*

*Santalum album—sandalwood.*

*Dillenia indica.*

*Begonia crenata.*

*Saraca asoca—ashoka.*

|   |   |
|---|---|
| 1 | 2 |
| 3 | 4 | 5 | 6 |

*Impatiens sp.*

*Rotala floribunda.*

*Pavetta.*

*Ipomoea.*

*Smithia sp.*

*Aeginetia indica.*

| 1 | | 4 | | 5 | 6 |
|---|---|---|---|---|---|
| | | | | | 8 |
| 2 | | | 7 | | 11 |
| | | | | 10 | |
| 3 | | | 9 | | 12 |

*Hitchenia caulina.*

*Bombax sp.*

*Lobelia nicotianaefolia.*

*Gnetum ula, female cones.*

*Gnetum ula, male cones.*

*Pimpinella.*

*Vanda tessellata.*

*Clematis.*

*Heterophragma quadriloculare.*

*Smithia sp.*

*Amorphophallus sp.*

*Actinodaphne hookeri—pisa.*

| 1 | 2 | 3 | 4 |
| 5 | 6 | 8 | |
| | 7 | | |
| 9 | 10 | 11 | 12 |

*Ficus racemosa.*

*Fermiana colorata.*

*Butea monosperma—palas.*

*Olea sp.*

*Cinnamomum.*

*Holoptelea integrifolia.*

*Zizyphus.*

*Erythrina sp.*

*Albizia sp.*

*Azadirachta indica—neem.*

*Pongamia glabra.*

*Helicteres isora.*

| 1 | 2 | 3 | 5 |
|---|---|---|---|
| 4 | | | 6 |

*Thelepaepale ixiocephala* or *wayati* flowers only once in three or four years.

*Strobilanthes* shrubs in the Western Ghats flower once in seven years and then die.

*Strobilanthes*; from Wallich, 1832

The undergrowth of *Strobilanthes* plants in the Western Ghats is a vital component of the forest ecology.

*Lantana camara.*

*Breynia retusa.*

## SHRUBS

Forest undergrowth ranges from a thick, impenetrable tangle, through sparse shrubs and climbers, to an open forest floor with a few small plants. Several forests have no shrub layer if the canopy is very thick and does not allow enough light to penetrate through for shrubs to grow below. Forest shrubs are of crucial importance for browsing mammals. Even grazers, such as elephants and chitals turn to browsing on shrubs when the grass begins to get tough and dry. Many of our forests have probably already developed a shrub layer which could well be very different from that of undisturbed forests a few centuries ago. Human activities in 'managed' forests have changed the forest floor, either by clearing the undergrowth for its timber, during forestry operations, or by the continuous collection of small timber and firewood, or by the action of repeated fires lit for enhancing grass growth year after year. It is rarely appreciated that weeds introduced accidentally can be as disastrous to a forest ecosystem as the deliberate planting of exotic timber species. To cite the most well-known example, a large number of our forests are now infested with *Lantana*, *Eupatorium* and other weeds, which have changed the original, highly diverse community of shrubs to a single species. This has altered the habitat of the forest for the fauna that utilized a variety of shrubs as food. Changes in community structure induced by such introductions of invasive shrubs can spell disaster for populations of certain animals that are specifically adapted to their natural habitat, eventually leading to their extinction. While the loss of 'naturalness' has serious implications on the ability of several herbivorous species to thrive, it favours those that are able to adapt to the exotic undergrowth of shrubs such as *Lantana*. The problem is serious, as removal of this thick thorny undergrowth is difficult and expensive. Its removal also leaves the area bereft of cover for species such as carnivores and small herbivores, which use it to hide in when the natural undergrowth has disappeared. Regrowth of the natural community of shrubs could take decades.

## CLIMBERS AND LIANAS

The shapes of large climbers or lianas ascending into the canopy in spirals form giant 'U'-shapes as they link one tree to another. This gives the forest a typical jungle-like quality. I have hundreds of pictures of climbers and lianas which, however, somehow never seem to capture the actual effect they create in real life!

There are many fascinating aspects of climbers that have always intrigued me. Climbers spiral in one direction in the northern hemisphere, and reverse in the southern hemisphere in relation to the earth's rotation. Lianas that bridge forest canopies can maintain the continuity of the canopy even if trees that support the liana age and fall. They make convenient bridges between the canopies of the trees and are used by arboreal mammals such as squirrels and monkeys to move through the treetops without descending to the forest floor.

Woody lianas and twining climbers that twist and turn through impenetrable forests are an important aspect of its structure. In plantations they are less abundant as they are frequently removed during forestry operations, thus reducing the naturalness of the ecosystem. There are an incredible number of climbers in a natural forest that not only add to its beauty, but form a significant part of its ecosystem. The wild pepper is a climber for which the Europeans came to India for its commercial value. They later developed techniques to grow it by stripping off all the other climbers and planting it along with other spice plants in the evergreen forests of South India. It was one of the earliest

changes that occurred in the exploitation of the forest systems. Later, the development of timber plantations led to a management system in which climbers were removed.

The lower part of the stem of woody lianas usually doesn't have leaves. The leaves and branches are produced after the plant reaches the forest canopy. This adaptation is due to the extreme competition for light in thick forests where the climber has to emerge above the canopy for sunlight. Lianas are also more abundant in dense forests, and disappear where degradation has opened up the forest canopy.

## THE GROUND FLORA

From the dank darkness of a thick forest floor covered with dry crackling leaves in a broad-leaved deciduous forest, to the strong fragrance of pine needles, each forest floor has a character of its own. In an evergreen, high-rainfall area, the ground is covered with ferns and epiphytes. In the drier areas, there are patches of rich diversity, with flowering herbs and innumerable species of grasses in the openings, in deciduous forests. The richness of species in the ground layer is an astounding feature of nature. I began to appreciate this while trying to unravel the nature of the less disturbed, as compared to the highly disturbed areas, in the forests of the catchments of Tata Power Company's dams from the Western Ghats in Mulshi and Mawal districts of Maharashtra. This has brought home to me not only the incredible diversity of plant species in terms of tree and shrub cover, but also the enormous variety and highly localized nature of the herbs of the open shrubby areas of the Western Ghats.

Plants such as rare ground orchids can be found either in very small, localized areas, or scantily distributed over wide areas. Both patterns of rarity need different management strategies if the extinction of such species is to be prevented. One can not define clearly the effects on these rare herbs of grazing and of repeated fires lit by grazers to induce fresh flush of grass and to burn off the old tough grasses. Even the Forest Department's strategy of planting fast-growing exotic trees such as eucalyptus and *Acacia auriculiformis* could

very well affect adversely the low level of abundance of a rare herb and drive it over the precipice of extinction.

Aparna Watve's work in the Western Ghats has shown the importance of natural open, grass-covered hill slopes on what is usually considered to be useless, highly disturbed, 'degraded' areas of the Western Ghats. There are probably more endemic and endangered species of plants growing in such open areas than within the forests themselves! It is these open natural areas, however, that are being encroached by human activity that make it difficult to define appropriate ecologically sensitive management regimes for tracts formed by a mosaic of different plant communities.

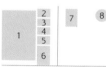

The trunk of a tree provides support for climbers, epiphytes, ferns and fungi.

Lianas have great twining stems as thick as branches of trees.

*Diploclisia glaucescens* creates bridges between treetops which are used by squirrels, monkeys and other animals.

*Diploclisia glaucescens* climbs into the canopy and flowers profusely.

Some climbers like *Clematis* have thin stems that twine through the forest canopy towards the light.

A climber twining around the trunk of a tree.

*Diploclisia* fruits.

Ground flora is rich in species. However, it can be easily invaded by exotic weeds.

| 1 | 2 |
|---|---|
| 3 4 | 5 |
| 6 | 7 |

The moist microhabitat of the forest floor is the niche for this *Sonerila*.

*Osbekia angustifolia;* from Wallich, 1832.

A carpet of flowers at the Himalayan foothills attracts large numbers of insects.

Plants have an enormous capacity for regeneration. Wind blown seeds can travel over long distances.

*Utricularia sp.*

Structural variations of flowering plants in the undergrowth link them to specific animal species.

Himalayan plants flower for a brief period.

| The Evolution of Plant Life | | |
|---|---|---|
| Species | Era | Time Period |
| Single cells, colonial, filamentous and multicelluar green algae | Pre-Cambrian | 4560–540 million years ago |
| Lichen | Cambrian | 540–500 million years ago |
| Plants with root-like systems | Devonian | 408–362 million years ago |
| Fern and gymnosperm features | Carboniferous | 362–290 million years ago |
| Gymnosperms, including conifers | Permain | 290–245 million years ago |
| Angiosperms | Cretaceous | 145–65 million years ago |

| | 2 |
|---|---|
| 1 | 3 |

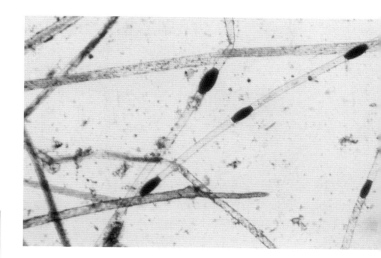

Seaweed has the potential to act as major source of food.

Algae.

Kelp forms the habitat for many marine creatures.

## THE EVOLUTION OF PLANT LIFE
### ALGAE

Algae evolved during an early period of the Earth's history. They are the simplest of all the forms of life and vary from different shades of green to blue-green, brown and red. The structure of these early species is given by cells grouped in a simple arrangement, which varies from tiny and brittle to powdery, while others are spongy or jelly-like. They range in size from microscopic unicellular protoctists to large seaweeds found in the ocean.

Algae are found almost everywhere. They live mainly in moist conditions, in the soil, in fresh water and in marine conditions. In aquatic ecosystems, they are vital primary producers on which several other forms of life are dependent. In forest ecosystems they grow on leaves, stems, the bark of shrubs and trees and moist rocks. Some of them are closely associated with fungi and form lichens. Algae reproduce vegetatively by division of cells or by spores formed inside the cell. They are used in industry, pharmaceuticals and agriculture. Various experiments are being carried out in an attempt to use algae as protein food for cattle and human beings. Some are being used as fertilizers.

In water bodies polluted with sewage or fertilizers, algal growth is facilitated due to an increase in nutrients. This results in massive algal growth, leading to eutrophication. This process, in turn, leads to an over utilization of the dissolved oxygen from the water, during the algae's respiration. Thus there is a lowering of the oxygen level, which kills off aquatic fauna such as fish and crustacea.

There are over 6500 species of algae in India (MoEF, 2002). The algal diversity of the Indian coasts alone is represented by 215 genera and 680 species (MoEF, 2002). Their diversity and great abundance in terrestrial as well as aquatic ecosystems is a significant part of life itself. The evolutionary processes that began as an alga-like form in the remote past of the earth's history will forever be an event representing a unique period for our planet.

The collections that were made to document Indian algae can be traced back to 1798. Marine algae were collected from the Andamans in 1822. Wight collected seaweed from the coasts of Cape Comorin and Pondicherry, along the eastern coast. Murray collected algal specimens from Karachi between 1881 and 1883. In the 1940s JA Murray, SC Dixit and PL Anand worked extensively on marine algae along the western coast of India (Biswas, 1945). Algae form the basis of several food chains, both in marine and freshwater ecosystems.

They support herbivores such as aquatic insects, crustacea, fish, reptiles and mammals—a fact that links them to the carnivorous species of the aquatic food web.

An overgrowth of algae, due to an abnormally high influx of nutrients from urban sewage for example, can change an aquatic ecosystem drastically. I have seen whole lake ecosystems change over a few years and rivers lose their fish and waterfowl. The Mula Mutha River, in Pune, turned into a sewer within a decade or two. A river once known for giant mahseer in the 1940s, now it cannot even support fish a few centimetres in size. The teeming wild fowl have been reduced to a small percentage of what were seen only a few decades ago. The masses of algae now consume all the oxygen and have killed the river.

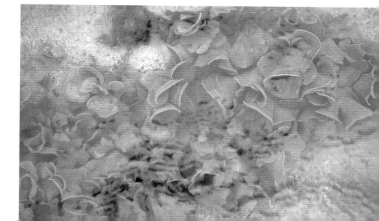

## FUNGI

This group of heterotrophic organisms— quite distinct from plant life—resembles plants in their reproductive mechanism and cell organization. They differ widely from green plants as they lack chlorophyll. Fungi can break down dead or living material to obtain nutrients for their growth. They are either saprophytic, and live on dead or dying plants and animals, or they are parasitic and live on living organisms. Fungi have fascinating variations in their structure.

In India, there are approximately 14,500 species of fungi reported, of which 24 per cent, or 3500, are endemic (MoEF, 2002). Fungi are found in different habitat types, ranging from moist evergreen forests to dry habitats. They are most abundant, however, in moist microhabitats. Fungi are an important part of the detritus food chain in the ecosystem, in which they maintain a balance by recycling nutrients. Fungi break down leaves, branches, trunks, roots, animal excreta and carcasses, converting them into simpler organic material and finally into inorganic salts. Their spores are found in air, soil, fresh and marine water. Some fungi cause allergic manifestations when they are inhaled by humans.

Fungi include diverse microscopic forms as well as large mushrooms, some of which are edible and considered a delicacy, while others are highly poisonous. It is difficult to differentiate between the fungi which are edible and those that are extremely poisonous. In the wilderness, even a small amount of innocuous-looking fungi can be fatal if eaten. While we would find it difficult to learn the difference, I have been out with tribal people who could tell the edible from the poisonous at a glance. Edible fungi are very rich in protein and have low carbohydrate content, and many species are used in the manufacture of enzymes and antibiotics. Some highly palatable mushrooms that are overharvested for food are becoming uncommon. Certain fungi are used by underground termites to grow fungal gardens on which they feed.

While the microscopic soil fungi remain hidden in the soil, it is their presence that helps plants to grow. Fungi form an association with the roots of plants and break down organic material in the soil that plants can absorb. We rarely realize this incredible linkage between plant life and the microscopic fungi in the ecosystem.

In the forests, the large fungi that grow on moist trunks of trees and out of moist patches of soft soil, have fascinating shapes. There are large brackets that are formed on tree branches, lacy or leaf-like fungi of different colours in the detritus of dead leaves and solid, ball-like shapes that emerge in moist places. Their colours vary from white and grey, gold to orange and even purple. I have seen fungi that are luminescent at night, changing the forests of the Bhimashankar Sanctuary into a glowing green mysterious world on a monsoon night.

There are fungi just about everywhere and they are an incredibly fascinating group, that plays an important role in the functioning of almost all ecosystems.

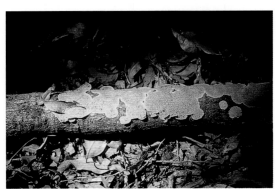

| | |
|---|---|
| 3 | |
| 4 | |
| 1 | 5 |
| 2 | |

Bracket fungi grow profusely in moist microhabitats.

India has approximately 14,500 species of fungi.

Mushrooms growing on a fallen log.

Mushrooms on the forest floor.

Drawing showing the enormous diversity of fungi in the Indian continent.

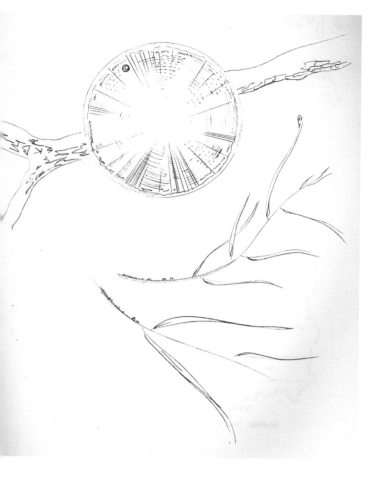

```
    2   8
1   3   9
    4
    5   10
    6
    7   11
```

Fungi are now not considered a part of the plant world but form a separate group. Several microscopic fungi have strong symbiotic relationships with plants. Others grow on dead or dying plant material, thereby recycling nutrients into the soil.

Profuse growth of fungi over a dead stump.

Fungi explode to release thousands of spores.

Fungi have the most incredible shapes and colours.

Lacy fungus in the Western Ghats.

Fungi thrive on dead wood.

Unusual red mushrooms in the undergrowth.

Bracket fungi.

Fungi can live almost anywhere.

Bright golden fungi make a splash of unexpected colour in the forest.

Many fungi are intimately related to the forest detritus.

## LICHEN

The rocks of an evergreen forest are covered with lichen that turn the rock into a mini living ecosystem. These tiny species cover even the rock surfaces. To a casual glance it is just one more simple species. But when one begins to understand its nature, one realizes that lichen is formed by an extremely interesting phenomenon, closely knit combinations of algae and fungi. Each is dependent on the other in this association that leads to the formation of a completely different-looking

structure—a tiny composite organism that covers the bare rock surface in the forest.

In this unique association of algal cells and fungi, the fungal partner dominates. The algal component produces food, which is used by the fungus. The fungus provides moisture for the algal form and is even involved in its reproduction. This symbiotic association benefits both the species. Each type of lichen is named after the specific fungal species that forms a part of this fascinating partnership. Some are powdery, others form a crust, while still others are fleshy and highly branched.

Lichen constitute one of the dominant life forms on earth estimated at about 8 per cent. There are about 2021 species of lichen present in India (MoEF, 2002). The Western Ghats are their richest habitat with 800 species, followed by the Eastern Himalayas with 759 species and the Western Himalayas with 550 species (MoEF, 2002). Lichen are found even in extreme conditions. They are the dominant forms in the Antarctic. They are pioneers that begin the process of succession in various types of barren areas. Their peculiar structure

allows them to grow by producing acids, which erode the rocky surface on which they spread. They can absorb moisture and other nutrients directly from the air. Some associations of species do not grow in polluted air and hence are considered to be indicators of the level of pollutants in the air.

Some types of lichen are likely to be so severely affected by pollutants that they disappear from polluted ecosystems. Lichens are used as food, medicine, spices, for extracting an essence and producing dyes.

## BRYOPHYTES
### MOSSES AND LIVERWORTS

A walk through a damp forest reveals its character created by the moss that covers rocks and tree trunks and hangs from the branches of the trees. This gives an impression of the moist nature of the ecosystem. I can never resist touching the velvety surface of a rock covered by moss in an evergreen forest. The moss on the tree trunks forms a microhabitat for a variety of insects, and it is here that insectivorous birds hunt for their food. And there are birds that collect moss to line their nests. The layer of moss favours

Lichen in the forest detritus.

Lichen is formed by an association of an algae and a fungus.

Lichen range from tiny barely discernable species to macroscopic forms

Bryophytes include mosses and liverworts.

the growth of epiphytic orchids and ferns. Moss forms a microhabitat covered with dewdrops, which acts as a specialized moist microhabitat for several species.

Bryophytes comprise an estimated 2850 species in India and are the second largest group of green plants in the country (MoEF, 2002).

Mosses (*Musci*) and liverworts (*Hepaticae*) form the group called Bryophytes. These are small, green, shade and moisture-loving species, which reproduce by spores instead of seeds. In evolutionary terms, they are considered to be somewhere between simple algae and more complex plants like ferns and angiosperms. There are about 14,000 species of mosses and 10,000 species of liverworts in the world. India has about 2000 mosses and 850 liverworts. They are abundant in the temperate regions of the world including the Himalayas, and in tropical ecosystems.

There are two distinct phases in the life cycle of bryophytes, first as a sporophyte and then as a gametophyte, each having a different chromosome number. The gametophyte is the conspicuous phase that resembles an alga with thin, delicate root-like rhizoids. The sporophyte is attached to the gametophyte throughout its life and is either partially or wholly dependent on it for nutrition. The sporophyte is well-differentiated into a 'foot', which is embedded in the gametophyte tissue by a 'seta' or stalk. It also has a capsule, which is the spore-bearing case. Water is essential for their fertilization.

Mosses are a group of comparatively more evolved bryophytes, with distinct root, stem, and tiny leaf-like structures, which are spirally arranged around a central axis. The structure of the sporophyte is similar to that of other bryophytes. When the capsule matures, it opens to release the spores from which new gametophytes arise.

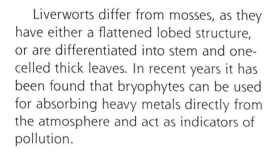

Liverworts differ from mosses, as they have either a flattened lobed structure, or are differentiated into stem and one-celled thick leaves. In recent years it has been found that bryophytes can be used for absorbing heavy metals directly from the atmosphere and act as indicators of pollution.

### PTERIDOPHYTES OR FERNS

Ferns are pteridophytes comprising a widespread group of plants of about 10,000 species. There are about 1135 species of pteridophytes in the Subcontinent. Nearly 17 per cent or 193 species of these are endemic to India (MoEF, 2002). Their habitats range from the Himalayas, to the Gangetic Plains and even the Thar Desert. The maximum diversity of ferns is found in the Himalayas. These beautiful plants vary in size from a hair-like creeping stem, bearing a few simple leaves, to tall tree-like forms. The stem or 'trunk' of these tree ferns can be a foot in diameter. The commoner species have stems that trail along the ground, or penetrate the soil and grow underground. When young, the leaf tips are coiled like a watch spring. A simple strand of vascular tissue runs through the stem and the leaves. Like most other plants they have conducting tissues—the xylem and phloem.

At one time ferns dominated the Earth's surface, till the more advanced angiosperms evolved and took over most of the habitats. Most ferns are associated with microhabitats that provide long moist periods and deep shade. Others grow in open areas or along the edges of forest patches. They grow in rock crevices, as epiphytes and as climbers in well-drained but moisture-rich habitats such as watercourses. Most forms multiply and spread by producing a very large number of spores. Ferns have no flowers, fruit or seeds, but some Himalayan ferns are edible. They are frequently used as decorative plants in homes and gardens. India is exceptionally rich in ferns, but few specific efforts have been made to preserve the rarer fern species by growing them in gardens. There is also a need to study the known areas where rare fern species are located, so that sanctuaries could be created for them. Ex situ programmes will have to be initiated where the rarer species can be grown in botanical gardens to preserve their gene pool.

Walking through an evergreen forest, one cannot help looking at the ferns that typify the moist nature of the ecosystem. Ferns are so habitat-specific that they grow only where light and moisture are at an optimal level. A bank of ferns may need a dark, dripping microhabitat. Another may act as the colonizer of a sunny opening in the forest, and be an indicator of change from a dryer, warmer habitat to a cooler, wetter one. This change that one can observe while climbing a hill or a mountain slope is so sudden that it shows how sensitive ferns are to habitat conditions. There is virtually a fern line, just as one can see a tree line in the Himalayas.

| 1 | | 4 |
|---|---|---|
| 2 | 3 | 5 |

Moss spreads by forming capsules which release thousands of spores.

Moss growing in a moist niche.

*Sphacropteris barbata*; from Wallich, 1830.

Ferns in the undergrowth are usually seen in moist areas.

Giant tree fern in an evergreen forest.

## GYMNOSPERMS

Gymnosperms, highly valued for wood and decorative purposes, are plants which have their seeds borne directly on the female organs. They have neither flower nor fruits and the male and female organs commonly form a woody cone as seen in the Pine. This group of plants, which produce pollen and seeds in their cones, evolved around 200 million years ago and are dominant mainly in temperate climates. In India, they are more common in the Himalayas, where Himalayan conifers like the deodar and the pine are well known. The tropical gymnosperms include the gnetum and the cycas species, which differ widely from those of the temperate region.

The species of coniferous forests differ in the eastern and western Himalayas. Of a total of 750 species of gymnosperms in the world, about 60 species occur in the Indian subcontinent. Within the boundaries of India, 48 species and 10 varieties of 14 genera grow in the wild (MoEF, 2002). Conifers are the dominant among the gymnosperms. *Pinaceae* is the richest family, represented by 17 species of 6 genera.

Male cones of *Gnetum ula*, a type of Gymnosperm.

## CYCADS

Whenever one sees an unusual or uncommon plant in a forest, one begins to wonder why it is uncommon. Take an example of the occasional presence of a cycad. Are the specific conditions it requires for growth and spread just too specific? Or is its growth or ability to multiply much slower, compared to other plants? Are its microhabitat needs more specific than those of other plants? Or is it an ancient species, which is now finding it increasingly difficult to compete with more recently evolved species and it is thus declining? I have seen cycas plants many times in different forests. But there have always been very few specimens in the area. It is species such as these that will disappear if left to themselves. They need both in situ and ex situ conservation efforts.

Cycads are gymnosperms which differ from the conifers in their palm-like appearance. They are among the most primitive seed plants, and have remained virtually unchanged through the past 200 million years. It was once believed that they were the link between primitive ferns and more complex seed plants. However current opinion from fossil evidence is that they are true gymnosperms. Cycas is the only genus native to India with five species.

An unusually branched cycad in the evergreen forest.

In India there are five species of Cycas.

Cycas is an ancient plant species which has remained unchanged for 200 million years.

## CONIFERS

The cold always seems sharper than the real temperature in a coniferous forest of the Himalayas, even at a lower level. The closeness of the trees, the darkness under their shade, the dampness of the dry needle-like leaves that form a thick layer on the ground, all add to this nip in the air. The tall, almost vertical, trunks and the symmetry of the branches of the conifers give the forest a rigid structure, most unlike the varied tree shapes and branching variability so obvious in a broadleaved forest. Both have a charm of their own, very different from each other but both, for me at least, are equally beautiful.

All Indian conifers are evergreen trees. Except for a single species, all the conifers are Himalayan and constitute a major part of the forests of the Himalayas and those at the foothills.

Coniferous forests of the Himalayas.

## ANGIOSPERMS

The flowering plants known scientifically as Angiosperms are the dominant group of plants in most terrestrial ecosystems and they have evolved about 120 million years ago. They are characterized by possession of a true flower with sepals and petals in addition to the male and female reproductive organs, and the seeds are enclosed in a fruit. These characters suggest that they are more advanced than the Gymnosperms and have, indeed, evolved from them. There are about 250,000 known species of Angiosperms, which are broadly classified into Dicots (with seeds having two cotyledons) and Monocots (with seeds having one cotyledon). The Dicots include familiar plants such as the pulses, while Monocots include cereals and palms. The further division of these two groups into families is based on the flower characters and may often confuse a layman. For example, plants that are commonly known as Palms in fact include plants from very distinct families. Coconut and arecanut are examples of the true palms while herbaceous and climbing palms seen in gardens are an altogether different group.

The composition of species of different trees and their abundance or otherwise in a forest provide the landscape with its distinctive features. Forests in hot spots of high diversity in India such as the Western Ghats can have over 100 species of trees. Shrubs, climbers, grasses and herbs add to this great diversity of flora. It is the rich evergreen plant communities that have fascinated me for years. In the Western Ghats around the Tata Power Company's lakes, I learnt to appreciate their incredible diversity and the great degree of patchiness that creates a wide range of plant communities. The patchy distribution of a tree species can be caused by such an enormous number of factors that it is almost impossible at times to explain this phenomenon except in the broadest of terms. Every species, from the few very abundant ones to the large number of uncommon species, are of importance in an ecosystem. However, it is the rarer plants that are most at threat as they are by nature few in number within the plant community. Species that are rare and used for a specific purpose are most highly threatened. Losing these species locally from several sites could ultimately lead to their extinction.

Some plants have a major role to play in the forest ecosystem and are considered to be keystone species. The most well-known of these are the ficus species that fruit all year round, providing food for frugivorous mammals, birds and insects when all the other tree species have no fruit. These species thus have a wider significance for ecorestoration in establishing a local conservation strategy of a degraded forest ecosystem. Appreciating the abundance and community structure of plants is important to establish a plantation based on sound ecological principles.

As most of our forests have been worked for timber over the last couple of centuries, their naturalness has been seriously affected by planting mainly economically important timber species. Clearing climbers and lianas and the removal of a large number of the less economically viable tree species to plant timber species have reduced the great biological diversity of many tracts of forests in India. In fact very little real undisturbed 'natural' forest can be said to exist today. Foresters love their straight lines of teak, sal or pine that they continue to grow wherever possible. I have seen teak plantations in the sal belt and pine trees growing in cleared

| 1 | 2 |
|   | 3 |

Flowering plants add colour to the forest floor.

*Careya arborea.*

Some species have an exceptionally short flowering period during the monsoon.

patches of highly diverse Shola forests in the southern Western Ghats, Nilgiris and Annamalais. Eucalyptus, *subabul* (*Leucaena leucocephala*) and *Acacia auriculiformis* are grown just about anywhere a plantation can be raised. The loss of plant diversity and forest naturalness is incredibly high. Grasslands of great value are converted into Social Forestry plantations, which are at times of rather dubious value for fulfilling the real needs of local people. Even highly threatened habitats, with endemic ground flora, such as plateau tops in the Western Ghats are planted with trees or bamboo, with no care for the large number of very rare ground plants that grow only on these rocky plateaus. The planted trees of course usually die, but the damage to these rare endemic species of small plants is likely to be permanent.

| 1 | | 4 |
|---|---|---|
| 2 | 3 | 5 | 6 |

*Hitchenia caulina.*

*Firmiana sp.*

Flowering plants are an important component of the forest biomass.

*Mappia foetida.*

*Ariopsis peltata.*

Brightly coloured flowers of *Melastoma malabathricum* attract butterflies.

| 1 | 2 |
|---|---|
| 3 | 4 |

*Emilia sonchifolia.*

*Sonerila scapigera.*

*Costus speciosus.*

*Rhynchospora wightiana.*

| 1 | | 3 |
|---|---|---|
| 2 | | |

White flowers usually attract night flying insects for pollination.

*Pinda concanensis.*

*Exacum tetragonum,* an attractive plant of the undergrowth.

White flowers are known to mainly attract nocturnal pollinators as well as insects and birds during daytime.

*Previous page*
Fragile lacy flowers commonly seen in the Western Ghats.

*Crataeva sp.* has delicate flowers.

The reproductive parts of an Angiosperm—stamens and pistils—are a distinctive feature of each species.

Wild roses from the Himalayas.

## PLANT DISTRIBUTION IN INDIA

The most abundant trees of a forest are frequently used to name the forest type within the more general ecologically related types of forests such as the coniferous forests and the broad-leaved forests of the Himalayas. The Himalayas are characterized by coniferous forests and broad-leaved forests which are related to the altitude at which a tree species grows. These forests have pines, cedars, birches, firs, junipers, cypress, yew, spruce, etc. in the Western Himalayas. Junipers, alders, fir, etc. are found in the Eastern Himalayas. The broadleaved trees are oak, birch, elm, poplars and rhododendrons. Rhododendrons are more prominent in the eastern Himalayas.

The thorn forests are located in western and peninsular India in the arid and semi-arid tracts of Rajasthan, Gujarat and Maharashtra. The dry belt of India has trees such as *Acacia, Salvadora, Capparis, Zizyphus* and *Anogeissus*.

Large parts of the Deccan Peninsula and of the Gangetic Plains have deciduous forests. To the west and south, the most abundant tree is the teak while to the northeast, the most abundant one is sal. The teak forests are generally dry deciduous, while most sal forests are moist deciduous. The plant species associated with teak and sal are generally different although some species occur in both types of forests. The other dominant trees in dry teak forests are *Terminalia, Anogeissus pendula, Anogeissus latifolia, Hardwickia binata* and *Cleistanthus*. Sal forests have dominant trees such as *Buchanania, Cleistanthus, Terminalia, Adina, Dillenia, Pterospermum, Syzygium* and *Toona*.

Evergreen forests are located in the north-east of India, Western Ghats and Andaman and Nicobar Islands. They have their own specific dominant species, such as the group known as Dipterocarps. The evergreen forests include species such as *Gordonia, Schefflera, Meliosa, Memecylon, Actinodaphne, Syzygium, Bridelia, Ficus, Dipterocarpus, Mesua, Palaquium*, etc.

Large sections of the coniferous and broad-leaved forests of the Himalayas have been degraded.

A typical thorn forest in Rajasthan.

1  2

3

Deciduous forests cover large areas of the Deccan Plateau and the Gangetic Plains.

Teak trees are generally found in deciduous and dry deciduous forests.

Sal is the dominant species of the moist deciduous and semi-evergreen forests.

The Nature of Biodiversity in India

The trees of the evergreen forest shed their leaves throughout the year, thus retaining their canopy in all seasons.

## HIMALAYAN FORESTS

In what is known as the alpine region, above 3600 metres in the Western and Eastern Himalayas, the dominant species are rhododendrons and junipers. In the temperate forests, between 1500 and 3600 metres, there are patches of conifers or broad-leaved forests. Broad-leaved forests occur in the Western and Eastern Himalayas between 1200 and 1800 metres. These consist of trees such as oak, chestnut, and maple. Mixed deciduous and sal forests occur in the tropical and subtropical parts, up to an altitude of 1000 metres.

The main difference between the vegetation of the Eastern and the Western Himalayas is that the eastern ranges have fewer conifers and more broad-leaved trees. There are more than 20 oak species in the east, as compared to 5 in the west. In the east, rhododendrons are more abundant, along with ferns and orchids, which greatly outnumber those in the Western Himalayas. Having travelled through the lower Himalayas over several years, I have watched forested tracts gradually disappear.

The typical shape and branching pattern of coniferous trees, such as pine and deodar with their thin leaves and cones, typify these forests of the Himalayas. The pine forests of the Himalayan foothills have a typical fresh smell and the dry pine needles on the forest floor form a thick cool moist carpet. It tends however to prevent the growth of a rich ground flora. The forest is remarkably silent until a flock of birds flits through the trees. Far away from an opposite slope a hill partridge begins to call. The haunting sound echoes through the hills. Other coniferous forests such as deodar (*Cedrus deodara*) are also similar. The tall stately trees give uniformity to the forest structure, producing wide vistas with the backdrop of snow-covered mountains.

The broad-leaved Himalayan forests are much more diverse, with rhododendron, which have bright scarlet red, pink or white blossoms, and oak trees (*Quercus sp.*), which turn gold and red as winter approaches.

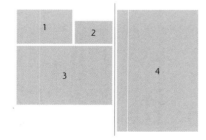

*Previous pages*
The extensive planting of the coniferous trees
has led to the depletion of deciduous trees in the
Himalayan Ranges.

Chir pine is seen between 1000 and 1600 metres.
Blue pine occurs at higher altitudes, above
1600 metres. The needle-like leaves of a conifer
are adapted for resisting heavy snowfall and
conserving water.

Pine trees have very diverse cones.

Pine cones produce spores for dispersion.

Coniferous trees have needle-like leaves.

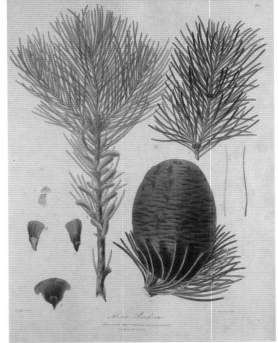

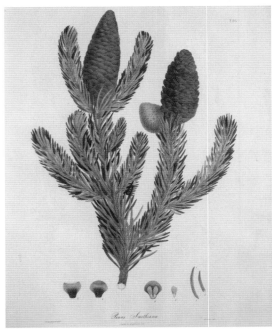

1 | 3
2 | 4 | 5

*Pinus quercus*; from Royle, 1839.

*Pinus brunoniana*; from Wallich, 1832.

*Abies*; from Royle, 1839.

*Pinus smithiana*; from Wallich, 1832.

Himalayan cedar or deodar is mainly found in the Western Himalayan coniferous forests at an altitude of 1600 and 1900 metres.

### GENUS *PINUS*

True pine trees, or the genus *Pinus*, are a group of about 100 species of evergreen conifers, of which 5 are found in India. Most are stately, pyramidal trees but a few are shrubs. The timber of pine trees is one of the most frequently used softwoods in construction, carpentry and the paper industry, while pine resin is used to make turpentine, resin, tar and pitch. Pine oils are obtained by distillation of leaves and shoots. Pines are extensively planted in the Himalayan region for timber as they grow rapidly and plantations are highly successful. This reduces the tree diversity of the Himalayan hill slopes and affects the integrity of this sensitive ecosystem. Pines are used for landscaping and as garden plants.

The *Pinus* species of the Western and Eastern Himalayas include specific groups of species akin to those of Europe in the west and those of the countries of South-east Asia in the east. For example, *Pinus wallichiana* and *Pinus roxburghii* are found mainly in the Western Himalayas, while *Pinus insularis* is found in the east Himalayas. Pine leaves are thin and needle-like, and they can be of two types, forming either bracts or adult leaves. Male and female cones are separate but occur on the same tree and male and female spores are produced in these woody cones. The dispersal of pollen is aided by the two wings each grain has. Wind pollination leads to seed development. The seeds have long wings and are dispersed by wind. As a group, they are one of the dominant trees of temperate Himalayan forests. These coniferous forests at high altitudes are interspersed by broad-leaved oak forests.

## GENUS *ABIES*

*Abies* is a genus of evergreen trees found in the Himalayan region. They are easily distinguishable by the erect cone breaking up at maturity. The needles occur singly, on a rounded, disc-like needle scar, which is not raised above the bark. Most species are valued for their fine ornamental stature. The softwood is easily worked and mainly used for simple furniture.

---

### *Abies sp.*—Firs. (Pinaceae).

A genus of about 49 species of evergreen conifer of the northern, temperate regions of Europe and Asia. Three species are found in the Himalayas.

---

## GENUS *CEDRUS*

*Cedrus* is a genus of stately evergreens found mainly in the Western Himalayas, of which deodar (*Cedrus deodara*) is the best-known species. All these species have long and short shoots, the latter with clusters of needle-like leaves. Male cones are erect, ovoid or conical, opening from September to November. Female cones are erect, borne terminally on short shoots. Fruiting cones are oval in shape. Usually trees do not bear cones till they are 40 or 50 years old.

The timber of the *Cedrus* is soft but durable, and widely used for construction and furniture. Its resin has been used for embalming.

*Cedrus deodara*, Himalayan or Indian Cedar, is a pyramidal tree when young and irregular when mature. It grows upto 60 metres in height with pendulous leading shoots and slightly drooping lateral branches with pendulous tips. Its cones are barrel-shaped with a rounded apex.

---

### *Cedrus deodara*—Himalayan cedar or deodar. (Pinaceae).

The only true cedar occurring in India, where it is native to the Western Hiamalayas. It was first described by David Don in 1824, in AB Lambert's monograph on the genus *Pinus*.

---

## GENUS *CUPRESSUS*

These are true cypresses comprising about 20 species, of which only one is indigenous to India, *Cupressus torulosa*. The branchlets are densely clothed with small overlapping scale-like leaves. Male and female cones are terminal, solitary and occur on separate branches of the same tree. The seeds are winged, aiding in wind dispersal. The timber of many of these species is valuable, being durable and easily worked. Its timber is also used in construction, carpentry and for posts or poles.

*Cupressus torulosa* is the Bhutan or Himalayan cypress, found in the Western Himalayas. The tree grows to a height of 50 metres. The branches are more or less flattened, curved and characteristially whip-like.

## GENUS *JUNIPERS*

Junipers are evergreen trees and shrubs, one of the commonest species in the Eastern Himalayas, although they are also present in the Western Himalayas. The juniper's leaves are of two kinds. The normal adult leaves are small and scale-like, while juvenile leaves are larger and awl-shaped. Cones are unisexual, borne either on different plants or separately on the same plant. Male cones are solitary or come in crowded catkins. Female cones consist of 3 to 8 fleshy, pointed scales, which coalesce to form a 'berry'. Juniper wood is durable and easy to work. The presence of oils is responsible for resistance to insect attacks. The timber is used in building, roof shingles, furniture, posts and fences. Junipers are slow-growing and hardy. A number of species are frequently grown as ornamental plants in parks and gardens.

## GENUS *TAXUS*

Yew is the popular name for *Taxus,* a genus of evergreen trees, shrubs and small plants. *Taxus baccata* is the only species of the genus *Taxus* with several varieties. The leaves are linear and more or less spirally arranged on erect shoots. Male and female cones are normally borne on different plants and are small and solitary. When ripe, the seed is nut-like and surrounded by a fleshy cup, conspicuous by its scarlet

colour. All parts of the plant except the scarlet aril are highly poisonous. The poison is a mixture of alkaloids collectively referred to as taxine. Yew poisoning, resulting in gastroenteritis and heart or respiratory failure, is extremely serious and can be fatal. Yews are used as ornamental plants, as they make excellent hedges. *Taxus baccata* is over-collected as it is used as an anti-cancer agent.

## GENUS *BETULA*

Birch is a species of the genus *Betula*, which consists of about 50 species, of which India has 3, mostly in the Western Himalayas. They are deciduous, wind-pollinated trees and shrubs known for their beauty and usefulness. The bark peels off in papery layers. Some species are characterised by trunks of yellow, orange, reddish-brown or almost black shades. Leaves are alternate and serrate. The flowers are borne in unisexual catkins, each with three flowers. Male and female flowers are found on the same plant. The fruit is a two-winged small nut, which is dispersed by the wind. The timber is used for furniture and firewood and the twigs and bark yield oil, is used as a preservative.

## GENUS *ALNUS*

Alders are characteristically found in cool climates and are moisture-loving. In India, they are found mostly in the Western Himalayas. Of the 35 species found in different parts of the world, India has only two. Alders are deciduous trees and shrubs with alternate simple leaves, usually serrate or dentate. Flowers are unisexual and occur in catkins with both sexes on the same plant. Pendulous male catkins are borne on the tips of the previous year's shoots, while female catkins are erect or pendulous, forming a characteristic woody fruit like a small pine cone. An important feature is the presence of large nodules on the roots of the symbiotic bacterium *Frankia alni* which fix nitrogen. Tannin obtained from the bark is used for curing hides and also for dyeing linen.

## GENUS *ULMUS*

Elm as a genus consists of deciduous trees. It is identifiable by two salient leaf characteristics: bilateral asymmetry and bidentate leaf margins. Flowers may be stalked or sessile, buds arising mostly in spring. The foliage of some species is used as cattle feed. The special characteristics of timber are that it is cross-grained and resistant to splitting, and to decay under waterlogged conditions.

### GENUS *QUERCUS*

Oak is a large tree and economically an important genus, including many trees known for their beautiful shape and their changing seasonal colours. There are 30 to 40 known Indian species of this genus found in the temperate areas throughout the Himalayas. More species of oak are found in the Eastern Himalayas than in the western part. Specimens have been recorded to grow up to 700 years old. Oaks are predominantly trees, but some are shrubs. They may be evergreen, semi-evergreen or deciduous. Leaf margins are usually cut or lobed in various ways. Male and female flowers are borne on the same tree. Male flowers are pendulous catkins; female flowers are solitary or form spikes of two or more flowers. The fruit is a large, solitary, characteristic nut (acorn). Oaks are wind-pollinated and interspecific hybridisation is extensive. Oaks provide the finest hardwoods of great strength and durability, used for building ships, bridges and furniture.

### GENUS *POPULUS*

Poplars belong to the genus *Populus* comprising 34 species of trees of which 6 are found in India in the Himalayan region, including the plains of Punjab and Sind. Mostly fast growing trees, they can grow to a large size. All poplars have resinous buds and alternate leaves with long stalks. Flowers occur in pendulous catkins, which open before the leaves, the two sexes occurring on separate trees, except in some specimens. Poplars are wind-pollinated and their fruit are capsules with numerous seeds, each surrounded at the base by long silky hair. The wood is soft, pale and without any smell. It is relatively non-flammable and does not readily splinter. Poplars have been extensively planted for the wood, which is used in the match industry.

Poplars are found in the Himalayan regions and spread into the plains of Punjab and Sind.

Oaks are found in the evergreen, semi-evergreen and deciduous temperate Himalayan forests.

## GENUS *RHODODENDRON*

This is one of the largest in the plant kingdom, with over 800 species. The highly diverse genus comprises mostly erect shrubs, which grow to a height of about 10 metres, but they may also form 30-metres tall forest giants or tiny alpine shrubs. Leaves vary in size, are alternate with entire margins, and may be evergreen or deciduous, and dark or light green. The undersides of leaves have glandular or non-glandular hair. The first flowers open at low elevations in midwinter carrying on into summer and fall. The size and shape of the bisexual flowers varies. The fruit is a capsule, and splits to release large quantities of very small and light seeds that are winged or tailed for wind dispersal.

Rhododendrons are classified into four groups: scaly rhododendrons, 'true' rhododendrons, azaleas and 'false' azaleas. They dominate plant life in the Himalayas, especially the Eastern Himalayas where 80 species are known, compared to 5 species in the Western Himalayas. Rhododendrons are mostly used for aesthetic purposes, though some have been used as medicinal plants. Few rhododendrons were known before Hooker visited Sikkim in 1849. The majority of species from South-east Asia were studied only between 1910 and 1950 and introduced into the West.

| | 1 | |
|---|---|---|
| | 2 | 3 |
| 4 | | 5 |

Rhododendron.

Rhododendron flowers provide splashes of colour in the Himalayan region. *Rhododendron niveum* is the state tree of Sikkim and *Rhododenrum arboreum* is the state tree of Uttaranchal. The flowers are also the state flowers of Himachal Pradesh, and Nagaland.

Rhododendrons are evergreen trees and shrubs frequently seen in the Eastern Himalayas and have a great variety of brightly coloured flowers.

*Oak acorn*; from Hooker, 1855.

Plant enthusiasts of the 1800s were interested in sending rhododendrons to the West for their gardens; from Wight, 1834.

### GENUS *JUGLANS*

Walnuts belong to the genus *Juglans* found in the Himalayan region and comprise mostly deciduous trees, with pinnate leaves which are aromatic when crushed. Male flowers come in unbranched catkins while female flowers are few in number and occur on the same tree. The fruit is a drupe with fleshy outer and inner nut, and a single seed containing oil. Several species with hard durable wood are timber trees used in furniture and veneers. Most species provide edible nuts. The common walnut is the most exploited and cultivated tree in this group. Its oil is used for food, soaps and paints. They also make magnificent ornamental trees.

### GENUS *CASTANEA*

Chestnuts or *Castanea* is a genus of fast-growing, long-lived deciduous trees, often growing to a great size, branching low and spreading horizontally. The trunk has a characteristic spirally-ridged bark. The leaves are elliptical, serrate, with a polished surface, which makes the tree identifiable even from a distance. Flowers are small and borne in catkins in the axils of leaves, with groups of male flowers on the upper part and female flowers below. It has three edible nuts enclosed in a prickly capsule. The timber of young trees is used for poles and barrels, but the wood of older trees is too weak. The bark is used in tanning. Some species are grown as popular ornamental trees.

### *GENUS MAGNOLIA*

The genus *Magnolia* is well-known in horticulture and magnolias have been used as popular ornamental trees and shrubs. They are named after Pierre Magnol, an early Director of the botanical garden at Mont-Pellier in France and Professor of Botany and Medicine. Magnolias have large, simple, alternate leaves and flower buds, which are enclosed in a single scale. The large showy flowers are solitary and borne terminally. The fruit is conical. The bark has been used as a tonic and general stimulant. Some species produce useful commercial timber.

*Magnolia*; from Hooker, 1855.

*Magnolia*; from Hooker, 1855.

## GENUS *ACER*

Maples, or genus *Acer*, consist of about 200 species. India has 15 species, two non-Himalayan, three in the Western Himalayas, six in the Eastern Himalayas and four that are common to both regions. They are deciduous trees, rarely evergreen or shrub-like with a scaly or smooth bark. The height varies from 6 metres to as high as 35 metres. The inflorescence is variable, usually bearing flowers of both sexes, with female flowers towards the base. Leaves vary in size, shape, margins, and may be entire or lobed, simple or compound. They are well-known for their brilliant autumn colours. The timber of certain species is used commercially.

Maple leaves; from Wallich, 1831.

Broad-leaved trees like the maple make the landscape gold in autumn.

## TREES

*FICUS SP.*

Wait at a fruiting Ficus in any forest in India and a large flock of birds of many different species will arrive sooner or later. It is the most favoured tree for insects, birds and mammals that are dependent on its figs, which ripen throughout the year. While most trees have edible fruit for only a few months during the year, the trees of a Ficus species fruit throughout the year. At any point in time, at least some of the trees of every Ficus species have ripe fruit. Thus, in the pinch period when other trees have no fruit, the Ficus trees that are fruiting support frugivores of all kinds. Ficus as a group is thus called a 'keystone' species. There are over 80 species of Ficus in India.

Ficus trees form a crucially important group of plant species for ecology. Each Ficus tree is a supporter of a complex web of life that consists of many different animals linked to each other in multiple food chains that are attached to it. The leaves of several Ficus species have many insect galls. The plant is linked with a large number of insects, birds, and small mammals in the ecosystem. There are many forests, however, where Ficus trees are not common, for instance in teak plantations for timber, where their absence is conspicuous and deliberate. The forest then lacks a major supporter of frugivorous animals and birds. Several Ficus species are the most spectacular trees in the forest as they have enormous canopies, beautiful adventitious roots, they develop a great girth and grow to a ripe old age. Old giants often have snags and deep holes in their branches, which are used as homes by birds such as hornbills, owls and animals like civets and jungle cats.

The Ficus fruit is not a fruit in the true sense, but a closely packed bunch of tiny male and female flowers covered by a skin. Gall wasps specific to each Ficus species penetrate the figs to lay their eggs. The larvae feed on it from inside. In return the plant requires the wasps and larvae for its pollination. This occurs inside the 'fruit'. Other insects also lay their eggs in the Ficus

The banyan tree has been a favourite of people in India from ancient times. The sages venerated it. The British planted it extensively along roads across India.

'fruit' but do not pollinate it. The Ficus fruit is thus a mini-ecosystem in itself.

The regeneration of Ficus trees is related to seed dispersal, most frequently attributed to frugivorous birds. They are also eaten and spread by mammals such as squirrels, monkeys and bats and it is possible that Ficus seeds that have been consumed and defecated germinate better than fresh seeds.

Most Ficus species produce a milky latex. Some species grow as epiphytes. When these epiphytes grow to a large

size they invariably strangle the host by spreading all over it so they are called 'strangler figs'.

Various Ficus species are found throughout India, except for the upper Himalayas. In most places, pipal, banyan and umber, the three most well-known ficuses of India, are not highly dominant and occur as isolated trees in many different regions as they are planted or protected for their religious significance. They are seen in evergreen, semi-evergreen and deciduous forests, as well as near human habitation. Some species produce fruit used by people and several species are used in local medicine. *Ficus racemosa* is traditionally considered an indicator of water in the vicinity. Many species like *Ficus benghalensis*, *Ficus religiosa* and *Ficus racemosa* are of religious importance and are considered sacred in India. Traditionally the pipal is considered to be the 'Bodhi tree' under which Buddha attained enlightenment. The banyan is encircled with thread once a year in Maharashtra by women who believe that it extends the life of their husbands. Tribal gods are frequently venerated near a large Ficus. It has thus been protected over many generations. Could the ancients have realized its crucial place in the web of life?

|   | 1 |   |
|---|---|---|
| 2 | 3 |   |

This strangler fig has killed the host tree on which it was supported for decades.

A strangler fig which has engulfed its host tree.

These trees could have led to ancient stories that plants were able to catch and strangle people.

## FICUS BENGHALENSIS—
BANYAN TREE, *VAD*

*Ficus benghalensis* is a well-known and much celebrated massive evergreen tree, with an enormous spreading crown supported by distinctive hanging stilt roots. The leaves are thick, large and dark-green in colour. The figs are red, soft, berry-like and up to two centimetres in diameter. It is a favourite of frugivorous birds that spread the tiny seeds. This is a keystone species in the ecosystem as it fruits all round the year when other species have no fruit, for insects, birds and mammals to feed on.

A well-known specimen in the Calcutta Botanic Garden covers a large area and is said to be more than 400 years old. Only the stilt roots now remain to support the giant canopy. Banyans are seen near almost all human habitation, but they occur only occasionally in natural forest ecosystems. They were previously planted along the roadsides as avenue trees as they are long-lived and have a thick shade-giving canopy throughout the year. Its utilization along roadsides where it was formerly common should be reintroduced for new avenues to support urban and rural ecology. In some cities a large number of these trees have been unfortunately cut down for road widening. They are being substituted by flowering exotics with a much lower ecological value.

When the banyans in Pune were all cut down in the late 1990s to widen the roads, many great-horned owls and barn owls found themselves homeless. The frugivores were also placed under great stress due to a shortage of food. Birds such as barbets, orioles and hornbills became less common. A great asset to the environment of the city has been lost and the local temperature along the exposed roads in summer makes travelling along the now unshaded roads unbearable.

### Ficus benghalensis—Banyan, Vad. (Moraceae).

This well-known and spectacular tree was first described by Linnaeus in 1753 based partly on the illustration in van Rheede's *Hortus Malabaricus*.

## FICUS RELIGIOSA—PIPAL

This sacred tree of the Hindus and Buddhists is one of the larger Ficus trees that occurs only occasionally in forests, but is frequently grown in towns and villages. It often occurs on rocks, precipitous hills and walls due to extensive dispersal by birds. It grows to 15 to 20 metres or more, has a smooth trunk and, occasionally, fibrous aerial roots. The leaves are shiny, bright-green and heart-shaped. The fruit is a fig, greatly relished by birds. Common all over India, this is a tree of great antiquity. Large specimens are believed to have lived for centuries.

### *Ficus religiosa*—Pipal. (Moraceae).

One of India's most famous trees, first (botanically) described by Linnaeus in 1753, based partly on the illustration in van Rheede's *Hortus Malabaricus*.

| 1 | 2 |
|---|---|
| 3 | |

Ficus is a keystone species. They are scattered all over the country in many different forest types. It provides food for animals, birds and insects throughout the year. *Ficus benghalensis'* fruit attracts a large variety of small birds and acts as a perch for this black-winged kite.

The *pipal* tree is also known as the Bodhi tree as it is believed that Buddha was born under its shade.

The banyan tree is the national tree of India and the state tree of Orissa.

India's
Floral Heritage

## FICUS RACEMOSA—GULAR

*Ficus racemosa* is one of the few Ficus species that occurs as a dominant evergreen in several forest types in the Western Ghats. It is frequently found near water courses and grows up to 20 metres in height. The trunk is smooth but may be gnarled when old. Figs occur in clusters on the trunk and main branches, are red when ripe and infested with insects. The bark is considered useful in indigenous medicine. A favourite species of frugivorous birds and small mammals, it is equally attractive to insectivorous birds, which look for insects associated with the figs.

### *Ficus racemosa*—Gular. (Moraceae).

This widespread south-east Asian species was first described by Linnaeus in 1753, based entirely on the illustration in van Rheede's *Hortus Malabaricus*, doubtless drawn in Kerala, where its bark and fruit are used medicinally. *Ficus glomerata Roxb.* is no longer regarded as being distinct.

## FICUS HISPIDA

This is a medium-sized evergreen tree, with large rough leaves arranged in pairs on the stem. The inflorescence, a fig, is globose with a short stalk. The figs are borne on special fruiting branches. Found throughout the Indian subcontinent, it is a species of semi-evergreen forest and it is found in degraded forest areas as well as in streambeds. The latex is used for mouth ulcers and as a purgative in local medicines.

### *Ficus hispida*. (Moraceae).

A widespread south-east Asian species first described by Linnaeus the younger in 1781 from specimens collected on Java by CP Thunberg, who visited the island on his way to Japan.

*Ficus racemosa* figs are a favourite food of many frugivorous birds and mammals. Wasps lay their eggs in the fig and pollinate the plant in the process.

A ficus fruit is like a mini-ecosystem, alive with insect life.

## TERMINALIAS

There are 10 Indian species of *Terminalias*, including species such as *Terminalia tomentosa*, *Terminalia paniculata*, and *Terminalia arjuna*. They are mostly found in deciduous forests along with teak. In some forests *Terminalia* is even more abundant than teak. *Terminalias* are dominant in Peninsular India and the Western Ghats, most frequently seen in Gujarat, Maharashtra, Karnataka, Tamil Nadu and Kerala.

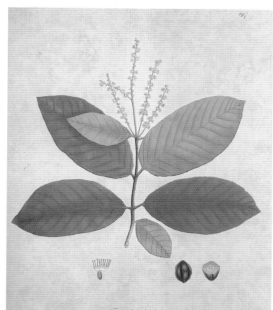

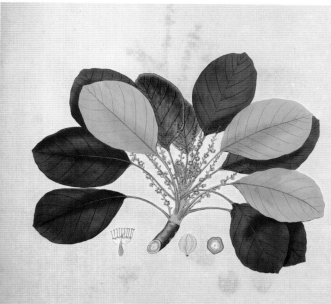

|   | 1 | 2 | 3 |
|---|---|---|---|
| 4 |   | 5 | 6 |
|   |   | 7 |   |
| 8 |   |   |   |

*Terminalia tomentosa*—ain or crocodile–bark tree, is a deciduous tree mainly seen in Peninsular India and the Western Ghats. It is also found in the dry deciduous forests of Maharashtra, Andhra Pradesh and Madhya Pradesh, frequently in association with teak.

*Terminalia arjuna.*

*Terminalia bellerica.*

*Terminalia* forms the dominant tree species in several forest types. They frequently grow in teak forests and are found in the forests of Tadoba, Pench, Bandipur, Mudumalai, Perambiculam, Koyna and Annamalais.

*Terminalia*; from Roxburgh, 1795.

*Terminalia bellerica*; from Roxburgh, 1795.

*Terminalia bellerica* seeds.

*Terminalia tomentosa* seed.

## TERMINALIA ARJUNA

This is a large deciduous tree commonly found on the banks of rivers and streams in deciduous and moist deciduous forest areas. The bark is smooth and white. Several knobs may be seen on the lower stem. The leaves are elliptic with two prominent protuberances on the lower surface near the base, and its yellowish-green flowers are borne in spikes. The fruit is five-winged and adapted for wind dispersal. The bark of this tree is said to have medicinal properties and is collected on a large scale in central India.

I was walking around a curve in a *nala* course in the forests of Melghat early one morning. As I turned the corner, there it stood beside the stream. A giant of a *Terminalia* tree. I spent the next half hour turning it into a picture story of its life and times. This *Terminalia arjuna* is a favourite of several animals and birds. The bark of this enormous tree is covered with vertical scars, as if a sharp knife has been repeatedly slashed into it. These parallel grooves are the unmistakable claw marks of sloth bears. They seem to have made this a habit as the marks have been made repeatedly. Some seem extremely fresh. High up in the canopy, the cause is evident. There are more than a dozen large beehives, the bear's most favoured food. A crested serpent-eagle uses its topmost branch as its lookout post. A snag in the trunk is home to an owl. Its lower branches have webs of several wood spiders. Woodpeckers tap at its bark for insects. It represents all the processes that one associates with a microhabitat. One feels like touching its bark, feeling the great tree's incredible strength, which has withstood the high winds and the floodwaters of the monsoon as the stream expands to angry proportions during each downpour. A similar ancient giant, but one with a hollow trunk, lies on the bank of the stream. It still survives and has developed several new branches that have grown out of its prostrate trunk. Life in the forest must go on. Even when a tree finally dies, its trunk and branches recycle nutrients back into the soil. Life processes all go on slowly but surely over several decades. This is so much a part of the great mystery of life itself.

### TERMINALIA TOMENTOSA—CROCODILE BARK TREE, *AIN*

*Terminalia tomentosa* has a typical, deeply cracked bark reminiscent of crocodile skin. At the base of the leaf there are two protuberances on a short stalk. It has small dull yellow flowers, which form an elongated bunch. The fruit has five brown wings for wind dispersal. The timber is used for various purposes including *rab* or wood-ash cultivation, which is prevalent in the hills of the Western Ghats.

### TERMINALIA CHEBULA—HIRDA

The myrobalan tree is common throughout India in moist deciduous and semi-evergreen forests. It is a medium-sized deciduous tree with tomentose young leaves. The mature leaves have slightly thickened edges near the base. Flowers are yellowish-green and come in spikes while the fruit is elliptical with faint ridges. The tender fruits are used for bad teeth while the mature fruits are collected and used in the tanning industry. The trees were lopped on a large scale in the past for making charcoal, leading to destruction of primary forests. Indiscriminate collection of fruit may have a negative effect on the regeneration of this species.

### TERMINALIA BELLERICA—BEHEDA

This is a very common tree in deciduous, semi-evergreen and evergreen forests. It is very tall often with a large buttressed trunk. The bark is smooth and pale brown. The leaves have a long petiole, rounded tip and are clustered near the ends of branches. Bright red young leaves develop from March to May. Flowers are yellowish-green in spikes. The fruit, which is used in the tanning industry, is elliptic and smooth.

***Mangifera indica*—Mango. (Anacardiaceae).**

One of the best known of all Indian fruits, the species was first described botanically by Linnaeus in 1753 in *Species Plantarum*, the starting point of all botanical nomenclature. Linnaeus based the name partly on an illustration in van Rheede's *Hortus Malabaricus*, doubtlessly made in Kerala.

### MANGIFERA INDICA—MANGO

This large, evergreen tree, which has been known in India for 4000 years, is found wild in mixed deciduous forests as well as in the evergreen forests, and is cultivated throughout the subcontinent. The tree reaches 20 metres in height and has a straight, stout trunk covered by rough bark, which develops cracks when the tree grows old. Its bunches of small flowers attract a large number of insects, which in turn attract insectivorous birds such as drongos and bee-eaters in cultivated areas and gardens, and babblers, thrushes and flycatchers in the forest. The wild mango has a small fruit with a relatively large seed covered thickly by fibres. While the pulp is not as sweet as that of cultivated mangoes, its tangy flavour is excellent. It attracts birds such as parakeets with beaks that can bite into the fruit. Squirrels, bats and monkeys also feed on it in the summer months.

## SYZYGIUM

*Syzygium* is a group of trees that includes *Syzygium cumini*, one of the common fruiting trees in several forest types including dry deciduous teak forests, where it remains green even when most other species are leafless. In moister sal forests, *Syzygium operculatum* is fairly dominant. In the evergreen forests of the Western Ghats, jamun, *Syzygium cumini* is seen in most areas. Its pulpy fruit is favoured by frugivorous birds and its small flowers attract ants, bees and other insects which pollinate it. The tender leaves and fruit are eaten by leaf-eating monkeys which drop the ripe fruit to the ground where they are picked up by the *chital* herds that follow the monkey troops in the forest.

## SYZYGIUM CUMINI—JAMUN

The jamun fruit vary from tiny berries to large pulpy fruit. Every frugivore in the forest uses this as food in the fruiting season. This large evergreen tree's trunk is covered with a peeling bark. Its leaves, a shiny bright-green when young, turn dark when older, and have a peculiar refreshing fragrance if crushed. It has small fragrant flowers in clusters and juicy, purple-black edible fruit, which attract large numbers of birds and mammals when they ripen. The tree is grown for its fruit all over India.

### *Syzygium cumini*—Jamun. (Myrtaceae).

This tree, producing edible fruit, is widespread in tropical south-eastern Asia. It was first described (in the genus *Myrtus*) by Linnaeus in 1753, based on specimens from Ceylon.

## CASSIA FISTULA—INDIAN LABURNUM

The brilliant splash of yellow in the distance surrounded by the green and brown of the deciduous forest cannot be matched by the paintbrush of an artist. It is simply vibrant. The blossoms form great bunches which can be those of no other tree but the Indian laburnum, the *Cassia fistula* tree. As one gets nearer the tree, one finds that it is buzzing with insect life. Several insectivorous birds flit through its blossoms. During the flowering season, with its slender sloping branches, it is a nature lover's delight. The seeds are dispersed mainly through the agency of animals such as monkeys, jackals, bears, and wild boar that break open the pod for the pulp and scatter the seeds, or swallow them and disseminate them on defecation. A common tree all over India, up to an altitude of 1500 metres, it is used in indigenous medicine.

### *Cassia fistula*—Indian Laburnum. (Leguminosae).

This beautiful flowering tree was described by Linnaeus in 1753 based, among other elements, on material from Ceylon, and an illustration in van Rheede's *Hortus Malabricus*. It is native to tropical south-east Asia, but is widely planted, and the pulp inside its long pods is a powerful laxative.

An early drawing of what was once called Mazagaon Mangoes; from Forbes, 1831.

*Terminalia* trees provide many important products that are used by local people. The trees are heavily lopped as a source of fuel wood and for wood ash to fertilize crops.

The mango tree is one of the best known fruit trees in India and is found in many forest types. Known from ancient times it has been cultivated and developed into many specific varieties grown in different parts of India. It is the state tree of Maharashtra.

*Syzygium*—jamun—is an evergreen tree found across the country which is well-known for its fruit. It is a dominant species in the Western Ghats and is often seen in the Protected Areas of the Western Ghats from Bhimashankar in Maharashtra, southward to Kerala.

Flowering *Cassia fistula* wrongly called Indian laburnum by gardening enthusiasts is popular as it has great bunches of bright yellow flowers. This deciduous tree is found in a variety of forest types. It is the state flower of Kerala.

## PALMS

### *COCOS NUCIFERA*—COCONUT PALM

This is a tall stately palm up to 25 metres in height which has a more or less straight trunk with circular markings. The base is surrounded by a mass of fine roots. Its leaves are pinnate with narrow tapering leaflets and its cream-coloured flowers appear in large clusters. It produces the familiar coconut, filled with liquid and a soft, white, edible, initially jelly-like material that later hardens into the edible material which is a common ingredient of food in India, especially in the south. It is extensively cultivated along the coastal regions and islands of India. Most parts of the tree yield several useful products such as broomsticks and fibre from the husk of dried coconuts.

### *Cocos nucifera*—Coconut Palm. (Palmae).

The source of a vast range of materials and products useful to man. It is now cultivated pantropically and its native home is uncertain, but was doubtlessly somewhere in the Pacific. It was first described by Linnaeus in 1753, based on several elements, but including the spectacular plates in van Rheede's *Hortus Malabaricus*, made by artists in Kerala.

Coconut palms are widely cultivated in the coastal areas and are a major economic resource.

## SHRUBS AND CLIMBERS
### ASPARAGUS RACEMOSA

This large shrub has sharp curved thorns that point in the reverse direction and seem to be grabbing your clothes as you pass through the forest undergrowth. The fine needle-like leaves give it an aesthetic appeal that has led to its extensive use in gardens. Small white inconspicuous flowers are present in the axils of the leaves, and the small, round, green berries become bright red on ripening. These plants are frequently located in degraded forest vegetation in most parts of India. As the tuberous roots are used in Ayurvedic medicine for making a tonic, it is extensively collected from the wild in many parts of India.

**Asparagus racemosa. (Asparagaceae).**

A widespread, Old World, sub-tropical species, occurring in Southeast Asia, Australia and Africa. First described by CL Willdenow in 1799, from specimens sent to him from South India by the Tranquebar Missionary JG Klein in 1797.

Wild asparagus is a lacy shrub or climber that has been extensively used in gardening.

### CALOTROPIS GIGANTEA— GIANT MILKWEED

A common shrub, which attains the size of a small tree if permitted to grow, this plant has a furrowed trunk and branches which are milky if broken. Its flowers are purplish-white. The shrub is common all over the plains, particularly on wasteland and it flowers throughout the year. It is considered sacred by Hindus, and is said to be a medicinally important species.

**Calotropis gigantea—Giant Milkweed. (Apocynaceae).**

This plant, which is used in medicine, was first described by Linnaeus in 1753, based on an illustration in van Rheede's *Hortus Malabaricus*.

*Calotropis* (in the foreground) is a familiar plant that grows where forests have been degraded.

## CARISSA CONGESTA—KARAUNDA

Though this is usually a shrub, it can climb up trees to a height of 20 metres like a climber. It has typical twin, branched thorns on the branches. The flowers are white and mildly fragrant and the purplish-black berry is sweet and has a typical flavour, though the taste may vary from one plant to another. The amount of pulp also varies, as some plants have large, pulpy fruit while others have a small amount of pulp. The plant is very common throughout plains and low hills.

### Carissa congesta—Karaunda. (Apocynaceae).

A spiny tropical South-east Asian shrub, often used for hedges. It was first described by Linnaeus in 1767, based on a plate in Georg Everhard Rumphius's book *Herbarium Amboinense*. This lavishly illustrated work describes the useful plants of the (then Dutch) island of Amboina in the Spice Islands of Indonesia.

*Carissa congesta—karaunda—*is found in forests in low hills and dry plains. It is a dominant shrub in several types of forests in the Western Ghats. Birds are attracted by its abundant fruits. Local people collect the fruit extensively from the wild.

*Gloriosa superba* is used in traditional medicine; from JBNHS, 1893.

*Gloriosa superba* produces splashes of colour in several different forest types and continues to grow in degraded forest tracts. It is the state flower of Tamil Nadu.

## GLORIOSA SUPERBA—GLORY LILY

The glory lily is a climber growing in clumps of shrubs in open areas and at forest edges. It climbs by means of its elongated thin leaf tips, which coil around any nearby support. It has beautiful bright yellow and red flowers with long stamens.

The seeds of the glory lily contain colchicin, which is used medicinally to arrest cell growth in the cancerous tissue at certain stages. While its tubers are highly toxic and can be lethal, the plant has long been used in Ayurvedic medicine and is now cultivated for colchicin. The glory lily has been nearly eradicated from many areas where it was once abundant, by over-harvesting.

### Gloriosa superba—Glory Lily. (Colchicaceae)

This extremely poisonous climber was originally described by Linnaeus in 1753, based in part on the illustration in van Rheede's *Hortus Malabaricus*. It is widespread in tropical Asia and Africa, but is also commonly cultivated for its beautiful flowers.

## ENTADA PURSAETHA

*Entada* is a woody liana found in the Himalayas, Nepal and western peninsular India. It grows by twining through large trees in moist deciduous, semi-evergreen and evergreen forests. It has a characteristically coiled stem resembling a giant spring and leaves that end in a forked tendril. The flowers are yellow and grow on old leafless branches from March to May. The pods are great, woody, flat structures with bulges where seeds are present. When cut, the branches exude a thin watery liquid which is potable. The *Entada* have unique large, smooth, reddish-brown oval seeds that are collected and used as ornaments, and can produce a lather which may be used as soap or shampoo. It is known to grow so extensively that the tree it grows on is crushed by its weight and falls down. Its spiral woody branches lie on the ground or stretch between adjacent trees giving the forest a jungle-like appearance.

### Entada pursaetha. (Leguminosae).

This large climbing legume was first described by Linnaeus in 1753, based partly on an illustration in van Rheede's *Hortus Malabaricus*. When Carl Sprengel transferred it to the genus *Entada* in 1825, he had to give it a new epithet. *Entada pursaetha* DC is no longer recognized as being distinct.

*Entada pursaetha* are found mainly in evergreen and semi-evergreen forests in Western Peninsular India and the Himalayas. The giant seed pod of an *Entada* climber can grow to a length of nearly a metre.

## THE GROUND COVER
### GRASSES

Grasses form the second largest group of flowering plants in the world. Their characteristic long and narrow leaf blades in which the veins run parallel along the leaf axis vary from a few centimetres to several metres in length. The stem may creep on the ground and produces roots at the nodes. The tiny flowers are usually arranged in a complex inflorescence of different shapes. Much variation is seen in size in different species, but the overall appearance of different species is the same. While grasses typify grassland ecosystems, they also grow in forests.

Tall and short grasslands are seen in various eco-regions all over India. In these, the dominating species are grasses along with many other herbaceous plants. Most grasses prefer sunny open areas and cannot grow in shady areas in the forest.

They are the single most important source of genetic wealth, as our major crops like cereals and sugarcane belong to this group. Certain species have industrial uses, for instance, in the perfume industry and the manufacture of paper.

Several grass species have specific habitat needs. Some are restricted to certain types of soils. A few are fire-resistant and regrow soon after a fire while others gradually disappear after repeated fires. Some species are favoured by domestic and wild herbivores and are thus extensively grazed. Others are not palatable and thus grow in spite of grazing.

| 1 | 2 |
| 3 | 4 |
| 5 | 6 |
| | 7 |

A *nala* course forms a specialized habitat in the hills for several grass species.

Flowering grass is wind pollinated and its light seeds are dispersed by wind to far-off locations.

Grasses form a large group of ecologically and economically important species that grow in a wide range of ecosystems.

Bamboos; from Roxburgh, 1795.

Different species of bamboo are found in tropical and sub-tropical regions in India. Large patches of Bamboo or isolated clumps are seen in the northeastern regions, the Western Ghats and their offshoots. Bamboo groves form superb habitats for India's wildlife. It is also an important forest product used in paper and other industries like basket making and housing. Bamboo shoots are edible.

A young bamboo clump that will someday become a major resource for local people.

*Andropogon*; from Wallich, 1832.

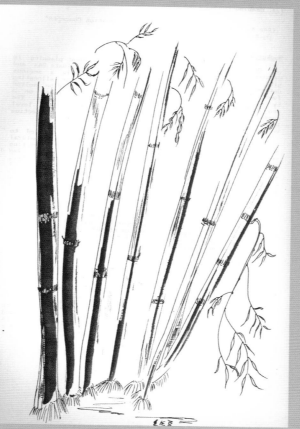

## BAMBOO

This common plant has 1250 reported species all over the world. It has tall, rigid, cylindrical stems, the insides of which are hollow, their colour varying from dark green to golden yellow. Bamboo grows in clumps in several different forest types. They also create large bamboo breaks in the forest, that form a favoured habitat for elephants, gaur and other herbivores to feed in. The thick cover they provide makes these spots a favoured place of rest for tigers and leopards during the heat of the afternoon. Bamboos are full of bird and insect life and form a preferred nesting place for several bird species. Flowering occurs at intervals, and may take up to 60 years or more for some species. All clumps in one area flower and fruit together and then die. When the bamboo flowers, there is an increased activity in rats and mice. The rodents get an enormous amount of food and reproduce in alarming numbers. Local people know from experience that in all probability such flowering will be followed by a year of famine in the area, due to the prolific increase in rodents that are sure to feed on crops once the bamboo is gone.

Bamboo of different types grows throughout India in dry deciduous, moist deciduous, semi-evergreen and evergreen

|1|2|
|3|4|

Bamboo groves are favourite habitats of the great cats of India.

Dead bamboo after cyclical flowering and seeding.

Bamboo plants flower after many decades.

Insectivorous birds frequent the bamboo clumps in the forest.

India's
Floral Heritage

areas. The diversity of bamboo species is highest in north-eastern India. Of about 125 species of Indian bamboos, 58 are found in the north-east (MoEF, 2002).

Bamboo is extensively used for a variety of purposes such as poles for construction, paper manufacturing and furniture making. It is very useful in tribal areas, where it is an essential resource for everyday life, e.g. in the construction of huts, in the weaving of baskets, as utensils for cooking and carrying water. The soft shoots of some species are edible, as are the large seeds of certain species. Bamboo is now over-exploited for use in the paper and pulp industry. A variety of commercial uses at highly unsustainable levels of extraction are leading to loss of bamboo from a number of forest areas across the country.

### ENSETE SUPERBUM—WILD BANANA
The wild banana plant is characterized by its non-woody pseudo-stem formed by a wide and long leaf base surrounding a flowering shoot. The true stem is underground and perennial. In nature, the banana is vegetatively propagated by stem budding. The inflorescence emerges out through the stem. The male as well as the female flowers are protected by large leafy bracts. Wild banana fruit bear seeds that are dispersed by the animals that eat them. It flowers through most of the year. It is partial to growing on rocky outcrops, *nala* courses, and even as an epiphyte on tree branches. It prefers to grow in shady areas. The fruit of the improved varieties of banana is edible and highly nutritious.

> **Ensete superbum—Wild Banana. (Musaceae).**
> This differs from the actual bananas (*Musa spp.*) in dying after flowering. It is native of the rocky slopes of the Western Ghats and was first described by William Roxburgh in 1811, from specimens growing in the Calcutta Botanic Garden sent from southern India.

### SENECIO GRAHAMII
This is a large annual herb with pointed leaves which have serrated margins. The lower surface of the leaves has silvery white hair. The flowers form large bright yellow masses, and the small black seeds have papery wings for wind dispersal. Distributed throughout the Indian subcontinent, it covers open grassy hill-slopes and scrublands.

> **Senecio grahamii**
> This species, which is endemic to the Western Ghats of Maharastra, was first described by Robert Wight in 1846, as *Doronicum reticulatum*, from material sent to him by JS Law, the Collector of Tanna. It was later renamed *Senecio grahamii* by JD Hooker, but that name was not justified, so it was given a new name by Balakrishnan in 1970.

Forest fires spread rapidly through dead bamboo.

*Senecio* grows in the ground cover of hilly slopes and scrubland.

*Ensete superbum*—wild banana—is a plant that grows in moist areas, *nala* courses or dry rocky areas. It can grow on the ground or as an epiphyte.

A hill slope in the Himalayan foothills covered with flowers.

The Himalayas are important sources of medicinal plants.

Ground flowers change every week.

*Digitalis purpurea* (Foxglove) is native to temperate regions. The presence of glycoside digitoxin makes this plant poisonous and can cause death in humans. But digitoxin in an appropriate dosage is also used to treat cardiac disease. In suitable conditions Digitalis seeds itself in partial shade and can become a minor weed. It is often cultivated as an ornamental plant due to its attractive flowers.

## BEGONIA CRENATA

Begonias are seasonal herbs that appear during the monsoon in areas of high rainfall, growing most often near *nalas* and waterfalls. The leaves are heart-shaped and taste sour. There are several species that are endemic to the Western Ghats. It is most frequently found to grow on moss covered rocks along streams and in moist shady places.

### *Begonia crenata.* (Begoniaceae)

Endemic to western India, where it was first collected by A.P. Hove in 1786 on rocks on the island of Salsette near Bombay. It was described by Jonas Dryander, librarian to Sir Joseph Banks.

## EPIPHYTES
### ORCHIDS

This is the largest group of flowering plants in the world, with 18,000 species reported in literature. Of these, 1500 species are found in India, making it one of the largest families in the country, with a maximum concentration of a staggering 700 species in the north-east (MoEF, 2002). Several new varieties are being constantly produced for floriculture. These plants are terrestrial or epiphytic herbs. Some species even complete their life cycle underground. In some orchids, the stem forms pseudobulbs of various sizes. Flowers show a range of bright colours and great variations in structure. In some species, one of the petals is distinct from the others and is called a lip or labellum. This colourful petal attracts pollinators. Pollination occurs through birds, bats, beetles, wasps, bees, and even nematodes in the case of the underground species. The flowers have several mechanisms

| 1 | 2 |
|---|---|
| | 3 |

*Begonia crenata* grows in moist areas and is often seen in the Western Ghats. It has been extensively used in gardens.

A large number of orchids are epiphytes.

A tiny button orchid of the Western Ghats.

for attracting pollinators. Different scents ranging from sickly sweet to that of rotting meat are produced. The lip has various markings to guide insect pollinators. Some of the orchid species have flowers with highly specialized structures to attract specific pollinators. The flower may resemble a female wasp with which male wasps engage in pseudocopulation and in the process pollinate the plant!

The capsules contain thousands of minute seeds, each of which has an embryo with its growth arrested at an early stage. Seeds are dispersed by wind and the embryo can grow only after developing a symbiotic relationship with a specific fungus. This limits the multiplication possible by seeds. In floriculture vegetative reproduction is the simplest way to multiply.

A great variety of orchids, both terrestrial and epiphytic are found in the Western Ghats, Andaman and Nicobar Islands, the north-eastern region and the Himalayas. Orchids are however seen in several ecological conditions, except for extreme conditions, such as very cold or very hot and dry ecosystems.

The major use of orchids is in the floriculture industry. Records of their collection from wild areas are available for at least the past three centuries. Tropical regions throughout the world were explored by collectors and thousands of specimens were shipped to the West, leading to

the extinction of several species in the wild. A large number of orchids are now under threat. The establishment of Nature Reserves and tissue culture ex-situ conservation programmes has been initiated for their conservation. India has done very little to try and maintain their population in the wild. Some protection is afforded by the network of National Parks and Sanctuaries. However, as orchids frequently have a limited range, there are likely to be several rare orchids that occur only outside Protected Areas. These are likely to become extinct more rapidly than those found in a Sanctuary where collection is prohibited.

Orchids form the largest group of flowering plants in the world. More than 1500 varieties are found in India, being specific to certain forest types and regions. Several species are found in warm, humid, tropical forest types.

*Dendrobium barbatulum.*

Some orchids have a beautiful fragrance.

Many orchids are highly endemic.

*Epidendrum sp.*; from Roxburgh, 1795.

*Epidendrum sp.*; from Roxburgh, 1795.

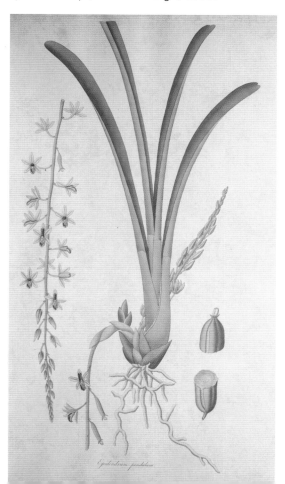

Vanda; from Hooker, 1855.

*Aerides crispum* is commonly found in the Western Ghats.

*Habenaria sp.* is a terrestrial orchid in the Western Ghats seen on the lateritic plateau tops.

A dainty *Habenaria* orchid.

## AERIDES CRISPUM

This is a common epiphytic orchid growing on large and medium-sized trees. The leaves are thick, leathery in texture and elongated, while the flowering shoot with clusters of flowers attracts small insects. The capsules are oval and have a large number of tiny seeds dispersed by the wind. This orchid flowers prolifically in May and June.

It is distributed all over the Indian subcontinent. It grows most abundantly on trees and shrubs in open sunny conditions, tree-savannahs and shrub communities. It is a fairly common ornamental species and is collected for sale in gardens. Most plants do not flower for years when translocated.

**Aerides crispum. (Orchidaceae).**
An epiphytic species first described by the great orchid expert John Lindley in 1833, from specimens collected by the Tranquebar Missionaries at Courtallum, at the southern end of the Western Ghats in the state of Tamil Nadu.

## DENDROBIUM BARBATULUM

This is an epiphytic orchid growing on small trees and shrubs and endemic to the Western Ghats. It prefers deciduous forests, shrublands and tree savannah habitats. The leaves are elongated, thick and leathery. The pale pink flowers appear in early summer on straight shoots. This species is locally abundant and is used as an insect repellent.

## HABENARIA MARGINATA—TOOTHBRUSH ORCHID

The toothbrush orchid is a small ground orchid with a rosette of leaves close to the ground. The flowers are bright yellow with frilly petals. The toothbrush orchid is distributed over the Indian peninsula in semi-arid and scrub areas.

**Habenaria marginata—Toothbrush Orchid. (Orchidaceae).**
Widespread in upland parts of India (Himalaya and the Western Ghats) and Burma, this small orchid was accidentally introduced to the Calcutta Botanic Garden where it was first noticed, naturalized in the turf, in 1814. HT Colebrooke sent a description of it to WJ Hooker in Glasgow, which was published in 1825.

## EVERGREEN FORESTS (THE NORTH-EAST, WESTERN GHATS AND THE ANDAMAN AND NICOBAR ISLANDS)

### TREES

#### DILLENIA INDICA

*Dillenia indica* is an evergreen, medium-sized tree, 10 to 20 metres in height, with a dense rounded crown. The trunk is erect with straggling branches with drooping ends. The large leaves arise at the ends of branches. Flowers are large, white, fragrant and solitary. *Dillenia* is found in moist evergreen forests of the sub-Himalayan tract and in the south in coastal regions.

#### SANTALUM ALBUM—SANDALWOOD

Sandalwood is certainly the most smuggled species in the country. Many of the forests in South India have been extensively damaged to the near exclusion of this species.

This is an evergreen, slow-growing tree. It has a dark brown bark, small reddish-brown fl owers, and pea-sized purplish-black edible fruit. Seed dispersal is aided by birds that eat the fruit and broadcast the seeds widely. The roots of the young plant are parasitic on the roots of other plants without which the tree cannot grow. The hard wood at the centre of the tree forms after the plant is over ten years old and is used for distilling the world-famous fragrant oil used in perfumes and soaps. Good quality oil is however extracted from trees over thirty years old.

After drying, the wood itself is extremely fragrant and can retain its fragrance for many years, making it a favourite wood for the manufacture of wooden artifacts. This tree is said to be endemic to the Timor Islands, but is probably indigenous to parts of south-western India as well, and is found in the Western Ghats, Mysore uplands, Coorg and Madras, Coimbatore, Salem and the Nilgiris. India is now the main source of sandalwood, which has been extracted illegally by the timber mafia. The notorious dacoit Veerappan was engaged in these illegal activities for years till at last he was ambushed and killed by the police.

> **Santalum album—Sandalwood. (Santalaceae)**
>
> The source of an extremely valuable fragrant wood, from which oil is extracted. It was first described by Linnaeus in 1753 based on earlier descriptions and an illustration published by JP Breyn in 1739.

*Dillenia indica* is often seen along with *Shorea* and *Pterospermum*.

*Dillenia indica*.

*Santalum album*—sandalwood—is an evergreen species found in evergreen, semi-evergreen and moist deciduous forest regions. It is most often seen in the Western Ghats.

### ACTINODAPHNE SP.—PISA

An evergreen tree, with leaves in whorls, with a typical silvery sheen on the lower surface, this tree has small flowers and small, red fruit when ripe. It is found in the Western Ghats and is common in semi-evergreen forests.

### MEMECYLON SP.—ANJAN

These trees frequently form a copse of the deepest shade, the canopy is so thick that very little light filters to the forest floor. These patches of forest, found in several parts of the Western Ghats thus have very little undergrowth even though the forest floor is thick with moist humus in these semi-evergreen and evergreen forests. There are, however, climbers and large lianas in the middle layer which give the *Memecylon* forest its great aesthetic jungle-like appeal. *Memecylon*, which occurs both in semi-evergreen and evergreen forests shares its habitat with species such as *Actinodaphne*, *Ficus sp.* and *Syzygium* in the hill forests of the Western Ghats.

This medium-sized, evergreen tree is identified by its dark green leaves and a pale translucent margin. It has bunches of purple flowers which grow directly on the old stems and small purplish black berries.

| 1 | 2 |
| | 3 |

*Actinodaphne sp.—Pisa—*is a common tree of the evergreen forest and is generally found in the Western Ghats. It is seen in Maharashtra in areas such as Koyna and Radhanagari.

*Memecylon* is an evergreen species found in evergreen and semi-evergreen forest types of the Western Ghats where it frequently forms low forest patches as shady groves with a thick canopy. It grows along with *Ficus*, *Syzygium*, *Bridelia* and *Actinodaphne*. Flowering *Memecylon* are bright purple in colour.

*Memecylon* leaves have a typical brightly-lit edge when seen against the light in the thick canopy of foliage.

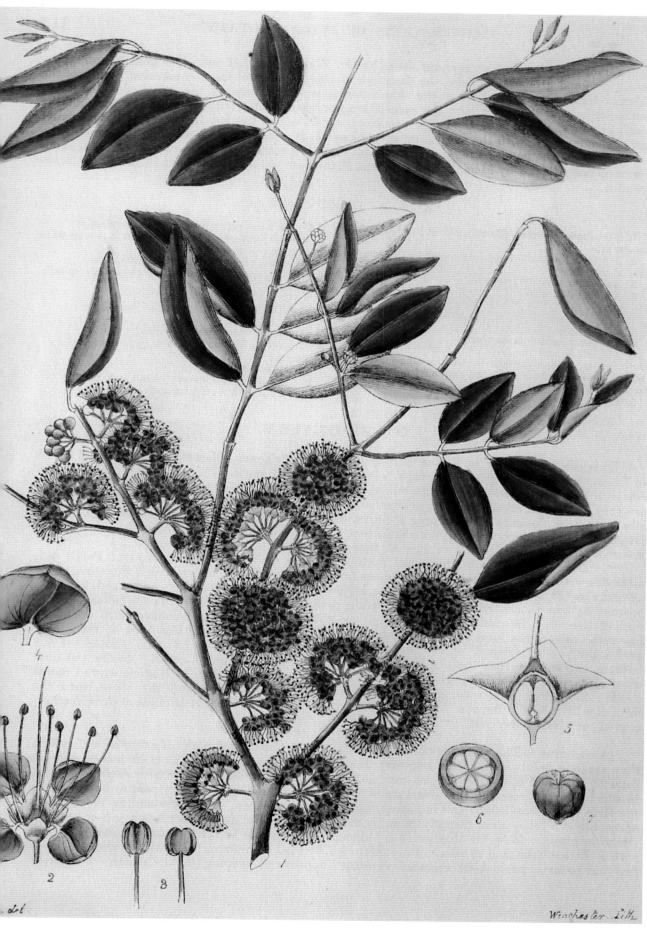

Memecylon; from Wight, 1838.

## PONGAMIA PINNATA—KARANJA

*Karanja* is an evergreen tree reaching up to 12 metres in height, with a spreading crown and a soft greyish-green bark. The compound leaves are pale green and produce a peculiar bitter smell when rubbed between the fingers. Its flowers are white and the fruit is a woody pod. This tree is common in the Western Ghats, chiefly found along stream banks and in coastal regions. It is also cultivated along roads as it has a large shady canopy. Oil extracted from its seeds is in high demand as a lubricant. There are future plans to use it as biodeisel and with petrol.

### *Pongamia pinnata—Karanja.* (Leguminosae).

A widespread South-east Asian species first described (under the genus *Cytisus*) by Linnaeus in 1753, based entirely on an illustration published in Leonard Plukenet's *Phytographia* in 1691. It is possible that the specimen illustrated had been sent to London from Madras.

*Pongamia pinnata* or *Karanja* is found very frequently in the Western Ghats. It is mainly an evergreen tree and has a very brief leafless period.

MESUA FERREA—IRONWOOD OF ASSAM
A mid-sized evergreen tree with a straight trunk that is found exclusively in Assam, it has characteristic leaves which are red when tender and large fragrant flowers which have have four petals with crinkled stamens, and a semi-woody fruit.

### Mesua ferrea—Ironwood. (Guttiferae).

As the vernacular name suggests, the wood is hard and has been used for railway sleepers; the flowers are large and beautiful. The species was first described botanically by Linnaeus in 1753, based on material from Ceylon and an illustration (doubtlessly made in Kerala) in van Rheede's *Hortus Malabaricus*.

## MICHELIA CHAMPACA—CHAMPAK

This is a tall evergreen tree, with spreading branches and greenish yellow flowers which give off a heavy fragrant sweet smell and are used for making oil. The fruit grow in bunches, globular and brownish in colour with small white spots. On drying they open to reveal scarlet or deep orange seeds. It is found in the Eastern Himalayas, Sikkim and the Western Ghats.

## MALLOTUS PHILIPPENSIS—KAMALA

The *kamala* is a medium-sized evergreen tree, 10 metres in height. It has many branches, with a thin grey, rough bark, and numerous flowers in spikes with male and female flowers on separate trees. It commonly occurs in scrub and mixed forests upto 1500 metres, and is widely distributed in the northern, western, central and southern India. The coloured powder covering the fruit is used as a dye and has purgative properties.

## SARACA ASOCA—ASHOKA

The *ashoka* tree is a medium-sized evergreen, which grows up to 10 metres in height, with bark varying from dark brown to almost black. The trunk has a warty surface. The leaves are compound and the colour of the flowers ranges from orange-yellow to red, occurring in dense clusters on the branches. It is usually found alongside streams or in the shade of evergreen forests. Though frequently cultivated as an ornamental tree, it is found wild in the Eastern Himalayas and Western Ghats. It is one of the trees held sacred by Hindus and Buddhists.

### Mallotus philippensis—Kamala. (Euphorbiaceae).

A widespread south-eastern Asian species; its fruits are a source of red dye. It was first described by Lamarck in 1786, based on specimens collected in the Philippines by the French explorer and naturalist Pierre Sonnerat.

### Saraca asoca—Ashoka. (Leguminosae).

This beautiful flowering tree is sacred to both Hindus and Buddhists. It was first described botanically by William Roxburgh in 1795, when he placed it in the genus *Jonesia*, named to commemorate his friend the great Orientalist Sir William Jones.

## DIPTEROCARPUS

The order *Dipterocarpaceae* contains 325 species of trees of 16 genera confined to the Indo-Malayan region. These are species of typically tropical evergreen forest formations which occur in the northeast of India, the south-western Ghats and in Andaman and Nicobar Islands. They form tall stands of trees with enormous girths. Typically, they have a seed with a propeller-like arrangement which allows the seed to whirl to other sites even on a slight breeze. The wood is used for boat building, dug out canoes and planking.

## DIPTEROCARPUS TURBINATUS—GURJAN

This is a lofty tree in the evergreen forests of Assam, Bangladesh, Andamans and Burma. These trees are some of the largest trees of our forests, growing to 60 metres in height, and yielding valuable red timber and gurjan oil. Its bark is light grey and the leaves are leathery and glossy, with stalks covered by a waxy bloom. The showy flowers have pinkish-white petals, and the fruit are spindle shaped and have two papery wings, characteristic of dipterocarps, and crucial to the dispersal by wind of seeds that are viable for a very short period.

## TREE FERNS

In the tangle of vegetation in the evergreen forest there is a lone distinctive plant. It has a trunk like a tree and a circle of radially directed giant lacy fern-like leaves. Its great symmetry due to the radial placement of its fronds and the fluid grace of the curve of each frond combine to give it an ummatched aesthetic appeal. Added to this is its rarity. Tree ferns are seen as isolated plants or small groups in very specific locations where light filters in patches to the forest floor in a humid part of the forest. The pictures of tree ferns I have taken never seem to bring home its incredible beauty, nor do the pictures demonstrate its uniqueness as one of the rare plants in the forest.

I have tried hard to capture the symmetry and vibrant green of the tree fern's large radial fronds, stopping often for one more picture, but the pictures seldom look as beautiful as the real plant with its superb lacy fronds.

Tree ferns are ancient large plants with a tree-like structure and fern-like leaves. The large fronds are produced at the tip of the stem in a rosette. One 150 to 200 million years ago, tree ferns were widely distributed but are now restricted to a smaller range in very humid evergreen forests. In the Jurassic period when dinosaurs roamed the earth, they formed the dominant vegetation on which herbivores lived. Fossils of these tree ferns have been identified in many parts of the world.

Tree ferns grow in the Western and Eastern Ghats and north-eastern India. They occur in the undergrowth of evergreen forests in these high rainfall tracts, their range restricted to residual patches of less disturbed evergreen forests, which are now under great threat. Even here one sees only a few of these plants, an indication that they are among our more endangered plant species.

*Michelia champaca—champak—*is an evergreen tree seen most often in the Western and Eastern Ghats.

*Saraca asoca* is an evergreen tree found frequently in the Western Ghats and Eastern Himalayas.

*Dipterocarpus* are large evergreen trees that are dominant in the tropical evergreen forests of the Western Ghats, the Sholas, the north-east and the Andaman and Nicobar Islands. Their winged seeds float through the air and eventually grow into giants of the evergreen forests. *Hollong—Dipterocarpus retusus—*is the state tree of Arunachal Pradesh.

Tree ferns are one of the most attractive plants in an evergreen forest. They are often habitat specific and are usually seen in the hill forests of the Western and Eastern Ghats and north-eastern India.

1
2
3 4

*Cycas* is an ancient species that grows sporadically in deciduous and evergreen forests of south India, Eastern Himalayas and Andaman and Nicobar Islands

A travellers' palm stands tall among the many tree species growing in the forests of the Western Ghats.

An uncommon *Strobilanthus* shrub which flowers only once in 13 years.

*Strobilanthus* are evergreen shrubs that grow on hill-slopes in evergreen and semi-evergreen forests. Large expanses of the Western Peninsula and Central India are covered by these shrubs which flower only once every few years. *Karvi* blooms once in seven years.

### CYCAS CIRCINALIS

Seeing this ancient species can transport one into a bygone age when prehistoric animals roamed the world, an age that has passed, leaving behind thousands of extinct plants and animals. Somehow this ancient species is present in forests even today. This prehistoric seed-bearing plant is said to have evolved over 200 million years ago and could be one of the oldest Gymnosperms on earth. *Cycas* trees look like palms with large leaves arranged in whorls around the main trunk. As the dry leaves fall off, the trunk is covered by a distinctive pattern left by the persistent leaf bases. The feathery compound leaves are produced at the tip of the trunk. Normally the stem is not branched. However, if the tip is destroyed, the plant tends to branch. There are male and female plants producing different types of cones. The male plant produces a woody cone. The female plant bears them on its woody reproductive leaves that mature into seeds.

The species is found in the deciduous and evergreen forests of south India, in the Eastern Himalayas, and the Andaman and Nicobar Islands, and are frequently observed in ravines. The male cones are varnished and sold in local markets as decorative articles while the fronds are used for expensive flower arrangements. *Cycas* plants are beginning to be rare due to habitat destruction. Their being used as expensive garden plants acts as an ex situ conservation strategy.

### CARYOTA URENS—FISHTAIL PALM

A tall, unbranched palm, generally 15 to 20 metres tall, but sometimes reaching upto 30 metres, the fishtail palm has a smooth cylindrical trunk with ring-like markings. The bipinnate leaves are large with leaflets serrated at the tip, giving them the appearance of a fishtail. The tree flowers only once every 10 to15 years, with flowers in large bunches of pendulous spikes, and the fruit is small, round and reddish, rather like a split arecanut. This palm is very common in evergreen forests throughout the warmer regions in India and is tapped for its fermented juice called toddy.

**Caryota urens—Fishtail Palm. (Palmeae).**

This large palm, which dies after flowering, was first described by Linnaeus in 1753, based in part on an illustration in van Rheede's *Hortus Malabaricus*. It is native of the Western Ghats, but is widely cultivated.

## SHRUBS AND CLIMBERS
### CARVIA CALLOSA—KARVI

*Karvi* is a large shrub with straight stems and nearly vertical rough and woody branches and large coarse leaves, while the bunches of distinctive purple and white flowers have a strong fragrance like that of balsam, which some people dislike and others, like myself, love! The perfume is retained even by the dry seedpods. The shrubs grow closely packed to each other, making the undergrowth quite impenetrable.

*Karvi* is seen throughout the western peninsula and central India, mainly on the hillslopes of the Western Ghats and its offshoots. It is a very common plant in the undergrowth and spreads in large patches, covering open areas and forest edges, in moist deciduous, semi-evergreen and evergreen forest areas.

Walking through a flowering hill-slope of *Karvi* in the Western Ghats is the experience of a lifetime—and for a person who may live about 70 years or so, it can only happen some ten times in a given region! This gregarious flowering is thus a rare event in one's life unless one goes in search of different flowering areas. Though the hills covered by the vivid sight of great masses of scented blue-violet flowers are spectacular, it is not just the visual experience that I find fascinating. The forest undergrowth comes alive with its pungent but pleasant perfume, and with the sound of thousands of bees and other flying insects that are attracted to the hill slopes. The shrubs are buzzing with insect life and insectivorous birds. Butterflies flit through the bunches of flowers that flash their diverse colours. Brushing through the undergrowth leaves the sticky pungent odour on one's clothes. Once the *Karvi* flowers wilt and die, the seedpods are formed on the plants. They leave a skeletal undergrowth of dead plants until the rain comes and the *Karvi* seeds pop open with a loud crackling sound, spraying seeds all over the forest floor. Another great event is to experience this in the mist and cold rain of the hills hearing the sound of tiny *Karvi* seedpods exploding, heralding the birth of a new generation of *Karvi* plants in the undergrowth! That new generation will take another seven years to mature. First, during the latter half of the the monsoon season, the *Karvi* seedlings create a bright green carpet of thousands of seedlings that begin the next seven-year cycle, taking two or three years to grow and mature. How is this long seven-year cycle primed? This event must have an incredible influence on forest ecology and regeneration. The growth of seedlings of several other species must wait for the year when the *Karvi* shrubs are dried out so that light penetrates through the otherwise closed shrub cover. Only when this happens can the seedlings of trees that the *Karvi* has shaded and also protected for seven years hope to become saplings. The bees that multiply even before the *Karvi* begins to flower must await this period of plenty, so that they can produce, once in seven years, an enormous amount of honey. Somehow they are primed to multiply miraculously just before the flowering occurs.

In the 1970s I found that *karvi* stakes were being extensively harvested to support a new type of climbing tomato plant. While these stakes have long been used by people in the Western Ghats to make covers for houses during the monsoon, to build and to produce various other household goods, this has essentially been a sustainable level of extraction, as *Karvi* can coppice well. However, this new commercial use for tomato stakes led to truckloads of *Karvi* being removed during the flowering season from areas such as Mahableshwar. My feeling was that this could be disastrous for the necessary quantity of viable seed material to support and reform the forest's undergrowth for the next seven years. This is a vital component of the undergrowth microhabitat. I therefore lobbied with the Forest Department to prevent extraction until the seedlings had sprouted in the next monsoon. A good senior Forest Official, who understood what I was getting at, saved the next seven years by allowing the *Karvi* to regenerate and support all its dependent animal species.

---

### *Carvia callosa*—*Karvi*. (Acanthaceae).

This large shrub, which flowers every seven years, covers large areas of the Western Ghats of Maharastra. It was first described by the German botanist Christian Nees von Esenbeck in 1832, based on specimens in the East India Company's herbarium. These had been cultivated in the Calcutta Botanic Garden from material sent by James Barstow in 1826 from Nagpur. It has sometimes been placed in the genus *Carvia*, but this is no longer considered worthy of recognition.

## COMBRETUM OVALIFOLIUM—
## ZELLUS (MADBEL)

A ground-spreading shrub, the *zellus* stretches out over clumps of vegetation. The flowers are small, yellowish-white and borne in spikes upto 10 centimetres or more in length. Its fruit has four bright red wings that help in dispersal by the wind.

It is distributed from Gujarat to Kanyakumari and is seen in degraded forest areas, frequently in moist deciduous and semi-evergreen ecosystems. It grows as a large climber in open areas of the forests.

### *Combretum ovalifolium—Zellus* (Combretaceae).

A large scrambling shrub, first described in 1832 by William Roxburgh, based on specimens introduced to the Calcutta Botanic Garden from the Coromandel Coast, in 1804.

### CEROPEGIA

The *ceropegias* are a group of uncommon plants. I know of three of these beautiful plants that grow in the Sahyadri Ranges in Mulshi taluka within a few kilometres of each other. Each species has highly distinctive flowers of intriguing shapes, with extremely varied coloration from white to bright yellow, green and brown. Many species are found in India and are endemic to particular areas. Their microhabitats may be the undergrowth of forests, shrubby thickets and open scrubland. Many species have edible tubers, a fact that is a major threat to their existence. Plants whose roots and tubers are eaten are destroyed more rapidly than those whose leaves or fruits are used. These uncommon plants are now incredibly rare and may be vulnerable to extinction.

*Ceropegias* are annual climbers and are thus seen only in the monsoon. The leaves are situated opposite to each other and are hairy. The flowers of some species have a complex distinctive structure. Each tubular flower has five lobes joined at the tip into an inverted cone-like funnel. This creates five openings that lead into the tube, which serves as an entrance to its insect pollinators. The pollinating insects are trapped inside the flower till the process is completed. They can, however, escape after the flower wilts.

### *Ceropegia hirsuta.* (Apocynaceae).

A rather variable climbing species widespread in southwestern India. It was first described by George Walker-Arnott and Robert Wight in 1834, based on specimens collected by Wight in the Nilgiri Hills.

### CEROPEGIA HIRSUTA

This is a small delicate climber with oval leaves. It grows annually from bulbs, which remain dormant during the dry season, and produces lantern-like, yellow flowers with crimson specks, their unusual shape being its most distinctive feature. It is a patchily distributed uncommon plant of the Western Ghats, growing in open scrubland habitats. Protecting such open areas is essential if this species is to be conserved, along with a number of other rare plant species. As the tubers are edible, this beautiful species in certainly under threat.

| 1 | | |
|---|---|---|
| 2 | | |
| | 3 | |

Seeds of *Combretum ovalifolium.*

*Combretum ovalifolium—zellus*—grows in moist deciduous and semi-evergreen forests. It is commonly found in the Western Ghats from Gujarat in the north to Kerala in the south.

*Ceropegia huberi* is an uncommon annual climber that grows in isolated patches. Several rare species grow in the Western Ghats.

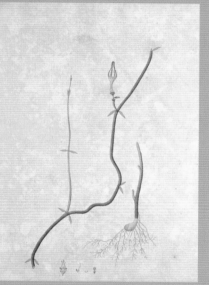

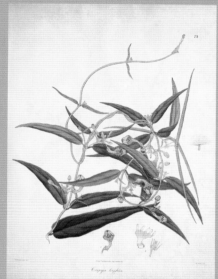

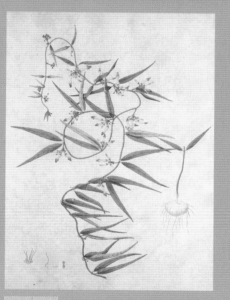

| 1 | 2 | |
|---|---|---|
| 3 | 4 | 5 | 6 |
| 7 | 8 | 9 | |

This incredible group of uncommon plants has a wide variety of flowers with unique structures.

Most *Ceropegias* grow from dormant bulbs every year.

*Ceropegia*; from Roxburgh, 1795.

*Ceropegia*; from Wallich, 1831.

*Ceropegia*; from Wallich, 1831.

*Ceropegia*; from Roxburgh, 1795.

*Ceropegia*; from Wallich, 1831.

*Ceropegia*; from Roxburgh, 1795.

*Ceropegia*; from Roxburgh, 1795.

## HOYA WIGHTII—AMBRI, DUDH-VEL

The *dudh-vel* is an epiphytic climber that climbs trees by growing small roots from its stem. It produces milky latex and the leaves are thick and glossy. The beautiful waxy white flowers form dainty round bunches with a pink centre and have a delicate fragrance. The fruit when dry has seeds with cottony hairs or 'coma', which aid in seed dispersal. The plant grows in western peninsular India on medium-sized trees in semi-evergreen and evergreen forests. It is, on the whole, an uncommon climber, and occurs sporadically. Iit may cover a whole tree and hang like festoons from the branches.

### *Hoya wightii—Ambri* or *Dudh-Vel.* (Apocynaceae).

A climbing species of the Western Ghats, first described by Sir Joseph Hooker in 1883, in his monumental seven-volume *Flora of India*. Hooker included in his species elements of a species that Wight and Arnott had called *Hoya pendula* from the Nilgiri Hills and Malabar, and for this reason Hooker chose to commemorate Robert Wight in his epithet.

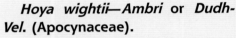

The *Hoya* climber is found in evergreen and semi-evergreen forests, mostly in the Western Ghats. This unique climber forms long strands that climb through the canopy.

*Hoya*; from Wallich, 1830.

*Hoya* flower.

*Impatiens*; from Wallich, 1830.

*Impatiens* is a common flowering plant, especially suited to moist microhabitats, and is found in several forest tracks throughout India.

*Impatiens acaulis.*

*Striga gesnerioides* is a beautiful flowering plant. It is a parasite which grows on roots of other trees.

The insectivorous *Drosera* is a small plant that grows in rocky areas where soil fertility is low.

*Drosera indica* traps ants and other insects.

## IMPATIENS ACAULIS

These are small annual herbs. The petioles are reddish in colour and the leaves are pointed and asymmetrical. The flowers, produced on erect shoots, are dark pink in colour with a capsule that is broken and bursts open at the slightest touch. Seeds are round and they are dispersed by water and wind.

These plants grow all over India, in very moist conditions. They usually occur on wet rocks near *nala* courses, along with ferns and moss. Their wide range in forest tracts may be decreasing due to the loss of the microhabitats it requires.

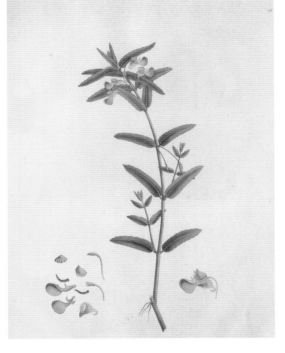

### *Impatiens acaulis.* (Balsaminaceae).

First described by the Scottish botanist George Walker-Arnott in 1836, based on specimens collected in Ceylon by Colonel and Mrs. Walker. The species also occurs in the Western Ghats.

## STRIGA GESNERIOIDES

This is a herbaceous root-parasite up to 30 centimetres tall, which sometimes grows on rocks. The plant has a bright crimson stem and small violet-purple flowers. Found all over the Indian peninsula, it is mostly seen in semi-evergreen forest areas.

**Striga gesnerioides.**
**(Orobanchaceae).**

A widespread tropical parasitic plant, occurring from Africa, through southwestern Asia, to India. It was first described (in the genus *Buchnera*) by the Berlin-based botanist CL Willdenow in 1800, using specimens collected by Benjamin Heyne in 1798, at Pondepillay in Tamil Nadu.

## DROSERA INDICA—INDIAN SUNDEW

The sundew is an insectivorous plant, about one to three centimetres tall. The leaves are long and narrow and covered by red gland-tipped hairs that secrete a sticky fluid, in which insects get trapped. All the hair on the leaf moves slowly and the leaf coils around the trapped insect. It is then digested by enzymes present in the fluid. Pink flowers appear after the monsoon, between August and October. The plant grows in moist conditions, in open grassy areas and is patchily distributed in areas where the soil depth and quality are poor, but moisture levels are relatively high. The whole plant is supposed to have medicinal properties. It is a rare species and is being further collected by botanists for their herbaria.

**Drosera indica—Indian Sundew.**
**(Droseraceae).**

This insectivorous plant was first described by Linnaeus in 1753, based partly on an illustration in van Rheede's *Hortus Malabaricus*.

## ANEILEMA SP.

It is an annual herb with fibrous roots. The leaves are narrow, long and grass-like. Its pale blue flowers grow on erect shoots and have three petals. The fruit is a small capsule, and the seeds are dispersed by wind. About 60 different species are distributed throughout the tropical and subtropical regions of Asia. It is a common group of species that grows in the monsoon and is found frequently near flowing water, in moist conditions in open grassy areas.

## ARISAEMA SP.—SNAKE LILY

The snake lily, whose distribution is relatively restricted, is one of the plants with tubers, which remain underground throughout the year. The leaves, usually one or two, are produced only during the monsoon and are large and shaped like the palm of a hand. The petioles are white or green or have brown blotches. The inflorescence or flowering shoot is produced on a stalk enveloped by a sheath which may be marked with green, purple, or pinkish lines. Both male and female flowers are produced on a cylindrical shoot. The fruits are small red berries.

## ZINGIBER CERNUUM

The *Zingiber cernuum* flowers in the middle of the monsoon and is a large herb with bright green leaves and stem. The flowers appear in July directly from the rootstock, and are buff-coloured, with one petal variegated with distinctive white and red marks. The capsules are a smooth yellowish-white outside, and bright orange inside, and the ripe seeds are red. It is endemic to the Western Peninsula and favours semi-evergreen and evergreen forests.

Snake lily—*Amorphophallus*—adds colour to the undergrowth.

*Zingiber macrostachyum.*

*Zingiber*; from Wallich, 1830. *Zingiber* is most frequently seen in the evergreen and semi-evergreen forest areas of Western Peninsular India.

**Zingiber cernum. (Zingiberaceae).**
Described by NA Dalzell in 1852, from the Ram Ghat. Theodore Cooke, author of the great *Flora of Bombay,* despaired of collecting this plant as it flowers in July—a time, he said, when the mountains were streaming with water!

## CURCUMA PSEUDOMONTANA—GAURI

This is a small herb with an underground rhizome. Leaves and flowers are produced only in the monsoon and the leaves look like those of the garden canna. The flowering shoot is erect and rigid, its flamboyant pink bracts bearing bright yellow flowers. The flowers produce splashes of colour of different shades. The plant is seen in open areas as well as forests and normally grows under the forest canopy but also in clearings in the forest. It is collected on a large scale, especially in Maharashtra, at the time of the Ganapati festival, to be used for decoration for Gauri Puja. It is becoming probably less common in some areas, as it is being extensively harvested. Oddly enough, it has not been tried as a garden plant even though it is extremely beautiful.

**Curcuma pseudomontana—gauri. (Zingiberaceae).**
Endemic to the Western Ghats of Maharastra, from where it was first described in 1839 by John Graham, Deputy Postmaster General of the Bombay Presidency. He reported that its tubers were used by local people as a kind of arrowroot.

## FREREA INDICA

This plant was first described in 1864 by Nicole Alexander Dalzell. Following this, it was documented in 1908 in the *Flora of Bombay Presidency*. In 1940, Charles McCann (1939) reported in the JBNHS, Volume 41 that he had collected it near the Shivneri Fort in Junnar, Poona District in 1938.

This plant is a small pendulous herb with fleshy branches. Its leaves are peculiar as they have purple-brown patches. It grows on bare-rock faces, at fairly high elevations in the Western Ghats and adjacent isolated hills.

| 1 | |
|---|---|
| 2 | 3 |
| 4 | |

*Curcuma pseudomontana* is one of the most flashy plants of the forest floor. This species flowers for a brief period during the Ganesh festival, when it is extensively collected for the Gauri ritual in Maharashtra.

*Curcuma cordata*; from Wallich, 1830.

*Curcuma*; from Wallich, 1830.

*Frerea indica* is a rare small, fleshy herb growing on bare rocks in the Western Ghats.

## MOIST DECIDUOUS SAL FORESTS—TERAI AND CENTRAL INDIA

### SHOREA

There are seven species of *shorea* in the Indo-Burma region, and they are mainly found in two regions, in central and northern India. Their fruit has three long wings.

### SHOREA ROBUSTA—SAL

The luminescent greens and yellow greens of recently matured, fresh sal leaves give the sal forest the most vivid colour. The tall stately sal has a shape that is unmatched. Sal trees generally grow closer together than teak, and the unbroken stands of sal trees, together, create an incomparably beautiful landscape teeming with wildlife. The sal of the Terai, across an expanse of water or tall elephant grass, leave an indelible impression on the memory; equally exciting are the sal patches interspersed with meadows of green short grass dotted with chital in the plains of India. And when one goes into the shady canopy of the sal forest with its lianas, climbers and ground flora, the experience is thrilling. The next tree may well have a tiger sleeping in its shade.

The sal is a large, sub-deciduous or semi-evergreen tree and is hardly ever totally leafless. It has a smooth bark, with fissures along the trunk and branches. When covered with its tiny flowers, it appears light cream or yellow. Found in moist deciduous forests and having a shorter leafless period than the drier teak forests of peninsular India, it grows mainly in the sub-Himalayan region and eastern parts of India, in Madhya Pradesh, Orissa, Uttar Pradesh, Bihar and Assam, forming large aggregations. Sal trees have straighter, less branched trunks than the teak. The timber was used for making railway sleepers, and is now used in construction work, while its seeds are used for making oil.

| | 3 | |
| 1 | 2 | 4 |

Sal trees grow profusely in semi-evergreen and moist deciduous forests. They are found in the sub-Himalayan regions, the Terai and the North-east extending southward to the forests of Madhya Pradesh, Orissa and Bihar. They constitute one of India's most well-known timber species and were used extensively by the British in their plantation programmes. Even today sal forms one of the mainstays of the Forest Department's plantation activities.

A flowering sal tree. Its seeds are used in making oil for cosmetics.

Bauhinia flowers are considered sacred in some parts of India.

Gmelina arborea is found in mixed deciduous forests.

During the British period, Sal was planted near pure stands of tall, straight, stately trees that led to a vertically-oriented crown, packed closely together so as to provide deep shade. Today several of these reserved forests have become our national parks and sanctuaries.

### BAUHINIA PURPUREA

There are over 30 species of *Bauhinia* in India: in the sub-Himalayan tract, Assam, Madhya Pradesh, Andhra Pradesh, Karnataka, Tamil Nadu and West Bengal. They all have a typical leaf, that is deeply cleft giving it a bi-lobed appearance. These trees have flamboyant flowers—ranging from pink and mauve to speckled white—

and elongated, flat, drooping seedpods. The flowers are edible in some species. It frequently forms a part of the understorey of the forest, lowering the level at which the trunks break into the canopy. This gives access to herbivores, which would otherwise find less food to graze on. A hardy, deciduous species that grows upto seven metres tall, *Bauhinias* are considered sacred in India.

### GMELINA ARBOREA—GUMHAR

This is a deciduous tree, 10 to 12 metres tall, with a straight trunk and horizontal branches. The flowers are greenish yellow and occur in terminal panicles and the fruit is fleshy, orange-yellow and date-like. The tree occurs in coastal regions, the dry deciduous regions of central India and in the Himalayan tract and Assam. It is a fast growing tree with excellent timber.

## *LAGERSTROEMIA SPECIOSA* OR *FLOS-REGINAE—JARUL*, QUEEN'S FLOWER

The *jarul* is a medium-sized, deciduous tree with a rounded crown, grey smooth bark, exfoliating in irregular flakes, and flowers of a bright mauve or purple, arising in large panicles. The fruit is an ellipsoid capsule. This is a well-known ornamental tree and is cultivated in gardens and by the roadsides. It is found to be a more common species in Bengal, Assam and South India.

*Lagerstroemia* with its flashy flowers is the state flower of Maharashtra.

*Lagerstroemia* is a deciduous tree found in the moist deciduous forests of Bengal, Assam and most of the Peninsular Deccan plateau and South India.

Deciduous forests have a large number of plant species. However, as more and more exotics are being planted in these regions, it is leading to a fall in biodiversity.

| 1 | 2 |
|---|---|

| 3 | 4 | 5 |
|---|---|---|

| 6 | 7 |
|---|---|

*Tecomella undulata*; from JBNHS, 1935.

*Colvillia racemosa*—Colvill's glory; from JBNHS, 1935.

*Gardenia resinifera*; from JBNHS, 1934.

*Solanum grandiflorum*; from JBNHS, 1935.

*Bauhinia variegata*; from JBNHS, 1934.

*Glyricidia*; from JBNHS, 1931.

*Plumeria rubra*—frangipani and *Plumeria rubra acutifolia*—pagoda tree.

*Tectona grandis*—teak—is a dominant species of deciduous forests in Peninsular India in areas where sal does not grow.

A hollow teak tree trunk with its drying leaves.

In 1795, Roxburgh had his artist paint the *Tectona grandis* flower. *Tectona grandis* has become one of the most valued timber species in the world.

## DRY DECIDUOUS— TEAK PENINSULAR FORESTS

### *TECTONA GRANDIS*—TEAK

The moon through the trellis work of dry branches looks nearly unreal in size. A cool breeze begins to blow the warm air of the evening away. A tiny rustle of dry leaves is followed by a loud click as a large, dry teak leaf falls from a nearby branch and wafts down to the dry, thick detritus on the forest floor.

Throughout the winter and summer, the dry, transparent net-like leaves of the great teak trees give the forest a typical appearance. The rustle of leaves and the buzz of mosquitoes as the night deepens create a sense of anticipation. The creatures of the night have silently begun to move through the skeleton of the dry deciduous forest. With the approach of the monsoon, this changes drastically as the large bright green leaves of the teak trees begin to form its thick shady canopy.

The dry deciduous forests in which the teak has been planted and replanted over the last 200 years create an attractive landscape even in the dry, leafless season. The undergrowth also lies dormant, so this is a period when its dependent herbivorous

animals are greatly stressed for food. Teak has been the forester's favourite ever since British times, when it was used for building ships, furniture and for the construction of houses. Teak is, even today, very much in demand for its valuable timber used for high quality furniture. The hard knots which develop on the trunk, are prized for making tobacco pipes. The most magnificent teak tree I have ever seen is an ancient giant that stands alone in a clearing in Perambiculam, dwarfing all the other large teak trees around it. Its fluted trunk ascends to the sky with a relatively small canopy at the top. When one stands below it, one feels dwarfed and tiny. Its age is written in every verticle projection of its great trunk. If only man had left some of the forests alone, there would undoubtedly have been more such giants.

The teak is a deciduous tree that grows up to 40 metres in height and is characterized by its large, rough, light-green leaves. It has big bunches of small white flowers and small round fruit. One of the few trees that flower during the monsoon, it has a wide trunk with an irregular pattern. When unlopped, the teak has a nearly spherical canopy. However, in forests where timber is extracted, its branches are lopped so that it develops a straight, wide trunk. Local people also lop its branches for wood-ash cultivation in many forests, which turn teak trees into straight totem poles. A tree of the peninsula, it covers many of the slopes of the Western Ghats and other hill ranges to the south of the Satpuras. Most of the sanctuaries in peninsular India are located in teak forests that were used for timber till the Protected Areas were notified. This is why even in sanctuaries we have trees growing in unnatural straight lines of teak, with only a few young trees of other species.

Teak occurs as a major dominant species, along with several other species, forming a variety of forest types in peninsular India. Extensively planted here from the British times, its proportion in many forests that were used for timber is much higher than would have been present naturally, before plantations were developed.

Teak occurs mostly in dry deciduous regions in Gujarat, Maharashtra, Karnataka,

The largest teak tree in the world is in Perambiculam.

Tamil Nadu and Kerala, as well as parts of Madhya Pradesh and Andhra Pradesh. The other dominant species in these forests include the *Terminalias, Anogeissus, Hardwickia, Adina,* and *Lagerstroemia*, which are mostly deciduous. However, there are also species that are evergreen in such forests, such as mango and *mahua*, which remain green when the rest of the forest is leafless.

### ANOGEISSUS

*Anogeissus* is a species of semi-arid and deciduous forest, dominant in both the very arid forests of Babul in Rajasthan, and in the teak forests of Gujarat, Maharashtra and Karnataka. It includes species such as *Anogeissus pendula* and *Anogeissus latifolia*.

### ANOGEISSUS LATIFOLIA— GHATTI OR DHAURA

This tree is beautiful even in its leafless phase due to its white bark that differentiates it from the rest of the trees in the forest. It is a mid-sized tree that grows up to 10 metres in height, quite gregarious, growing on the upper hill-slopes in the deciduous forests. Its distinctive pale-grey bark has patches that peel off the trunk. The stem has alternate leaves of a light green colour. The flowers are dull yellow and occur in dense clusters. This tree is characteristically found in dry deciduous forest systems throughout India. The trunk yields a gum called *dhavda*, used in textile printing.

### EMBLICA OFFICINALIS—AMLA

This deciduous, medium-sized tree grows to a height of 10 to 15 metres. It usually has a crooked trunk, spreading branches and a greenish-grey bark that peels readily. The small leaves are a bright green, arranged in two planes on either side of the stem, and small, greenish-yellow flowers in clusters. The fruit itself is greenish yellow, sour and rich in vitamin C. It is used as a medicine, in pickles and for dyeing and tanning. Frequently referred to as 'the Indian olive,' to which it has no similarity either in appearance or taste, it is found throughout the subcontinent up to 1300 metres.

*Emblica officinalis—amla—*is a deciduous tree growing throughout India. Its fruit is extensively used.

### MADHUCA INDICA—MAHUA

There is a strange but sweet smell in the air. The giant tree in the grassy opening in the forest, surrounded by a carpet of creamy-white flowers, is an ancient *mahua* tree. Chitals quietly eat the flowers strewn around it, guarded by a noisy group of monkeys which are feeding in the canopy. As the flowers ripen, they ferment, and wildlife such as wild boar, chitals and sambars are unable to resist it and are known to get high on the alcoholic content. In the adjacent area, the trees are lopped severely for *rab*—wood-ash cultivation—and many trees have been cut. But in the Dangs, the tribal folk preserve the mahua tree, as they use its flowers for food and to brew a potent alcohol.

This is usually a medium-sized, deciduous tree, 15 metres in height, with a large leafy crown. Its bark has multiple cracks which, when stripped, display the red inner bark and release a milky latex. It has thick leathery leaves and large bunches of drooping, cream-coloured, fragrant flowers. *Mahua* seeds are used to extract oil for making soap.

*Mahua*; from Forbes, 1813. This deciduous tree is found in different forest types. Its leaves and flowers are used by the tribal people as a vegetable and to make a potent alcoholic drink.

### HARDWICKIA BINATA—ANJAN

This deciduous tree has wide-spreading branches. Its leaflets are deeply cleft and tinged reddish when young. It has flat seedpods, narrow at both ends, which open at the apex, each containing a single seed. The leaves are used as fodder. The wood is very hard and durable. It is seen in the dry parts of central- and south-India.

### DIOSPYROS MELANOXYLON— TENDU, EBONY

A mid-sized, deciduous tree, up to 15 metres in height, the *tendu* tree is common in dry deciduous forests throughout the subcontinent. There are around 50 Indian species. Its bark exfoliates in large rectangular scales, and it branches profusely, forming a dense crown. The leaves are elliptical and leathery and the young ones are extensively used for making bidis. The fruit is brownish-yellow and astringent. *Tendu*-leaf collection necessitates burning undergrowth and slashing the branches of the trees to get at the leaves. The resulting disturbance to wildlife is a serious issue in Protected Areas.

### AZADIRACHTA INDICA—NEEM

The *neem* is one of India's most well-known trees, found in the dry and semi-arid regions of the Deccan. It grows into a large evergreen tree, up to a height of 15 metres, has a dark grey-brown bark with long oblique fissures, and leaves with a serrated margin and a very bitter taste. Its small, white flowers are faintly scented and attract a large number of bees. The greenish-yellow fruit are oval and relished by birds. It is considered sacred and health-giving chiefly because of its insecticidal and medicinal properties. It is suited to dry climates and semi-desert or scrubland conditions, as it has very deep roots and is a preferred tree for plantations in the semi-arid regions of India. It has been used for a variety of purposes in India for generations. The recent excitement over the Intellectual Property Rights issue has to do with the fact that its utilization as a non-toxic pesticide has been investigated outside India and been rated highly. Older tree-trunks exude a bitter gum.

## ADINA CORDIFOLIA—HALDU

This stout, deciduous tree, which grows up to 20 metres in height, is found in dry forests throughout the hilly parts of the country. It has horizontal branches with a thick furrowed bark, large round leaves with a short pointed tip and small yellowish flowers in bunches.

## ERYTHRINA INDICA—
## INDIAN CORAL TREE

Come February and the coral trees in the forest burst into a deep scarlet-red, attracting several species of birds. For the birds it is nectar time. Even birds like crows take to this pattern of feeding usually associated with nectarivores such as sunbirds and mynas. The nectar is, however, of greatest interest to great flocks of jungle mynas, which have a specially designed apparatus of thick erect feathers over the bill, that readily pollinates its flowers. Rosy pastors, orioles and sunbirds flit through the scarlet red clumps for three months gorging on its blooms every morning. Squirrels feed on it by day and fruit bats flit through the branches at night.

There are about seven Indian *Erythrina* species. This medium-sized deciduous tree grows up to about 20 metres in height and looks best when it is in flower, as it is completely leafless. The smooth stem is covered with prickles. The leaves are distinctive, as they are compound and trifoliate and shed in November and December, after which the profuse flowering occurs from January onwards in most parts of India. The deep-scarlet flowers are seen at the tips of the leafless branches. The seedpods are black when dry and remain hanging on the plant almost throughout the year and often into the next year. The dark red-brown, smooth, shiny seeds are bean-shaped. The plant germinates easily and grows well through pole planting.

Another species of *Erythrina* is common in gardens and along roads. It has a light greyish-green bark, its stem is without prickles and it grows very rapidly from poles. It is found across the Indian subcontinent, south of the Himalayas, in east India and in the Andaman and Nicobar Islands, most often in moist deciduous and semi-evergreen forests. It is popular with birdwatchers and with people who fancy bright-coloured flowering trees for their gardens. The wood is soft and used for making such things as boxes and toys. It is commonly planted as a support for vines like pepper. It is said to have medicinal value and is used against worms. A comparatively rare white-flowered variety is also seen.

*Azadirachta indica—neem—*is an evergreen tree found in dry deciduous forests. It commonly grows in semi-arid regions and is seen in the Deccan scrublands. There is now a worldwide interest in *neem* for its properties as an insecticide. It is the state tree of Andhra Pradesh.

*Adina*; from Roxburgh, 1795. *Adina cordifolia—Haldu—*are deciduous trees found mainly in dry deciduous forests all over India. They often have a horizontal branching pattern.

*Erythrina* flowers in February and March create great splashes of scarlet that attract numerous nectarivorous birds.

*Erythrina indica* is also called the Indian coral tree. It is a deciduous tree found in several types of deciduous forests; from JBNHS, 1930.

## BOMBAX CEIBA—
### SILK COTTON TREE, SEMUL

One of the great giants of the deciduous forest, its nearly horizontal branches and short thorns that cover its bark give it a distinctive appearance. Walk through a deciduous forest when the *Bombax* trees are in full bloom and one can see here every bird species that uses flower nectar as a source of food. The large, cup-like, red flowers are spectacular and advertize the nectar, so that birds will pollinate the tree. It forms large pods of seeds covered in fine silky material, one of nature's mechanisms to transport the seeds far and wide on even a slight wind.

This 25-metre tall, deciduous tree frequently has a buttressed base once it grows to its full height. In a young specimen, several branches emerge circumferentially from the trunk at the same level. This makes identification simple even from a distance when it is leafless. The bark, which is covered with small conical prickles, develops vertical cracks with age. The leaves are compound with five leaflets spreading like the fingers of a hand and its large red flowers appear directly on the terminal branches after the leaves fall off in early summer. The flower has many stamens and is loaded with large amounts of pollen and nectar, which attract insects, birds and small mammals. The capsules are dark brown and woody. The seeds, encased in soft light cotton, can disperse over long distances. It colonizes open areas. The Tata Power Company's hydel lakes were built in the early 1900s. There are islands in the lake that had been cleared, which are now covered with a large number of *Bombax* trees. *Bombax* is, however, less abundant in the old forests around the lakes. The tree-cover on the islands might be a result of wind dispersal, which led to te bombax spreading faster to the islands than other tree species that are spread by birds or mammals.

Bombax is distributed all over peninsular India in most deciduous forests up to 1300 metres. The silky, hair-like, snow-white material from the pods is used for filling pillows and mattresses, while the wood is used for making matchsticks.

| 1 | 4 |
| 2 | 3 |

Flowering *Bombax* or silk cotton trees grow throughout India and are often seen in the Himalayan foothills where they can grow to a height of 1300 metres.

*Bombax*; from Wight, 1838.

*Bombax*; from Wallich, 1830.

*Bombax* is a deciduous species in a variety of forest types. The striking red flowers against the stark summer landscape attract birds and insects.

## MIXED DECIDUOUS FORESTS

### BOSWELLIA SERRATA—
### INDIAN FRANKINCENSE, SALAI

This is a deciduous middle-sized tree. The leaf margin is crenate and the leaves are fragrant when crushed. The flowers are tiny and the fruit is roughly triangular in cross section. This tree is found throughout India, except Assam.

### GARUGA PINNATA—KHARPAT

This medium-sized, deciduous tree grows to a height of 10 metres and sheds its leaves in winter. The bark peels off in large flakes. It has pointed leaflets with an oblique base, an arrangement that makes the compound leaf asymmetrical. The flowering shoots at the ends of branches are highly branched, bearing small yellow flowers and fleshy, edible, black fruit. The seed has a membranous wing and the leaves are used as fodder. The tree is found in many parts of the lower hills and plains throughout India.

### BRIDELIA RETUSA

This is a medium-sized, 10-metre tall, deciduous tree found in deciduous forests all over India. Its grayish bark has long spines when young and its leaves are bright green and leathery. The flowers are greenish-yellow and occur in crowded clusters with purplish-black, pea-sized fruit.

### BUTEA MONOSPERMA—
### FLAME OF THE FOREST, DHAK

Butea monosperma creates a splash of colour on the hill-slope covered in different shades of green, interrupted by patches of flaming-orange flowers. A mixed flock of birds are calling from the nearest orange-coloured leafless tree which is full of blossoms. The forest floor is covered with the flowers that the birds have dropped during their frantic feeding session. Bees buzz actively around the tree. It is like a tiny hot-spot of biological diversity—a spot of unmatched beauty.

The medium-sized, 10 to 20 metres tall, deciduous tree with irregular, frequently crooked branching habit, has a rough bark. Each compound leaf bears three leaflets. Its flamboyant flowering starts around February, when large, velvety, heavy, orange flowers containing a large amount of nectar are produced. They are a favourite of several insects, birds and mammals. In some forests where it occurs, it is infrequently seen, while in others it acts as a rapidly expanding colonizer of open areas, starting the process of natural succession, to the near exclusion of other species. An open patch of sal can soon be covered by the slow-growing shrubs of Butea that begin to increasingly dot the grassy open meadows.

It is thus a regionally-common plant of many deciduous forest types, dry and moist. It does, however, occur sporadically in several other habitats, where it is found in abundance. The tree is more abundant in certain areas where it has been planted. A tree earlier used for lac, its leaves are now commonly used for making large leaf plates, while the flowers yield a yellow dye. Gum is obtained from the bark, leaves, and flowers, while the seeds are said to have medicinal properties.

| 3 | |
|---|---|
| 4 | |

| 1 | 2 |
|---|---|

The flowering of a Butea monosperma attracts pollinating insects and birds in great numbers.

Butea flowers; from JBNHS.

Butea monosperma; from Roxburgh, 1795.

Prolific flowering of a Butea monosperma, often called the Flame of the Forest.

### DALBERGIA

There are between 30 to 40 species of *Dalbergia* in India, several of which are shrubs.

### DALBERGIA LATIFOLIA—ROSEWOOD

Rosewood is a 20-metre tall, straight, deciduous tree, with a straight trunk and greyish-brown bark, marked by irregular longitudinal cracks, which peel off on the trunk. The tree has compound leaves and small, white flowers. It is indigenous to south India, Madhya Pradesh, the Western Ghats and the lower Himalayan ranges. In northern India it tends to be a low, branching tree. Rosewood is the most extensively planted timber tree after teak, as it is fast growing, adaptable and able to withstand temperatures from below freezing to 50 degrees Celsius, and it is often cultivated as a shade tree for its dense foliage. It yields a valuable, hard, deep red-brown timber used for woodcarvings, the colour giving the artifacts a superb smooth polished finish.

### TAMARINDICUS INDICA—TAMARIND

One of the best-known Indian trees, the tamarind, an evergreen tree with spreading branches and a cracked, rough bark, grows to a large size and is known to live for over 200 years. The compound leaves taste sour. Its small yellowish flowers appear in loose clusters from May to June and its familiar fruit is a curved pod with sour pulp containing a number of squarish seeds. The pulp in the fresh fruit is either green or red. As it ripens, it turns sticky and brown and separates itself from the skin. The tree is commonly cultivated as a shade tree as well as for its edible sour fruit. The wood is used as timber as well as fuel. This tree is indigenous to tropical Africa, but cultivated all over the tropics. Brought to India by the Arabs, the name is derived from the Arabic *tamar-e-hind*, meaning 'date of India'.

## THORN FORESTS

### ACACIAS

The acacias comprise over 20 Indian species, including *Acacia nilotica* (*babul*), *Acacia senegal* and *Acacia catechu* (*khair*). Thorn forests have a typical appearance. Unlike deciduous forests, they continue to have leaf cover in winter and summer, while deciduous trees become totally leafless. The crowns of an Acacia forest have a typical dome-like symmetry and if heavily browsed by wildlife, they look like umbrellas, as they are hemispherical with a straight lower surface. The other species which are frequently encountered in Acacia forests are *Capparis*, *Anogeissus pendula* and *Anogeissus latifolia*. Thorns act as a defence against browsing and lopping, but several species can still browse on its young shoots when the thorns are soft.

### ACACIA NILOTICA—BABUL

The babul is a small, evergreen thorny tree, usually less than seven metres tall, indegenous to Sind and Deccan. It has a characteristic umbrella-like crown, the small leaves give the canopy a lacy appearance at the edges. The bark is dark with deep furrows. It has long pointed spines near the leaves, which are compound and have small leaflets, and the tiny, bright-yellow, mildly fragrant flowers are grouped together to form globular clusters. The pods are narrow, resembling a chain of beads, and may be seen hanging from the tree almost all year round. Found throughout arid regions in India, it is a dominant species of thorn forests, scattered irregularly in open savannah-like areas, as well as in dry deciduous forests. It is favoured as a browsing tree by the nilgai and other herbivores of the thorn forests, while in grasslands it is browsed by the blackbuck.

Its reasonably hard wood is used to make agricultural implements and the tree is commonly seen growing near agricultural fields. The gum is edible and has medicinal properties. The bark and pods are used for tanning.

**Acacia nilotica—Babul. (Leguminosae).**

Native of tropical Africa, and probably an ancient introduction to India, where it is naturalized in drier parts. First described by Linnaeus in 1753, as belonging to Egypt. Used for timber, its bark for tanning, and leaves for forage cultivated.

## ALBIZIA

These are either shrubs or trees growing 15 to 25 metres in height, usually deciduous but occasionally evergreen and common to the forests of peninsular India and Deccan. The leaves are bi-pinnate, with many pairs of small leaflets or a few large leaflets, bearing conspicuous glands on the stalks. Flowers are often showy, pink, yellowish or white and occur in axillary globose heads or clustered at ends of branches. Several species yield a hard, dense, easily workable dark wood. The soft-wooded species are used to make matches. Several species are a source of gum and resin.

### *Albizia lebbeck*—Siris. (Leguminosae).

A widespread, tropical South-eastern Asian leguminous tree, also introduced to the Caribbean and Africa. First described by Linnaeus in 1753, as belonging to the upper Egypt.

| | | 3 | | |
|---|---|---|---|---|
| | | 4 | 5 | |
| 1 | 2 | | 6 | |

Tamarind; from Curtis. *Tamarindus indica*—tamarind—is an evergreen tree of mixed deciduous forests across India. The tamarind fruit is used in nearly every form of cooking.

*Acacia*; from Wallich, 1831.

Thorn forests of Western Ghats and the dry peninsular plateau are dominated by the *Acacia nilotica*—the *babul* tree.

*Acacia nilotica*—*babul*—is a xerophytic thorny tree found in thorn forests and dry deciduous forests all over India. A shrike sits on its favourite perch in a thorny covered *babul* tree.

*Ziziphus* is a species of trees or shrubs found across the dryer parts of India. The fruit of *Ziziphus mauritiana*, ber, is consumed by people and animals. It is predominant in the Wild Ass Sanctuary in the Rann of Kachchh.

*Albizia* are found in the dry deciduous and thorn forests of the Deccan and southern India.

## ZIZIPHUS

These typical trees and shrubs of the arid and semi-arid areas are stunted, thorny plants and form a prominent part of shrublands or medium-sized trees. They also colonize degraded areas of deciduous forests. *Ziziphus mauritiana* is the most frequent species. Commonly browsed species by both wild herbivores and domestic animals, these trees are also a favourite of frugivorous birds. They fruit in summer and support a variety of birds and mammals such as sambar and chital. The plants form thorny trees or shrubs and cover open areas in forests, in the form of thick scrub, which is a favourite resting site for tigers, leopards, jungle cats, jackals, and other animals. Such tracts of scrub are an important microhabitat for mammals and birds in various types of arid and deciduous forest types. Unfortunately, many of these areas have been taken over by *Lantana*, which has limited food value, as most browsers will not eat it. Berry-dependent birds are its most prominent dispersal agents and transfer its seeds to other sites. It has small flowers that are pollinated by several insects. *Ziziphus* is frequently covered by ants that climb all over its shrubs.

## ZIZIPHUS MAURITIANA—BER

*Ber* is a small evergreen, thorny tree, which can grow up to 10 metres in height, with a cracked rough bark. It is found both wild and cultivated, throughout India. The edible fruit is a drupe, oblong in shape and orange-yellowish in colour. The tree's characteristic umbrella-like shape gives it a distinctive appearance in heavily browsed thorn forests.

### *Ziziphus mauritiana*—*Ber*. (Rhamnaceae).

This spiny shrub, with edible berries, was first described by Lamarck in 1789 based on specimens collected on the island of Mauritius by Pierre Sonnerat. It had been described previously (in 1753) by Linnaeus as *Rhamnus jujuba*, based on earlier descriptions and specimens from Ceylon, but for technical reasons this epithet was not available for transfer to the genus *Ziziphus* specimens collected by Wight in the Nilgiri Hills.

## STERCULIA URENS—KARAYA GUM

This is a medium-sized, deciduous tree, about 10 metres in height, with a white, papery bark and large, velvety, five-lobed leaves. The tree blooms when it is leafless, and its clusters of starry flowers have a strong smell. The fruit is woody, with five fruitlets, which look like starfish with bristly hair. Commonly found in most jungles, it frequently grows on rocky precipices. Birds feed on the fleshy covering of the seeds. This is a common tree in northern and central India, in Deccan and Rajasthan.

### *Sterculia urens*—*Karaya* Gum. (Sterculiaceae).

This small tree with papery bark is widespread in India, in dry rocky places. It was first described from the Eastern Ghats by William Roxburgh in 1795.

| 1 | 3 | | |
|---|---|---|---|
| 2 | | 4 | 5 |

*Sterculia*; from Roxburgh, 1795.

*Sterculia urens* is a deciduous tree found in northern and central India, as well as in the Deccan. It has a distinctive white bark.

*Firmiana colorata*; from JBNHS, 1930.

Wild date palm.

Mangroves are constituted by several species of *Avicennias* that grow in salt or brackish water whose roots are inundated at high tide.

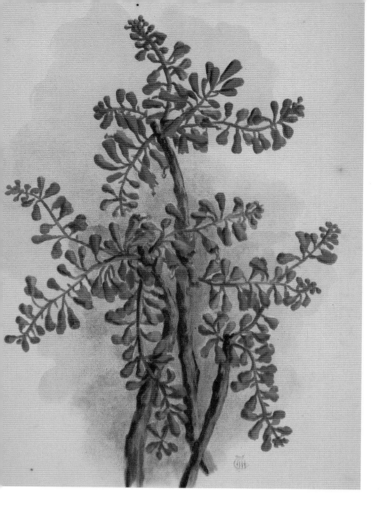

## CAPPARIS APHYLLA

This is a much-branched shrub or small tree of open, dry, scrub forests in Punjab, Sind, Rajasthan, Gujarat and drier parts of the peninsula. Associated with *Prosopis spicigera, and Acacia,* it has a mass of slender, thorny, green, leafless branches, and small leaves which grow mainly on young shoots. The tree is conspicuous in early summer when covered in red flowers. The round, pink, fleshy fruits are eaten by birds.

## PROSOPIS CINERARIA—KHEJDI

This is a moderate-sized, thorny evergreen tree with light foliage and slender branches, occurruing in dry and arid regions of Sind, Punjab, Rajasthan, Gujarat, Deccan and drier southern India. The branches have conical prickles. The wood is very hard and is used as fuel and charcoal. The pods are used as cattle feed.

## PTEROSPERMUM ACERIFOLIUM

This large, handsome, evergreen tree with a thin grey smooth bark is found in the sub-Himalayan tract, Bengal, Chittagong, Manipur, in the Khalsi Hills, Burma and North Kanara. The wood is moderately hard and reddish. It is used for carpentry and sometimes for planking.

## PHOENIX SYLVESTRIS—WILD DATE PALM, KHAJUR

This tall, unbranched palm grows up to 15 metres in height and has a rough trunk typically covered by prominent persistent leaf bases. Leaflets are pointed and sharp. Its flowering spikes are enclosed in a boat-shaped bract, while the fruit is reddish, sweet and edible. The tree is indigenous to many parts of India, growing on wastelands, barren hills, both wild and cultivated. The trunk is tapped for a sweet drink called *nira,* which ferments into a strong alcoholic toddy. The leaves are used to make brooms.

### *Phoenix sylvestris*—Wild Date Palm, *Khajur.* (Palmae).

A conspicuous feature of the Indian landscape, and useful for its sap which is tapped and used to make sugar and fermented into liquors. It was first described botanically (under the genus *Elate*) by Linnaeus in 1753, based in part on an illustration in van Rheede's *Hortus Malabaricus,* probably made in Kerala.

## MANGROVES

There are 58 principal salt-tolerant or halophilous species known in India. Species of such plants as *Rhizophora* and *Avicennia* form mangrove forests in river deltas and along the western and eastern seacoast. The greatest concentration of mangroves is seen in the Sunderbans of West Bengal and Bangladesh, with a total area of about 100,000 square kilometres. Other incredible patches of mangrove in an undisturbed form are seen in the Andaman and Nicobar Islands.

The lush green trees of these varied species are a vital component of shallow brackish water, deltas and highly productive coastal communities. They can tolerate moderate to high levels of salinity and occur most frequently in the intertidal zone, their prop roots reducing the force of tidal currents on the mud banks on which they grow. They act as breeding grounds for a large variety of marine fish and crustacea. Seeds of these plants germinate while still on the tree, a process known as vivipary. The seedlings drop off and float on the water until their well-developed roots take hold in shallow water elsewhere.

## AQUATIC PLANTS

### NELUMBO NUCIFERA—LOTUS

The lotus, considered a symbol of wisdom, is an aquatic floating herb with a large rhizome rooted in mud. Its leaves are circular and flat, covered with a waxy coating which protects them from water. The flower grows on an erect stalk and it has several petals ranging from pink-violet to white. The fruit is a spongy cone with multiple round seeds.

The lotus is widely distributed in wetland habitats such as shallow, marshy areas and plays a major role in the habitat for aquatic birds such as jacanas, and moorhens whose long feet enable them to use the leaves to walk on while hunting for their food. The rhizome, stalks of leaves and seeds are considered delicacies. The fruit is used for dry decorations. The flower has been a traditional motif in Indian art.

Mangroves have evolved special roots for breathing, as they grow in muddy silts that lack aeration. These roots are called pneumatophores and are negatively geotropic, that is, they tend to grow away from the ground. These roots have numerous pores all over the surface, known as lenticels, through which gaseous exchange occurs. Specialized glands, called chalk glands, are present on the leaves through which the excess salt is removed in the form of a precipitate.

Mangroves have been used for timber, firewood, charcoal, and as a source of tannin. Mangrove forests are frequently converted into large open saltpans. They are, however, important as they stabilize coastal areas. Mangrove plantations aid in the reclamation of degraded saline destabilized soil on coastal areas.

> ### Nelumbo nucifera—Sacred Lotus. (Nelumbonaceae).
>
> One of the best-known and most beautiful Indian plants, extensively used in Hindu and Buddhist iconography. Although first described botanically by Linnaeus in 1753, based partly on illustrations in van Rheede's *Hortus Malabaricus*, for technical nomenclatural reasons it was renamed by Gertner in 1788.

1
2
3

Mangroves are highly productive ecosystems.

*Avicennia*; from Wallich, 1832.

Floating vegetation in a wetland.

## UTRICULARIA STRIATULA— BLADDERWORT

These are small, insectivorous herbs, ranging from extremely minute species, barely half a centimetre in height, to 15 centimetre high varieties. The tiny leaves are attached to a horizontally spreading stem and some of them are converted into bladders. The trap is a hollow bag, with a small entrance surrounded by bristles that guide insects towards the entrance. The entrance is closed by a valve with four hairs. When the insect touches the hair, the valve is triggered and a rush of water drags the insect into the trap. These species relish habitats with a continuous slow trickle of water as well as open, sunny, but cool ones. Most of the species have blue or mauve flowers that are borne on erect shoots. Flowering occurs throughout the monsoon and continues for a brief period while the hill streams are flowing.

A large number of species are found in different forests, several of them endemic to the Western Ghats, but they are probably less common than they used to be, as their microhabitats of perennial *nala* courses and cascades are disappearing due to the deforestation of hill-slopes.

The lotus is India's national flower and the state flower of Haryana, Jammu and Kashmir, Karnataka and Orissa.

*Utricularia* is found in very specific habitat conditions in wet areas in the ground cover of forests. It catches aquatic insects in its tiny bladders.

Utricularia in a waterfall.

*Utricularia* in a waterfall.

*Utricularia purpurascens* forms a large bed in the flowing water of a hill stream.

When a stream dries, a *Terniola* leaves a pattern over the rock.

*Terniola* just before it dries.

## TERNIOLA ZEYLANICA

This is a minuscule aquatic herb which grows in the shallow patches of rapidly flowing water, usually in hill streams with rocky, smooth beds. The stem is truncated and ribbon-like, the leaves are moss-like, and the flowers very small and green in colour, with petals conspicuous by their absence. Pollination is done through the flowing water. Its capsules are formed on erect shoots, one centimetre in length and the seeds are dispersed by water. The plant remains in a dried condition on rocks in *nalas* after the monsoon. Flowering occurs only when the *nala* is flowing.

Frequently found in western peninsular India, in *nala* courses, it is generally considered to be a rare plant as it is found only in *nalas* that flow for a long duration. Its range is limited by the specific conditions it requires for its growth.

## EXOTIC PLANTS AND WEEDS

While biodiversity loss was ascribed to poaching by local people and later to habitat destruction, again by local people who had lost their stake in managing community lands, this has gradually shifted to understanding that the present impacts of unsustainable development are due to major development projects—dams, mines, roads, industrial growth and urbanization—which play an ever-growing role in the threat to biodiversity. The least appreciated is the loss created by the large number of weeds introduced into natural habitats. *Prosopis juliflora* was introduced from Mexico to India in the early 1920s; *Lantana* came in as a garden plant to overrun forest undergrowth; and Hyacinth entered India from South American rivers, invading a large number of rivers, lakes and wetlands.

*Lantana* can grow either as a shrub or climber. As it is an exotic, it spreads prolifically in the forest.

Water hyacinth—*Eichhornia crassipes*.

*Parthenium* is an aggressive weed that has spread widely all over India

### *Eichhornia crassipes*—Water Hyacinth. (Pontederiaceae).

This floating plant is native to tropical South America but has been widely introduced and is now a problematic pantropical weed. It was originally described from Brazil in 1823, by the German botanist Carl Friedrich Philipp von Martius, the great authority on palms and on the flora of Brazil.

### *EICHHORNIA CRASSIPES*— WATER HYACINTH

The water hyacinth is a herbaceous aquatic plant which floats on water and has rounded glossy green leaves. The petiole has a prominent bulge of spongy tissue and its bright lavender flowers are borne on erect shoots. It is insect pollinated and produces a large number of seeds, which are dispersed by wind and water. Originally from freshwater habitats in north-eastern Brazil, it has extensively invaded water bodies in South Asia, Africa, Australia and North America, and grows in all climatic zones including warm temperate, dry, subtropical, tropical and arid regions. A prolific freshwater weed, it grows rapidly to form large floating mats of vegetation. The plant, however, cannot tolerate water temperature more than 34 degrees Celsius. Its vegetative reproduction is rapid and it extends over large water surfaces, restricting the growth of other aquatic plants and animals. Its rapid root growth and decay of dead parts reduces the oxygen present in the water and it lowers water levels through its high rate of transpiration. It grows well even in polluted waters and has a tendency to accumulate heavy metals. Attempts are being made to use this plant in the water-treatment processes. There are no simple measures to eradicate this weed. Most of the water bodies have to be cleaned manually. Even if large areas are treated chemically, re-invasion from seeds is seen to occur. Biological control using a beetle *Neochetina eichhorniae, Warner coleoptera- curculionidae* has been successful in some areas. Inoculation of plants with the fungus *Cercospora rodmani* may improve the success of insect control. This weed has damaged aquatic systems all over India and should be eradicated, as it reduces the biological diversity of aquatic ecosystems. My fear has been that if it is found useful, it would stop being considered as a weed and would then be cultivated in all our rivers and wetlands, leading to the destruction of aquatic ecosystems and a serious loss of biodiversity.

# India's Rich Faunal Heritage

India has always been associated with her rich variety of wild creatures. No one can think of this country without reference to the world of the tiger, the elephant, and the peacock. And yet, hardly a fraction of the forests of bygone days is still left, and the population of animals and birds that live in the small residual islands of the Indian wilderness is being rapidly depleted. Perhaps the only exceptions are the animals that are protected in our Sanctuaries and National Parks, which form a small part of India's land. Even here the pressures of population growth and development in and around the Protected Areas are increasing and could well lead to early extinction of the more sensitive species. Several of these species have only a single home; external impacts in these situations can lead to early extinction. The loss of a single species can have serious effects on the dynamics and functioning of the ecosystem.

There is an overt concern for the decline in the numbers of most of our glamour species that excite the imagination, such as the tiger. While this is an indicator of the deteriorating status of these species, the decline in their population also suggests that other less-known components of biological diversity are equally or perhaps even more at risk. There could well be a large number of species we still aren't aware of and they could be vanishing

India's rich faunal heritage has been part of its culture since ancient times. This has included small and large creatures most of which were either used for food, were considered dangerous, or had religious significance. The mouse is portrayed as a vehicle of Lord Ganesh.

The elephant has been venerated and used in India over many generations.

even before they are documented by plant and animal taxonomists. Increasing fragmentation and degradation of our different forest types has seriously affected most wildlife species. The ones that are adapted to life in the wet evergreen forests are more sensitive to changes in their habitat and are undoubtedly at greater risk. Several forest tracts are indeed being fragmented and as these fragments get increasingly isolated from each other, the ability of several plant and animal species to cross from one patch to another is lost. Isolated small populations of a species cannot be expected to survive in the long term. The species confined to the ecosystems that cover a small proportion of the earth's surface, such as wetlands, are affected much more seriously by a shrinkage in the extent of their habitat. Wetland species are also affected by water pollution, changes in surrounding land-use, and draining done to reclaim more land. Equally at risk due to land-use changes are animals of the grassland plains of India. Species of the desert are at risk due to expanding irrigation that destroys their habitat. Wilderness habitats everywhere now face a growing threat from tourism. The Himalayas and hill stations are an important example of this new threat. Marine animals are threatened by an unsustainable increase in fishing and by pollution from industrial and other activities on the adjacent seashore. The Andaman and Nicobar Islands face a growing threat from several activities, which can rapidly lead to the extinction of the endemic species that live in this most fragile of ecosystems.

During the last 40-odd years I have seen forests being converted into urban areas; grasslands being changed into intensively used agricultural tracts and industrial belts; wetlands and percolation tanks vanishing; hillsides being severely eroded; and rivers turning into sewers in urban areas. Their rare, specialized creatures, as well as many familiar forms of life are being threatened by a variety of unsustainable human activities. The residual wilderness is decreasing in species-richness and the composition of their plant and animal communities is altered. But while I have been saddened and indeed frequently

astounded by the incredible rate at which these changes occur, I am even more apprehensive of the plight of the unseen and unknown creatures that are rarely—if ever—observed. There are many species that we do not know about. One cannot expect to know them all. They are just too many for scientists to even begin to identify them in the near future.

There are several species with which, for one reason or the other, I have been more deeply concerned than with others. While many of these are indeed the more eye-catching, fascinating species, there are several less-known plant and animal species that I have photographed and observed in the wilds of this incredible country. Many of them are being pushed towards the precipice of extinction, towards a terrible, permanent oblivion.

## VANISHING WILDLIFE

Wildlife in India is increasingly getting confined to Protected Areas, both as a result of rapid shrinkage of wilderness areas, as well as of the increasing poaching pressure on several species. While the pressure on some well-known species is frequently reported in the press, the growing extraction of species of medicinal plants such as *Mappia foetida*, for its anti-cancer properties, is less heard of. We do not know how its disappearance could affect linked species of fauna. In the minds of most people, wildlife still conjures up an image of major mammals or beautiful birds and does not include the large variety of plant-life, or the less glamorous species of reptiles, amphibians or insects.

Animals such as corals, produced by polyps, starfish or sea urchins, are far removed from the conscious world for most of us. Of even less concern are microscopic plants and animals and the incredible world of fungi, which are not really plants. Fungi are linked both to plants and to a large number of animals in nature. Several species such as the tigers now live mainly in Wildlife Sanctuaries and National Parks, where their habitat and prey species have been protected. Outside these Protected Areas their rate of decline, though obvious, is less overt and remains essentially unquantified. Animals such as the elephants have been forced to move

out of their habitat due to a loss of their natural movement corridors. They have come into increasing conflicts with the neighbouring human communities, with disastrous consequences for both humans and animals.

In a book of this nature, it is virtually impossible to include all our rich diversity of species. The species selected are thus more or less a random selection and they are frequently those for which I have developed a special interest, whatever may be the reason for that. In the recent past I have become increasingly concerned about the future of several of these species. While most people are familiar with the taxonomy and characteristics of these species, they are unaware of various aspects of their behaviour, ecology, or of the factors that threaten their existence. It is these specific aspects that I have dealt with in this book.

## THE ANIMAL WORLD

We often don't realize the large diversity of animals that live in our natural habitats. While we are aware of the glamour species, essentially large mammals and several types of birds, we rarely appreciate the fact that there are several species of animals, such as the invertebrates and the marine animals, that we do not know of. It is this hidden world of animal life that we do not see or hear, that constitutes a large proportion of the earth's biological diversity.

There are 90,000 species of fauna that have been identified from India. India has 4 to 12 per cent of the global species of lower faunal taxa (MoEF, 2002). If a certain species is endemic to a particular region which is gradually destroyed, that species is at grave risk of vanishing altogether. Vertebrates such as amphibia have a high rate of endemism; more than 50 per cent of amphibia are endemic, mainly to the Western Ghats. Freshwater fish and reptiles also have high endemism levels, reaching 30 per cent or more. Endemism among mammals, however, is low—probably less than 10 per cent. Similarly, bird endemism is relatively low and could be only 10 per cent. A high number of sub-species of birds occurs in the Andaman and Nicobar Islands. We know too little about the endemism among lower forms of life such as invertebrates, but it is estimated at 10 or 20 per cent.

Loss of individual species has been found to affect the energy flowing through an ecosystem. Those ecosystems that have a large number of food chains would inevitably have a more complex food-web and more interrelationships. Severing these threads could well be disastrous.

Invertebrates and lower vertebrates are more patchily distributed than mammals or birds and are thus more vulnerable to human pressure. Well-known recent extinctions include species like the cheetah, the mountain quail and the pin-headed duck. The restricted distributions of several other species and fragmentation could rapidly add to this list.

Protozoa are unicellular animals of various shapes. A large majority are microscopic and are found in aquatic habitats in freshwater and marine ecosystems. These unicellular animals multiply by division. They have a simple mechanism for feeding, called phagocytosis—engulfing their food material. Protozoa are either herbivorous or carnivorous and they form an important component of food chains in aquatic ecosystems.

Parazoa are several primitive, multicellular organisms—such as sponges—which are found in marine habitats and which form polyp-like animals and other motile organisms in aquatic ecosystems.

Metazoa are higher multicellular animals with complex tissues and organs. A large number are invertebrates, while higher forms are vertebrates. The most basic forms of invertebrates are *Coelenterata*. Most of these are aquatic polyp-like animals, with a stalk and many fronds. Several form coral; others are sea anemones. Worms are either parasitic or free-living. Molluscs are soft-bodied ancient animals. Arthropods include crustaceans, spiders and insects. Echinoderms consist of starfish and allied species. The vertebrates include fish, amphibia, reptiles, birds and mammals. Fish are a diverse group found in fresh and marine habitats. Amphibians form another ancient group. Reptiles that once ruled the earth still have a large number of species. The most highly evolved are the warm-blooded birds and mammals.

## INVERTEBRATES

The invertebrates consist of a variety of taxa that inhabit both aquatic and terrestrial ecosystems. Together they constitute a great proportion of life on earth, both in terms of the richness of their species as well as in terms of their incredible abundance. The most primitive were the protozoa, now separated into a different group called protoctista. The zooplankton, formed by microscopic animals, is one of the bases of the important links in the food chains in various aquatic habitats. The marine ecosystem consists of enormous numbers of polyp-like animals, that form rich colonies of coral. Coral reefs are said to be nearly as rich as tropical forests in their component species. There are thousands of different kinds of animals in the shallow seas. Worms include a great diversity of species. Many of these are parasites on other

animals and live within the alimentary canals of their specific hosts. Molluscs are very ancient species that live in oceans as well as in freshwater. Several of these are hermaphrodites, their eggs being laid by an individual that acts as a female as well as a male. Arthropods are ancient species that include spiders and scorpions. There are more than 20,000 species of actual spiders. Crustacea are primitive species that inhabit different types of aquatic habitats; they include crabs and lobsters. The antennata are a specific super-class of animals that include centipedes and millipedes.

This astounding world of invertebrates forms a major sector of the earth's animal life. We are rarely conscious of this great abundance of less-known, unfamiliar species. Frequently we refer to these species as pests. Without them, however, the earth's living ecosystems would die.

Snails are ancient forms of life.

The diversity of the invertebrate world is an astounding feature of nature.

| 1 | 2 | | 6 | |
|---|---|---|---|---|
| 3 | 4 | | 7 | 8 |
| 5 | | | | |

A large squid.

Marine crab.

The dollar is an ancient marine animal.

Sea cucumber.

Sea-shells on a coast.

Stick insect.

Lunar moth.

Moths have a great ecological significance.

## PROTOZOA

These are mainly unicellular, primitive forms, that are now included in an ancient group of species formerly classified as part of the animal world. Zoologists now include them as heterotrophs, belonging to the same group as the algae. This primitive group of species that was present on earth before the evolution of plants and animals is called *protoctista*.

The zooplankton was studied in 1936 by B Bhatia for *The Fauna of British India, Ceylon and Burma*. Volume I, *Protozoa (Ciliophora)* was a detailed analysis of what was known so far on these tiny creatures.
AK Mandal (1987) worked on *protozoa*.

## PARAZOA

*Parazoa*
In 1911, Nelson Annandale, wrote on 'Freshwater Sponges, Hydroids and Polyzoa' for *The Fauna of British India, Ceylon and Burma*. Annandale's work has been one of the great reference materials for these less-known species for decades.

### JELLYFISH

These organisms are transparent and glossy, with their tentacles and internal organs brilliantly coloured. Some forms are phosphorescent. They can measure up to a metre in diameter. This bell-shaped colony of *Coelenterates* floats near the surface of the sea and in backwater areas. A few genera live attached to rocks, mud-banks and weeds. All jellyfish are carnivorous and feed on crustaceans, fish and other small sea animals. The shape of the bell differs with the species. Some are shaped like a goblet, others are like four-sided cups, or conical, or saucer-like or flat discs.

### SPONGES

This group includes the most primitive multicellular animals. Sponges belong to the order *Porifera*, meaning porous animals. Most sponges are found in marine habitats and have a most fascinating structure.

## METAZOA
### SEA ANEMONES

Sea anemones are like coral but usually single. They have numerous contractile tentacles with fine hair called 'cilia'. The contractile tentacles have stinging cells which help them to capture their prey and transfer it to the mouth. Sea anemones come in a variety of colours and shapes, either stalked or flat. Growing to a size of 10 to 30 centimetres, they are found in rocky pools, mud-banks and shallow seas along the western and eastern coasts of India and around the islands. They live in tidal pools and reefs. Sea anemones slowly slide along the bottom of the sea and catch passing prey by stinging and engulfing them through a central mouth. They eat small fish, Molluscs and crustacea that float past them. They are threatened due to habitat loss.

```
      3
      4
   2

1
```

A giant jellyfish.

Sea anemones come in all shapes, sizes and colours.

Coral.

Coral and sponges from important links in the ecosystem.

### CORAL

Look into a crystal-clear, shallow zone of the sea around the Andamans or Lakshadweep Islands and an incredibly vivid world of shapes and colours will form an aquatic paradise in front of your eyes. The colours are an incredible rainbow, with flashing movements of fish and slow movements of thousands of coral.

Coral are polyp-like organisms and are grouped with *Coelenterates*. Most of them form large colonies and secrete calcareous skeletons which develop a large variety of fantastic shapes. The polyps of the coral have multiple tentacles and are frequently brightly coloured. They can vary from extremely tiny, pinhead-sized animals to fairly large polyps and they are found in clear warm shallow coastal waters, especially in gulfs and the shallow seas around the islands. They can live only in marine habitats, with clear shallow water, where they are fixed to the seabed. In many species, the arms of the coral wave slowly, enhancing the colony's ability to catch passing food. They feed on small organisms like algae, zooplankton, tiny worms, crustacea and molluscs that move past them. They are highly threatened due to trawlers and collection of corals as artefacts, as well as due to global warming, which has already warmed tropical seas and has led to the massive death of coral. Unless the global climate conditions caused by human activity—such as the release of carbon into the atmosphere—are improved, coral will continue to die. Reducing the other destructive impacts on coral, such as pollution and siltation due to degradation of mangroves on the adjacent land, can prevent further loss of coral reefs. The species that form coral reefs are themselves a diverse group of organisms. They form, however, a highly specialized habitat for thousands of other marine creatures such as fish, crustacea, starfish, octopuses and other micro-flora and fauna, and are believed to be as rich in species as evergreen forests. Their loss will lead to an enormous fall in global biodiversity.

## MOLLUSCS
### SNAILS (SINGLE-SHELLED MOLLUSCS)
Snails form the largest group of molluscs. Each snail has a single shell, and each species has a different kind of shell. Taken together, they offer various sizes, shapes and colours. Snails are grouped into terrestrial, freshwater and marine species. Land snails, which have a round spiral shell, have slime-coated bodies, and they leave a slimy trail behind as they move.

The head bears two pairs of tentacles of different lengths, a short one, behind which there is a longer pair, with an eye at each tip. Many snails can completely withdraw these tentacles, which are sensory organs, into a hollow in the head. Land snails are vegetarians. A simple aperture with an arched jaw forms the mouth of these snails. Snails are highly moisture dependent. In the monsoons they can be seen in large numbers creeping over moist stones, moss-covered surfaces and many different plants. During the hot, dry summers they withdraw into their shells with a tightly closed lid. They bury themselves under loose earth or conceal themselves in thick debris. Snails aestivate gregariously.

Terrestrial snails are hermaphrodites. Sperms and ova are produced at the same

time but in different chambers and are led by separate ducts to a common genital opening. Snails lay only a few eggs, compared with other molluscs.

Pond snails differ from land snails in the position of their eyes and the number of tentacles. Aquatic snails have only one pair of tentacles, at the base of which the eyes are situated. The tentacles are contractile but cannot be withdrawn completely. Aquatic snails deposit their spawn in irregular gelatinous masses, under water-plants and other debris.

Certain snails can survive in polluted or brackish waters and sulphureous springs. Although they live in water, they are lung-breathing animals and have to come to the surface to breathe. During summer, when the ponds dry, they aestivate buried in mud and remain there until the next monsoon comes and fills up the pond.

Molluscs were studied for the *The Fauna of British India, Ceylon and Burma* by G K Gude (1914–1921), who was concerned with land molluscs and H Preston (1915), with freshwater molluscs.

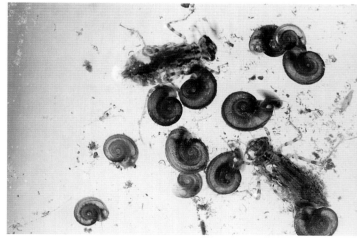

Snails feeding on a clump of moss.

Snail feeding on a leaf.

Snails are an important component of several aquatic ecosystems.

### OCTOPUSES

The octopus is a *Cephalopod* which has eight strong tentacles armed with suckers and a hard, beak-like mouth. Giant octopus species, found in tropical seas at different depths, can grow to a length of 14 feet. The octopus attacks its prey—fish, molluscs and crustacea—by using its strong tentacles and crushing it with its hard beak. It is threatened due to habitat loss, marine pollution and over-harvesting for food.

### ECHINODERMS
#### BRITTLE-STAR

Brittle-stars are included in a group called Echinoderms. Found in the sea, in different types of habitats, they are star-like in shape and have a central disc with five very slender radiating arms. On the lower surface there is a mouth. The brittle-star is protected by a number of calcareous plates which are loosely joined to each other. Some brittle-stars have sharp spines, which act as a protective device. They are found along the western and eastern coasts of India and in the sea-bed around the Andaman and Nicobar Islands, at various depths of their marine habitats. The arms of the brittle-stars grow back if detached. It crawls along the ocean floor, using its radiating arms. Brittle-stars are threatened due to habitat loss and pollution.

### WORMS
#### EARTHWORMS

Earthworms are characterized by a segmented body. They move by contracting and relaxing their body segments. Earthworms hatch from a cocoon, the size being variable with the species. There are several common species seen around houses and gardens, near wet and damp places. The earthworm plays a very important role in the detritus food chain by feeding on organic waste, and in the process releasing nutrients, which are returned to the soil. Earthworms are now successfully bred through a process called vermiculture. Vermicompost is today a very valuable bio-fertilizer.

Worms were categorized for *The Fauna of British India, Ceylon and Burma* in the 1930s by H Baylis.

J Stephenson (1923) and JM Julka (1988), wrote on earthworms and freshwater worms.

H Mehra, with additions from CS Srivastava (1980) wrote on parasitic flatworms and flukes.

RP Mukherjee (1986–1992) wrote on flukes.

| 1 | |
|---|---|
| 2 | 3 |

The octopus has eight tentacles with multiple suckers, a powerful beak-like mouth and can release a black inky material to defend itself.

Echinoderms, including brittle stars, are found in a variety of ocean habitats, especially coral reefs.

Earthworms.

## CRUSTACEA
### BARNACLES

Barnacles are small, mollusc-like species, protected by a very hard, calcareous, dome-shaped crust. They are stationary and remain attached to the rocky substratum in the highly changeable inter-tidal zone, and they feed on zooplankton. They are found in various marine environments along the coasts of India. Colonies of barnacles can most often be seen on rocky seashores. The inter-tidal zone, the barnacle's habitat, shows a gradation that creates a physically stressed environment. Part of the time it is exposed to the atmosphere, but it forms an aquatic environment when the barnacles are submerged in water and have to face predation.

### CRABS

Crabs belong to an ancient group of crustacea. They have five pairs of legs, the first of which is modified into claws and not used for walking. Most crabs have a large shield on their backs, covering the breathing system which is adapted in certain species for drawing oxygen from water. Land crabs absorb oxygen from moist air. A crab's eyes are at the tip of two extended stalks, which it can swivel 360 degrees to look for its prey and warn it against the predators around. Crabs vary in colour from dull to extremely bright, variegated patterns. They live in a variety of aquatic habitats and are found all over the country. Each species is adapted to a different ecosystem. These range from seashores with microhabitats varying from rocky or sandy coasts and brackish environments such as mangroves, to shores of lakes and banks of rivers. Crabs also use

man-modified landscapes such as paddy lands. The habits of different species are closely linked to the microhabitats they live in. Most are scavengers. They burrow holes in soft mud or sand. Marine crabs use a variety of empty seashells to live in, to protect themselves from predators. They walk and run sideways, and are omnivorous, feeding on small animals, insect larvae, worms, snails and a variety of plant-life. Crabs are eaten by humans and therefore over-harvested in certain areas.

## ARTHROPODA
### SCORPIONS

Scorpions are arachnids with a pair of very large claws, four pairs of legs, and a long mobile tail with a painful, poisonous sting. They vary from 1.3 to 18 centimetres in length, and hide during the day in crevices of rocks or under loose stones. Most species are nocturnal hunters of insects, which they paralyze by their sting. The females eat the males once mating is complete. Scorpions are viviparous and the young are looked after by the mother till they grow up.

RI Pocock, a meticulous researcher, described seven new species of scorpions from India in 1897. He published this in the JBNHS in the same year. He presented a detailed description, according to distinguishing characteristics such as colour, trunk, tail, chelae, legs, pectinal teeth, length locality, etc. They belonged to three genera: *Prionurus*, *Buthelous* and *Buthus*.

BK Tikadar and D Bastawade (1983) wrote extensively on scorpions.

|   | 2 | 6 |
|---|---|---|
|   | 3 |   |
| 1 | 4 |   |
|   | 5 |   |

Barnacles.

A crab displaying its large claws.

Crabs are ancient animals adapted to fresh water and marine ecosystems.

Crab in the detritus.

Crab.

Scorpion stings are painful but not life-threatening.

## SPIDERS

Spiders belong to a group called arachnids, having a head, thorax and abdomen, and four pairs of legs. They have four pairs of eyes. Spider webs are made from organic, thread-like material secreted by a specialized organ in the abdomen.

They vary considerably in size and are adapted to a wide variety of habitats. Indian spiders are harmless. Smaller spiders prey on flies and mosquitoes, and are a useful means of controlling pest populations. Large spiders catch bigger insects, butterflies, moths, grasshoppers and even dragonflies. Female spiders are dominant and larger than the males. As with scorpions, in some species of spiders the females eat the male after mating. They also care for their young by building a special protective web and guarding them till they mature. Some spiders build cocoons of different shapes for their eggs and young.

What has always fascinated me is the variety of ways in which different species of spiders build their webs. Several spiders have distinctive microhabitat needs, living either in the canopy, shrubs, grass or under detritus. Their living quarters vary from the tunnel webs on the forest floor to those in the shrub layer. Community spiders live

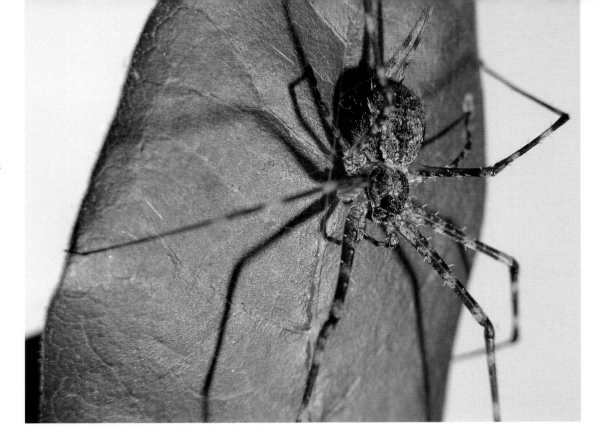

together in masses. The well-known orb web is built in the tree canopy which, with its ribs and linking threads, forms architecturally perfect structures among the branches of trees in the forest.

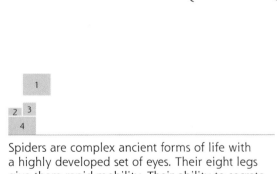

|   | 1 |   |
|---|---|---|
| 2 | 3 |   |
| 4 |   |   |

Spiders are complex ancient forms of life with a highly developed set of eyes. Their eight legs give them rapid mobility. Their ability to secrete material to create a structure of great strength is a wonder of nature.

Spider.

The long legs of this unique animal give it the common name of 'daddy long legs'.

The spiders' webs are intricate mechanisms for assisting predation. It is incredible that nature has been able to provide spiders with a capacity to create such an efficient structure.

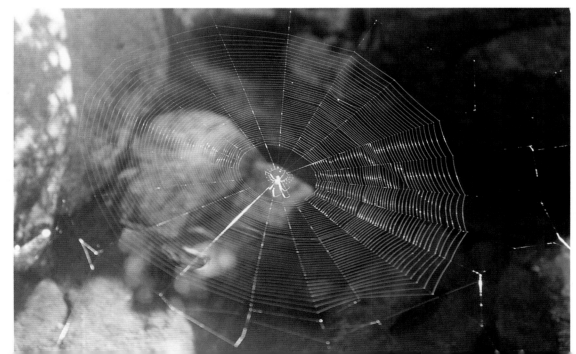

It is a mystery why the signature web spider signs its small extra-visible sign on its web.

A spider eating its prey.

A signature web spider guarding her young ones.

### Megalomorphic spiders

These are a nocturnal spiders usually having a brown, squarish cephalothorax (head and thorax). During daytime, these spiders remain hidden under rocks or in holes lined by silken thread. Some build tube-like tunnels, with a trap door, underground.

### Arachnomorphic spiders

This group has several families. The *Erisidae* are colony formers and can number hundreds in a nest, which is an irregular, shapeless mass, with an inner chamber accessible through multiple openings.

A lacy spider's web with dew drops that sparkle in the sunlight is a delightful early morning sight in the forest.

## Orb-weaving spiders

This group has several species, varying considerably in size and colour. The well-known web has radial threads and a spiral that forms the familiar circular, vertically-placed web in the canopy or shrub layer. Some species add zigzag lines or debris in them; others are shaped like domes suspended in the foliage.

Some of these are elongated spiders, with long legs placed in line with their bodies. The more familiar species, such as the wood spider, have radial legs. Some species are tiny and insignificant; others are multicoloured, with prominent designs or spines.

A tiny orb-weaving spider awaits its prey.

The female wood spider is much larger than the male. She is known to kill and eat the male after they have mated.

The **giant wood spider** of the Indian forests is familiar as it builds large webs that are frequently a metre in diameter. The female is a giant among spiders. Watching these creatures is as interesting as watching a carnivore like a tiger, as their feeding behaviour is an example of nature's complex food chains. The female wood spider has black and white stripes on its back, orange spots on the lower side, and yellow spots on its black legs. In contrast the male is a tiny, brown, somewhat insignificant spider. The female builds the irregular mooring strands, then the radial arms, and finally weaves its fine spiral.

A group known as *crytophoras* build nests close to each other, but they capture their prey independently. Their dome-like webs have a fine mesh within multiple, haphazardly-placed, mooring threads.

*Attidae* are known as 'jumping spiders'. They are found in different microhabitats, adapting well to a variety of conditions including human homes. Commonly seen on walls, this brown or black spider with subtle designs has rather hairy legs. Those species that live in trees are green or metallic blue. Some mimic the appearance and behaviour of a tiny dangerous scorpion. Others look like ants.

The enormous diversity of spiders makes spider-watching a fascinating experience.

Spiders from different parts of the country were studied. Despite that, there are probably even today, several unknown species. As interest in spiders grew, it became evident that they were important links in the web of life. New species were thus being continuously identified.

*The Fauna of British India—Arachnida* was published by RI Pocock in 1900.

He described three new species of spiders from India, namely, *Teragnatha cxlestis, Orisnome marmore* and *Argyroepeira beata*, according to their characteristic colour, head, abdomen, measurement and length in detail. (Pocock, 1901).

BK Tikadar worked on different groups of spiders in 1982.

Spiders that build sheath webs in the grass often live close to each other.

A spider with its case from which its young emerge.

| | 2 |
|---|---|
| 1 | |
| 3 | 4 |

A brightly coloured signature web spider devouring its prey.

This spider's web is home to its large number of young which are carefully guarded.

A tunnel web superbly built to catch unsuspecting prey on the forest floor.

A spider eating a moth much larger than itself. Spiders have learnt to colonize houses and can live in the most unlikely places.

## CENTIPEDES

Centipedes have elongated, segmented bodies and multiple-jointed legs. A pair of poisonous fangs under the head, fed by a poison gland, gives them a painful but not deadly bite. They prefer moist areas in detritus, crevices in tree barks and gaps under boulders. These carnivores feed on insects such as crickets, cockroaches and earthworms, and are active at night.

## MILLIPEDES

Among the several species of millipedes, there are the large ones, usually seen singly, and the much smaller reddish-brown species that frequently form large masses and move in groups, like a loose colony, separating and aggregating while they forage through the moist forest floor. They are great detritivores. I have observed millipedes break down the pellet droppings of a hare, a clear demonstration of animal waste being rapidly recycled into the soil.

RI Pocock wrote on millipedes in 1899 in Volume 12 of the JBNHS.

| 1 | 2 | |
| | 3 | |
| | 4 | |

The centipede has a vicious bite, which is not fatal.

A millipede rolled into a coil can become a round ball, exposing only its hard surface.

A millipede with its superbly coordinated legs can go over every obstacle in its path.

Millipedes mating.

## INSECTS

A vast majority of the species in the animal kingdom are insects, the most abundant animals on earth. More than a million insect species are known to science, and it is estimated that five out of six animal species in the world are insects. The number of insect species identified by entomologists continues to grow every day! The number of insect species that have not yet been identified could be three times the number of known species. India is rich in insect life and what is known about their lives is only the tip of a giant unknown iceberg. Understanding insects is as fascinating as studying large mammals or beautiful birds.

Insects are the most diverse creatures on earth. There are over a million species, many of which have adapted themselves to specific habitats.

A bright green, shiny jewel beetle uses its colour to ward off predators.

Tiny beetles emerging from their eggs.

Beetles are the most species-rich group of animals in the world.

Beetles come in all sizes, shapes and colours.

The incredible value of insects in maintaining the balance of nature in ecosystems is rarely appreciated. Insects have linkages with a great variety of other forms of life and they inhabit a wide spectrum of ecosystems. Closely associated with human life, they have both beneficial as well as serious negative impacts on our existence.

Insects are pollinators of a wide spectrum of flowering plants and act as agents of seed dispersal. They assist in the spread of wild plant species and play a vital role in the production of crops. The history of insects goes back to the carboniferous period, and they have since colonized almost all parts of the earth. The wide variety of insects have great variations in their structure and habits to enable them to live in specific microhabitats. Some insects that are generalists have adapted to a wide variety of habitat types.

Structurally, the typical insects have the head, thorax and abdomen covered in several plates, forming an external skeleton. They also have a wide spectrum of colours and shapes. Several have incredibly beautiful markings.

The varied behaviour of insects in nature provides fascinating insights into how the different complex ecosystems are all dependent on their insect life and its great diversity.

The absence of specific data on threats to this diverse group of species makes it difficult to assign the majority a clearly defined conservation status, but it is probably true that many insects are on the verge of extinction. As global warming increases, insect life will have to move northwards, as well as upwards into mountain regions. With wetter conditions in some areas and drier conditions in others, the insect life will have to move to areas where they are not present today. If their predators do not respond at the same time, there may be a hyper-abundance of insect life in the newly colonized regions of the world. There are several groups of unique insects. For example *Mallophaga*, feather lice, are specific to bird species and feed on decaying parts of the bird's feathers. Others live unique lives. One species of moth is known to live on the lacrimal secretion of the sambar deer and it spends most of its time near the sambar's eyes. Insect life is one of the most fascinating aspects of nature.

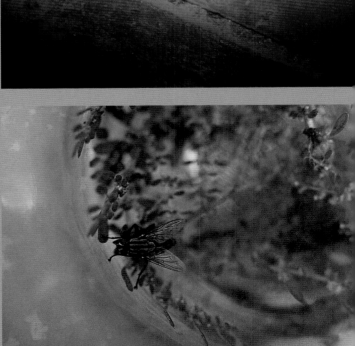

Some species of beetles live together in colonies.

A butterfly with translucent wings.

An unusual predatory insect walks through the forest undergrowth.

The fly is one of the insects that favours man's habitation where it can feed on food, garbage and waste material.

An interesting group of insects from the BNHS Journal demonstrates the detail with which old drawings were made; from JBNHS, 1903.

Lace-wing.

A moth with a mosaic pattern on its wings.

The *Fauna of British India—Insects* has a large number of amateur, and later professional zoologists, documenting insect life in India. There are still new species being discovered, that have not been seen by scientists. Most of the work done for the volumes of *The Fauna of British India* were put together by various authors in the 1900s.

- G Hampson et al (1892–96) wrote Volumes 1–5 on moths, including silk moths, hyspid moths, tiger moths, day-flying moths and others.
- WL Distant (1902–18) wrote extensively on insects such as true bugs, cycads, hoppers and aphids.
- CT Bingham wrote on ants, bees and wasps (1903), and butterflies in Volume 1 in 1905.
- C Gahan (1906) worked on beetles.
- Jacoby et al (1908–36) wrote four volumes on leaf beetles (1908).
- M Burr wrote on earwigs in 1910.
- G Arrow (1910–31) wrote on stags and scarabaed beetles.
- W Fowler (1912) worked on beetles.
- E Brunetti (1912–23) wrote on flies.
- C Morley (1913) wrote on ants, bees and wasps.
- Marshall, G. (1916) wrote on weevils.
- S Maulik worked on beetles from 1919 to 1936.
- J Stephenson (1923) wrote on earthworms.
- Andrewes H (1929) wrote on ground-beetles.
- M Cameron wrote on beetles in the 1930s.
- SR Christophers (1933) wrote on flies.
- PJ Barraud (1934) wrote on flies.
- FC Fraser (1933–34) authored the volumes on dragonflies and damselflies.
- Bell & Scott (1937) wrote on moths.
- G Talbot (1939–47), worked extensively on butterflies.
- A Ghosh (1984) wrote on cycads, hoppers and aphids.

Recent work on insects in India has been carried out by AK Ghosh, between 1982 and 1993, SK Gupta (1986), MS Mani (1989) and ML Roonwal and OB Chhotani (1989–97).

### GLOWWORMS—*LAMPIRIDAE*

As a schoolboy, I was extremely fascinated by the twinkling of fireflies. I cannot recall exactly when I caught my first firefly, but I distinctly recall that during several monsoons I would wait for them to appear in the garden after the first rains and trap them in a matchbox. After everyone else in my family had gone off to sleep, I would release them near my mosquito net and induce them to fly around by moving the net to disturb them. One day, I found that while there were none inside the house, there were several blinking away at the edge of the compound, where it was damp and bushy. I decided to sneak downstairs with my matchboxes. The first blinking light over which I put my hand in the dark felt very strange; it wriggled. I put it into the matchbox and when I opened it, I found, to my utter surprise, a glowworm!

Many years later I observed that fireflies had all but disappeared in Pune, except for two or three locations at the edge of the city. I decided to try to understand more about these curious creatures. When I read through the literature, I was surprised to learn that both these incredible creatures, the firefly and the glowworm, were one and the same species! They begin life as a worm-like larva, with a slowly glowing signal under the tail, and then, after a long period as a dormant underground pupa, they mature into female glowworms or adult male fireflies. They are active in the monsoons and signal to each other using their lighted tails during the night. While the female is an active, long-lived predator, with a voracious appetite for soft-bodied snails and worms, the male is short-lived and has no intestinal tract for feeding. Another interesting point about these insects is their linkage in the ecosystem. As the larvae and females are primarily snail eaters, they aggregate near their food sources. Snails need water in their habitat, while the drainage of ponds, pools and stagnant water kills off the glowworm's food supply and makes it disappear.

A fire-fly.

### DAMSELFLIES—*ODONATA*

The damselfly has four extremely thin, translucent wings and a very long and thin abdomen. Several of the species are highly coloured. Damselflies are usually smaller than dragonflies.

They are found in wetlands, ponds and moist grasslands, and have a different flight pattern from dragonflies. Swift and agile fliers, they normally rest with their wings together over their backs. Their breathing organs, found at the tip of the abdomen, are much more noticeable than those of dragonflies. Damselflies have small eyes, placed apart from each other on the lateral sides of the head. They feed on small insects.

Damselfly.

## DRAGONFLIES—*ODONATA*

Dragonflies have four membranous wings with complex venation, and very large compound eyes set close together. Their legs are tilted forwards, to enable them to catch objects on which they settle or to grasp their prey, and are not used for walking. When perched on a vantage, point the wings are held horizontally on either side. Dragonflies undergo incomplete metamorphosis, the larvae taking from one to five years to complete their development. The nymphs are predators of aquatic fauna and have pincer-like extensions of the lower lip, called the mask, which they use to catch their prey. There is no pupa stage. When nearly mature, they climb up a plant stem out of the water, shed the last larval skin, expand and dry their wings and fly off as adults. Dragonflies vary in length from four to eight centimetres. The adults perch on vegetation with wings spread out, usually near a water body with grassy banks. Dragonflies are predators that spend most of the day on the wing. They are capable of flying at high speed, of rapidly changing direction or of hovering at the same spot in mid-air. This agility in flight helps them to feed on small insects caught during flight.

| | 1 | 2 |
|---|---|---|
| 3 | | 4 |
| 5 | | 6 |

A dragonfly perched on a pneumatophore root of a mangrove.

An immature dragonfly emerging from the water; from JBNHS, 1899.

Dragonflies are insectivorous.

Dragonflies fly at inecredible speeds.

A green dragonfly lays its eggs on water, where its early forms live.

A dragonfly can hover like a helicopter.

**Dragonflies are predators. They have the ability to hover at one spot as well as to accelerate rapidly.**

### CRANE FLIES—*TIPULIDAE*

These insects have thin bodies, narrow wings and long fragile legs. The wings of the females are reduced in size or absent. When disturbed they take off with a low, dancing flight, their long legs dangling beneath them. Hundreds of small eggs are deposited in the soil. The tough-skinned larvae live in the soil and eat the roots of grasses and other plants. They pupate in the earth and some weeks later, the slim, horned pupae push halfway out of the soil for the adults to emerge. This is one of the largest and most widely-distributed families of flies, usually found resting on foliage in damp, shady places. Some species are crepuscular.

### TERMITES

The anthills of the Indian forests are in fact built by termites, which are very different from the ant family. The termites either live as a colony in dead wood or construct the giant mounds so frequently seen in forest clearings and grassy openings. Each species makes a specific type of mound, but two common patterns dominate. One has multiple small chambers in which the termite grows fungus as food. The other variety has a single hollow chamber, or a few large hollow chambers, with multiple buttresses. The life history of the termite is fascinating. There is a queen and a king for multiplication, a few soldiers and a large number who comprise the working section of the colony. The queen lays thousands

of eggs, supplying the colony with all its workers and soldiers. Just before the monsoon, some of the termites capable of breeding start developing and grow weak wings. When a mound of termites erupts, all the insectivores, which include various birds, reptiles and mammals, feast on the emerging termites. A few, however, escape to form new colonies. Termite mounds are sometimes covered by a mushroom, which arises out of the fungus and emerges above the surface. Some of these are said to be edible. Termite mounds could well be 50 years old and harbour an estimated 5 lakh insects!

Thousands of termites emerge during the monsoon.

A grey tit feeding on a termite mound as it erupts.

### GRASSHOPPERS AND MANTIDS

Grasshoppers and mantids are an ancient group of species that have adapted to a wide range of habitats. These species will probably outlive humans on earth. Locusts have been known to cause serious famines over the last few centuries.

### Grasshoppers—*Orthoptera*

Grasshoppers have long rear legs that enable them to spring long distances at high speed. Their species vary in colour and in the patterns on their bodies. The bright-yellow upper wings covering the abdomen make the painted grasshopper a conspicuous insect. This could be used to scare off predators. A broad black band runs across the body between the thorax and abdomen. Several grasshopper species that are green in colour are capable of a high level of camouflage and not easily detected by predators.

Grasshoppers rub their forewings against each other; this or the friction of the ridges on the hind legs produces that high-pitched sound so familiar in forests and grasslands. This is more pronounced in males and is linked with courtship. Sizes range from two to eight centimetres in different species.

Grasshoppers of different species occupy specific types of habitats. Some are ground-dwelling insects, while others live in trees. Several species are semi-aquatic and live close to wetlands, pools, rivers and paddies. They live singly, either on the ground or in various types of vegetation, and are the prey species of several insectivorous birds especially during the birds' breeding period. A large number of insect parasites live on grasshoppers, which are active during the day as well as at night.

The different grasshopper species are carnivorous, herbivorous or omnivorous. Adults as well as nymphs frequently feed on plants such as *Calotropis*. Most are common species that extensively damage crops, which are sprayed with insecticides to keep their population in check.

**Grasshoppers and mantids. This highly adaptable group of species live in a variety of ecosystems.**

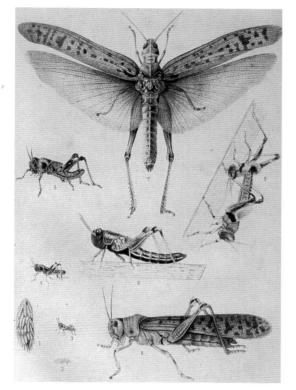

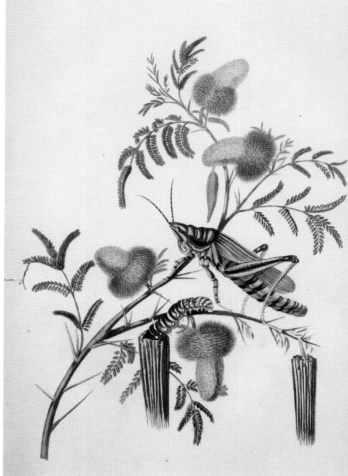

|   |   |   |
|---|---|---|
| | 1 | |
| | 3 | 4 |
| 2 | | |
| | | 6 |
| 5 | | |

Crickets and grasshoppers come in a variety of shades.

An old BNHS drawing showing the structure of a locust; from JBNHS, 1891.

A stick insect, well camouflaged in a thorny tree.

Blue locust; from Forbes, 1813.

A pair of painted grasshoppers.

Skeleton mantis; from Forbes, 1813.

## Mantids

Mantids are large, solitary, predatory insects, their forelegs armed with spines, which help them to catch and hold other insects that form their main food. The forelegs are usually held upright in a peculiar posture that resembles a person in prayer. Even the most devout human can never hope to spend as much time praying as a mantid! The mantis god must indeed be thrilled with his subjects who never ever seem to stop praying in total silence, slowly moving from side to side with folded hands!

Both adults and nymphs are of several shades of green and brown, which camouflage them perfectly. They are weak fliers, even though they have well-developed wings. Females of most of the mantid species are wingless. Some mantids have very brightly-coloured hind wings,

which are folded and hidden behind the forewings when stationary. In flight, this striking bright colour scares off predators. Each species has habitat preferences ranging from very hot and dry areas to extremely moist forested tracts.

Mantids deposit eggs in an oval structure that is attached to tree-trunks, stems, rocks or walls. They also deposit their eggs in the soil or on grass.

## Orchid Mantis
### —*Gongylus gongyloides*

The rare orchid mantis is a unique praying mantis, resembling a bright flower, but easily camouflaged by its shape, which is similar to dry leaves. The thorax is stick-like, with bright purple and violet extensions near the head. Brown, circular, leaf-like discs on the joints of its long stick-like legs camouflage them among the leaves. It can vary in length but can grow to a size of 10 centimetres. It is distributed over much of the Indian peninsula. Walking up to the highest point of the Dang forests of Gujarat, I thought I saw a strange brightly coloured flower in the grass. To my surprise, it was one of the most beautiful creatures I have ever come across. It was, in fact, a highly cooperative orchid mantis and I have a series of pictures of him posing for my camera! Though usually spotted in the grass, they can be seen on branches of trees and shrubs. They are predatory insects and feed on other insects such as grasshoppers, butterflies and moths.

## BUGS

Bugs belong to the order *Hemiptera*, one of the dominant insect groups, primarily dependent on plants. Some have piercing mouth-parts to suck plant fluids, while others, such as the giant species *Belastoma* are carnivorous, feeding on animal juices and blood, as well as decaying matter. Several of their body parts are used to make sounds not unlike those made by grasshoppers and crickets. Their defense mechanisms include camouflage, mimicry and glands that secrete poisonous fluids.

Based on their habitat, bugs are divided into three subgroups: aquatic or littoral bugs, bugs that live on water surfaces, and those that are mostly terrestrial.

| 1 | |
|---|---|
| 2 | 3 |
| 4 | |

Katydid is a strange leaf-like species.

Crickets and grasshoppers form an important link in the grassland food chain.

A leaf-insect camouflaged itself by mimicking a leaf.

A tiny mantis can make itself look dangerous by waving its forelegs and creating a threatening posture.

Bugs feed either on plants or on animals.

This beautiful mantis has a purple thorax and leaf-like circular, brown expansions near the joints of its legs, which make it look like a clump of small dry leaves.

## CICADAS

When I think of a forest, the first sound I imagine is the high pitched, stereophonic waves of the cicadas. The sound begins suddenly at a low volume and moves in a rapid crescendo, as all the cicadas begin to add their own screech to the overall sound. Then gradually, the volume seems to diminish till a palpable silence descends on the forest. The sound of cicadas makes one an integral part of the forest. Unseen, these insects are obvious only from this incredible waxing and waning sound.

## BEETLES

Beetles have the largest number of species in the insect world. Each species has very specific characteristics. There are beetles that can live in several different types of ecosystems and others that are habitat-specific. Beetles, due to the richness of their species, contribute to a large number of food chains in nature.

### Dung-Roller Beetle

I have often watched dung-roller beetles with interest while they were working with frantic energy making a home for their young. It is a complex activity that this tiny insect has been primed by evolution to do over several thousand years. The dung-roller is a large ground beetle, about three centimetres in length, with a jet-black shining exoskeleton and a wide shovel-like head. Widely distributed over the semi-arid and arid regions of India, it favours grassland and scrubland ecosystems. It is usually seen crawling for long distances over dry ground, but it occasionally flies from place to place. Adults scoop out the dung of large mammals using their shovel-like heads and roll it into a ball. Considering their small size, the ball is enormous and the beetle's strength could well be compared with that of a bulldozer pushing a ball larger than our giant bulldozers are capable of. Pushing the ball backwards using their hind legs, often for distances of up to half a kilometre, they bury it in a moist warm place. The female then lays her eggs in the centre of the ball, where the grubs hatch and feed on the dung until they mature. Adults feed on leaves and nectar from flowers.

### Blister Beetle—*Mylabris pustulata*

Blister beetles have colourful, elongated soft bodies, with a bent head and a narrow neck. Their common name comes from the fact that their body fluids contain cantharidin; when disturbed, they release the fluid as an oily, yellow or orange liquid that causes painful blisters on contact with human skin. They are distributed all over India, preferring sunlit areas in a variety of habitats, and appear suddenly in large numbers with the first rains, before disappearing until the next monsoon. They often visit flowers and are agents of pollination for several plants.

*Opposite page*

| | |
|---|---|
| 1 | 2 |
| 3 | 4 |
| 5 | 6 |

A beetle which usually lives in trees and shrubs.

A beetle with extremely long antennae.

Beetles that live in the detritus break down dry leaf material into small fragments that add to the nutrients in the forest floor.

A brightly coloured beetle in the forest floor.

A scarab beetle rolling a dung ball much larger and heavier than itself, to create a home for its larvae.

Dung-roller beetles roll a ball of dung into a safe place for their young to mature in.

Cicadas make waves of sound in the forest.

Cicadas leave their exoskeletons behind and form new ones.

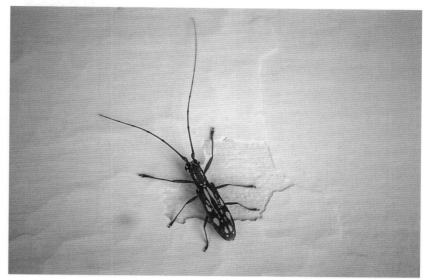

Beetles form the largest number of species on earth and thus contribute significantly to the 'web of life' in different ecosystems.

## Whirligig Beetle—*Dytiscus*

If one sits by a quiet pool in a forest, the surroundings are usually very still. The only constant movement is the rapid, frenzied, circular movements of a myriad of shiny flat beetles on the surface of the water. They are common, small, oval-bodied aquatic beetles. They have short antennae and compound eyes, divided into an upper half for vision in the air and a lower half for vision under water. The middle and hind legs are short and function as paddles.

There are many species adapted to varied conditions, with a worldwide distribution. They inhabit shady water bodies and stagnant or slow-moving water in pools formed in *nala* courses, where they aggregate in large groups. If disturbed, they promptly dive under the surface. They are ferocious predators and feed on small aquatic animals, plants, algae and decaying organic matter.

Wasps; from JBNHS, 1908.

Hundreds of whirligig beetles form large aggregations on the surface of the water.

## BEES AND WASPS—*HYMENOPTERA*

While most species are brown, some bees have bright, striking colours. Their body is covered with branched hair. In most of the species, the females bear a sting that is absent in males. Bees form a very large group of pollen and nectar dependent insects, a group that has evolved along with flowering plants. Several examples are present in nature to show that some flowers have peculiar shapes and are specifically pollinated by specific bees. Even though the majority of bee species are solitary, the honeybee, *Apis sp.*, is a universally known social insect. Bees collect nectar from the flowers along with the pollen and convert the nectar into honey by partially digesting and concentrating it. Some antiseptic preservatives are added and it is stored as honey in the comb. Bees form large combs on trees, rocky ledges and tall buildings. They have a complex social organization. The colony has a queen-bee, a few male bees and thousands of sterile worker bees. The queen-bee is the sole reproductive female. After fertilization, the queen may return to the same colony or form a new nest. There are special cells for the queen-bee in the lower portion of the hive. A few of the larvae are fed with a special food called royal jelly. These larvae mature into queen-bees. The other larvae get ordinary food and become workers. The queen controls the whole colony and their communication is based on pheromones.

The workers usually hunt for nectar and perform a special dance on the surface of the hive, by rapidly moving in circles, to inform other bees about the location and distance of the food source from the hive. This enables the rest of the workers to easily locate aggregations of flowering plants they can visit, several kilometres from the hive. Honey serves as food for the adults as well as for the young. Honey is a favourite of bears as well as of several birds which have learnt to break open hives. Human beings have learnt to include honey in their diet for generations. Several tribal people have evolved their own ways of getting honey without being severely stung. Aviculture has become a thriving occupation.

|  | 1 | |
|---|---|---|
| 2 | 3 | |

A bumble bee.

A wasp's nest, with its complex internal architecture, is more precise and functional than the houses that modern architects design.

A wasp's nest with its grubs.

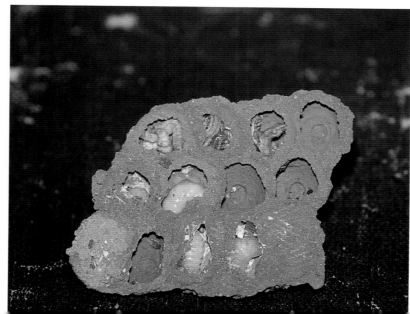

## MOSQUITOES—*DIPTERA*

A large variety of mosquitoes live in different habitat conditions. Some of these spread human diseases such as malaria. Their species vary in size. While moving in the forest, one realizes the great abundance of mosquitoes that inhabit these ecosystems. One becomes most aware of this when mosquitoes begin to bite. Part of the life-cycle is aquatic, while the rest is terrestrial. The female mosquito lays its eggs in either a stagnant or a slowly-flowing water body, and the larvae develop in the water. Both larvae and pupae are active swimmers. They live near the water surface and dive under water when disturbed.

While some mosquitoes feed on plant saps, others are mainly dependent on the blood of animals, including that of humans.

## ANTS
**Harvester Ants**

*—Holcomyrmex / Pheidole*

Harvester ants include a number of common small-ant species with specific behavioural patterns. Distributed throughout India, they inhabit every forest, grassland and semi-arid tract.

|   | 1 |   |
|---|---|---|
|   | 2 | 3 |
| 4 | 5 |   |
| 6 | 7 |   |

Ant colonies are highly specialized communities. They live together and use their territory as common property.

An ant colony built to prevent water from seeping into it during the rains.

Ants with their aphids that play the same role as domestic cattle play for us.

A nest of crematogaster ants.

Black ants shifting their eggs to a new location.

Red ants constructing their nest by joining leaves.

Black ants moving in a long line, using a forest branch as a bridge.

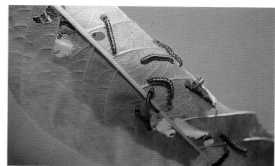

In each harvester ant colony there are gynaecoid workers, who are capable of becoming queens if well-nourished. Some of the ordinary workers, usually sterile females, act as soldiers to protect the colony. These soldiers have big heads, terrible jaws and very sharp teeth. The harvester is commonly seen in grassy areas and near agricultural fields, collecting mature seeds of the grasses around their nests and taking them down into their underground storage places. The nest has small circular mud walls. If it is on a slope, the wall towards the higher edge is higher than the wall on the opposite side, to prevent rainwater from entering the colony. How these tiny insects have been primed by evolution to perform these complex behavioural patterns, including setting up colonies, has always been a source of great wonder for me! One can spend hours looking at these incredible creatures that build architectural marvels.

### Red Tree-Ant, Common Indian Ant or Fire Ant—*Oecophylla smaragdina*

The red ant is typically a forest species, which is widely distributed in various forest types in the country. These bright red ants make a nest by sticking leaves together, using silken threads secreted by their larvae. Worker ants hold the larvae delicately in their jaws and move them up and down, then back and forth to weave the nest. These ants defend their nests ferociously. They collect dead insects and sometimes attack living ones near the nest. They bite viciously and squirt a fine jet of formic acid when disturbed. The ants practise animal husbandry, rearing mealy bugs in the nest. They feed them regularly and milk them for their sweet secretion called honeydew. These ants are omnivorous and eat anything and everything that is available. Due to their enormous population, ants can influence their ecosystem more than most other species. Thus, they maintain several processes that operate in the ecosystem and maintain its complex functions.

| 1 | 2 |
|---|---|
| 3 | |
| 4 | |

Caterpillars avoid predators by congregating together to simulate the bark of a tree.

Caterpillars feeding voraciously on their host plant.

Caterpillars of butterflies and moths feed on specific host plants. It is remarkable how nature has taught these insects which plants their caterpillars will survive on.

Some caterpillars move in groups in search of food.

## MOTHS

Important insects of the night, like this large group, act as a major pollinator of nocturnal flowers. While a number of species are dull-brown for camouflage, others are brightly coloured.

**Evolution has designed a great diversity of moths**

| 1 | 2 |
|---|---|
| 3 | 5 |
| 4 | |
| 6 | |

The pattern on this moth resembles bark and acts as camouflage on the tree.

Moth displaying false eyes to frighten off its predator.

Moths are important pollinators of plants.

A brilliantly white moth makes a striking contrast with the dry leaf on which it sits.

Moths must lay a large number of eggs, as their caterpillars are subjected to severe predation.

Moths have extremely good night vision.

| | 1 | |
|---|---|---|
| 2 | 3 | 4 |
| 5 | | |

This moth is difficult to distinguish from the dry leaves.

The feathery antennae of the moth are very sensitive to smell.

An owl moth displays two false eyes to scare off predators.

This moth can conceal itself on its perch, but if spotted by a predator, it tries to scare it off by rapidly flapping its bright scarlet wings.

A moth which has newly emerged from its chrysalis.

### Atlas Moth

The atlas moth was an insect that I had desperately wanted to photograph for several years. While common in Pune, during my box-camera days, by the time I had graduated to the sophistication of a 35 millimetre with macro lens, this species was locally extinct. It was when I was trying to document insect diversity in Lonavla, in the Western Ghats, that I met up again with this spectacular species. In fact, when I did find it, the moth was not in the forest, but was attracted by a lamp light in the Tata Power Company's guesthouse in Lonavla! I put one stool on another and climbed up precariously to get a close-up. Before I could press the shutter button, it flew off and flapped its way slowly into the dining room, where it flopped onto the floor and I took several pictures. Finally, it flew off and dropped into the lake from which it was fished out with great difficulty! The same year I saw a large specimen in the headlights of my car in Radhanagri. I took several pictures by climbing precariously on the top of the car, as the moth flew from one low branch of a tree to another.

### Lunar Moth

This is a spectacular species of the night. Its silvery shine and large size, its elongated spirals, which form twin tails, give it a highly distinctive appearance. Always uncommon, it is now very rare. I have seen it several times in the Western Ghats, in intact forest tracts of Maharashtra.

### BUTTERFLIES

India is rich in butterflies. There are an estimated 1000 species of butterflies in India. Several aspects of the behaviour and the ecology of butterflies considerably influence an ecosystem. They are great pollinators, assisting the propagation of several angiosperms while they flit from one flower to another. While each species pollinates many different flowering plant species, the caterpillars of each of them feed on only one or a few host plants. This may be an evolutionary mechanism preventing each species from competing with others for food for their caterpillars to grow and multiply. It would also mean that, as only a single or a few species of caterpillars are dependent on a single plant host, this restricts and controls the defoliation to a level that does not damage the plant growth. Thus, there has been a constant increase in the number of butterfly species found in India.

Edward Blyth's *Butterflies of the Indian Regions* was published in 1860.

Maj GFL Marshal and Charles Lionel de Niceville's *The Butterflies of India, Burma and Ceylon* was an important document written in 1889.

Atlas moths are the giants of the moth world and look like birds flitting through the forest at night. They are becoming rare.

| 1 | 2 |
|---|---|
| 3 | |

Lunar moths frequent undisturbed forest areas.

It is estimated that there are about 1000 species of butterflies in India.

Baronet butterfly.

**These delightful insects with their bright flashing wings are some of the most spectacular creatures in the world.**

Several amateur scientists made large collections of butterflies from India. Some workers dealt with specific regions. A list of butterflies of the Konkan was published by EH Aitken and E Comber in the JBNHS of 1903. About 130 butterfly species were described, with their classification, occurrence, distribution and the season in which they are seen. They also described how to recognize some of the rare species.

TR Bells, IFS, was a keen butterfly observer and regularly reported occurrences on new or unknown species of butterflies. In 1909 he described five species of butterflies. The species, namely *Techinia violex*, *Telchinia violex*, *Danais algea*, *Danais chrysippus*, *Euplexa* core are found in the Indian plains.

### Blue Tiger
*—Tirumalal limniace*

The blue tiger is a common butterfly found all over India. The forewings are slightly beaked, and the hind wings have a broad, forked black streak. Though the scales are transparent, they look bluish due to the refraction of light through the wings. Males have a sack-like scent pouch on the hind wings.

The blue tiger frequents open forests, plantations and gardens. Its slow and jerky flight is characteristic of those butterfly species that birds avoid eating because of their unpalatable nature. It is frequently seen in wet areas of the habitats, such as moist mud, from which it sucks salts. Blue tigers are often seen roosting together in shaded patches of forest. During seasonal migrations, they are seen in hundreds. In Lonavla, in the Western Ghats, a large number of them were seen aggregating among a thick grove of trees, year after year, for four years. Why they selected this specific spot remains a mystery, as it appears no different from other patches of forest. Their caterpillars feed on *Dragea*, which is their sole food plant.

### Blue Mormon
*—Papilio polymnestor*

This large butterfly always attracts one's attention in the forest, sporting, as it does, a vivid colour and a typical, meandering flight pattern. The hind wings have a prominent, shiny, pale-blue patch

The blue mormon looks distinctive as it flies with slowly flapping wings.

Great eggfly.

that extends along the margins of the forewings, becoming narrower towards the apices. Its wingspan makes it larger than most other butterflies. It is more frequently observed in undistributed, heavily-forested areas in peninsular India. A strong, swift flier, it prefers to fly through forests with closed canopies and frequents the banks of perennial streams. The caterpillars feed on *Atalantia racemosa* trees, which are its specific food plant. Once common, this species is no longer seen as frequently as in the past, because it prefers relatively intact forest ecosystems.

### Tawny Angle
—*Ctenoptilum vasava*

The upper sides of the forewings of the tawny angle show white spots, except on the margins. The hind wings also have white spots, grouped together close to the body. The wings have three beaks with dull undersides and markings similar to those on the upper wings. Females are larger than the males. The moth has a very swift flight and is difficult to track once disturbed from its resting place. The caterpillars feed on species of grass or bamboo.

### Great Eggfly
—*Hypolimnas bolina*

The male eggfly has conspicuous, bluish-white, egg-shaped markings on the wings, which give it a distinctive appearance in flight. The female is a perfect mimic of the common crow butterfly, *Euploea core*, which is an unpalatable species for insectivorous birds. This prevents predators from attacking the female, even though it is, in fact, edible! The female is generally larger than the male. The species is distributed in moist, well-wooded regions throughout India. The male is highly territorial and is frequently seen chasing other males. Its caterpillars feed mainly on *Portulaca*.

## VERTEBRATES

We are very familiar with what are known as glamour species, mostly mammals and birds. A great diversity of vertebrates is found on land as well as in aquatic ecosystems and in various marine and fresh-water environments. The vertebrates include mammals called *amniota*, which have a special membrane covering the embryo. This arrangement replaces the aquatic environment in which the larvae of fish and amphibia develop. Most of us are invariably fascinated with the commonly known species of mammals. Among these animals, the powerful carnivores and swift herbivores of large size are the most well-known. We are frequently oblivious of the large diversity of small creatures. The most widely known mammal and bird species are those that shikaris hunted for sport or food. The less known are documented and studied mainly by zoologists. But this information rarely finds a place in the reading material that most interested readers are likely to access. The linkages between assemblages of species and their habitat, are perhaps the most fascinating aspect of biological diversity, which encompasses both species and ecosystems. There is an increasing tendency to publicize rare and endangered species of animals and birds. Thus, literature that is frequently available for an interested reader often neglects the interesting aspects of behaviour of our commoner species. The diversity of life is a march of evolutionary processes from the miraculous early forms to mammals and primates, of which man is just one more species—an account, in other words, of our earth's history. Much of this has remained a mystery to modern science even today.

There are over 1400 marine and estuarine species of animals in India. Only three per cent of our marine and coastal shallows are included in our Protected Area Network. This is extremely inadequate. Even these Protected Areas in the Marine National Park in Gujarat, and in the Andaman and Nicobar Islands, are under serious threat from activities such as ship-breaking yards and, more recently, oil installations, onshore industry, salt works, urbanization and a host of other issues. Marine reptiles such as turtles, and mammals such as dolphins and dugongs are under serious threat from both accidental catches and purposeful poaching.

## FISH

Fish are aquatic, cold-blooded creatures which breathe through gills and have fins. They are one of the most ancient vertebrate groups, having evolved some 500 million years ago. There are an estimated 20–30 thousand species worldwide. In waters around the Indian subcontinent, there are 2000 fish species, of which 130 are said to be endemic to India, mainly the southern parts. Fish are either oviparous or viviparous. They are the commonest vertebrates found in nature.

They can be divided into freshwater and marine fish.

The abundance of fish in both marine and aquatic ecosystems is falling due to increased fishing. Several fish species that use streams as their habitat in the Indian subcontinent could be on the verge of extinction, as more and more perennial streams are running dry due to deforestation of the mountains and hills. Recent work on freshwater fish, by Ranjit Daniels and several others, has shown the serious depletion in fish diversity in many of our rivers.

The diversity of freshwater fish in India is seriously affected by the introduction of exotic varieties such as tilapia, which has led to the extinction of indigenous fish species. Fish diversity has been seriously affected by the introduction of exotic species ever since 1847. There were five species of carp that were introduced into

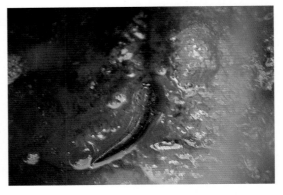

| | 1 | |
|---|---|---|
| 2 | 3 | |
| | 4 | |

*Cyprinus mosal*; from Gray, 1830.

As many as 2000 species of marine fish are found in Indian waters.

A well camouflaged mudskipper in a muddy mangrove.

A fish catch like this from a freshwater ecosystem can now fetch a high price.

Indian waters, followed by several others around 1939. The tilapia is from Africa and zealously guards its progeny in its mouth till they grow up. Thus it is a highly successful fish that competes with native ones, which begin to gradually disappear where tilapia are introduced. Some marine fish need to enter brackish water for breeding; others need to move upstream to small clear-hill streams to breed. Another threat appears to be from the introduction of imported aquarium fish in our rivers. Ranjit Daniels has identified introduced gouramys and platys in some rivers in south India. Check dams along hill streams and rivers are another serious problem for fish, as they cannot migrate to their natural breeding grounds upstream. A serious new threat will occur through the proposed project to link river systems across India. With the loss of natural barriers between river systems, the loss of diversity of aquatic fauna could be disastrous.

Many fish are dependent on micro-fauna and flora, which they use as a sole source of energy. Others feed on larger forms of life, that live mainly in the benthic layer.

A large number of coastal and freshwater fishing communities depend on fish from these ecosystems for their livelihood. Increased mechanized, deep-sea fishing has reduced the abundance of fish along our coastal waters. River and lake pollution from both urban sewage and industrial effluents has converted streams and rivers into sewers and lakes and ponds into dirty pools of water in which fish cannot survive.

Marine fisheries at the consumer level were worth 20 thousand crores between 1999 and 2000. This is now distinctly unsustainable. India is the largest exporter of sea horses. This is said to account for 1.3 million animals per year—that is 30 per cent of the global sea-horse trade, even though this is a highly endangered species! Sea-horses will soon be threatened by extinction.

Fish

The early work on fish in India was documented for two volumes of *The Fauna of British India* in the late 1800s, by Francis Day (1889).

R Beavan (1877) wrote *A Handbook of the Freshwater Fish in India*.

Raj Tilak (1987) wrote mainly on fish.

AGK Menon (1987–1992) wrote extensively on fish fauna and its management.

G Ramakrishna worked on Crustacea —Crayfish (1995).

PK Talwar worked on fish (1995).

**Mahseer**—*Tor spp.*

The Mahseer is one of our largest freshwater fish, all three species of which are on the brink of extinction. Once world-famous as a game fish, it now inhabits only some of the least polluted rivers in India, Pakistan, Bangladesh, Burma and Sri Lanka. Despite the former abundance of Mahseer, their number and size are declining at an alarming rate in India.

The different species of Mahseer inhabit a variety of freshwater ecosystems, ranging from tropical waters to sub-Himalayan regions, from streams at sea level to ones up to a height of 2000 metres. They are omnivores and useful in controlling aquatic weeds and epiphyton. They also feed on crabs, molluscs and other benthic forms of life.

The Tata Power Company has a major ex situ breeding programme for these endangered fish in Lonavla, in the Hydel

Over-fishing has depleted the fish population in coastal India.

Mahseers have been successfully bred in the Tata Power Companies fish farm. Here, a demonstration catch is being done to study their growth rates. They have now been reintroduced into the Tata Lakes at Mawal and Mulshi in Maharashtra.

lakes of the Western Ghats. This effort over the last three decades has led to the survival of this fish. Mr SN Ogale has worked all his life to save this fish from extinction and has the unique distinction of employing a low-cost, low-tech fisheries unit to successfully breed this fish. It has been introduced in the four Hydel lakes where the species is thriving and they have grown to a phenomenal size. We have introduced some fingerlings into a tank at the Bharati Vidyapeeth Institute of Environmental Education and Research (BVIEER) where they are thriving. It is an incredible sight to see a shoal of rapidly swimming Mahseer come to the surface to feed to the sound of clapping. I have seen even small Mahseer jump to a height of six feet out of the water at incredible speed. It looks like a torpedo emerging from the surface!

**AMPHIBIA**

Amphibia are species that have two patterns in their lives. This vast number of species of the less known animal world require both terrestrial and aquatic ecosystems for their survival. Some of the distinguishing characteristics of this class of animals are: a body generally covered with moist skin without scales, fur or feathers; soft toes with no claws; external fertilization of eggs and the process of metamorphosis by which they gradually completely alter their appearance before they reach their adult form. Amphibians were the first land animals. They are link species in the many food chains, forming bridges between aquatic and terrestrial habitats. Frogs, which spend most of their time in water, are the prey species of several predators from the terrestrial ecosystem. Their eggs, however, are eaten by aquatic

insects and fish in the water. Tadpoles are caught by birds, fish, dragonfly nymphs and water beetles that use aquatic habitats to hunt in. On land, adult frogs are eaten by snakes and are a major source of food for several birds of prey as well as storks and egrets. They are also hunted by mammals such as the lesser cats. I have once observed a leopard catching frogs in a riverbed in the Dang forests of Gujarat. India is rich in amphibian species. The Western Ghats are rich mainly in endemic amphibia not found elsewhere.

Amphibians are divided into three orders, the commonest of which is *Silientia*, which includes frogs and toads. *Ranaidae* or 'true' frogs are characterized by their fairly smooth moist skin. They usually lay their eggs in loose clumps and breed in almost any kind of water body. These are the frogs that are most commonly used as food.

The toe tips of the *Rhacophoridae*, or tree frogs, are expanded into discs, which enable them to hang on to twigs and tree trunks. They are found in the undergrowth as well as in the canopies of trees. A third family comprises frogs with narrow mouths, called *Microhylidae*. The *Microhylidae* are the commonest amphibians of dry arid areas.

A hundred and ten new species of amphibians have been recently identified in the Western Ghats. There could be several more cryptic species that no one has ever looked at closely enough.

Boulanger wrote on amphibia of India in 1890, reporting 77 species. In the 1980s, JC Daniel suggested that Robert Inger and Sushil Dutta write a review of amphibian fauna for the JBNHS Volume 83. By this time Indian amphibia numbered 181 species. Of these, 165 were

frogs and toads, 15 were caecilians and one was salamander. During the last few decades, surveys especially in the Western Ghats and the north-east have continued to yield species that were not identified earlier. Endemism is high, with at least 60 species endemic to India.

The overall amphibian endemism, along with a few neighbouring countries, could be as high as 75 per cent. Of these, 84 of the endemics occur in the Western Ghats and 20 in the north-east, where there are high concentrations of amphibian species. However, more work has been done in the Western Ghats than in the north-eastern states. Structurally complex habitats such as the ones in these evergreen forests, have the largest number of microhabitats that harbour amphibia.

FROGS

India is exceptionally rich in frog species. As a medical student I refused to jab spikes into a frog's brain and perform ridiculous experiments on the poor creature! I was called in by the Dean of the College and in a shaking voice I explained that I thought it a useless and unnecessarily painful experiment for the frog and an equally painful experience for me! Strangely enough, I was excused. Years later, when Maneka Gandhi was the Minister in the MoEF, the BNHS was asked about the need to kill frogs for physiology practicals. JC Daniels requested me to respond and eventually several of these experiments that provided no real learning experiences were removed from the work curriculum of medical graduate students.

Humayun Abdulali (1985) emphasized the need to curtail the export of frog legs in Volume 82 of the JBNHS. He

**Amphibians, including the ancestors of frogs and toads, were the earliest terrestrial animals. India is rich in endemic amphibian species, many of which are found only in the Western Ghats.**

| | 2 | 11 |
|1| 3 | 12 |
|4| 8 | |
|5 6| 9 | |
|7| 10 | |

A well-camouflaged small tree frog.

Frogs eat huge quantities of insects.

Frogs constitute a link between terrestrial and aquatic ecosystems.

Toad.

Tree frog in Southern India.

Frog from the Western Ghats.

Tree frog.

Most frogs lay their eggs in water. However some use a frothy nest where tadpoles can mature and from where they can drop into water.

Tree frog.

Toads can survive in very adverse habitats.

Toad.

Tadpoles form large masses underwater, as frogs breed prolifically.

estimated that 3–4 tons of frog legs were exported every year. This would mean the destruction of at least 6000 tons of frogs. He suggested that frogs eat the same quantities of insects or other animal foods everyday. Thus, in a three-month period during the monsoon, these frogs would have eaten 5.4 lakh tons of insects. He concludes that this would have prevented the use of many tons of insecticide. His efforts finally prevented the export of frogs.

A recent threat to frogs is likely to be due to changes such as global warming, as well as increasing UV radiation, especially at high altitudes. The Wildlife Institute of India scientists believe that frogs that were present only a decade or two ago in Ladakh have now vanished. This needs further study.

An early study of amphibia for *The Fauna of British India* was done by MA Smith between 1931 and 1943.

### Indian Bullfrog—*Rana tigerina*

The bullfrog has a moist skin, with markings of different colours, a long tongue and large bulbous eyes. Growing to a length of 30 centimetres, it is distributed all over India. It inhabits moister areas within a variety of different terrestrial ecosystems and is associated with aquatic systems ranging from ponds and *nalas* to large wetlands, the shores of lakes and riverbanks, and paddy fields.

In drier regions, bullfrogs emerge during the rains and aestivate during summer. When threatened, a bullfrog will inflate its lungs and bow its head, puffing itself up and appearing larger than it really is, to deter predators such as snakes.

### Tree Frog—*Rana temporalis*

Tree frogs have a coloration that mimics the bark of the trees on which they sit. As it is capable of flattening itself on the branch, it is very difficult to spot. Other species of tree frogs are a bright green, which serves as camouflage in the surrounding foliage.

The tree frog inhabits evergreen, semi-evergreen and moist deciduous ecosystems, never straying very far from a particular area, and capable of jumping from one branch to another with great dexterity. Its diet consists mainly of nocturnal insects. The tree frog of southern India has a peculiar call, 'pit-pit-pit', which is not associated with its mating calls and appears to be some sort of territorial marker. Tree frogs are gravely threatened by habitat loss.

Humayun Abdulali of BNHS fought for decades to ban the export of frogs' legs from India and finally succeeded.

### REPTILES

Reptiles evolved after the amphibians and have developed a scaly skin. They either lay eggs or give birth to live young. Reptiles evolved during the carboniferous period, 260–300 million years ago and they were the dominant forms of life 120–140 million years ago, in the Mesozoic era. Several of the large reptiles, such as dinosaurs, then disappeared and the age of the reptilian dominance came to an end. There are several theories on how this happened, a phase that can be looked upon as a major evolutionary hiccup.

*The Fauna of British India—Reptiles* was written by ACLG Günther in 1864.
George Albert Boulenger, in 1890, wrote *Reptilia and Batrachia*.
The earlier work was followed by *The Fauna of British India* volumes on reptiles and amphibia by Malcolm A Smith, (1931–1943) in three volumes.
Maj Gen Thomas Hardwicke wrote extensively on snakes between 1778 and 1823.
Lt Col J Stephenson wrote *The Fauna of British India—Reptiles and Amphibia* in 1931.

The *Rana tigerina*, or common Indian bullfrog, was once extensively exported to the West for frog's legs, which are considered a delicacy. Export is now banned.

This tree frog is difficult to detect in the foliage.

Reptiles include snakes, lizards, turtles and tortoises. This lizard looks like a snake because it has extremely tiny limbs.

However, this could well have led to the age of the mammal and thus to man himself.

Reptiles have a lower metabolic rate than birds and mammals and control their temperature by using sunlight. Reptiles are divided into three groups—lizard-like forms, cylindrical forms, like skinks and snakes, and turtles and tortoises, which are enclosed in a bony shell. Reptiles inhabit both terrestrial and aquatic ecosystems and are adapted to many habitat types.

There are 238 species of snakes in India, 150 species of lizards, 26 species of freshwater turtles and tortoises and 5 species of marine turtles inhabiting our coastal waters.

### Crocodile—*Crocodylus palustris*

India's largest reptile can grow to a length of up to 3 metres, and is said to live up to 100 years! It has powerful jaws and a highly developed sense of smell, hearing and sight. Its body is covered in scales, rather like a suit of armour.

Once found all over India in rivers, lakes and wetlands, the crocodile is now highly endangered due to its prized skin, which has led to its extermination across the country. It is estimated that there are only 3–5000 in the wild. However, several ex situ breeding programmes are taking place.

Crocodiles feed on fish, mammals and birds and they also scavenge on dead animals. They hunt at night and bask in the sun all day.

Romulus Whitaker has developed a very successful breeding programme in the Crocodile Bank in Chennai and there are a number of other highly productive breeding programmes in India, but there are few, if any, safe habitats where they can be reintroduced into the wild.

From April to August 1975, Romulus Whitaker conducted a survey of major freshwater streams and associated tidal creeks in the Andamans. The crocodile population was depleted mainly due to hunting in the past, and human settlements along almost all the fresh water streams and associated nesting habitats of the saltwater crocodile.

R Whitaker (1978) wrote a preliminary survey of the saltwater crocodile (*Crocodylus porosus*) in the Andaman Islands in the JBNHS, Volume 75-.

### Gharial—*Gavialis gangeticus*

The gharial is a greenish-brown, slender reptile, six to seven metres long. It has an exceptionally long snout, which is bulbous at the tip in males. Now confined to small stretches in the Indus, Ganges, Brahmaputra and Mahanadi Rivers, it is highly threatened in the wild, but has been successfully bred in ex situ programmes and is being reintroduced into the wild. The present wild population is estimated at only 2000. Gharials live in groups dominated by a single male and require undisturbed sandbanks for nesting and basking in the sun. They predominantly feed on fish but also catch birds and small mammals. Gharials prefer areas in the river that flow very slowly. While taking pictures of gharials in the Ramganga River in the Corbett National Park, I found that one of them had a short lower jaw. Nearly three fourths of it was missing. It appeared, however, to be little hampered by the loss of its razor-sharp teeth and its prey-killing mechanism.

The gharial was first described by Gmelin in 1788 (Whitkar and Basu, 1982). Several records of the early 1900s showed that they were common on the Indus River, the Gandak River, Bhramhaputra, Mahanadi and parts of the Kosi River. However, by the 1970s, Whitkar and others showed that it had become extremely rare. In the mid-70s, the largest remaining concentration was observed at Katerniaghat in Uttar Pradesh and in the Chambal River. In 1978, Whitkar and Daniel estimated their population in the wild to be less than 200. Subsequently, captive breeding and reintroduction programmes led to a gradual build-up of populations in the wild (Whitkar and Basu, 1982).

### TURTLES AND TORTOISES

There are 16 species of freshwater turtles, six species of soft-shell turtles and four species of land tortoises in India.

Turtles are commercially exploited as food in most parts of India, packed along with fish for clandestine sale in metropolitan markets. They are also prized for their medicinal properties in Unani and other alternative systems of medicine. The pet trade endangers the existence of tortoises. The Indian star tortoise is commonly seen in homes both in India and abroad. It is reported that thousands are exported.

---

Crocodiles that were once very common in India are now confined to very small areas. Their continued existence is due to strong captive breeding programmes. However, the places where they can be released are very limited.

---

The gharial, a rare fish-eating crocodile, poached extensively for its skin has been brought to the brink of extinction.

## Freshwater Turtles

The turtle is venerated as an incarnation of Vishnu, the Creator of the Universe in Hindu mythology. The flat turtles at the doorsteps of temples idolize this beautiful creature. Yet they are killed, their eggs are eaten and they are tortured to provide blood to people with asthma, a completely unfounded belief with no medical support whatsoever.

### Indian Mud or Flap-Shell Turtle
*—Lissemys punctata*

This turtle is a symbol of Lord Vishnu and is said to be his second incarnation. The olive-brown carapace is oval in shape and covered with a smooth skin. Its front and rear edges have skin flaps that are bent downwards to hide the head and limbs when they are retracted. It has an oval head, prominent tubular nostrils and a short tail. The digits are fully webbed, a fact that makes it an excellent swimmer. The female grows to around 27centimetres, while the male is much smaller and does not grow more than 10 centimetres in length.

The flap-shell, our commonest turtle, is distributed all over peninsular India, south of the Gangetic plains. It inhabits lakes, ponds and tanks which may or may not be connected with river systems. It uses shallow, weed-infested, aquatic habitats and basks among aquatic vegetation where it lies buried in the mud and snaps at passing prey.

This turtle is omnivorous and feeds on water plants and small animals such as

frogs, fish, snails and crustacea and on dead animals. It can aestivate and remain dormant in the mud for several months. It is evidently long-lived and I know of one that was known to have quietly lived in a small fountain for at least 60 years. No one even fed the creature and it seemed none the worse for this lack of attention! The flap-shell is less common than it used to be, as it is frequently caught for food.

## Marine Turtles

Lakshadweep used to export a large number of turtles till 1976. Wildlife Institute of India research points to an increasing amount of kills, after 1997–98, of all the species of marine turtles on the eastern Coast.

Marine turtles are affected by trawling for fish along the coast and around our islands. A large number of sea turtles are killed each year. To prevent this, a new device has been developed, that gives the turtles a chance of escaping, but this leads to a drop in the fish catch by six to seven percent.

The largest Olive Ridley sea turtle nesting site in the world is at Gahirmatha beach in Orissa. The beach is a 35-kilometre stretch on which thousands of turtles lay their eggs. Since 1975, this has been given sanctuary status. The few major arribada sites, where hundreds of turtles lay eggs, are much better documented today.

Turtles approaching nesting sites are caught in fishing nets in thousands due to the increasing numbers of trawlers. Pollution due to oil spills is another serious concern. Changes in land-use on and around nesting beaches affect the breeding success. Even lighting up a beach at night can lead to a fall in population, as hatchlings tend to move soon after hatching towards the light instead of the open sea. With global warming and a rise in the sea level, it is possible that their nesting success will be jeopardized even further.

## Star Tortoise—*Geochelone elegans*

The star tortoise has a thick, hemispherical carapace with multiple small hexagonal humps. Each hump has a yellow patch in its centre, radiating yellow and brown streaks fanning outward. Each hump also has thin ridges that run in a hexagonal pattern. Small irregular shields cover the head. The hind limbs are cylindrical and club-shaped with large scales, and the tail has a spur-like scale at its tip. The length of the carapace is approximately 28 centimetres. The female is much larger than the male. They grow extremely slowly and are known to have long lives.

Distributed across Western India, in Rajasthan and Gujarat, and in peninsular India in Karnataka, Tamil Nadu, Andhra Pradesh and Orissa, they are partial to shady tracts in semi-arid regions and coastal scrubland. They are most active during the monsoon and remain dormant during winter. They are becoming increasingly rare, mainly due to the pet trade and slaughter for their shells, which are used as artefacts.

Many years ago I had five pet star tortoises in my home. They were extremely friendly and recognized the people who fed them. They would even extend their necks to be petted and would frequently follow people around the house. I gave them away to the Snake Park as I felt it was inappropriate to keep the endangered animals as pets. I have seen them in the wild in the Rann of Kachchh and in Gir where they are still quite common.

## Travancore Forest Tortoise
### —*Indotestudo forstenii*

HS Fergusson was the first to draw attention to a tortoise near Trivandrum. Later, in 1906, Bonlenger confirmed it to be a new tortoise species, in the JBNHS.

This rare tortoise is known from only a few locations in South India. It is distributed in the semi-evergreen and evergreen forests of the Western Ghats. The species is endemic to India. The IUCN has included it in the Red Data Book. It is a dirty-yellow, with one black blotch on each scute of the carapace.

My brief encounter with this animal took place in the forests of Thattekad, on the banks of the Periyar River. Surprisingly, this rare species frequented the compound of a small interpretation centre.

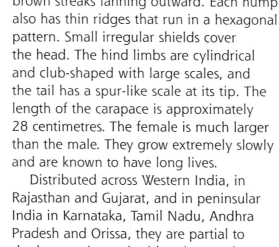

**Most snakes found in India are non-poisonous.**

## SNAKES

Most snakes in India are non-poisonous. The recognition of poisonous species is of key importance as those that are neurotoxic or haemotoxic can kill. Snakes are crucial in the biological control of rodent pests.

|   |   |
|---|---|
| 1 |   |
| 2 | 4 |
| 3 | 5 |
|   | 6 | 7 |

Many cobras are killed each year in both urban and rural settings.

Snakes display a variety of camouflage mechanisms.

Snakes are important predators in most ecosystems.

Cobra; from Forbes, 1813.

The rather uncommon coral snake may be occasionally found even in towns and cities.

The coral snake's tail gives it its name, as does its bright pink colour. The snake rolls the tip of its tail into a ball and waves it around as a warning sign to predators.

The cobra, the best-known snake in India, is considered sacred by several peoples; from JBNHS, 1912.

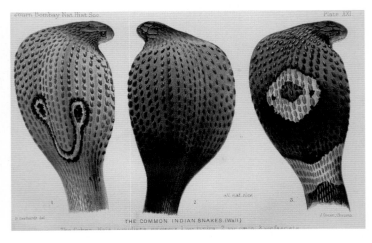

Several medical men and army officers during the British period became interested in snakes. New species were identified and described.

In 1908 Major Wall CMZS described several new species of snakes in the Himalayan and Assam Ranges in the JBNHS Volume 18.

Joseph Ewart (1878) published his work on *Poisonous Snakes of India*. Even today, new species are being described, especially from the north-east of India.

**Russell's Viper**—*Daboia russelii*

The Russell's viper is a large, poisonous snake with vertical pupils and rough scales. It is brown or yellowish, with large, dark-brown, diamond-shaped spots in three rows that are edged with white and black. This usually forms a distinctive chain-like pattern. An interesting feature is its colour variation, the colour changing in different regions. Its underside is white in Western India, partly speckled in the South-eastern India, and heavily speckled in the north-east. The average length varies from 1 to 1.5 metres. It is easily mistaken for the non-poisonous Indian python and is distributed all over the country, frequenting open areas in hilly landscapes as well as the plains. It lives in agave

plantations and scrub jungle bordering farmlands, and shelters in termite mounds and rat holes or crevices.

The viper looks deceptively sluggish, but when provoked is capable of lightning speed. It has a loud warning hiss. Snakes, lizards, mice, gerbils, land crabs and probably scorpions and other arthropods form its diet. It has been persecuted due to its highly poisonous nature and also collected for its skin for the export market. I was once trying to take a picture of a huge specimen in Melghat when it moved aggressively towards me. It could have been my last photograph!

**Green Tree-Snake, Whip-Snake or Vine-Snake**—*Ahaetulla nasutus*

The vine-snake is bright or dull green, which makes it difficult to spot in foliage.

Its slender body has a long tapering head and a pointed snout. A thin white or yellowish line separates the scales on the back from those on its belly. It has horizontally placed, elliptical pupils, a unique feature among Indian snakes. Its mouth opens widely, exposing the bright-pink colour of its palate to threaten predators. Averaging about 1 to 1.5 metres in length, it is fairly common in the Western Ghats and in the southern and eastern parts of the country. An arboreal snake, it is seen on low bushes and scrub, in and on the periphery of forested areas. If undisturbed, it is fairly placid, but it is also capable of striking furiously with a wide-open mouth if irritated. It is, however, non-poisonous. It feeds on lizards, small birds and occasionally rats and frogs. The pit viper, which is very poisonous, can be easily mistaken for a vine snake. Its pupils are vertically oriented. But you need to go rather uncomfortably close to differentiate the pit viper from the vine-snake.

| 1 | 4 |
|---|---|

| 2 |
|---|
| 3 |

The Russell's viper can be aggressive and is highly poisonous.

The vine snake scares its prey and its predators by displaying a pink oral cavity.

A vine snake coiled in a tree, waiting for passing prey.

An Indian rock python in readiness to grab its passing prey. It is known to catch even large mammals.

**There are 150 species of lizards currently documented in India.**

Blue LIZARD and NEVA Tree.

| | | | |
|---|---|---|---|
| 1 | 6 | | |
| 2 | 7 | | |
| 3 | 8 | | |
| 4 | 9 | 10 | |
| 5 | 11 | | |

Blue lizard; from Forbes, 1813.

A lizard which has adapted well to living in the undergrowth.

A fan-throated lizard with its bright blue flap closed.

Lizards form an important link in food chains, between insects and larger animals.

A male forest calotes turns bright red and black during territorial and courtship displays.

An obviously aggressive calotes displaying its bright colours.

The garden lizard has adapted to urban environments

A lizard adapted to life in the extremely harsh climatic conditions of the Thar desert.

This lizard displays its ability to camouflage itself on the rocks.

A pair of geckos.

An unusual gecko in the Western Ghats.

### Indian Rock Python—
*Python molurus molurus*

The Indian rock python is a large, heavy-bodied snake with blotched marks, as opposed to the chain-like markings of the Russell's viper. It has a lance-shaped mark on top of its head.

It grows to a length of six metres and is distributed in peninsular India, from Rajasthan to Bengal in the east. Though usually a jungle dweller, it is also found in open forests, rivers and jheels. It can be diurnal or nocturnal, arboreal or terrestrial. In the north, pythons hibernate during the cold season. They feed on mammals, birds, amphibians, and other reptiles. The python mates between December and February and the eggs are laid between March and June. Hatching takes place in approximately two months. The python is highly endangered, due to habitat loss and poaching for the illegal skin trade.

### LIZARDS AND GECKOS

This is an ancient group of species which plays a great role in the control of pests. These common reptiles include several rare species.

### Common Garden Lizard, or Bloodsucker—*Calotes versicolor*

This common, grey-brown lizard has a large oval head and a laterally compressed body. The males have prominent cheeks. There are two distinct spines just behind the tympanic membrane on each side. There are larger scales on the dorsal side, which are directed backwards. The tail is long and cylindrical and swollen at the base in males. The males sport a distinctive dorsal crest of lens-shaped scales from nape to the spot above the vent. These lizards are capable of rapidly changing their colour to suit their surroundings, turning from a dark grey-brown to a sandy light-brown. Males during aggression change to a fairly deep red on their head and neck and they are generally longer and heavier than females. Widely distributed throughout India, this reptile is commonly seen in garden hedges, along boundaries of agricultural plots and in scrubland as

well as all types of habitats, ranging from dry desert to thick forest. It is arboreal and diurnal. Creatures such as insects and small birds, nestlings and frogs, form its diet.

### Southern Green Calotes
—*Calotes calotes*.

This is a thin, showy, bright grass-green lizard, with whitish or cream-coloured transverse bands over its body, the colouring matching perfectly with its surroundings. The dorsal side has a single row of scales, which are pointed backwards and upwards. It measures around 20 centimetres in length, including the tail. It is widely distributed in the southern peninsula of India and is commonly found in several forested tracts. Insects, especially ants, form its staple diet. It also feeds on small birds, nestlings, frogs and other small animals. This lizard has been frequently

| 1 | |
|---|---|
| 2 | 4 |
| 3 | |

Lizards are ancient reptiles that have survived tens of millions of years.

Common garden lizard or bloodsucker.

Two aggressive garden lizards in a territorial fight.

A *Sitana* with a bright blue flap is a common species of the semi-arid ecosystems.

seen with local medicine vendors and is therefore likely to have become less common than in the past.

### Fan-throated Lizard, or Sita's Lizard—*Sitana ponticeriana*

This remarkable lizard has a distinctive fan-like expansion under its neck, that can be retracted or expanded. The male frequently displays its bright blue, orange and black flap during the breeding season to attract the female. The only Indian lizard with four toes on its hind legs, it is widely distributed throughout India, occupying a variety of habitat types, with the exception of areas with very heavy rainfall and extremely arid deserts, preferring semi-arid grasslands, scrub and sandy areas. A ground-dwelling diurnal lizard, it has long hind legs that enable it to run rapidly. It rests under shady bushes and climbs onto exposed rocks or branches of shrubs to bask in the sun and often has a favourite rock or other vantage point from which it displays its colourful flap and feeds on ants and other small insects. Once fairly common, it may be less abundant today, as a result of the increasing use of pesticides in agricultural lands. The habitat of these lizards is being destroyed by digging soil for construction sites and other changes in the land-use of their grassland habitat.

### Chameleon—*Chameleon zeylanicus*

This incredible lizard has a laterally-compressed body, covered with granular scales and a prominent conical casque on top of the head. Its most remarkable feature is the large pair of eyes covered by granular lids, which leave only the pupil exposed. It can move its eyes in all directions, and each eye can be moved independently of the other's movement. This enables it to scan an almost 360 degree area without moving its head. The prehensile tail helps it to grasp twigs while moving through the foliage and is sometimes held in a tight coil. The lizard can camouflage itself completely by blending with its background and can change from a dull green-yellow to a dark green and black. The change in colour is a response to light, heat, its emotional state and the colour of its surroundings. Distributed throughout the Indian peninsula, this arboreal species requires well-wooded habitats with moderate rainfall and is also found on the edges of semi-desert areas. Within deserts, it is restricted to oases. It is a diurnal, slow-moving lizard, especially adapted to arboreal habitats, making a hissing sound when disturbed. The chameleon is unique in its feeding habits, flicking out its long, sticky, club-shaped, extensile tongue to capture its prey. I have watched it sitting motionless in a shrub and rotating its eyes about till it spots an unsuspecting prey. Then in a flash, the tongue is shot out and retracted with the prey sticking to its club-shaped tip. The whole action is extremely rapid and, if necessary, is quickly repeated to capture its prey. This species is under threat as it is believed to provide medicinal products. This has no documented scientific value.

### Skinks

Skinks are generally ground-dwelling lizards. They live in burrows in the soil or remain hidden under rocks. Their short limbs and long glistening bodies lead them to be sometimes mistaken for snakes. Skinks are striped, cross-barred or spotted. They do not change their colour but the males acquire an orange or red colour during the breeding season. Small skinks have a red tail which, if attacked, splits away from the rest of the body and wriggles furiously. The red colour then attracts the predator so that the skink can escape.

Skinks live mostly in burrows, but hunt in the undergrowth and in and under forest detritus. Some species lay eggs while others are viviparous. Insects of the forest floor form the chief constituent of their diet.

1

2  3

A *Sitana* displays its large yellow flap to warn off other males.

A chameleon displays its aggression by opening its large red mouth and hissing loudly.

The common skink can disappear rapidly into grass or dry leaves as soon as it feels threatened.

## Common Indian Monitor
—*Varanus benghalensis.*

This large reptile is olive-grey or brownish with black spots. The head has lighter spots, and the temples have a dark streak. It is found all over India, in all biotopes ranging from evergreen forests, deciduous forests and scrublands to the fringes of the desert. It is a diurnal lizard, more active in the early mornings and late evenings, very shy, ready to disappear into a crevice if disturbed. This carnivorous lizard feeds on small mammals, birds, reptiles and crabs. Frequently trapped for its supposed medicinal properties, there is now a gross depletion in its population from many of the areas where it was abundant till only a few years ago. The monitor is now becoming an increasingly rare species.

## Water Monitor—*Varanus salvator*

The young water monitors are black above with yellow spots arranged in transverse rows, a pattern that fades with age. Its length is 2.5 metres, the female being generally smaller than the male. It is found in Orissa, Bengal and Eastern India, in fresh as well as saltwater habitats. It can readily climb trees and lays eggs in holes in banks, in tree holes or in termite nests and feeds on crustaceans, molluscs, and frogs. The water monitor is endangered by the illegal trade in reptile skins. Unless the demand for reptile skins diminishes on the international market, lizards will continue to be trapped for the money they bring in.

1

2

3

4

A large monitor lizard walks through dry detritus searching for prey.

The giant *varanus* or monitor lizard, is a formidable predator.

A large Indian monitor perched across a dead tree, waiting for its prey.

A water monitor lizard emerges from the water to clamber into the mangrove forest in the Sunderbans.

## BIRDS

Birds evolved 150 million years ago and are divided into 27 orders with very specific characteristics. All birds are characterized by wings, which are the modified forelimbs enabling them to fly, feathers that perform a variety of functions including insulation, and hollow bones and airsacs which make them lighter. They are egg-laying, warm-blooded, feathered bipeds. Birds are divided into birds of prey and those that are dependent on various parts of plants like fruit, flowers and seeds. While most bird species are arboreal, several are adapted to living in aquatic habitats. Terrestrial birds are either generalists, able to use various habitat types, or specialists that use specific habitats such as forests, grasslands, deserts, wetlands, and coastal areas.

As a schoolboy in Pune, I lived in a house in the middle of the cantonment, with a big garden full of trees. The plot adjacent to the house was a jowar and bajra field. Dr. Salim Ali frequently came to visit and we would go down to the well in the farm to look at the bayas. I had been given a 'Salim Ali Book' and spent many hours reading it, until I knew it by heart and could recognize every garden bird. Even when we went on a holiday to Mahableshwar, I could spot and identify nearly all the birds that I saw there for the first time, without even referring to the book.

|     | 3 |
|-----|---|
| 1 | 2 |
| 4 | |
| 5 | 6 |

Birds evolved 150 million years ago and are divided into 27 orders.

Scarlet minivet.

Birds are either generalists, able to live in diverse habitats, or specialists linked to specific habitats.

Many species of birds are endangered by human activities.

A scarlet minivet splashes colour over an arid landscape.

Crows gathering at sunset, before going to their roost.

**Ornithology as a study has been primarily done by non-professional birdwatchers.**

In later years I became more involved with the conservation of water birds as a result of my repeated visits to a small shallow section of the Mula-Mutha River close to the Bund gardens, a kilometre from my house, a favoured wintering place for thousands of waterfowl and waders. The river is now unfortunately degraded to a sewer and my favourite bird-watching place is depressingly dirty. The number of birds is much lower and many species, especially the waders, have disappeared altogether or are rarely seen. Grassland birds became yet another focus of interest for me as I saw their habitat rapidly disappearing through Maharashtra's economic 'development'.

In its concern with birdlife, the BNHS has identified eight bird species as being critically endangered in India. There are 79 species that are threatened and another 57 that are 'near threatened'. While it is

TC Jerdon's *Catalogue of the Birds of the Indian Peninsula* was published in the 1840s, and *Birds of India* in 1862. John Gould's *Birds of Asia* appeared in 1883.

AO Hume's Journal of ornithology for India, *Stray Feathers* in 12 volumes was put together between 1873 and 1899.

Eugene Oates wrote *The Fauna of British India—Birds* in 1889–90.

WT Blanford wrote for *The Fauna of British India—Birds* in the 1890s, in four volumes.

EC Stewart Baker wrote on birds for *The Fauna of British India* in eight volumes, from 1922 to 1930.

Salim Ali and Dillon Ripley completed *The Handbook of the Birds of India and Pakistan* in 1974, after decades of extremely hard work. This is the bible of ornithology of the subcontinent and an irreplaceable work.

important to take measures to prevent these from getting extinct in the country, it is equally important to appreciate that even common species are suffering a precipitous fall in their populations.

A number of research workers across the country have shown that several avifaunal populations have been decreasing over the last few decades. These figures have helped me to corroborate my personal observations. Over the years, I have noticed trends indicating that certain bird species are disappearing at an increasingly rapid pace. Among the many such species, vultures appear to have been severely threatened by a precipitous fall in their numbers. They have all but vanished through most of their range during the last six or seven years. I found that the king vulture and the Egyptian vulture, which were always less common around Pune, were the first to disappear. It was only a matter of time before the white-backed vulture I used to once see in hundreds became locally extinct. This serious disaster that gradually spread all over the country took only a decade!

Other bird species, such as floricans and bustards, which have always been rare, are now on the verge of falling off the precipice of extinction. Some of the less documented reductions in numbers are species such as owls and nightjars, perhaps as a result of increasing pesticide use, as they feed on a large number of insects.

Birds such as the jungle fowl, the partridge and the quail continue to be poached. In most areas their populations have shrunk, while in some areas where they were found a decade or two ago, they have become locally extinct. These local extinctions isolate existing populations from each other and constitute an added threat to these species.

In Karnataka, the population of spot-billed pelican fell from an estimated 2000 to only 330, over a mere 30 years. Sarus cranes in Bharatpur have decreased from 27 breeding pairs to five or six pairs. This decrease has been ascribed to the use of Aldrin as a pesticide.

While the depletion of many species can be simply ascribed to habitat loss, in other cases, the reasons are highly cryptic. The rapid decline in the population of some species is related to the high levels of disturbance in breeding areas, especially for those species that nest in colonies. In several towns and cities, sparrow populations have dropped drastically during the last seven or eight years. No specific cause and effect phenomenon has been identified.

Some insectivorous birds are known to consume up to 2000 insects per day. Within the ecosystem, this control over the most populous group of species on earth, which damages our agricultural yield, is of great importance. Hypothetically, without insectivorous animals and birds, the growth of plant-dependent insect life would rapidly defoliate every forest, grassland, agricultural and horticultural system, and in fact all plant life, leaving a skeleton of the earth's producer-base. As the use of insecticides increases, the buildup of these toxic chemicals in the metabolic systems of insectivorous birds will continue to deplete their population and eventually destroy nature's own method of keeping insect populations at an appropriate level.

Birds are crucial links in regenerating forests, as they pollinate flowering plants and transport seeds. This leads to a mosaic of different plant species in the forest landscape. The microhabitats formed are an important aspect of natural vegetation, creating ideal habitat conditions for a large number of faunal species.

Observing the fascinating behaviour and intricate relationship of birds to their habitat has been one of my favourite pastimes. I have also frequently used bird-watching as a tool for turning many young people into nature-conservation enthusiasts. While it is true that bird-watcher groups have sprung up in many towns and cities in India over the last couple of decades, this is still, on the whole, an uncommon and purely urban pastime, and in terms of India's population, a miniscule one. In the west, bird-watching is an extremely common activity. I was once in the countryside in the UK when we found ourselves in a long traffic jam, caused, we were told, by large numbers of bird-watchers who had sighted a rare bird! There were so many people that I never got to see the much sought-after species. Encouraging bird-watching at the school level would initiate a great interest in nature, which could lead to pro-conservation action.

## AQUATIC BIRD SPECIES
## WATERFOWL
### GREBES—*GENUS PODICEPS*
**Great-crested grebe**—*Podiceps cristatus*
**Black-necked grebe**—
*Podiceps nigaricollis*
**Red-necked grebe**—*Podiceps griseigena*
**Little grebe**—*Podiceps rufficollis*

Among the four grebes found in India is the tiny dabchick. Diving like a flash under water when disturbed, it usually surprises the bird-watcher by reappearing at a completely different spot after a fairly long period. This is done by expelling air from its body and feathers, thereby increasing its specific gravity, which then permits it to virtually disappear and swim with only its head exposed above the surface.

I once found a pair of dabchicks completing their small floating nest. It was only three or four metres from the water's edge. Even though I moved away very quietly to get my camera, when I returned five minutes later, the dabchicks had floated the nest with its clump of hyacinth into deeper water, several metres from the edge of the river.

EC Stuart Baker was a well-known ornithologist of the early 1900s. He frequently wrote reviews of various birds from the Indian subcontinent. In 1915, he wrote a review on the Indian swan, in the JBNHS, Volume 23, identifying four species, the Bewick swan, Alpheraky's swan, the whooper, and the mute swan, describing in detail the differences in the colour and shape of their beaks. Today these birds have vanished from India.

Little grebe—'Dabchick'.

Pelicans are highly fish-dependent.

## PELICANS
There are three species of pelicans found in India.

### Spot-billed or Grey Pelican
*—Pelecanus philippensis*

This is a large, greyish-white bird, with a brown crest, a gigantic pinkish bill with blue spots and a pouch that has purple and blue markings. They are now patchily distributed and specific to only certain water bodies with plenty of fish and expanses of open water. They move in a line to drive fish into the shallows and trap them in a small area. In flight, they make a V-formation or soar in the sky in large circles. As these pelicans are almost exclusively fish-eaters, their population is dependent on the abundance of fish in a water-body. They nest in large colonies at traditional sites, year after year. Only a few such breeding colonies remain in India.

The species is highly threatened, as it has a limited distribution in only a few favourite areas and there are few large nesting colonies. The spot-billed pelican's population in India, as tentatively estimated by BNHS scientists, is down to only 3000 birds in 2002. Their breeding success is highly dependent on a successful monsoon.

## CORMORANTS
There are four species of cormorants in India: the large cormorant, the Indian shag, the little cormorant and the pygmy cormorant. A glossy, black bird, the cormorant's bill is long, slender and sharply hooked at the tip. In the breeding season, the Indian cormorant gets white feather tufts behind the eyes. The sexes are alike.

They are found throughout India, but not at higher elevations in the Himalayas, and are locally migratory, living in shallow lakes, jheels and river ecosystems in several landscape forms.

Cormorants are gregarious and form large flocks. They hunt in parties by driving a shoal of fish, hemming them into a small area where they are caught underwater. They are frequently seen stretching out their wings to dry after a dip.

As they eat only fish, the presence of these birds is an indicator of fish abundance. They normally nest in trees, from July to February, though I have observed a colony nesting on a small rocky island in the Andhra Lake in the Mawal taluka in Maharashtra. The nest is similar in size to a crow's nest. Cormorants breed in small colonies or as part of a larger mixed heronry. Three to six pale, bluish-green eggs are laid in a clutch, and are incubated by both parents. This highly abundant species is now being affected by falling fish populations, due to river and lake pollution.

## HERONS, BITTERNS AND EGRETS

There are 17 species of herons, four species of egrets and seven species of bitterns in India. These long-legged birds fly with their long necks folded in an S-shape. When they descend, their neck extends, so that they can survey their immediate vicinity for worms, insects, frogs and fish. It is interesting to watch how they hunt for their food. Perfectly still like a statue, the bird remains in position till it spots its prey, and then, by slowly moving its head it takes perfect aim. The unsuspecting prey finds that it is pounced on in a lightning flash. Most of these birds breed in great mixed colonies, on tall undisturbed trees. Heronries are still found in rural areas, close to human habitation, if they are not disturbed. Heronries in most urban settings, frequently seen till a few decades ago, have disappeared almost everywhere. The linkage between wild herbivores, domestic cattle and the cattle egrets is well-known all over India. They also follow farmers when they plough their fields, to catch disturbed insects.

| 1 | 2 |
| 3 | 4 |
| 5 | |

Cormorants generally nest in trees. This unusual colony has built its nests among the rocks on an island.

The paddy bird frequents ponds, river-fronts and wetlands.

A cormorant beside its favourite fishing pool.

The grey heron consumes great quantities of fish, amphibia, crustacea and molluscs.

The grey heron is one of the largest herons in India.

India's Rich
Faunal Heritage

## Little Egret

Egret feathers were much in demand in the late 1800s and early 1900s and egrets were extensively trapped and killed for their plumage especially in Sind. When the trappers were prohibited from engaging in this activity, local people started domesticating the egrets, which were also bred in captivity. The bird's eyes were sewed up to prevent escape. Eventually this was stopped by using the *Prevention of Cruelty to Animals Act*. These egret farms supplied plumage in large quantities to the west for several years, until fashion changed.

Egret plumes were very popular for hats in the 1800s and early 1900s. In 1922, CG Chevenix Trench reported on egret farming in India. He found that 'egret plumes were valuable and so easily smuggled out of the country that no amount of prohibitive, but unintelligent legislation will prevent the export trade in aigrettes, which continues as it has done in the past in spite of the Plumage Act.' To save the egret he suggested that 'egret farming of the bird be undertaken in every possible way and the export of only farmed plumes be permitted under license' (Chevenix Trench, 1922).

## STORKS

There are nine species of storks in India. These large, thick-billed birds are now highly endangered. Until the 1950s, storks could be seen circling the sky in thermal currents all over the country, often accompanying vultures. A possible explanation for their decline is the disturbance of their nesting colonies. The rarest of them is the greater adjutant stork. The black-necked stork, the white-necked stork and the painted stork, once much more common, are now hardly ever seen. In the 1970s, I photographed white storks in a saltpan adjacent to the Mumbai-Pune road. Dr Salim Ali was thrilled to see these pictures taken so close to Mumbai. When I also showed him pictures of a black stork taken near Pune, he was even more surprised. In the last 30-odd years, even the very common open-billed stork has become uncommon near most urban areas.

| 1 | |
| 2 | |
| 3 | 4 |

This rare white stork was photographed in 1982, near what is now Navi Mumbai.

Black-necked stork at Bharatpur.

Egret feathers were once a major item of export. Egrets were killed in thousands for their feathers which were considered fashionable till the early 20th century.

Painted storks soar through the air effortlessly in spite of their large size and weight.

## IBISES AND SPOONBILLS

These are ancient species, that evolved some 60 million years ago. The Egyptians venerated the ibis 5000 years ago and mummified them before putting them in their tombs, with other objects that they valued. The three common species in India are the white, black and glossy ibis. Spoonbills hunt in flocks by wading in the water with their bills open. Both spoonbills and ibises feed on crustacea, insects, worms, amphibia and fish.

| | | 4 |
|---|---|---|
| 1 | 5 | 6 |
| 2 | | |
| 3 | | |

White-necked storks either live alone or in large groups.

Storks in flight.

Lesser adjutant storks are becoming increasingly rare.

The Ibis has been known from ancient times. There are three species commonly found in India—white, black and glossy.

Ibis; from Smith and Doyle, 1828.

White ibis.

## FLAMINGOES

The Maharao of Kachchh first reported the flamingo breeding colony of Kachchh in 1892 (Lester, 1893). The first photographs of flamingoes nesting in the Great Rann of Kachchh were taken in 1903. In 1938, Charles McCann published pictures of a deserted flamingo city from the same area, in the JBNHS. Salim Ali described the Flamingo City in detail and made a film, which he showed in the Fergusson College in the 1960s. When the film projector got jumpy and made a burring sound, I distinctly recall Salim Ali's quip that he had not recorded those sounds and asked for the sound to be shut off. He then went on to give a live commentary that was much more fascinating than what we had heard in the first half of the film.

In the 1950s, I followed the Maharaja of Bansda through a swampy area near the Pashan Lake in Pune, where he was filming a small group of lesser flamingoes. Their incredible pink against a backdrop of blue water, surrounded by green babul trees, was a memorable sight. Today Pashan is polluted, urbanized, and has lost most of its spectacular birdlife. The memory of my early exposure to this glamorous species was rekindled when I found a flock of greater flamingoes in a lake on the Pune-Solapur road in the 1980s. With several active bird-watchers in Pune in those days, the story hit the press and several cars would descend on the small lake every Sunday. The birds then moved to the backwaters of Ujjani Dam, where they were joined by more and more greater flamingoes over the next few years. The local fisher-folk soon became ardent field guides. Not satisfied with stills, I got the Educational Media Research Center (EMRC) of the Pune University to produce a video film on *The Changing Nature of a Wetland* for the University Grants Commission's Open University Programme. Over the next three years, a number of video clips were put together to show how the ecosystem of the newly created wetland changed through the eutrophication resulting from fertilizers used by local farmers. The greater flamingo's open mud-bank habitat was overrun by *Paspalum* grass, and finally by great masses of *Ipomea* shrubs. The feeding areas of the flamingo shrank and the 2–3000 flamingoes were reduced to a few hundred.

The Flamingo City was first reported in 1896, 10 kilometres north of Mir, in the Great Rann. Charles McCann visited the Flamingo City in 1935, and Salim Ali first visited it in 1943. In those days it was reported that there were possibly as many as 7–8000 flamingoes in the Great Rann. He recorded that there were

1

2

3

Spoonbills are usually seen in flocks.

Spoonbills nesting.

The lesser flamingo has a pink tinge all over.

| 1 | | |
|---|---|---|
| | 2 | |
| | | 3 |

Greater flamingoes are white and have deep scarlet wings that flash prominently in flight.

Flamingoes are highly specialized filter-feeders.

Flamingoes at dawn, in a wetland.

A long line of greater flamingoes flying through a cloudburst.

great fluctuations in the breeding success and attributed this to changes in yearly water levels in the Rann (Ali, 1945). He requested Maharao Vijayraji of Kachchh to have guards patrol the area to protect the flamingoes. He also recorded that successful breeding occurs only once in three to four years. McCann suggested that Indian flamingoes breed as far away as Spain.

In 1945, when visited by Salim Ali, there were abundant nests, and he estimated the total population to be about half a million birds. Salim Ali found that rosy pelicans used the old unused nests of flamingoes. In 1973, Phillip Kahl, who visited the Flamingo City, estimated that it had 10,000 nests. He also took incredible aerial photographs of the colony. That same year Salim Ali again visited the Flamingo City and for the first time observed the lesser flamingo breeding in India along with the greater flamingo. The estimated figure for lesser flamingo in the area was about 2–5000 birds, while the greater flamingo could have been anywhere between 25,000 and 30,000.

Greater flamingoes feed from the muddy bottom of their aquatic habitat on a wide variety of foods, including vegetable matter such as the seeds of the Ruppia plant. The lesser flamingo feeds by skimming the surface of the water. It has a more complex beak structure and feeds on much finer particles, especially blue-green algae.

The flamingo's beak has a unique evolutionary design, linked to its complex feeding pattern. Inverting its head below

water, it uses the bill and tongue as a sieving mechanism. This permits it to separate the mud from tiny crustacea and vegetable matter on which the bird feeds. Algae, diatoms, protozoa, worms and molluscs are eaten from the rich organic soup that collects at the bottom of the mud-bank under the water. Flamingoes can use both marine and freshwater ecosystems.

Flamingoes are a magnificent sight, both in the water where they feed together in large flocks, and in flight, when they form long strings of scarlet and white. However, their real beauty is seen when they raise the feathers on their backs during their breeding display. They also spread out their wings horizontally, in flashes of brilliant scarlet. I have seen these noisy, spectacular displays on several occasions at Bhigwan over the years.

AH Marshall, a nature lover serving in the Indian Police, wrote about the occurrence of the pink-headed duck in Punjab. He shot one of the ducks. It was Blanford and Oates who confirmed that it belonged to that rare species called the pink-headed duck (Marshall,1917).

## DUCKS AND GEESE

Many years ago, on a wetland bird-watching expedition, I asked an assorted group of people who were new bird-watchers, the names of the ducks they could identify. A small boy immediately responded 'Donald Duck!' An old gentleman who had joined the group recently, looked up from the bird book he was engrossed in and asked, 'Where is it? I can't find it in the book.' I have also seen amateur bird counts documenting pink-headed ducks. Unfortunately, this species is almost certainly extinct in India! Most records of the early 1900s are from the north-east and Bengal.

Ducks are an exciting group of species for most bird-watchers. A long V-formation flying through a golden morning sky is a sight almost everyone finds thrilling. Tell a new bird-watcher that these birds could well be coming in from Siberia and most of them get hooked on birds for life. There are 17 species of ducks in India and several species of migrants that come through the high Himalayan passes every winter, as their summer breeding habitat is bitterly cold and snowbound. Others are local or migrate only within our subcontinent.

I find that most ducks can adapt, as waders cannot, to some level of changes in their habitat. Most waders are less adaptable. The disappearance of wild ducks from a water-body therefore indicates high levels of disturbance or serious pollution. Ducks feed either primarily on aquatic and semi-aquatic vegetation, or on crustacea, worms, insect larvae and other forms of life. Some species use both types of food. Only a few ducks—such as the Merganzer living along the rivers and wetlands of the north-eastern states of India—live on fish. Duck species specialize in feeding on different sources of food. Some dabble in the shallow water, reaching the muddy floor of the water-body with their necks stretched and their tail ends sticking out of the water in a sort of *sirsasan*. Diving ducks feed at a deeper level. Other species are surface feeders, and feed on the floating food found in the upper layers of the water. Mixed parties of ducks form a sort of loose feeding guild, which permits each species to optimize the amount of food it can get from the various microhabitats of a wetland.

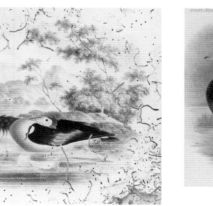

| 1 | 2 | |
|---|---|---|
| 3 | 4 | 7 |
| 5 | 6 | |
| | 8 | 9 |
| | 10 | |

Bar-headed goose; from Hume and Marshal, 1880.

Bar-headed goose; from JBNHS, 1899.

Shovellers.

Coots chasing each other.

Combed ducks; from Hume and Marshal, 1880

Shoveller; from Hume and Marshall, 1880.

White-fronted goose; from JBNHS, 1898.

Ducks—'Nakhta'; from Smith and Doyle, 1829.

White-winged wood duck; from JBNHS, 1908.

The population of ducks has decreased considerably over the last 20 years.

EC Stuart Baker, FZS, a well-known ornithologist and collector of the early 1900s, wrote extensively on Indian ducks and their allies. He presented his documentation on Indian duck species before the BNHS on 18th November 1896. His work was later published in the JBNHS in 1898. He described their habitat, enemies and allies, nesting and eggs, male-female differences and distribution (Stuart Baker, 1898).

## Ruddy Shell-duck or Brahminy Duck—*Tadorna ferruginea*

The Brahminy is a large orange-brown or cinnamon-brown duck, with pale head and neck and a prominent metallic-green speculum on the black wing, with a white wing patch in front of it. In overhead flight, its orange-brown body, the white underside of its wings and its black quills make it easily identifiable. Its loud call, reminiscent of a goose, also makes its presence clear even before it is sighted. Mainly a winter visitor breeding in Ladakh, the Brahminy is found all over India, but is less abundant in the south.

The Brahminy ducks live in large open lakes and rivers. Less gregarious than most other ducks, they are usually seen in groups of a few birds or in small parties. Flocks of 20 or more are less common. They are aggressive and intolerant of feeding competitors of their own and other species. They graze on dry riverbanks and grassy lake margins, pecking at grain, tender shoots and tubers. They also hunt for crustaceans, molluscs, aquatic insects and small reptiles. At the Telco guesthouse in Pune, they were fed every day at the same time. The Brahminis had learnt to land at the edge of the water just before their feeding time was due and call to be fed. If delayed, they would set off a cacophony of angry, demanding calls.

## Pintail—*Anas acuta*

The pintail is a large duck with long, pointed central-tail feathers, which give it its name. It is the size of a large domestic duck. The males have a characteristic dark-brown head, with a prominent white band that runs down the neck to join the white breast and abdomen. The dorsal plumage is greyish and finely stippled, and there is a bright metallic green patch on the wing when closed. The female is mottled with various shades of brown.

Pochard; from Baker, 1908.

Red-breasted Merganzer; from JBNHS, 1901.

Pink-headed duck; from Finn, 1915.

The Brahminy ducks found all over India during winter, breed in Ladakh in the summer.

Brahminy ducks; from Hume and Marshal, 1880.

Great aggregations of pintail ducks have been migrating for centuries to India. Over the last few decades their numbers have been falling.

In some areas, pintails are the most common migrant ducks.

The long thin tail feathers are prominently seen in flight in both sexes. It is widely distributed throughout India in winter, inhabiting wetlands where it feeds on both underwater and emergent vegetation. It is also seen in rivers and coastal belts.

The pintail migrates to India across the Himalayas in September and leaves again in March. It nests north of the Himalayas in summer.

These ducks feed along the edges of water-bodies, in reeds or move into paddies. They dabble at the bottom of the muddy floor of the water-body for aquatic vegetation. In paddies they feed on molluscs, worms and aquatic insect larvae. The pintail is one of our commoner migrant aquatic species and bird counts in several states have shown that they occur in large numbers, accounting for a fairly high percentage of the duck population in several wetlands.

The BNHS has records of birds ringed in Siberia that were recovered in India. These incredibly long and obviously arduous annual to and fro movements are a survival strategy that is linked to evolutionary changes and geographical configurations developed over thousands of years.

### TEALS

The well-known teals are the common teal, the gargany teal, the cotton teal, the lesser whistling teal, and the greater whistling teal.

The gargany and the common teal are among the commonest ducks that migrate to India. One or the other dominates the mixed community of ducks in most of our wetlands. The common teal is primarily vegetarian, while the gargany feeds on both vegetable matter and small aquatic animals. The male common teal has a distinctive green patch going from the eye to the back of the head and a green patch on the wing. The gargany has a blue patch

on the wing, which is more prominent in flight. The males have a prominent light stripe over the eyes.

The Andaman teal is endemic to a few islands in the Andamans. Its population is estimated at around 500 individuals, which makes it one of the world's most endangered waterfowl species. It uses several aquatic ecosystems, including small freshwater pools in the forest clearings and brackish-water areas near the coast. I have observed a flock of these birds feeding actively in shallow, brackish water near a busy road just outside Port Blair.

| 1 | 2 |
|---|---|
| 3 | 4 |
| | 5 |
| 6 | |
| 7 | |
| 8 | |

Pintail; from Hume and Marshal, 1880.

Gargany teals are found in several wetlands along the river courses.

Male and female gargany teals.

Gargany teal; from Baker, 1908.

The rare Andaman teal; from Baker, 1908.

Common teal; from Hume and Marshal, 1880.

Cotton teal; from Hume and Marshal, 1880.

Cotton teals.

### Spot-bill or Grey Duck
*—Anas poecilorhyncha*

The spot-bill is a large duck with a scaly, patterned, light and dark-brown plumage, white and metallic green wing-bars and bright, orange-red legs. The dark bill, bright yellow tipped, has two prominent orange-red spots on either side near the forehead. The spot-bill is distributed throughout India, where it is resident in some areas but frequently migrates locally. Spot-bills live in pairs or small flocks. Their favoured habitats are jheels and percolation tanks. Less frequently, they live in slow-flowing, shallow rivers. They are surface feeders, but also feed by 'up-ending' to reach the mud in the bed of the wetland.

The call is a hoarse, wheezy note by the drake and a loud quack by the duck. Its nesting season is not rigidly defined, but it usually occurs between July and September. The nest is made of a pad of grass and weeds in the marshy margins of tanks and may contain six to twelve eggs, greyish buff or greenish-white in colour. The spot-bill is increasingly affected by loss of its habitat and disturbances to its breeding grounds. Watching a train of ducklings following the mother as they swim near the bank of a wetland is an indicator of the health of an aquatic ecosystem.

### CRANES
This group of seven species is disappearing more rapidly than most of the other endangered species. Once seen in thousands, they are severely affected by water pollution as well as by habitat loss due to the conversion of wetlands to other uses. A recent development has been a rise in the number of incidents in which farmers have poisoned them to prevent crop damage.

### Black-headed Crane—*Grus nigricolli*
The black-headed crane is the only alpine crane of the world. Its well-known wintering ground in India is in the Apa Tani Valley in Arunachal Pradesh. It also breeds in the Chang-Thang region of Ladakh, where I observed several pairs with their chicks. The earliest record of this beautiful bird in India was made by F Ludlow in 1919, followed by Osmaston in 1925 and Meintertzhagan in 1927, from Ladakh. In the 1970s, Salim Ali and Hussain, and later Prakash Gole, surveyed Ladakh and other regions to study this highly endangered species. In recent years, there have been several studies to bring about conservation strategies for the crane, as part of projects undertaken by BNHS and WWF-I. The most recent assessment has been done by Pankaj Chandan of WWF-I. The survey accounts for about 60 birds.

1
2

3 5
4

Lesser whistling teal; from Baker, 1908.

Lesser whistling teals.

Spot-billed duck; from Hume and Marshal, 1880.

Spot-billed ducks are among the commonest ducks breeding in India.

Black-necked crane.

**Sarus Crane**—*Grus antigone*

This distinctively tall, grey bird, with its bare red head was once a common sight in many wetlands in India as far south as Gujarat; but its distribution has shrunk severely in the recent years. In 1890, Murray observed that it was widely distributed. The 1969 map by Ali and Ripley reduced this range considerably, but it could still be considered to have had a fairly wide distribution up to the early 1970s. Studies by the Wildlife Institute of India in 1999 have shown that its range is now extremely patchy. The southernmost limit, where I saw a pair of sarus about 10 or 12 years ago, was at a small wetland off the Mumbai-Ahmedabad highway near Daman. The wetland itself has now disappeared. There is no objective data on the rate of loss of these small but optimal habitats. Loss of wetlands could however account for more frequent sightings of Sarus in unlikely habitats. I know of three Sarus cranes that have been consistently observed in Bandhavgad feeding in grassland patches that have very little water. I last saw two of them in 2002.

BC Chaudhari and his co-workers from Wildlife Institute of India have shown that the breeding success of Sarus is higher in an area where there is a mosaic of wetland and grassland habitats. Their home range in a wetland area is smaller as each pair can find a sufficient quantity of food within a shorter time. As their habitat disappears, we will never be able to see a pair of these magnificent birds dancing in the morning haze over the wetlands of India.

Prakash Gole has been observing crane populations for over 30 years and documented in the 1980s that there was a serious drop in sarus crane numbers all over India. In 1998–99 the Wildlife Institute of India did a national survey in 11 states which showed serious crashes in population in several states. For instance, Bihar, which used to have a large number of cranes, had no sightings. At present Uttar Pradesh has the largest number of sarus sightings.

The Wildlife Institute of India researchers have documented that the sarus have now begun to nest increasingly in fields, which is a reflection of the loss of wetland habitats that they once used. Nesting success in wetlands that dry up is obviously low and those that nest in agricultural land have even less chance of success.

Heugh S Symons recorded the presence of sarus cranes in Bombay, at Panvel, in 1897 and Santa Cruz, in 1908 (Heugh, 1909).

Sarus cranes are known to pair for life.

Sarus cranes; from Smith and Doyle, 1928.

Sarus cranes feeding in a marshland. It is the state bird of Uttar Pradesh.

### Siberian Crane—*Grus leucogeranus*

The Siberian crane is a magnificent, large white bird with a bare red face. A migrant to India from Siberia, it was known to winter only in the Keoladeo Ghana National Park in Bharatpur over the last several decades.

Siberian cranes feed on aquatic vegetation by persistently probing the underwater vegetation with their long bills. Rhizomes of *Scirpus tuberosus, Cyprus rotundus* and *Nymphaea* are their favourite food item, but they also feed on aquatic insects, molluscs and worms. Studies on this bird done by the BNHS have shown that, as emergent weeds increasingly spread over the water surface in Bharatpur, it became difficult for the birds to locate the food they liked under the water.

It was our most critically endangered species, with a count of only two wild birds in 2000. In 1985–86 there were 37 adults and six young. This precipitous decline has occurred most rapidly in the last decade, inspite of the knowledge that it was critically endangered and required urgent conservation action. During the last two or three winters there have been no more sightings of this beautiful species from Bharatpur. Their story in India has come to an unfortunate end.

### Demoiselle Crane—*Anthropoides virgo*

The Demoiselle crane is a graceful grey bird with black head and neck, long feathers on the lower part of the neck that fall over its breast and a distinctive white tuft behind the eye. It is mainly a winter visitor to India, with a range extending from the Himalayas to Karnataka. Its habitat in the wetlands extends into surrounding agricultural areas, especially wheat fields. In the past it used to come to the wetlands of Maharashtra and Karnataka in greater numbers, especially in years when Gujarat had a drought.

I first photographed this species at the Veer Dam near Pune in the 1980s. The birds used to rest on sandbanks along the edge of the shallow lake, and every day the flock soared in large circles at a great height to descend on an unattended field. The loud, musical, high-pitched trumpet could be heard right across the large lake. Subsequently local farmers began to poison the birds, as they damaged their wheat fields. The number has reduced significantly as the area has been increasingly industrialized in the recent years.

Siberian crane; from Hume and Marshal, 1880.

Siberian cranes were last sighted in India in Bharatpur, in 2002.

F Waller Photo and Lith 14 Hatton Garden London

M. Herbert

Demoiselle cranes; from Hume and Marshal, 1880.

Demoiselle cranes make large flocks. They damage wheat crops.

| | | |
|---|---|---|
| | 1 | |
| 2 | 4 | |
| 3 | | |

Pheasant-tailed jacana uses its large feet to walk on floating vegetation.

Pheasant-tailed jacana.

Purple moorhens are commonly seen in wetlands.

White-breasted water hen; from Gould, 1850.

### JACANAS AND MOORHENS

This group requires floating vegetation or thick mats of underwater reeds, which they use to walk on the surface of the water. This is how they are able to hunt for frogs, worms and molluscs in a microhabitat in which waders and ducks are relatively uncomfortable. This specialized niche is rich in aquatic fauna. India has two species of jacanas and four species of moorhens.

1 Crab plovers are generally seen on seashores. This is an unusual sighting inland at Kolhapur in Maharastra.

2 A large flock of waders on a muddy shore.

3 The long legs of a black-winged stilt enable it to wade in deeper water than most other waders of its size.

4 Waders living in the polluted Mahim creek in Mumbai.

## WADERS

The waders include a large number of species that have long legs and use the shallow edge of water bodies to find their food. Waders with longer legs are able to access food such as worms and crustacea at a greater depth than those with relatively shorter legs. The latter are restricted to the extreme edge of the water body. Species such as the black-winged stilt, the redshank and the godwits use a depth of 15–20 centimetres, while sandpipers can wade in water that is about four or five centimetres in depth.

While some waders specialize in using fresh water systems, others use coastal areas where the ebb and flow of the tide gives them access to the exposed food material in the sand or mud-banks at low tide. Estuarine species congregate in large numbers on several beaches and saltpans. In the mosaic of microhabitats used by aquatic birds, such as open water, reed beds and mud-banks, the waders' habitat, which consists of very shallow water with a muddy floor, is limited to a very small proportion of the ecosystem. It is also most easily disturbed by human movement, pollution of both the water and the banks, and the type of changes in the habitat

that are bound to occur when the water is surrounded by buildings, as happens when urban centres spread around water bodies. One rarely realizes how critical this habitat is until these birds suddenly disappear. I have observed that this does take several decades to happen. Aquatic ecosystems have a resilience that allows birds to feed until a threshold is reached, after which they may desert their habitat within a couple of years. I have noticed this in the rivers around Pune, where the population of waders suddenly decreased in the 1990s, as pollution levels soared.

### Black-winged Stilt
—*Himantopus himantopus*
Stilts are distributed all over India, from the Himalayas to Kanyakumari, inhabiting wetlands and riverine tracts with a muddy floor. They are capable of using all types of aquatic ecosystems including marshes, jheels, village tanks, salt pans and tidal mud flats, where they are seen probing the squelchy mud, looking for worms and molluscs. They also catch aquatic insects on the surface. The stilt's flight frequently appears to be weak and flapping, but the bird is, in fact, a strong flyer and migrates long distances. Its squeaky 'peep-peep-peep' call is uttered when it is alarmed or just before it flies off. With aquatic habitats getting increasingly polluted, this species is disappearing from village ponds and urban rivers.

The black-winged stilt is a striking black and white wader with a straight, slender black bill. For its small size, it is an unusually tall wader with long, thin, red legs giving it a distinctive appearance.

In 1984 I wrote an article for *Sanctuary* magazine, as the editor, Bittu Sehgal, liked my pictures of this very common species. I remember that he was hesitant to publish the article, as the magazine had not portrayed a common species in its earlier editions. My pictures were mainly from the Mula-Mutha River in Pune, which even in those days was not exactly an attractive place. Today the population of this bird has been depleted in this river, which now acts as the city's sewer, as a result of serious levels of water pollution from untreated sewage and industrial effluent.

### SANDPIPERS
A group of 12 species, sandpipers are birds that specialize in using the edge of a water-body. Muddy or squelchy edges are the microhabitat in which they prefer to probe for worms, insect larvae and other cryptic forms of life. Their ability to hunt for their food below the mud is quite a surprising feat of sensory perception. These small waders appear to be more sensitive to habitat changes than ducks or egrets. It is possible that in a polluted habitat, their prey species disappear earlier than those eaten by dabbling ducks, which can use deeper water.

### GULLS AND TERNS
Gulls and terns are associated with both freshwater and saline habitats. There are 10 species of gulls and 27 species of terns found in India. Their ability to adapt their primary diet, from fish and amphibia to floating garbage helps them survive in moderately polluted habitats. They are thus the last species to disappear from an increasingly polluted river or tidal area. In the 1970s I observed a sudden increase in immature river terns in Pune. I felt they must breed somewhere, and eventually, Pradumna Gogate, who worked with me on the ecology of a newly-created irrigation dam 100 kilometres downstream at Bhigwan, found them nesting on islands that emerged from the water in summer.

| 1 |
| 2 |

| 3 |

Spotted sandpiper.

Sandpipers are among some of the commonest waders.

River terns patrol up and down the banks, diving into the water when it sees a fish.

| | 1 | | |
|---|---|---|---|
| 2 | 3 | 4 | |
| | 5 | | |

A river tern taking off from its nest.

There are 10 species of gulls found in India.

A river tern feeding its chick.

Black-bellied tern; from Gould, 1850.

Sea gulls feeding at Chowpaty Beach in Mumbai on food waste.

There were hundreds of nests on the ground in little depressions of human and cattle footprints. The risk of crushing an egg or a chick has prevented me from revisiting this incredible nesting site. Over the years I made serious attempts to request local fishermen not to use these islands for drying their nets. The number of nests reported over the last few years has been decreasing.

## KINGFISHERS

There are 14 kingfisher species in India that feed on fish and aquatic insects, both in fresh and brackish water. The white-breasted kingfisher, the small blue kingfisher and the pied kingfisher are the three well-known species. The latter has a distinctive way of hovering over a shoal of fish before diving straight down like a stone into the water.

Gulls now find themselves using highly polluted water.

A pied kingfisher hovers before diving into the water for its prey.

**There are 14 species of kingfishers found in India.**

| 1 | 3 | 5 |
| 2 | 4 | |
| | | 6 |
| | 7 | |
| | 8 | 9 |

A rare three-toed kingfisher; from Jerdon, 1847.

A three-toed kingfisher.

The white-breasted kingfisher is the commonest species of kingfishers. It is the state bird of West Bengal.

White-breasted kingfisher.

White-breasted kingfisher; from Gould, 1850.

A common blue kingfisher.

Pied kingfisher.

A pair of common blue kingfishers.

Black-capped kingfisher; from Gould, 1850.

## WAGTAILS

There are 19 species of wagtails in India, most of which are winter migrants. The pied wagtail is, however, a local species and is seen in summer as well as winter. It uses the extreme edge of the habitat between land and water. While hunting for their food, the pied wagtails persistently wag their tails rapidly up and down, and zigzag their way along the muddy area of the waters' edge, looking for insect larvae, worms and molluscs.

## BIRDS OF PREY IN AQUATIC HABITATS
### OSPREY

This is one of our most exciting birds of prey that frequent wetlands and lakes. It sits on a favourite old pole or tree from which it makes sorties over the surface of the water and dive-bombs a fish. It can pick up even large fish from the water. The osprey was never a common species, but it is increasingly threatened now.

| 1 | 3 | |
|---|---|---|
| 2 | 4 | 5 |
| | 6 | |

Yellow-headed wagtail; from Gould, 1850.

Great pied wagtail; from Gould, 1850.

Deccan wagtail; from Gould, 1850.

Wagtail.

Pied wagtail.

Osprey.

## GREY-HEADED FISHING EAGLE

The grey-headed fishing eagle is a large, prominent bird that frequents wetlands and is capable of picking up its prey with great dexterity. It has a loud, piercing call.

## WHITE-BELLIED SEA EAGLE

A large fishing eagle found in coastal India, this is one of the most magnificent birds of prey. It is an extremely powerful bird, which can dive into the water to lift a large fish.

## FOREST AVIFAUNAL SPECIES

Forest birds can be grouped according to what they feed on: birds that feed on flower nectar, fruit, insect life and birds of prey, that form the apex of the food pyramid. Birds share the food resources of the forest by using different microhabitats as well as one or more types of food. Each species has a microhabitat in which it locates its preferred food. Insectivorous birds, such as drongoes and bee-eaters, specialize in catching insects while on the wing. Others, such as babblers, thrushes and jungle fowl, catch insects that live in the dry detritus of the forest floor. These birds also catch caterpillars and worms. Still others, such as woodpeckers, tap on tree trunks and large branches to disturb insects, which they then catch as they emerge from the bark. Sunbirds and flower-peckers feed on flower nectar. They opt for plants that have brightly coloured flowers. Others such as mynas and orioles also use flower nectar. Among the frugivorous birds, there are those like parakeets that use their curved beaks to gnaw at the fruit. Bulbuls feed on small berries which they swallow whole. Hornbills catch lizards and other kinds of small prey and feed on fruit as well. Raptors, at the top of the food chain, are being increasingly affected by pesticides.

Insectivorous birds play a crucial role in every ecosystem by controlling insect populations. They are also one of the worst affected by pesticides. These toxic chemicals are concentrated in these birds, as they form the second-order consumers in the ecosystem.

| 1 | 4 |
| 2 | |
| 3 | 5 |

Nest of a grey-headed fishing eagle.

Grey-headed fishing eagle.

White-bellied sea eagle in flight.

The grey hypocolleus is a rare species. The bird was observed to have migrated three successive years to the same location, at Lonavala in the Western Ghats.

Some forest species are generalists and can use diverse habitats, while others are specialized, using specific habitats such as the Himalayas, the Western Ghats and the semi-arid thorn forests.

| | 1 | |
|---|---|---|
| 2 | 3 | 4 |
| 5 | | |

While some birds live independently, others like the bee-eaters form a family party and live together.

Green bee-eater; from Gould, 1850.

A common, green bee-eater with its prey, seen in open forests.

A flycatcher, one of the many species that link birds to the world of insects.

The shrike is a pugnacious bird which frequents thorn and scrub forests. It feeds on insects, worms and occasionally on small reptiles. It is commonly seen in thorn forests.

| 1 | 2 |   |
|---|---|---|
| 3 | 4 |   |
| 5 | 6 | 7 |

Species such as the Himalayan treepie are habitat specific.

The common Iora is frequently identified by its long, melodious whistling call.

Pheasants are indicators of a healthy Himalayan ecosystem.

Many migrants return to the same area, year after year. This redstart used the same branch of a shrub for many winters.

The tailor bird can stitch leaves together to make its nest.

Magpie robins; from Gould, 1850.

The Indian robin is a common species adapted to various habitats.

1 | 2

3

Indian fairy blue bird; from Gould, 1850.

Ash-coloured tit; from Gould, 1850.

Grey tits are found in many different types of forests.

Bengal *pitta*; from Gould, 1850.

Gold-backed redstart; from Gould, 1850.

The Indian roller is commonly found in thorn and deciduous forests.

The Indian roller; from Gould, 1850.

The shama is one of India's famous songsters.

PHEASANTS

The pheasants are mainly found at the Himalayan foot-hills. Many of them are threatened due to habitat loss.

### Peacock

The peacock was declared the National Bird of India on January 31st, 1963. Its food includes seeds, fruits, leaves, and insects, as well as small vertebrates like frogs, snakes and lizards. Adult males are territorial.

In India, there is no bird as well-known as the peacock, which has been mentioned in folklore and mythology for centuries. It adapts to a variety of forest types. Watching the males dance is one of the most colourful sights in the forest. An interesting feature of these large birds is their ability to vanish into tall grass or undergrowth and move around completely unseen. Though venerated, the peacock is prized for its feathers and is poached for them as well as for its meat. It is now protected both through religious sentiment and as a result of its status as our National Bird. In some cities, such as Delhi and Ahmedabad, it has adapted itself to living in urban green belts.

| 1 | 3 |
|---|---|
| 2 | 4 |
| 5 | |
| 6 | |

Peacock; from Smith and Doyle, 1829.

The dance of a peacock is one of the most spectacular sights in the forest.

Peacock.

A pair of peacocks.

The peacock, India's national bird, has fascinated the world for generations. It is also the state bird of Orissa.

Peacocks have adapted to living in various Indian towns.

## JUNGLE FOWL

There are two species of jungle fowl in India. The red jungle fowl is found in Northern India, from the Himalayas to the Panchmari hills, along the banks of Godavari in North-eastern Andhra Pradesh. This is said to be the ancestor of all our domestic poultry. The grey jungle fowl is found in peninsular India and has a distinctive call. Once these calls were commonly heard in nearly every forest in the Deccan, but poaching has seriously depleted their numbers.

Grey jungle fowl; from Hume and Marshal, 1880.

Grey jungle fowl are found in the southern parts of India.

The red jungle fowl, found in North India, is the predecessor of domestic poultry.

Red jungle fowl; Hume and Marshal, 1880.

## PARAKEETS

Parakeets live on fruit and nest in holes formed in the trees or in small crevices in rocky cliffs and roofs of old houses. There are 21 species of parakeet found in India. The number of rose-ringed parakeets still being captured for the pet trade is enormous. The tiny lorikeets are not seen as frequently as they used to be. They could be increasingly threatened.

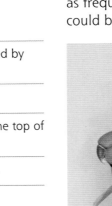

| | 1 | 5 |
|---|---|---|
| 2 | 3 | 6 |
| | | 7 |
| | 4 | |

Jungle fowl populations are being depleted by poaching.

Grey jungle fowl; from Baker, 1930.

A female grey jungle fowl peering from the top of a tree.

Blue-winged parakeet; from Gould, 1850.

Lorikeets; from Smith and Doyle, 1829.

Blossom-headed parakeet; from Gould, 1850.

Parakeet; from Smith and Doyle, 1828.

## NIGHTJARS

Nightjars are a group of species that usually prefer open scrub or grassland habitats. However, a few are specific to forest environments. There are eight species in India.

**Common Indian Nightjar**—*Caprimulgus indicus*—also known as the little Indian nightjar, was once commonly heard all over India, in open scrub jungle, till fairly recently. Nightjars are primarily nocturnal and feed on insects that are active at night. Mottled-brown, sleek birds seen sitting on the ground in the middle of a road, or superbly camouflaged on a transverse low branch of a tree or shrub, they are becomingly increasingly rare and have

disappeared from areas where they were once commonly found. Humayun Abdulali wrote in the JBNHS, in 1947 that he had noted that nightjars along roads around Bombay were becoming less common and ascribed this to the asphalting of roads. In Pune, even in the 1980s, one could drive out of town at night in any direction and nightjars would take off from the road at least once in every kilometre. In the past 20 years, they have become so rare that one can drive along the same roads for 20 or 30 kilometres without seeing a single bird. The beautiful and varied night calls of these species that I recall from my childhood are gone. The nights feel dead silent without them.

| 1 | |
|---|---|
| | 3 |
| 2 | 4 |

Nightjars are probably becoming uncommon due to the use of pesticides.

A nightjar in flight.

A nightjar and a bird of prey; from Smith and Doyle, 1828.

Nightjar; from Gould, 1850.

### Hoopoe—*Upupa epops*

The hoopoe is resident throughout India and is usually found in grassland habitats, especially near water. It is a striking bird with a large fan-shaped crest and black and white zebra markings on its back, wings and tail. It feeds on insects, grubs and pupae and is thus beneficial to the agriculturist. Its call is a soft, musical 'hoo–po–po' which gives it its name.

### HORNBILLS

India has nine species of distinctive and easily identifiable hornbills. They are primarily frugivorous and are an important species for seed-dispersal in the forest. The larger hornbills are associated with thicker forests. Here, the loud whooshing sound of their wings heralds the appearance of these magnificent birds.

Their curious nesting behaviour is very fascinating. The male closes the female into a hole in a tree by creating a wall of mud and keeps only a small, slit-like opening, so that she can poke her bill out for him to feed her until the chicks are ready to fly.

During nesting, the seeds defecated by the female and her chicks collect around the base of the nesting tree. Perhaps this can explain the concentration of certain tree species in patches in a forest. Ficus is one of their favourite fruits, especially when other trees are not fruiting. The hornbill thus aids in the dispersal of ficus seeds, which are a keystone species in the ecosystem. These linkages that one is usually not aware of are vital to the health of a forest ecosystem.

The grey hornbill—*Tockus birostris*—a brownish-grey bird with a large, yellowish-grey, curved bill with a pointed casque over it, is the most frequently observed hornbill throughout India. It is found in forests as well as in agricultural and urban areas. The Indian and Malabar pied hornbills are much larger and are restricted to undisturbed patches of forest.

| 1 | 2 |
|---|---|
| 3 | 4 |

A hoopoe displaying its brilliant crest.

India has nine species of hornbills. It is the state bird of Arunachal Pradesh and Kerala.

Hoopoe; from Gould, 1850.

Common grey hornbill.

## BARBETS

There are 10 species of barbets found in India, of which the best known is the crimson-throated barbet or coppersmith of urban areas, and the small green barbet of the forests and some urban settings. Both are known better by their typical calls that go on and on throughout the day, giving an otherwise silent ambience an audio signal that one forever associates with forest habitats all over the country.

## WOODPECKERS

There are 30 species of woodpeckers in India, of which the golden-backed woodpeckers include four species. The commonest is the lesser golden-backed woodpecker—*Dinopium benghalensis*—which is frequently seen in well-wooded areas throughout peninsular India. It has a distinctive red crown and occipital crest and is partial to large mango trees and old growth forest. The woodpecker's knocking on wood serves a dual purpose. It dislodges insects that hide in the crevices of the bark of trees and creates nesting holes that are safe and inaccessible to predators. The lesser golden-backed mainly feeds on insects and occasionally on ripe fruit and flower nectar. The pied woodpeckers form another group of common woodpeckers, characterized by their black and white patches. Several species in this group have a red patch on the head or the back of the neck.

```
        7
    1     8
    2   4
    3   5
        6
```

The crimson-throated barbet or coppersmith has a distinctive repetitive call.

Green barbet; from Jerdon, 1847.

The Himalayan barbet is region-specific.

Brown-capped pygmy woodpecker with a termite in its beak.

A commonly seen woodpecker in peninsular India is the Maratha woodpecker.

Golden-backed woodpecker.

There are 30 species of woodpeckers in India. This golden-backed woodpecker drums on a tree to flush out insects.

A woodpecker feeding from an *Erythrina* tree.

India's Rich
Faunal Heritage

## ORIOLES

This is a beautiful group of birds, with 11 species found in India. Both the well-known species—the golden oriole and the black-headed oriole—have loud, musical calls. Besides, the black-headed variety mimics the calls of a large number of other species. How mimicry has evolved is one of the enigmas of the natural world. I have heard the black-headed oriole call like a crow, a drongo, a treepie and a variety of other mixed groups of calls, within the span of a few minutes.

## DRONGOES

India has 21 species of drongoes. Among the most pugnacious of birds, the common black drongo is seen in forests, scrublands and grasslands. The racket-tailed is more frequently heard than seen in the forests. When it flies, one is tempted to think that two bumblebees are on its trail. The racket probably acts like a pair of stabilizers, helping it in making rapid twists and turns in flight. All drongoes are insectivorous species that catch their prey while on the wing.

## TREEPIES

The 10 Indian species of these noisy, spectacular birds are found in forests. They adapt to nearly all types of forest patterns and are often one of its more obvious species. The large size, bright colour and long tail give prominence to the bird during any bird-watching experience.

|   | 3 |
|---|---|
|   | 4 |
| 1 |   |
|   | 5 |
| 2 |   |

Golden oriole.

The black-headed oriole is a wonderful mimic and songster. Its call can be heard from a great distance.

India has 21 species of drongoes. The commonest is the black drongo or king crow.

A drongo feeding on nectar.

The black-browed treepie is found in the Himalayan forests.

## CUCKOOS

The Indian cuckoo's call through a deciduous forest is one of the most distinctive and haunting sounds one hears on a quiet morning, echoing over the hills. Each of the 25 species of cuckoos has developed a capacity to fool other bird species into bringing up their young.

In August 1934, MS Suter reported a purple-rumped sunbird being parasited by what was probably a plaintive cuckoo, near the Turf Club in Pune. The editors of the BNHS Journal wrote that this was the first instance recorded. It was known that violet and emerald cuckoos of the Himalayas are parasitic on the sunbirds (Suter, 1945). I have, on four occasions, observed in Pune a sunbird raising the young of plaintive cuckoos that are two or three times their own size. The normal host of the plaintive cuckoo is either the Ashywren warbler or the tailorbird. Why they also use the much smaller nest of sunbirds in Pune, where the usual host is quite abundant, is inexplicable.

How nest parasitism could have evolved and why a bird should give over its eggs for incubation to a completely different species is a fascinating enigma. I have seen koels being chased by crows, which indicates that the koel destroys their eggs. What the crow does not seem to understand is that the koel does this after it has laid its own eggs in its nest. The avidity with which a young koel will follow its foster parents to be fed, while the crow's own young placidly wait to be fed makes, I am sure, the koel's young grow faster than the crow's own fledglings.

| 1 | | |
|---|---|---|
| 2 | | |
| 3 | 4 | |

The Indian treepie.

A male koel enticing a female with a berry.

A male koel. The koel is the state bird of Jharkhand.

A female koel.

## BULBULS

Although there are 42 species of bulbuls in India, we usually see only two of the commonest ones: the red-vented and the red-whiskered species. This bird is evidently highly successful. If one counts the bird species in several of our forests and scrublands, bulbuls are frequently among the most abundant species. I recall sitting in a workshop in Hawaii, at the East West Centre, a few years ago and listening to the calls of a bird that sounded like a bulbul. On confirming this with a local ornithologist, I was told that this species was not Hawaiian, but it had been brought to the island decades ago and had become one of their most abundant species.

### Gold-fronted Chloropsis, Green Bulbul or Gold-fronted Leaf Bird
*—Chloropsis aurifrons*

This is a slim, bright, grass-green bird with golden forehead, purple and black chin and throat, and a curved bill. The female is paler and duller than the male. The juvenile has a small diffused yellow patch on its fore-crown. Pairs or parties of these birds frequent nectar-producing trees such as *Erythrina*, *Butea* and *Bombax*, which are actively pollinated while they are feeding. They hunt for insects and spiders in the foliage where they are well camouflaged. It is more easily heard than seen, and mimics calls of other birds like the bulbul, the drongo, the shrike and the magpie robin.

### Crow Pheasant
This aggressive bird is commonly known as 'Bharadwaj'. It is a great hunter of reptiles, insects and bird eggs or chicks.

| 1 | |
|---|---|
| 2 | |
| 3 | 4 |

Crow pheasant.

A red-whiskered bulbul at its nest.

Red-vented bulbul; from Forbes, 1813.

There are 42 species of bulbuls in India.

## BABBLERS AND THRUSHES

India has about 100 babbler species and 60 thrushes, found in our forests and scrublands. The most common species are the jungle babbler and the common babbler. Both move in noisy family parties, helping each other to locate prey. They frequently huddle together on a branch and preen each other's wings.

Among the thrushes, the Malabar whistling thrush is the most beautiful songster of the Indian forests. No music can enchant one as much as the long melodious song that emerges from the mists, at dawn, in a cloud-covered evergreen forest, with the background sound of a watercourse as it tinkles down the hillslope.

| 1 | 2 | |
|---|---|---|
| 3 | 4 | 5 |
| 6 | | |

A chloropsis pair; from Gould, 1850.

Gold-fronted chloropsis, also called the leaf bird, is found all over India.

Common green bulbul; from Jerdon, 1847.

India has 60 species of thrushes. The white-throated ground thrush is found all over India.

Blue rock thrush; from Jerdon, 1847.

White-cheeked bulbuls are found in the Himalayan foothills.

## FLYCATCHERS

Out of the 63 species of flycatchers found in India, the common ones are the Tickell's flycatcher, which has blue wings, white breast, and a typical call, and the fantail flycatcher, which is identified by its brown colour and its habit of fanning out is tail and calling loudly while foraging for insects in the canopy.

The black-naped blue flycatcher or black-naped monarch is one of our distinctive forest flycatchers, a small bright-blue bird with a whitish abdomen, a prominent black patch on the nape, which forms a short tuft, and a black gorget at its neck. The females are brownish-blue, with grey and white underparts and they don't have black marks.

As deforestation progresses, several forest flycatchers appear to have partly shifted to tree-covered gardens in small towns and village wood lots. With the growth of these towns into concrete high-rise building areas with a low level of foliage, the insectivorous birds disappear altogether.

Typically, flycatchers hunt for insects singly or in pairs and also join mixed foraging parties of other birds. Some species frequent the middle and lower storey of vegetation. Others use the canopy, while a few descend to the ground to catch insects in the detritus.

|   |   |
|---|---|
| 1 | 5 |
| 2 | 6 |
|   3 |   |
| 4 | 7 |

The blue rock thrush frequents scrublands and rocky regions.

Yellow-eyed babbler; from Baker, 1922.

Fantail flycatcher; from Jerdon, 1847.

Black-naped flycatchers.

There are 62 species of flycatchers in India. Of these, the fantail flycatcher is one of the most common.

Fantailed flycatcher feeding its fledgeling.

Red-breasted flycatcher.

| | 2 |
|---|---|
| 1 | 3 |
| | 4 |
| 5 | 6 |

Paradise flycatcher; from Gould, 1850.

Paradise flycatcher; from Smith and Doyle, 1828. The paradise flycatcher is the state bird of Madhya Pradesh.

Tickell's flycatcher; from Jerdon, 1847.

Tickell's flycatcher.

With the degradation of forests, the more adaptable flycatchers are moving into urban gardens.

Verditer flycatcher.

## SUNBIRDS AND FLOWERPECKERS

Nectarivorous birds such as the sunbirds and the flowerpeckers are an important group, as they are major pollinators of the forest system. The tiny Tickells flowerpecker not only pollinates the *Loranthus* parasite, but transports its sticky seeds from one tree to the next, so that it can spread when the flowerpecker cleans its back. Among the 13 species of brilliantly coloured flowerpeckers and 26 species of sunbirds in India, the most frequently observed are the purple sunbird and the purple-rumped sunbird. Sunbirds feed in two ways. They either poke their beak through the base of the flower or get at the nectar by hovering over the flower directly. Watching a pair of sunbirds build their fragile pendant-nests that mimic a cobweb can be a rewarding experience for nature-watchers.

The Nature of Biodiversity in India

| 1 | | 5 | 8 |
|---|---|---|---|
| 2 | | 6 | 9 |
| 3 | 4 | 7 | 10 |

A pair of purple sunbirds at a water tap.

A sunbird at a water tap in summer.

A male purple sunbird just before it turns into its glossy purple colour for the breeding season.

Asiatic sunbird; from Gould, 1850.

A male purple rumpled sunbird feeding chicks.

White-eye.

A Tickell's flower pecker at its nest.

A purple sunbird feeding on *Erythrina*.

Purple rumpled sunbird; from Gould, 1850.

Purple sunbird; from Smith and Doyle, 1828.

## DOVES AND PIGEONS

These species are adapted to grass, scrubland or open forests. The most common is the blue rock pigeon, that has adapted itself to urban areas and cityscapes. It has learned to flock around streets and live on ledges of concrete buildings where it nests.

The common doves of scrubland are the little brown dove and the ring dove. They look for seeds and insect life on the dry sand and strut around in funny zigzag fashion searching for food.

Green pigeons prefer forested tracts and their flocks search for fruiting trees. Ficus is their favourite fruit.

|   | 4 |   |
|---|---|---|
| 2 | 5 |   |
| 3 | 6 |   |
| 1 |   | 7 |

Green pigeon; from Smith and Doyle, 1829.

A little brown dove building its nest.

The emerald dove, one of the most spectacular doves found in India, is the state bird of Tamil Nadu.

Spotted dove.

A little brown dove.

The green pigeon's colouring affords it nearly complete camouflage when it sits among the foliage in the treetops. It is the state bird of Maharashtra and Tripura.

Green pigeon; from Jerdon, 1847.

**Birds of prey are gradually disappearing from India.**

```
    2  3
 1     4
       5
```

1 Brahminy kite.

2 A juvenile black-shouldered kite surveys its surroundings from a tall perching site.

3 An eastern steppe eagle displays its great wing span.

4 A kestrel.

5 A shikra watching its prey before it swoops down on it.

# BIRDS OF PREY AND SCAVENGERS
## VULTURES

Vultures use a large number of habitat types. There are 10 species of vultures. The better known species include the Egyptian or scavenger, the white-backed, the long-billed and the king vultures.

A decade ago I felt that the vultures in the sky were decreasing in number around Pune and other urban areas. None of the well-known bird-watchers believed me. I then began to look at vulture populations outside the urban sector. Here too I observed that the once numerous birds circling in the sky were not as common as in the past. I wondered where they had gone. The well-known ornithologists looked at me with disbelief when I said that the vulture population was on the verge of disappearing.

Vultures, which were once a common sight, have now decreased drastically in number. This is due to feeding on carcasses of cattle that had been treated with Diclofenic.

White-backed vulture.

White-backed vulture in the Rajasthan desert.

Vultures at a carcass in Rajaji.

Pheros chicken at their nesting site.

A large group of white-backed vultures in Pune, 1988.

However, when they did agree that the numbers had begun to fall drastically, they ascribed this to a theory according to which the vultures were being shot by Airport Authorities and the IAF. When I pointed out that they had become less common even in areas where there were no airports, they were completely confused. It is now apparent that there is indeed something seriously wrong with vultures all over India. It has taken only a few years for the drastic fall in their population to become highly obvious. Numbers first fell more rapidly in the southern part of the peninsula and this trend appeared to be spreading gradually northwards. It is believed that this could be due to a viral disease. The current view is that their deaths are due to feeding on carcasses of sick cattle that had been treated with Diclofenac as an analgesis or anti-pyretic.

Interestingly, I have seen the population of sparrows in Pune crash and recover after a few years. One hopes that this is what will happen with our vultures. A few years ago, I had taken pictures of white-backed vultures at a small breeding colony within the Wildlife Institute of India, outside Dehra Dun. Within a year or two they

1 | 2 4
  | 3
  | 5

King vulture photographed in Bandhavgarh.

Do the vultures stand a chance of survival in India?

Egyptian vulture, also called 'Pheros chicken'.

A sick vulture affected by kidney failure as a result of ingesting meat containing Diclofenic.

King vulture; from Gould, 1850.

disappeared. I did, however, find small groups of Egyptian vultures outside Delhi, on garbage heaps in 2000. In 2002, I saw a large number of vultures in Bandhavgarh Wildlife Sanctuary where they seem to be breeding. The group of about 30 or 40 birds included king vultures, Egyptian vultures and white-backed vultures. There were a few in Kanha circling around in 2002. There have been reports of several dead vultures found in the Kanha Tiger Reserve during the last two years.

India has 10 species of vultures, all of them now likely to be under this new threat from which they may or may not recover. The BNHS has included the white-backed, the long-billed and the slender-billed vultures in its list of critically endangered species.

Vibhu Prakash of the BNHS has worked on raptors and vultures for the past 20-odd years. The rapid decline in vulture populations observed by his team is indeed a matter of the greatest concern. Vultures, in all probability, will become extinct in India in the course of the next few years. While I feel that vultures have become extinct locally in most regions outside Protected Areas, there are some birds left in a few of our National Parks and Wildlife Sanctuaries, where a small number are still breeding. Vibhu's work has shown that populations have declined by around 90–95 per cent even in most Protected Areas.

The team of BNHS scientists working on this discovered that in most areas where some nesting is still occurring, a large proportion of the fledglings die. The symptoms appear to be due to kidney failure, dehydration and electrolytic changes, which probably manifest as a drooping neck. Most birds that show this abnormal behaviour die in a month's time. The BNHS now has a captive rehabilitation centre set up in Rajasthan.

One of the important effects of the depletion in vultures is the enormous rise in rotting cattle carcasses in rural areas. The vultures used to clean up the carcass within a short span of time, leaving only clean bones. Today, the major scavengers are village dogs. Since both the white-backed and the long-billed vultures, which used to be seen in hundreds, consumed a large amount of food, the dogs are now having a free-for-all and are probably increasing in number.

The BNHS has excellent vulture data from early 1993, when the raptor survey counted vultures in several Sanctuaries. Jaldapara had 993 in 1993, out of which only eight were left by 2002. Buxa had 300 in 1993 and none in 2002. Kaziranga, which had 390 in 1993, had only 20 birds in 2002. Thus most areas have seen a 90–100 per cent decline in less than 10 years.

In 1978, Robert B Grubh studied the field characteristics of some Indian vultures for JBNHS, Volume 75.

He has written about 5 species:
1. The white-backed vulture;
2. The long-billed vulture;
3. The fulvous griffon vulture;
4. The king vulture;
5. The Egyptian vulture.

He described the vultures on the basis of the plumage characteristics and the colour of bare parts that can be observed on the birds perched or sitting on the ground. He also documented the flight and wingspan of each vulture, to which it can be identified from the ground with diagrams. This data has been used to understand the pattern of bird strikes that damage aircrafts.

## EAGLES

Thirty-one species of eagle exist in India. They are difficult to identify, especially when one sees them soaring high up in the sky. Once one learns their key identification features, watching them is a fascinating experience.

Until a few years ago, one could see eagles even in semi-urban or agricultural landscapes and on garbage dumps. In these situations they are now obviously less common. The species which are more easily identifiable include the white-bellied sea eagle, Bonelli's eagle, the crested-hawk eagle, the crested-serpent eagle, the black eagle, the lesser spotted eagle, the tawny eagle, the golden eagle, the eastern steppe eagle and the imperial eagle.

No sight is as exciting as that of one of these birds of prey swooping down on its quarry from high up in the sky. I have seen an eagle move so rapidly to alter its line of descent as it finally catches its prey, that it is difficult to believe this large bird can be so incredibly agile. The Palla's fishing eagle, the greater spotted eagle and the eastern imperial eagle are considered vulnerable.

In 1987, I spent many days sitting beside a Bonelli's eagle's nest, watching the birds bring up their young. They had become so used to me that they would go on with their routine of feeding their chicks, or tidying up their nest even if I was at a short distance. I can never forget the sight of the first chick trying to fly, ending a long period of being carefully looked after by its parents. The Bonelli's eagle—*Hieraetus fasciatus*—is a slender-built, medium-sized, resident eagle, inhabiting lightly wooded hill ranges.

pesticides that reach them through their food chain. The spotted owlet is still our most frequently seen owl. It is a small, grayish-brown bird, with tiny white spots, seen around villages, towns and cities. These birds inhabit all types of landscapes except heavy forests and are distributed throughout the country.

The Indian barn owl is mid-sized and has a flat, heart-shaped face with a ruff around it. It is seen in varied landscapes from urban areas to forests. It is beneficial to the farmer as its chief source of food is rodents.

The Indian great horned owl—*Bubo bubo*—and the brown fish owl—*Bubo zeylonensis*—are less common. The former is easy to identify by its large size and its prominent 'horns' of long feathers. It feeds on small animals and is an important control for field rats and mice. The brown fish owl prefers dense foliage near water-bodies and feeds on fish and other aquatic life. It is increasingly endangered and is now mostly seen in Protected Areas.

The forest owlet is the rarest of our owls, rediscovered after 113 years! Studies by the BNHS have shown that it is present in an east-west belt in north Maharashtra and Madhya Pradesh. It prefers teak forests and has an extremely small and fragmented population.

## OWLS

Owls are birds I have been observing with great interest for years. As an apex bird species of the night, our owls have no parallel. It is strange that there has been so much superstition surrounding them. I have been involved with saving owls from being driven out of their nests for years by people who considered them inauspicious. In fact, having owls around the house could rid the place of rodent pests.

There are 63 species of owls in India. Of these, the Indian barn owl—*Tyto alba*—and the spotted owlet—*Anthene brama*—were common urban species till a few decades ago. These are now becoming rare due to loss of roosting sites and toxic

The owl's hunting expertize is based on its incredible eyesight, a feature of its large eyes, and its acute sense of hearing. It is thought that its flat, disc-like face is a parabolic device that concentrates sound to its ears. The owls are thus able to home into their prey by the sounds that they make. Owls are a major control mechanism for rodents in ecosystems ranging from forests, grasslands and agricultural areas to towns and cities. They nest in hollow trees. When the ancient massive banyan trees were felled to widen roads in Pune, a large number of displaced barn owls and great horned owls were found dead or injured. Till this happened, one hardly ever noticed that there were so many of these great birds of the night in the city.

The forest owlet was officially recorded after 11 decades, in the 1990s, by a team of BNHS scientists from several locations.

| 1 | 2 | 3 |
|---|---|---|
|   |   | 4 |
|   | 5 | 6 |
|   | 7 | 8 |

Spotted owlet at its nest.

The Eurasian eagle owl has a large wing span.

A Eurasian eagle owl.

A barn owl peers out of its hole.

Barn owlets at their nest a few days before learning to fly.

A Eurasian eagle owl near its nest among a group of rocks.

Barn owl.

There are 63 species of owls in India.

| 1 | 3 | |
|---|---|---|
| 2 | 4 | 5 |
| | 6 | 8 |
| 7 | | |

The brown fish owl is one of the few owls that hunts by day.

A young Eurasian eagle owl. Owls have been persecuted as they are considered inauspicious by some Indians.

A Eurasian eagle owl among the Marble Rocks of the Narmada River.

Owl; from Gould, 1850.

Barn owl; from Gould, 1850.

Horned owl; from Smith and Doyle, 1828.

Red scops owl; from Jerdon, 1847.

Scops owl; from Gould, 1850.

## SWIFTS, SWALLOWS AND MARTINS

The 17 species of swifts, 14 species of swallows and nine species of martins in India all seem to have extensively decreased. Once hundreds hawked for insects over grasslands and flew over every water-body in their rapid to and fro flight pattern. Urban areas, which had bungalow-type houses, had large numbers nesting in their tiled roofs. The present pattern of high-rise buildings does not give them suitable apertures and overhangs to build nests. Insecticide is a likely reason for their fall in numbers, as all of them are only insectivorous.

### Edible Nest Swiftlet—*Collocalia unicolor*

The edible nest swiftlets build nests by using only their saliva. These nests are used in Chinese food and medicine, and consequently over-exploited. Nests fetch 2–4000 dollars per kilogram. This ranks the nests as the most expensive food item in the world.

In the Andamans, using local experts as guides, Ravi Sankaran of SACON found 286 active caves containing swifts, of which edible swiftlet colonies were present in 249. The total number of nests counted was about 4600. Local collectors harvest nests every two to four days. It is estimated that only three to five nests per season can be harvested if the output for the market is to be maintained at sustainable levels. At the present rate of collection, only 0.3 per cent of all nests had eggs even at the peak of the nesting season. Partially

built nests sell at Rs. 3000 to 5000 per kilogram. Implementing protection appears to be next to impossible on these remote islands. Ravi Shankaran suggests using the techniques known to local people in Indonesia by training nest collectors in the Andamans. This would bring about alternative ex situ breeding colonies, which could be used to harvest the nests. The supply could well reduce the pressure on the few wild colonies that are left on the islands.

In Indonesia, the edible nest swiftlet trade is based on setting up breeding colonies within houses which have roofs in which the birds nest. The nests are harvested sustainably, so that each household maintains a colony of these birds without depleting their population. This is done by collecting the eggs of the edible nest swiftlet from the wild and introducing them into the nests of non-edible swiftlets in local houses. A colony of the edible nest swiftets is thus developed in the nest collector's own home.

Ravi Sankaran worked extensively on edible nest swiftlets through a SACON project and has been able to get local support to breed this highly endangered species in the 1990s.

|   | 3 | 5 |
|---|---|---|
| 1 | 4 |   |
| 2 |   |   |

Crested tree-swift incubating its egg in its tiny nest on a precarious branch.

Swallow; from Gould, 1850.

Crested tree swift; from Gould, 1850.

Swift; from Gould, 1850.

There are 17 species of swifts, 14 species of swallows and nine species of martins in India.

## CROWS

Crows are the most adaptable of the bird species, continuing to change their behavioural patterns along with man. There are 13 species of crows in India. In the last three or four decades, crows in urban areas have started using steel wire instead of twigs to build their nests. Clearly, there is a shortage of twigs and an abundance of steel wires, which crows, like most mechanical engineers, possibly prefer.

## MYNAS

In this large group of 27 species, the commonest are the common myna, the brahminy myna, the jungle myna, the pied myna and the bank myna. The linkage between the pollinating efficiency of the jungle myna's tuft of feathers on its beak—that fits perfectly into a pollinating position of the *Erythrina* tree—and the shape of the flower is an interesting evolutionary feature.

## WARBLERS

About 150 species of India's 2546 species of birds are warblers. This accounts for 5.9 per cent of the bird species in India. Several of these are known to the casual bird-watchers as 'LBJs', or 'little brown jobs'. They are, in most instances, difficult to differentiate in the field. Often they are brown splotchy birds that flit around in scrub, grassland and reed beds.

The hill myna is one of India's great song birds. It is the state bird of Chattisgarh and Meghalaya.

Mynas include several species some of which are uncommon.

White-headed myna; from Jerdon, 1847.

Ashy wren warbler.

Tailor bird nest; from JBNHS, 1890.

There are 150 species of warblers in India and they constitute five per cent of all bird species. Tailor birds are one of the commonest warblers.

## GRASSLAND AND SCRUBLAND BIRDS

The birds of the open grasslands and scrublands are adapted to living on the ground. There are species that live on the abundant insect life of these habitats, as well as on worms and other invertebrates. They include lapwings, plovers and coursers. A number of species feed primarily on grain, such as munias, partridges and quails. These are now increasingly adapted to living on crops. The birds of prey comprize those that are specific to open plains, such as the black-winged kite, the kestrel and the white-eyed buzzard. Eagles use both grassland and forested habitats. Changing these dry-land habitats into irrigated farmland is leading to a serious shrinkage of this rich and highly specialized habitat. On the Deccan Plateau in Maharashtra, I could, until the 1970s, drive along any road in the rural areas and see a raptor sitting on at least one of every four or five electric or telephone poles. Now, one cannot see a raptor after crossing even 20 or 30 poles. Of course, the poles have multiplied in the last two decades or so, but it is evident that there is a serious fall in raptor populations in the grasslands. The reason is probably the bio-magnification of pesticides in the bodies of these apex species. This affects their breeding and can even lead to their death.

The hunting technique of the black-winged kite is perhaps the most interesting. The bird hovers in the sky like a helicopter, rapidly beating its wings while its beautiful red eyes scan the grassland below. It does this repeatedly, systematically surveying the area. Once it spots its prey, it drops like a stone, lifts its prey with dexterity and flies off in one long, fast, graceful dive.

1

2

3

Eastern steppe eagle.

Black-winged kite.

Sand-grouse are found in semi-arid and desert ecosystems.

## BUSHCHATS

There are 21 species of bushchats, insectivores of the grassland ecosystem. They perch on the top of shrubs or small trees, surveying the grass for all sorts of insects.

## BAYAS

Our common baya or weaverbird builds colonies of complex nests out of strips of grass, or crops that they cut away and weave into their nests. They are migratory birds, the males arriving earlier than the females to build their nests. Females, which arrive later, select the males that are most active and have built the stronger nests. One male may have a harem of females in the colony, one after another.

The rarest of our bayas is the beautiful bright-yellow Finn's baya, a great favourite of Dr Salim Ali, who made several excursions to look for it and finally rediscovered it. It is probably trapped extensively for the pet trade and its habitat has been rapidly converted to industry and sugarcane. This baya builds a globular nest without a tube, on a bare tree. Its nestlings are extensively preyed on by house crows.

## MUNIAS, FINCHES AND BUNTINGS

The 15 species of munias are easy to differentiate. The only brightly-coloured species is the red munia. All the munias are netted for the pet trade in large numbers. I have occasionally bought and released them. The rise in price is not an effect of increasing demand, but rather an indicator

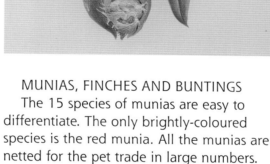

Salim Ali's early work in the 1950s led to a greater understanding of the behaviour and breeding biology of the baya.

Baya; from Forbes, 1880.

Male weaver bird or baya, building its nest.

Tailor bird at its nest; from Gould, 1850.

There are 15 species of munias in India, most of which are found in grasslands. They are extensively trapped for the pet trade.

Rose finch from the Himalayas. This is one of the 56 species found in India.

The crested bunting has a musical call.

Red munia.

of a fall in their wild populations. The 56 Indian species of finches are all caught for the caged bird trade. Buntings, which include 21 species, are more difficult to identify. The spectacular crested bunting is a beautiful bird and more frequently seen among rocky areas and hills.

### RAPTORS OF THE GRASSLANDS

The birds of prey are apex predators that swoop from the sky to capture their prey. The order includes birds which are grouped into eagles, kites, falcons and allied species, all of which are increasingly under threat in India. All of them are slow breeders and take great pains to raise their chicks.

Rishad Naoroji and other BNHS scientists worked on a nationwide Raptor Project that led to an understanding of their precarious status.

### FALCONS

There are 21 species of falcons in India. The more frequently seen falcons in any semi-arid tract include the shikra, the sparrow hawk, the kestrel, the hobby, the merlin, the peregrine, the shaheen and the Lagger falcons.

On several occasions I have watched a shikra twist and turn at high speed through the branches of forest trees, towards its unseen target, till a fluff of feathers bursting from its prey tells the tale of its assault on the unsuspecting bird. The precision notwithstanding, there are occasions when the quarry gets away unscathed. During and after

the attack, every other bird sends alarm calls ringing through the forest. After the dive, there is a stunned silence and then slowly, very gradually, the birds begin to sing again.

### KITES

Of the six species in India, the most common is the pariah kite. This is the raptor that has adapted to all human habitats. It thrives most effectively on the garbage of the urban sector and on agricultural areas. Once these birds shared the thermal currents with vultures, eagles and storks. Today, in most thermals, the only bird circling the sky is the common kite.

The black-winged kite, seen frequently on telephone wires, has the dexterity to remain motionless in a light breeze with a minimal fluttering of wings. On other occasions it beats its wings rapidly before diving for its prey.

### HARRIERS AND BUZZARDS

In India, there area six species of harriers and six species of buzzards. The pale harrier, the marsh harrier and the pied harrier are the commoner harriers among the six species found in different habitats. A common buzzard is the white-eyed buzzard that lives in grasslands of various types. These birds live on rodents, insects, reptiles and frogs. The marsh harrier is partial to catching fish and frogs, but also hunts an occasional waterfowl.

| 1 | 2 |
| 3 |
| 4 |

Buntings include 21 species.

Falcon; from Gould, 1850.

Black-winged kite; from Gould, 1850.

Birds of prey; from JBNHS, 1900.

| 1 | 4 |
|---|---|
| 2 | 3 |

Raptors of the grassland are apex species. Their population has fallen drastically due to the extensive use of pesticides in areas converted from grasslands to agricultural lands.

Bird of prey; from Jerdon, 1847.

Shaheen falcon; from Jerdon, 1847.

Gould's birds of prey are masterful works of art. During this period, falconing was a popular sport and there was a great interest in the hunting abilities of different species of raptors.

| 1 | 2 |
|---|---|
|  | 3 |
| 4 | 5 |

Common sand-grouse; from Hume and Marshal, 1880.

Sand-grouse; from Hume and Marshal, 1880.

Painted sand-grouse; from Hume and Marshal, 1880.

A yellow wattled lapwing guarding its chick.

Yellow wattled lapwing sitting on its nest.

## PARTRIDGES

There are 23 species of partridges in India, of which the most familiar are recognized by their distinctive calls. The common grey and the painted partridge are two examples. The painted partridge's call sounds like 'chick chick chick chicker'. The calls of the common grey—*Francolinus pondicerianus*—differ in the male and the female. The male's call is a loud 'kateetar-kateetar-kateetar', while a female's reply is 'tee-tee-tee' or 'kila-kila-kila'. Partridges call from a vantage point to proclaim the extent of their territory to the neighbours. A call usually sets off the neighbour, which is followed by neighbour after neighbour across the open plains. Both these common species are found in peninsular India, in habitats consisting of dry, undulating open country and thorn scrub, and both have adapted to cultivation. They live in pairs or family parties of four to eight birds, on a diet formed mainly of weed seeds and grain, grasshoppers, termites and maggots. They are now much less common than in the past because of extensive poaching both by shooting and trapping, and they are seriously threatened by habitat loss. The most remarkable call, however, is that of the hill partridge, which echoes through the grassy hill slopes of the Himalayan foothills. The painted partridge is more prominently marked than the common grey.

Black partridge at sunrise in Corbett.

Black partridge; from Smith and Doyle, 1828.

Olive partridge; from Gray, 1830.

Grey partridge; from Hume and Marshal, 1880.

One of the commonest species is the grey partridge, which frequents thorns, scrubs and cultivated tracks.

### Great Indian Bustard
—*Choriotis nigriceps*

The Great Indian bustard is one of our most magnificent birds. Its enormous size, strong flight and fascinating behavioural pattern make watching this bird an unforgettable experience. The adult alpha males can weigh up to 14 kilograms; females are much smaller and weigh only three to six kilograms. This great difference in size between the sexes is peculiar to bustards. My first sighting of a big male in 1981 was at a little known village called Nanaj, close to Solapur. My father knew this area well and in the 1940s had seen enormous herds of blackbuck and a large number of bustards here. When I visited the area, it had not yet been declared a sanctuary and there were no restrictions on driving over the dirt tracks through the bajra and jowar fields with areas of open grazing land, which is the bird's favourite microhabitat. We moved through the open grasslands in my small Standard Herald, bumping the low differential on the rocks several times. On my return, I spoke to the Forest Department, and gave them my pictures for their publications on the promise that a sanctuary for the bustards would be notified at Nanaj. When this finally happened it was in the shape of a totally unviable giant paper-sanctuary, which I insisted was not necessary. As no one knew their precise distribution and range, a whole taluka and parts of adjoining talukas had all been included in this unviable sanctuary, covering some 8500 square kilometres. I felt this had no rational basis. History has proved my feelings right. The inappropriate decision led to one conflict after another between the local people and the Forest Department. Ironically, I was later asked to investigate this, and was appointed in a committee to rationalize the boundaries of the sanctuary more than 20 years later. The sanctuary has now been reduced in size, from over 8500 square kilometres to about 400 square kilometres in multiple patches.

There are four species of bustards that are endemic to India and Pakistan. The Great Indian Bustard was once a popular game-bird and was extensively shot. In addition, it was a favourite of Middle-Eastern rulers who used it as a target for

| 1 |
|---|
| 2 | 3 |

Jungle bush quail.

Asiatic bush quail; Gould, 1850.

Bush quail; from Hume and Marshal, 1880.

### QUAILS

The 25 species of quail range from abundant to rare, and include both generalist and specialist species. They generally live in small parties, a protective mechanism against predatory activity. When a flock of quails is disturbed, they fly off noisily in a highly coordinated burst in different directions, startling even the stoutest predator. I myself have been repeatedly startled by the noisy burst of birds from a thick patch of grass at my feet. Quails are still being killed and snared all over the country. They are sold illegally and even reach the tables of five star hotels where they are stamped as being legally obtained from captive-bred stocks of exotic Japanese quails.

falconing. The BNHS Journal quotes *Oriental Sporting Magazine* which recorded the killing of 961 bustards between 1809 and 1829 near Ahmedabad by a single shikari. At present only five to ten birds are recorded here occasionally. The residual population is thus one per cent of what was shot 200 years ago.

Blanford had reported that the bustard was extensively distributed from Punjab to Madurai and eastwards up to Sambalpur. By 1878, Fairbank had already begun to notice that it was becoming rarer.

In 1946, Shri Yuvraj of Jasdan wrote in the JBNHS that the Great Indian Bustard was vanishing from Kathiawar, even though local rulers had previously prohibited its shooting. He advocated urgent protection measures and suggested that without them the bustards were likely to become extinct. The editor's note in the 1952 Journal of the BNHS points to the fact that the numbers had been seriously depleted by habitat loss, and recommends 'most urgent and effective action.'

In the 1940s and 1950s, my father had seen a number of bustards a few kilometres east of Pune. By the 1960s, they had all but disappeared. Farid Tyabji, writing in the journal of the BNHS in 1952, recalled having seen 200–300 at a single location near Nagpur. In 1966 it was already thought to be rare. In the 1980s, BNHS estimates ranged between 650 and 900 birds in India. In 1990 this estimate varied between 770 and 1920 birds. In the last 10 years, however, the population appears to have crashed and present estimates show that the population could be less than 500. It has even disappeared from Bustard Sanctuaries such as Karera and Sorsan.

From an analysis of these reports it appears that during the 1950s the population began to crash. The BNHS took up its studies on the Great Indian Bustard only in 1981, leading to an increasing concern regarding the plight of this species. Several sanctuaries were then created to protect its dwindling habitat, which led in turn to an increase in

other species as well, like the blackbuck. However, this has led to hyper-dense populations of blackbuck that damage crops around the Protected Areas. Thus the strategy used to protect the Great Indian Bustard has led to a complex set of conflict issues with local farmers, largely because of the hyper-abundance of blackbuck. In 1981, I first observed a large bustard in Nanaj. It was the alpha male in the area, and it characteristically displayed its neck feathers and its wings to other birds several times during the next couple of hours. He had selected a low mound close to the favourite, undisturbed grassland patch as his territory. He was strutting along the highest point in the otherwise flat plain and displaying continuously. He extended his enormous gular pouch which hung from his neck more than halfway down to the ground. Tail erect and wings lowered, he made a strange sound. This mound remains a favourite display area of alpha males even 20 years later.

Great Indian bustard; from Baker, 1921.

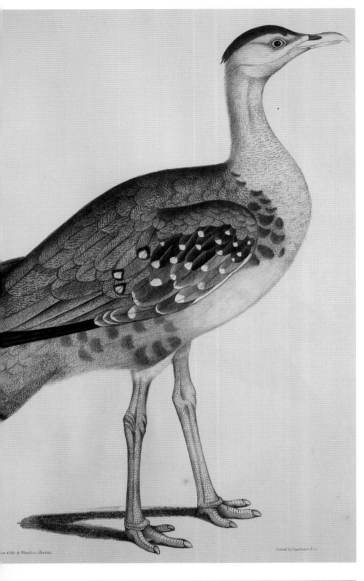

Great Indian bustard; from Gray, 1830.

Great Indian bustard; from Hume and Marshal, 1880.

A great Indian bustard at a water hole. The great Indian bustard is the state bird of Rajasthan.

The decline of the bustard has been noted in nearly every state where it once lived. The last one I saw in 1997—in the semi-arid grasslands where they were frequently seen four decades ago—was a single bird which I observed near Pabal, just outside Pune. Others have reported sighting three birds in different parts of the Pune District, in 2000 and 2001. These sightings show that bustards occasionally stray widely from their well-defined home ranges around Nanaj, which is 240 kilometres from Pune. Extensive bustard surveys were undertaken by BNHS in the 1980s. Rajasthan was the only state with a viable estimate between 500 and 1500 birds. The estimated countrywide total population was only between 770 and 1920 birds. Considering its extensive range and the scattered, but highly localized, fragmented nature of its residual habitat, this bird is now under very serious threat.

At Sadasari, in the Desert National Park, in 1987 I saw two males display to each other at the waterhole. The larger male had a more prominent pouch. When the smaller one began puffing out his pouch and raising his tail, he was firmly evicted from the water's edge. The big male then folded his legs and sat there imperiously before beginning to drink, as if to demonstrate that he owned the waterhole. He kept an eye on his retreating rival but permitted large flocks of sandgrouse to continue to drink from the pond at his feet.

The bustard's major source of food comprizes grassland insects such as grasshoppers and beetles. The bird frequently joins a herd of feeding blackbuck, which disturb insects that attract the bustard's attention as it stalks and catches them when they resettle. It also catches reptiles and feeds on grain and *Zizyphus* fruit. BNHS scientists have found that *ber* can form as much as 75 per cent of its diet during the fruiting season.

Shamita Kumar, who is doing her PhD at BVIEER with me on the semi-arid grasslands of Maharashtra, has worked on several aspects of the bustard's habitat, to identify appropriate management techniques for grassland Protected Areas. The work has demonstrated that grassland Protected Area management must be different from that used in Forest Department Kurans that are developed for increasing the grass biomass, a strategy that in no way retains the grassland ecosystem's naturalness. As the bustard's major food item is insect life, the BVIEER team compared a burnt and an unburned patch of grassland for insect abundance over three years. While the burnt grass regenerated fairly rapidly and was green soon after the fire, the insect population was rebuilt more slowly, taking over two years to attain its full complement of insect species in adequate numbers. Burning grasslands extensively as a management practice may thus benefit the blackbuck, by producing a rapid flush of grass, but is inappropriate for bustards, which need insects!

Karera and Ghatigaon in Madhya Pradesh were declared Bustard Sanctuaries in 1981, through Dr Salim Ali's personal intervention with the Government. BNHS recommendations led to the notification of Kundanpur in Rajasthan and Rollapadu in Andhra Pradesh in 1985. Over 13 Sanctuaries in India had been established by 1988 to afford protection to the bustards. Interest in grassland fauna suddenly found a place in conservation circles. Several conservation gains were made due to this newly-found enthusiasm.

Asad Rahmani has worked with bustards for well over 30 years. Presently Director of the BNHS, Asad is constantly preoccupied with bustard conservation, which has taken him over thousands of kilometers into the semi-arid and desert tracts of India. He believes that the Great Indian Bustard's range is only 10 per cent of what it used to be a couple of centuries ago. Asad estimates that about 50 per cent of its population has been lost in the past 10–15 years, even though this is the period when awareness of the imminent extinction of this species became apparent. He points to continual habitat loss, mismanagement of grassland Protected Areas and increasing conflicts with local people, as wild ungulates such as blackbuck and nilgai increase with protection.

The under-representation of grasslands in our Protected Areas network is still an important concern. In Maharashtra, among the several well-known threats to the bustard, there is the added threat of rapid change in land-use. The increasing development of sugarcane farming and sugar factories has destroyed vast tracts of bustard habitat. So-called wasteland, which is in fact a rich semi-arid grassland ecosystem, has been rapidly replaced by intensive forms of land-use. The residual patches of natural grassland are small and cannot support adequate populations of its flora and fauna. Can the bustard survive the relentless onslaught of development?

## COURSERS

The coursers are primarily grassland and scrubland species. There are three species of coursers found in India. The Indian courser is a distinctive, sleek, long-legged bird, which can camouflage itself by remaining perfectly still. It is a strong flyer and is seen singly, in pairs or occasionally in a small flock of six to eight birds.

### Jerdon's Courser

Presumed extinct in the early 1900s, the Jerdon's Courser was rediscovered by Bharat Bhushan of the BNHS in 1986, in the Lankamalai hill ranges at Cuddapah in Andhra Pradesh. It is primarily nocturnal, which is why it had not been spotted for several decades. Local people, however, knew all along of its existence. This courser feeds mainly on termites. Bharat worked for years to get this species protected and finally succeeded in saving one of our rarest birds, when the area where it was located was made into a Protected Area at the behest of the BNHS. In 2002, the BNHS team detected three new places, some distance from the original areas identified by Bharat Bhushan in 1986.

Indian courser; from Gould, 1850.

The Indian courser is a fairly common bird of grass and scrub country.

Bharat Bhushan of the BNHS rediscovered Jerdon's courser after a gap of eight decades, in Andhra Pradesh in 1986.

1 | 2
3
4

Yellow wattled lapwing at its nest.

Great stone plover.

A yellow wattled lapwing.

Swallow plovers—small Indian pratincole.

## PLOVERS

Among this large group of grassland birds, there are several fascinating species with clearly defined habitat needs. They live either primarily inland, often close to water, or on the shoreline of saline aquatic ecosystems. Of India's 23 species, the most common plover of the dry area is the red-wattled lapwing, commonly known as the 'did-you-do-it' bird. It is identified by its call, when it protests angrily after being disturbed. The yellow-wattled lapwing is less common and has a high-pitched, softer call.

In 1984, I observed an unfamiliar flock of birds flying rapidly over the Rankala tank, just outside Kolhapur. I was with a group of bird-watchers who insisted they were black-winged stilts. As they were fast

## LARKS

Grasslands are full of birdcalls, especially during the pre-monsoon breeding period. Many of the songs are those of larks, of which India has 39 species. The well-known species, seen almost in all grasslands, are the crested lark, identified by its crest; the distinctive ashy crowned or black-bellied finch-lark, which is the only species with a black belly; and the rufous-tailed finch-lark, which has a bright rufous patch better seen in flight. Several larks are specific to a region and are not easily identifiable. While recording birdcalls for the BNHS cassette, I was listening to a crested lark and adjusting the sound. Suddenly I heard the distinctive call of a yellow-wattled lapwing and a red-wattled lapwing. With headphones on, it is difficult to judge where the sound is coming from without swinging the microphone from side to side. It took me a while to realize that the multiple calls were all made by the crested lark. I recorded a variety of bird calls, all very real, coming from this tiny mimic during the next five or six minutes! Several larks have a song that goes with a superb aerial display, in which they hover and then dive steeply, descending finally.

strong flyers and were circling the tank in a very tight flock, I felt that they must be some other species. I took a series of pictures and showed them to Dr Salim Ali, who quipped, 'Let's consult a "good" book.' As I wondered which book he was referring to, he walked up to his shelf and pulled out a volume of his own book! Flipping through the pages, he confirmed that the birds I had seen were indeed crab plovers. As this species is a seashore bird, which is normally found only north of Mumbai and restricted to the coast, he insisted that I immediately sit and write a 'note' for the BNHS journal. This was how he encouraged amateurs to write in scientific journals. He then went on to explain the enormous value of the data that is to be found in the *Notes* section of the BNHS Journal. Years later I realized that there is a fund of information in these short notes that is not documented in major scientific papers.

1

2  3

Black-bellied finch larks.

Spur-winged plover; from Gray, 1830.

Crested lark with an insect in its beak.

## MAMMALS

There are 390 species of mammals in India, accounting for 7.6 per cent of mammals worldwide. Indian mammals are linked through evolution to those of Europe, South-eastern Asia and Ethiopia.

Large mammals include a majority of our 'glamour species' that wildlife tourists hope to see during a visit to a National Park or Sanctuary. Among the carnivores, the great cats, especially the tiger, are what attract people to a Protected Area. Most large mammals were hunted by shikaris until the mid-1900s. As a result, they remained extremely shy till Protected Areas were notified and wildlife tourism increased after the 1970s. In many Protected Areas, it is now possible to watch an animal going about its routine activities undisturbed by human presence, an exciting experience indeed for the serious wildlife enthusiast. Animal behaviour alters in response to interactions with people. In Protected Areas in which there are large numbers of visitors and the protection levels are high, animals have learnt to tolerate human interference. It is now possible, for example, to observe for prolonged periods of time tigers which would have vanished in a flash at the sight of a human a few years ago. Surprisingly, leopards are still shy of people. Wild elephants will tolerate familiar researchers, but have frequently chased me off for no apparent reason.

Most mammals are fairly specific to different habitats. Deer are primarily forest species, while antelope-like animals prefer grasslands and semi-arid tracts. Mammals such as otters are highly dependent on fish and live near aquatic ecosystems. Many of our mammals are more active during early morning and at sunset; many species are highly nocturnal and are rarely seen during the day. For the average tourist it is the big cats that are most fascinating. But to a discerning wildlife-enthusiast, an animal like a pangolin or ratel is a mammal worth seeing.

It is likely that there are several species of small rodents and bats that have yet to be identified. New bat species that have not been identified till recently are still being found. These interest the serious wildlife researcher.

The Fauna of British India—Mammals was written by RI Pocock (1939–41) and has been published in the volumes Mammalia I and Mammalia II.

JR Ellerman (1961) worked on Mammalia—Rodentia.

TC Jerdon published Mammals of India in 1867.

WT Blanford wrote Fauna of British India—Mammals between 1888 and 1891.

Captain J Forsyth wrote on mammals in his book, Highlands of Central India, in 1889.

RI Pocock wrote for the second edition of The Fauna of British India—Mammals, in 1901.

Dunbar Brander wrote his book Wild Animals of Central India, in 1923.

SH Prater wrote The Book of Indian Animals in 1948.

EP Gee's The Wildlife of India was published in 1964.

### CATS

The great cats of India include the tiger, the leopard, the snow leopard and the lion. The smaller species include the Felix chaus, or the jungle cat, and the much less frequently seen caracal, the leopard cat, the golden cat and the fishing cat. There are also some extremely rare cats such as the clouded leopard and the rusty spotted cat.

Whereas the tiger prefers thicker jungle and requires larger tracts of intact forests, the leopard can survive in less dense jungle and even in scrubland, where it adapts to living on small prey and livestock. These great predators were once found nearly all over India, except in the arid zones. In the upper reaches of the Himalayas, the apex of the food pyramid is occupied by the elusive snow leopard. In the arid, open grassland region there once lived the Indian cheetah, the predator of the blackbuck and of the chinkara of the plains. Divyabhanusinh Chavda, who has studied the cheetah's sad tale of extinction, found that the last known sighting of the cheetah was from Korea, in Madhya Pradesh in 1947, when three of them were shot.

A kitten of the very rare rusty spotted cat.

Strangely, one keeps hearing of cheetah sightings in Madhya Pradesh even today! All of them are unconfirmed. The ghost of the cheetah still lives on, half a century after the last one was shot. The lion was a common animal during the Mughal times, and was found in the environs of Delhi. Its favourite habitat extended throughout the thorn forests of Western India and the plains of the Ganga. It is now restricted to only one Sanctuary in the Gir Forests. All the lesser cats, such as the common jungle cat and the beautiful leopard cat, are now seen less frequently. Of the several species of lesser cats found in India, I have had a special interest in a very small species called the rusty spotted cat, which is extremely rare and perhaps on the verge of extinction. Caracals occupy the dry belt of semi-arid land and are very uncommon. They too could well be close to extinction. I have seen a pair only once, in Sariska in 1987.

All the cats are apex species in the ecosystems in which they live. As major predators, they are at the end of several food chains that constitute the web of life of the ecosystem. Since a food pyramid can support only a limited number of predators, tourist sightings of these species are less frequent and thus much more exciting than sightings of the herbivores forming their prey base. When a big cat is on the prowl, the jungle comes alive with alarm calls. Monkeys give alarm calls from the treetops and begin to crash from branch to branch. They carefully watch the predator, which one can spot by observing the direction in which they persistently stare. The chitals and the sambars start giving alarm calls as soon as they spot the predator stalking them. The rest of the forest sounds are hushed. Birds stop calling, and one feels the palpable sensation of imminent danger. And while the tiger quietly stalks its prey and makes its final rush, the forest erupts into a crash of hooves as the chitals run helter-skelter in every conceivable direction and dive into the cover of the forest. The jungle then returns to normal whether the tiger has made its kill—or not. There are many aborted charges before the tiger catches its prey and brings it down.

Divyabhanusinh Chavda chronicled the history of the cheetah from ancient times up to its extinction in the country in the 1940s (Divyabhanusinh, 1996).

| 1 | 2 |
|---|---|
| | 3 |
| | 4 |
| | 5 |

The tiger is India's national animal.

Tiger; from JBNHS,1930.

Lions which were once found all over India are now restricted to Gir.

*Felix chaus* is the most common lesser cat in India.

The jungle cat is highly adaptable and is found in many forest ecosystems.

## Tiger—*Panthera tigris*

The thrill at the sight of this most magnificent predator has to be experienced to be believed. One invariably feels a prickle up one's spine when a tiger is close, a primeval sensation elicited in every human being by the sheer power of this animal.

A big male tiger appears much larger than one expects. It can exceed three metres in length, from the nose to the tip of the tail, and it can weigh around 200 kilograms. It is incredible that this enormous animal can be close at hand in a patch of grass, and at the same time remain completely camouflaged. Individual variations in markings help in identifying tigers. Individuals are also identified by the size of their pugmarks. Plaster casts of pugmarks are used extensively to study tiger populations, by identifying individual tigers that one can never see. In the recent past, camera traps have been used to photograph tigers along forest trails. There have been serious debates among experts regarding the appropriate methods for a census of the tiger populations. Traditionally, the Forest Department has used the specific characteristics of a tiger's pugmarks, such as their size and configuration, to differentiate one animal from the other. Several scientists have, however, felt that this is too subjective and that using portraits of tigers taken with camera traps is a more accurate method. Recent work by the Wildlife Institute of India seems to suggest that in experienced hands, the accuracy of the pugmark method is likely to be in the region of 92 per cent.

It is believed that the tiger came to India from the colder climes of Asia, in the prehistoric period. The habitat suited to the tiger is thus one where there is enough ground cover to protect it from intense heat. In summer, tigers frequently take to water to cool off. Though this species is our most well-known predator, we still do not know enough about its needs in all the different and varied habitats in which it lives. The tiger has adapted to the conditions at the foothills of the Himalayas, in Terai forests, in the deciduous forests of the plains, the dry thorn forests, the wet evergreen forests, and the mangrove swamps

of the Ganges Delta, and it has even been reported occasionally up to an altitude of 3000 metres in the Himalayas. Its wide— but now highly fragmented—distribution thus includes a remarkably large variety of ecosystems.

An idea of the former abundance of tigers in India and Nepal can be estimated from the enormous number of tigers shot by several shikaris during the 19th and 20th centuries. Schaller, in his book *The Deer and the Tiger* (1967) recounts some of these tragic figures. Gordon Cumming shot 73 tigers in one district along the Narmada River in 1863 and 1864. He once shot 10 tigers in five days, along the Tapti River. Forsyth shot 21 tigers in 31 days in Uttar Pradesh. The British monarch George V and his party shot 39 tigers in 11 days in Nepal in 1911–12. Rice shot or wounded 158 tigers, including 31 cubs, in Rajasthan between 1850 and 1854. The Maharaja of Nepal and his guests shot 433 tigers, as well as 53 Indian rhinoceros, between 1933 and 1940. Colonel Nightingale shot over 300 tigers in the former Hyderabad State. The Maharaja of Udaypur shot at least 1000 tigers during his lifetime. The Maharaja of Vijayanagaram had shot 323 tigers by April 5th, 1965. The Maharaja of Surguja shot 1150. The tiger population crashed.

Corbett estimated that only 2000 tigers survived in India by the mid-1940s. In 1964, Gee placed their number at only 4000. This indicated the need for a strong conservation programme if the species was to survive in India, leading to the implementation of Project Tiger and a gradual increase in its population. In its early years, the programme was supported by Indira Gandhi, who personally kept track of the tiger population.

The tiger population in India, which was estimated to have been well over 50,000 in the early part of this century, had thus fallen to a meagre 1800 by the 1960s. The establishment of Project Tiger in 1973 resulted in a gradual upward trend in their population. The 1997 census showed that there were 3500 tigers, of which 1500 were in Tiger Reserves and 2000 outside. The sudden rise in tiger poaching, for its bone used in Far Eastern traditional medicine, has once again brought its

population down to dangerously low levels. The opening up of China and more porous borders in the region has increased the demand and thereby boosted the highly profitable illegal trade. In the late 1990s this new trend sent shivers up the backs of most conservation people. Numbers were falling. The Government began to take notice of this only in 2005, when a press-report that all the tigers from Sariska had been poached sent shock waves through conservation circles. Prime Minister Manmohan Singh made statements to the effect that protecting the tiger was now a crucial issue. The country was woken up to the fact that we have failed as a nation in protecting our national animal.

The tiger is primarily a hunter of the night. However, it frequently hunts by day. Stalking its prey with great skill, it makes a final deadly charge. Its prey primarily consists of large herbivorous animals, such as deer, nilgai and wild boars, as well as small prey such as porcupines and langurs. When driven by hunger it is also known to stalk birds, fish, and reptiles. In the absence of wild prey, it perforce takes to killing cattle, bringing it into conflict with local communities that live in nearly all our Protected Areas.

Ulhas Karanth has estimated that adult males need 2000 to 2500 kilograms of meat per year and females 1850 to 2300 kilograms per year. This would mean that each tiger requires about 40 to 50 large prey animals per year, or approximately one per week. Females with cubs could need 60 to 70 prey animals per year to feed her cubs, which means that they need one large herbivore every five days. It has been estimated that tigers can catch only about 10 per cent of the total number of prey present in an area. Thus one tiger needs a prey base of about 400 large herbivores in the area to get an adequate amount of food. This has been estimated by Ulhas Karanth, who has worked intensively on tigers in Nagarhole, for over 10 years. While this could vary substantially in different ecosystems and for a different composition of prey species, it is evidently a very sensitive balance.

The tiger population in a Protected Area is related to a large number of factors. Tigers carefully scent-mark the boundaries

of their own territory with urine. This is to make other tigers avoid their areas. This indicates that large Protected Areas would have a larger number of tigers. A quick look at the tiger populations in the Tiger Reserves shows that small Reserves of less than 800 square kilometre have less than 50 tigers. However, large Reserves do not necessarily have a larger population of tigers, which indicates that the size of the area is not the only limiting factor that controls their numbers. The other limiting factor could be the abundance of their prey species. However, this also does not correspond with tiger populations, as prey may be concentrated in only a certain part of the habitat. It is a combination of all these factors—and the superadded effect of poaching—which is responsible for the number of tigers in an area.

A tigress produces about three cubs every two and a half years. Recent work suggests that tigers in the wild have an average life span of only three to five years, as young animals have a high mortality rate. Many tigers, however, probably live for about 15 years.

Tigers from different areas appear to selectively choose different preferred prey species even when the other species are available. The favourite prey of tigers in Nagarhole are gaurs and sambars. In Kanha, the favourites are chitals and langurs. These differences not only reflect the abundance of different prey species, but also the characteristics of the habitat. For example, while in most areas tigers stalk their prey from a short distance and then make a final, rapid leap, in Ranthambhor at the edge of the forest, they chase the sambars from a considerable distance while they are feeding in the lake.

Tigers frequently have large home ranges, but in Protected Areas where prey is abundant they have much smaller ranges. Thus, the creation of a viable Protected Area for tigers must take into account the density of prey animals and their distribution.

Tigers need heavy shade to sleep in and pools of water, as they frequently spend the very hot part of an afternoon submerged in water. They are also strong swimmers.

The use of tiger bone is driving tigers to the brink of extinction.

A tiger cleaning up after a meal.

The tiger population which had crashed to about 1800 in the 1970s rose due to the success of Project Tiger. However it has declined again due to the increase in the illegal export of tiger bones to China and other East-Asian countries for its use in traditional medicines.

Two young tigers rest under the shade of a tree.

Tiger scratching itself. Even the king of the jungle is disturbed by the tiny creatures that inhabit his kingdom.

A fresh tiger pugmark provides a feeling of anticipation.

Tiger family crossing a forest opening.

Tigress with her cubs resting in a *nala* course.

A tiger closely watching the approach of the author's elephant from the bank of a *nala*.

In terms of conservation of this superb species, India implemented a very successful Project Tiger over nearly two decades. This collapsed in the last few years, as we have not been able to generate effective action at the global level to prevent the growing trade in tiger bone. No local efforts can reverse this rising trend in tiger poaching in India. Policing is simply not feasible. It is difficult to get a clear picture of the exact nature, extent and utilization of tiger bone and other tiger products. This illegal trade is similar to the trade in drugs, and what is known is probably only the tip of the iceberg. AK Jha compiled a list of the uses of tiger bone in 1993. Chinese medicine uses it for a variety of purposes such as ulcers, joint and muscle pain and fever. Twenty-five Chinese drugs are said to include tiger bone in some form or the other. Among the more fantastic uses, tiger bones are believed to ward off evil spirits when placed on a rooftop. The penis and other parts are reputed to be aphrodisiacs. In Vietnam, bones, skin, teeth and claws are used for a different set of ailment cures, including a commonly used medical balm. In Laos the nose is used as a sedative and the teeth are used for dog bites and fever. With so many unconfirmed uses, the pressure on the tiger is enormous. Poaching cannot be effectively prevented, for with each kilogram of tiger bone priced at over 400 US dollars, the gains for a poacher far outweigh the risk of getting caught.

Among the many tigers I have seen in the wild, the most memorable was a tiger known to people in Bandhavgarh as Charger. He was the dominant tiger that roamed the central area where there was a high density of prey and he ruled the forests of this Sanctuary for several years. He was known to have made innumerable false charges at jeeps. KK Singh recalls how he experienced the first of his charges several years ago. Later, this characteristic behaviour became a well-known pattern in Bandhavgarh. When I saw Charger in 1997, he was ageing but still magnificent.

The largest tigers I have ever encountered were two incredibly powerful males, one in Manas Wildlife Sanctuary and the other in Kanha. The tiger in Manas, which I saw one early morning,

appeared gigantic. He was known to the Forest Staff but was seen infrequently. The Kanha tiger was the one filmed by Belinda Wright and Stanley Breeden for their well-known film *Land of the Tiger*. He was a powerful, photogenic animal in his prime and a major source of excitement for visitors to Kanha in the 1980s. Of the many tigers I have seen, I will never forget a small one-year-old female cub in Bandhavgarh, who repeatedly snarled at the visitors whenever someone moved in the jeeps parked around her. I have now begun to dislike these tiger shows. They not only cause a disturbance level that changes the tiger's behaviour, but also prevent people from having a true wilderness experience with the tiger behaving naturally.

There have been several champions of the cause of tiger conservation in India during the recent past. SP Godrej frequently had a black tag on his sleeve which he wore for several causes, one of which was to bring home to people the 'sad plight of the tiger.' The Tiger Cell at WWF-I in Delhi, formerly led by Dr MK Ranjit Singh and now under Shri PK Sen, has taken several positive actions for tiger conservation. Valmik Thaper of Ranthambhor Foundation has supported the cause of tiger conservation in a variety of ways throughout his life. Though there has been much work done, the threat to our most magnificent predator grows relentlessly. Can we let the exciting roar of the tiger be silenced forever in the jungles of India?

**Leopard**—*Panthera pardus fusca*

Often incorrectly called a panther, this is our commonest great cat. Its superb rosettes camouflage it beautifully. My first close encounter with a leopard was on the outskirts of Pune. My father's driver, Genu, was a great hare-hunter and would walk off on foot for miles with me as his torchbearer. With his 12-bore, we approached, from a distance of a few metres, what he thought was a hare behind a shrub. A leopard emerged with a great 'umph' and charged past me in one clean bound to disappear into the nearby lantana scrub. I have never forgotten the fleeting image as it rocketed past me.

A leopard watches suspiciously from a clearing in a forest.

On April 9th, 1888, JD Inverarity read an interesting note on the tiger at the Society's meeting. It was related to the tiger from Western India, its habitat use and food patterns (Inverarity, 1888).

A large number of shikaris made it possible to get a better understanding of tiger behaviour, turning it into the most well-documented and celebrated species in the country. It also became the species on which several books were written in the 1980s and 90s.

In 2005, it was reported that all the tigers in Sariska Tiger Reserve had been poached. Initially, most people thought this was on overstatement. This just could not have happened in a well-known Tiger Reserve in a few months. Then the rumours began to seem justified. In April 2005, the Prime Minister, Dr Manmohan Singh appointed a Tiger Task Force. The members were Sunita Narain, Samar Singh, Valmik Thapar, HS Panwar and Madhav Gadgil who are currently also members of the National Board for Wildlife.

I once came across a large male leopard in Gir, one that was completely invisible behind a straggly bush barely 10 metres away, until it bounded away into the forest. On several occasions I have seen leopards vanish into thin air once they enter even relatively thin grass or scrub.

Leopards adapt to a wide variety of habitats, including agricultural areas. Their adaptability extends to prey species. I was travelling in a jeep one starry night in the Dang forests. As we bumped across a small bridge over a nearly dry riverbed, I saw a slight movement in the riverbed below. On crossing the bridge, I slowly turned the jeep around. Right in front of me there was a leopard apparently unconcerned about the glitter of the jeep's headlights. He moved slowly along the edge of the water and swiped at something before he realized he was being watched and bounded off into the nearby forest in a flash. The next morning, I stopped by on the bridge and walked down to the riverbed. The story in the sand and mud near the edge of the river was written in a long trail of leopard pugmarks. En route, he had left behind the remains of several crabs. A leopard with a taste for crustacea! Or was it the serious decrease in prey species forcing the big cat to find alternate small prey? Domestic animals are the most common and the easiest animals to stalk and catch. Cows, goats and village dogs have become a part of its staple diet in the Dangs.

Its ability to adapt to a variety of habitats brings it into frequent conflict with people. Its stealth is remarkable. As a young college student, I have been present in a rickety machan built on the ground to wait for a man-eater that had reportedly killed 11 children belonging to a wide circle of villages in the Dangs. We tied up a goat as bait. Nothing happened all night—or so we thought. At dawn, Thomas, the local expert and shikari who had bagged many leopards over the years, and who had sat in the hide with us and coughed quietly all night, showed us a set of very fresh pugmarks a few metres from the hide. We had not heard the leopard even though the ground was strewn with large, dry teak leaves. Unseen and unheard, he had probably been watching us and the goat

we had tied as bait. He had decided not to make a kill.

The increasing conflicts between humans and leopards are directly related to factors such as the expansion of human settlements into the leopard's habitat and the loss of its natural prey species. In the Sanjay Gandhi National Park at Borivalli, now engulfed by Mumbai's growing urban sprawl, the number of people mauled and killed by leopards is increasing.

There are areas in the Garhwal where the incidence of livestock lifting, as well as man-kills by leopards is inordinately high. During the 1990s, the Wildlife Institute of India reported as many as 62 people killed from a cluster of villages in a small section of these hills. As a result, 40 leopards were killed by irate villagers, or at least the dead animals were discovered under circumstances that pointed to them having been killed.

In 2000 a leopard walked into Pune, penetrating several kilometres into the heart of one of its most densely populated areas of Erandwana. I first heard about this at 9 am from Aparna Watve, a botanist who is a keen wildlife enthusiast. Her neighbours had called her grandfather around midnight to report they had seen a leopard in her small garden. The old man thought it was a prankster and put the phone down. In the morning, a number of other neighbours confirmed the sighting. She asked me if it was really possible, and wanted to know if it was safe for her nephew and niece to play in the garden. Not really believing this story, I told her in a light vein that it would be safe as by now the leopard must have already had breakfast, as leopards are early risers! That afternoon I got phone call after phone call, as the animal was sighted near a school, a church and finally in a large pipal tree at the edge of a slum. Later in the day, the Forest Department requested me to come to the site. When I reached the area, the roads were jammed with parked cars. Crowds of people had gathered around the tree. The animal was terrified. It carefully hid among the leaves of the pipal tree, above hundreds of shouting people who were unwilling to go away even when the police threatened them with a lathi charge! Firecrackers were set off in the

neighbouring slum. Finally, after dark, he descended to the ground, was darted by a tranquilliser gun and sent off to a forest 100 kilometres away. Such episodes are bound to multiply in the future.

In the recent past, leopards have begun to take shelter in sugarcane farms. During the last couple of years, about 60 to 70 leopards have been trapped by the Forest Department outside the Bhimashankar Wildlife Sanctuary in Maharashtra, which is now surrounded by sugarcane farms. Managing this conflict has become a serious issue for the Forest Department.

In spite of these interactions and close encounters, there is very little work on this superb species. All the attention has been hogged by the larger cat—the tiger. The old records on leopards all come from the pens of shikaris who documented their habits; several of them noted the way in which leopards scare langurs, which drop to the forest floor in their crazed excitement and are quickly dispatched.

Every time I see a leopard, its handsome rosettes make me realize what an incredibly beautiful animal it is. Indeed, as beautiful as the tiger.

**Snow Leopard**—*Uncia uncia*
Peter Pallas first described the snow leopard in 1779. Its habits and status have, however, remained essentially a mystery despite the fact that in recent years several scientists have worked on this elusive species living on steep slopes and crags in the Himalayas. Its favourite prey species is the bharal or blue sheep of the Himalayas. R.S. Chundawat, who has worked recently on the snow leopard, estimates that to support 50 snow leopards, a Protected

Snow leopard; from JBNHS,1935.

Area should include 1275 square kilometre of habitat, with some 2200 Bharal as prey. Living as it does in the remote, snow-covered mountains, we still need to know more about its status in different parts of the Himalayas.

This elusive animal is adapted to living in the cold Himalayan snows. It moves up and down the mountain range seasonally, synchronizing its movements with the migration of blue sheep, which form its chief prey. The Wildlife Institute of India has had a major project to understand its behaviour and the conclusion was that only two per cent of the snow tiger's food consists of livestock.

### Asiatic Lion—*Panthera leo persica*

My first experience with the lions in Gir left me rather disappointed. They were obviously used to a large number of tourists even in those days. One has now got used to the idea that even large predators such as tigers in some of our Protected Areas have become accustomed to cameras clicking, video cameras whirring and noisy children, but this was not the case in the 1970s, and the semi-tame, placid-looking lions left me feeling that this was like a zoo. But the lions in Gir are known to be dangerous and unpredictable. The lion was India's national animal until the 1970s, when it was decided to change our flagship species to the tiger.

The Asiatic lion has a scantier mane than its African counterpart, a fuller coat, a longer tassel of hair at the end of its tail, and a more pronounced tuft on the elbow joints. The mane varies from light yellow to dark buff. The cubs have ill-defined spots or stripes. The average length of the adult, from the nose to the tip of tail, is 2.75 metres, which is a shade smaller than a big male tiger.

Once distributed over the whole of northern and central India, as far south as the Narmada, lions frequented all the thinly-wooded areas with stunted trees and an undergrowth of shrubs mixed with open grasslands.

MA Wynter Blyth examined the distribution of lions for the BNHS in 1948. He noted that considerable numbers had been observed in several areas in 1822, reported from Saharanpur, Ludhiana,

northern Rohilkhand, Moradabad and Rampur. In 1847, they were still found in Sagar and around the Narbada. In 1866, they were recorded near Allahabad! In 1931, there were still some lions found in Haryana. Within 200 years, their widespread distribution has shrunk to a single Sanctuary—the Gir.

In 1935, the number of lions in the Gir was reported to be below 100 (Cadell, 1935). By the mid-1940s, the once widespread Asiatic lion had vanished from other southern Asian countries and from the rest of India and was found only in the Gir forest of Gujarat. Lt Col LL Fenton described the gradual disappearance of the lion and sightings of lions outside the Gir in 1909. In a paper in Volume 19 of the JBNHS, he suggested that for better preservation of the lion, their indiscriminate slaughter in the Gir should be prevented. He suggested that 600 square miles of the Gir should serve as a Sanctuary for the lion as well as for other wildlife.

Its population in the Gir, which had dwindled to less than 30 animals, has gradually risen to around 304 in 1995 and 330 in 2002. Several lions are now straying outside the Protected Area, leading to serious conflicts.

The single relict population in the Gir would have become extinct if it weren't for the efforts of the rulers of Junagadh, who protected it as royal game. A single population in a restricted area is a precarious situation for any species. It can be lost forever through an epidemic or some other catastrophe.

The Gir lions are known to be cattle lifters and have frequented the Maldhari settlements for decades. The Maldharis have been known to kill lions occasionally, by poisoning their kills. Livestock had become the lion's major source of food by the 1960s if not earlier. Paul Joslin, a Canadian researcher, pointed out that the estimated 6000 wild prey of the lion in the Gir could not sustain the lion population within the 1500 square kilometre of protected habitat. SP Sinha found that there was a gradual change in the lion's diet, from 75 per cent domestic and 25 per cent wild prey in the 1960s, to a 50-50 percent situation by the 1980s. This shows

| 1 | | 4 |
| 2 | | |
| 3 | | 5 |

A lioness and her cub at dusk.

A lion stalking its prey.

The members of a lion family show a great deal of affection for each other.

Two lions carefully watch for the approach of the prey.

The lion is the state animal of Gujarat.

that their natural prey base, mainly chital, had grown. Ravi Chellum, a scientist at the Wildlife Institute of India, has recorded a complete reversal in the diet of the lions in the mid- to late-1980s, from what he had observed in the 1970s. Scat analysis revealed that the lion's major prey species shifted to wild ungulates, estimated by him to be around 75 per cent. Domestic livestock, however, still constitutes 25 per cent of their diet. His radio-telemetry studies on radio-collared lionesses in the Gir have shown that they have home ranges of about 85 square kilometre in summer and 67 square kilometre in the monsoon, but as the area used changes with the different seasons, the total home range required by a lion could be in the region of 200 square kilometres for males and 120 square kilometres for females.

A census of the lion population in Gir in 2001 reported that about 50 were living on the periphery of the National Park, an indication that Gir's capacity to support the present population is now inadequate. Translocation to an alternate habitat has become an urgent issue, not only because of the need for a second breeding population, but to prevent further dispersal of lions into agricultural areas surrounding Gir.

There has been a long controversy about the need to relocate a few lions to some alternate site, so that there can be at least two locations in case of a natural disaster hitting Gir. The alternate site suggested at present is in Madhya Pradesh, but the Government of Gujarat refuses to give up 'its lions' to another state. The project has thus been on hold for several years.

A proposal by the Gujarat Government to shift some of the lions to Barda in Gujarat instead of the Palpur Wildlife Sanctuary in Madhya Pradesh, is yet to materialize.

NB Kinnear described the past and present distribution of the lion in south-east Asia in 1920 in the JBNHS, Volume 27. An extract from his description makes interesting reading even today:
'There is no evidence to show that the lion inhabitated Afghanistan or Baluchistan within historic times, but it was formerly found in Sind, Bahawalpur and the Punjab, becoming extinct round Harina in 1842. It was however extinct in Sind earlier and the last record showed that it was shot near Kot Deji in 1810. A single record was documented of one lion being killed in the Palamau district, Behar and Orissa in 1814, but whether this was merely a straggler is not known. In 1832 one was killed at Barado while further north it was comparatively common round Ahmedabad in 1836. The occurrence of the lion in Cutch is doubtfully recorded. The lion probably was found in Cutch at one time but the records are not satisfactory. Lt. Dodd mentioned that Burns about 1830 wrote that lions as well as tigers, bears and wolves were found north of Bhooj but that none except the last was found, a solitary lion was shot near Bela on the Runn which was supposed to have been a straggler from Gujrat. In Rajputana they became extinct about the same time and in Jodhpur by 1872. The last four are stated to have been shot near Jagewantpura about 1872. The lion is still found in small numbers in the Gir forest but occasionally stray over the border into neighboring states where it is not long before they are shot.'

In 1931, RI Pocock tried to establish the former distribution of the lion in Europe and Asia in the JBNHS, Volume 34.

Ravi Chellam of the Wildlife Institute of India began his work on lions in the Gir in 1985. While one of the main objectives of this long study was to lead to trans-locating some of the lions to another safe home, nothing has happened yet. Does this majestic animal have a future unless this is done?

### THE LESSER CATS
**Jungle Cat**—*Felis chaus*
This is the most familiar small cat of the Indian jungle. It lives on small prey and is mostly nocturnal. Surprisingly, I once saw one stalk a group of chitals and make them scatter. Perhaps it was after a small fawn which I could not spot. Once a very common animal that could be seen around villages, it has now all but vanished from most agricultural lands.

Lesser cat; from Gray, 1830.

Jungle cat on the prowl.

### Leopard Cat—*Felis benghalensis*

The leopard cat is a small, very secretive cat which one rarely sees. My last sighting was in Ukhimath, near the Kedarnath Sanctuary, on the periphery of the town. Its beautiful fur makes it a target for poachers, and its beautiful dark rosettes are more distinctive than those of the leopard.

Leopard; from JBNHS, 1935.

### Rusty Spotted Cat—*Felis rubigionosa*

Jerdon wrote that, 'This very pretty little cat frequents grass in the dry beds of tanks and occasionally drains, in the open country and near villages, and is said not to be a denizen of the jungles.' In 1846 he had a pet rusty spotted cat which had become quite tame. Humayun Abdulali reports that he shot a rusty spotted cat in 1941, in Suriamal, 70 miles north of Bombay, where he recorded having seen them several times (Abdulali, 1945). I became interested in the conservation of this species in the 1960s when I read E.P. Gee's book, which emphasized its rarity. I scoured the Dangs at night with the Maharaja of Bansda who had seen them on several occasions and we did spot three or four of them over the next three or four years. Twenty years later, repeated visits to the Dangs left me fearing that habitat loss could have wiped out this beautiful little wild cat. I convinced Dr MK Ranjitsinh, who was then in the Ministry of

Environment and Forests, that we should try to look for it again and work on its habitat needs. As I was a guide for PhD at the School of Environment Sciences of Pune University, Sejal Worah took this as part of the topic for her PhD thesis. Thanks to a small grant from SANCF and later from the MoEF, we began to understand more about the habitat needs of various species that were threatened in this region. A surgeon colleague, the late Dr SV Bhave, had a small Beechcraft from which we studied the fragmentation of the forest and documented and photographed the mosaic of vegetation and different patterns of land-use. These were the early days of Geographical Information Systems (GIS) and this led to the first GIS study done in India for ecological monitoring. It helped to successfully locate the rusty spotted cat four or five times, by surveys at night which Sejal did over the next two years.

Several years after our work, a Forest Officer in Gujarat photographed a rusty spotted cat in Gir. Shri Walke, another Forest Officer in Maharashtra, found two young ones in a rat trap in Borivalli. While the project created an awareness of this species and showed that it is more widely distributed than we thought, it is so rare that it is probably on its way out forever.

The rusty spotted cat was observed in the 1940s by Humayun Abdulali. EP Gee thought it extinct in the 1950s, but it was reported by the Maharaja of Bansda in the 1960s. EK Bharucha and S Worah had sightings of it in the Dangs in 1989. Following this, it was reported from a few sites including Gir and Borivilli.

### Cheetah—*Acinonyx jubatus*

The Indian cheetah was once the apex predator of the grasslands of India. It is strange that local people frequently call the leopard a cheetah in several parts of the country. This shows that the memory of a particular species remains in the minds of people for a very brief period. Nowadays, most people do not know the difference between these two very different species. Divyabhanusinh Chavda, one of

> IN MEMORY OF THE CHEETAH—1968. HOW MANY OTHER SPECIES WILL FOLLOW?

India's well-known wildlife enthusiasts, has worked extensively on the history of the cheetah. Divyabhanu chronicles the story of the disappearance of the cheetah in his detailed study done over several decades. He writes that cheetahs were tamed in India about 2000 years ago, and that by 12th Century CE, using them for hunting blackbuck was an established royal sport. Thousands of cheetahs have been removed from the wild over the centuries. Emperor Akbar had 1000 cheetahs, as documented in his memoirs. He is reputed to have collected 9000 during his reign of 50 years. Apart from depletion in the wild, they are difficult to breed in captivity. Their grassland habitat was the first to come

A kitten of the rusty spotted cat caught in Sanjay Gandhi National Park near Mumbai in August 2006.

The rusty spotted cat is one of India's rarest lesser cats—Dangs, Gujarat, 1989.

under the plough as a result of increasing human population. Since they run down their prey, with the vanishing of grasslands, it became difficult for them to hunt successfully.

In the last 200 years, they were extensively hunted. The British paid bounties for their destruction. Cheetahs were killed in 1918–19 in the Mirzapur District. Three were shot in Melghat in 1890, and one in 1894. A female and four cubs were shot in Rajkot in 1894 (Editors JBNHS, 1935).

In 1947, the last three cheetahs were shot. In 1952, KM Kirkpatric reported the sighting of a cheetah in the Chitoor District in the JBNHS, Volume 50. In 1968 we have the last credible sighting report from India.

A superb predator, which could have been saved, had there been a high level of public interest, has quietly disappeared from the grass and scrubland of our country forever.

### CIVETS

Several species of civets are found in India. Some, like the small Indian civet and the palm civet, are found all over the country. Others like the Himalayan

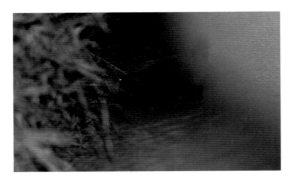

palm civet and the binturong of North India are found only in localized areas. The brown palm civet is found only in a few areas of the southern part of the Western Ghats. One was, however, caught in a marketplace in Pune, about a decade ago! It is supposed that it jumped out of a vegetable and fruit truck that was being unloaded in the marketplace. It is possible that some of our rare nocturnal small species still survive, unseen and unheard, in a few small pockets in thickly forested areas. We need far more detailed surveys to locate them if conservation measures are to be instituted.

> RI Pocock, FRS (1933), observed various species of civet cats in Asia. He wrote on their general distribution and gave a brief description of their habits in the JBNHS, Volume 36.

### CANIDS

The wolf, hyena, jackal, fox and the dhole or wild dog represent the dog family in India. Of these, jackals and foxes are still found over most of the country, although their numbers appear to have dwindled during the last decade. The population of wild dogs has not been carefully estimated. In British times it was considered a serious danger to populations of 'game' species. Its large numbers must have contributed to a serious loss of those animals that the shikari wanted to maintain in appreciable numbers. A price was thus paid to kill the beautiful wild dogs, which led to a serious depletion in their population. It

now appears to be recuperating in a few Protected Areas. While the dhole is a forest animal, jackals and foxes are also found in scrub country and near human habitation. The wolf has become very rare. In the few pockets in which it still survives, it has become increasingly dependent on livestock. Hyenas act as scavengers and carrion eaters and play an important role in the ecosystem. They frequently feed on tiger or leopard-kills, after the big cats have left. I once saw a dead half-eaten hyena near a leopard's kill in the Dangs, which could well have been due to a mistimed approach to eat from the kill, while the legitimate owner was still in the vicinity. However, such occurrences are rare. I have also observed a rather terrified, but obviously very hungry jackal steal a bone from the remains of a tiger kill in Sariska. Canids play multiple roles in several ecosystems. Foxes and jackals are important control mechanisms on the population of highly voracious, super-active and rapidly breeding rodents, whose super-abundance would otherwise destabilize the intricately balanced web of life. The wolf is the only predator which controls over-abundant blackbuck populations in grassland Protected Areas. The dhole pack is said to drive out even tigers from the area in which they live. Their role as apex predators is frequently not as obvious as that of the great cats. Several are increasingly threatened. There are very few good studies on canids done in India, except for those on wild dog, by Johnsingh and the ones on wolf, by Jhala.

### Wolf—*Canis lupus*

The colour of the Indian wolf is extremely variable, ranging from grey to buff. In the plains, it has a sandy or fawn coat, stippled with black. Wolves from Tibet, Ladakh and the northern slopes of the Himalayas may have almost black coats. Himalayan wolves have a longer coat than those of the plains and develop a dense grey or bright buff undercoat in winter, to protect them from the intense cold.

The wolf varies in height from 65 to 75 centimetres. Bare open lands are favourite habitats of the wolves, but they are occasionally also encountered in thick scrub or in wooded areas. They are distributed over the region from Ladakh and parts of Kashmir to the desert zone, and are patchily found in the dry, open grasslands and scrublands of peninsular India. In the Deccan Plateau, each pair excavates several dens on hill-slopes among rocky outcroppings. I have also seen dens dug in the sand dunes of the Desert National Park and near Jaipur in the small sanctuaries notified for protecting the blackbuck. In most regions, they hunt both by day and by night. They hunt either in small groups or alone, preying on sheep, goats, blackbuck, chinkaras, hare, other small rodents and even birds.

They are known to attack people occasionally, perhaps when driven by extreme hunger or due to aberrant behaviour caused by unknown reasons. There is a possibility that some attacks have been caused by diseases such as rabies. However, these episodes seem to occur only sporadically and then stop completely for many years. Himalayan wolves probably feed mainly on rodents and smaller animals in summer and switch to wild sheep and goats in winter.

---

*Opposite page*
Palm civet.

---

A palm civet which was run over by a vehicle.

The wolf is a rapidly disappearing species. In many parts of India the wolf has become highly dependent on shepherd's flocks.

In 1982, SP Shahi described the status of the wolf in India in Volume 79, JBNHS. His map showed that there were eight isolated pockets across the country, the largest being in Rajasthan. Shahi also described their aberrant behaviour in occasionally attacking children. He described their increasing dependence on sheep and goats which is well documented by several researchers. Jhala's work on the wolf in Velavadar brought about a greater understanding of its behaviour in the 1990s. The author's work on wolves in Phaltan, Maharashtra, has demonstrated that they migrate along with shepherd's flocks for over 50 kilometres.

The pack is a small family party of two to nine individuals. Each pack may make a kill once every three or four days. Dr Jhalla of the Wildlife Institute of India has radio-collared wolves in the Vellavader Sanctuary in Gujarat and found that their home ranges are enormous. Lone wolves in the Wildlife Institute of India study had ranges that extended up to 227 square kilometres! Packs, however, have a range averaging half this size. Territories are smaller in areas where there is a higher density of blackbuck, their most frequent prey.

This animal is now highly endangered, both due to habitat loss and a serious decline in the population of its larger wild prey. Its dependence on livestock has brought it into serious conflict with shepherds, who wage a relentless war on its residual population. Its skin is also traded for its fur and it is probably still hunted as a trophy.

The current estimate of the wolf population in India ranges from 1800 to 3000, which is perhaps lower than our current tiger population. I have been seriously concerned about the fate of one of the last breeding populations of wolves on the Mann Plateau near Phaltan in Maharashtra. Here, the Dhangar shepherds frequently corner and kill wolves as they attack sheep. Five years ago, I asked Wasim, a young schoolboy from Phaltan, to find out more about the wolves. He found that they followed the Dhangars' flocks over their long migration routes. One pack went all the way to the Western Ghats, while another went eastwards as far as Osmanabad! While migration of wolves is well known in North America, where they follow the movement of their wild prey, wolf migration has to my knowledge never been documented before in India.

My earliest chance encounter with a wolf was in the 1980s, when I tried to remove thorny branches and rocks that local shepherds had placed at the mouth of a wolf den near Phaltan. After I had stuck my arm deep into the den and cleared it of the brush that villagers use to burn the wolf alive, I turned to pick up my camera to take a picture. As I turned back to the den, I found myself face to face with a wolf. It stiffened and looked straight into my eyes. I froze instinctively. We stared at each other for several seconds. Then in a flash it turned, dashed up the ridge and disappeared. It cleared forever, in my mind, the myth of wolves being dangerous. That animal could have torn my arm off in seconds when I put it into the den! Ever since then, wolves have greatly fascinated me. They are incredibly intelligent animals. Their ability to disappear into their sparsely covered open habitat, vanishing into thin air, is astounding. I have seen a wolf lope gracefully behind a group of small rocks on the side of a hill and just vanish! It took me a while to appreciate how the wolf manages this disappearing act. Once behind cover, instead of emerging where one expects it to, the wolf runs up towards

wolf whelps in there! I put my camera into the den and blindly took several pictures. They all turned out to be a bit out of focus, but one can just make out the tiny cubs. While this ten-minute episode was in progress, we had thought the adult wolves must be out hunting. But when we had finished, we found that the alpha male, a thin, tall animal, had been carefully watching us from the crest of the hill. As soon as he saw that we had spotted him, he moved off quite openly. It appeared that he wanted us to chase him so that our attention would be diverted from his cubs. Next day, the wolves moved the cubs to another nearby den and we placed Forest Guards to watch over them until the cubs grew up. A year later, the big alpha male I used to see frequently was probably killed by shepherds. My friend Bon Nimkar followed the progress of the cubs for several years. Unless we compensate for sheep lifted by the wolves periodically, the Dhangar will continue to kill these beautiful animals.

In 2005, the conflict between wolves and shepherds in this area worsened. Every few days there are reports of wolves killing sheep. We are now attempting to get the sheep insured against wolf kills.

### Jackal—*Canis aureus*

The colour of the jackal's coat varies according to different seasons and different localities. It is mostly grey and has patches of light buff on the shoulders, ears, and legs. Jackals are distributed throughout India and can adapt to almost any landscape, from humid forests to dry open plains and are even found in the desert. I have seen one chasing flamingoes on a saline marsh in the Marine National Park in Gujarat! They are found at the foothills of the Himalayas, but are most frequently encountered in the plains and among low, hilly tracts. They are also found on the periphery of cities, towns and villages. They are less frequently observed now around urban landscapes, as there are few open woodlots around major cities and towns. They also frequent cultivated areas, where they shelter in holes in the ground, among old ruins, or in dense thickets in grass or scrub. They usually move about at dusk and retire at dawn, hunting alone or in a

the crest of the hill, carefully keeping the rocks in line with the person it is running away from, until it disappears over the hilltop.

I once found an apparently empty wolf den in Phaltan. Hearing a slight sound, I tried to look inside. As the opening was too small, I let my daughter Jeroo, who was then six or seven, look inside the den with a torch. She excitedly counted seven young

Wolf on the prowl.

A large alfa male guarding its den.

group of two or three animals, and have also been known to hunt in a small pack, chasing young deer or antelope. They feed mainly on small animals as well as on carcasses, offal and fallen fruit such as ber. Near human settlements, they frequently depend on garbage. Jackals make a long-drawn, eerie howling sound at dusk and I recall most vividly hearing them sing choruses outside the forest guesthouse in Bharatpur. The Wildlife Institute of India has studied jackals by using radio-telemetry in the grasslands of Gujarat. This has shown that they have a home range of about 15 square kilometre. While the ranges of individual animals overlapped considerably, the core area of each jackal's range was exclusively used by a single individual.

### Indian Fox—*Vulpes benghalensis*

A short, slender animal, with a bushy black-tipped tail, the Indian Fox is greyish in colour, with rufous-brown legs. Those in the Himalayan foothills grow a thick winter coat.

They are distributed throughout India, from the foothills of the Himalayas to Kanyakumari, over a variety of landscapes ranging from wasteland and cultivation to rocky hills and scrub country. They live in burrows that they dig in open ground or under shrubs. Typically the burrow has several openings, some blind, others communicating with a central chamber, 60 to 90 centimetres below the ground. The fox's tail, which frequently trails over the ground, is carried horizontally when walking slowly. When trying to escape,

foxes run rapidly in zigzag. The tail is held vertically to help it balance as it twists and turns at high speed. Its call is a chattering bark, or a sharp yelp, repeated three or four times.

I once got to observe a fox that lived in a small shallow depression at the edge of a contour bund in the Rehakuri Blackbuck Sanctuary. It usually lay along the length of the depression in full view, but one could only spot it if one knew where to look. I was out taking pictures with Dr MK Ranjitsinh, who was keen to photograph blackbuck. As we approached the bund, I asked him if he wanted to take a picture of a fox. He looked at me as if I were crazy, but got his camera ready. I told him that if he stayed where he was a fox would run past him in a few minutes. I walked behind the foxhole quietly. The fox, however, saw me approaching, gave me a long stare and dashed towards the place where Dr Ranjitsinh was standing. It passed so close to him that I doubt if he was able to get a picture at all! The fox lived there for three or four years and I could predict what he would do and where he would hide if I got too close. He soon learned to ignore me if I was quietly watching blackbuck.

One of the reasons for fox poaching is the attraction of its tail for people. Taxi drivers and truckers often hang the tails behind their windscreen. The tails look so much more attractive when the foxes wave them in the air, twisting them from side to side, meandering with great agility through the scrubland. The late Mr. Humayun Abdulali of the BNHS and Mr. Shaikh of the Forest Department once went around Mumbai, several years ago, arresting people who had fox tails hanging in their cars. This led to a reduction in the number of tails in taxicabs for quite some time. Small acts of pro-conservation action sometimes go a long way in protecting a species.

AJT Johnsingh (1978) identified several aspects of the ecology and behaviour of the Indian fox—*Vulpes benghalensis*.

Johnsingh published a brief report on the Indian fox in the grassy plains and rocky areas lying to the north-west of Nanguneri, in Tirunelveli district. He described the dens of the Indian fox in rocky areas, its hunting habits and prey, as well as the cubs' behaviour. He stated that the future of the Indian fox is safe in such rocky areas (Johnsingh, 1978).

The jackal is a common predator in many ecosystems.

The desert fox can be identified by its large ears.

Bengal fox; from Gray, 1830.

## Asiatic Wild Dog or Dhole
### —Cuon alpinus

This animal lives in forested areas, in packs of five or six animals. A maximum of 20 to 25 have been seen together by some observers. AJT Johnsingh's work on the dhole suggests that there have been several misconceptions about their behaviour. For instance, it is believed that while hunting, they chase animals for long periods in a sort of relay system. Johnsingh reported that in fact they catch prey through a short sprint of 500 metres. Recent work done by him in Kanha showed that their most frequent prey is the chital. Dholes live in burrows that are about a metre depth.

I have seen dholes walk intently in single file through the trees in Bhadra. They were obviously hunting and yet, mysteriously, we saw no signs of any of its prey species in the vicinity. It is believed that the presence of a pack scares off its prey species. Dhole populations have fluctuated due to changes in the human attitude to its presence. Considered as an undesirable animal that took a toll on the shikari's game in British times, it is today seen as an important part of the ecosystem in which it lives. One would especially like to see it increasing in numbers where there is obviously a super-abundant population of chitals in Protected Areas such as Kanha.

Home-range sizes vary considerably in the several studies done from different areas. Johnsingh's studies had indicated that they use 15 square kilometres in Bandipur and 83 square kilometres in Mudumalai. Recent studies by the Wildlife Institute of India show that in the Pench National Park, the range increased to 218 square

AJT Johnsingh of the Wildlife Institute of India has worked exensively on the dhole's behaviour over the last several decades.

JD Inverarity read a description of the Indian wild dog before the BNHS, on 17th April 1890.

He had made several observations of the species, suggesting that the wild dog is of a separate genus and differs in some remarkable respects from the canids, especially when it comes to its dentations (Inverarity, 1895).

kilometres, when a collared female moved out of its range and shifted to a new location.

These studies show that Dhole home-ranges can vary from very small to very large areas. The dhole's favourite prey in Pench shows that 90 per cent of kills are chitals, the rest being sambars and wild boars.

### RODENTS

Rodents are among the strangest of creatures. From the glamorous giant squirrel to the tiny field mouse, they are voracious feeders, linked to several food chains, but rarely acknowledged as being important components of wilderness ecosystems. The Malabar giant squirrels of the Western Ghats, the porcupines that live in a variety of forests, the hare in the grasslands and the gerbils of the Thar, all provide insights into the food chains in these varied ecosystems. It was reported in 1980s, for instance, that porcupines in the Sariska National Park had suddenly decided to extensively chew up the bark of a few particular species of trees, leading to a serious mortality of these species over a brief two or three years. Why this happened no one really knows. Was it due to a population explosion of porcupines leading to a shortage of their normal food?

I recall spending frustrating times trying to get pictures both of gerbils in the Desert National Park and of mice in the Dangs, with no really good results. Sitting

The wild dog is feared even by large herbivores due to its lethal group hunting practices.

A field mouse nosing its way through the undergrowth.

The hare, once found everywhere in large numbers, is becoming uncommon.

Indian mouse; from JBNHS, 1900.

A very young hare seems paralyzed with fear.

Pika is a rodent found in the Himalayas.

A porcupine emerging from its burrow.

| | | 5 |
|---|---|---|
| | 2 | 6 |
| 1 | 3 | 4 7 |

on the balcony of the Forest Resthouse at Mahal one night, I saw a tiny dark shadow running back and forth on the railing. It took me a while to appreciate that the shadow was a mouse that was rather curious about the humans sitting soundlessly on the balcony in complete darkness! I tried to take its pictures in the dark, with a flash, but it was a no-win situation. Silhouetted against the moonlight, the mouse finally stopped to peer at me. I slowly stretched out my hand and placed it where I guessed his tail would be. And sure enough I had him! I lifted him slowly towards Sejal Worah, the field scientist in the Dangs, who was sitting across from me and told her to put on her torch. In the sudden glare we saw the little mouse hanging by its tail with all four legs spread out to their maximum length. I will never forget Sejal's scream! The mouse, now terrified too, was instantly released and scurried away down the balcony at an incredible speed and jumped off at the opposite end. The attendant, usually dead-drunk at this time of night, came running out asking what had happened. For Sejal, who was not worried about leopards, to admit that a tiny mouse had frightened her was, according to her, simply not on. We settled for 'no problems, nothing to worry about!'

In 1978, while in Kaziranga, I met Willheim Boruvka, a Czechoslovakian taxidermist who would frequently disappear into the forest all by himself. The Wildlife Warden thought this was strange and asked me to keep an eye on him and observe what he was up to. I discovered that he had a set of small traps with which he was catching mice for the museum in Opava! He always smelled strongly of civets, as he used their jungle paths to set his traps. His argument was simple. If the civets used these trails, the mice just had to be there too. And he was right. He caught several rodents during the two days I was asked to 'look after him.' The Forest Guards, however, thought he was crazy. Why should anyone in his right mind take the trouble to trudge through marshland and forest to catch mice?

Rodents, through their numbers alone, play an important role in the ecosystems in which they live. They are fruit eaters, grain eaters, insectivores, and outnumber most of the other mammals in several ecological setups. While some are highly adaptable species, others occupy a narrow niche and disappear if their habitat is disturbed. Giant squirrels have disappeared from many parts of the Western Ghats in the past few decades. Their presence is thus an indicator of less disturbed tracts of forest.

### Squirrels

There are several species of squirrels found in India. Of these, some of the most threatened are the grizzled squirrel, the flying squirrel and the Malabar giant squirrel. I have seen the grizzled giant only in the Chinar Sanctuary in Kerala, where several of them live along a riverine patch of forest among a grove of tamarind trees.

Our common palm squirrels have delighted me since my childhood. I once reared a tiny, abandoned one with an ink dropper for several weeks during my vacation, after which it ungraciously disappeared! A brown species found in the north-east has no stripes. I saw these in Kaziranga, where they scuttled around the forest rest house.

Along with primates, tree shrews and bats, this is one of the groups of mammals that live in the canopy of trees. Squirrels are pollinators of several tree species which have an abundance of flower nectar. They are important seed-dispersal agents in the forest ecosystem.

### Giant Squirrels
### Indian Giant Squirrel
—*Ratufa indica indica*
### Grizzled Giant Squirrel
—*Ratufa macroura dandolena*
All the giant squirrels belong to a single genus, *Ratufa*, and are among the largest squirrels in the world. *Ratufa* in India are considered an ancient species, as they are similar to the earliest known fossils of squirrels from the Oligocene, 35 million years ago.

| 1 | 3 | 4 |
|---|---|---|
| 2 | 5 | 6 |
|   |   | 7 |

A palm squirrel carries away a ficus fruit to its den.

The palm squirrel is the commonest squirrel in India.

A Malabar giant squirrel, the state animal of Maharashtra, seen at Bhimashankar Wildlife Sanctuary.

A Malabar giant squirrel at the Mudumalai Sanctuary.

A Malabar giant squirrel at the Kalakad Mundantharai Sanctuary readies itself to leap from one branch to another.

The grizzled squirrel is a rare species found in the Chinnar Sanctuary.

The Indian giant squirrel lives in the forests of Central India.

WT Blanford, FRS, described a large Indian squirrel (*Sciuris indicus erx.*) and its local races of sub-species in 1897. He noted that it was seen in the Western Ghats and in patches along the Ganges and the Godavari river, east of longitude 80° (Blanford, 1897).

There are two species of Giant Squirrels distributed within the peninsula. These are the Indian Giant Squirrel and the Grizzled Giant Squirrel. There are several races of the Indian Giant Squirrel (Daniel J. C and Humayun Abdulali, 1952, Volume 50, page 469-473, JBNHS). *Ratufa indica indica* is the main race of the Indian Giant Squirrel. The term Malabar Giant Squirrel is applicable to the race which occurs in the Western Ghats of Kerala and up to Coorg. There are different colour variations that occur within the species. Seven varieties which have distinctive colours occur from North to South in the Sahyadris.

The Malabar race of the giant squirrel was studied by several workers including Prater and Humayun Abdulali in the 1940s. In the 1980s, Renee Borges and others brought about a greater understanding of this species.

The head and body of the giant squirrel varies from 35 to 40 centimetres in length, with a bushy tail of up to 60 centimetres. Giant squirrels are exclusively forest dwellers, living in the treetops and only occasionally descending to the ground. They jump from tree to tree and are capable of long leaps with their limbs outspread, using their tails as an effective balancing tool. They can cover as much as six and a half metres in a single bound. Their distinctive, loud alarm call makes their presence known in the forest, especially in the early hours of the morning and in the late evenings. They live alone or in pairs, building multiple globular nests of twigs and leaves. An individual may build several nests in different trees within a small area of jungle. These are used as sleeping quarters, and one of them becomes a nursery. Squirrels are partial to some patches of the forest and establish strong territorial rights around their nests. There are frequent territorial skirmishes and noisy chases from one tree to another. They feed on fruit and seeds of specific plant species.

The Malabar giant squirrel has several colour variations in the Western Ghats, mostly different shades of brown. From Bhimashankar to Goa, they are a light rust-brown and off-white, with a white waistband and a darker rump. Much darker red-brown sub-species inhabit the evergreen vegetation in the south, through Goa up to the Nilgiris. They are nearly black in the Anamalais.

The Malabar giant squirrel has sizeable populations in the Bhimashankar Wildlife Sanctuary in the Sahyadris of Maharashtra. Much work has been done on this species by Renee Borges, who has documented their nesting, territorial behaviour and feeding habits, with special reference to the tree species they use as food. They feed mainly on flowers and fruit, but take to feeding on leaves and bark in lean seasons, memecylon and mangifera being their favourite feeding trees. Malabar giant squirrels are territorial and use only a part of the territory for feeding every day. The yellow-brown giant squirrel once found in the Dangs, appears to have become extinct in the 1940s and 50s. Sejal Worah and I searched all over the Dangs for this pale golden giant squirrel in the 1980s. Local people said that perhaps there might still be some left in the Mahal area known as 'Kot-nu-jungle'. Although we searched persistently for a year, there were none. A few older tribal people were able to

variegated in colour, with patches of dark and light brown.

In a few hill ranges of the south, there are small populations of the highly-threatened grizzled giant squirrel. It is distinctive in having the back and tail grey or brownish grey, more or less grizzled with white. During surveys by the BNHS in the 1920s and 30s, these squirrels were found in several places in the Eastern Ghats and in the rain shadow areas of the Western Ghats in south India. In surveys by the Wildlife Institute of India in the 1980s by Johnsingh, it was seen in the Algarkail valley in Srivilliputtar, in the Grizzled Squirrel Wildlife Sanctuary and in five other small areas, as well as in Palavi and Chennar Wildlife Sanctuaries in Kerala. It lives primarily in riverine tracts. Johnsingh estimated that in the 1980s there were only 50 to 75 left in Chennar and about 200 in Megamalai, in Tamil Nadu. They feed mainly on seeds of young fruit and on fruit, seeds, flowers, and shoots. Among the trees they use as food, *Terminalia indica* is their favourite; others include the tamarind—*Albizia lebbeck*—and the jamun—*Syzygium*.

The Malayan giant squirrel lives north of the Ganges in Nepal, Sikkim, Bhutan, and Assam.

**Flying Squirrels**—*Hylopetes sp.*
These squirrels have acquired the ability to sail or glide through the air on a flap of skin stretched between their front and rear legs and used like a parachute. When the squirrel is at rest, this flap is hardly noticeable. Only when the animal leaps from tree to tree is it expanded. The squirrel can glide smoothly for a fair distance, but this is just a prolonged leap and not continuous flight. The body is steered by altering the position of the limbs and the parachute. In India, flying squirrels are grouped as large or small species. They are patchily distributed throughout the forests of India and are becoming increasingly rare due to habitat fragmentation. Flying squirrels are essentially forest animals and, unlike other squirrels, are nocturnal. They feed on the fruits and nuts of various trees.

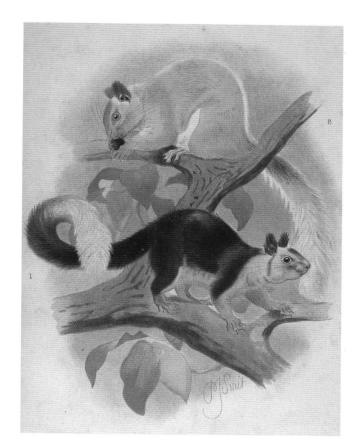

Skins of Malabar giant squirrels from different parts of the Western Ghats, in the BNHS Museum.

Giant squirrels; from JBNHS, 1898.

Giant flying squirrel.

Giant squirrels; from JBNHS, 1898.

Flying squirrel; from Gray, 1830.

The eyes of a nocturnal flying squirrel reflected in the flashlight.

## BEARS

Of the three species of bears found in India, the commonest is the sloth bear, which is found in many different kinds of forests. The Himalayan black bear is found at an altitude of between five and ten thousand feet, while the Himalayan brown bear occupies the inhospitable snows at a higher altitude, frequently even climbing above the tree line.

Bears are the only species that one has to be wary about in a forest. I had a rather nasty experience with a Himalayan black bear in Dachigam, and another close but rather unusual encounter with a sloth bear in Melghat. The variation in behaviour, from highly aggressive to almost placid, makes them extremely unpredictable animals.

### Sloth Bear—*Melursus ursinus*

This is the most well-known of our bear species, with a long, coarse, typically black coat. The face and muzzle have short off-white or brown hair. Some animals have a light V-shaped mark on the chest.

They vary from 130 to 180 centimetres in length, and from 65 to 100 centimetres in height at the shoulders. The sloth bear is patchily distributed over peninsular India, found in several forested tracts of the Deccan plateau and in evergreen, deciduous and thorn forests, and frequently in caves and rocky outcroppings.

The sloth bear hunts for food both during the day and at night, though in some areas it is mainly nocturnal. An omnivore, it is dependent on fruits, roots, and termites, its favourite food being honeycombs, for which it nimbly climbs the tallest trees. Its poor eyesight is supposed to be responsible for its unpredictable behaviour, a fact that makes encounters with it dangerous. The Wildlife Institute of India has studied bear-related problems in Bilaspur in Madhya Pradesh. Out of 178 villages in the area, 122 were seriously affected. Between 1973 and 1998, there were an astounding 395 attacks on humans! These attacks have been attributed to a serious loss of bear habitat.

Its range and distribution has shrunk due to the live animal trade in which the bears are killed for their bile, which is supposed to have medicinal properties.

Reginald Gilbert wrote a note on the Indian Bear—*Melurus ursinus*. He was concerned about the decline in this species and claimed that this bear was, however, still found all over the Indian peninsula, although its population was gradually decreasing. He wrote that 20 years earlier it was very common throughout the Bombay Presidency. In several districts in which they were formally shot they were rarely or never to be found by 1890. In wild and rocky districts, he had reports that far away from the railway lines they existed in good numbers and frequented the same jungles year after year (Gilbert, 1897).

### Himalayan Black Bear—*Ursus tibetanus*

The Himalayan black bear is larger than the sloth bear, has a broad head and extremely powerful jaws. Its short, smooth, shiny coat and black claws distinguish it from the more common sloth bear. It has a tan or brown muzzle and white or buff chin and a characteristic V-shaped mark on the breast, which may be white, yellow or buff. It varies in length from 140 to 165 centimetres. It is distributed patchily in the Himalayas, from Kashmir to Assam, inhabiting steep hillsides in coniferous, deciduous and evergreen forests. In summer it lives in the mountains above 3000 metres and in winters it descends to 1525 metres or lower, to hibernate.

The Himalayan black bear spends the day sleeping in a cave or in the hollow of a tree and is said to have an excellent sense of smell, but very poor eyesight and hearing. It emerges at dusk to hunt for food and retires after sunrise. It feeds on wild fruit, berries, nuts, roots, tubers, honey, insects, termites and the larvae of insects, as well as rodents and young birds.

In the JBNHS, Volume 52, RC Morris and Salim Ali (1955) said that black bears had increased considerably in some parts of Kashmir. They mention that in the past a reward of Rs. 15 was offered for shooting black bears. In fact they recommended that the black bear should be considered 'vermin' for 5 years.

Its present population shares the habitat with the very rare Himalayan brown bear of the upper reaches of the mountains, and with the much more common sloth bear of the plains. It is seriously affected by habitat loss and poaching, killed for its gall bladder which is supposed to have medicinal value, and also traded for domestic use in bear shows and in the international market for zoos and circuses.

Sloth bear

A Himalayan black bear.

### PRIMATES

The two most common groups of primates in India are the macaques and the langurs. The rhesus macaque mainly occupies the Indo-Gangetic plains, while the larger bonnet macaque lives in southern parts of peninsular India. The Assamese macaque is found only in the northeast. The rare lion-tailed macaque is a beautiful monkey, with glossy, black hair and a hairy, grey mane fringing its small dark face. It lives in the evergreen Shola forests of the southern part of the Western Ghats. This species requires a very special rain forest habitat and is one of the most endangered of macaques.

The common langur is found all over India, while the capped langur is found only in Assam. The Nilgiri langur is seen only in a few hilly tracts in South India. The rare golden langur is restricted to a very small area on the Bhutan border, along the banks of the Manas River and a small patch of forest at Chakrashala in Assam.

C McCann, (Assistant Curator BNHS) documented his observation on Indian Langurs in 1933. He described four species of langur from India, the common or Hanuman langur, the Himalayan langur, the Nilgiri langur and the capped langur in the JBNHS, Volume 36.

| 1 | 2 |
|---|---|
| 3 | 4 |

The common langur adapts itself to forests, villages and even towns.

Capped langurs are found only in North-eastern India.

The Nilgiri langur appears like a silhouette due to its black coat.

Bonnet macaques are one the commonest species of primates in India.

### Lion-Tailed Macaque—*Macaca silenus*

Many years ago, I was given a lion-tailed macaque to look after, one of two monkeys that had been doomed to die. The Forest Department felt that it was best that I look after them temporarily, till they could decide what was to be done with them. This took six or seven years, by which time the two monkeys had passed away.

It was through Pippa, the lion-tailed macaque, that I learnt how incredibly intelligent these primates are. They are, in fact, so like us. Pippa loved my daughter Jeroo, then only three or four years old, and who grew up being loved by this monkey, who always wanted to mother her. When I went into her large enclosure, she would be ecstatic and then no one dared approach this otherwise placid, sweet-natured monkey. Pippa frequently tried to get to the broom that the keeper used to clean her cage and would be very angry if she could not secure a broomstick. Once she had pulled out a broomstick, she would quietly settle down and conceal it in her fur. One day, after the excitement of grabbing a broomstick had died down, I found Pippa quietly approaching the drain, which was usually moist. There she settled down with her stick and put it carefully through the grating to extract tiny termites, which she promptly licked up! Years later, I read Jane Goodall's book where she mentions that her chimpanzees were using a similar tool for a similar purpose. Pippa had pre-dated the chimpanzee discovery, but I had not realized the significance of this tool using ability of primates in those days.

The lion-tailed macaque has a jet-black silky coat, a mane of long grey hair around a dark face and bright, orange-brown eyes. The tuft of hair at the end of the tail resembles the tail of a lion.

In 1859, Baker first recorded this macaque as appearing in the Western Ghats, as far north as Goa, but only in lonely dense forests. Blandford, in the 1880s, wrote that the lion-tailed macaque was sparingly distributed throughout the evergreen forest and he described it as a quiet monkey. In Travancore, according to Hill, it was not found below 2000 feet, its favourite altitude being usually from 2500 to 3000 feet. Like other macaques, it was known to be gregarious and lived in parties of 12 to 20 individuals or more.

Pocock (1939) in *The Fauna of British India*, refers to Baker's record of the lion-tailed macaque occurring in the Western Ghats as far north as Goa.

It is now distributed in a few patches of undisturbed evergreen forests in the Western Ghats in North Kanara and Kerala. I have also sighted a few around tea plantations in these areas. They normally inhabit dense, evergreen tropical forests between 600 and 1000 metres, where there are several types of trees on which they feed in troops of 12 to 20 animals. The call of the male resembles the loud 'coo' of a pigeon. They move slowly and deliberately through the dense canopy of tall trees, frequently walking along branches and clambering from tree to tree along bridges formed by the lianas high-up in the canopy.

They feed on a wide variety of fruit, berries, seeds, flower nectar and insects like caterpillars and spiders. Unlike other monkeys, they do not eat leaves and are dependent on a wide range of food plants, most of which are only seasonally available. They live only in evergreen forests where some form of food is available throughout the year. Their home range is about 1.25 square kilometre in lowland forests and 5 square kilometre at higher elevations. Ajit Kumar of SACON, who has been working on the lion-tailed macaques intensively for several years in the Annamalais (Indira Gandhi Wildlife Sanctuary) estimates that there are only about 4000 left in scattered groups which are restricted to a few Sholas and adjacent plantations where there are giant trees. The destruction of its sensitive habitat and poaching for zoos makes it one of our most seriously endangered species.

GU Kurup (1978) wrote about the habitat and status survey of the lion-tailed macaque—*Macac silenus*—described by Linnaeus in the JBNHS, Volume 75.

He identified the distribution range of the lion-tailed macaque as restricted to the southwestern face of the Nilgiris down to the Kalakkadu slopes in the Agasthya Ranges of southern spurs. A tentative estimate of the lion-tailed macaque population was about 50 troops of 570 individuals. Habitat conversion and eventual destruction and direct decimation were identified serious concerns.

The rare lion-tailed macaque is found only in the Anamalai Hills and in southern parts of the Western Ghats.

### Bonnet Macaque—*Macaca radiata*

Many years ago, in the 1970s, I was given a monkey to look after, which was otherwise going to be put to sleep by its owner who was going abroad. Chicko was a domineering fellow, who was shifted to a large enclosure made in our garden. As he was often smarter than the keeper who looked after his cage, we frequently found him outside, jumping noisily on the trees in our compound. Chicko's sworn enemy was our neighbour's rather stupid Pomeranian-Spitz. Whenever the arrogant, yapping dog passed Chicko's cage, he would look disdainfully in Chicko's direction and bark aggressively. One day, Chicko managed to unscrew the bolts of his cage, came out and began looking for the nasty dog. Chicko searched and found the dog on the first floor of our neighbour's house. The encounter resulted in a Pom that was scared to death. Whimpering but untouched, the Pom ran under beds and cupboards leaving a long trail of urine behind it.

I was operating when I received a phone call saying that I'd better come home as soon as possible, as the neighbour had complained that Chicko had almost given her pet a heart attack! We had many such adventures, Chicko and I, including the one where he bit my arm when I tried to catch him, pulled off my car's wiper blades, and

once had to be given a kilogram of toffees one by one to entice him back into his cage.

The bonnet is a familiar, large macaque, with a stocky body and a pale-pinkish face, and a crown of long hair, which radiates from the centre of its head to form a cap-like whorl. Its coat varies from lustrous olive-brown, with a whitish abdomen in the cold season, to buff grey, losing its shine and becoming scraggly in summer. The bonnet averages 60 centimetres in size, and has a much longer tail than other macaques.

It is distributed across the southern part of the Indian peninsula, from Mumbai in the west, along the Godavari River, down to the East Coast. It is a common monkey of both rural landscapes and the jungle, living in highly organized troops of about 20 to 30 animals, which are controlled by a core of a few highly-dominant males. They feed both on the ground and in the trees, but are more arboreal in habit than most macaques. They eat fruit, berries, leaves and shoots, as well as insects, grubs and spiders.

The bonnet is a common species associated with urban, rural and wilderness landscapes, though it is less adapted to living in major modern cities than the langur and the rhesus. It is commonly captured for the pet trade in South India.

### Rhesus Macaque—*Macaca mulatta*

The rhesus is the most common monkey of North India. Smaller in size than the bonnet macaque, it is also differentiated by its short tail. This and the hair on its crown, which is directed backwards, differentiate it from the bonnet. The loin and rump have a distinctive orange-red patch not seen in other Indian monkeys.

It is distributed extensively over North India, from the Himalayas to Assam, as far south as the Tapi in the west and the Godavari in the east. It lives in large troops that frequent towns and villages. A large male dominates each troop.

The rhesus mainly feeds on the ground, on a variety of plants as well as on insects and spiders. Its large population has decreased, as it was extensively trapped and exported for laboratory experiments. This has now been banned, but it is still trapped for the pet trade.

A bonnet macaque baby clings to its mother's belly as she bounds away.

Rhesus macaques were used extensively for research in the past.

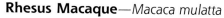

### Common Langur, or Hanuman Monkey—*Semnopithecus entellus*

This monkey is one of our common and most widely distributed animals in India, living in forests, village surrounds and even in urban settings where there are large trees. Langurs are vegetarian and eat fruits, flowers, buds, shoots and leaves. They raid crops, gardens and orchards. Their large, specialized stomachs help them digest mature leaves and this gives them the colloquial name of leaf monkeys. The average troop size is 18 to 25 animals in the north and about 15 in the south. Occasionally they form all-male groups. The home range of a langur group varies from 1.3 to 13 square kilometres, with adult males leading and co-ordinating the group. Interactions to establish dominance are milder than among the rhesus macaques.

On sighting a predator or a threatening human, they produce a distinctive guttural alarm call that alerts the troop, which then breaks into a frenzy. The 'whoop' call is made when bounding from tree to tree, or when separated, probably to re-establish contact.

Well adapted to urban areas, they are disappearing in most city environments, where there is too little tree cover to support them.

## Golden Langur—*Trachypithecus geei*

The history of the discovery of the golden langur started when some shikaris and Forest Officers noticed a cream-coloured monkey near the boundary of Bhutan and India (Gee, 1961). Probably the first to do so and report it was EO Shebbeare in 1907. Several subsequent references to this langur can be found in the 1940s, leading to EP Gee's visit to the area and discovering the species. The cream coat of the golden langur appears bright gold in sunlight. The hair is longer and darker on the flanks, and is lighter in summer. It has a black face, which contrasts sharply with its shiny coat. Its young and females appear silvery white to golden yellow. It feeds mostly on flowers, fruit and leaves.

It is to be found in Assam, in the region between the Sankosh and the Manas Rivers. Its range extends into the Bhutan forests up to an altitude of 1600 metres. It inhabits undisturbed evergreen forests in small troops of about nine animals. My only experience of this monkey was in 1978, on the Bhutan border in Manas. As both sides of the Manas River in Bhutan and India now have a protected status, the animal has a better chance of survival.

This rare species was first described in detail by EP Gee, during the 1950s, when he sighted it on the banks of the Manas River.

## Indian Elephant—*Elephas maximus*

During my visits to National Parks and Wildlife Sanctuaries, both in the south and in Corbet and Kaziranga, I have come to understand elephants more intimately than any other animal. This is because they seem to single me out for a chase. Being with BNHS scientists to understand how they studied elephants, I decided to make two films for EMRC's Open University Television Programmes. This led to several visits to Madhumalai and Bandipur, the main sites of these frantic elephant chases, each of which left me with the feeling that this could have been my last visit to a sanctuary on earth. But elephants are not malicious animals and invariably leave one alone once they know that they have made you run. We made two films, one on elephant ecology and another on radio-collaring. We had parked our old jeep, whose bonnet had once been squashed by an elephant, close to a herd of elephants. The boys decided to get a better view of the animals over the thick, tall, *Lantana* shrubs. In hushed voices, they proposed that the large TV camera be placed on the jeep bonnet. I felt this was unsafe, but Ramesh, who had been working with the elephants, said he knew the old female in the herd was safe! I sat in the jeep to change the film in my camera while they crowded around it and climbed onto the bonnet. Suddenly we heard the sharp squeal of a young elephant calf. It emerged from the *Lantana* and charged across the road. At that moment I realized that we had elephants on both sides of us. We had put ourselves in a really dangerous situation! Within moments, and before the cameraman could jump down from the jeep, the old female was on the road. With ears spread, she charged the jeep. The camera crew and the BNHS team yelled at her and ran for it. I was left in the back of the jeep, with the elephant menacingly moving towards me. She stopped a couple of metres away, raised her trunk and sniffed for a long time. Then she decided to back off in reverse gear. I have several exciting pictures of the charge, which could have been my last photographs but for the elephant's good nature. I have never seen a group of people dismantle heavy camera equipment and get into a crowded jeep as

quickly as they did after this memorable experience.

Elephants have been used in ancient India as a fighting machine for warfare and for hunting in royal shikar. During the British period they were domesticated for forestry operations.

Babur (1526–1530) records the presence of elephants in Kalpi and notes that there were higher densities to the east of his territory. Akbar (1556–1605) captured elephants in Narwar. Jehangir (1605–1627) caught elephants in Dohad in the Panchmahals. In 1867, due to the decrease in wild elephants and an increase in price, it was suggested to the Government that a breeding depot be started in the Anamalais. The acting Commissioner General of Madras endorsed this, but it was thought to be too expensive. Legislation was however made to protect them from being shot. EP Stebbing, in 1922, wrote that if it weren't for this rule, the animals would have become extinct in the wild.

From the vast tracts of land which constituted elephant habitats, there are now only five isolated populations in the country. These are: in northwestern India—Dehra Dun, Nainital (Uttar Pradesh); a southern population in the Western Ghats—Karnataka, Kerala, Tamil Nadu (north of Palghat); a southern population—south of Palghat; a central Indian population—Bihar, Bengal, Orissa; an eastern population—North Bengal and Assam and other northeastern states. Even within these areas their populations are highly fragmented. Nair, Sukumar and

The fixed gaze and alarm calls of langurs indicate the presence of a tiger.

A langur and her infant.

Grooming each other is an important part of the langur's social behaviour.

A langur feeds on young leaves and buds from a hanging branch.

A langur troop in Sariska drinking water.

The golden langur was first identified by EP Gee.

**The elephant has been domesticated in India over the last several centuries. Its numbers in the wild have declined as a result of habitat loss and poaching for ivory.**

Gadgil documented that the elephants south of Palghat were in eight separate areas in the late 1970s. During the last 30 years, each of these areas has fragmented into smaller areas isolated from each other by dams, roads, tea and coffee estates and urban areas. The corridors elephants once used to move between different types of forests are gone.

Habitat loss, habitat degradation, destruction of forest corridors, poaching for ivory, conflicts due to crop damage, attacks on humans that end in our killing innocent as well as errant elephants—all have a strong impact on elephants.

Hydel projects, roads, railways, and urbanization have created new impediments to elephant conservation. With this large number of human impacts, it is evident that this animal is under severe threat. Even within Protected Areas, there are several dams in south India for generating hydro power. A major cause of habitat loss is the spread of tea, coffee, rubber and cardamom plantations. Tea and coffee, first planted in the 1850s, and teak plantations that were raised by clear felling natural forests in the 1860s, have expanded enormously at the expense of elephant habitats over the last 150 years.

Between 1987 and 1992, the BNHS did intensive research on the ecology of the Indian elephant in Bandipur, Mudumalai and Nagarhole. One of the important findings was that, due to their enormous size, even a small number of elephants require great quantities of food. This has an important limiting effect on the vegetation profile of the forest. Browsing on the foliage of trees increases in summer and in the second rainy season, as the grass is too high and thick. The studies showed that elephants frequent grassy openings especially after a fire, when the grass is 50 to 70 centimetres in height.

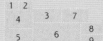

Elephant in Mudumalai.

Radio collaring by the BNHS team has helped in recording the range each herd covers as it moves through the forest.

A young elephant charging through water. The elephant is the state animal of Jharkhand, Karnataka, Kerala and Orissa.

Elephants at a waterhole which acts as a limiting factor for the population of animals in an area.

Studies on the Indian elephant have been done by the BNHS team led by JC Daniel and AJT Johnsingh and by Sukumar of the Center for Ecological Studies, Bangalore.

An elephant scenting the air.

One of the few large tuskers in Bhadra.

This large male elephant charged the jeep.

An elephant herd feeding quietly in the forest.

A detailed analysis of the tree cover showed that between 1986 and 1988, a high percentage of trees preferred by elephants for browsing were destroyed.

The Indian or Asian elephant is the second largest terrestrial animal in the world, the largest being the African elephant. In India, only the males have tusks, while in Africa both sexes can have tusks. There are tuskless males or *makhnas* in India, very large animals having extraordinarily well-developed trunks. The Indian elephant has smaller ears than the African elephant. It has a concave back unlike the African species whose back in more convex. The Indian elephant has four nails on each hind foot, while the African has three. The Indian elephant's trunk ends in a single lip, while the African elephant has two equal-sized lips. The head of the African elephant is elongated, with a flat forehead, while the Indian species has two distinct domes on its forehead.

The average height of adult males is about 2.75 metres with females averaging 2.45 metres. They weigh up to four tons. Its distribution is mainly in areas covered with tall forests, where the ground is hilly or undulating and where bamboo grows in profusion.

There are an estimated 30,000 to 50,000 wild Asian elephants in south and South-east Asia, of which half are in India. Nine to twelve thousand live in the northeastern states, 5500 to 7000 in south India, 500 live in the north, around the Himalayan foothills and 1600 to 2300 in Central India.

Elephants live in small, matriarchal family groups of closely related animals, and have now adapted to living in degraded forests. In many areas they have become increasingly dependent on crops. In the dry season, the herds keep to denser forest tracts, but during the rains they live in open grassy glades or enter cultivation. Elephants usually sleep during the hot hours of the day, as they are uncomfortable in the sun. They feed early in the morning and again in the evenings, and need large quantities of water to drink as well as to cool their large body surface. In summer, they drink as much as 200 litres of water per day. Large males have periods of excitement connected to their breeding behaviour known as musth. During the musth, a gland on the temple secretes a fluid, which indicates that the elephant can be unpredictable during this period.

Elephants feed on grasses and leaves of their favourite trees and also on stems and leaves of bamboo and the bark of a few selected types of trees. A full-grown adult can eat from 270 to 320 kilograms of green fodder per day.

BNHS studies indicate that elephants alter their own habitat quality and change the species composition of trees in the forest by their feeding habits. As habitats shrink, the elephant's feeding pressure can affect the ecosystem severely. When their food becomes scarce, elephants begin to feed on the bark of their favourite trees, killing them in the process. They also knock down trees to get at inaccessible foliage. These trees may or may not grow back. The elephant is thus a major keystone species in the ecosystem. They open up forest habitats and create grazing land which is used by smaller herbivores. In the absence of elephants, these grasslands would be gradually re-colonized by trees, resulting in a loss of habitat for grazers such as the chital, and in a favouring of browsers like the sambar. Trees which are uprooted by elephants also bring fruit within the reach of small herbivores, thus adding to their food supply. Elephants feed on a variety of fruit, and as they range widely, they disperse seeds of these fruit trees. Dung beetles and flies settle on elephant dung, using this as an important source of their food. The dung is also a source of nutrients for plant seedlings to germinate on. As elephants move through the forest, they open up trails which smaller animals use. Thus a large number of plants and animals in the forest ecosystem are linked to the elephant's behaviour and its movements.

During studies on elephant habitats in Mudumalai, BNHS scientists showed that out of 97 marked *Grewia tiliifolia* trees in 1986, there were 91 that were uprooted and killed by elephants in the sanctuary within the brief period of the study. The combined effects of elephant damage and fire appear frightening. Saplings of *Acacia catechu* and *Zizyphus xylopyrus* almost vanished over a nine-year period in the permanent study plots in the thorn forests. Repeated fires killed off a large proportion of regenerating saplings of several species that elephants feed on. Once the preferred species have been destroyed and their densities are lowered, the elephants switch to another set of species. These long-term monitoring studies by BNHS, SACON and other institutions have thus thrown new light on the need for preserving large tracts of land if the elephant's future is to be secured.

Domestic elephants, which are kept in habitats where they do not normally occur, can do serious damage around the elephant camps, destroying the forest and making it look as if a devastating storm has blown through it. Trees are uprooted, branches are torn away, barks are peeled off trees, bamboos are stripped of leaves and uprooted and the grass is severely trampled into the ground. I have observed this around many domestic elephant camps in the Protected Areas where they are used for sighting wildlife. Areas of Bandhavgarh have seriously affected sites where domestic elephants have been permitted to graze in the forest.

There is a serious problem due to feral elephants in the Andaman Islands. Elephants that were used for logging in the past are now living in a wild state. They swim across the sea between islands and cause serious havoc to the evergreen vegetation.

Elephant herds need large tracts of forests in which they can access different habitat types in each season. They migrate over a wide range, and each herd has a fairly constant territory through which they zigzag over the year. As development of roads, dams and tea and coffee plantations have increasingly disrupted their migration routes, the animals have begun to frequent surrounding croplands. This conflict has only been partially addressed by developing elephant trenches and installing electrical fences, which have had only limited success in controlling the movements of wild elephants. The man-elephant conflict is an increasingly alarming issue with few practical solutions.

The General Assembly of the IUCN in 1978 called on the Government of India to include a countrywide programme for the conservation of the elephant and its ecosystem. This led to initiating Project Elephant in 1992, for 11 Elephant Reserves. The project areas include Protected Areas and Reserved Forests where there are sizeable elephant populations.

Thirty per cent of elephants live outside the Protected Area Network. Menon and Kumar (2001) have estimated that between 1996 and 1998, 253 elephants were poached in India.

In North Bengal it appears that elephants die due to pesticides that enter their watering places from tea estates. Mortality due to train hits on the Delhi-Dehra Dun routes is another frequent problem. Elephants are also hit by trains in the Dudhwa Tiger Reserve in Uttar Pradesh.

The Wildlife Trust of India took up a study on the accidents leading to the death of elephants along railway tracks and reported that most accidents occur at night, especially during the summer months. This indicates that most accidents occur while crossing the tracks for getting to scarce water sources. Rajaji has seen a number of unfortunate accidental deaths over the years.

Elephant poaching is a serious concern. The number is staggering. It is rampant and appears to be spreading to most elephant habitats.

On July 7th, 2003, a young tusker was found dead in Bhadra, with its tusks sawed off professionally. Watching this on TV took me several years back to the time when I went looking for tuskers in Bhadra because they were nearly finished off in other Protected Areas such as Mudumalai and Bandipur. In 2001, a poached elephant was found in Palamau. In Corbett, 5 elephants were poached over a short period of 2 months in 2001. Elephant poaching is also a problem in Corbett, where 5 tuskers were reported killed between December 2000 and February 2001.

Elephant deaths are also due to the conflicts between humans and animals that arise when crops are raided. Various ways, such as electrocution, have been devised by farmers to kill elephants in Karnataka. Illegally electrified fences are erected to prevent elephants from raiding crops—a method that people appear to have learned from the genuine use of electrified fences which only give animals a nasty shock. This illegal method of using electricity is low-cost and kills the unfortunate animal on the spot. In Arunachal Pradesh, several elephants have been poisoned by local people after their crops have been repeatedly destroyed. I have seen croplands raided by elephants which were totally devastated. This conflict has to be resolved by compensating people for the loss of their crops.

Dalma has increasingly serious conflict issues related to elephants, even though their number appears to be constant. In 1997, there were 79 elephants, which increased marginally to 82 in 2001. The elephants come to the edge of the Protected Area and live close to human habitation on the fringes of Jamshedpur.

In the forests of Orissa, 151 elephants were reported to have been poached between 1991 and 2001. This high figure has been reported by the Evaluation Committee on Project Elephant. A large amount of ivory is still being used, mainly in the Far East, for making artifacts, charms and jewellery. Unless this is considered improper and a criminal, punishable offence, elephant poaching will kill off the few residual great wild tuskers of our country.

AJW Milroy (1923) described elephant catching in Assam. Some excerpts from his description are of interest today:

'Elephants were caught in Assam by two methods, mela shikar and kheddas. The former consists of pursing the wild herds with tame elephants carrying nooses. This method has been practiced from very ancient times.

'Three or four koonkies, tame elephants, usually operate together at shikar and it is considered desirable that one of the elephants should be a large male of known courage, in case the wild elephants prove aggressive. Mela shikars lead to a number of wild elephants being unavoidably strangled, and it is fortunate that this form of death is very instantaneous on account of the structure of the elephant's windpipe.

'Kheddas in Assam worked on a less pretentious scale than those organized in Mysore. Very rocky ground is avoided because of the difficulty in sinking the posts to the requisite depth and it would obviously be impossible to build a sufficiently strong enclosure on marshy soil. Stockades varied in shape according to the locality, drop gates are present but they were difficult to lift up and heavy swing doors 10 to 12 feet High, similar to an ordinary, English, five-barred gate were used'.

The first systematic census of elephants in Uttar Pradesh was carried out during the years 1966–67. The data collected was statistically analyzed and the results were published as a paper in Volume 66 of the JBNHS (Singh, 1969). After 10 years, a census was carried out to know the changes both in the extent and in the quality of the elephant habitat. The census showed about 500 elephants, consisting of 28 per cent males, 49 per cent females, 20 per cent calves and 3 per cent lone tuskers.

VB Singh wrote on the status of the Elephant in Uttar Pradesh in the JBNHS, Volume 75, in 1978.

## BOVIDS

The bovids include the gaur or bison, buffalo, goats, sheep as well as domesticated animals.

The gaur, traditionally known as the Indian bison, lives in the forests that cover hilly areas in different parts of the country. The wild buffalo lives in the moist Terai swamps and in grassy openings in the forests in the northeast. Their ranges were much wider in the past. A few lived around the Indravati River until a decade or so ago.

All the wild sheep and goats are Himalayan species, except the Nilgiri *tahr* of South India. Wild sheep and goats must compete with large herds of domestic sheep, goats and cattle for grazing, particularly in seasons when grass is scarce. This has become a problem throughout the Himalayan pasture lands. Added to this is a continued pressure from poaching, placing these species under serious threat.

### Gaur or Indian Bison—*Bos gaurus*

The massive bulk of a big male gaur is what makes it exciting. I have found myself in so many harrowing experiences in the old days, when it was still an acceptable practice to photograph them on foot in many of our sanctuaries. With the increasing number of wildlife tourists, this is not possible any longer. From the safety of a jeep, the gaur seems especially benign, until one sees a male displaying its strength by uprooting shrubs and smaller trees to establish its position in the herd. I have once been in the path of an awesome young male and even had a herd flash by me with only a few metres separating me from the thundering mass of animals! Both incidents could have been fatal and on both occasions it was no fault of the gaur! Rather it was my somewhat careless assumption that nothing can go wrong in the forest if you know your wildlife. In both cases, the gaur behaved differently from the accepted norms of behaviour. Which is why wildlife is *wild*! It is unpredictable. Which is why one must anticipate that animals make exceptions in behaviour when one least expects them to.

The old bulls are jet-black, with an ashy forehead and yellowish or off-white legs. The young animals are fawn-coloured.

They average 175 to 180 centimetres at the shoulders. The cows are a good 10 centimetres shorter and have a smaller build.

Gaurs require both forest and open grassy patches and are distributed in the Western Ghats, the hill forests of central and southeastern parts of peninsular India and West Bengal. In the Himalayan foothills, the gaurs climb to about 1800 metres.

Gaurs are usually seen in small parties of four to six animals, but occasionally herds of 40 animals have been observed. Large males are frequently solitary. The gaur has an acute sense of smell, but is said to have poor eyesight. These animals graze on grasses, herbs, leaves, fallen fruit and bamboo in the dry season, but turn to browsing on shrubs and low branches of trees after the monsoon. In Pench, studies on gaurs by the Wildlife Institute of India have shown that the gaurs use as many as 77 different food plants. The Wildlife Institute of India researchers monitored radio-collared gaurs in Pench in 1997–98 and found that the average summer home range of the males was 7.6 square kilometre, while the females had a range of 13.8 square kilometre. Of the 820 gaurs counted, there was approximately one male to 1.5 females. The group size was shown to vary in different seasons, with an average group size of three in summer, five in the monsoon and seven in winter.

Gaur herds migrate seasonally through the forest looking for the best tracts of grass. In several areas, foraging village cattle come into contact with them. The cattle, which are carriers of diseases such as rinderpest, have been known to spread disease to the gaur, leading to a serious crash in their population. During one such epidemic at Kanha in the 1980s, half the gaurs died within a year. Another epidemic has killed a large number in Bandhavgarh in 2002. I have not seen a single one since then.

In many regions, the animal is now threatened by the rapid destruction of its habitat. In January 2000, a young bull came to the outskirts of Pune and decided to hide in our small nature trail set up at BVIEER (Bharati Vidyapeeth Institute of Environment Education and Research).

This occurred during the inauguration of the Environment Forum of the prestigious Indian Science Congress. Early that morning, our gardener informed me in a frantic voice that a gaur, which he described as an enormous animal, had attacked a man and had torn up his thigh. I

hastily started off to check this unbelievable story when I got a call from my surgery housemen at Bharati Hospital that a wild animal at the Environment Institute had seriously injured a man who had been brought to the Casualty Ward of our hospital. By the time I got there, hundreds of people had surrounded our nature trail in which an angry gaur was knocking down our precious young indigenous trees planted with great love and affection. I called Mr Shaikh, our DFO-Wildlife to bring his tranquillizer gun. At first he thought I was only pulling his leg. Sunderlalji Bahuguna, who was invited as the Chief Guest for the opening of the session on Environment at the Science Congress, saw the gaur and used this to illustrate the various issues related to the serious loss of habitat in the country. The animal, during an attempt to tranquillize it, charged the DFO-Wildlife and broke four of his ribs! As the closest gaur herd lives in Koyna and Mahableshwar, more than 100 kilometres away, this animal must

have wandered this very long distance looking for a suitable patch of forest to live in! I have studied the forested tracts of this region on satellite images and could trace his course to this unlikely destination by observing that there are good forest patches with small corridors between them in the Western Ghats, through which this animal must have had to travel to come to our nature trail. He was finally successfully tranquillized several hours later and released into the Chandoli Wildlife Sanctuary. We can only hope that he is alive and well and does not plan to travel again. It is a wonder that no one in the unruly mob was gored and killed that day. Another old gaur lives at Authur's Seat Point in Mahableshwar and feeds on the corn coverings discarded by the corn vendors. Such animals tend to lose their fear of people and are extremely

| 1 | 2 |
| | 3 | 4 |
| | 5 | 6 |

The gaur is the state animal of Bihar and Goa.

Gaur is the largest bovid found in India.

Gaur herds move through the forest in search of food.

A herd of gaur feeding in an open plateau top in Radhanagari.

A gaur watches from the edge of the forest before dashing into the undergrowth.

A gaur cleans her calf's ear.

dangerous even though they appear placid.

The threat faced by the gaur indicates the need to not only protect patches of forest, but also the corridors between them, for their long-term survival.

**Wild Buffalo**—*Bubalus bubalis*

A wild buffalo resembles a domesticated buffalo for which it can be mistaken. Its legs are a dirty-white up to the hocks and the knees. The enormous horns are either curved upwards, in a smooth circle with the tips being separated by a small gap, or are spread outward horizontally from the head and curve slightly upwards and inwards near the tips. Both types of horns may be found in the same herd and there are several intermediate shapes. A large bull may reach two metres at the shoulder, weighing up to a ton.

They are patchily distributed in the Terai and the plains of the Brahmaputra in North-eastern India. A few probably still survive in parts of Orissa and adjoining Madhya Pradesh. The herds inhabit patches of tall grass in jungles and reed brakes in the neighbourhood of swamps. They require pools of water and mud wallows to lie in. The herds feed chiefly on grass, but may also enter croplands. Wild buffaloes occasionally mate with domestic animals. These males are generally young mature bulls that have been driven from the wild herd by a dominant male during the rut. The wild buffalo is seriously affected by habitat loss. I have observed them in Kaziranga and Manas, their last strongholds since 1978. Old bulls are known to be bad-tempered. A large male I saw in Kaziranga refused to get off the road for over half an hour. He was an enormous individual and aggressively inclined. Local people and Forest Staff kept out of his way.

All the domestic varieties of buffalo used in south and southeast Asia came from their wild buffalo ancestors in India. Interbreeding between the wild and domestic buffalo is a serious threat to the genetic strain of the true wild stocks left in India.

In 1988, when I was on the SANCF Committee, I was concerned about the status of the Asiatic buffalo in the wild. The SANCF thus funded a survey by Bharat Bhushan and HK Divekar, of the southernmost distribution of buffaloes in Madhya Pradesh. They found that only about 125 buffaloes were left around Raipur and Bastar. They identified that the decline was due to heavy poaching pressures. The estimated 125 animals were distributed in four isolated populations in the Indravati National Park, in the Bhairamgarh Sanctuary, in the Pamed Sanctuary and in the Uddanti Sanctuary. Their present status should be ascertained.

SHEEP AND GOATS
**Bharal or Blue Sheep**
—*Pseudois nayaur*

The bharal inhabits high altitudes, in the range of 16,000 feet (4880metres) in summer to 12,000 feet (3660 metres) in winter. This is an extremely sure-footed animal, that skips up even steep precipices, and extremely shy, probably as a result of persistent poaching. The structure and habits of the bharal show that it has linkages to both sheep and goats. Its horns are rounded and smooth, and curve backward over the neck. They graze usually on the undulating grassy slopes. They can climb the most difficult and inaccessible precipitous cliffs, and tend to gaze down from a cliff-edge to survey the valley below.

In 1886, RA Sterndale, FZS, described a new species of ibex—spp. *Capra Dawvergnii* or a variety of *Capra sibirica* in the JBNHS, Volume 1.

|  | 4 |  |
|---|---|---|
| 2 |  |  |
| 1 | 3 |  |

The wild buffalo is now found only in north-eastern India. It is the state animal of Chattisgarh.

Blue sheep from Ladakh jump across a steep precipice.

A herd of blue sheep.

Nilgiri tahr is the only species of wild goats and sheep found south of the Himalayas.

### Nilgiri Tahr—*Hemitragus hylocrius*

The Nilgiri tahr is the only wild goat that is found south of the Himalayas. It is dark yellowish-brown in colour, with a paler belly. Adult males differ from females in that they are a darker shade of brown. After the age of five, the brown bucks become almost black and begin to develop a well-defined, light-coloured saddle mark on the back. The large males, referred to as saddlebacks, have a very deep brown, almost black coat, with a distinctive light patch on the loins. The horns are almost in contact at the base, they rise parallel for some length, then diverge and sweep downwards. They are thick and deeply wrinkled. The Nilgiri tahr is slightly larger than the Himalayan tahr and stands 100 to 110 centimetres at the shoulder. The percentage of saddlebacks in different studies shows that they range between two and nine per cent of the population.

At the end of the 1800s, there were very few Nilgiri tahrs left at the western end of the Nilgiris. These small pockets grew to about 300 animals by 1963. Till 1963, the large male saddlebacks could still be shot. The Nilgiri Wildlife Association then took an active interest in preventing poaching, and along with the Forest Department, initiated conservation measures in Munnar, which led to a further growth in the population. In 1963, ERC Davidar wrote in the JBNHS that the Kundah Hydro electric scheme and other development projects were leading to serious impacts on tahr populations. He also felt that wattle and eucalyptus plantations of the Forest Department deprived the tahr of their feeding grounds. He writes that, 'the future of the tahr will depend upon what is left for it to eat.'

The tahr is now patchily distributed over the hills of the Nilgiris and the Anamalais and southwards along the Western Ghats, at elevations from about 1200 to 1800 metres. Its habitat is restricted mainly to scarps and crags which rise above the forest in the Shola grasslands.

Tahrs are active animals and are incredibly sure-footed even on precipitous slopes. They graze in herds on the rolling hills, nibbling on the upper part of the fresh grass shoots. Flocks usually consist of about six to eight animals, though I have seen 30 or 40 grazing together early in the morning and again in the late afternoon in Eraviculum. During their hours of rest, one or more of the females stands guard and watches for the approach of predators or human activity, which makes them dash across the open grasslands at incredible speeds. I have seen the tahr in large groups, medium-sized groups and occasionally just a male and female. I have observed that if a group is disturbed, the dispersed animals flock tightly together. They all point in the direction of the disturbance and finally charge off.

Males are known to fight occasionally when they rear up on their hind legs, circle each other and finally bang their heads together with a loud crack. This can go on for as long as half an hour.

Their numbers have decreased due to the rapid disappearance of Shola grasslands, which are degraded by repeated fires and overgrazing by livestock. Their distribution is now restricted mainly to the Annamalai Wildlife Sanctuary in Tamil Nadu, the Perambiculum Wildlife Sanctuary and the Eraviculum National Park in Kerala. Together, these account for

The Nilgiri tahr is the state animal of Tamil Nadu.

Large male tahrs are now a rare sight.

The population of Nilgiri tahrs is increasing due to better conservation action.

Wild goats are very sure-footed animals.

Goral are goat antelopes found in the Himalayas.

Goral on a hill-slope in Chail.

about 1500 animals. In February 1963, the Nilgiri Wildlife Association did a census of Nilgiri tahrs in the region. ERC Davidar, the Hon Superintendent, estimated the number to be around 400. He felt that the number had been increasing, but in other areas they had been wiped out. JC Daniel studied the tahrs in the High Range in Kerala and the southern hills of the Western Ghats in 1970. This survey was organized due to the concern that the state's plan to nationalize the tea industry could affect the habitat of the tahrs.

Their numbers have increased since the 1970s, when their population was extremely low. The species however remains at risk as their herds are isolated from each other. Wildlife tourism itself can have unforeseen disastrous consequences for wildlife. At Eraviculum, tahrs congregate around the Forest Department hut, where salt is kept to attract them. Tourists have been known to crush glass bottles and scatter the glass pieces, which look like salt. This has killed several tahrs! These thoughtless acts of vandalism can only be changed if wildlife is increasingly valued in our country. Only a mass awareness movement for wildlife conservation can bring this about.

GOATS—ANTELOPES
**Goral**—*Nemorhaedus goral*
The goral is one of the goat-antelopes of the Himalayas. It has distinctive backward sweeping, conical horns, with well-marked ridges, and foot glands of the kind seen in sheep. The coat is coarse and it develops a small crest on the neck. In Kashmir the race is greyish, while in the eastern Himalayas it is brown. Similar in size to an average domestic sheep, but lighter in build, it is a sure-footed animal that lives on steep precipitous slopes. It is distributed over the Himalayan ranges, usually from 1000 to 3000 metres, but ascending even to 4000 metres. It feeds on grassy hill slopes, interspersed with patches of scrub and forest, forming small feeding groups of four to six individuals, which dexterously jump from one steep crag to another. Shy and easily disturbed by the slightest movement or human voices, it dashes for cover or runs up steep cliffs, over which it disappears. The species is increasingly threatened by habitat loss due to deforestation and by extensive overgrazing by livestock.

## DEER

The commonest deer in India is the spotted deer or chital, found in various types of forests, where there are open grassy clearings. The north-Indian races are heavier and sport the largest antler spreads. Though the number of chital is increasing in several sanctuaries, their populations outside the Protected Areas are declining. Our other common deer is the sambar, which is frequently found in hilly tracts. This is a browser and frequents tree-covered areas that are in fruit or have tender leaves at a low level. With the increasing human threat to hill forests, their habitat has been seriously degraded. The barasingha is an animal of the Terai swamps. However, a small segregated subspecies is seen in the Sal forests of Kanha in Madhya Pradesh, where they have been brought back from the brink of extinction. The hog deer is a stumpy, short animal, found in the Terai Sanctuaries. The muntjack or barking deer is a small deer found all over the country in the past, living in forests and woodlands. It was so common 20 years ago, that it could be found in patches of vegetation close to many major cities, but one hardly ever sees them in the vicinity of urban areas today. Rare species of deer include the hangul, which is also called the Kashmir stag, the musk deer and the chevrotain or mouse deer, which is the smallest of the forest-dwelling species of deer found in India.

Deer shed and re-grow their antlers each year. Unlike antelopes of the plains, forest-dwelling deer live in small herds. The chitals that frequent open grassy areas within the forest live in larger herds than the sambars.

Deer constitute a major part of the prey base of the big cats. In the large areas of forest that existed before human civilization converted them into agriculture, the predators must have been able to control and regulate the number of prey, bringing about a balanced situation. In the course of the last few centuries, however, herbivores were decimated due to shikar. Even today, in habitats where one can expect a large number of deer, there are still too few to support large carnivores, which thus begin to kill cattle, which are easier prey. In a few Protected Areas, however, the deer populations have expanded enormously due to good protection, but the population of predators has not kept pace with the prey base, probably because the small size of many Protected Areas itself limits the number of major predators. An over-abundance of deer leads to overgrazing and an increasing level of conflict with local grazers for fodder. The open grazing grounds begin to deteriorate and there are few satisfactory methods to rehabilitate these grassy areas in the presence of large herds of deer. Kanha has become an example of overgrazed meadows during the last decade.

**There are eight species of deer found in India.**

1
2
3

The hard-land barasingha has been pulled back from the brink of extinction in Kanha.

Chital is one of the most common species of deer in India and lives in large herds.

Sambar live in small herds in various forest types.

## Sambar—*Cervus unicolor*

The sambar is the largest deer found in India, nearly 150 centimetres at the shoulder. It is dark brown with a yellowish or greyish tinge, a pale area near the abdomen, and a coarse and shaggy coat. Large stags are frequently very dark and have a short mane. The brow tine is set at an acute angle with the main beam. At its summit, the main beam is forked. The fully developed antler, with three tines, is developed when it is four years old. Sambar feed mainly at night, on forested hillsides, on grass, leaves and various kinds of wild fruit and in croplands adjacent to the forest.

It is distributed in the wooded areas of India, especially in hilly forested tracts, which include coniferous, evergreen, deciduous and thorn forests. Sambars can move silently even through dense jungle, but dash off noisily once they are disturbed. They require water frequently and are strong swimmers, feeding on aquatic vegetation when available. Stags

are known to fight to obtain rights over a favourite valley. The stag's harem is limited to four or five hinds, though at times there are eight to ten females with a big stag. Large aggregations have been observed occasionally. I have seen one such enormous group on the border between Bandipur and Madhumalai. I watched them quietly grazing in a small opening in the forest for over half an hour. This, however, is an uncommon phenomenon.

Once a very common deer all over India, the sambar is now less frequently seen outside Protected Areas.

JD Inverarity (1906) described the different shapes of sambar horns from the collection of the BNHS in Volume 17 of the JBNHS. The object of this paper was to illustrate the different types of antlers carried by the sambar, all of them from the large collection of the BNHS.

A treepie on the head of a sambar, looking for pests.

A magnificent sambar stag.

Sambar from 'Deer of all Lands' by Lydekker, 1898.

Two sambar stags face each other aggressively at a water hole.

A sambar herd.

A sambar stomping its front leg in alarm.

Sambar showing its unique set of vertical antlers.

A cautious sambar hind.

An unusually large herd of sambar in Mudumalai.

### Chital or Spotted Deer
*—Cervus (Axis) axis*

The sight of a herd of these rust-brown animals profusely dotted with white spots, grazing quietly in a forest clearing is superb. While the spots are irregularly distributed over most of its body, those along the spine are in neat rows. Old bucks have a darker-brown coat, which makes them stand out prominently in the herd. The chital stands 90 centimetres at the shoulder. Its antlers grow to a length of 85 centimetres and have three tines, with a long brow tine set nearly at right angles to the main beam, which branches into two at the end.

Chital are distributed throughout peninsular India and the Gangetic Plains, mainly in deciduous forests, which have a patchwork of openings that form grazing land and have a plentiful supply of water. They are also seen in semi-evergreen and thorn forests.

They aggregate in grassy forest glades, in herds of 10 to 30 or more. Two or three stags, along with several hinds, graze in these openings moving from one patch of grassland to another, frequently entering adjacent cultivated areas. Chital commonly associate with groups of feeding monkeys. Less nocturnal than the sambars, chital graze in the open until late in the morning. In some Protected Areas like Kanha they have multiplied into hyper-abundant populations and are now seriously affecting their own grassland habitats. They have been introduced into the Andaman and Nicobar Islands, where they have also bred prolifically, as there is no natural predator, and they have seriously damaged the local vegetation.

| | | |
|---|---|---|
| | 2 | 6 |
| | 3 | 7 |
| | 4 | |
| 1 | 5 | 8 | 9 |

Chital is the commonest large deer found in India.

A chital herd at a waterhole in Gir.

A chital stag.

A chital herd feeding in a meadow.

A chital stag in Sariska.

Chital from 'Deer of all Lands' by Lydekker, 1898.

A chital on a misty morning in Kanha.

Chital herd.

A chital hind.

## Swamp Deer or Barasingha
### —*Cervus duvaucelii*

The magical sight of a herd of this golden deer seen through the swirling mist at dawn is thrilling. Their antlers move in a symmetry that is difficult to describe.

Located in two distinct ranges, separated by hundreds of kilometres of the Gangetic plain, the swamp-dwelling or *Duvaucelii* is found in the Terai marshlands of Uttar Prahesh and Assam and was formerly common in the Sunderbans. It has splayed hooves and a larger skull. The *Branderi* race is found only in the hard, open, grassy meadows of Madhya Pradesh, in the Kanha National Park. It has smaller, well-knit hooves, and a smoother coat.

Swamp deer stags average 135 centimetres at the shoulder. The females are smaller in size. Their coats are almost woolly in texture, with shades varying from brown to yellowish and they are frequently covered by the swampy mud in which they wallow. Stags have manes and are darker in colour, while the young are spotted. There are wide variations in the shape of the antlers. There are usually 10 to 14 points (tines) on the pair of antlers, though there may be as many as 20. Average antlers of the big males measure 75 centimetres.

Barasingha, as swamp deer are called locally, are highly gregarious and less nocturnal than sambars. Like the chitals, they feed mainly on grass.

Claud Martin (1972) in reviewing the status of the barasingha in Kanha mentions that, in 1938, there were 3023 barasingha in the Kanha region, according to the census of the Forest Department. His estimate in 1971 was barely 70–80 animals.

JH Burnett (1959) mentions that the Kaziranga Wildlife Sanctuary was one of the few strongholds of the swamp deer left in Assam. He felt that by 1959, the swamp deer, earlier seen in groups of three or four, had increased to herds of 14 to 30 animals. He thus felt that in the preceding 20 years they had increased substantially in number. There are only about 400 of the animals left in Madhya Pradesh. They are now threatened with extinction even in the Terai grasslands, where they are restricted to only a few Protected Areas.

| 1 | 2 |
| 3 | 4 |
| 5 | 6 |
| 7 | 8 |

A herd of swamp deer in Kaziranga.

A barasingha stag in Kanha.

Swamp deer is the state animal of Madhya Pradesh and Uttar Pradesh.

Barasingha in Kanha. MK Ranjitsingh from the MoEF and HS Panwar from the Forest Department have been mainly responsible for the survival of the barasingha in Kanha.

A barasingha early in the antler-growing season.

The hard-land barasingha is one of India's rarest deer species.

A swamp deer from '*Deer of All Lands*' by Lydekker, 1898.

Swamp deer from Kishanpur.

### Kashmir Stag or Hangul
*—Cervus elaphus hanglu*

On a cold grey evening, as the sun sets over Dachigam, an unbelievable call rings out and echoes across the mountain sides. A hangul stag is challenging another male. In the fading light, the coat of the hangul ranges from light- to dark-brown, with off-white patches on the lips, chin, belly and rump. The rump has a broad dark stripe extending down to the tail. While a big stag is dark or rufous-brown, the females are lighter and the fawns are spotted. Old animals are frequently covered with white flecks. The hangul is 120 to 125 centimetres high at the shoulder. Its great spreading antlers are a metre in length and have a variety of shapes. Normal heads have five points on each antler, though antlers with as many as eight points each have been recorded. I have seen a large stag in Dachigam that had 13 points.

Lt Col AE Ward described the wildlife of Kashmir in the JBNHS Volume 28, in 1922. He mentions that the Maharaja had created local game reserves called *rukhs* and had introduced game preservation laws to protect this deer. Ward believed that while the population of the deer appeared to be on the increase at that time, it was not possible to stop the rampant poaching of the hangul. He also wrote in Volume 30 of the JBNHS (1925) that though it was patchily distributed, the hangul was still found in many valleys of Kashmir. Today this has shrunk to a single population in Dachigam.

In 1947, Gee estimated that there were 2000 hanguls left in India. He believed that by 1957 only 400 survived, and in 1965 there were only 180 left. However, the figures of the Forest Department were much higher (Schaller, 1969). George B Schaller recorded observations of hangul in the JBNHS Volume 66, in 1969. This rare deer is now restricted to the Dachigam Sanctuary near Srinagar. It is believed that a few may perhaps still survive in some of the adjacent valleys. It is a hill-forest animal, found singly or in small parties, grazing in grassy openings in the high altitude forests and migrating to lower elevations during the winter.

This species is highly endangered due to its restricted distribution in a single population. Excessive poaching has reduced their numbers considerably. Its present status is unclear due to the inaccessibility of Dachigam Valley in a politically unstable area. However, Shri Wani, the Chief Wildlife Warden of Jammu and Kashmir, estimates that there could be 350 to 400 animals at present. The number outside Dachigam remains unconfirmed, but it is evidently too small to have much long-term conservation significance.

The hangul or Kashmir stag is the state animal of Jammu and Kashmir.

A female hangul.

Hangul from '*Deer of All Lands*' by Lydekker, 1898.

Hangul on a steep hill slope in Dachigam.

### Barking Deer or Muntjack
*—Muntiacus muntjak*

A loud sharp bark in a forest is more likely to be the call of a barking deer than a village dog. This small deer, though common to most habitats, is seen much less frequently than chital or sambar. Its shy nature and the fact that it is usually single and hides easily gives one only a fleeting glimpse before it dashes off into the undergrowth and disappears. When most animals in tourist zones in Parks and Sanctuaries get used to tourism, this animal tends to retain its shy nature.

The small antlers have a short brow-tine and an unbranched beam. They are set on hair-covered pedicels, which extend down each side of the face as bony ridges. Excluding the pedicel, which may be up to eight to 10 centimetres long, the antlers rarely exceed 13 centimetres. Old males are dark brown. The upper canines of the male are well developed and are used by the animal in self-defence. An adult male is 50 to 75 centimetres in height.

It is widely distributed in India and frequents thickly wooded hills. It is found up to a height of 2450 metres, singly, in pairs, or in small family parties. It feeds on leaves, grasses and wild fruits.

It is less frequently observed than in the past, as it has been shot and decimated in all forested tracts outside Protected Areas.

### ANTELOPE AND ANTELOPE-LIKE ANIMALS

India is relatively poor in antelope and allied species in comparison to Africa. However, the species found in India are more or less endemic to the South Asian region. The Indian antelope or blackbuck is endemic to India. There has been a drastic reduction of its once vast herds that lived in our extensive grassland tracts. However, its population has increased in a few small grassland Protected Areas during the last couple of decades.

The chinkara or Indian gazelle is a species of open scrubland and low hills. Moving with effortless bounds, chinks can disappear from sight at incredible speeds. It seems to have vanished from many areas during the last 30 years.

The four-horned antelope is a tiny animal found in some open forests and scrublands in different regions. They used to live in varied habitats, but are now rarely seen.

The nilgai or blue bull is a large, antelope-like animal that lives in open areas as well as in dry thorn and deciduous forest tracts. Its habitat extends from north India, through the central plains, into the Deccan Plateau. At one time it was regarded as vermin and extensively shot, which reduced its population drastically. At present its numbers have grown in a few areas in Gujarat, Rajasthan, Punjab and Haryana, where it has become more abundant; this in turn leads to serious problems of crop damage. Only the name 'nilgai', which translates into 'blue cow' gives it sanctity, perhaps the only factor that prevents it from being killed off by angry farmers.

The barking deer or Muntjack is a solitary common deer found in different forest types in India.

A four-horned antelope is one of nature's curious ungulates that has two pairs of horns.

Four-horned antelope.

## Blackbuck or Indian Antelope
### —*Antilope cervicapra*

A blackbuck herd, as one after another of these lithe animals hurtles through the air in a graceful curve, is one of the most spectacular sights the grasslands of India offer.

The blackbuck is the sole representative of the genus *Antilope* in India. Males have a striking black and white body, which makes them stand out in a herd of fawn-coloured, hornless females. The stark white belly, neck-front and rings around the eyes give the antelope a striking, spectacular appearance. In the south, adult bucks are rarely black and their coat remains a dark brown. Adults stand 80 centimetres at the shoulder, with horns up to 65 centimetres long. The horns develop as small spikes after the first year. A large open spiral is developed during the second year, and after three years, four spirals are developed. The dark, nearly black coat of the males also develops at this time. The blackbuck has keen eyesight. One or two in the herd in rotation constantly watch for predators. In the past, its main predator was the cheetah, now extinct in India. Its only predator now is the wolf, although jackals and village dogs also catch fawns.

They live in open grasslands covered with scrub or cultivation. The fallow agricultural lands, which once covered extensive tracts in the plains of India, before irrigation spread through the semi-arid regions of the country, supported enormous herds. After the conversion of these open flat plains into intensive agriculture for growing cash crops such as sugarcane, the blackbuck's habitat has been severely affected. The blackbuck is now restricted to small pockets in residual areas of semi-arid grasslands and has adapted to using degraded wastelands and the few areas of rain-fed croplands. In some areas, protection has led to hyper-dense populations resulting in the escalation of the level of conflict with local farmers.

They are seen in herds of 20 or 30 feeding on grasses, herbs and cereal crops. They browse on stunted trees and shrubs when fresh grass is not available. The herds graze until noon and again in the late afternoon.

1
2
3
4

The blackbuck is the state animal of Andhra Pradesh, Hariyana and Punjab.

A large herd of blackbuck usually has three or four males and 15 to 20 females.

Male blackbuck often form bachelor herds.

The blackbuck is the only true antelope found in India.

| | |
|---|---|
| 1 | 2 |
| 3 | 4 |
| 5 | 6 |
| 7 8 | 9 |
| 10 | 11 |

Two blackbuck males sparring.

Blackbuck running across open grasslands in Maharashtra.

Blackbuck bachelor herd at Rehkuri in Maharastra.

Blackbuck; from Gray, 1830.

Blackbuck being chased off an agricultural plot by local people.

Blackbuck are the fastest runners among Indian ungulates.

A dominant male blackbuck guarding his territory by marking it with a dung pile.

In Maharashtra, blackbuck have adapted to living in drought-prone area development plantations.

Blackbuck sparring with each other to establish their dominance in the group.

Racing blackbuck.

Blackbuck in a grassland.

One of the most exhaustive studies on the blackbuck was undertaken by MK Ranjitsingh in the 1950s. He studied its behaviour and ecology, leading to a better understanding of its conservation biology.

NLNS Prasad (1983) studied seasonal changes in the herd structure of the blackbuck in the JBNHS, Volume 80.

Five herds of blackbuck consisting of a population of over 50 animals were observed during 1987–80 at Mudnal, in Andhra Pradesh. He identified four categories of social grouping:

1. Mixed herds consisting of loose aggregation of males and females of various age groups.
2. Herds consisting of only males—the bachelor herds.
3. Herds of females only.
4. A single territorial male occasionally accompanying several females.

The minimum and maximum herd size observed was two and 36 respectively. The various factors contributing to the changes in the herd structure were noted down.

Nilgai at a water hole.

Nilgais are most frequently found in semi-arid and thorn forests.

The nilgai or blue bull is a large antelope- like animal.

They live in a mixed herd of a few males and several females. Large territorial males, which are the breeding bucks, live as solitary animals and establish their territories by marking them with a series of dung piles and urine. Frequently, several big males have their territories adjacent to each other in a favourite patch of grassland.

Blackbuck are illegally shot for crop protection and for so-called sport. In some areas they are still trapped by local trappers such as the Vaidus in Maharashtra. The meat is sold in villages and is cheaper than goat's meat! While their fate is being slowly sealed by development of intensively irrigated farmland and rural industry, there are still 'wildlife experts' who suggest that they should be culled. We need to look at alternate methods to compensate for crop damage, if this species is to have a future in the wild. Divyabhanu Chavda reports that there may be only some 30–40,000 blackbuck left in India, out of an estimated four million before 1947! He attributes the decline in numbers in the 1950s and 1960s to excessive shooting pressure due to the large number of crop protection guns issued to farmers. Now the next imminent crash in their population is due to changes in land-use, irrigation, spread of sugarcane fields and industrialization of the semi-arid grassland tracts of India.

Salim Ali writes in his autobiography *The Fall of a Sparrow* (1985) that he used to see large numbers of blackbuck 'almost anywhere,' from a little beyond Pune and up to Sholapur and beyond in the 1920s. By the 1940s, he writes that they were completely wiped out.

### Nilgai or Blue Bull
—*Boselaphus tragocamelus*

At a small tank of water, late one evening, a herd of blackbuck suddenly charge into the scrub for cover. A wolf appears silently out of the shrubs at the other end of the clearing and settles down, carefully watching the waterhole. There is another movement at the far side of the tank. A large male nilgai appears, freezes and looks fixedly at the wolf for a long two or three minutes. He then moves a few steps towards the wolf, which then gets up and disappears.

The nilgai is the largest antelope-like animal of India. They are usually seen in groups of four to ten. Occasionally, large males are loners and mark their territories with dung piles. The largest dung pile I have seen was in Sariska, which was over three or four metres in diameter!

The coat of the nilgai is short and smooth, with distinctive white spots on the side of the head and on the fore-legs. The large males are bluish-grey, giving the animal its name—nilgai or blue cow. Females are fawn-coloured. Nilgai have relatively short but powerful spike-like horns.

The nilgai grazes and browses, feeding on leaves and the fruit of *Zizyphus* (ber) and other trees. It can reach higher branches than most other herbivores of the thorn forests, thanks to its height and it is said to be able to go without water for prolonged periods of time.

Like the blackbuck, they severely damage crops and are a cause of serious conflict with farmers. In certain areas where they have been protected, they have grown into hyper-dense populations, leading to a serious conflict issue with local farmers.

### Chinkara or Indian Gazelle
*—Gazella bennettii*

As a medical intern in the early 1970s, I chose for my rural posting a remote site outside Pune, where no one else wished to go. There were two other young doctors with me, who soon began to point out birds so that I could tell them their names. I had selected the site, however, because it was known to have a few chinkaras. One morning, as the jeep bumped towards a remote village, one of my colleagues said, 'look at those strange goats.' Twenty metres away were three sleek gazelles which began to bound away gracefully across the plain. During those six months, we saw chinks on three or four occasions, and this was in a place where 20 years earlier my father had seen them frequently. Thirty years later, there is not a single chinkara left in this area. It is locally extinct.

The chink is a small gazelle, light-chestnut in colour, with white under-parts, flanks and buttocks. A white streak runs down each side of the face, and there is a pale patch above the nose. The horns average 25 to 30 centimetres. The horns of the male appear almost straight when seen from the front; in profile they take a graceful S-shaped curve, with 20 to 25 rings. The horns of the females are smaller, straighter and smoother. A full-grown male measures about 65 centimetres at the shoulder.

It is seen among the less disturbed plains and low hills of North-western and Central India, extending up to the Krishna River. The arid thorn scrub is its favourite habitat. It lives in the wastelands broken up by *nalas* and ravines, scattered bush and sand hills of the desert zone. Chinkara go without water for long periods, live in small herds, the average group size being three. Males are territorial and hold territories of about 200 metres in diameter. These are demarcated by dung piles used repeatedly by the male to indicate territorial rights. It feeds on grass, leaves and fruits of shrubs, as well as on crops.

It has disappeared from many regions in which it was quite common till a few years ago. It appears to be less easily adapted to changes in land-use than the blackbuck.

Nilgais occasionally move in small groups.

Nilgai with young.

Chinkara or the Indian gazelle form small groups in semi-arid grassland and thorn scrub.

Nilgai damage crops extensively..

Chinkara is the state animal of Rajasthan.

An aggressive large wild boar is avoided even by tigers and leopards.

A sounder of wild boar at a water hole.

Wild boar live in nearly every forest type in India.

## PIGS

### Wild Boar—*Sus scrofa*

This common, highly adaptable species is seen all over the country in a variety of habitats. They are often the last large mammals to be seen in degraded forests after other species have disappeared and they are usually seen at night as they forage from one area to another, living on all sorts of food, including grass, fallen fruit, a variety of roots and even carrion. They frequently devastate crops. Farmers shoot, poison and bomb them. In the Western Ghats, I have seen a complex trap built to catch them in forest clearings. Built out of large rocks, the animal is attracted to the trap which when sprung releases a number of big rocks on the animal. The males can become enormous and have large tusks and bad tempers. A big boar is even avoided by a much larger predator. Their prodigious breeding capacity maintains their large saunders even in areas where they are being poached.

### Pygmy Hog—*Sus salvanius*

The Pygmy hog is one of the rarest pigs in the world. It is a small boar found only in Manas and perhaps in a few other locations in Assam. It is a critically-endangered species, thought to be extinct, until rediscovered in the 1970s in the Manas National Park. The Pygmy hog was recorded in 1847 by BH Hodgson in the Journal of the Asiatic Field Society, Bengal. Hamilton in 1921 had observed droves of about 50 animals during a shooting expedition.

William Oliver and Goutam Narayan set up the Pygmy Hog Project in 1996. They caught six Pygmy hogs in Manas, two males and four females and began a highly successful captive breeding programme in Gauhati.

The Pygmy hogs in Manas are known to live in small saunders. They feed on a variety of food and build nests to live in the grassland, and larger ones for breeding. They are specific to the tall-grass Terai ecosystem in Manas. An extensive, but rapid survey of several areas in the northeast where the Pygmy hog was known to occur in the past yielded a negative result. This makes their survival in the wild highly precarious.

## HORSES AND RHINOCEROS

### Asiatic Wild Ass—*Equus hemionus khur*

The Asiatic wild ass is a magnificent animal belonging to the horse family and is characterized by its single hoof. The general colour of its coat varies from reddish grey to fawn or pale chestnut, with the lower parts being whitish. The erect, dark-brown mane is continued as a dark brown stripe extending over the back to the root of the tail. Males are larger than females. The height at the shoulder varies from 110 centimetres to 120 centimetres.

The wild ass had a fairly wide range, at least up to the 1600s. Emperor Akbar hunted wild ass in Sind in 1571. Now found solely in the Little Rann of Kachchh, the wild ass population has reportedly grown from about 500 to 2500 in the past few decades, after it has been protected. However, increasing pressure from salt-works and transportation of salt is a growing threat to this species.

In 1946 and 1960, Salim Ali surveyed the Little Rann for the wild ass and studied its ecology. In his autobiography, Salim Ali (1985) mentions the ingenious way he weighed the wild asses by tying the carcass at one end against the weight of three people who hung onto the other end of the improvised weighing scale.

EP Gee surveyed the wild ass in 1962. He was prompted to do this survey as South African Horse sickness, a viral disease, was reported to be spreading in that part of India. He reports that previous estimates of wild ass were in thousands, but he though there were only 800 animals left. Epidemics, he said, had led to high mortality in 1958, 1960 and 1961.

Wild Asses frequent 'bets'—flat, raised islands from where the water recedes, covered with a luxuriant growth of grass. They graze between dusk and sunrise, on scrub and grasses on the edge of the Rann, spending the day roaming over the barren sun-scorched desert in herds of 10 to 30 animals. There are also groups of two or three, or solitary individuals. They can maintain a speed of 45 to 50 kilometres per hour, over a considerable distance.

The Wild Ass is now a highly endangered species, as it survives only in this single pocket. If a disease of domestic horses affects it, extinction could rapidly follow.

> While investigating a carcass of a young wild ass from Kachchh, VS John Henry Steel, AVD, described parasites in the animal. His observations, from the stomach to the rectum of the animal, revealed that most of the parasites were Ascaris species. The carcass was given to him by Sterndale and Phipson (Steel, 1887).

### Kiang or Tibetan Wild Ass
*—Equus hemionus kiang*

The kiang is the wild ass of Tibet and Ladakh. It roams over the cold desert, completely indifferent to the –40 degree Celsius temperature. It is now very uncommon. At one time persecuted by the Army, it is now actively protected. When followed in a Gypsy, kiang tend to run alongside and then accelerate and cross over in front of the vehicle.

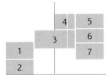

The Asiatic wild ass represents the horse family in peninsular India.

Once widely distributed, the Asiatic wild ass is now found only in the Little Rann of Kachchh.

A kiang can survive at temperatures of –40 ˚ C.

The kiang or the Tibetan wild ass represents the horse family in Tibet and Ladakh.

In ancient India the rhino existed across the entire Indo-Gangetic Plain.

The Terai grasslands are the favourite habitat of rhinos.

The rhino population has declined as the rhino is poached for its horn which is believed to have medicinal properties.

## Indian Rhinoceros

*—Rhinocerous unicornis*

Rhinos were once widely distributed throughout the plains of India. Timur is recorded to have killed rhinos around Kashmir in 1398. LC Rookmaaker has made the most extensive studies on the distribution of the rhino in ancient India and collected evidence to show that three species existed in prehistoric times. In the 16th century, rhinos were found nearly throughout the Indo-Gangetic plains. Harappan and Mohenjo Daro seals depict rhinos.

Ibn Bhattuta, an Arabic traveller and writer, saw them near the Indus River in 1334. They were still there in between 1505 and 1530, for we know that Babar killed them around the Indus River.

In the Mughal period, rhino hunts were said to be numerous. Akbar's reports on rhino hunting are from Sambhal in Uttar Pradesh. The rhino disappeared from the plains, except in the northeast during the 17th and 18th centuries, and by the 19th

century they had small residual pockets in eastern Uttar Pradesh and Bihar. This rapid decline in a mere 200 years demonstrates a growing pressure on wildlife through habitat change and hunting pressures. Perhaps the rhino's medicinal horn could have spurred its collapse faster than other species.

By the 1950s, the rhino had become restricted to Kaziranga. At present, there

are approximately 1500 rhinos in India, nearly all of them in Kaziranga, in Assam. It is estimated that 700 have been killed over the last 15 years alone. In 1953, Gee estimated that there were 350 rhinos left, of which 50 were in Nepal, 58 in Bengal and 240 in Assam. He got the then Prime Minister, Jawaharlal Nehru, interested in conserving their habitat in Kaziranga. TRAFFIC, the organization that

The emperors of the Mughal period hunted rhinos in Uttar Pradesh. By the mid-20th century, the rhino population had dwindled significantly and was restricted to Kaziranga in Assam. EP Gee advised Jawaharlal Nehru to notify Kaziranga as a Protected Area.

Rhinos frequently wallow in mud.

monitors trade in wildlife, has recorded the population of rhinos from 1966 to 1996. Between 1966 and 1986, the population increased from 530 to 1334. After 1986 the growth rate slowed down from 1334 in 1986, to only 1512 in 1996. The exact count for 2005 is not known. Apart from the great one-horned rhinoceros, it is possible that the lesser one-horned survived in the Sunderbans till the early 1900s (Ansell, 1947).

The Indian rhino weighs around 1800 kilograms and grows to an average height of 1.5 metres. The distinctive single horn is about 200 millimetres in length and occurs on both males and females. The rhino's thick skin acts as a shield, studded with masses of round tubercles.

The rhino is a solitary animal living in swamps and moist grasslands, feeding on grass and marking its territory by its large dung piles. Adults need up to 150 kilograms of fodder a day. Males defend their territory from other males, often resulting in serious battles. The rhino is partial to water and I have seen one swim rapidly across a river in Kaziranga, like an amphibian tank. They frequently roll around in a favourite mud wallow. I once experienced a terrifying charge at my jeep from a mother who was tending her calf.

The horn of the rhino is believed to have medicinal properties, for which the rhino is extensively poached. This practice is now driving this animal rapidly towards extinction. The belief that rhino horn has aphrodisiac properties has no scientific proof. While its population has increased after protection measures have been taken, the rhino will never be safe unless this false belief is corrected.

Though Kaziranga is one of our oldest Protected Areas and was created to protect the rhino, one cannot, in the long run, expect to protect the rhino in a single site. Kaziranga was notified as a Game Sanctuary way back in 1926 and was made into a Wildlife Sanctuary in the 1940s. This makes measures to protect the rhino one of the longest conservation programmes in the country. However, we still have only one major viable population and the level of threat through poaching still persists. This demonstrates that when the market price for a wildlife product is very high, conservation action becomes next to impossible and protection measures fail miserably. The most appropriate conservation tool is, thus, creating awareness among its users of the dubious value of such products. Another possible tool is translocation to a new home. A few rhinos have been shifted from Kaziranga and Nepal to Dudhwa, where they are breeding successfully. Some of them have been kept in a large enclosure, as the free-ranging rhinos move into adjacent croplands where they are likely to be poached.

A report in the Assam Tribune in Sept 2001, quoted in the Protected Areas Update 34–35 estimates the number of rhinos poached since 1985 to be a staggering 485! This would make the rhino one of our most endangered species today. There is said to be a linkage between poachers and militants who supply the arms to the poachers.

## MONGOOSES
**Common Mongoose**
—*Herpestes edwardsi*
**Small Indian Mongoose**
—*Herpestes javanicus*
**Stripe-necked Mongoose**
—*Herpestes vitticollis*
**Ruddy Mongoose**—*Herpestes smithi*
This predator can tackle even a large poisonous snake with its superb speed and agility. It preys on a wide range of animals, but also feeds on plant material such as fruit and roots.

The rare ruddy mongoose has a black tip on its tail. I have seen it only once in the Annamalais. The stripe-necked mongoose is larger than the common mongoose. While it is also rare, I have observed it on several occasions in Bandipur.

The mongoose's ability to catch a snake is meticulously taught to the young ones by its mother. I once observed their fascinating teaching-learning method, and saw that it fits in well with our modern

concepts of activity-based learning for school students. The mother snapped at the neck of the snake, shook it up and threw it into the air, but carefully left it alive. She then invited her young ones to repeat this on their own. They approached the snake gingerly at first and one of them, probably the boldest, jumped on it. The mother then repeated the attack several times before finally leaving the nearly dead snake for the young ones to play with. They then used it for a tug of war.

### BATS

The only mammals capable of true flight, bats are divided into frugivorous and insectivorous species. The largest bats, which are incorrectly referred to as flying foxes, as well as the several smaller insectivorous species, are much rarer than they used to be. The large bats form giant colonies, with several hundreds aggregating in a group of large old trees. They were once equally at home in urban as well as forested habitats. Urban colonies are disappearing in most cities.

The decline in insectivorous bats is even more apparent. This is likely to be related to the increasing use of pesticides, which reach these bats through the insect-linked food chains. Pesticides are stored and concentrated in the bats' tissues, finally killing them. The natural mechanism in the food web for the control of insect populations is thus disrupted beyond repair.

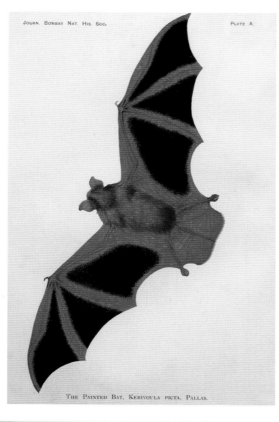

THE PAINTED BAT, KERIVOULA PICTA, PALLAS.

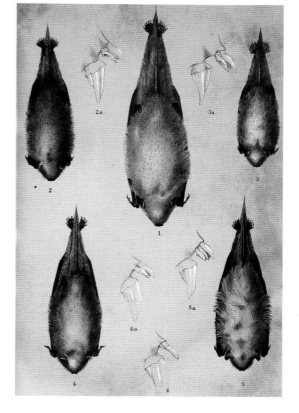

Several species of mongoose are found all over India.

The most favoured prey of the mongoose are snakes.

A stripe-necked mongoose in Bandipur.

Ruddy mongoose.

Bats live in colonies. They frequent caves from which they emerge in hundreds at dusk.

A tiny bat hangs from its daytime roost.

Flying foxes.

Painted bat; from JBNHS, 1912.

Bats; from JBNHS, 1900.

*Following pages*
A drawing of a shikar party using cheetahs; from Forbes, 1813.

# National Parks and Wildlife Sanctuaries of India

Part II

Page 369: Evergreen forest canopy at dawn.
Pages 370–371: Raptor diving for its prey.
Pages 372–373: Tiger!

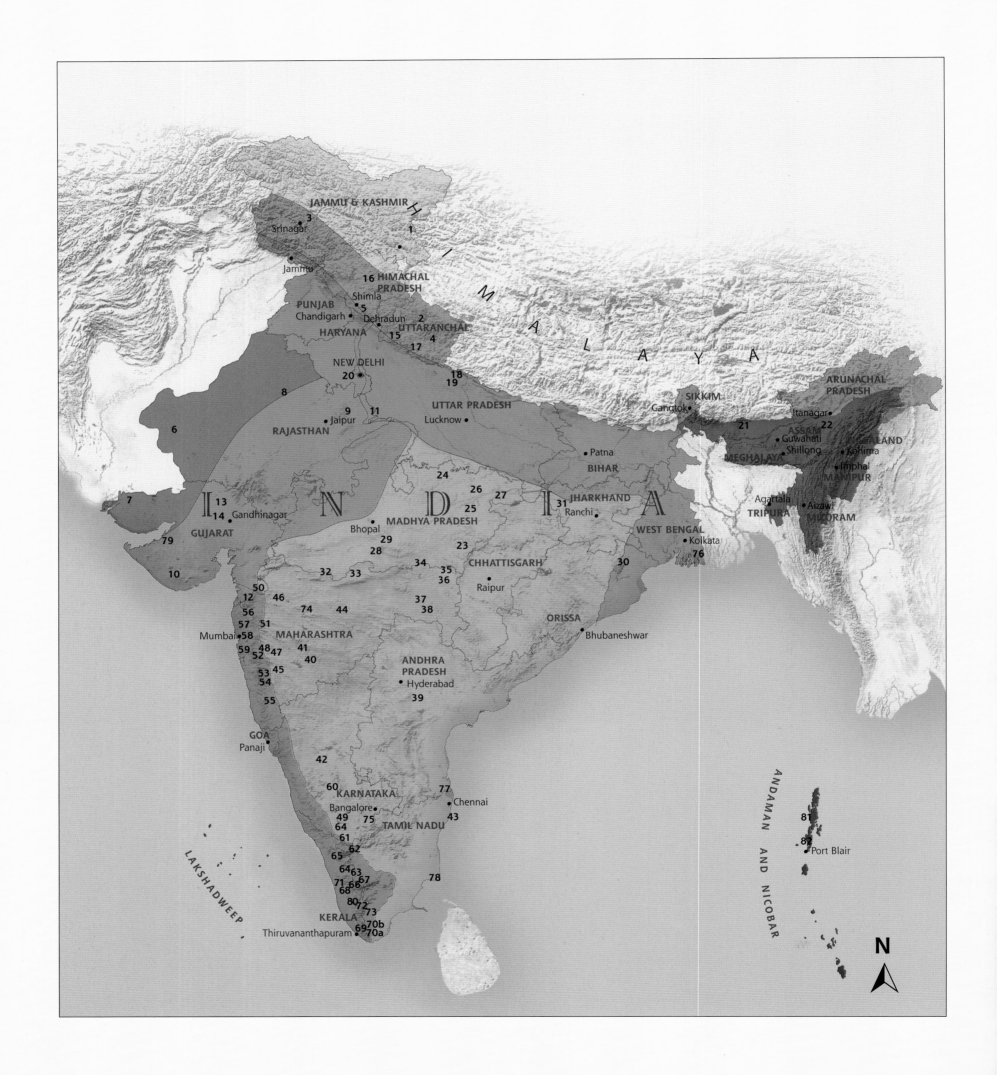

JAMMU & KASHMIR

1

Srinagar

3

Jammu

16 HIMACHAL
PRADESH
PUNJAB Shimla
Chandigarh 5
Dehradun
HARYANA 2 UTTARANCHAL
15 4
17

NEW DELHI
20 18
19

8 UTTAR PRADESH
9 11 Lucknow
Jaipur
RAJASTHAN

Patna

BIHAR

SIKKIM
Gangtok

ARUNACHAL
PRADESH
Itanagar
21 22
ASSAM
Guwahati
NAGALAND
Shillong Kohima
MEGHALAYA Imphal
MANIPUR
Agartala Aizawl
TRIPURA MIZORAM

24

26
27
25
31 JHARKHAND
Ranchi

13
14 Gandhinagar
GUJARAT
79

I N D I A

MADHYA PRADESH
Bhopal
29
28

23

CHHATTISGARH
Raipur

WEST BENGAL
Kolkata
76

7

6

10

50
12 46
56
57 51
58
MAHARASHTRA
Mumbai
59 48 47
52 41
45 40
53
54
55

32 33

34
35
36

37
38

30

74 44

ORISSA
Bhubaneshwar

ANDHRA
PRADESH
Hyderabad
39

GOA
Panaji

42

60 77
KARNATAKA
Chennai
Bangalore 43
49 75
64 TAMIL NADU
61
62
65
64 63
71 66 67 78
68
80 72
73
KERALA
69 70b
Thiruvananthapuram 70a

LAKSHADWEEP

ANDAMAN AND NICOBAR

81
82
Port Blair

N

N

# WILDLIFE SANCTUARIES

## BIOGEOGRAPHIC ZONES

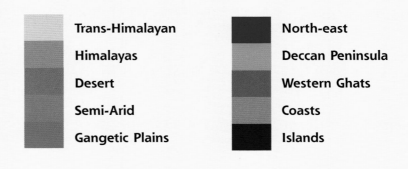

Trans-Himalayan
Himalayas
Desert
Semi-Arid
Gangetic Plains
North-east
Deccan Peninsula
Western Ghats
Coasts
Islands

Based upon Survey of India maps with the permission of the Surveyor General of India.
Responsibility for the correctness of internal details on the map rests with the publisher.

OODAMPORE. 4 MARCHES FROM JUMMOO.

A painting of Udampur near Jammu from the British period.

Gulab Sinh's fort in the hills with a caravan of camels and mules.

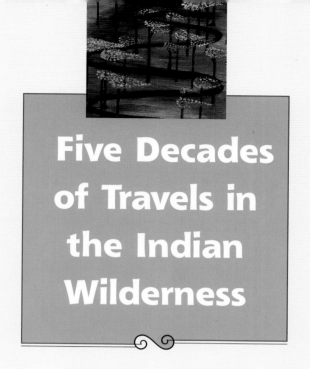

# Five Decades of Travels in the Indian Wilderness

> 66 Travelling through the narrow tracts of a Sanctuary is an incredibly diverse and exciting experience. 99

The wilderness is like an addiction. The more you see of it the more you love it and yearn for it. In time, the grandeur overpowers you. The intricacies of nature begin to increasingly fascinate you. And its wildlife draws you back again and again, to learn more about it.

The story of my own obsession with the wilds of India goes back to my childhood and it is sometimes difficult for me to recall what really triggered it. But I know it just grew over time into a passion that made me want the wilderness to live forever. I began to travel across India's national parks and wildlife sanctuaries and later started documenting India's nature through photography. The journey has been a long one. And it ended after four decades in putting it together for this book.

## FIFTY YEARS IN THE NATIONAL PARKS AND WILDLIFE SANCTUARIES OF INDIA

In retrospect, the 1950s when I was in my teens were a watershed period in the wildlife protection scene in the country. It was a time when individuals who were interested in shikar observed that there was an alarming decline in the mammals and birds they had been shooting. As a young boy in school, I read and heard about this from people around me. I was lucky to

have grown up in such an environment both at home and, to a certain extent, at school. There were many sportsmen shikaris who had given up their weapons around me. Conservationists began to voice their fear that at the rate at which habitat loss was occurring and given the increase in illegal hunting, there would soon be nothing left to conserve. The sword of extinction dangled over several glamour species. Most experts did not even perceive that this was the tip of an iceberg, as the pressures on the less glamorous species were undocumented. India had too many other priorities to deal with. Alleviation of abject rural poverty, creation of arable agricultural land, adequate water for irrigation, the development of a health-care system and education for all—till then accessible to only a very small segment of society, were priorities of a newly emerging development strategy. This did not take into account the fact that, in our traditional setting, Western models of unsustainable land and resource use patterns, would lead to a very rapid loss of wilderness and an unprecedented decline of wildlife populations whose value had been till then only envisioned by most people as 'sport' for the rich.

After independence, shikar became an activity that had prestige value for the neo-rich and neo-powerful. After all, India was

My visits to the National Parks and Sanctuaries left behind memories that could not always be captured on film.

the dangerous jungles they had never seen. So as a scout running around unafraid in the forests of Mahableshwar, I was considered either very brave or simply mad by my fellow scouts.

My father's deep interest in the wilds and in wildlife was turning gradually towards a concern for its future, one which influenced my thinking as well. Even as a college student, I knew a number of prominent conservation people such as Dr Salim Ali (Salimbhai for our family and 'uncle' for me), who visited us in Pune frequently; Dinshaw Pandey, a close friend, who was in the Bombay Natural History Society (BNHS) Executive Committee; the Maharaja of Bansda, who took me to the Dang forests in Gujarat every Diwali; and Professor Nadkarni, my zoology teacher at college, who influenced me throughout my college days. They were rather appreciative of my serious and growing interest in Nature and were surprised at the amount of Natural History I had read and personally experienced both in my garden and in the surrounds of Pune, on my bicycle. I had begun to develop strong views about conservation by the time I had become a medical student. At home, however, my 'bird-watching' was seen as something that was keeping me away from my studies.

In college, I took my friends for excursions to the Western Ghats. While they thought this was exciting, they obviously felt that I was a rather strange fellow to have developed this great fascination for the wilderness. I became popular at college parties, as I could send shivers up people's spines, especially girls', with thrilling and wild stories based on factual experiences. I must admit that in those days I took the liberty of exaggerating a bit, a practice I certainly have had to give up now as a writer.

In the 1950s, many of the roads around Pune were mere cart tracks and I learned to negotiate the big Chevrolet 51 through boulder-strewn *nalas* (streams) and open fields in search of the animals my father occasionally shot. I would take carloads of young people at 80mph in the Chevrolet out into the countryside. Once out of the town we would frequent the less known cart roads and when these also vanished, we would trek through the hills around

now a democratic country! Added to this were the shikaris who were bureaucrats, foresters and officers of the armed forces, all of whom felt this was their newly acquired right as powerful administrators of an independent nation. Who had the right to question them about their actions? The use of crop-protection guns by the farming community (whose guns were not necessarily used only to protect their crops) was commonly believed to be responsible for the decimation of tigers, leopards, deer and other major mammals from the forests, as well as antelopes from grasslands and game birds from both wetlands and grasslands. How could anyone question the starving farmer for killing an animal that wiped out his only crop? While all this did take its toll, the realization that habitat degradation and loss was an ever-growing, serious issue was only perceived

several years down the line in the 1960s. Even the diehard shikaris I knew in the 50s were beginning to wonder if what they were doing as sportsmen was really sportsmanlike. My father, for instance, stopped shooting altogether. Many of the maharajas who had shot game as a sport began to join and lead conservation organizations such as Bombay Natural History Society (BNHS) and later the World Wildlife Fund (WWF).

The 50s, when as a schoolboy I was first introduced to wildlife and bird-watching, were indeed an exciting time for a youngster to grow up in. I was unofficially appointed the story-teller for a group of interested, wide-eyed schoolboys. I would tell them of exciting encounters with wildlife that I had observed in remote wild places where my father took me on shooting trips. They believed that wildlife was all about

Pune. I discovered nature for myself and was happy to share my experiences with whomsoever took the slightest interest in wildlife. Unfortunately, in later years, as I read more of Natural History, I found that the observations I made had been documented decades ago! But I know today that it was this sense of discovery that made my interest grow into an obsession.

There were no BNHS field trips for Pune-ites and WWF did not exist. I learnt my field identification from books by Salim Ali and Prater. But most of all, I experienced Natural History by trudging through the scrublands around Pune, or by cycling a few miles out of Pune into the hills. I also learnt Natural History just gazing out of the window at the trees around my home on Bund Garden Road. I was trying to take pictures of nature with my box camera and later with a twin lens Yashika. But neither wildlife nor bird photography was feasible with the cameras I owned. It was many years before I became the proud owner of a secondhand Exacta and my first tiny 100mm tele-lens which was purchased by my father as a gift. I finally changed to an old secondhand Pentax and later a series of Nikons.

By the end of the 1950s, I was making it a point to visit the BNHS whenever I was in Bombay. I often went in only to say hello to Dr Salim Ali. I spent a lot of time in those early years satisfying my wanderlust in the lush forests of Mahableshwar during holidays and in the dry open deciduous forests of the Dangs in Gujarat with the Maharaja of Bansda. Like my father, he too had changed from a sportsman shikari to an ardent conservationist, protecting what was left of the gigantic trees of the Dangs on his ancestral property at the Sadad Devi farm that became his unending passion. He fought for years to make the forest he once owned into a National Park. He succeeded only after many years of battling with the Government of Gujarat, which, given the smallest chance, would have felled this glorious tract of forest for its magnificent timber. Today this grand personality, who saved a whole forest from being cut down, also cuts paper napkins into four pieces before handing them to his important guests at the breakfast table—'to reduce the wastage of paper that comes from forests'—much to the embarrassment of his two college-going granddaughters. For me, this represents the role of a conservationist par excellence. An individual who is responsible for having saved a whole forest can still think of saving even that last bit of forest resource that goes into making a single paper napkin. If only there were more conservationists of this magnificent calibre in our country!

My growing fear for the well being of wildlife and wild places was emerging as a concern in more ways than one. People whom I met in various spheres of life had begun to see the drastic changes that were beginning to devastate the wild lands in the country. Slowly the 'conservation people' were beginning to increase in number. However, it was primarily an urban, educated, elitist lot, mostly ex-shikaris and ex-rulers of Princely States. I got to know several of these great conservation-minded individuals.

My father took me to places which later became National Parks and Wildlife Sanctuaries. Bhimashankar, Koyna, Bandipur and Mudumalai are early childhood memories. This is where I learned my Natural History. It was for me a period of discovery.

## THE 1960s

The 60s were my Wadia College days in Pune. I took many of my college friends for night drives spotting wildlife. And my early obsession with camera and lens was beginning to bear fruit. As the 60s saw the further decline of wildlife, a greater interest in conservation was becoming apparent among a handful of people around me. Articles appeared in magazines and the press on the need for conservation. Several brilliant black-and-white wildlife photographers were increasingly getting their pictures into magazines such as the *Illustrated Weekly of India*. Awareness levels were certainly growing. But this did nothing in terms of active conservation, to reverse the trend of degradation that continued unabated. It was still the early days of warning that all was not well with nature, for the chital in many forests were still sending out alarm calls that the tiger was on the prowl. A few kilometres from most urban areas, like my hometown in Pune, one saw open wilderness with several birds and animals if one knew where to look for them. But this was rapidly reaching a breaking point. Wetlands in the percolation tanks, once the home of thousands of wintering waterfowl, were showing signs of a lowered population of migrant birds. Grasslands were turning into agricultural land. Forests began to disappear, turning into fuel wood for rural people and charcoal for urban kitchens. I was soon reading old books on wildlife whenever I could lay my hands on them. The library at Bansda was a great source. These were the books by Forsyth, Brander and Whistler, and of course, Jim Corbett. Then came the books presented to me by my parents—Gee, Schaller, Sankhala and a few others that appeared after a long gap. Having read these, my growing interest made me go back to the two older superb books by FW Champion. They came as presents to me from the Maharaja of Bansda. I had, of course, acquired Salim Ali, Prater, Brander and Whistler that I read and re-read. Surprisingly, I could identify birds that I had never seen before because I had read about them and carefully looked at their pictures in Salim Ali's book time and again. While the pictures in the earlier edition that I owned were not great, his description would vividly remain in my mind's eye. I needed no other nature guide or interpreter to identify species for me. Ornithology had become instinctive. My visits to the Dangs and the forests of Purna, which later became Purna Wildlife Sanctuary, were exciting adventures during the summer or Diwali holidays in Bansda over a period of several years. Visits to the wetlands around Pune became an annual winter feature. I knew most of the forts around Pune that were full of bird life. And I knew many secret small footpaths in Mahabaleshwar which were rarely used by tourists. It was on these paths that I realized the intensive labour that local people had to put in gathering fuel wood and taking water to their homes. I soon began to appreciate the difficulties they had living in their forest villages. I also learnt about wildlife from my father's friends and I was taken with them for shikar trips. I can

❝ I was fascinated with the red-gold of the Flame of the Forest tree (*Butea monosperma*), which I observed in many Protected Areas. ❞

of Bandipur and Mudumalai, Kaziranga and Manas, taken three decades ago, appear in the sections related to the Terai forests and the hills of South India.

In these years, there were many changes in the way people began looking at wildlife. Legislations relating to conservation appeared and research into wildlife was moving from taxonomy, to species behaviour, to habitat studies and finally to ecology and conservation biology. The BNHS had several ecosystem-oriented research projects. I frequently had the opportunity to visit these sites and interact with the field scientists at Bharatpur, Point Calimere and at the Elephant Project in Bandipur and Mudumalai. In spite of a growing conservation consciousness, the downward trend in wildlife populations could not be reversed, and only the late 70s saw serious legislative steps being taken that began to halt this decline. Salim Ali became a household word both as an ornithologist of international repute and as a conservationist. Humayun Abdulali, JC Daniel, and several others were instrumental in working on conservation issues through the BNHS. I would meet them frequently at the Society. The erstwhile rulers of Kachchh, Dhrangadhra, Jamnagar, Baroda, Mysore, Bansda, many of whom were known to me as my father's patients, had become a part of the conservation movement. People from different walks of life became leaders of a gradually growing band of conservation conscious people, most of whom were BNHS members. There was a growing number of wildlife-oriented Forest Officials without whose commitment no conservation action would have ever been possible on the ground. In every Protected Area I visited, I would invariably not only meet the Officials, but also the frontline staff from whom I learned a great deal about the Protected Areas' wildlife. During these years a number of large and small conservation-oriented NGOs, which fought for a variety of interrelated conservation issues, from species to habitats, to the rights of wilderness-dwelling tribal communities, were initiated.

Many of these early 'conservation people' had to fight against a tide of development pressures, as the conflict

never forget sleeping through a cold winter night out in the car and finding the fresh pugmarks of a leopard that had circled the car during the night!

## THE 1970s

I believe this was the golden age in the conservation history of India. It was also the decade in which I began going to the Protected Areas from every bio-geographic region. They were all brief visits. Unlike most people, I was using photography to depict ecosystems. I thus evolved a system of documenting habitat characteristics,

and many of the plants and even the less glamorous animal species I saw. I used these images in slide presentations. As people who saw my pictures wanted to put them into a book I worked towards it for four decades. This book is however not organized according to the period in which I have taken the pictures, but has been presented spatially, more or less from North to South as major ecosystems. Thus pictures I have taken recently may have been placed early in the book, and Ladakh, which I visited as late as 2004, opens the section on ecosystems. My earliest pictures between unsustainable development and the loss of wilderness was growing. I became increasingly concerned at this time with what I saw as growing differences between those who supported the needs of poor people and those who championed the cause of wildlife preservation. While I had not picked up conservation jargon such as 'conflict' and 'biodiversity', my early slide-shows and small-time WWF funded research projects looked mainly at conflict issues. I was soon being identified as a sort of oddball on account of this interest in 'conflict'. I gave slide-shows on these issues—blackbuck and crop damage, wolves that killed Dhanghar's sheep, and pollution of the local river and its aquatic ecosystem that had begun affecting the population of aquatic birds. These were my earliest attempts at studies on conflict and in trying to evolve possible strategies that could be used for their management.

The NGO groups gradually brought many like-minded people together. These small bands of people began to form groups mainly in Bombay and spread to Pune and other cities. Like several others, I joined the BNHS and WWF. Similar initiatives to set up independent nature-related NGOs were beginning to emerge across the country. In Delhi, it was Kalpavriksh, in Bombay the Bombay Environmental Action Group. There were just too many for me to name them here. Many did not survive over the next few decades. Others were highly successful.

By the mid-70s, I had a fairly large collection of exciting wildlife pictures, and was presenting my slides from the many National Parks and Wildlife Sanctuaries I had visited to various audiences. There were times when I would address at least three audiences in a month.

Travelling along the wilderness tracts of India in the 70s was much more difficult than it is today. On my meagre salary as a Government Lecturer of Surgery, I had to use the cheapest mode of transport, or there would be no money left to buy film! Just getting there and back would eat up all my small savings for the year. I thus made it a point to read a paper at every Annual Conference of the Surgeons of India so that I got a Government-sponsored third class train ticket! The conference was always in December and I would find information on the closest Protected Area to the Conference venue and make a beeline for it by bus as soon as the conference was over.

I recall that the bus to Darjeeling ran off the road, down a hill slope, and stopped, perched over a fairly big drop. And the one taking me to Point Calimere veered off into a boggy ditch to avoid a rather intoxicated man who decided to run across the road. It was the election day and we were lucky not to hit him.

I got to Kaziranga when the local unrest had just begun. On the second day of my visit I was politely requested to give up my room temporarily as the Forest Minister was expected. I forgot my

> For me,
> the loss of a great tree
> became
> as important as
> the poaching of
> an animal.

footwear in the room, and the Minister noticed this and asked if anyone was occupying the room. On my return he sincerely apologized and said he had used the verandah as he felt it would not be appropriate to deprive me of my room. One cannot ever expect this today anywhere in the country. On the last day I took a short walk. The village nearby was deserted. When I got back all the tourists were moving out. I stood in a bus all the way back to Guwahati. The disturbances that have rocked Assam for the last three decades had begun in earnest.

Among my many nearly disastrous trips for taking wildlife pictures, was the aftermath of my visit to Kaziranga, Manas and Sunderbans in December 1978. The photographic studio in Pune in those days had to send colour film to Bombay for developing. Imagine my anguish when I was told the building where my film was processed had fallen down precisely when the boxes were being picked up. The courier had left them on the counter to save his life! 'Don't worry, we can see your film is safe on the counter through a chink in the door, but as the building is not properly insured, the police won't let anyone in at present.' I got my film back, with the boxes half-eaten by rats some three months later! The pictures were safe.

### THE 1980s

In the 1980s I worked as a Committee Member of the Pune Division of the WWF, for which I was also Principal Investigator of research projects on blackbuck ecology and problems due to crop damage in the Rehekuri Wildlife Sanctuary, and I was responsible for monitoring the Wetlands at Bhigwan in the backwaters of the Ujjani Dam. I made a film for the Open University Programme on *The Changing Nature of a Wetland* that was one of the first efforts to show a wildlife film to University Students. In 1986 I joined the BNHS as a Member of the Executive Committee at the behest of Dr Salim Ali.

Conservation was changing from Natural History into a new science. A less emotional and a more pragmatic approach to wildlife was becoming apparent. It was no longer the done thing to be dubbed a 'Natural History Conservation' person or an 'environmentalist'. We now had 'animal behavioural scientists' and 'ecologists' systematically 'studying' wildlife rather than watching and documenting whatever they saw. The element of fun in watching nature was slowly disappearing. Conservation and environmental activism was becoming serious business. At first, the formal ecological scientist looked down upon the amateurs of the period as dabbling with things they did not know about or understand. But it was the amateurs who seemed to have access to political powers to influence the conservation policy. The NGO groups gradually grew increasingly strong and influenced Government decisions more frequently than the scientists or the officials of the Forest Department.

My role in the BNHS as an Executive Committee Member and through the Salim Ali Nature Conservation Fund (Salim Ali had told Dilnavaz Variava to ask

“ My visits to wetlands and other aquatic ecosystems left a deep impression on my mind. I hoped these wilderness systems could last forever. ”

me to be a part of this after his death) led to my organizing closer interactions between the Wildlife Institute of India (WII) and the BNHS, as I had friends in both organizations. My friends at WII were Alan Rodgers, HS Panwar, Johnsingh, Jhala, and many others. They called me to Dehra Dun for several meetings and workshops. The network I became a part of was growing. Shekhar Singh from the Indian Institute of Public Administration (IIPA) became a close friend who greatly influenced my thinking. He has been my sounding board on conservation issues ever since. I had now visited and photographed wildlife and the diverse ecosystems in many important Protected Areas from nearly every eco-region of the country.

Some of the Protected Areas I visited have left pleasant memories of people I met and episodes that I will always recall even though I have been there only once. On my way to Zainabad in Kachchh in 1984, I landed at dawn in Ahmedabad only to find the streets deserted and strewn with stones and broken glass. There had been rioting the evening before. A curfew had been declared and the army had been called out to patrol the streets. A friend, whom I luckily managed to trace, was influential enough to send an Army Major to pick me up. He arranged for a state transport bus to drive me and two other passengers to the edge of town under an armed escort of three trucks and a jeep to Zainabad. Then we found out that the bus driver had never been to Zainabad and did not know the route. He had agreed to drive us only because he wanted to get out of Ahmedabad! He got us eventually to a deserted Zainabad late in the evening and I had to find my way to the house of Shabir Malik, one of the most enthusiastic and experienced wildlifers in the Little Rann. The strange, tired-looking, dishevelled man at the gate of his house was scrutinized carefully before being reluctantly allowed into the compound. I did not fit into the regular pattern of guests to Shabir's tourist outfit—besides I had come on foot!

I have been in forest rest houses in the most idyllic places. But there are others I recall not for their beauty but the events that left living memories. I have so many different memories of my days in a small forest rest house in Rehekuri in which I spent several days over many years, when I went there to watch and study blackbuck throughout the 1980s. It was invariably hot and dry, and the taps rarely had water in those days. But one hot, dry, pre-monsoon day, as I sat on the verandah, a dark cloud crept up behind me and burst with a clap of thunder. The rain was ice cold! Small hailstones littered the darkening verandah like so many stars. The thirsty scented earth, as it swallowed up each large drop of rain, created wisps of vapour. I walked out as the thundercloud rolled past to open the sky up with a pale gold evening light. The background music befitting this could only have been Beethoven's *Pastoral Symphony*. On my return, my feet were clogged with mud. I recalled there was no shoe-scraping device, as on a previous visit with MK Ranjitsinh he had remarked that this old-fashioned device was not required anymore since Forest Officers rarely walked about in the wilderness. I left my muddy shoes outside and discovered the next morning that they had become home to a frog during the night. Probably his first night out after a long dry spell—for him the rain must have been as exciting as it was for me.

By the last years of the 60s I had been to more than 50 Protected Areas, several on many different occasions, in different seasons and over the previous decades. The changes I observed were both a rise in pressures, especially as a result of development, and, in some places with good protection, a surprising increase in wildlife populations. Increasing tourism was now beginning to lead to a variety of new pressures. Plastic bags, noise and the loss of a real wilderness experience have been some of the consequences. People now dominate the wilderness landscape— both the tourists as well as the growing local human population.

## THE 1990s

I consider this a black period in the conservation history of India. This has been a time when, on the one hand, there was greater knowledge, but on the other, a lowering of political and executive desire to 'do' things for conservation. It was however at this point in time that the Judiciary appears to have become an active trigger of environmental protection, arresting the loss of forests, blocking the impending destruction of sensitive coastal tracts and of fragile hills and mountains. While State Governments were trying to exploit Nature for its revenue, the Courts began to see this as an unsustainable practice. In no other country has the Apex Court been so proactive towards conserving a country's natural assets. No amount of praise can be enough for their foresight and their staunch resistance to a wave of anti-conservation actions by Government and the 'development' lobby that only looks at short-term economic gains. In spite of this, land use changed from wilderness to cash crops and industrial development has grown, rapidly engulfing what was left of the residual wilderness of India. This has adversely affected the environment in economically affluent states, with the growth of enormous industrial belts such as those in Maharashtra and Gujarat, more seriously than states such as Madhya Pradesh and Uttar Pradesh, where it is still possible to envision a more sustainable form of development in the future. Most conservationists feel that there is now a growing nexus between institutions that are looking at rapid economic returns and the Ministry of Environment and Forests (MoEF) itself. The MoEF appears to have lost its teeth and unfortunately, passes projects that will lead to the loss of India's biological wealth.

In 1993 a chance event led me to initiate the Bharati Vidyapeeth Institute of Environment Education and Research-(BVIEER), with the strong backing of BVIEER's dynamic founder, Dr Patangrao Kadam. Dr Kadam loves ceremonial tree planting and during one of these occasions I was also asked to plant a tree. When I said that I did not like planting eucalyptus trees as it was ecologically unsound, he responded that environmentalists only talk but rarely do anything. He then said I should start an Institute to spread awareness and educate people about conservation issues. I was given several reminders to write this up as a project. We started with the background of my experience with BNHS, WWF and the School of Environmental Sciences of Pune

" I spent a lot of time
visiting remote villages of India,
where I appreciated the issues
that led to people-wildlife conflicts. "

University which I had helped establish. Once we started the Institute, it rapidly grew from early school teacher training programmes on environment education, to starting an M.Sc. course. This took a brief six months! This Institution now runs Ph.D., M.Sc. and B.Sc. courses, a Diploma in E.E. for in-service school teachers and a large number of research programmes related to biodiversity conservation. All this has greatly influenced the text for this book. I had by now visited over 70 Protected Areas across the length and breadth of India, many of them several times over. My collection of pictures had become very large—in fact, too large to fit completely into the pages of this book.

I realized that there is no real wilderness without people left in our country except in some remote areas in the lofty rugged Himalayan ranges and some of the tiny islands in the Andamans. Most forests have had scattered small human habitations for centuries. Their numbers have now grown enormously. In previous generations the number of tribal people who were the main inhabitants of the wilderness depended solely on hunting and gathering, along with a small amount of farming in openings in the forests. They lived different lives that were far below the poverty line in those days. Today their own essential needs have increased, their population has expanded and their horizon has legitimately expanded as

well, to take in and mimic the lifestyles of people living outside their own semi-wilderness ecosystems. Their way of life is further compromised by the need to compete with communities living just outside their wilderness ecosystem in highly man-modified environments. In many instances people from outside have in fact migrated to these places, which are now less inhospitable than in the past. Enhanced communication, education, health care and other development measures have unfortunately changed tribal life from a highly sustainable way of living into an unsustainable pattern.

The natural forests, grasslands, mountains and coasts of India have thus inevitably succumbed to increasing local human population growth. I have come to realize this increasingly over the past 30-odd years. As the so-called 'backward' areas have become more and more accessible, the last of the remote areas of my childhood have all but vanished.

There are many types of forests I have visited during the last few decades. But each time I have left the wilderness with an increasing sadness, a feeling of trepidation that on my next visit, if and when I return, it may not be the same. I have observed that forests have changed in their structure due to several human interventions. This has happened much faster than most people believe. And as the habitat changes, the populations of their component wild species alter drastically in number and composition. The more sensitive species that are more easily affected by habitat changes decrease alarmingly in number, while in many situations the more robust generalist species or the exotic species introduced purposefully or accidentally from outside the ecosystem, increase in number. The 'naturalness' and unique aspects of the forest ecosystem vanishes forever.

The development strategy we have used for the people who live close to their local natural ecosystem has been thrust upon them in such a way that it is like a malignant disease—a cancer—that relentlessly kills a patient by growing within the body unchecked. The legitimate human rights of people living in the Protected Areas to develop their economy remain unquestionable. However, the mode and approach to enhancing their livelihoods, to the level of those living outside the wilderness, has left them in fact increasingly resource-poor. Development has itself added to the unsustainable practices now forced upon an unsuspecting group of people who have been marginalized for generations.

For years now I have been talking to people from all over the country belonging to tribal cultures and otherwise dependent on the natural ecosystem. While all of them understand their current plight through a world view of their own traditional knowledge systems, they are ill equipped to find solutions to problems that are not of their own creation. My respect for their knowledge of their surroundings has grown year after year during the last three decades. What is rarely documented is that development pressures due to activities such as changes in land use from forest to agriculture, or plantations, or dams for hydel and irrigation projects, or roads, all lead to far greater and more lethal degradation of the wilderness than the gradually growing pressure from the activities of the poor and vulnerable local inhabitants.

It is these changes in land use from wilderness to highly productive areas that are a prime factor in the loss of ecological security and biodiversity. Only enlightened and sensitive policy makers can make a difference. They will only be elected if the average man on the village street and the urban roads of India begins to elect 'green' politicians.

## BEYOND 2000

By the year 2000 I had completed a CD-ROM on India's biodiversity and had begun to plan writing a book on my experiences in the vanishing wilderness of India. I realized that for completeness I would have to add areas that I had not visited or had not enough pictures to use for the book. I thus visited the Protected Areas of Ladakh and Kedarnath in the Himalayas. I went to Kalakad and Mundantharai, the southernmost evergreen forests of India and the Andamans on several occasions.

The last few years have begun to emerge as a new challenge for conservation. The NGO groups fighting for conserving resources seem paralyzed at the onslaught of unsustainable development. Others have been frustrated trying to support the needs of tribal people who are still forest dependent. One of the greatest pro-conservation inputs has again come from the Apex Court, which has brought Environment Education into school and college curricula. I believe this will lead to the creation of a 'green' movement through which the people of India will vote for politicians and political parties that have a 'green' agenda. It is the common people of India alone who can save our biological wealth for posterity.

" Rural people have had to fell trees to eke out a living. Conservation cannot succeed without their participation "

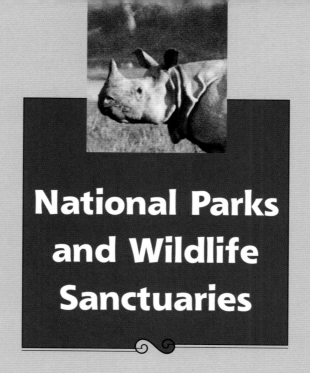

# National Parks and Wildlife Sanctuaries

Several hunting reserves of Princely States were converted into Protected Areas.

In the 1950s wildlifers persuaded the Government to create Protected Areas. EP Gee induced Jawaharlal Nehru to protect Kaziranga and safeguard the rhino.

The word 'park' comes from the old European word 'parc', used to demarcate a hunting area. In ancient times, between 550 and 350 BC, royal hunting reserves were used by Persian ruling families in Asia Minor. In more recent times in the mid-1800s, London had Royal Parks, which were recreational areas. The first National Park, as we understand the term today (areas preserved in a natural state or instituted to protect endangered species), was the USA's Yellowstone, created in 1872. Its focus, however, was to protect natural grandeur. Canada's Banff National Park in 1885, Australia's Royal National Park in 1879, and New Zealand's Tongaro National Park in 1894 followed in due course. In the 1920s the former USSR had created Zapovedniki or 'forbidden areas', where endangered plants were strictly protected and only ecological studies were permitted. A second line of National Parks was created in Russia in the 1960s, for recreational purposes. By the 1960s African National Parks had become a major source of earning foreign exchange. Currently there are about 1400 National Parks in the world, of which about 92 are in India. This accounts for six per cent of the world's National Parks for a country that should have at least double the number.

During the two decades of the 1940s and 50s, many of India's hunting reserves that had belonged to rulers of Princely States or used as shooting blocks organized by the British mainly for sahibs were converted into Wildlife Sanctuaries. Shooting blocks were created by the British to maintain an adequate number of animals for shikar. Hunting was thus kept at sustainable levels. Still other areas were ther Reserved Forests, which had retained major mammals and thus became Protected Areas. None of these were created to preserve biodiversity, nor were they conceived as representatives of a network of different wildernessecosystems.

Even after Independence, Gee, Corbett and Lt. Col. RW Burton, who were great 'wild-lifers' and writers, contributed to the cause of setting up National Parks and Wildlife Sanctuaries in Independent India in the 1950s. The erstwhile Maharajas, once ardent shikaris, now took it upon themselves to protect wildlife.

The first time I came across the use of the term 'Protected Areas' for both National Parks and Wildlife Sanctuaries in Indian literature was in the *JBNHS* (1954), Volume 52, where KS Dharmakumarsinhji, in his article on wildlife preservation in India writes the following: 'I have come to the conclusion that it is essential for the States to inaugurate 'Protected Areas' where Sanctuaries in the strict sense cannot be established as early as possible, and

In the 1970s and 1980s several Protected Areas were created in grasslands, wetlands, rivers and coastal areas.

with the aid of the Central Government, create National Parks immediately.'

The sub-committee for setting up National Parks and Wildlife Sanctuaries in 1951 had considered several issues. These included legislations, selection of areas, forestry operations, and management of the Protected Areas. The policy was gradually evolving. The individuals spearheading this were wildlife lovers, frequently ex-shikaris, who had begun to feel that the wilderness and its denizens should be urgently protected. In contrast, there were those who felt this was contrary to the economic aspirations of poor farmers in an essentially poverty-stricken, starving nation. In 1952 the Central Board for Wildlife had its first session in Mysore and recommended that

its name be changed to the Indian Board for Wildlife (IBWL). It suggested far-reaching changes, for instance that the IBWL be considered in the Constitution as an 'institution of National importance.' The Board envisioned trade controls on wildlife and wildlife products, considered the setting up of National Parks and Wildlife Sanctuaries as a means of promoting public interest in wildlife, and recommended the establishment of State Wildlife Boards. The need to place National Parks, till then a State subject, on the concurrent list of the Government, was pointed out by the IBWL around 1952, then again suggested in 1955. The Board also suggested the creation of a Bill for this purpose in 1957 and 1959 and recommended interim measures. It took

several years to make this change. Thus in the 50s the Board had begun playing a major advocacy role through its members who were private citizens of great eminence. In the recently appointed Board in 2004 there are very few non-governmental organizations (NGOs) and non-governmental individuals (NGIs), and their voice has been clearly overruled.

## THE GROWTH OF INDIA'S PROTECTED AREAS

From Independence to 1964, when Jawaharlal Nehru was Prime Minister of India for three terms, several new Protected Areas were created. In 1970, however, there were only 4 National Parks and 61 Wildlife Sanctuaries that were notified. Indira Gandhi's first term as Prime Minister

Several tiger reserves were created in the 1970s which were funded through Project Tiger.

between 1968 and 1977 saw an increase to over 100 Protected Areas. The new Government lasted for three years and the country voted Indira Gandhi back into power in 1980.

The Tiwari Committee set up by Prime Minister Indira Gandhi in 1980 included non-government experts such as M Krishnan. He stated the following (Thapar, 2003):

'I suggested 5% of the total land is to be preserved in perpetuity… The committee is reluctant to recommend any specific percentage. The reasons for this reluctance are not clear, and are probably rooted in an apprehension of the procedural difficulties involved. I submit that in a matter of such National importance, a more dynamic and constructive response should be made.'

He further noted that in 1980, though there was about 2.3 per cent of land in the Protected Area network this was inadequate; he referred to this as the 'so-called' wildlife preserves. He went on to remark that if this was raised to five per cent, in reality only 1.2 to 1.5 per cent would ultimately remain. Many experts were pointing out the difference

between what the International Union for Conservation of Nature and Natural Resources (IUCN), referred to as a National Park, and a Wildlife Sanctuary (WLS), which was not practical in a developing country. A quarter of a century later in 2005, we can see how prophetic Krishnan's words were. With about 4.7 per cent of land now in the Protected Area network there are high pressures from development to reduce the size of the Protected Areas to make way for dams, roads, industry, etc.

The decade between 1970 and 1980 saw an increase in the Protected Areas across the country by 129 bringing the total to 194. In the 1980s every state had begun to see the need for establishing Protected Areas in non-forest ecosystems. In Maharashtra, notifying non-forest areas such as grasslands, wetlands, rivers and marine ecosystems was seen as an urgent need over three decades ago. An amorphous group of bird-watchers held meetings and lobbied with the Forest Department to notify Nandur, Jayakwadi and Mayeni as wetland sanctuaries for waterfowl. Similarly, in several states, non-forest landscapes were gradually introduced into the Protected Area network.

This unfortunately came too late to save many of these unique ecosystems, which were under-represented in our Protected Area network until the late 1970s. Over 100 of the small islands in the Andamans were notified as PAs during this period. The 1970s also saw several Protected Areas being converted into Tiger Reserves.

Indira Gandhi was killed at the peak of her power and popularity in 1984 and Rajiv Gandhi became the next Prime Minister. The interest that she had initiated in notifying new Protected Areas continued, however, after her. New Protected Areas thus continued to be notified over the next few years. Rajiv Gandhi's era, from 1984 to 1989, saw the Protected Areas continue to increase, selected on the basis of Rodgers and Panwar's document on India's Protected Area network that was completed in 1988. Rajiv Gandhi lost the elections in 1989. During the 1980s, India notified 294 new Protected Areas, the sharpest increase that we have seen so far.

In the 1990s, Chandrashekhar, followed by PV Narasimha Rao, led the country for about five years. In 1990, there were 71 National Parks and 417 Wildlife Sanctuaries. By 2000, their number had

Areas with rich communities of plants such as the North-east, the Andaman and Nicobar Islands and the Western Ghats were recognized for their high biodiversity values. This was in response to Rodgers and Panwar's study on the Wildlife Protected Area Network in India.

It was realized that more areas such as the Western Ghats should be notified as Protected Areas.

increased to 86 and 480 respectively. Thus in this decade, only 78 Protected Areas were added. A sudden slowing down of additions to Protected Areas shows evidently a lack of political will and a lack of new possibilities. This is also a result of rapid increase in all the other land use changes, which had a negative impact on conservation initiatives.

From 1991 to 2000, only 78 new Protected Areas were notified, most of them being selected as a result of the document *Planning a Protected Areas Network for India*, by Rodgers and Panwar from the Wildlife Institute of India. This period has seen the slowest additions to the Protected Area network as compared to the three earlier decades.

From 2000 to 2005 there were about 584 notified Protected Areas, covering only about 4.7 percent of India's landmass (Mathur, 2005), a grossly inadequate figure to protect one of our most valuable resources. These areas are especially important for the country's long-term sustainable development.

Today, of the roughly 600 Protected Areas in India, 100 are small islands in the Andaman and Nicobar. Nation-wide, many of the Protected Areas are subjected to enormous pressures from human habitation and rapid degradation due to present patterns of economic development—including roads, dams, mines, timber extraction, fishing and industrial growth which are spreading around the Protected Areas and have serious impacts on conservation values.

Dams and roads have even been developed within their boundaries! Saw mills have been illegally established on the boundaries of Protected Areas. Townships are growing on the boundaries of Protected Areas and industries are mushrooming around them.

Even today, Protected Areas in forest ecosystems disproportionately outnumber those in other ecosystems such as wetlands, grasslands, hills, mountains, deltas and coastal areas. Certain key areas with high

### The Protected Area Network of India

Number of National Parks and Wildlife Sanctuaries in India.

| Year | 1950 | 1960 | 1970 | 1980 | 1990 | 2000 | 2003 | 2005 |
|---|---|---|---|---|---|---|---|---|
| National Parks | | | 4 | 30 | 71 | 86 | 89 | 92 |
| Wildlife Sanctuaries | | | 61 | 164 | 417 | 480 | 500 | 500 |
| Total Protected Areas | 22 | 23 | 65 | 194 | 488 | 566 | 589 | 592 |

*Source:* W A Rodgers, Hemendra S. Panwar and Vinod B. Mathur (2000). *Wildlife Protected Area Network in India: A Review* (Executive Summary). Wildlife Institute of India, Dehradun, NBSAP and personal communication with Dr V B Mathur, (2005).

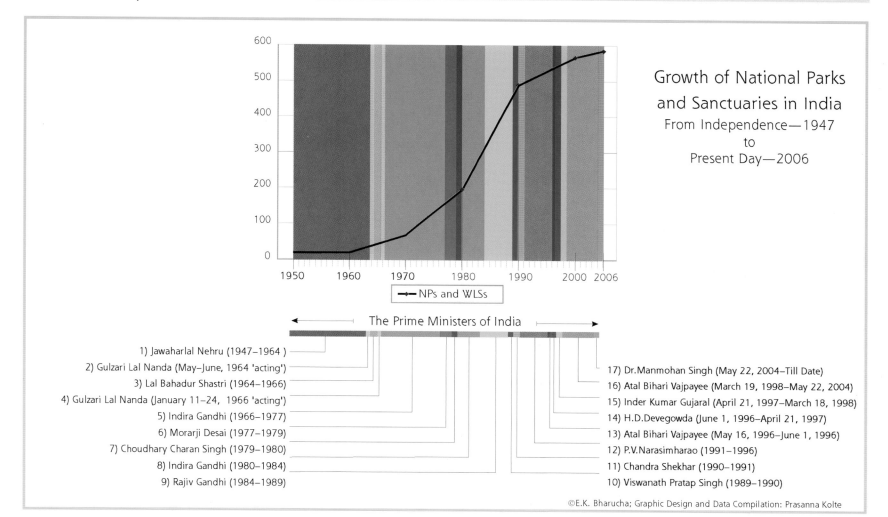

## Growth of National Parks and Sanctuaries in India
From Independence—1947
to
Present Day—2006

→ NPs and WLSs

← The Prime Ministers of India →

1) Jawaharlal Nehru (1947–1964 )
2) Gulzari Lal Nanda (May–June, 1964 'acting')
3) Lal Bahadur Shastri (1964–1966)
4) Gulzari Lal Nanda (January 11–24, 1966 'acting')
5) Indira Gandhi (1966–1977)
6) Morarji Desai (1977–1979)
7) Choudhary Charan Singh (1979–1980)
8) Indira Gandhi (1980–1984)
9) Rajiv Gandhi (1984–1989)

17) Dr.Manmohan Singh (May 22, 2004–Till Date)
16) Atal Bihari Vajpayee (March 19, 1998–May 22, 2004)
15) Inder Kumar Gujaral (April 21, 1997–March 18, 1998)
14) H.D.Devegowda (June 1, 1996–April 21, 1997)
13) Atal Bihari Vajpayee (May 16, 1996–June 1, 1996)
12) P.V.Narasimharao (1991–1996)
11) Chandra Shekhar (1990–1991)
10) Viswanath Pratap Singh (1989–1990)

©E.K. Bharucha; Graphic Design and Data Compilation: Prasanna Kolte

Vedanthangal was one of the earliest bird sanctuaries to be given legal protection.

Up to the 1950s wildlifers persuaded the Government to create Protected Areas. EP Gee induced Jawaharlal Nehru to protect Kaziranga and safeguard the rhino.

biodiversity values need special emphasis. These include the Western Ghats, highly impacted by new forms of land use; the Protected Areas of the north-east seriously disturbed due to political unrest; and the Andaman and Nicobar Islands threatened by strategies to increase tourism.

## THE HISTORY OF PROTECTED AREAS IN INDIA

The first area to be given legal protection in modern India (1898) was the Vedanthangal Bird Sanctuary, an incredible aquatic ecosystem in Tamil Nadu, teeming with bird life. When it was first closed for hunting no one could have imagined that, just 100 years later, there would be very few similar large nesting colonies of birds left in this vast country. If a similar level of protection had been afforded to a larger number of breeding colonies of birds such as storks, pelicans, spoonbills, ibises, and egrets, there would have been much larger breeding colonies today.

Kaziranga was declared a Sanctuary in 1928, as it was clear that the continual poaching of rhinos for their horns would soon drive it to permanent extinction. Thus the first formal Protected Area was notified to protect a single species from being exterminated. In the 50s, EP Gee took personal interest in supporting conservation initiatives in Kaziranga and took Prime Minister Jawaharlal Nehru on elephant back to see rhinos. Later, in 1985, Kaziranga was declared a World Heritage Site, one of the first natural heritage sites in India to be so declared, along with Manas and Keoladeo.

Corbett National Park (initially called Hailey National Park) was the first National Park in the country to be notified in 1936 and was aimed at preserving one of the best known habitats of the tiger in the country. It was part of the great forests in which Jim Corbett shot so many man-eaters, and was thus renamed after him. This park is also one of our first Tiger Reserves which was expected to protect the entire range of major fauna and preserve their habitat as an intact ecosystem.

In the post-Independence era there were several instances in which individuals lobbied to create Protected Areas. This was no easy task. Tolaram K Mirchandani

(1956), a Forest Officer in the 1950s, wrote in the Journal of Bombay Natural History Society (JBNHS) that: 'All Indians who are interested in the protection of nature are grateful to the Society for the sustained effort it is making to foster public interest in the preservation of the fauna and flora of our country.' He explains how he initiated moves to notify Dandeli as a Sanctuary: 'In 1942–43, when I was Divisional Forest Officer, Kanara North Division, I selected an area of approximately 100 square miles suitable for a wildlife sanctuary in that Division. By an executive action, signboards were put up at all road entrances and exits, prohibiting shooting within the area and the Conservator of Forests, Southern Circle, declined to issue shooting block permits for the shooting blocks included in the proposed Sanctuary. Later, when I was the Conservator of Forests in charge of this Circle, I closed all shooting in this area by a notification under Indian Forest Act and submitted detailed proposals to Government to constitute this area into a National Park. For this purpose it was necessary to remove 2 or 3 hamlets within the area affecting about 500 persons (100 families). For the rehabilitation of these persons, the proposal included the creation of a model village near Dandeli, cost of which would be met from selling the forest crop on the proposed site for this village.'

The following extract from the diary of Father. H Santapau would appear to show that no effective action had been taken until 1954. The sanctuary which he observed across the river had monkeys, some domesticated buffaloes and they could hear jungle fowl and an occasional woodpecker. From the above it should be realized how difficult it was for State Governments to effectively manage any proposals when local interests were not sympathetic. It explains the progressive diminution of wildlife all over India in spite of protective laws. Mirchandini's article referred to above demonstrated how in several cases it took years for a Protected Area to be so designated. It required an interested group of people and a sensitive administration to be located in the area at the same time. This lucky chance did not happen too often!

In 1947 in the JBNHS , Volume 47, Burton, writing on the importance of notifying National Parks remarks that, 'those who have knowledge of the subject are of the opinion that India is not yet ready for these.' He writes that the Hailey National Park conforms more to conditions laid down for a Sanctuary. This is undoubtedly an insight that we appreciate today more than ever. Our National Parks will never be as inviolate as one would like them to be. Nevertheless, there is a need to protect the more important areas if our highly threatened species and critical habitats have to be protected in National Parks. The National Parks' higher conservation status and better management than a Sanctuary enables them to develop a core and buffer surrounds, the former being of greater significance for protecting wildlife in the long term.

Burton also mentions the need for a separate Wildlife Department that could work hand in hand with the Forest Department. He observes that wildlife cannot be preserved unless enough money is allocated for this purpose, and suggests the need to develop propaganda programmes through the All India Radio. 'The Education Department could cause all governing bodies and educational institutions to issue pamphlets, organize lectures, lantern slide talks and issue leaflets to all colleges, schools and primary schools.' We have been unable to do this even now though we have been talking about it for over 50 years! By the 1940s and 50s, it had already become apparent that India needed to protect its wild species and their habitats, which was a clause included in our Constitution itself. By the 1960s it also became apparent that protection was required on two levels. Areas that would be considered of greater importance were to be notified as National Parks and it was planned that these should have inviolate cores and a surrounding buffer. The less important areas would be notified as Wildlife Sanctuaries. The initial growth in the number of Protected Areas was extremely gradual, but it increased rapidly once Indira Gandhi became the Prime Minister of India in 1998.

In 1956, EP Gee in an article on India's National Parks and Wildlife Sanctuaries

Fantail flycatcher—Jerdon, 1847.

published in the JBNHS wrote that the Environment Commission and the Indian Board for Wildlife had documented that 'it was not an essential condition of National Parks that there should be no human intervention.' Only a sanctum sanctorum may in some situations be created, which was to be left undisturbed. He refers to the real needs of a 'land-hungry' people with a growing population. He also wrote that 'unless we can produce evidence of the economic or tourism value of our Wildlife Sanctuaries, the other values (ethnic, recreational, scientific and biological) may not be sufficient to tip the scales in favour of their maintenance and continuance.'

The 1960s were a stressful period for India. The economy was in a poor shape, drought had led to serious food shortages and wheat was in precarious supply. The wars with China and Pakistan were major concerns. Wildlife protection thus took a backseat. One of the indicators that provide the level of interest in conservation is

to follow the trend in the notification of National Parks and Wildlife Sanctuaries in the five decades following Independence. It is an indicator of political will in furthering the cause of conservation. The policy-level changes were linked with legislative changes, which are indicative of the Government's interest in conservation over the last 50 years. From the late 1960s to 1977, there was a period during which conservation was rapidly strengthened. Indira Gandhi, at the helm of the Indian Board for Wildlife, held regular meetings herself and took a deep interest in the Environment Department, and later in the Ministry by holding the portfolio herself. Her address at the Stockholm Conference in 1972 was an important step in the understanding of environmental concerns in the developing world. Throughout her Prime Ministership, Indira Gandhi backed a number of pro-environmental decisions. The 1980s, however, were the most progressive decades for conservation

planning and the Five Year Plan developed during this era supported environmental management. The growing awareness of the economic potential of biodiversity began to emerge as a more convincing way to notify more areas as National Parks and Wildlife Sanctuaries.

The Wildlife Protection Act of 1972 became an instrument to bring conservation to the centrestage of governance in India. While it was the Forest Department's duty to look after their management, it was expected that the Revenue Department would sort out the rights and privileges of the local people before the final notification. This process has been one of the stumbling blocks for the notification of Protected Areas. Another problem was that in the 1970s, Protected Areas were not selected through carefully designed scientific studies. While India did manage to increase its number of Protected Areas in the 70s and 80s, new Protected Areas began to be selected more carefully only after Panwar and Rodgers wrote *Planning a Protected Area Network in India* in 1988.

## SELECTING AND NOTIFYING PROTECTED AREAS IN INDIA

If one looks into the history behind the creation of a network of Protected Areas in India one finds that several interested individuals and often chance events have led to their notification. I have seen several non-government individuals championing the cause of creating a Protected Area, and even leading to the notification of a number of Protected Areas. Earlier attempts by individuals to notify Protected Areas came soon after Independence when EP Gee galvanized the Government into establishing several Protected Areas. This process began with his efforts to save rhinos. Gee supported the cause of Kaziranga when Jawaharlal Nehru visited the area, which became one of the last well-protected homes of the threatened rhino population. In the 1950s, the most obvious areas to be notified as Protected Areas were those where large mammals had been protected as 'game' for organized shikar, many of them, erstwhile private shooting reserves of the Maharajas of various Princely States. For

The fight to preserve the Silent Valley in Kerala has been one of the most celebrated victories in conserving biodiversity in India.

example, Bandipur was the well-managed and carefully-guarded preserve of the State of Mysore. Kolhapur State had a bison-shooting area in Dajipur, which became the Radhanagari Bison Sanctuary. Bharatpur had the most celebrated waterfowl shooting reserve of Keoladeo where Salim Ali's efforts led to the notification of a Sanctuary that was later upgraded to the status of a National Park. The Alwar State's famous shooting reserve later became Sariska National Park and Tiger Reserve with a high population density of ungulates.

By 1975, when I became seriously involved in wildlife conservation, there were still only 5 National Parks and 126 Wildlife Sanctuaries in the country. By 1983 these had increased rapidly to 19 National Parks and 210 Sanctuaries. This was the period during which I, like so many others, became increasingly concerned about the well being of many species in the country. I began to seriously question if creating more Protected Areas alone could help conservation. The legitimate needs of local people and the methods used to protect wildlife came into

a head-on collision course. Conflict issues were increasing rapidly. It also became obvious that there was no public support either from the people at large or from the press, which usually preferred stories about how people were being killed by tigers.

The best-known controversial and much publicized battle to notify a Protected Area was indeed Silent Valley, a struggle that was anything but silent. It rocked conservation circles, so much so that a large number of conservationists entered the fray, and today one finds that several individuals lay claim to having either initiated, furthered, or finalized the process that led to stopping the development of a dam and establishing the valley as a National Park. Most people, however, acknowledge the role played by interactions between Salim Ali and the then Prime Minister, Mrs. Indira Gandhi.

There are however several unsung stories. For example Koyna Dam had some of the best patches of forest left in the northern part of the Western Ghats around the lake. People had already been moved out of the dam site during its construction. Shri Walke was the District Forest Officer

(DFO) of Satara in 1987. He enjoyed watching wildlife and walking into the forest and had begun taking National Service Scheme (NSS) students to this area where the forests around the Vasota Fort were still thick and undisturbed. He had attended my talk with slides on National Parks and Wildlife Sanctuaries and called me to address a gathering in Satara to discuss the need for a Protected Area in Koyna. Walke had already been trying to notify the valley and now requested me to help strengthen his cause. I went on a boat with him on the lake to look at the area. Finally, after I had made several visits to some of my friends in the Government to lobby on his behalf, Koyna did become a Protected Area. Koyna's forests remained protected for the next two or three dacades. However, in 2004 there was a major project proposal to create a new tourist township on its eastern banks, on the slopes of the adjacent Khas Plateau. This would destroy the serenity and the unique nature of this area. The plateau has already been changed by the presence of hundreds of windmills, the impact of which on the ground flora of the rocky plateau is not well understood. The new township, proposed to be built on the slopes overlooking the lake at the edges of the forest, will in no time destroy the fragile vegetation that forms the most undisturbed semi-evergreen forests in this region.

In Madhya Pradesh, MK Ranjitsinh began moves in the 1970s to create several Protected Areas. When he moved to the Department of Environment (DoEN), in Delhi these matured into a number of proposals that were supported by Indira Gandhi. Several of the Protected Areas of Madhya Pradesh owe their existence to his persistent pressure on the Government, both at the State and National levels.

During her Prime Ministership, Indira Gandhi wrote to the State Governments to create more Protected Areas, and Chief Ministers all over the country took serious steps to please her by doing so. In Maharashtra, Shri Kopikar, who was a Conservator of Forests and had just returned from his position as Director Project Tiger in Delhi, was asked by the State Government to spearhead moves in response to a letter from the Prome Minister asking the Government of Maharashtra to create new Protected Areas. As Mr Kopikar knew I had travelled all over Maharashtra, he called me to select new areas. We brainstormed several possibilities during which I suggested that it was important to select ecosystems other than forests such as grasslands and coastal areas. As Maharashtra already had deciduous teak forest Sanctuaries in the northern belt of forests, I suggested that the Western Ghats, known to be exceptionally rich in plant life, should receive priority during the selection of new areas. I also suggested a Protected Area for bustards and Mr Kopikar asked the BNHS where the birds lived. I knew of Nanaj, but the early BNHS recommendation was to cover a larger area and a huge Protected Area of 8496 square kilometres containing the city of Solapur within it, was proposed, much to my personal dissatisfaction.

A chance piece of information provided by a clerk during my discussions with Mr Kopikar led to yet another Protected Area. When I suggested creating coastal Protected Areas, one of the Forest Department's clerks said he had seen an old file written over a decade ago suggesting that an area called Phansad near Janjira on the coast should be notified as a Sanctuary. No one knew of this area which was once the private shooting reserve of the rulers of Janjira State. A Range Forest Officer (RFO) was asked to go there and check it out. On his return the next day, he reported that there were some residual coastal forests in the area and Phansad was suggested as an additional Protected Area. Years later, the World Bank Forestry Project, for which I designed the Conservation Plan for Maharashtra, suggested that this Sanctuary should be singled out for extra support on account of its unusual ecosystem and floral diversity. These discussions I had with Mr Kopikar thus led to several steps in the decades that followed, resulting gradually in the birth of several new Protected Areas in Maharashtra.

In the 1970s, a group of amateur bird-watchers in Maharashtra banded together to organize annual meetings in different towns in the state. Its active supporters were Jay Samant from Kolhapur and my very old friend Dr Ramesh Bidve, from Pune. Ramesh was my senior in the medical college and the supervisor of our rural internship programme. I gave him my copy of Salim Ali's book of Indian birds and he became an ardent bird-watcher. Over the years his interest in birds led to organizing several public awareness programmes on bird life that have awakened public opinion on the need for conserving important bird areas in the state. He did all this in a unique unassuming way, never coming into the limelight of the conservation efforts in the state. Ramesh was bird-

Bhigwan, in the back waters of Ujjani Dam, is a wetland of key importance in Maharastra. Unfortunately, it has not been notified.

watching in Nicobar when a tsunami struck and he disappeared from one of the remote islands—a great loss to the bird-watching enthusiasts of Pune. The *Pakshi Mitra Sammelans* he helped organize were meetings that were held by different local groups of bird-watchers every year. One of the earliest meetings where I was asked to give a presentation of places with good birding areas in Maharashtra was held in Panhala near Kolhapur. This was organized by a group of bird-watchers from Kolhapur who had caught people hunting waterfowl at a small tank called Mayeni. I was taken to visit the lake the next day and the Forest Officials were requested to take action to notify the area. In the following years, bird-watchers at Solapur invited Salim Ali to see the Jaikwadi Dam and had it notified as a Sanctuary. Nasik bird-watchers followed by getting the Nandur Madhmeshwar Dam made into a bird sanctuary. Thus there were many such initiatives taking place all over the country, spearheaded by individuals who had a personal emotional stake in an area rich in wildlife.

The first and perhaps only well-organized move to rationalize the notification of Protected Areas came only after the WII undertook a project to develop a document on *Planning a Protected Area Network for India* in the 1980s. Rodgers and Panwar made an incredible effort to get information on potential sites from the State Forest Department personnel, NGOs and interested individuals. Rodgers wrote and phoned me on several occasions about possibilities of creating new Protected Areas in Maharashtra and to understand the status of existing Sanctuaries so that some could be upgraded to National Parks.

Rodgers and Panwar asked for suggestions for new areas from across the country. Their work also led to the concept of bio-geographic zones and smaller provinces which helped creating a rational basis for selecting more sites. The document took over two years of very intensive work to compile and was a hit even before its final form was printed. A large number of new Protected Areas were created all over the country based on its recommendations. No document has done as much for the country's Protected Area network.

In 1992, when one of the earliest World Bank Forestry Projects was initiated in Maharashtra, I was asked to work on its conservation aspects. By then I knew most of the important sites that needed protection. I set about motivating the World Bank team to apportion a larger budget than they had proposed for conservation by giving their team slide-shows of Maharashtra's wildlife and taking several Bank consultants to exciting Protected Areas in the state. What followed as a part of the Project was the much-needed strengthening of the Wildlife Wing in the state. It also pushed for several new Protected Areas and capacity building through a series of workshops and seminars for Forest Department Staff on conservation issues and Protected Area management. Research into several conservation aspects hitherto neglected was funded, and the formation of a long-term strategy for conserving biodiversity in the state was initiated. During that period, however, Maharashtra was rapidly being changed into a giant, sugarcane-dominated, highly irrigated area, undergoing industrialization and urbanization faster than any other state in the country. If the steps taken by the Forest Department during this period had not been initiated, the unplanned development would indeed have spread into the residual wilderness much more rapidly. There is no doubt that Maharashtra would have been much poorer in its biological inheritance but for this effort through the World Bank's Forestry Sector Project. Unfortunately, after this Project ended, the Government cut budgets on conservation and downsized the recently developed Wildlife Wing. Protests fell on deaf ears and much of the gains made during this period were reversed.

There are many such episodes where ups and downs of fortune in constituting our Protected Area network led either to net gain or to a serious loss of conservation efforts. In Maharashtra, I had induced the then Chief Minister, Sharad Pawar, into creating a high-powered Wetland Advisory Board at the state level that would help notify Protected Areas in wetlands. Once the Government changed, the Board disappeared into thin air. I took the then Chief Secretary, Mr BG Deshmukh, to visit

Maharashtra's most important wetland in the backwaters of Ujjani Dam to show him flamingos. He was completely fascinated. At Bhigwan we had arranged meetings with villagers for whom I had been giving talks and slide-shows on the wetland and its wildlife for the past several years. The villagers agreed to support a Protected Area if fishing was allowed in selected parts of the lake. This was agreed to by the Chief Secretary. BG Deshmukh went on to being nominated as the President of the BNHS and after his retirement was one of Tata's executives who helped fund several conservation projects. I frequently wonder if the flamingos he saw at close quarters at Bhigwan had something to do with furthering his interest in wildlife conservation! Unfortunately, in Bhigwan, an NGO began to spearhead moves to prevent fishing, and took tourists to see the bird life in boats. A conflict began between the NGO and the people and the Protected Area never saw the light of day. My entire effort towards the near-creation of an important Protected Area was lost through one small error of judgment by the actions of an NGO. Even today, the best wetland in the state remains unprotected.

During the period 1998 to 2000 I was a member of Maharashtra's Wildlife Advisory Board. I suggested that there was an urgent need to create new Protected Areas in the Western Ghats, to prevent or at least curtail the unsustainable development beginning to mushroom around Pune. The Forest Department and the Chief Wildlife Warden agreed and I helped the Conservator Wildlife to prepare the necessary documents. Around the same period, I was asked to go to Delhi to the MoEF's Committee as an expert to suggest ways and means to reduce the impact of the proposed Mumbai-Pune Expressway. I suggested adding tunnels and the creation of two Protected Areas north and south of the proposed alignment as a mitigating measure. The two areas were demarcated by doing a study through satellite imaging and ground truthing. I carefully overlaid the intact vegetation seen on satellite images on maps of the Reserved Forests so that the *malki* lands (land owned by the tribal people) where local people had farms could be avoided altogether. However, at the last meeting when the Wildlife Board of Maharashtra was to recommend the notification, a Board Member asked if the local people had been consulted. I tried to explain that since this area was already Reserved Forest, asking people for their views in this case was irrelevant, as their lands would not be affected in any way. However, the Minister, who obviously wished to take a populist view, insisted that the local people should be consulted in any case. The process was blocked. Though I got the necessary agreements signed by local Sarpanches, the two areas in Mulshi and Mawal talukas have been left out of the Protected Area network and are being converted into major urban centres for holiday homes. A golden opportunity to protect these forests as a corridor between the Protected Areas of Bhimashankar and Koyna in the Western Ghats has been lost. In conservation action one learns that one can win some and lose many more battles. One just has to go on chipping away, lobbying, talking to policy makers and administrators, researching ecological and social issues so that conservation happens. Research must provide the data that can convince administrators. The BVIEER team in Pune

is now well known for its work in the Western Ghats and the semi-arid grassland tracts of Maharashtra. Unfortunately, in the recent past the political will to settle conflict issues has taken a backseat. The Protected Areas are increasingly threatened by unsustainable development of their surrounds.

In the late 1990s, the Supreme Court set up a Centrally Empowered Committee to look into several environmental concerns. In most instances the Protected Areas had not completed the processes of notification due to local political agendas that were spearheaded by moves towards a variety of unsustainable development options.

The absence of full and final notifications of many of our Protected Areas led to a Public Interest Litigation in the Supreme Court which ordered the Government of India to see that the Forest Departments from each state complete the processes necessary by law for notifying their Protected Areas. In 2001, on the order of the Supreme Court, regional committees were set up to help states rationalize the boundaries of their Protected Areas and complete their notifications. Dr MK Ranjitsinh, Dr Asad Rehmani and I looked at the contentious issues that had blocked

the notifications in Gujarat, Madhya Pradesh, Maharashtra and Goa. This process itself took over a year. We fought to maintain the sanctity of Protected Areas. While political pressures were attempting to reduce the size of several Protected Areas. We strongly resisted such requests unless totally justified on ecological grounds. Where absolutely necessary and where conflicts were very high, we asked for better alternatives to compensate for areas that would be de-notified. We spent several days at these meetings and went into the field to study areas that had the most complex boundary issues. As this was a rationalization process, we were willing to look at changing boundaries only if it would help manage the Protected Areas better. In no case would we permit a decrease in the area unless adequate adjacent 'good' habitat was added on to compensate for what was lost.

In several cases it has been evident that the initial notification had included unviable areas. For instance, the Great Indian Bustard Sanctuary in Maharashtra accounted for half the area under National Parks and Sanctuaries in the State! This was unviable, as no rational District Collector would attempt to notify the Solapur City

Two Protected Areas that were to be created North and South of the Mumbai-Pune expressway, as a mitigating measure for its environmental impact, have not been notified even though they are situated in a hot spot of plant diversity.

itself as a Protected Area. We went into a rationalization process by including multiple Reserved Forest patches covering some 400 square kilometres but requested the formation of new grassland Protected Areas in Maharashtra in exchange for what was lost in the Great Indian Bustard Sanctuary. Thus a paper sanctuary became a more viable area of multiple areas that were already Reserved Forests.

For Gir, the Task Force recommended an increase in the size of the Protected Area by 55 square kilometres and asked the State Government to urgently address the issues facing Maldhari grazers. Similarly, our deliberations led to a 2000 hectare increase in the size of Velavadar's grasslands to support species such as the lesser florican, wolf and blackbuck. Another special case was Kachchh Desert Wildlife Sanctuary, which the Forest Department wanted to reduce in size by 122 square kilometres. The Committee did not accept this and alternative measures were suggested. The presence of salt works in the Little Rann of Kachchh, the last habitat for the wild ass, became a contentious concern. Could an embankment to improve transport facilities separate the connection with the open sea from the Rann? We felt it could seriously alter the nature of the periodic changes due to tides and seasons that occur in the area. Much of the habitat-specific biodiversity is dependent on an intricately balanced and constantly fluctuating salinity.

The large and unviable Marine National Park of Gujarat, with the existing industries, ship-breaking yards, oil jetties and fishing activities, led to a serious conflict with the conservation needs of coral atolls of incredible beauty and diversity. With its present size and with the uncontrolled pressures, nothing can ever remain except a seabed of dead coral. How can one rationalize these concerns?

Chief Wildlife Wardens who are in charge of the network of Protected Areas, and experts from several states met at the WII for the Annual General Body Meeting in December 2001. Several pointed to increasing conflict levels due to crop damage by elephant, nilgai and blackbuck. While the problem was serious, the suggested solutions of eliminating the animals implied that we could no longer live with wildlife!

with wildlife! This is against the very grain of the Indian ethos where the sanctity of all forms of life is deeply held and revered. We need to look at methods to live with this growing problem by suggesting ways to protect crops, provide compensation for losses and a variety of such methods. We do not do away with cars because road accidents kill people! Nor do we suggest getting rid of roads! No one talks about crop damage by insect pests that damage crops each year. But the damage caused by wild mammals and birds is constantly targeted in the press. How is it possible that experts from the Ministry of Environment and Forests at the meeting could suggest measures such as culling, which must remain an unacceptable or at least last-resort solution? This could well lead to the extermination of several species at the local level and eventual extinction at the national level, of some of our most threatened species. While we can no longer neglect to address the rights of local people, we cannot forget altogether the rights of our fellow creatures that inhabit mother earth. They are also her denizens, like we are. All of them contribute to this great web of life in the thin and very limited biosphere on which the well-being of mankind is completely dependent.

Several other issues have to be decided based on 'good' conservation principles. We need to support the largest possible, and the most viable Protected Areas in our country with extra funds so that our rich biodiversity is preserved in all its grandeur. Our species diversity must be protected for all time. We need a stronger research base to make this happen. The possibility of long-term conservation of genes, species and ecosystems remains bleak, unless 'people pressure' supports conservation and elects 'green' governments with an agenda for conserving biodiversity as a national asset.

After 2000 the MoEF began to look at landscape level initiatives. It gave a directive that a 10 km belt around Protected Areas be treated as an Ecologically Sensitive Zone. This led to my undertaking a study to understand this issue. In Maharashtra; the results are frightening. Most of the Protected Areas are now surrounded by

sugarcane fields and sugar factories. The Maharashtra Industrial Development Corporation has suggested new areas around several Protected Areas to set up small-scale industries. While this brings income for local people, these small-scale industries are unable to handle their waste appropriately. Wastage and soil pollution could have serious impacts on the Protected Area and its surrounds. Proposals for roads, new spreading townships and other forms of unsustainable development have reached the fringes of PAs, which need buffers to conserve their sensitive biological diversity. With this background, is there a future for the existing Protected Areas in a developed state such as Maharashtra? These Protected Areas will in the near future have no buffers between intensively developed land and the wilderness. Eventually the wilderness and its wildlife must inevitably lose. In the process, as wildlife moves out from the Protected Areas into highly urbanized sectors or sugarcane fields, predators are bound to hurt people. And wild herbivores will damage what is left of the crop lands.

While the MoEF has created these Ecologically Sensitive Zones, the State Government has suggested creating new townships where special privileges will be given to developers in the same regions. The reasons are obvious. These are the only regions in which the forests continue to provide a year-round source of water, labour is still cheap and the areas which till recently were inaccessible now have a network of roads. Another sinister move to develop high levels of tourism which will damage even the sensitive ecosystems around the forests of Mahableshwar and Panchgani, will kill the last possibility of maintaining a corridor between the Protected Areas of the Western Ghats. This is inspite of the hill stations being considered to be a special Ecologically Sensitive Zone by the Court!

Looking back between the 1970s and 1980s, 129 new Protected Areas were added. The number thus increased threefold in a decade. This was a great achievement. Form 1980 to 1990, there were 294 newly created Protected Areas, which was an even greater step forward. However, between 1990 and 2000, only

78 new areas were notified. This shows that it is increasingly difficult to identify new areas that can be included in the Protected Area network. There is also a lack of funds and a fall in the political will to develop more Protected Areas.

A set of new circumstances have risen during the last few decades, as 'people issues' resulting from the curtailment of resources have become an increasingly critical concern. While a few successful efforts have been made through eco-development initiatives, tribal people are still impoverished. This has led to a backlash in which a Tribal Bill is being formulated, that will give them land. This could lead to disasters of a new, serious nature, for conservation. This will eventually not benefit the tribal folk but others, who will exploit their new-found assets. The loss will affect the nation's conservation initiatives.

## THE MANAGEMENT OF PROTECTED AREAS

Managing Protected Areas primarily concerns managing impacts of people and preventing the damage caused by 'development' processes. It is less concerned with the direct management of wildlife or their habitat needs. If the human pressures on wildlife habitats are managed sensitively, the wild flora and fauna of these areas have a better chance of being effectively protected. It is not only the local people—traditional inhabitants of the Protected Area—that are involved, but also the new settlers, tourists, land grabbers, industrial developers, urban development planners, constructors of roads, dams, mines, etc. Conservation is not about managing wild animals, it is about sustainably managing 'development'!

Having conflicts between the needs of preservation versus the use of resources is not a recent phenomenon of India's Protected Areas. Medieval peasants in Europe were constantly battling against hunting reserves maintained for upper-class hunters. Indian Princes and Mughal rulers metted out punishments to farmers who killed wildlife for food. However, the conflict levels have grown considerably over the last two or three decades, as increasing population pressures and the awareness of local rights and privileges to the use of resources is more clearly appreciated at the local level.

Pressure from tourists who 'love nature' is an inevitable outcome of a growing awareness of the beauty of a wilderness experience. This increases the number of people who wish to explore the wilderness and experience it for themselves. While, on the one hand, we need a public awareness movement to generate the steps to protect biodiversity, the large and ever-increasing groups of people visiting such areas create a growing problem. The high levels of disturbance, traffic, noise, and growing numbers are all signs of the success of the tourism department. They have already exceeded the level of tourists that several of our Protected Areas can handle. The nature lovers and the less discerning wild animal viewers are, in effect, killing off the object of their love. Managing this aspect is as complex as managing the needs of resource collection by local people.

Species and wilderness ecosystems are increasingly at risk. Only a general mass awakening to the urgent needs of biodiversity-conservation can save what is left. This would require a conceptual change regarding the objectives of creating Protected Areas—a shift from seeing them as places for the viewing of wild animals, to the more important and urgently required understanding of the need to preserve biological diversity.

Although the number of Protected Areas in our country has been increasing steadily over the last several decades, a large number of them are unfortunately extremely small in size and may not act as a viable mechanism to protect biodiversity in the long term. New sanctuaries need to be created in different ecosystems and existing ones may have to be made larger or converted to National Parks wherever possible. Most of them are surrounded by human habitation or have people living within their boundaries. These wilderness ecosystems have been a part of the 'resource collection areas' of local people for generations, and to this day, a large number of people collect all their daily needs from them. Alternate resources for local people need to be generated if local pressures on the Protected Areas are to be mitigated. For successful conservation, local people must become party to conserving the biodiversity of these areas. This can only be done through a locale-specific eco-development programme.

The majority of India's Protected Areas have a large number of settlements both

Management of Protected Areas must deal with the rights of local people to use resources that they have traditionally been using.

on their boundaries and within them. Their ecosystems provide resources such as fuel wood to cook food and much needed fodder for livestock, resulting in a conflict between resource-use and the needs of conserving biodiversity. These growing impacts are a fact of life. And they continue to increase with our growing population. Good planning and management of these Protected Areas can reduce this conflict. It requires more funds, more expertise and more manpower, but also the formation of graded zones of utilization of resources around the Protected Areas.

While the land included in our Protected Areas covers only about five per cent of the geographical area of India, much of the forest in Protected Areas includes old plantations of sal or teak, which are often relatively poor in diversity, and have a low level of 'naturalness'. Man-made bodies of water in the backwaters of hydroelectric or irrigation dams have been included in Sanctuaries as these are often the only aquatic ecosystems that are left! Overgrazed wasteland in areas which were once flourishing grasslands have also been notified as Protected Areas. The real, natural, undisturbed grasslands have been unfortunately converted into tree plantations, and this has had serious consequences for grassland biodiversity.

The history of our Protected Areas and their effectiveness for conserving biodiversity is closely linked to the way land use has been altered, especially through the development processes over the last three decades. It is the rapidity with which changes in the areas around the Protected Areas have occurred, especially in highly industrialized States such as Maharashtra and Gujarat, that has led to a staggering loss of biodiversity. There has been little effort on the part of the State Governments to see that selecting sites for industrial complexes does not adversely affect biodiversity within the Protected Areas. No alternative development strategy is made available for the fringes of Protected Areas. The local people are bound to feel disadvantaged in villages where industrial development is prevented. The MoEF has laid down, 'Siting Rules' for Industries that need Environmental Impact Assessments (EIAs) if they are situated on the periphery of Protected Areas. This broadly covers different types of industry. In 1998, these norms were restated and expanded. However, development still continues to spread around the fringes of many Protected Areas.

## THE FUTURE OF PROTECTED AREAS

The notification of wilderness as Protected Areas in our National Parks and Wildlife Sanctuaries was essentially done on an ad hoc basis. While these Protected Areas have provided some level of security for the wild species in each of our bio-geographic zones, they need to be developed into a more rational and interlinked group of Protected Areas with each area networked into an Integrated Protected Area System (IPAS). Each Protected Area should be rated in terms of its relative importance within this IPAS both at the national and at the state level. Providing all these Protected Areas with their due proportion of financial support, manpower and infrastructure alone can lead to the preservation of relict ecosystems and their endangered flora and fauna.

State-level networks of Protected Areas must be developed to provide an adequate representation in each bio-geographic zone in all the states. These must include not only the network of Protected Areas but other Multiple Use Areas that constitute a second line of reserves. For administrative purposes each state must develop its own IPAS which gives greater importance to those ecosystems located only within the State and not present elsewhere in India. This must emphasize the protection of areas that have high levels of biodiversity, those with a large number of distinctive, endemic or endangered species, and those that are highly fragile or sensitive to human interference.

It is essential to rationalize the boundaries of existing Protected Areas and select new sites where Protected Areas can be created. Ecosystems that are poorly represented in the Network of Protected Areas need to be surveyed and new National Parks and Sanctuaries urgently notified wherever possible in the prioritized areas. Time is now running out for this. The present spread of unsustainable development makes it difficult to notify more areas as wilderness. Rapid unsustainable economic growth must be rationalized so that the long-term goals of preserving biodiversity can be met. It must inevitably include a local development strategy that is labelled 'eco-development'. In this concept ecological protection is linked with sustainable economic development, in which local people's needs are met with and their impact on biodiversity is minimized.

The World Conservation Union, previously the International Union for the Conservation of Nature and Natural Resources, stipulates that 5 to 10 per cent of every ecosystem must be protected to conserve biological diversity. For Ecologically Sensitive Areas it is expected that this should be at least 10 per cent. It will be difficult to achieve this target in our country, where the pressure for land is increasing and resources are diminishing. It will be even more difficult if our development strategies do not start to conform to the need for ecological security. How then can we manage to preserve these threatened ecosystems and their wild denizens? These are complex issues and have no simple solutions. In many instances the answer lies in a trade off between eco-development and conservation. This will only be possible through a national conservation movement in which all of us must play an active role.

Conservation in India can only be brought about if public awareness grows to a level in which the country begins to elect 'green' politicians and administrators. It is not 'government apathy' that ails conservation in India; it is 'people apathy' that comes from a lack of information on the need to protect biological diversity. This lack of public awareness results in an indifference to conservation. It is only if we can create a mass conservation movement, a heightened concern for protecting biodiversity, and a willingness to act and lobby for preserving wilderness that biodiversity conservation will become a reality.

The Wular Lake, Kashmir—Hardinge (1847).

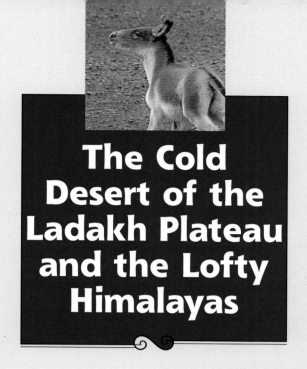

# The Cold Desert of the Ladakh Plateau and the Lofty Himalayas

The lofty Himalayan ranges extend from Ladakh to the north-eastern states and constitute a unique habitat for plants and animals.

The plateau of Ladakh includes a large number of wetlands.

The Himalayan massif, stretching from Kashmir in the West to Assam in the East, is formed by spectacular ranges of snowcapped peaks. The upper reaches of this inhospitable land with arctic conditions support very specialized forms of plants and animals that can survive in the perpetual snows. The Ladakh plateau with its great ridges, river valleys and wetlands has an important role to play in conserving India's biodiversity.

Plant life begins just below the snowline at a height of 5000 to 6000 metres. The grasses and herbs have a variety of attractive flowers, blossoming sequentially on the hill slopes, which burst into patches of various colours. These grasslands constitute the grazing grounds of wild sheep and goats that wander in search of fodder on the steep slopes.

A belt of 'elfin' forests with twisted, stunted trees occur at a slightly lower elevation. At the tree line, stately coniferous forests of pine, fir, deodar and spruce begin, the forests alternating with grassland. At places the vegetation consists of rhododendron or oak forests, and several types of miscellaneous forests, depending upon soil and climatic conditions. Mountain streams with ice-cold, crystal-clear water rush down from the melting snows during the summer. In winter several feet of snow cover the forest in an unbroken white mantle.

The migration of forests in the distant past of the earth's history has resulted in marked differences in the plant species of the western and eastern Himalayas. The pattern evolved, on the one side, through the spread of the forests of Europe from the West, and on the other from Indo-China and beyond in the East. This was the result of tectonic plate movements that attached India to the southern coast of the Eurasian landmass. The variations in floristic patterns are dependent on climatic factors, such as more snowfall and less rain to the west of Sikkim, whereas less snowfall and heavier monsoon rains occur in the east. The western Himalayas thus have a higher proportion of conifers, whereas the eastern part supports more oak forests.

The animal and bird species that live here migrate up and down the mountainside seasonally, looking for food. The high altitude grasses, which are lush green in summer, are the home of many specialized herbivores not found elsewhere in the country. Serow, *markhor*, yak and ibex are found here, as well as deer species such as the *hangul*, which must have had a wider range in the past. The musk deer, another Himalayan species, is becoming rare as it has been extensively killed for its musk gland, used in the manufacture of perfume, and illegally exported. The breeding of this deer in small numbers in

A drawing of a Himalayan animal done by Major John Luard on stone and said to be a shawl goat.

captivity has not reduced poaching substantially. The very rare snow leopard is the largest predator of the mountains. Unfortunately it has been much hunted for its beautiful fur and is increasingly hard to find. The bears of the mountains are larger than the common sloth bear of the rest of India. The brown bears are found at a higher elevation, often well above the tree line, whereas the Himalayan black bear is seen more commonly in the oak and coniferous forests lower down.

The high valleys attract a large variety of brilliantly coloured butterflies flitting through the forest during the short period when the flowers are in bloom and pollinating several tree species. This linkage is of great importance for the regeneration of plants in the forest. The undergrowth in the forests is full of other insects, which are pollinators of shrubs and undergrowth species. Several species of Himalayan hill birds such as pheasants, partridges, quails, snow cocks, treepies, and barbets are not found elsewhere in India. Many of these are exceptional songsters.

To the south of the mountains lies a long belt of low hills. From these foothills the awe-inspiring rugged beauty of the mountains can be seen on a clear day from a great distance. The view in the foreground has a unique beauty of its own. The youthful bubbling mountain torrents swell into mature rivers; the Himalayan flora undergoes a gradual transition, conifer and oak give place to a new dominant, the sal tree, that grows in gregarious patches all along the hillside and down into the Terai belt in the plains to the south.

Here, the snow leopard gives place to the tiger and the leopard of the lowlands. The herbivore 'niche' filled by the *hangul* and musk deer in the mountains is occupied by the sambar of the hills, the chital of the plains and the swamp deer of the marshes. The twitter of the bulbul changes in character as the hill bulbul disappears and the red-vented bulbul of the plains makes its appearance. And in the place of the pheasants the morning is full of the crowing of the red jungle fowl.

The mountains are a place where myths have been born for centuries. There are stories told by holy men who have lived alone in the desolate regions high up in the snows, of a half-human creature known as the Yeti or snowman who is supposed to walk through the deep snows leaving giant human-like footprints. Local people believe in its existence and mountaineers have even said that they have seen its footprints. These unconfirmed rumors are difficult to discredit. While a few of the sightings appear authentic, they could well be of bears that have been mistaken for a human-like animal. I know that the snows can play tricks on one's eyes in a misty environment where everything is covered by a mantle of white. I have also experienced the flights of fancy that the mind can produce if one is not fully acclimatized to the rarified air of the high mountains. So the snow man remains one of the greatest of Himalayan enigmas.

A variety of pressures have resulted from an ever-growing human population in the mountains. Increasing land-hunger has lead to terracing of even the steeper slopes of the Himalayas. Fuelwood has become a major issue, going back to the famous Chipko Movement, a forerunner of several NGO action groups that are now active over the rest of the country.

The Himalayan vegetation is characterized by the high biological diversity of flowers that bloom seasonally in its valleys. There are 60 species of balsam that are not found elsewhere. Grasslands alternate with forests of birch and rhododendrons around 5000 metres above sea level. Below 3500 metres the forests have maple and walnut or giant stands of conifers such as deodar, pine, spruce and fir. The foothill forests are characterized by trees such as chirpine and banoak.

The Forest Department's replacement of oak forests with pine over the last 30 to 40 years has created a major change at the landscape level and poses a threat to the ecology. Livestock grazing has a serious impact on the system and the enormous flocks of domestic sheep and goats as well as cattle at lower elevations compete for fodder with the wild ungulates, which are already in much lower densities than a few decades ago. Livestock grazing also has an impact on ground flora which, once overgrazed, could take years to return even if afforded protection. Species such as rare ground orchids could be destroyed totally and several species may already be on the verge of extinction.

Ecological work in the Himalayas has been done by the WII for the last 15 years. This has focused on habitat ecology, ungulates, the snow leopard, bears, birds, flora, vegetation mapping and socio-economic aspects. The snow leopard is the main apex predator of the mountains, and WII has shown that only two per cent of its prey consists of livestock. To survive, it moves seasonally with blue sheep, also called *bharal*, to the higher altitudes in summer, and descends to lower elevations once the winter begins. The ibex is now one of the highly threatened wild goats of the Himalayas, and the major conservation issue is that it must compete with large herds of livestock for the same grassy mountain slopes. There has been a theory that livestock grazing may not adversely affect grassland habitats, and to an extent may benefit some wild ungulates. While this may be true in certain grassland ecosystems, livestock grazing in the Himalayan pastures has now reached levels that not only create a food crunch for wild ungulates, but are likely to wipe out endangered flora, including very rare and threatened ground orchids.

The tall stately coniferous forest is found below the snowline.

# CHANGTHANG COLD DESERT SANCTUARY
CHANGTHANG, LADAKH

| State | Jammu and Kashmir | Zone | Trans-Himalayan (Ladakh Mountains) |
|---|---|---|---|
| Area | 4000 sq km | Ecosystem | Cold Desert |
| Year of Notification | 1987 | Visited | Sep, Oct 2004 |

It feels strange that I should be writing this chapter of the book last. Over the past 35 years I have travelled with my camera to Sanctuaries and National Parks in most of the wild ecosystems of our country, but never to the rooftop of India. For years I have wanted to experience this remote land on India's border. And as I went through the writing of three volumes of text and the selection of over 1500 pictures taken all across India, I realized that our greatest wilderness could not be left unrepresented.

My short early morning nap on the flight from Delhi to Leh is broken by the stewardess asking if I would like breakfast. It is 6 a.m. I glance out of the aircraft window at the silhouetted peaks as the sun peeks out over them. And then within minutes the aircraft is flying over range after range of rugged, snow-covered mountains, their tips glowing red-gold in the low rays of the sun. Their jagged, linear angulations contrast sharply with the curving sweeps of glaciers, as the snows descend from their mountain birthplace to form the rivers that feed the plains below with life-giving water. I suddenly realize the stark difference in the landscape from most other places in India. There are no signs of human life down there, no signs of human habitation, no farmland, no dammed rivers, no townships. Just smooth snows and empty spaces. Wispy clouds turn from gold to a brilliant fleecy white. It is a wonderful world here at the northernmost corner of India.

My last-minute decision had left me no time for planning or organization. On arrival at Leh I was told to take three days off for acclimatization, but that way I would lose half of my trip time! So I worked on this book on the first day and went off to get permits and reach Army contacts the next. I was not breathless, had none of the headaches, I was told to expect at this

The Changthang Cold Desert Sanctuary is a rugged, inhospitable land, with highly ecosystem-specific plants and animals.

altitude, which I frequently get in Pune at low altitudes. Here in Leh, I literally felt on top of the world!

Ladakh is situated in the Trans-Himalayan belt, some 1,00,000 square kilometre of rugged plateau ranging from 2500 to 7500 metres in altitude and criss-crossed by rivers. Bordered by the Himalaya and Karakoram ranges to the North and South, it comprises the mountains of Zanskar and Ladakh and the basin of the Indus River. Parts of the region are cold desert with little rain and desert flora; other areas contain high altitude lakes, some of which are saline; and a system of wetlands rich in birdlife and home to the rare black-necked crane.

Below the craggy snow-covered peaks and boulder-strewn lower slopes, the valleys are full of old glacial features that have left their rounded boulders in a loose substratum. Here lie the small settlements of Ladakhi farmers, and the high grazing lands of nomadic people who have for generations herded their flocks of sheep, goats and yaks across this rugged land. And then there are the army camps, where the jawans and their officers spend months in isolation from the rest of the world. It is a tough life; I can hardly imagine how they survive the winter with temperatures dropping to minus 30° Celsius. Their housing looks as if it could well do with some modern building material that would be warmer. In each of the camps I visit they gave me hot tea and biscuits and welcoming smiles. I could only feel a sense of guilt that I was giving them an added chore to do.

On the first day out of Leh, I had a tough six-hour ride along the precipitous banks of the Indus River. As we ascend towards Chiang La, the third highest pass in the world, the air turns thin, dry and cold. The lack of oxygen does strange things to one not accustomed to these altitudes. I have only had two days of acclimatization in Leh; too short to prevent headaches for which, now that we are at higher altitude, I have to take Brufen tablets with hot cups of tea. The wind pierces through my body. The pass has a small army post, where some half a dozen

The habitat of the Tibetian wild ass extends from Ladakh to Tibet.

| | 2 |
|---|---|
| 1 | 3 |

Goats—Luard. The people of Ladakh have used both domestic and wild animals for their wool.

The perennial snows form glaciers from which Himalayan rivers flow and provide the plains with water.

The geologically young mountains formed by unstable rocks crumble easily, resulting in landslides.

The wide expanse of Ladakh includes pasture lands, wetlands and mountain ranges.

As winter approaches, streams rapidly freeze into conical ice formations.

The early course of the Indus river forms a giant 'U' loop in Ladakh and Kashmir and goes through a series of deep gorges.

soldiers supplement their defence duties by rescuing tourists whose vehicles have broken down. Descending towards the Tibetan border a splash of blue appears. Pangong Tso reveals itself as a huge brackish water body hemmed in by steep sides. Even though the sky is overcast, the lake is an unbelievable turquoise blue. Beyond are the snow-covered peaks that feed it with fresh water and maintain its pH balance so that life can exist. The temperature is dropping even in early September, and at one point on the side of the road, the water trickling out of a fissure has formed metre-long ice sculptures. As I take a picture of the glittering ice, the sun sets. The melting period of the day is over and the freezing night will act as the sculptor for nature's artwork of tomorrow.

On my second day the road through the mountains from Leh to Diskit passes through the most extraordinary terrain of coloured rocks, ranging from yellow-grey to reds, greens and black. Contrast this with the silver white of the snows and you have a landscape that is truly out of this world. As we ascend, the vegetation of scrub and ground flora changes and eventually disappears at the pass into Nubra, at 5700 metres, the highest in the world. Nothing

moves on those freezing, barren slopes. Descending again into the Nubra Valley, a different world appears. The river is another shade of unbelievable blue, between banks of pale cream. Its wide floodplain is covered in sand dunes. It is as if we have been transported suddenly to Rajasthan, and the picture is completed by the dromedaries, brought here as the most suitable beasts to work this unique ecosystem.

The township of Disket is surrounded by fields and with a tree cover that attracts a huge number of different kinds of birds to this oasis of green. There is a famous old monastery built here, into a gigantic cleavage in the rock face next to a spring. Five hundred lamas live here; where the tenets of Buddhism are taught to aspiring monks. The young boys in maroon robes run up and down the steep hill. Later, I hear them chanting their evening lesson in a faraway singsong manner. The world and time seem to have stopped in some distant era of the Buddha. The magnificence of the valley and the mountains on the other side set me reflecting on the feeling for the wilderness that the monks must gain by experiencing it every day. This is the last of the wilderness areas with a very small

The mountain roads of Ladakh pass through three of the highest passes in the world.

The rarefied air in the highest pass in the world creates light-headedness and severe air hunger.

High-altitude lakes seasonally support a large number of aquatic birds.

One thinks of the cold desert of Ladakh as being snow-covered peaks, but there are also wide expanses of sand.

Several lakes and wetlands are saline in nature.

human presence, left in this country. The Nubra Valley and its river are still relatively untouched. These monasteries are the last refuge in India of the Buddhist tradition of protecting all forms of life, a tradition that long ago spread to this serene spot in Ladakh from the plains below.

This is one of India's most fragile ecosystems. The youthful mountains, which arose out of the seabed in recent geological times through the shift of tectonic plates, crumble easily. Sharp cut rocks slide dangerously down from cracks and fissures on the mountainside. The area was heavily glaciated during the Ice Ages, but at present the glaciers are receding rapidly because of the effects of global warming. There is other evidence of climate change: recent reports blame the disappearance of some species of frogs on skin damage due to increased ultraviolet radiation resulting from the thinning of the

The monastery high up in the mountains is a refuge and a place of learning ancient Buddhist traditions.

A group of happy young lamas after their evening chant.

ozone layer; local people say they receive more rain and less snow than they used to and complain that the rain washes away rapidly in the rivers, while the melting snows used to give them water throughout the year. Are these early warning signs of a great disaster to come and the beginning of the end for this distinctive ecosystem?

Ladakh was once a hunting ground for the toughest of British shikaris, and one imagines that the Buddhist Ladakhis must have regarded their hunting with horror, seeing it as immoral and unnecessary. Today, the political instability on the borders of Ladakh has turned the area into an army camp. Many of the army personnel hunted animals until very recently, but have now been instructed to protect the remaining wildlife and even apprehend poachers. There is evidence too of increasing levels of grazing by local

farmers' yaks and cattle and the nomadic shepherds' sheep and goats. Most accessible areas have been grazed down to a point where the remaining vegetation is almost invisible! Yet in places where the vegetation has been protected by the Army and Forest Department, many of the shrubby species have grown into miniature trees with wide girths.

On my third day out of Leh, driving along the Indus towards Manali, we finally see the wildlife for which I have come so far. Pankaj, who works on the Black-necked Crane Project of the WWF, is taking me to the wetlands of the Changtang Cold Desert Sanctuary, notified in 1987 and covering 4000 square kilometres. He has promised me black-necked crane, *kyang* (Tibetan wild ass) and blue sheep. And there they are! Across the river three herds of blue sheep watch us curiously before retreating up the

| 1 | |
|---|---|
| 2 | 3 |

An old couple collecting subsistence resources from the wilderness.

A pair of black-necked cranes with two young ones feeding in the wetlands. Usually only one chick survives.

The yak is a multipurpose domestic animal that all Ladakhis depend on.

sheer cliff face, jumping from rock to rock with sure-footed agility. By mid-afternoon we reach the wetlands at the bottom of a bowl-like valley surrounded by multicoloured precipices. A small group of *kyang* are moving away from the herds of sheep and pashmina goats of the nomadic herdsmen. Heavy, golden-brown animals, they give us imperious, challenging stares from a safe distance. And then at the water's edge, three cranes—two adults and a young one—appear as if from nowhere. Pankaj is distraught. This pair had two chicks till only a week ago! There is a deep sigh of relief as the second chick appears from behind its parent. The Black-necked crane is the rarest of the crane family worldwide, restricted to a few wetlands on the eastern edge of the Tibetan plateau. They are shy and easily disturbed, especially when raising young, and I decide not to pursue them for a close-up. They move off gracefully, picking their way like ballet dancers through the grasses and out of sight.

We get our parathas heated by a nomad who has his Gypsy jeep parked outside his tent. He wants money for letting us take pictures of his cute kids with their delightful but dirty faces. It is cold and windy. We eat by a brook that feeds the wetland. It is a metre or so wide, with a rapid flow of crystal water. Marmots have built colonies on its banks and periodically throw dirt out of one hole and take a quick peek at us from another. The peace is mind blowing, more powerful than the cold blowing wind. I feel strangely at home. The cloth tents of the nomads are strewn several hundred metres apart from each other over the desolate plain ringed with distant mountains. As a Parsi descended from an old stock of Iranian pastoral herdsmen, am I perhaps connecting with my ancestral roots?

On our way back to Leh we are trapped in a snowstorm. It rapidly leads to a complete 'whiteout'. The jeep slithers and stalls repeatedly through the heavy snow, now knee-deep. We do, however, reach the

A flock of sheep returning home after grazing in the high mountains.

|   |   |
|---|---|
| 1 | 3 |
| 2 | 4 |

Majestic *kyangs* canter across the cold desert.

The black-necked crane is one of the rarest cranes in the world.

A flock of blue sheep approach the river to quench their thirst.

Blue sheep are extremely wary.

Children of Ladakhi pastoralists.

The first snowfall of the season.

Within two hours of the first snowfall, the pass was closed.

pass from where an Army Major helps us back to Leh.

Sadly I must leave Ladakh already. I have no time to pursue the few wolves, foxes or elusive Snow Leopards that a century of hunting has almost eliminated from the region. They are still recorded occasionally from below the snowline, preying on the varied species of wild sheep and goats that are unique to the area, or on the rare *chiru* (Tibetan antelope). All these must compete now for grazing with the ever-increasing herds of domestic animals. I must leave now without visiting Hemis, Ladakh's National Park (notified in 1981 and covering 4000 square kilometres), home to the ibex and the brown bear. I leave too without having been able to identify a single species of the low ground-hugging plants! Ladakh's ecology is so distinct from that of the rest of the country, that a botanical amateur from the plains like myself would have to re-train completely to become familiar with its flora, let alone devise strategy to preserve what is left of it!

The rapidly approaching clouds herald a snow storm.

Dry plains covered by sparse over-grazed grass become wetlands after it rains.

| 1 | 2 |
|---|---|
| 3 | |
| | 4 |

Himalayan vegetation has evolved in order to survive in the extremely low temperatures.

Most ground flora remains dormant through winter.

The last Himalayan flowering plants of the season.

Photographing Himalayan plants at high altitudes is difficult because it involves climbing in the rarified atmosphere.

# KEDARNATH WILDLIFE SANCTUARY

KEDARNATH

| State | Uttaranchal | Zone | Himalaya (West) |
|---|---|---|---|
| Area | 957 sq km | Ecosystem | Alpine Region, Oak, Rhododendron and Pine Forests, Mountain Streams and Rivers |
| Year of Notification | 1987 | Visited | Apr 2005 |

Most people in India know of this part of India as the origin of our most sacred river. The Ganges is dotted with religious places of worship, an obvious result of an ancient appreciation of its ability to sustain the lives of millions of people who live off the agricultural lands of the plains. This great religious fervour becomes evident the moment one gets off the train at Haridwar. I had been asked by the India Canada Environment Facility to visit Ukhimath to work on environmental issues with an NGO—Alternate Technologies India. (ATI).

Surprisingly, as I got off the train my bag was grabbed by a man in kurta-pyjamas and with a mala and a large tikka, who greeted me warmly. He did not fit the NGO type I expected. The holy man then insisted on collecting my camera bag as well. No protest was possible. I relented. Probably my expression showed that something was wrong and he finally asked 'Where you from?'—'Pune,' I said. 'Maharashtra, yes, yes,' he said. 'Come, come, we go!' he insisted. By now it was becoming evident—I was being virtually

kidnapped due to a mistaken identity. When I asked if he was from ATI he looked shocked. Wasn't I the MLA from Maharashtra? —'No, no,' I said. I was quickly abandoned in preference of another bearded but portly man, emerging from the railway compartment. He was obviously on a pilgrimage. I dread to think that I would have had to visit a religious centre and take a bath in the polluted river instead of carrying out ATI's work with the struggling people of the hills. On locating the ATI taxi, a sleepy-looking cabby with a

The mountain ranges of the Kedarnath Sanctuary have attracted thousands of pilgrims.

rather well used Indica took off for Ukhimath. He looked dazed after the first four or five hours and he was all too happy to allow me to drive. A little later the engine overheated and after several long eventful hours we got a lift in an ATI car passing by. The view of the Ganges was spectacular all the way to Ukhimath at the edge of the Kedarnath Wildlife Sanctuary.

Mukul Prakash runs ATI. They involve local people in sericulture, silk weaving, dairy development, honey, and a variety of other economic activities such as ecotourism which are aimed at bringing about economic development that could lead to conservation of natural resources. Mukul and his team drive me through the whole region. The local people are either harvesting or looking after new crops—tilling and weeding. The women work, the men smoke the ganja that grows everywhere, drink home brewed alcohol and play carom.

Beyond the agricultural lands terraced over extremely steep hill slopes with a minuscule layer of soil, are degraded hill slopes. The farms form layer upon layer of narrow terraces. On a clear day, the Himalayan range in the distance sparkles in the sunlight. Local people affirm that it has begun to rain more and snow less. They shake their heads in dismay. It is a bad time, they say. The scientist pundits say this is global warming. Whatever the reason for change at the global level, the local issues are obvious. A growing population's hunger for arable land must naturally spill over into the adjoining forests. This canopy begins to open up, blanks appear and regeneration is nearly non-existent. What is remarkable is the resilience of local people. Their nearly impoverished lifestyle is still interspersed with smiles of welcome. Another community of people are the thousands of sadhus with no worldly possessions wending their way up and down several kilometres a day from one holy spot to the next. And they all smoke cannabis and their eyes mist up into another world. The most hallowed of the sites is in Badrinath and the whole region is infested by religious-minded people who want to go straight to heaven by praying at this site. It is a whole economy based on religious fervour which not only

supports the lives of the priests and provides free food to the sadhus, but provides also the support for local shopkeepers, dhabawallas, taxi drivers and mule owners among several others. If one has to work on resource economics one has to consider this silent cryptic revenue that the region receives from pilgrimage tourism. A new form of five star tourism—with adventure related activities such as river rafting and river crossing on the banks of the Ganges—is adding to the trekkers and rock climbers that have been increasing over the last 30 or 40 years. They too have led to ecological footprints that time cannot erase.

A few hundred metres from the edge of an agricultural plot finds one in a forest ecosystem that is replete with plant diversity. A local guide, Yashpal Negi is recommended to me by ATI. He takes me bird-watching. He is amazing. He knows not only the names of every Himalayan bird we spot but knows their calls and behaviour. He uses the Bird Call Cassettes I have made for the BNHS and is thrilled to meet the person who has made it. He shows us nests of the paradise flycatcher, the Himalayan tree pie, an ashy drongo, all within a few hundred metres. I am invited to take pictures from the roof of his tourist hut which is surrounded by large peepal trees in fruit. Black bulbuls, flycatchers, parakeets and several species of barbets are busy having their morning meal in the

nearby leafless tree. On the roof a level below is a large male lizard which consistently chases smaller ones.

To appreciate local environmental concerns ATI sends me off to see Sari village, which is being developed as an ecotourism resort. It is an ideal setting nestled at the foot of a steep slope. A local guide walks with me up the steep gradient for 2.5 kilometres. He emphasizes how the lopping of the trees for fodder is cycled every three years so that the canopy has time to regenerate. The village is inside the Sanctuary but its people are completely forest-dependent. Around us the hillscape is dotted with far off village settlements with their agricultural lands. The top of the hill is said to be sacred. Devaria Tal is a small natural depression with an algae-rich water body that retains water throughout the year. Here the first presence of the Forest Department makes its appearance by asking for Rs. 40 as entrance fee! The water is full of life. Fish, tadpoles—but surprisingly no waterfowl.

During a brief night drive two kilometres out of Ukhimath, a flash of gold and black dashes across the road in the jeeps headlights. The leopard cat stops to look at us before disappearing into the darkness. My day is made. I finally got to see one after two decades. These lesser cats have become so rare. There is a large trade in their very beautiful skins which should be prevented.

On a moonlit night, as the full moon emerges over the crest of the hills, the distant mountains are sketched on the dark sky shimmering a pale electric blue. If it weren't for the fact that one knows they are the distant mountains they could be passed off as a mirage, a figment of one's imagination. A single nightjar is calling from the opposite hillside—one more group of species that seems to have gotten unaccountably rarer during the last few decades. And no one seems to be worried about this species which was once so common. Most professional ornithologists first feel skeptical when I bring this up. One needs to realize that the abundance of some species is dropping faster than others. When I brought up the reduction in the population of vultures over a decade ago, it was looked upon with the same skepticism. Now the same ornithologists are fighting over why vultures have vanished. One group blames Diclophenac, used as an antipyretic for sick cattle, from which it reaches vultures through the food chain. Another group feels it is an infection of some kind, probably a virus. A third group says that the Air Force is systematically shooting them out of the sky to prevent air strikes of their costly jet fighters. No one is sure as yet, but while the controversy continues, vultures keep dying. During this trip to Kedarnath I asked about vultures. I see six king vultures hovering around in wide sweeps awaiting a thermal current to carry them off upward on their effortless wings. It is heartening to see that there are still some vultures left in these remote areas.

To get to the boundary of the Sanctuary the road twists and turns over the hills. One travels several hours up and down a valley only to find oneself only a few kilometres away as the crow flies. The forest is exceptionally beautiful. Patches of large oak and rhododendron covered with epiphytes and mosses. The undergrowth has several species of dwarf bamboo. Tiny streams trickle down the steep slopes, sparkling in the bright sunlight. A monal crosses the road. Birds flit through the trees, their calls resound through the hills. A great Himalayan barbet calls incessantly from an adjoining hill slope.

What makes this region memorable is the power of the great Ganges. Its tributaries have fascinating names steeped in folklore and myth. The torrents froth with a green blue transparency as the waters swirl around the boulders that make the bed of the stream. As the rivers grow in size, they meander downwards, cutting the bank on one side of the curve and depositing fine off-white sand on the other, alternately. It is a fragile, complex system in which the snows of the mountains melt to supply life-giving water to the plains throughout the year. The forests bind the loose boulders and rock faces which have a meagre layer of soil. The still growing Himalayas are a young mountain range and its loose earth and loose rocks give way easily. Destabilize the precariously balanced mass of the mountain slope by a natural calamity like an earthquake and it all comes down into the river, forming a steep slope of rubble on its bank. The landslides are everywhere—large ones in deforested areas smaller ones in the forest. But they are an ever present phenomenon. The recent advent of the Himalayas in the long geological timescale of our earth, is a result of the collision of two gigantic masses of land forming the mountains. The climate of India would not have had the monsoon rains that support the growth of her forests. And the rivers would not have flowed throughout the year from the melting snows high up on the peaks where perennial snows are maintained by Nature's great cycle of water—an endless cycle that supports all forms of life on our subcontinent.

A small lake with its surrounding forest is considered sacred and has been traditionally preserved.

There are varied forest types between the foothills and high ranges of Kedarnath.

Orchids, ferns and climbers abound in the foothills.

The people of Kedarnath are agriculturists who depend on forest products—fodder, bamboo for construction, herbs and medicinal products. Some are pastoralists, travelling with their sheep, goats and Bhutia guard dogs. Sadhus also roam the area from one sacred site to another.

A traditional old wooden home in the hills. These houses are now giving way to concrete structures.

Removing weeds in the farm is a laborious activity and it is generally done by women.

Many sadhus from different parts of the country have settled permanently in these regions.

An old lady in traditional dress.

An old lady with her harvest.

Livestock are considered family.

Women de-husking the harvest.

Different types of Bamboo are used to make a variety of artifacts. Bamboo collected from the forest provides an important resource.

Large amounts of fodder need to be collected and carried long distances to feed the cattle through winter.

The family harvest being supervised by a senior member of the household.

The forest provides all the energy needs for the community. Collecting fuel wood is a time consuming activity.

The forest is a major source of fruits, nuts, roots and medicinal products.

| | | 3 |
|---|---|---|
| 1 | 2 | 4 |

| 5 | 6 | 7 |

An iridescent fern patch at the edge of a watercourse provides a microhabitat for many species of insects.

Brightly coloured flowers are pollinated mainly by butterflies.

The life cycle of Himalayan plants is complex and is closely linked to seasonal changes.

Some Himalayan plants can grow in very small quantities of soil among the rocks from which they derive their nutrients.

Several flowering plants are endemic to the Himalayan region.

The Himalayan ground flora flowers sequentially for brief periods of time.

*Erythrina* is pollinated by both birds and insects.

The colour of the ground flora changes as different species of flowers begin to bloom.

The Himalyan Rose was a favourite of Mughal Emperors.

The fragrance of a Wild Rose attracts large numbers of insects.

Himalyan treepie.

Green pigeon.

The Ganges flowing through the Himalayan foothills provides life-giving water.

# DACHIGAM NATIONAL PARK

DACHIGAM, LADAKH

| State | Jammu and Kashmir | Zone | Himalayan (North-west) |
|---|---|---|---|
| Area | 141 sq km | Ecosystem | Coniferous and Broad-leaved Forest |
| Year of Notification | 1981 | Visited | Sep 1982 |

The Dachigam Valley is a picturesque area from which the waters melting off the snowy peaks around Srinagar flow into the Dal Lake. I visited Dachigam in September 1982. As one climbs from the Sanctuary gates on the lower slopes at 1500 metres to the high mountains beyond, the forest begins to change. The lush vegetation of the valley gives way to the high altitude vegetation of the Himalayas. Poplars, elms, oaks, willows and walnut trees grow thickly on either side of the road. Higher up, this changes to coniferous forests. The peaks are still snow-clad in September.

As autumn is approaching, the greens are turning into various shades of yellow, orange and gold. The air begins to get cooler as one drives up through the forest. Along the banks of the heavily canopied streams there is a pronounced nip. Trickling around the oval boulders, polished by hundreds of years of rapidly flowing water, the rocks in the streams are organized into a range of sizes all rounded off and smoothed down into spheres. The water seems to be made of crystal clear glass. The stream flashes with the movement of fish, reflecting the light of the bright sun. The air is so clear that from a sunlit forest glade the hills all around appear to be within arm's reach. At the top of the valley the mountain peaks around Upper Dachigam appear and disappear through the rapidly moving clouds at 4000 metres. The tall coniferous trees form dark belts of forests on the higher slopes while on the lower slopes the forest is broken by open grassland. There are patches of deodar, spruce, blue pine and silver fir. The upper grasslands are covered with a profusion of multicoloured flowering plants that bloom and disappear rapidly one after another during the flowering season.

Mir Inayatullah was the Chief Wildlife Warden and helped us to stay overnight at the Fisheries guesthouse. He introduced me to Johanna Von Grusson who was photographing *hanguls* at the time. Johanna agreed to look after my daughter while we went off for walks in the forest. She has remained a friend all these years.

| | 3 | |
|---|---|---|
| 1 | 2 | |

Upper Dachigam with snow-covered peaks and coniferous forests.

Stream in Lower Dachigam with broad-leaved vegetation.

Stalking this shy *hangul* stag was a long, difficult task.

I walk into this idyllic forest with a young boy who was the son of the local Forest Guard. As we walk along the edge of a stream, a sudden challenging sound rings across the hills and echoes through the valley. The call of the *hangul* (Kashmir Stag) seems to ricochet from the hills all around us. It sounds so loud that one expects it to be around the next corner in the path. In reality it is way up in the hills. The rutting call is the haunting challenge to other stags of one of the most endangered deer species found in India. It is immediately answered by a challenging stag from across the valley. As the sound echoes through the hills, one realizes that this is the only place in the world where this call can still be heard as this deer is only found here. Even in this last valley, it is now increasingly threatened and the effect of the terrorist ridden areas around the valley on *hangul* populations remains unclear.

Dachigam once typified the exuberant nature of an unspoiled Himalayan Valley. The area had been traditionally preserved by the rulers of Kashmir, who were keen to keep the waters that flowed out of the snows down this forested valley into the Dal Lake, unpolluted by human activity. In more recent times, it was realized that though it is so close to Srinagar, it is the last refuge of the *hangul* and was thus notified as a National Park. Attention was first drawn to Dachigam and its *hangul* by EP Gee who visited it in 1957 and 1960. He convinced conservationists in India that the *hangul* was highly threatened and required urgent protection. This deer is an exceptionally wary creature. It has been hunted for generations for its incredibly beautiful, twelve-pointed antlers. Consequently, it has developed a deep-rooted fear of human beings that frequently overpowers its inquisitive nature, making it crash off into the forest as soon as one approaches it. In 1953 the Government of Jammu and Kashmir asked the BNHS to study the status of wildlife in Dachigam. The team that did the study comprised Salim Ali and Ralph Morris.

The Dachigam River was first stocked with trout by Francis James Mitchell who also helped founding the Kashmir Trout Fishing Club. He personally brought the trout over when he went on a visit to England and taught local people how to develop trout hatcheries. These are present even today.

I have never forgotten walking through the valley in 1982. On hearing the rutting call of the *hangul* on the adjoining hill we crossed the ice-cold stream. My young guide was at first rather reluctant. He was worried about bears. The guard himself could not come as it was a holiday and the reluctant youngster was deputed to join me because I was extremely keen on taking pictures of one of these superb stags.

I had only two days to spare. As we followed the call, it initially sounded as if the deer was close at hand. This peculiar ventriloquial quality of the *hangul* call is probably accentuated by the sound echoing off the neighbouring hillsides. Following the frequently repeated call, we crossed several meandering ice-cold streams, and climbed up the steep hillside for several hundred metres. As we approached the grassy area from where we had last heard the *hangul* calling, he must have spotted us, for he seemed to vanish into the thin cold air. Though we carefully searched the grassy clearing for more than half an hour, we could not spot him in the tall grass. We settled down behind some bushes to wait for him to show up. Another uneventful quarter of an hour passed by. Disappointed, we headed back down the steep slope. The deer must have seen us moving away as we forded an open stream. We had barely got to the opposite bank, when he sent out a challenging call, which stopped us in our tracks. We decided to try and stalk him again. We re-crossed the water further downstream, hoping that the spot was out of sight from his vantage point. Again we climbed the steep slope making as little noise as possible. Yet again he must have spotted us because, before we could get a glimpse of him, he had hidden himself in the grass. Another half-hour's wait yielded nothing. Disappointed, we descended once again through the thick woods scratching our hands and knees in the thorny scrub. Shortly the deer began calling again. I decided to make one final bid, though it was late in the evening and the light was fading.

This time I went ahead and asked the boy to keep a good distance between us and to walk as quietly as he could. For most of the climb I was on all fours, moving cautiously up a steep small rocky waterfall to provide cover. As I ascended further, I saw that the origin of the stream was on a nearly perpendicular slope. The rocks were slippery and moss-covered. I had thought the gorge would act as good cover but had not anticipated how difficult it would be to climb through the ice-cold spray. Creeping up the slippery trickle was extremely dangerous, as there was very little to hold on to. As I climbed up the watercourse out of breath and carrying my heavy camera, a small rocky outcrop gave me a chance to stand up and look over the ledge above. The deer must have been just over the crest of the rocky hillside. But this time he had not been able to see me. With his remarkably good sense of hearing he

probably knew there was something in the stream below, but perhaps mistook this for a challenging stag. At first he cautiously appeared over the ridge, his superb antlers silhouetted against the sky and peered over the grass down the slope suspiciously. I froze and waited. Gradually the magnificent creature emerged over the top of the precipitous slope. I nearly forgot to take pictures for several seconds, then I took several, feverishly, my hands shivering with cold. He was now alerted by the click of my camera shutter. Repeatedly he raised his head to scent the air and gave a peculiar snort. It was one of the most memorable sights I have ever experienced. The stag was beautiful, with huge antlers and a broad neck. He stood on the edge silhouetted against the sky, stamping his forefoot in challenge. Antlers pointed forwards, he looked fixedly downwards in my direction. I ran out of film as he came further forwards and stood broadside on the crest of the grassy slope and raised his head to scent the air carefully. My frustration at having no more film in the camera made me scramble to reload. Instantly he began to move away through

the grass. Crouched precariously on the slippery rocks, the icy water flowing past me—I tried to get at a spare film in my camera bag. The deer kept repeatedly turning around to watch the *nala* course suspiciously. By the time the camera was operational again he was standing behind a small bush. Only his fabulous antlers showed above the thick foliage. As I moved cautiously into the grass, he played a game of hide-and-seek keeping the bush always between himself and the camera, until the light was too low to take any more pictures.

In the dark the descent from the hill was a painful combination of grazed knuckles, knees and elbows. My feet felt as if my boots were made of ice. But my acute discomfort became obvious only after the incredible excitement of taking the photographs was over. Those photographs were some of the most hard-earned but most rewarding I have ever taken! They may not be photographically superb but have nevertheless caught those never-to-be-forgotten moments and frozen them in time.

Dachigam Valley sports a large number of other interesting species. The Himalayan

Being charged by a Himalayan black bear can be a terrifying experience.

Dachigam is a bird-watcher's paradise.

black bears inhabit the lower valley and are still to be found in quite large numbers. They can be seen climbing into trees looking for honey and fruit. Green walnuts and mulberries are also favourites. Bears are unpredictable creatures. I had a close encounter with one of them another day. Walking through the forest with the guard's son, there was a rustle in the bushes on the opposite side of a clearing, about ten metres away. The large round rump of a bear slowly made its appearance out of the foliage. We froze. The bear turned around and peered at us with a rather silly shortsighted look on its face. Suddenly rising up on its hind legs, it let out an ear splitting snarl, baring a set of enormous teeth. As it moved towards us with short menacing steps, now barely three or four metres away, the boy looked terrified and raised his cane and I, my camera, with its 300 mm lens. From the corner of my eye I could see that the boy was about to make a

dash for it. I am sure he would have been able to rapidly climb a tree. And I could envision the bear pulling me down even before I could start climbing! To my relief, it suddenly seemed to change its mind, went down on all fours and scampered away into a nearby bush. Once it had disappeared, the boy's bravado promptly returned and he said that had it come any closer, he would have swatted it over the nose! He was even more confident of this while telling the story back at the tourist lodge. I have always regretted not having had the presence of mind to get a picture of the bear, standing in front of me with its mouth wide open and snarling angrily less than four metres away! I cannot help recalling how the previous day my six-year-old daughter had said that the bears were as appealing as her toy teddy bear. She had seen them amble quietly past our jeep, unconcerned and deeply intent on hunting for food on the ground.

This idyllic valley is exceptionally fragile. Any changes made by human beings are bound to adversely affect the whole ecosystem. A sheep-rearing farm has been set up on its outskirts. It would be disastrous if a disease that affects the sheep spread to the small *hangul* population, the only one left in the world. In the years after my visit, tourist activity increased rapidly in the valley. Now, terrorist activity has reduced the tourism pressure, but as no census of the *hangul* or bear populations has been attempted in the recent past, there is no clear indication of their present status.

This valley is one of the natural treasures of Kashmir. Several of its other species, such as pheasant, *chukar* and hill partridge, are also important species in need of urgent protection. And the *hangul*, quite apart from being a flagship species in Dachigam, is India's most critically endangered deer species. Its survival is of national, even global significance.

# BINSAR WILDLIFE SANCTUARY
BINSAR

| State | Uttarakhand | Zone | Himalayan (North-west) |
|-------|-------------|------|------------------------|
| Area | 45.59 sq km | Ecosystem | Coniferous and Broad-leaved Forest |
| Year of Notification | 1988 | Visited | Nov 1995, Dec 1996, Apr 2001 |

Not far from the township of Almora in Uttarkhand is a Sanctuary that affords the most stupendous views of the Himalayan Ranges. On a clear morning, the individual tall peaks light up one by one, as the rays of the rising sun strike the snows, making them glow in incredible shades of pink and gold. Later, the unbelievable whiteness of the snow emerges and range after range of mountains creates a vista on the horizon that appears to be endless. From deep down in the valley the incessant, haunting call of a jungle fowl reminds us that a new day has begun.

The forests of Binsar are teeming with bird life. Trees such as pine and deodar alternate with beautiful clumps of oak and rhododendron. Fluorescent green velvety moss covers the tree trunks.

Trekking through the hills at Binsar in the cool of the clear air, listening to the calls of Himalayan birds as they move in large feeding droves through the forest, is a rewarding experience. The fact that no major wildlife is sighted does not distract one from the pleasure of this ideal setting. In fact, it adds to a quiet feeling of total aloneness in the forest, until one hears the

At sunrise, the distant Himalayan ranges from the Binsar Sanctuary appear much closer than they actually are.

sound of a woodcutter's axe. Suddenly one is faced by the real-life experience of the existence of 'man'—and the all too real needs of people who must use the resources of these forests for their very survival.

The tourists who visit this Sanctuary are mostly picnickers who have no real appreciation of the unique biodiversity that surrounds them. It is in Sanctuaries such as Binsar that there is an urgent need to develop Interpretation Centres and visitor-friendly information services.

I have come to love the forest paths that wind through the forest. I have learnt each turning and have in fact found myself photographing the same trees and the same vistas from the few vantage points that open out suddenly as I walk along the path.

The scent of pine and ban-oak in this forest that is like an island surrounded by terraced farmland, has made me want to go back there each time I visit Almora where my friend Lalit Pandey runs a unique NGO—the Uttarakhand Seva Nidhi (UKSN). Its programmes include helping school students to understand resource-use issues and the value of their soil, water and forest resources. Lalit knows of my fascination with Binsar and has made it possible for me to visit the Sanctuary every time I go to UKSN. And each time I leave Binsar I wonder when I will be able to get back and whether it will have survived.

Hill-slope vegetation at Binsar.

1 | 2
3 | 4
5

Binsar has an abundance of climbers.

Moss and epiphytes cover tree trunks in the low Himalayan forests.

A variety of grasses and herbs grow where there are openings in the forest.

Ferns at ground level need very specific habitat conditions to grow.

Golden autumn leaves at Binsar before snowfall.

Flowering rhododendrons in the forest.

There are many fruiting plants in the shrub layer.

Rhododendrons are one of the species that the British plant collectors wanted for their gardens.

1

2

3

Flycatcher.

Butterfly pollinating a flower.

Sunset at Binsar.

# CHAIL WILDLIFE SANCTUARY

CHAIL

| State | Himachal Pradesh | Zone | Himalayan |
|---|---|---|---|
| Area | 108.54 sq km | Ecosystem | Coniferous and Broad-leaved Forest |
| Year of Notification | 1976 | Visited | Jun 1997 |

A goral looking down from the crest of a steep precipice in Chail.

Dawn in the Himalayan foothills of Chail produces a sharp nip in the air. The cold air is so clean that my urban lungs can hardly believe their luck! The climb is steep and rather risky. Far away in the distance the call of a hill partridge echoes off the steep hillside. It is a haunting, never-to-be-forgotten sound. The forest path opens onto a precipice and begins to feel dangerously crumbly below my feet. Tiny dislodged pebbles skitter down the slope. We are looking for goral, the goat-like antelope—or an antelope-like goat—of the Himalayas. Have we made too much noise scrambling along the path?

Evidently we have…on the slope beyond there is a brown form skipping upwards from one narrow ledge onto another until it reaches the crest of the hill. There it stops as if mesmerized by the small groups of curious people looking up at it. It is a superb male goral silhouetted against the misty pale sky. It watches for several minutes before disappearing over the crest of the precipice. Further down the path there is a movement near a clump of shrubs. A group of four gorals emerge hesitantly in single file, only to scuttle away down the *nala* course. They are all too far away for good photographs.

The next morning seems to draw a complete blank until we begin to walk back towards Chail. As we move cautiously around a blind corner in the path, there he is! The goral keeps behind the shrubs in a thick patch of grass, and slowly turns to look towards the sound it has heard, before dashing for cover. It was stationary for only a few seconds; hardly good enough for a rapidly taken picture.

That morning returning down the path was a disaster. My knees were badly scraped. A lens cap was lost. And worst of all, around the last corner, bang on the path, was a Himalayan marten. The camera beeped—the film was over. There was no chance of a picture! Consolation: several sightings and two fairly good pictures of *kaleej* pheasants crossing the main road that I had never seen before. These increasingly rare birds are not only being protected in the Park, but efforts are being made to try and breed them in large enclosures in Chail.

Chail has been an important focus of conservation efforts over several decades. Bernard C Ellison describes the Maharaja of Patiala's early efforts at conserving wildlife in Chail (Vol 33). This included attempts at the introduction of English pheasants! He mentions that around Chail there were black bears, musk deer, barking deer, gorals and other animals. He observed *chukor*, *cheer* (*Catreus wallichi* or Wallich's pheasant), *khaleej* (pheasant) and, occasionally, monal pheasants.

One of the major issues in Chail relates to the fact that when the Sanctuary was created it included the township of Chail. It is estimated that the 15,000 people who live in the township of Chail and have lived there for several decades have no rights to their land that lies within the Protected Area. This has become a serious and contentious issue in the recent past.

The landscape of Chail.

A goral watches cautiously before dashing off into the forest.

1 | 2
1 | 3

Flowers of the undergrowth.

The ground cover has a fascinating variety of plants.

Spot the butterfly!

| 1 | 2 |
|---|---|
| | 3 |

Spot the nightjar by looking for its shiny red eye!

Two young nightjars superbly camouflaged among dry leaves.

A pheasant darts across the road.

Sunset at Chail.

Stack of timber from the coniferous forest. Deforestation leads to soil erosion. The resulting landslides block the rivers in the valley and may subsequently cause flooding.

Himalayan foothills from Mussourie—Luard.

## THE BHABAR FORESTS AT THE FOOTHILLS OF THE HIMALAYAS

These are the forests on the slopes of the foothills that have undergone a constant and expanding level of degradation as they have been terraced for farming and used by local grazers for sheep and goat grazing. The fragile slopes, once deforested, undergo severe soil erosion. The soil that loosely binds the large volcanic rocks into a crumbly near-vertical wall is eroded each monsoon. The Bhabar is a belt that divides the vegetation of the Himalayas and that of the Terai planes. Bhabar forests have both a Himalayan and a Terai component of plants and animals, containing chir-pine as well as sal-dominated patches, a fact that gives them a distinctive character. Corbett and Rajaji are Protected Areas with both Bhabar and Terai elements.

The Himalayan foothills and lofty ranges beyond are a memorable sight.

# The Himalayan Foothills, the Terai and the North-east

# RAJAJI NATIONAL PARK
RAJAJI

| State | Uttaranchal | Zone | Gangetic Plains |
|---|---|---|---|
| Area | 820.03 sq km | Ecosystem | Bhabar Forest |
| Year of Notification | 1983 | Visited | Apr 1990, Mar 1997, Dec 1998 |

The still beauty of a Japanese-style landscape painting, with unbelievably sheer slopes scattered with loose bare rocks and interspersed with tall trees and thick shrubs and traversed by rapid cascades that seem to bring this ideal scene to life—this is the Rajaji National Park.

Rajaji contains some of the most spectacular remaining patches of Bhabar forest. The steep mountain slopes look as if they could crumble at any moment. In fact, if you venture to climb onto these steep hillslopes, you immediately appreciate what I meant by a fragile ecosystem! The hillslope disintegrates under your feet, loosening the ancient, smooth, nearly spherical rocks that clatter down the slope towards the river below. The autumn colours of the forest provide splashes of vivid yellow, orange and brown with a few scattered coniferous trees that remain green. While the Sanctuary is a refuge for its incredible wildlife, the forest is unfortunately also a constant battleground as the local Gujars graze their enormous cattle herds here. The 'nesses' in which the Gujars live are scattered virtually throughout the National Park. Cattle dung lies everywhere, an ever-present evidence of the high level of conflict. How can one find answers to this complex issue concerning the needs of people versus the needs of wild creatures?

Nomadic Gujars first came to this region from Kashmir about 100 years ago. A majority of them have now settled in Rajaji and do not migrate, as they once did, to the Himalayas. This constant year-round grazing pressure is one of the factors that prevent an adequate regeneration of the forest. In the past, due to a seasonal

1

2 3 4

Gujar villages are found throughout the Rajaji National Park.

Macaques grooming.

Treepie in flight.

Hornbills are more easily heard than seen.

reduction in grazing, the forest had a relief period with very little pressure from domestic animals.

The forests of Rajaji were used for hunting by the Mughals, and during the British period, the area was divided into shooting blocks. It was left without any active protection up to its notification in 1980. In 1984, the three Sanctuaries of Rajaji, Motichur and Chilla were merged to form the 820 square kilometre Rajaji National Park, the name being a tribute to C Rajagopalachari, the first Indian Governor-General. MD Chaturvedi, Chief Conservator of Forests, Uttar Pradesh, writes in the JBNHS (1949): "In Uttar Pradesh, it was at the initiative of the Forest Department that the first National Park in India was constituted (the Hailey National Park, which later became Corbett National Park). This year I succeeded in creating the Rajaji Sanctuary in the Siwaliks, which comprises shooting blocks once reserved for the Governor General."

Chaturvedi (1949), also suggested that a Board for the Preservation of Wildlife in Uttar Pradesh be created, with the Minister, two Members of the Legislative Assembly (MLAs), enthusiasts from sporting circles, the Chief Conservator of Forests, the Director Agriculture, the Director Veterinary Services, a senior Commissioner and the Provincial Wildlife Officer as Secretary. It took several years to bring this about.

More than two-thirds of the forest is dominated by sal trees. Other trees include *Terminalia tomentosa*, *Terminalia balerica*, *Anogeissus latifolia* and *Mallotus philippensis*. The last, along with bamboo, are the favourite browsing species of Rajaji's elephants. Other species that herbivorous mammals depend on include *Zizyphus mauritiana* (*ber*), *Phyllanthus emblica*, *Semicarpus anacardium* and *Aegle marmelos* (*bael*).

There are about 400 elephants and 40 to 50 tigers in Rajaji according to recent census figures. Leopards are more numerous than tigers. An uncommon species is the Himalayan yellow-throated marten. Small herds of goral are also seen. The Himalayan bird species found in the chir-pine forests include the *kaleej* pheasant. The home ranges of male elephants in Rajaji varied from 188 to 407 square kilometre and for females between 183 and 326 square kilometre as reported by AJT Johnsingh and his team. This gives an indication of the need to reduce cattle pressure if wild herbivores are to get enough food out of the 820 square kilometre sanctuary. One of the serious issues in Rajaji is the number of accidents that wild elephants meet with because of the trains passing through the Protected Area. Over several years, pleas to the railway authority to ask their drivers to slow down their trains have fallen on deaf ears.

Tracking wild animals offers an intimacy with forest creatures that one cannot get by sitting in a jeep or riding on elephant-back. The risks of course are ever present, and even the most experienced naturalists have bungled into dangerous situations in which they should never have placed themselves. Walking with AJ Johnsingh, one of India's most famous wildlife scientists, one gets a feeling of security. At the end of the jeep track there is a small Forest Resthouse near the bank of a river. A small *nala* course meanders through the Rajaji valley to join the main river. Above, the steep hillslopes are covered with stately sal forests. Johnsingh, and I walk up this *nala* course early one morning in the hope of seeing a goral. There are chital and sambar tracks everywhere. Then, close to the edge of the forest, there are signs of a scuffle having taken place near a small pool of water. There is a very small patch of reasonably fresh blood and sambar hoof marks and then we see the pugmarks of a large tiger in a patch of highly disturbed sand. We follow the fresh pugmarks meandering towards the bank and drag marks of sambar hooves stretching across the sandy riverbed to the opposite bank. We anticipate that the kill should be in the vegetation on the side of the stream. But instead the tiger has dragged it up the steep hillslope. The undergrowth has been heavily disturbed, boulders have been dislodged. The tiger has evidently been able to drag his prey up this sheer slope, which we can barely climb. Its might and surefooted ability to do this makes us wonder at the sheer power of this astounding predator! He is indeed the king of the jungles of India. In this ecosystem humans are so much less efficient, so much smaller. We quietly turn around and head back to the Forest Resthouse.

# K A N A W A R

KANAWAR

| State | Himachal Pradesh | Zone | Gangetic Plains |
|---|---|---|---|
| Area | 61.57 sq km | Ecosystem | Bhabar Forest |
| Year of Notification | 1954 | Visited | Jun 2000 |

A short drive from Manali brings one to a valley with tall coniferous forests and mountain streams. The views are stupendous. Kanawar has a small steep path that takes one up into the hills. The forest is cool and fragrant. There are birdcalls and sounds of insects all over the forest. An old man walks past us, grinning a toothless welcome. The guards accompanying me wave to him and walk on. The light filtering through the trees creates a mosaic of green patchwork in the ground cover. The rocks are covered with moss. It feels cool and damp with the early morning dew.

Kanawar, in the Himalayan foothills is an extremely fragile ecosystem. Changes induced by human activity easily destabilize both the abiotic and the biotic aspects of the ecosystem.

A high diversity of flowering plants is found in the undergrowth.

Certain plant species grow in small patches where the microhabitat provides them with specific habitat needs.

A cleared area or landslide has left a scar on the hillslope. Boulders have hurtled down the slope along with tons of soil. It could take decades for the system to stabilize itself and gradually acquire a cover of plant life in which the fauna can live. The steps towards rehabilitation can be accelerated by a carefully done re-vegetation, but this cannot go through the natural process of succession that will bring back slowly but surely a natural diverse secondary forest.

As we climb higher, the thin clean air is exhilarating. The sharp light allows me to pick out the small plants of the undergrowth. The diversity is astounding, the colours brilliant. The flowers flash a message to the insects that buzz around each flowering herb and bush.

The water in the waterfall is crystal clear and ice cold, and one can taste the freshness of this living, gurgling, unpolluted stream. The fatigue of the rapid ascent seems to vanish as the water quenches my deep thirst. Each Himalayan valley has a character of its own. Every one that I have walked through has been a new, distinctive experience.

Forest loss in the Himalayas is the result of decades of timber extraction, exacerbated by the needs of the local people who use the forest for fuelwood, fodder and several non-wood forest products. It is the extraction of timber for commercial purposes that led to the Chipko Movement of the 1970s. Led by the charismatic Sunderlaljee Bahuguna, the movement banded together local people, especially women, to prevent logging in the forests around their homes. Sunderlal links deforestation with issues that are connected to the forest's control on the local water regime and to the prevention of soil erosion so eloquently that the logic becomes irrefutable. Other impacts arise from mining, hydel dams, roads and a variety of development projects. The growth of mountain tourism, with its garbage strewn over every popular Himalayan trail, is a problem that has meant expensive clean-up projects as has been done for Everest. How many can one afford? With all these pressures, Himalayan Protected Areas, as well as the valleys where there is no formal protection, are precarious refuges for Himalayan wildlife.

## THE TERAI

The Terai is the low-lying region where the Himalayan rivers disgorge themselves into the Indo-Gangetic plains. The beautiful forests of this area grow on relatively higher ground, whereas the lowest-lying areas are covered by tall elephant-grass, which grows thick and luxuriant in the boggy soil. The depressions form some of the most incredible wetlands left in the country, still teeming with life.

Over the millennia many of the animals which evolved here have adapted so well to their niche that they are hardly seen anywhere else in the country. Thus the Terai represents a mosaic of habitat types, which together form a landscape that is full of life and activity. Several primates are specific to the area: the Assamese Macaque, the Capped Langur and the rare Golden Langur. Some beautiful cats, like the Golden Cat and the Leopard Cat are also found here. Hogdeer and swamp deer are also endemic to this region. Elephants and rhinos are its largest herbivores.

The marshy, shallow waters are covered by migrant aquatic birds in winter, which make Terai their first halting place as they come across the Himalayas. Many,

A typical Terai landscape, with tall forests alternating with elephant-grass and wetlands. Note the elephant in the tall grass.

however, stop here throughout the season as the aquatic life that forms their food material is plentiful. The ecosystem includes a large diversity of beautiful butterflies and other insect life.

In this mosaic of forest and elephant-grass habitat, certain species, such as primates, occupy only the forests. Others, such as swamp deer and rhinoceri, frequent only the marshy elephant-grass, while animals like the elephant use both zones, moving from one habitat type to another in different seasons. The elephant browses on the leaves and fruit in the forest, often breaking down several trees, and in the process opening up the canopy so that the young trees are given a chance to grow. This gives the forest a varied structure. When grass is tender and green, the elephant uproots it, cleans off the sticky soil by beating the roots against its leg, and eats the juicy long stems. The elephant thus makes use of this dual habitat alternately, as it requires enormous quantities of food.

Within this shrinking forest and swampland are several National Parks and Wild Life Sanctuaries. In the past this tract of Terai forests was much more extensive. Indiscriminate draining of its wetlands for agriculture, felling of its forests and grass-burning have modified the balance between forest, grasslands and marsh. The swamp is an important component of the habitat, supporting several animals and birds that are not found elsewhere. Unless urgent conservation measures are taken, changes in this landscape could herald the end of a variety of highly specialized species. Humans have, in the recent past, degraded this ecosystem beyond repair for the sake of short-term gains and opted to perform the most grave and thoughtless acts against nature in the region. The shrinking Terai is an example of the unsustainable land-use practices that are so widespread in our country.

| State | Uttaranchal | Zone | Upper Gangetic Plains |
|---|---|---|---|
| Area | 520.82 sq km | Ecosystem | Moist Sal Forest |
| Year of Notification | 1936 | Visited | Apr 1992, May 1994 |

Elephant herd emerging from the mist to cross the Ramganga River at dawn.

King vulture in 1994. Probably very few now remain after a sharp decline in numbers in the late 1990s.

The Ramganga River is home to crocodiles and gharials.

Elephant with its calf.

Corbett has a special flavour that is woven around the name of the famous shikari/naturalist. Initially called Hailey National Park, the area was notified a National Park in 1936 and was the first National Park in India. It was then re-named Ramganga National Park after Independence, and it finally became the Corbett National Park in 1957. Jim Corbett's home at the foot of the hills, near Nainital, evokes visions of the wildlife of yesteryear. The images of great tigers roaming through the uncharted wilderness that once covered large tracts of the India of a past era, can never return in reality. Today we can only imagine what it must have been like—the splendour of sheer isolation. Today the tiger population at

Corbett has stabilized at about 140 and an estimated 750 elephants still roam in its forests. In 1997, the population of sambar as estimated during the tiger census was 5727, and the barking deer population was 2229 (Jain, 2001).

The Corbett National Park contains both Terai and Bhabar forests, and patches of short alluvial grasslands. The sal forests contain trees such as *Angeissus latifolia*, *Terminalia tomentosa*, and great clumps of bamboo. The Bhabar forest has coniferous trees and broad-leaved species such as *Lagerstroemia parviflora*. In the low alluvial areas there are *Salmalia*, *Adina cordiflora* and *Dalbergia sisoo*. As one ascends into the upper regions, the chir-pine forests of the Sivaliks cover most of the steeper slopes of the foothills.

My visits to Corbett have left indelible memories of the scenic beauty of the Ramganga River as it flows through hilly terrain and down into the wide valleys. Early one morning, the mists were swirling over the riverbed. It was like a monochrome photograph with a pale blue wash. I was on elephant back, moving slowly along the bank. On the other bank, a herd of elephants moved out of the forest. They suddenly decided to crash across the river. The swirling mist and the spray as they thundered through the water brought the silent, misty-grey dawn to instant life. It is in moments such as these out in the wilderness that one's bond with nature is suddenly rekindled.

In 1994, I spotted one of Corbett's few remaining king vultures. When I last visited Corbett I knew that all over the country vultures were becoming increasingly scarce. The king vulture has always been less abundant than the other species. It was reported that the Park still had a few vultures, which had become increasingly difficult to spot. Turning around a corner in the road, a dark shadow landed effortlessly in a distant tree. It was a king vulture, still too far away for a really good picture. After a long circuit we got close enough to the tall tree to enable us to take its picture.

Perhaps my most enjoyable afternoon in Corbett was spent sitting besides a waterhole in a watchtower and viewing a large herd of elephants as they moved in single file slowly past me to the water. After they had drunk, sprayed themselves with showers of water and left to feed in the nearby forests, the waterhole was visited by a wild boar, a herd of chital, a pair of eagles, a broad-billed roller and a variety of other smaller birds. The elephant herd continued to feed for the next two hours, concealed in the foliage nearby. The grand finale of the day was the sight of the elephant herd stampeding past the tower when it was disturbed by the approach of a domestic elephant that was returning to pick me up in the evening.

Gee visited Hailey National Park in April 1954 and mentions that it was more beautiful than he expected after reading EA Smythies and FW Champion's descriptions of this region. He describes how he and Hailey had fished in the waters of the Ramganga in the 1920s. Now that it is a National Park, fishing is banned. There is a story of how Shri Negi, who was the Director of the Tiger Reserve, caught a Minister red-handed catching a fish in Corbett, confiscated the catch, auctioned it at the local marketplace as prescribed by law and fined the Minister. No amount of pressure changed Negi's purpose! Few Forest Officials would dare to do this; Negi had a single-minded approach to protecting his Tiger Reserve through a personal dedication to the cause of conservation.

Corbett is rich in its variety of birds of prey. Driving through the forest we came across a tall, rickety wooden structure. It was Rishad Naoroji's hide, built to photograph the nest of a bird of prey. The structure looked unstable and dangerous. Wildlife photography has its risks! We bump into Rishad on his way back from his hide. He is ecstatic; he says he has got the most incredible pictures during the day. His knowledge of birds of prey is second to none in the country, and his dedication to nature photography is obsessive. I have always enjoyed talking to him about wildlife and conservation. Why can't there be more Rishads?

The forest and its teeming wildlife have changed since the time Corbett stalked tigers through these forests, when he had to trek from one tiny hamlet to another on

A tusker threatens the parked jeep, before turning away into the grass.

Chital at dawn.

foot in search of the dangerous man-eaters of that era. My experience of tigers in Corbett after several trips has been limited to two brief encounters, barely three or four minutes apart. From the jeep I spotted a highly agitated monkey giving alarm calls repeatedly. The crashing of branches was occurring higher up, on a hill slope. The whole troop appeared to be in a state of panic. This just had to be a sign that a tiger was in the vicinity. Two elephants were brought to the site and we had to scramble onto the large animals as best we could. It took 15 minutes to go around the hill slope in a long circuitous route to the top. The elephants were brought quietly to the edge of the slope. Just then a tiger flashed past between the two elephants a few metres away so rapidly that there was not even time to see it through the camera viewfinder. But the monkeys were still alarmed; something was clearly still agitating them. As we peered downwards through the grass, a tiny movement I perceived with the corner of my eyes, attracted my attantion. There, peering around the edge of a boulder barely 10 metres away, was the half-hidden face of a tiger. He was watching the elephant with one eye. There was a sudden 'umph!'

and a flash of gold and black dashed past us, so close that it made our elephant spin around and charge off through the bamboo for a good 20 or 30 metres. Hanging on for dear life as we crashed through the foliage was all we could think of! The tiger was gone. I may never get a good photograph of a tiger in Corbett. The 1400 square kilometres of forested land around Corbett should be able to support 100 tigers. It also supports, however, 200 Gujar families who use enormous quantities of fuelwood and graze their cattle, and this conflicts with the food availability for the tiger's wild prey. The pressures from habitat loss and poaching have both accounted for pushing this glorious animal towards the brink of the precipice of extinction. Only public opinion can force the Government to implement laws to prevent poaching for the skin, and more recently, for its bones. The amount of poaching that we hear about is only the tip of the iceberg. The illegal trade fetches enormous sums of money and is as difficult to eradicate as the drug trade. The flame in the eyes of this glorious animal, the 'Tiger, tiger burning bright in the forest of the night,' may remain a poetic verse, for the light in its eyes may soon be extinguished forever.

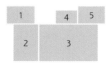

| 1 | | 4 | 5 |
| 2 | 3 | | |

A tiger peers from behind a rock before charging my elephant which turned and ran.

The largest sal tree in India.

This spur-winged plover is difficult to spot among the rocks.

Elephants in the grasslands of Corbett.

A gharial on the bank of the Ramganga River.

| State | Uttar Pradesh | Zone | Upper Gangetic Plains |
|---|---|---|---|
| Area | 680 sq km | Ecosystem | Terai Forest |
| Year of Notification | 1977 | Visited | Jun 2004, Dec 2004 |

The roar of the storm moving rapidly through the forest canopy could be heard from far away, from the bridge over a small *nala* course in the depths of Dudhwa. When it reached the bridge, pandemonium broke out. The silence that had preceded the storm for the last 15 minutes was broken by a shattering wind that bent the trees and cracked their branches like matchsticks.

Thousands of leaves floated into the sky. A few glorious moments passed before the dark grey cloud burst and rain began to descend in torrents. It was one of the first few rains of the season and the parched earth and the forest road sent puffs of water vapours wafting through the trees. The rain came pouring through the canopy and down the sal trunks, disappearing into the thirsty ground. As the roar grew in intensity and darkness brought on thunder and sharp lightning, I began to feel as if I could not only see and hear the storm, but sense it in my innermost being. Then, as the wind dropped in intensity, the air was filled with the sweet scent of wet earth that had been waiting for the rains through the long dry months.

I will never forget the two elephant rides that I had with Nama, an old, bearded mahout. This grand old man's long quiet conversations with his elephant sounded more as if they were with a young family member than to a pet or working animal. I remember how, when the elephant's occasional desire to eat a choice branch made it stop in the middle of the forest, he would explain in a quiet but firm voice what was expected of it. Once, when she refused to proceed, in a loud, exasperated tone, he exclaimed, 'Now if you go on doing this, I will start breaking your skull!' There was instant obedience! The elephant always gives me a sense of awe with its controlled power, as well as its ability to

Dudhwa has fascinating vegetation. It includes sal and mixed forests, the great grasslands and the aquatic vegetation of its wetlands.

Boggy areas that are extensions of the wetland spread into the forest.

The early morning mist floats from the wetlands into the forests.

The ecotone between the forest and wetland is rich in plant species.

A large monitor lizard in the grassland.

My favourite elephant and its mahout at Dudhwa.

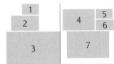

Portrait of a macaque.

Fruiting plants in the shrub layer provide food for insects, birds and mammals.

Exceptionally tall termite mounds are found all over the Dudhwa forest.

A rhino with her calf.

The grasslands of Dudhwa require urgent protection.

A rhino displays its magnificent horn.

Rhinos were trans-located here from Kaziranga and later from Nepal.

A large strangler fig tree in the forest.

A machan built by farmers to protect their crops from being damaged by wildlife.

Croplands at the edge of the forest.

The railway that runs through the forest has been responsible for the death of a large number of wild animals, including elephants.

This wetland near Dudhwa supports several species of aquatic birds.

| 1 | 2 |
|---|---|
| 3 | 4 |
| | 5 |

Ferns form a thick patch in the undergrowth.

A flowering plant in the marshland.

The grasslands are periodically burned to prevent forests encroaching into them.

A chital stag rests in the shade during the afternoon.

Chital hind.

think and know what its mahout wants. One of those I rode in Dudhwa had a two- or three-year-old baby with tiny tusks following along behind. This youngster just had to play with everything in sight, tugging at his rope to get what he wanted: to break a stick to a convenient length to hold in his trunk and scratch himself with; to strip bark, knock down ant hills, or simply frolic to and fro during the long walk. One morning he must have been woken up too early. Before we could get up onto his mother, he had curled up on the ground to have a snooze. He was such fun to watch when there was no wildlife about!

Dudhwa's grasslands are composed of tall elephant grass and a great diversity of short grasses, which were in flower. We searched for the Bengal florican and hispid hare, two highly endemic Terai species, but the grass was just too high. The enclosure where the reintroduced rhinos are kept makes it easy to observe rhinos. But even in the large wild enclosure, they are difficult to spot unless one patiently rides an elephant through the grassland. In a wetland nearby, groups of 20 or more swamp deer were feeding quietly. Once they had spotted our vehicle, they kept at a relatively long distance, as if they were aware of being threatened by poachers. If so, the poachers must be using high-powered rifles and not shotguns.

Perhaps what irked me the most were the trains that roar through the Protected Area day and night at top speed, blowing their horns to keep wildlife off the tracks. Last year, three elephants were tragically killed by trains and there are reports of pythons being bisected and many other animals crushed to death. And still the Railways do nothing to slow down these roaring monsters as they snake their way in a wide curve through the Tiger Reserve.

A giant tree supported by great buttress roots towers over the canopy of forest trees.

# KISHANPUR WILDLIFE SANCTUARY

KISHANPUR

| State | Uttar Pradesh | Zone | Upper Gangetic Plains |
|---|---|---|---|
| Area | 204 sq km | Ecosystem | Terai Forests and Wetlands |
| Year of Notification | — | Visited | Jun 2004, Dec 2004 |

This sanctuary is a part of the Dudhwa Tiger Reserve. It was established in 1972, and brought under Project Tiger in 1987–88. A great expanse of swampy land with open water and emergent vegetation, it harbours India's largest single population of barasingha, endemic to the Terai region. The centre of the lake is dotted with their orange-red graceful forms, grazing or following their leader from one end of the wetland to another, and even swimming out into deeper water. The lake is full of fish of a wide range of species and numerous snails. The most stunning feature for me was the largest concentration of waterfowl, ducks and waders that I have ever seen in India in the recent past. These alone make this a reserve of national importance. It is vital to protect it, now, from the township growing at its border.

Swamp deer at Kishanpur.

The Kishanpur swamp has one of the best residual populations of the swamp deer and teams with wild fowl.

The forest and grasslands of Kishanpur provide optimal habitat for wildlife.

| State | Assam | Zone | North-east India |
|---|---|---|---|
| Area | 500 sq km | Ecosystem | Terai Forest, Tall Wet Grasslands, Shallow Marshes |
| Year of Notification | 1937 | Visited | Dec 1978 |

As the jeep bumps over the crest of the top of a small rise in the forest, a breathtaking sight unfolds. Down below flows a sparkling river of a most unbelievable deep turquoise. Its banks are covered with perfectly smooth, round, pale-coloured rocks, which the torrent has brought down from the hills up-stream over the last several thousand years, perhaps even during an earlier glacial era. On the opposite bank, the slopes are thickly clothed with a semi-evergreen forest, interspersed with patches of moist deciduous forest. The river emerges from the hills, meanders sharply around a picturesque narrow bend and flows swiftly past in a great, gradual sweeping curve that is broken by several rapids. Further downstream it flows into the distance, broadening as it approaches the plains, and seems to disappear over the distant horizon as if it were flowing over the edge of the earth. The riverbanks are covered alternately by forest and wide expanses of elephant grass that form large tracts of alluvial grassland. This is the Manas River on the border of India and Bhutan, which has some of the most magnificent scenery in the world.

The sal forests of the Protected Area lie along the northern flood plains of the River, which overflows its banks periodically, flooding the plains and raising the water level in its surrounding wetlands and thus absorbing some of the force manifested downstream. Manas is the land of rivers and over 10 tributaries run through the Protected Area southwards, to flow into the great Brahmaputra; of these, the Manas River is one of the most important. It flows out of the hills of Bhutan and its crystal-clear water creates one of the most spectacular riverscapes I have ever seen. Its banks are a complex mosaic of habitat types ranging from the stately sal forests and tall elephant-grass, to riverine tracts, savanna grasslands and sal forests.

There is a difference of opinion regarding the date when this area was made into a sanctuary. It was probably given protection from 1905 onwards; and the sanctuary has been in existence since 1928. The rulers of the States of Gauripur and Cooch Bihar used these forests as private shikar areas. Over the years, the sanctuary has been extended several times. Finally, in 1990 it was decided to re-designate it as a National Park.

Manas was not only one of the first areas to have been designated a Tiger Reserve under Project Tiger, in 1973, but it was also acknowledged as one of India's important Natural Heritage Sites under the World Heritage Convention, an International Treaty that recognises areas of global conservation significance. At least 20 animals found here are highly endangered and listed in the IUCN's Red Data Book. The number of rhinos in 1952 was not clearly known. Estimates varied from 100 by the Conservator to only eight or nine by Salim Ali. There were 250 elephants, 500 buffaloes and 100 bison.

In 1988, Manas had an estimated 92 tigers, in 1993 numbers were falling and there were only 81 left (*PA Update* 30–31).

The forest guesthouse in the Tiger Reserve is a wooden structure built on the edge of a steep slope, with windows overlooking the river and the forest beyond the river in Bhutan. A mere minute's walk from the house takes one to the depths of the Terai forest. During a short walk along the river, I tried to get through the forest into a nearby clearing where I had heard the unmistakable sound of the wing-beats of a large hornbill. The bushes were so thickly covered by climbers that they were impenetrable. Abandoning the search for the bird, I waited for the Forest

## THE NORTH-EAST

This region is a hotspot of global importance. Its Protected Areas are of great value to mankind. They form the habitat for a large number of endangered and endemic species. Apart from the well known notified Protected Areas, several small areas are being increasingly protected by local people. These areas are now included in a new network of Community Conserved Areas (CCAs).

In this World Heritage Site, the Manas River flows from the foothills of Bhutan into the plains of India.

Department elephant, while beautiful golden-backed sunbirds hovered over my camera lens in large numbers, flitting around in the bushes from flower to flower.

The cow elephant allotted to me in the Manas Sanctuary was a most remarkable animal. She had an innate sense of what her mahout wanted her to do. On the first day I fed her some bananas and on subsequent days she invariably singled me out of the group of visitors, extending her trunk and blowing her wet breath all over me. She was small and had an interesting personality, being most curious about everything and eager to explore places and people around her. Her mahout was an experienced old hand in the Forest

Department. He sat stiff and upright like a soldier and gracefully parted the branches overhead with his iron spike, which he rarely ever had to use to guide his mount. He told us several stories of the wildlife of Manas and of the more colourful visitors he had taken into the forest through the years.

While climbing up a steep bank of the river on elephant back there was a sudden crash among the branches. A family of capped langurs had been disturbed while feeding on the flower buds of a *Bombax* tree. Further uphill, a small group of chital rushed off into the forest. There was a loud crack of breaking branches nearby. The wild elephant feeding on bamboo seemed already aware of the presence of the domestic elephant, and was carefully scenting the wind. Turning around, it moved rapidly into the forest. Our elephant remained unconcerned.

She had many surprises for me. One morning we had spotted a group of wild buffaloes in the distance on the riverbank and were moving towards them, cameras ready, when she suddenly stopped. The mahout's quiet voice ordered her to move forwards which she refused to do. Then turning around he whispered—'Have you dropped anything, saheb?' 'No,' I answered. 'Just look carefully, I think you have,' he added. Turning around I asked my friend Gerard Ewald, who was sitting behind me, if he had dropped anything. Feeling around in his pockets he realized that his lens cap was missing. The elephant moved backwards a couple of steps, and picking up the lens cap with her trunk, handed it to the mahout. I never found out how she knew that something had fallen down and should be retrieved.

I recall another time when the mahout, in his quiet way, indicated that he thought she had spotted something in a nearby bush. She was stalking the area carefully, apparently needing no guidance. Slowly she circled an isolated patch of bushes. Then suddenly she moved backwards a few paces and began scenting carefully. None of us, not even the mahout with his keen forest-dweller's eye, could see anything. He tried to get her to move on with a little prod, when I saw a tiny movement behind a bush very close by. It was the flap of a deer's ear. I could then just discern through

1

2  3

Swamp deer in tall grassland at dawn, watching the approach of a tiger.

The golden langur was first identified by EP Gee.

The Manas river is deep turquoise blue and contrasts with the pale round rocks on its banks.

Taking pictures from this elephant's remarkably steady back was unusually easy. One of the problems of taking pictures from elephant back is that they constantly move their great weight from one foot to another, rocking from side to side slowly. This causes immense problems for the wildlife photographer. The swaying movement appears to be multiplied several-fold while using a long tele-lens. Unfortunately this usually blurs only the most exciting pictures due to 'camera shake'. I try to expose pictures during the short pause while the elephant swings from one foot to the other.

Jeeps and cars often present a similar problem. The engine has to be put off to avoid vibrations. Other excited animal-watchers in the vehicle have to be told to avoid making sudden movements, to prevent the vehicle from rocking on its suspension. They rarely ever comply!

Of my several jeep rides in Manas, I will always recall the last one as being the most thrilling. We had started off before sunrise on the New Year day of 1979. It was cold and the misty air was rushing past the open windscreen. Driving along the narrow mud track, through the tall elephant-grass, we could see the sun rising. A large male wild buffalo with one of its horns missing moved off the road into the grass. The forest guard in the back of the jeep mumbled that this was an omen. He did not specify whether it was a 'good' or a 'bad' omen, and I never did find out exactly what sighting a one-horned buffalo is supposed to foretell. However, irrespective of the local superstitious beliefs, it seemed to have given us a lucky start. Five minutes later, we spotted a large animal moving along the road in the distance, keeping to the middle of the track. The dark shape silhouetted in the morning light was a huge tiger. I took a series of unremarkable pictures of the majestic animal walking casually along the road with his back to us. He must have been aware of us, but paid no attention, as we drove cautiously behind him and stopped about 30 metres away. It was only then that he paused to glance over his shoulder and watch us briefly. He then turned to move off into the elephant-grass—the low golden rays of the rising

the foliage two suspicious eyes peering at us. As I pressed the camera shutter the little creature bounded away. The elephant had stalked it unobtrusively and without disturbing it. She moved nearly soundlessly through the undergrowth of the steep hill forest, and seemed to feel equally comfortable through the marsh, or while moving through tall elephant grass. She was as much at home in the water, while swimming across the fast flowing Manas River, as on land.

One evening, at the end of a long and backbreaking ride, a large animal seemed to have parted the tall grass. Further on, there was a little muddy pool. In the mud were the unmistakable wallow marks and spoor of a rhino. The elephant persisted in following the trail until we got her to abandon it at sunset. I am sure we must have disappointed her keen interest in the chase!

Capped langurs are restricted to the north-eastern states.

Portrait of a well-known aggressive wild buffalo of Manas.

a picture of a pair of powerful haunches and a long tail! I seem to have lost many of the best possible pictures by running out of film at the wrong time. It is a familiar story similar to the tales woven by shikaris of yesteryear whose largest trophies always seemed to escape!

Turning the jeep around, we then attempted to head the tiger off along another jungle track, but we never saw him again. What we did spot was a very nervous-looking family of swamp deer. At first they hardly paid any attention to the jeep, as they were too preoccupied peering into the dry elephant grass, where we had last seen the tiger. Perhaps we were responsible for having saved the life of one of these beautiful creatures that day, as one of them could well have become the tiger's breakfast.

Later that day we crossed the river into Bhutan. The forest has several narrow pathways meandering up the hillside, which is covered by exceptionally tall trees. Although we walked as quietly as possible, the loud insect sounds were suddenly silenced at our approach. A movement in the treetops made us look upwards. Suddenly a flash of gold seemed to erupt from one tall tree to land noisily on a neighbouring branch, bending it acutely

sun reflected off his shiny coat. This was my first chance to get a really superb picture of a very large tiger. In fact, the largest I have ever seen. The light was just right. The setting was perfect, with the tiger framed by tall grass. With mounting excitement I wound the camera shutter only to find I had run out of film! I watched in utter dismay as this incredibly powerful animal slowly began to move into the grass. I made a dash for fresh film and reloaded the camera as fast as I could. I was left with downwards. On the swinging branch sat a beautiful golden-yellow primate, staring at us through a pair of glistening eyes shining on its black face. Its long tail swung wildly as it balanced precariously on its unsteady perch. Another, and yet another golden flash moved through the foliage of the giant trees. Quickly the troop of golden langurs began to move away from us. We had spotted one of the most beautiful monkeys found in India, a species that is indeed very rare.

At midday we got into a small boat and poled into the middle of the river. The current began to carry us swiftly downstream. As we approached the first few rapids, I was rather worried. The boat swayed up and down, tilting dangerously from side to side, and bumping its bottom on the rocks below.

My apprehension, however, evaporated as I saw a group of merganser ducks streaking over the water past the boat. The sleek merganser is a fast flier. The duck has a serrated bill, used to catch fish. On the Manas River, several animals and birds prey on the abundant fish. There were several fishing eagles. One chased a merganser, which had a fish in its beak. The frightened duck dropped its catch, which the eagle caught in mid-air. A small family of eagles sat among the boulders in a rocky cove, sharing a shiny fish, two-feet long.

Further downriver I heard the Forest Guard, who was sitting in the back of the boat, cursing under his breath. There was a large black shape in the distance, and as we got closer it turned around to face us. It was the largest wild buffalo I have ever seen. The guard quietly explained that the buffalo was a loner and had been known to attack people in this area, as he considered this stretch of river to be his own territory. He had also taken the liberty of upturning a couple of boats in the water. If he decided to be nasty today there would be no chance of even climbing a tree. What troubled me was how I could save my precious camera and even more precious exposed films! Though worried, I could not resist standing in the boat to take several pictures of him as we passed downstream safely. The huge animal stared fixedly at us till we were out of sight, pawing the ground and snorting angrily.

The river with her changing moods carried the boat lazily around bends or quickly through small rapids. It was an unforgettable experience. The clear water allowed glimpses of the rocky riverbed where shoals of fish flashed by. Pied kingfishers hovered over the water. The shores were covered with incredible forests and tall grassland. As we reached 'civilization' again at Barpeta Road, one could not have imagined that only a few years later local political instability would make Manas nearly inaccessible. Its forests have been degraded, its grasslands burnt and its wildlife threatened. And this is the Sanctuary that India has included and proclaimed a World Heritage Site! Its species includes some of our most threatened major mammals: the pygmy hog, our smallest wild boar, the golden langur, the swamp deer, the rhino, and birds such as the rare florican.

This was where I first met Deb Roy when he was the Director of the Tiger Reserve. We remained close friends until his death a few years ago. His passion was Manas and he told stories of his great days in this idyllic site to anyone willing to listen. Many years later, as a reviewer appointed by Project Tiger, I was asked to visit Manas once more. The Field Director, however, refused to let me come, as he feared that I would be kidnapped! My pleas that I was not worried did not convince him and I have regrettably never returned again to this enchanting Tiger Reserve.

It is to the credit of Deb Roy and several of the other field directors at Manas that they have been able to manage this sanctuary throughout the period when it has been disturbed by the unfortunate political events that have occurred in the region. While the tiger is the apex predator of this ecosystem, there are several other species of highly endemic mammals and birds, which require intensive protection in this all-important World Heritage Site. Militant activity has been a problem in Manas for over a decade. However, in the late 90s, this has been significantly reduced. The problem seems to have escalated again after 2000.

A merganser duck in flight.

| State | Assam | Zone | North-east India |
|---|---|---|---|
| Area | 430 sq km | Ecosystem | Terai Forest |
| Year of Notification | 1908; NP 1974 | Visited | Dec 1978 |

Kaziranga is one of India's earliest National Parks. It was created specifically to save the endangered rhino.

Kaziranga was created in 1908 as a reserve and closed for shooting to protect rhino. It became a Game Sanctuary in 1928 and was opened to visitors in 1937. In 1940 there were an estimated 300 rhinos. A number of rhinos died of anthrax in 1947. The population in 1952 was estimated to be 150. EP Gee writes that, 'it costs very little money to plan new Sanctuaries, and these are urgently needed before it becomes too late.' His efforts to save the rhino and its natural habitat in Kaziranga have succeeded in saving the species and this all-important site in Assam.

Kaziranga is a WorldHeritage Site. It had about 1550 one-horned rhinos and 1666 wild buffaloes in 2001.

When a wildlife sanctuary has been in existence for a long time, it acquires a special character of its own. The animals in old sanctuaries begin to regard human intrusion as a minor nuisance and do not retain their normal fear of human beings. Sanctuaries of this type are often rather like a zoological park, and though one does enjoy the close proximity of several animals, it also produces a certain sense of disappointment at this loss of 'wildness'

in its wildlife. The total number of tourists in Kaziranga in 1950 was 46! By 1955 this had increased to 900 per year. By the 1980s it had grown several-fold. The large numbers of tourists with whom the animals are familiar at Kaziranga makes viewing wildlife extremely easy. The swamp deer at Manas had been wary and alert, while here they went on grazing nonchalantly, like the antelopes of the East African Parks. The wild buffalo that give intimidating stares at Manas, ambled over unperturbed towards the domestic elephants, with several noisy tourists on their backs. Rhinos that had done a rapid disappearing act in Manas were totally at ease with the visitors here. However, this is only true of the viewing area close to the tourist complex. Further afield the animals are as shy as anywhere else in the Terai.

The sanctuary is covered with semi-evergreen sal forests, large belts of elephant-grass and shallow marshland. Several rivers zigzag through it, with large trees and palms growing down to the edge of the water. There are about 200 wetlands of great biological value in Kaziranga. It is possible that these are being gradually silted up during the repeated floods.

The most exciting animal of 'Kazi' is undoubtedly the Indian rhinoceros. This creature is the amphibian tank of the animal world, perfectly adapted to the Terai swamps. In the past they were also found in other types of forests where water was plentiful, such as the swamps of the Ganges delta. In 1999, the count of rhinos in Kaziranga had risen from a few dozen, when the Park was notified, to 1552. This shows that creating a Protected Area even when the population is down to near extinction-levels can be successful if intensively managed.

Much of the rhino's day is spent wallowing around in muddy pools of water. Rhinos are territorial in nature and I saw the same animal occupying a small area for several days. They are known to defecate at the same spot and there were several such mounds scattered around. They are temperamental and at times dangerous. Trying to make a rhino more accessible for the camera, our driver had got fairly close to a female rhino with a calf. She was quietly grazing until she suddenly decided

that she had had enough of this intrusion and made a charge at the jeep. At the last moment she turned away, only grazing its rear end as she passed. The impact however was sufficiently powerful to push the jeep sideways.

Killed over generations for the supposed aphrodisiac and medicinal properties of their horns, the rhinos of Kaziranga had all but disappeared during the early part of this century, but they multiplied considerably after the establishment of the sanctuary in 1928. However, there are now fresh reports of rhino poaching. It is vital that some of them be trans-located to other Protected Areas from where the species has disappeared as a result of human interference. A small number were reintroduced into Manas and Dudhwa a decade ago.

At dawn, near an open *jheel* (lake), large flocks of bar-headed geese flew overhead in great 'V' formations. Several settled down in the nearby marsh. I thought it a good opportunity to get pictures of them on the ground. Guarded by an old Assamese Forest Guard with an even older 12-bore gun, I plowed my way towards them, knee-deep in mud. After the first few pictures, the guard, whom I had instructed to keep well behind me, gesticulated wildly for me to return. Looking around I saw the cause of his anxiety. While we had been watching the geese, a group of wild buffaloes had emerged from the elephant grass and were watching us suspiciously.

As I joined the guard and headed for the nearest patch of tall grass, a single buffalo pushed its head out of the grass barely five metres away! Nostrils flaring, it snorted loudly at the sound of the camera shutter before disappearing. The wild buffalo, though best suited to the Terai, had a much wider range in the past and used a similar niche in other types of habitats. Their distribution has been gradually reduced over the recent past as man drains swamps for agriculture, and the animals' microhabitat needs disappeared from other types of forests, leaving only small pockets in the Terai.

Large flocks of pelicans are attracted by the easily accessible fish in the marshlands of Kaziranga. In flight, they look like the large seaplanes of the 1940s. In the water, they form a small fishing party shaped like a 'U' to drive their prey into the shallows, storing fish in the large pouch in their beaks. The birds move from one marsh to another, often working each area systematically. Changes in the water-level account for these movements, as they prefer to hunt where the water is conveniently deep. The pelicans have a large nesting colony in a patch of very tall trees surrounded by marshland in a remote part of Kaziranga. I was keen to see the Pelicanary at dawn, before most of the birds had moved off to their feeding areas. Unfortunately, on the way we came across a male wild buffalo that refused to get off the road. He kept staring at us, tossing his head menacingly and wagging his tail. We had to wait for more than half an hour before he moved off into the forest. The Forest Officials with me said that this buffalo was a mean old animal and very unpredictable. A little further, we came across some trees lying across the road. An elephant herd had passed through the area. Large branches were strewn all over. By the time we could clear the road and proceed to the Pelicanary, most of the birds were out feeding. The nests were built in a very inaccessible place beyond a shallow river and the trees were covered with guano. Some juveniles were flapping around in their nest. An occasional parent flew into the colony with its bill heavy with fish, which led to a frenzy of movement. A large elephant was quietly uprooting grass under the trees. And further upriver, a barking deer cautiously descended to the edge of the water for a drink.

During my stay at Kaziranga, I repeatedly went for walks in the hope of photographing red jungle fowl. They invariably flew off before I had a chance to take a picture. The driver and guard, knowing that I had had no luck with them over several days, were excited when on our way back a beautiful cock and several hens flew across the road and took cover in the nearby bushes on a river bank. I stalked them very carefully to a distance of a few feet, ready to get a picture of them as they flew off. Behind me, there was a loud splash in the water. Turning around in surprise, I found I had cornered a rhino on the riverbank between the jeep and myself and had inadvertently forced it into the river. As it swam across, I got a few pictures of it splashing noisily. But my carefully stalked jungle fowl had eluded me again!

Some of my favourite pictures at Kaziranga are taken from elephant back. Elephants prefer to walk in single file through the swamp. Each animal follows exactly in the footsteps of the preceding one. Perhaps this makes it easier for them, as the suction effect of the mud is reduced. The sanctuary is a paradise for wildlife photographers, especially those who expect quick results with little effort.

1

2

Herd of swamp deer.

Brown palm squirrel.

Few sanctuaries in India can give as many opportunities for close-up pictures of various animals as Kaziranga.

Every few years the mighty Brahmaputra River rises in spate to inundate Kaziranga. In 1998, one of the bad years, rhinos, swamp deer and other animals moved out of the Protected Area and several were drowned in the rising waters, or were killed outside the area. In 2000, it is reported that 48 rhinos were killed by the floods. Studies on the Brahmaputra and its floods point to the fact that this leads to severe erosion effects on Kaziranga, which could well have lost several square kilometre in the last 30 or 40 years. There is also a problem caused by the excessive silting of the wetlands in the Protected Area. These are also being covered by hyacinth, which is adding a serious dimension to the wetland biodiversity conservation.

While extremists in the North-eastern states were considered a threat to wildlife, in a recent development, there are reports of extremist groups supporting the cause of wildlife conservation and even threatening to take severe action on poachers and the timber mafia operating around Kaziranga.

| 1 | |
| 2 | |
| 3 | 4 |

Wild buffalo in the grasslands of Kaziranga.

Rhinos are strong swimmers.

A rhino with its young. This female charged our jeep.

Bar-headed geese feeding in the wetland.

| 1 | 2 |
|---|---|
| 3 | 4 |
| 5 | |

A red jungle fowl with its harem of females scuttles across the road.

Barking deer.

A hog deer on the forest road.

Forest, tall elephant-grasslands and wetlands constitute the Terai ecosystem.

Assamese children warm themselves at a fire on a cold morning at the edge of Kaziranga.

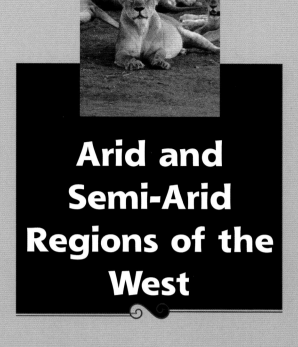

# Arid and Semi-Arid Regions of the West

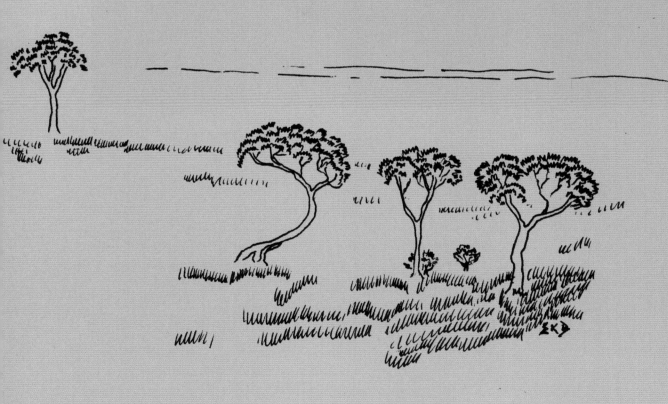

Desert landscape with xerophytic trees that are protected by the local people.

This bio-geographic zone has several ecosystems, which are home to a variety of wildlife species adapted to these harsh conditions. The summer days are incredibly hot, the winter nights bitterly cold.

When it rains, the desert is transformed temporarily into grassland. Animals like the blackbuck and the *chinkara* rapidly move into such areas then, to feed on the fresh growth of grass. The desert has its specific predators such as the desert fox, distinguished by its very large ears, and the caracal, a rarely encountered cat, which is the most ill understood predator. In the semi-arid areas one can find the wolf. This animal hunts *chinkara* and blackbuck and several smaller mammals and birds. It lives in small family groups, and when it cannot find its natural prey, depends on sheep and goats. As a result it is persecuted persistently by local shepherds and is considered a highly threatened species. The nilgai, blackbuck and *chinkara* are the most common herbivores of semi-arid and arid zones. Birds common to both the desert and semi-arid scrubland are the sand grouse, courser, plovers, and the great Indian bustard. This ecosystem is the habitat of a variety of desert reptiles, lizards, snakes and tortoises.

Among these arid landscapes, the Rann of Kachchh is a unique ecosystem. The Great Rann is famous for its breeding colonies of flamingoes. The Little Rann is the

A temporary water pool collects in the desert after a brief shower of rain.

last habitat of the Indian wild ass. These areas change from a salt desert with a few shrubs and sparse groundcover in summer and winter, to a marsh during the rainy season. The Rann is then dotted with small islands known as bets and the lowland is inundated with brackish water.

Grasses, herbs and several animals of diverse species are the specialized components of this ecosystem in which the rainfall is insufficient to support a forest, but just enough to prevent the formation of a desert. Its plants die after the rains and lie dormant until the next rainy season. In the desert and semi-arid tracts, trees such as the babul and the *khejadi* have always been preserved by local people, who also use palm trees and *ber* as a source of food.

The desert is a sensitive ecosystem, permanently under severe stress due to the erratic nature of the rainfall. Disturbances such as over-grazing seriously affect its species diversity. The introduction of an exotic plant from abroad, *Prosopis juliflora*, has rapidly changed the nature of the desert ecosystem by converting it into a thorn forest. Similarly, bringing in canal water has destabilized the system and produced saline areas due to rapid evaporation of the excess water from the sandy soil. Conversion to agriculture from a low-density grazing area only produces a short-term gain for local people. And there is also the long-term loss of its biological value.

The thorn-forest belt that lies adjacent to the Thar Desert supports a plant-life that is similar to that of Africa. Its best-known trees are *Acacia nilotica* (babul) and *Zizyphus* (*ber*). The Aravalli Ranges support *Acacia-Anogeisus pendula* forests.

A large population of angulates abounds these semi-arid thorn-forest ecosystems. Protected Areas in this ecosystem have always been rich in wildlife and were once the shikar areas for the various Maharajas of Rajasthan. Many of these private shooting reserves have ended up being notified as some of our most important Sanctuaries and National Parks.

| State | Rajasthan | Zone | Desert |
|---|---|---|---|
| Area | 3162 sq km | Ecosystem | Desert |
| Year of Notification | 1981 | Visited | May 1987 |

The narrow sand track disappears into the distance. The wide expense of featureless land with scrub and intermittent dunes bears no likeness to the traditional picture of a desert formed by a sea of sand dunes. The ecosystem of the Thar Desert is full of life and responds dramatically to the occasional showers of rain that are so unpredictable and patchy. Sadasar is a small, enclosed area in the desert, which has been well protected for years. It is now an island of arid grassland surounded by desert. The only waterhole in the area has a small hide. At dawn flock after flock of sand grouse begin to settle at the water's edge. The noisy beat of their wings seems to be endless. Great Indian bustards come for a long morning drink, followed by small groups of *chinkaras*. As the sun moves up into the sky two bustards move to the waterhole, the larger male chasing the smaller one away from the water repeatedly. Behind me in the hide, I notice a movement. There is a scorpion sitting beside me! I look around and discover two more! I decide to ignore them so I can continue with the photography.

One of my most memorable experiences is that of sleeping out in the desert on a clear starry night. The stars appear so close that it is as if by stretching my hand I can catch one. They are incredibly bright. I hear the wind, which begins to blow from out of the darkness; cold, biting. The sand which is whipped up, stings. As the *andhi* or desert wind dies down, the night's soundless hush

Only a small part of the Desert National Park has typical sand dunes.

seems ever deeper, until the wind begins to blow again. Then from the darkness of the night sky, large drops of rain begin to beat onto the parched sands. The thunderstorm thrashes the sands for half an hour and ends as suddenly as it began. The sun rises on a crystal-clear dawn. The dry watercourses of the previous day are filled with water. The desert is alive. Within a few days the dry stumps of grass will spring into lush green patches. All the desert animals will then move into them. Bustards have an uncanny ability to discover water in the desert. Driving through the Desert National Park I came across a bustard drinking water from a tiny leakage in a pipe. How could this bird locate this resource in the wide-open expanse of the desert!

The Thar seems endless. Kilometre after kilometre, the horizon all around becomes a giant flat disc of space. As the day advances, shimmering mirages begin to emerge over the horizon, creating the most unimaginable spread of luminescent water.

It is unbelievable that the shining water in the distance is unreal. It appears clearer than a real lake.

Only a few patches of large sand dunes are found in the western parts of the Thar. Som is an area of large wavy dunes with their characteristic wind-blown shapes. There is evidence here of prehistoric hunter communities who have left behind stone tools, a sign that the desert once supported a great abundance of wild animals that they could hunt.

At the edge of the Desert Sanctuary near Jaisalmer, there is an area covered with ancient tree fossils, showing the changes that have taken place in the ecology of the region over time. The ancient nature of the Thar must have been very different from what it is today. However, the rapid changes in the desert's ecosystem caused by human intervention have begun to have a much greater impact in the last few years than through millions of years of evolutionary processes.

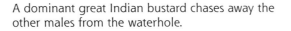

A dominant great Indian bustard chases away the other males from the waterhole.

Lagger falcon at the waterhole.

1

2 3

This sub-adult lagger falcon demonstrates its dexterity during flight.

A chinkara rests in the shade of a shrub to keep away from the scorching afternoon sun.

Thousands of sandgrouse arrive wave after wave to drink at the waterhole.

| State | Rajasthan | Zone | Desert |
|---|---|---|---|
| Area | 7.90 sq km | Ecosystem | Thorn Forest |
| Year of Notification | 1971 | Visited | May 1987 |

Just outside Jodhpur in Rajasthan, there are several sanctuaries created to protect the desert and the semi-arid land and its fauna. But this is not a relatively recent conservation strategy. In fact wild animals and their habitats, especially the *khejdi* trees, have been traditionally protected by a local sect known as the Bishnois for many decades. The Bishnois claim that this tradition to protect their trees was strengthened when a local ruler ordered his people to fell trees in the region. The Bishnois are said to have laid down their lives to protect their trees, which they valued as a sustainable natural resource above their own lives. The king is said to have later repented. This seems to have inspired the famous Chipko

Movement of Sunderlal Bahuguna in the Himalayas, where the local people also clung to their trees in the foothills when threatened by timber exploitation.

Today, blackbuck and *chinkara* walk around in the small sanctuaries in Rajasthan, apparently fearlessly at the edge of small Bishnoi villages, unconcerned with the approach of a tractor. The many years of protection afforded by the Bishnois have made these animals feel secure. As I walk along the dusty road, a doe and her young fawn continue to graze without even looking up.

At sunset, as I sit near a small water tank, a nilgai cautiously emerges from the scrub forest beyond. It persistently peers at a patch of nearby trees. As it approaches

the water's edge, there is a small movement in the scrub; a wolf emerges and ambles down to the water. The nilgai jumps in the air and flees into the forest. For its size and weight it is extremely agile on its hooves.

The neighbouring scrubland has several wolf dens dug into the sand, under the thorn scrub. There are several old kills strewn over the sand, mostly the remains of *chinkara* and a few blackbucks. Wolf tracks can be seen all over the sands. The marks left by the wolf's paws tell the story of how this superb predator of the open country stalked its prey, pulled it down, and dragged it over a long distance where the rest of the family joined it for a meal at the edge of a dry *nala*. The wolves appear to

Blackbuck roaming fearlessly at the periphery of a Bishnoi village in 1987.

have dug holes in the dry streambed. Is this done to see if water trickles into the hole? The Forest Guard thinks this is what wolves do when they are thirsty.

The Bishnois around Talchhappar were interested in understanding my own fascination with blackbuck and my concern for its survival. Their obvious appreciation culminated in one of them taking me to his home, introducing me to the rest of the family, asking me to take their pictures and providing me with cups of tea, and ended up by telling me of their life in the desert. The hospitality has left a memory of friendship that I have long cherished.

Their concern has continued, over the years, to lead to strong conservation action. In 1998, the popular film-star Salman Khan was apprehended by Bishnois for shooting blackbuck. In 2006, the courts have sentenced him to be jailed for one year and to pay a fine of Rs. 5000. His lawyers have now appealed to a higher court, but the message is clear. No one, not even the popular film actor, can now kill an endangered species and get away with it without being punished! The exposure this event has received in the press and electronic media has led to a heightened public awareness about poaching.

Chinkara with a backdrop of *khejadi* trees around a Bishnoi village.

Blackbuck moving gracefully in the Gudda Wildlife Sanctuary.

A wolf track in the sand shows it is dragging a chinkara or blackbuck across the sand dunes.

Local women filling earthen pots for their daily requirement of drinking water.

The remains of a wolf kill.

Two Bishnoi women were my hosts in the village.

A Bishnoi hut constructed from local material.

# SARISKA NATIONAL PARK

SARISKA

| State | Rajasthan | Zone | Semi-arid |
|---|---|---|---|
| Area | 273.80 & 492 sq km | Ecosystem | Dry Deciduous and Thorn Forest |
| Year of Notification | WLS 1958; NP 1982 | Visited | May 1987 |

There are few thorn forests in the country that are as rich in wildlife as the *Acacia, Ziziphus* and *Anogeissus* forests of Sariska, once the private shooting reserve of the rulers of Alwar State before Independence. Hunting was prevented by the Forest Department after 1955 and Sariska was notified as a Sanctuary in 1958 and converted into a National Park in 1982. The rulers of Alwar had a large hunting lodge at the edge of the forest, which is an indication that this area was rich in 'game species.'

In 1987, the BNHS requested Alan Rodgers, who was working in the Wildlife Institute of India, to train BNHS members and staff in assessing the status of wildlife habitats. We selected Sariska for the training session. This was a memorable experience for all those who participated in the exercise. Interestingly, a small but significant paper was published in the JBNHS, as an outcome of the data collected during the workshop on the Algual Spring, a small *nala* in the Tiger Reserve. It demonstrates the habitat values of a perennial spring and its influence on wildlife. I personally learned an enormous amount of field ecology from this brief visit. Alan is an amazing teacher.

A group of BNHS members, Alan and I went out on a field visit to a nearby village to study local biotic pressures on the vegetation. As the vehicle turned a corner of the degraded landscape at the periphery of the Park, I spotted a cat at the very edge of the road. I felt it looked very unlike a *Felix chaus*. We stopped and scanned the hill slope. As soon as I spotted the animal through my lens I realized to my utter surprise that it was a caracal. I'd never seen one before but its tufted ears were

The thorn forest of Sariska.

unmistakable. Then someone said there was another behind a nearby bush. In my excitement I took a quick picture as soon as I saw it enter an opening in the scrub, after which I found that as usual I had run out of film. While everyone else had a good look, I was busy reloading. As I closed the camera, both the animals disappeared. My great disappointment was when I got the film developed. The only caracal picture I managed to take has a large green leaf, which is out of focus, covering the caracal's face! In 1997–98 Goyal, Johnsingh and Shomita Mukherjee of the Wildlife Institute of India worked on small carnivores in Sariska and found that the caracal's habitat was the open scrub where we had sighted it and that they were highly dependent on small rodents. Happily, the caracals were still around ten years after I first sighted them. I wonder if this rare threatened

animal still survives now with the growing pressures around the Park?

In 1987 the number of porcupine in Sariska was enormous. These rodents had begun to selectively debark their favourite trees, which were drying up in large numbers. There is very little work in India that documents the effect of such population changes, so disastrous to an ecosystem. It appears that such rapid increases in population, especially among rodents, drops spontaneously after a certain period of time, but the change in the ecosystem can persist for a long period thereafter.

The census figures indicate that between 1991 and 1997, the tiger population increased from 18 to 24, the *sambar* population from 4839 to 5600, while the nilgai population increased from 3830 to 4780, the wildboar population from 2193

to 2900 and the chital population remained static around 2900 (Jain, 2001).

The high population-density of herbivores becomes obvious as soon as one passes through the gates of the Sariska Tiger Reserve. The flat plains are covered by dry *ber* or *Zizyphus* shrubs, and there are nilgais feeding in the bush every few hundred yards. Further into the sanctuary, there are wooded tracts of *Acacia senegal* and *Acacia eucophobia*. There are so many *chital*, sambar, nilgai and domestic livestock browsing on the lower branches of the trees that the trees have a straight, flat, leafless line to show the point beyond which they cannot browse. Thus one can see under the canopy deep into the forest, nearly throughout the Sariska forests. Climbing

| 1 | |
|---|---|
| | 2 |
| 3 | |

Two male nilgais engaged in a show of strength.

A large male nilgai.

Sambar doe with fawn.

into the low hills, the forest changes into a more dry deciduous pattern. The hill forest has *Anogeissus pendula*, *Boswellia serrata* and *Terminalia tomentosa* trees. Here sambar cross the road repeatedly and chital graze in the small openings.

Sitting at a waterhole at the first light, in Sariska, in October 1986 was a rewarding experience. There were few tourists who opted to sit in the hide so early in the morning in those days. I sat there all by myself. At dawn peacocks began to call and the forest began to slowly come alive with the twittering of its abundant bird-life. A nilgai brought her young fawn carefully to the water's edge. This was soon followed by a herd of chital, a troop of playful langurs, three jackals and two warring male nilgais. The tussle between these two large animals appeared to centre around chasing the weaker animal away from the waterhole, probably to maintain this important resource of the dry ecosystem within the territory of the more dominant animal.

Suddenly the forest becomes hushed. A tiger could well be on the move, but it refuses to appear in the clearing. The palpable silence in the small hide is suddenly shattered by a harsh loud sound. The sharp squawk is the call of a semi-tame, jungle babbler that, along with its flock, demands food from tourists in the

hide. It sits in the small hole in the wall of the hide, with one glaring eye fixed on the articles lying inside, expectantly awaiting a scrap of food. Unfortunately I have only my camera bag. Another bird from the flock soon chases it away to take its place. Finally the flock flies off to a nearby tree, obviously disgusted with a tourist who has no food to offer! The forest sounds are now slowly returning. A treepie is calling in the nearby trees. A chital gives an alarm call some distance from the hide. A hesitant nilgai slowly approaches the water. The tiger has probably moved away.

An evening in another hide higher up in the forest was another great Sariska experience. One soon realizes the immensely important way in which water determines life in this dry land. Here at the waterhole there is a constant stream of visitors. Herd after herd of chital and sambar appear at the waterhole to drink. The only time that this persistent parade is interrupted is when a large male feral buffalo decided to drink. Its sudden appearance made even the wild boar vanish into the forest in haste. It could be dissuaded from having a long wallow in

the pool only by waving a tripod out of the hide to drive it off. Sitting alone in the hide in the silence of the forest, watching the wild animals use this life-giving resource and quietly disappear to give place to another group, makes one realize that water is a serious limiting factor that determines the abundance of wildlife populations the ecosystems can sustain.

The linkages in the lives of different species of wild animals in a forest ecosystem are at times demonstrated in the strangest of episodes. I observed a sambar hind standing in a small clearing in the forest in a curious posture. It seemed to be poised on three legs. From under the raised rear leg emerged a treepie which flew onto the sambar's back and then hopped onto its head between the antlers. It continued to sit there till the sambar suddenly raised its other hind leg. The treepie then swooped onto the raised thigh and pecked at the sambar's abdomen, probably to catch insect pests to feed on! Another interesting association is a species of moth that feeds on the lacrimal secretions from the gland near the eye of the sambar. The moth can be seen at night hovering around the animal's head till it alights near its eye. The sambar are apparently unconcerned and make no effort to drive off the insects.

At the apex of the valley where the river narrows into a small stream, there is a famous temple that attracts a large number of pilgrims. On a quiet evening it is a delightful place. No wonder that it was considered a hallowed spot.

The dry thorn-forest ecosystem is broken by belts of vegetation along the *nala* courses that are surprisingly green even in the dry season. The Algual Spring is one such *nala*. Traversing the stream along a

Nervous jackals at the waterhole. It was probable that there was a tiger in the vicinity.

Two sambar stags confront each other at one of the few waterholes in Sariska.

1

3

2

A jungle cat peers through the grass at dusk.

Even a tiger feels threatened by a big wild boar.

A jungle babbler waits for food at the window of a tourist hide.

small path one soon realizes how diverse the vegetation is. The edge of the stream is lined with palm trees and a few other plant species that can survive under waterlogged conditions in the monsoon. Even in summer the shrubs are green. Wildlife must live only around the pool and depend on the last green browsing material during the summer pinch period. On the hill slope there is a great big dung pile left by a nilgai. A tiger has left its pugmarks on the path. It is a vital area for the well-being of Sariska's wild creatures. It is however frequented by cattle from neighbouring villages as well as the wildlife that drink from its quiet pools.

This has been a constant cause of conflict between the people who live in the villages around Sariska and Wildlife Managers. Both have strong viewpoints. Can one resolve these issues? Complex problems cannot have easy solutions. They require an equal understanding of human and wildlife needs. Constant debate and locally relevant solutions alone can generate a clear perception of the importance of conservation. This cannot happen without local support. And local

support cannot be elicited without providing alternate sources of resources and additional income for local people. The local people living around Sariska have been exploring these alternate avenues over the last several years.

There are other impacts that need to be considered which have even greater implications for conservation in Sariska. A Public Interest Litigation has been issued against the use of NH13 that passes through the Protected Area. An alternative route is possible outside Sariska but is not used. Thus 2500 vehicles pass through the Protected Area in a day. This is likely to continue to escalate unless the route through Sariska is closed to traffic.

During the last few months of 2005, Sariska has been in the news. It has suddenly come to light that all the tigers of Sariska have been killed by poachers. This is a national disaster that has occurred in one of our prime Tiger Reserves. Several inquiries have been instituted. The Prime Minister has taken serious steps to probe the issue. Unfortunately it is too late for Sariska if all its tigers are gone. But steps need to be taken in other areas both within and outside Tiger Reserves to see that poachers do not annihilate tigers from other Protected Areas.

| State | Gujarat | Zone | Desert |
|---|---|---|---|
| Area | 4953.70 sq km | Ecosystem | Seasonal Dry Desert and |
| | | | Saline Wetland |
| Year of Notification | 1973 | Visited | Dec 1984 |

The Little Rann, also known as the Wild Ass Sanctuary, is an incredibly changeable ecosystem. It appears like a wetland or saline marsh-like ecosystem in the monsoon and dries up rapidly to become a dry desert-like ecosystem in the summer months.

The flat open space is often erroneously labelled a 'wasteland'. Its sparse scrub and grass cover, the cracked earth, the nearly blinding light of the vast sky, and the scorching heat may appear inhospitable to most people. For me it was an amazing experience. And to the wild ass it is its only remaining home in India. The wild ass is usually chased in jeeps by tourists and wildlife photographers. Walking towards a small group of wild ass, far from any other living creature in the wilderness, is a very different experience. The wild ass is indeed better adapted and more comfortable in these harsh surroundings than humans can ever hope to be. The wild ass is a superb creature. Its speed, agility and ability to live under these difficult conditions are astounding. Food is scarce and cover is negligible. Once a widespread species, it now has just this one habitat left in the country. Any disease that affects horses could easily wipe this species off the face of the earth. Can this superb creature survive in today's changing world? Salt works and other development activities now increasingly threaten the Rann, making survival increasingly difficult for the wild ass.

The adjacent Great Rann of Kachchh is the only known place where flamingoes breed in India. Dr Salim Ali first filmed *Flamingo City* during the 1950s and I saw the film in 1952 in Pune. As the sound did not work and the film kept jumping up and down, Salim Ali related his experiences in the Rann himself. His talk has left an indelible impression on my mind. Flamingoes have fascinated me ever since, and the first time I saw them at close quarters, years later, in Bhigwan near Pune, led to my first small research project. When Salim Ali heard this he was delighted and was surprised that that I could recall what he had said so many years ago.

Parts of the Rann are also of great value as a habitat for estuarine and other waterfowl. It is a highly sensitive and complex ecosystem, which requires careful protection from being over-exploited.

In 1860s, Dr Ferdinand Stoliczka, a geologist, collected bird specimens in Kachchh and wrote about them in the *Journal of the Asiatic Society of Bengal*, in 1872. Maharao Khengarji of Kachchh discovered that the greater flamingo bred in the Great Rann of Kachchh in 1893. Later this was visited by Salim Ali and Charles McCann. Salim Ali wrote on the birds of Kachchh in 1943. Between 1942 and 1948 Salim Ali took up bird studies in Kachchh. He describes an area he visited in the Little Rann in 1946 where the Banas River enters the Rann. The area described in his *Fall of a Sparrow* must have been an

incredible sight. He says that there were 'duck by the million darkening the water for miles' (Ali, 1985). He also saw 80 rosy pelicans, three to five lakh lesser flamingoes and countless waders, common and demoiselle cranes. This was, he explains, a major collecting site for waterfowl during their outward migration. The BNHS instituted bird-ringing camps in Kachchh for several years.

Kachchh was one of the Society's major long-term ringing stations. Some of the early studies in the 1850s were done to find out if birds spread viral diseases by carrying parasites from one continent to another. The studies were done in collaboration with the Virus Research Center, now known as the National Institute of Virology, Pune.

Two species that I recall from my visit with Shabir Mallik in the Little Rann are the starred tortoise and the soft-shelled turtles. The tortoises were everywhere, mostly resting in the shade of thorny shrubs. The turtles in a small tank had found that domestic buffaloes are good safe animals onto which they can clamber when they come to the water to keep away the heat of the sun. While the buffaloes use the tank to cool off, the turtles use the buffaloes to take in the warmth of the sun. These inter-species relationships between the two animals are another fascinating aspect of nature.

Asiatic wild ass in the Little Rann of Kachchh.

# GIR NATIONAL PARK
GIR

| State | Gujarat | Zone | Semi-arid |
|---|---|---|---|
| Area | 258.71 sq km | Ecosystem | Dry Deciduous and Thorn Forest |
| Year of Notification | 1965; NP 1975 | Visited | Dec 1984 |

Gir's dry deciduous and thorn forests are interspersed with riverine vegetation along small *nala* courses and open grassy clearings in which small prides of lions can be seen in their last home in our country. The lions laze in the sun, unconcerned with the groups of tourists. There is a feeling of quiet power in their eyes. No threat, no fear. The fact that they are used to people and are semi-tame makes them in fact more dangerous. Their innate fear of humans has nearly disappeared. Predation on the livestock of the local Maldharis has become a serious issue, which can only be solved with a greater level of sensitivity to the needs of both the King of the Forest and the people who have increasingly encroached on his shrinking domain. Gir is home to over 36 species of mammals, 450 species of plants, 30 species of reptiles and nearly 300 species of birds.

Gir's very dry teak forests of *Tectona grandis* include a variety of deciduous and thorny species such as *Terminalia tomentosa*, *Dalbergia paniculata*, *Acacia catechu* and *Zizyphus*. The degraded areas have *Euphorbia* scrubland and open savanna-like grassy areas with *Acacia* and *Themeda triandra*.

The emperor Jehangir is said to have shot a lion near Malwa in 1617. Lions were found in Bihar up to 1814 and in Haryana up to 1834. Lions were recorded in Central India in 1872, and in several parts of Gujarat in 1880. The lions in Gir were protected by the Nawab of Junagadh. He is said to have officially stated that only 12 or 13 lions were left in Gir, and this persuaded Lord Curzon in the 1890s to encourage their preservation

| 1 | 2 |
|---|---|
|   | 3 |

Sleeping lions.

Deciduous forest in Gir.

Thorn forest in Gir.

rather than shoot them (Gee, 1964). Their decline was put down to large-scale hunting.

It is possible that historically Gir has undergone great fluctuations in its wildlife populations. In 1912, CA Crump was conducting a mammal survey in this region and reported that wildlife was extremely scarce (JBNHS Vol 22, 1913). He ascribed this to a famine that had occurred and due to which thousands of cattle were let into the Gir forest and grass-cutting was organized on a large scale, leading to the clearing of forest cover. He felt that a large number of animals might well have been killed during this period.

In the 1930s, several supplements in the BNHS journals focused on the need for Preservation of Wildlife in India (JBNHS Vol 37). One of the articles written by Sir Patrick Cadell focused on the preservation of the lion. He mentions that in the District Gazetteer of 1880, Colonel. JW Watson had estimated that there were not more than a dozen lions left in the Gir forests. When Lord Curzon was to visit Gir to shoot a lion, a well-known citizen of Bombay wrote to the press pointing out that there were only a dozen of these animals surviving in the Gir. In response to this plea, Lord Curzon directed the Junagadh Durbar to protect the lions and refused, despite his earlier intention, to shoot the lions as his predecessors had done. Strict preservation

following this led to the increase in lions to about 50, which probably grew to 100 and then to 200 by around the 1930s.

Habitat loss and population growth is likely to have been a major factor since the 1940s. MA Wynter-Blyth conducted a lion census in 1950 in the Gir and felt there were only 219 to 227 lions left and up to 250 in the whole region. In 1955, the Gir was a Reserved Forest with several small human settlements. Gee mentions that even though people live in the area, it could be made a National Park. He quotes examples of National Parks in Africa, which have herds of livestock grazing in them. As early as the 1950s, he recommended that if people could not be moved, at least grazing could be restricted, controlled, and regulated after a careful study of conditions and in conformity with a wise policy of effective land use.

A Sanctuary was effectively created in 1965 and upgraded to a National Park in 1975. However, there are still two highways and the Visavadar-Veraval railway passing through the Park.

I first went to the Gir in December 1984, accompanied by Taej Mundkur who was working on a variety of ornithological issues . Even then there were hordes of tourists, but certainly not a fraction of the numbers that throng to see the lions now. In the past lions were drawn to the site by tethering a goat or calf to a tree as a bait,

a practice stopped by Indira Gandhi when she was Prime Minister.

In 1989 a serious drought led to wildlife being affected by foot and mouth disease spread from the herds of domestic cattle that moved into the Protected Area. In 1995 the census figures showed that the lions had increased to 304.

During the last few years lions have strayed outside the Protected Area leading to conflict issues with people. Over the years it has been felt that a few lions should be translocated to an alternate site as protecting a single population could put the whole species at risk. A natural disaster or a disease can devastate such a single pocket. But Gujarat state is unwilling to provide its most unique species to any other state. One wonders how this sentiment can take precedence over the urgent needs of conservation.

The Asiatic lion is restricted to the Gir Sanctuary in India.

A partridge scuttles for cover.

| 1 | 2 | 3 |
|---|---|---|
| | 5 | |
| 4 | 6 | |
| 7 | | |

A peacock calling at sunset from its roost.

A palm civet is a nocturnal animal.

Lioness at dusk.

An alert nilgai inches its way past a pride of lions.

A flock of quails.

A maldhari takes his herd home for the night.

Sambar.

Drawing of a tiger shikar by Williamson and Howitt (1807).

# The Sal Forests of Central India

$S$al forests are found south of the Himalayan foothills, extending across the marshy Terai belt and the plains of the Ganges and of the Brahmaputra systems, from the north-eastern part of India up to the central highlands. South of this region, the dominant tree of the deciduous forests changes to teak. The demarcation line between the sal- and the teak-bearing areas is related to factors such as soil and climate rather than to latitude. In a small belt in the Satpura ranges these two species occur in the same forest. In contrast to the teak, sal is semi-evergreen with a very short leafless period—barely a fortnight at the beginning of the summer. The canopy in the sal forest is fairly dense throughout the year, whereas the longer leafless phase of teak opens up the canopy for a prolonged period.

In most natural teak forests several other trees that are fairly common along with the teak are found scattered throughout the forest. The sal, however, is more gregarious in nature and frequently occurs as pure stands. Whereas teak seems to grow best in hilly regions, the best stands of sal are often in valleys and along watercourses. In some areas sal grows along with trees such as *Terminalia*, *Bauhinia* and *Lagerstroemia*, and in the Terai forests grows alongside large tracts of elephant-grass. In the southern part of its range, the open areas are covered by short grasses that form small glades or, at times, larger patches of grassland maintained by repeated fires. Bamboo is less common in sal forests than in areas dominated by teak.

The timber of the sal tree has been used for hundreds of years to build houses, and in more recent times, for railway sleepers and scaffoldings. Sal seeds are used in the manufacture of oil and chocolate. Its growth has thus been encouraged by the Forest Department and sal was planted in preference to other species in these areas. It dominates the landscape in many of the Protected Areas, which were once timber-producing Reserved Forests.

These forests are the home of carnivores such as the tiger, leopard, hyena, wild dog and jackal. The herbivores found here are the *chital*, and in the hilly regions, the *sambar*. Smaller herbivores include the common barking deer and the less frequently seen four-horned antelope. Bird life is abundant and consists of feeding parties of several forest species.

Some forms of semi-evergreen forest such as those in Simlipal are considered to be among India's most threatened forest types. These Toona-Garuga forests are not found elsewhere.

The sal forests of Central India are located in the Eastern sector of the central highlands. Other species that grow with the sal are *Terminalia*, *Bauhinia* and *Lagerstroemia*.

| State | Madhya Pradesh | Zone | Deccan Peninsula |
|---|---|---|---|
| Area | 940 sq km | Ecosystem | Moist Deciduous Forest |
| Year of Notification | 1955 | Visited | May 1983, Jul 2002 |

Some of the most beautiful residual continuous tracts of moist deciduous sal forests are found in the Banjar and Halon River valleys, which emerge from the Maikal Hills. These forested ranges are offshoots of the main Satpura Range in Madhya Pradesh. This area forms the southernmost extent of the distribution of sal trees and is just north of the transition zone between the moist sal and the drier teak forests of the central highlands. These forests have always been known for their high concentrations of wildlife, and their animals were described in great detail during the 1880s by Captain Forsythe (1871) in his book *The Highlands of Central India*. Subsequently AA Dunbar Brander visited the area several times and wrote *Wild Animals in Central India* (1923), which remains a masterpiece of wildlife literature. According to Schaller, who worked in the region in the 1960s, Kanha's large meadows represent abandoned village sites, perhaps permanently deserted after a major famine in 1874. Prior to this, the Baigas cultivated the land until the Land Settlement Act of 1868 prohibited agriculture. In 1935, the Banjar Valley Reserve Sanctuary was created. However, parts of it were still used as shooting blocks till the 1940s, to reduce the chital population, which were said to affect the regeneration of sal seedlings. Shikar continued throughout the 1940s. The Maharaj Kumar of Vijayanagaram shot 30 tigers between 1947 and 1951. Sal was felled for railway sleepers and other purposes from 1864 to 1959. In the 50s, the size of the sanctuary was increased every few years and it was finally turned into a National Park in 1955. In the same year Gee wrote: 'this is one of the best potential National Parks of India, provided that good access roads can be made, the forest village at Kanha removed or kept under stricter control and a few of the difficulties caused by its remoteness overcome.'

With the advent of Project Tiger, an area of about 2000 square kilometres was constituted into the Kanha Wildlife Sanctuary. About half of this forms the core area. The Banjar Valley, having been protected from an earlier date, harbours a much larger wildlife population than the Halon valley.

After it became a Tiger Reserve, several villages were relocated, the grazing pressure of the livestock was reduced, the water sources were bunded, and the forest fires controlled. The wild ungulates rapidly increased in number. The tiger population grew to over 100. There are, at present, an estimated 300 of the rare barasinghas and 2000 chital. A natural forest ecosystem full of life has been rejuvenated. But this has taken over 30 years!

In the 1960s Schaller's studies on the tiger's behaviour and habitat needs in Kanha led not only to a better understanding of the conservation action needed to support the tiger but also to his book *The Deer and the Tiger* (1967), which rapidly became popular reading. This was followed by Sankhala's books on the tiger in the 70s. Much research work had been done in Kanha so that these books could be printed for interested people. After a long quiescent phase, the Breeden film on the tiger once again focused its attention on Kanha. This was being filmed during my own visit in 1983. Important visitors were invariably taken to Kanha to see tigers as they had gradually become used to tourists. Not only were the mahouts experts at locating the big cats, but the elephants had also quickly learned what was expected of them.

|   | 2 |
|---|---|
| 1 | 3 |
|   | 4 |

Forsythe, in 1871, and Brander, in 1923, studied the wildlife in this area and wrote extensively about the animals in this region.

The Kanha forests spread for many kilometres across the valleys of the Banjar and Hallon rivers, from the crest of the Maikal hills into the valleys.

The sal forest at Supkhar has patches of meadows which were once farmland and later abandoned.

Young tigress marking her territory.

HS Panwar, who was the Field Director in Kanha, recalls the fact that the creation of the National Park in the 1950s was a response to the shooting of a large number of tigers in the area. The public outcry that resulted from repeated reports of tiger shikar eventually resulted in positive conservation action. In the early days of Project Tiger, HS Panwar tried many innovative ventures to make conservation possible in the Tiger Reserve. With great sensitivity he shifted villages, encouraged research and did a great deal to popularize Kanha as the flagship Protected Area of the Project. It was while he was Director that the sanctuary was extended. He successfully translocated some of the villages away from the core zone and was one of the first Forest Officials to address the issue of local people's needs, realizing that unless they were provided with an alternate source of economic support, conservation would become impossible. This single-minded action of a committed and resourceful official has contributed enormously to the conservation of the biodiversity of this superb sal forest.

In 1964 when Schaller studied tigers in Kanha, the park area was only 277 square kilometres and he estimated that the tiger population was around 10 to 15. By the year 1997, the population of tigers in Kanha was estimated at 106 in 1945

square kilometres (Jain, 2001). While it is unrealistic to compare these two figures in terms of absolute numbers, it shows that the density of tigers in the central part of Kanha when Schaller did his study was 0.054 per square kilometres and at present it is 0.05 per square kilometre. The estimate of prey species in 1997 according to the census figures amounted to 20.250 chital, 3.598 sambar, 1.130 barking deer and 1.190 gaurs. According to the Madhya Pradesh wildlife census of 2001, Kanha and surrounding forests have 192 tigers.

Kanha is an unforgettable experience. Each jeep-ride through its forested tracts and grasslands has left me with special memories. In 1923, Brander wrote that in one evening he could count '1500 head of big game, consisting of eleven different species.' And even in 1983 I was able to observe that there were hundreds of chital. They were totally unconcerned at the approach of our jeep. Though their numbers seemed to exceed one's wildest expectations, it was obvious that the concentration around the central part of

the core area of Kanha is far higher than the population in neighbouring areas such as Kisli and Supkhar. By 2001 the high population of herbivores had begun to seriously overgraze the central meadows.

While most people know of the research work in Kanha by Schaller done in the 1950s and by Sankhala in the 1970s, few know about PC Kotwal. When I reached Kanha in 1983, I was already down with a terrible stomach upset. As usual I had no medicines with me and asked if I could get some. I was referred to Dr Kotwal through a wireless set. The tablets reached me that night with a message that the doctor would visit me the next morning. He did—it was only then that I realized that he was not a medical man but a Ph.D. He was equally surprised that his wildlife

leg outside the overcrowded bumpy jeep for hours. I recall that he stopped on the main road on seeing a dead langur which had been run over and examined it very carefully. He was deeply concerned about the well-being of Kanha and its wildlife.

There are several fascinating features that are of special interest in Kanha. The tops of the hills are flat grasslands, called 'dadars'. Descending from the 1950 metre-high crest of the ranges, the grassy plateaus change to a mixed vegetation, with a fairly open canopy. Many giant lianas stretch between the trees, and flowering shrubs cover the ground. Further downhill, bamboo makes its appearance. The shallow soil supports large trees with great buttress roots. The giant sal trees intermingle with the miscellaneous vegetation, which

contains a variety of trees. The lower slopes and the valleys, 450 metres above sea level, are covered by stands of nearly pure sal. These large forests are dense and the straight trunks of the trees show that several are very old. To a Forest Officer they are an evidence of a tradition of years of watchful care and are a source of great pride. However, the plantations still retain their straight lines demonstrating that most of this area is planted vegetation and not a 'natural' forest formation.

The lower plains have open grassy areas where periodic fires seem to have kept the adjacent sal forest from spreading. The belief that these are the sites of ancient villages and their surrounding farms, abandoned mysteriously to the deer that live here in large numbers, has found

|   | 1 |   |   |
|---|---|---|---|
|   |   |   | 3 |
| 2 |   |   | 4 |

Kanha is one of the most successful of the Tiger Reserves.

In May 1983, this was the dominant male tiger in Kanha. It was possible to approach him on elephant back.

This tiger would sometimes permit the elephant to come within a few feet of him and thus became a favourite of many photographers.

This tiger was the star of the famous film on tigers made by Stanley Breedan and Belinda Wright.

photographer patient was a medical man! Kotwal's work on grasslands in Kanha was indeed a landmark in those early days of understanding the management and ecology of these critically important maidans of Kanha. We spent a lot of time together watching the most magnificent tiger as we drove through Kanha and spent the night in the wonderful old forest bungalow at Supkhar where he had released barasingha. It was through him that I got the chance to visit a Baiga village outside Kanha, in a remote area. The roads were terrible and I travelled with one

The survival of the barasingha is the result of good management of the Tiger Reserve.

One of the unique features of Kanha is the barasingha, which is otherwise found only in the Terria region. In 1923 Breedan had reported the presence of the barasingha in several areas outside Kanha.

As the grasslands dry in summer, the barasinghas lose weight.

With the onset of rains, fresh grass begins to grow. The barasinghas put on weight and develop a new coat in readiness for the breeding season.

It is possible that the rapidly increasing chital population in Kanha may create a shortage of food for the barasingha.

little objective evidence to support it. In a country where population pressure has been growing, an abandoned village with open farmland and a fairly abundant supply of water would be an especially attractive place for the surrounding people to move in and resettle in a short time.

An unusual feature of Kanha is the diversity of its herbivorous mammals. Along with the more common chital, sambar and barking deer, there is the beautiful barasingha. This subspecies of the better known Terai swamp deer is now highly endangered and found only in Kanha. The barasingha sports twelve tines on its majestic antlers. The stags group together, while a single large male is frequently seen with the hinds, mainly in the meadows. Even though their numbers

have been increasing considerably, they refuse to climb over the hills into adjacent areas. Perhaps the fact that they subsist almost entirely on grass and do not browse on trees or bushes keeps them from moving across the forested hills. The fact that they confine themselves to a single area means that a disease could easily wipe out their whole population. Evolution has brought about a change in the deer by adapting its splayed hooves, evolved for the swampy Terai, to a narrower structure, more suitable for the hard ground of the sal forests in Kanha. The presence of deer in Kanha indicates that in the distant past barasingha must have been found extensively from the foothills of the Himalayas through the Indo-Gangetic valley and south to the Vindhya and

Satpura ranges. Why they disappeared completely except in Kanha remains a mystery.

Brander (1923) did an exhaustive study of barasingha in the early 1900s. In his time there were large herds of this deer in Kanha. However, he also reported that some were found in Balaghat, Bilaspur, Raipur, Bastar, Bhandara and South Chanda, places in which they have now completely disappeared.

To start a new herd, the Forest Department tranquillized a few barasingha and transported them to an area located at Supkhar, across the Maikal Ranges. In the Halon River valley there is an old bungalow, built on the edge of the forest, overlooking a large grassy clearing. From the balcony one can observe the trans-

A peacock calling at sunset from its roost.

The last herd of blackbuck photographed in Kanha in 1983.

located deer in the nearby grasslands. The house is unforgettable. Built in the early 1900s, it has a large verandah and a high thatched roof. The dining room sports a large cloth fan, which stretches from one end of the room to the other. A rope was used to move it from side to side by an attendant who would sit on the adjacent verandah.

Around the house, the British had cleared the forest and grown a plantation of pine trees. It was strange to see these stately old trees growing beside the natural sal forests. There is hardly any regeneration of these trees. Very little underbush was in evidence and they were devoid of the orchids seen in the adjacent sal forest. The plantation demonstrates how man-made changes remain stamped on an area over prolonged periods of time. Walking through the pines in the evening, I came across peacocks, red jungle fowl, golden-backed woodpeckers and racket-tailed drongos. A small group of sambar dashed up the adjacent hillside. In the plains beyond, a small group of barasinghas were grazing quietly. As dusk approached, a deep sense of solitude and of the striking beauty of the forest descended upon me. Heading back to the house I felt as if I had been transported into a bygone era a century ago, when this part of the country was still considered an incredibly remote wilderness. Sitting on the open verandah of the old forest guesthouse, listening to the

call of an owl and the sound of the wind blowing through the pine needles, I had a feeling of anticipation. At dusk, through the darkening sky, the roar of a tiger deep in the forest seemed to fulfill that feeling. The King of the Forest is on the move...It thrills one so completely that one never forgets its reverberating sound. Night had arrived.

Another mystery was the presence of the blackbuck in this forested area. How were these meadows, separated from the surrounding open grassland areas by thick sal forests and hilly tracts, colonized by an antelope of the grassy open plains? How did the blackbuck find their way over several ranges of hills covered by thick forest to find these grassy meadows? Kanha is an unlikely spot to encounter this animal

of the open dry plains. In the 1983, Kanha had a small group of blackbuck; by 2002 I could not locate a single one.

The noisy passage of bounding langurs on the roof ushers in the dawn. A bird calls from a huge eucalyptus tree in the garden, its glorious song heralding the imminent sunrise. In the grey light, the bird is invisible. Suddenly there is a cawing from the same tree. A crow must have woken up as well. As the sky brightens and the top of the eucalyptus tree becomes more visible, only one small bird can be seen perched on the treetop. The whistling song and the crow cawing that are heard alternately are both in fact made by a black-headed oriole! Why this bird that can sing a superb melody imitates the raucous caw of a crow remains beyond our understanding.

At dawn, on a cold and frosty morning, dewdrops cover the grass with a million sparkling droplets as our open jeep climbs a steep road in the hills. In the adjoining field a group of sleepy chital look cold and wet. Driving over the top of a small hillock, a barasingha stag stands motionless in the morning light. Its antlers are not fully-grown. It stands erect, watching the approach of the jeep, one foreleg curled beneath it.

A herd of gaur still grazes in the same place where it was spotted the previous night. As we approach the forest, the sun is rising above the adjoining hillside. The gaurs, like dark shadows, are clustered close to the edge of the sal trees. As we move gradually towards them they look up and watch suspiciously. There are about a dozen of them. The large black male suddenly walks over to a nearby bush, and swings his great horns from side to side. He begins thrashing the shrub as a display of his dominance. The other smaller males pay careful attention to this show of strength in acknowledgment of his leadership. A cow carefully licks the back of her young calf's ear while watching the now stationary jeep from the corner of an eye. The big male has finished his demonstration and follows the herd as they quietly move into the forest.

The sun rises over the hillside, bathing the valley in a bright golden light. As we climb further into the hills on the rough jeep track, we come upon a lone male langur sitting on a rock in a forest opening. The low rays of the sun shining through his pale grey hair give him a bright halo. A jungle fowl crows lustily nearby. As we drive round a sharp, steep bend in the road, it takes off from just beneath our front wheels.

It was on the way back from Supkhar that one of Kanha's magnificent tigers decided to provide me with some of the most memorable moments in my life.

The tiger is India's most sought-after animal by today's nature photographers, just as, in the past, it was the most sought after trophy of the hunter. To shoot one on film is as exciting for the photographer as bagging one was for the shikari. The monarch of India's jungle is very much in evidence here. In fact the lives of all the animals as well human beings seem to revolve around his majestic presence. The Forest Department officials and the tourist guides talk endlessly about the tigers, the areas where the latest sightings were recorded and the time and place where recent kills have been found. When was a particular tiger seen last? What is the condition of a particular tigress's cubs? Kanha is one of the most well known Tiger Reserves for wildlife tourism. The conservation effort has been rewarded by

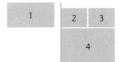

A herd of gaurs in the Supkhar Range.

Chital stag with hinds.

A large chital stag at dawn.

A chital hind at dusk.

an increase in its tiger population. This has however brought in an ever-increasing number of tourists.

At the gate of the tourist area in Kanha, there is a palpable excitement in the air. Visitors converge on the gate. A radio message informs us that a tiger has just been sighted four kilometres away. Several cars are released at the same time leading to a mini car-rally spewing dust to get to the waiting elephants.

The close-up view of the biggest tiger in Kanha from the proximity afforded by an elephant's back is an incredible experience. The elephant meanders towards the tiger that has settled down in a depression of wet earth under the cover of thick grass, close to a pool of water. In the hot summer afternoon his breathing can be clearly heard. As our elephant approaches, the magnificent animal glances up casually. Several times he slowly gets up and moves from one spot to another on the edge of the moist patch of grass. His belly sags with the weight of a large meal he has had the previous night. When he moves into the grass, he seems to miraculously vanish. His camouflage is so perfect that it takes several minutes before he is sighted again only 10 or 15 metres away. When our elephant moves in too close, the tiger gives a soft deep growl in his throat. This is enough to make the elephant retreat a few steps. This time the tiger looks up more threateningly before moving away into deeper cover. I can never forget that last, deeply penetrating stare. Its expression was unfathomable. There was no anger, no fear, no malice—none of the usual emotions that human beings seem to project on to wild carnivorous animals. He was at home and content with his own world. The only expression I could discern from that look was one of quiet power.

The chital, which is the commonest herbivorous species in Kanha, forms the tiger's most frequent prey. Surprisingly, the analysis of tiger faeces has shown that the second most-common prey species is the langur. How the tiger catches them has been speculated upon frequently. It is believed that the tiger approaches a tree full of monkeys and snarls loudly, making the nervous monkeys jump from branch to branch in panic, during which one of them

loses its grip and falls off the tree, where it is quickly dealt with. However, this may be unnecessary, as troops of langurs frequently move on the forest floor along with herds of chital. At such times a tiger failing to catch a fleet-footed deer, probably makes a swipe at a nervous, bungling langur instead. Perhaps the Kanha tigers have acquired a special taste for primates. Fortunately they have not begun sampling the other common primate now seen more and more frequently at Kanha! If they decide to do so, the concentration of tigers will soon shift from the core area towards the Khatia and Kisli Tourist Complex where the noisy tourists congregate in ever larger and ever more unruly groups!

Dusk is heralded by the calls of the peacock. In the rays of the setting sun the males dance, their long trains shimmering green and gold. A lone langur sits atop a large anthill surveying his world. Up in the hills a sambar calls. A jackal answers from the nearby riverbed. A call that sounds like 'doko-toko' is heard repeatedly as an Indian cuckoo comes closer and closer through the trees.

As the sun sets, the inhabitants of the day rest, giving place to those of the night. The nightjars are calling from the riverbed. At the top of a large dead tree a great-horned owl sets up a loud hooting. A tiger roars in the hills as another night descends upon the sal forests of Kanha.

My second visit to Kanha was in 2002, after a gap of two decades. Nitin, who had been my MSc student of Environmental Science, was a naturalist at an ecotourism camp and was extremely persistent that he take me around himself. Nitin loves wildlife

and his interest in understanding Kanha is an asset. I was told a series of recent stories of tiger sightings and kills, and that his boss had found a Russel's viper in his bed one morning. My first wildlife sighting on reaching Nitin's camp was when I was going to bed. By the flickering light of the candle I saw a slight movement below the bed cover and I was imagining a snake in my bed because of the recent story. But in fact the bed covers were moving. When I threw the sheet open, a tiny shrew looked at me, its nose quivering to smell what was up! I thought it best to take a picture as I did not have a picture of a shrew, but it vanished beneath the pillow. It then poked its head out and peeped at me, nose briskly moving. But it would hardly make a good shot. I decided to slowly pick up the pillow and press the shutter release with the other hand. But when I lifted the pillows there were two shrews, and as I wavered over which one to focus on in my surprise, they both disappeared under the bed and did not show up again for two days. Not a great beginning for a wildlife photography session after a 20 years' gap in Kanha.

Twenty years is a long time between two visits to a Sanctuary. Many things change. During my first visit to Kanha in 1983, the number of tourists was much less than in 2002. I recall that in 1983 there were only five to six vehicles racing to get to the elephants to see tigers at close quarters. Now, even at the fag end of the season, after the monsoon had set in, there was a string of Gipsy cars at the gate waiting to get there. Unfortunately my second visit was with an overcast sky, squalls of rain, and worst of all, a visit by the Principal Chief Conservator of Forests for which the Park was closed to visitors in the evenings! Even so it was fantastic. Early in the morning, as the Gipsy passed a *nala* course, I saw a tiger looking up straight into my eyes. It was a fleeting glimpse, as the jeep passed within 3 or 4 metres of her. By the time I got the Gipsy driver to reverse, she had already begun to move away. But that look of power in her eyes is something I will never forget. I felt no fear or shock at being so unexpectedly close to her face. I only regretted not having taken a picture of her superb eyes, as she gazed lazily at the Jeep above her. We turned around, anticipating that the direction in which she was strolling would lead her to a nearby road. We saw her again walking down a path in the pale morning light. Keeping a proper distance so as not to disturb her, we followed her for a full 25 minutes. She would walk from tree to tree, scenting it and then marking it with urine before moving on. Occasionally she glanced over her shoulder to see that we were keeping an appropriate distance. Finally she moved off the road and disappeared into the bamboo clumps on the side.

Everyone I met asked me the same question. What difference had I observed after this gap of 20 years? Perhaps the most strikingly obvious change was the enormous number of chital as compared to 1982. I have never observed any herbivore population like that in the 75 Protected Areas I have visited over the years. Another feature was the thinning of the grass cover in parts of the grassy meadows. The Forest Department now creates rather unsightly ex-closures to keep the chital from overgrazing the whole meadow. I don't know how effective this is, as the area accessible to the chital is now relatively smaller and thus will undergo even further overgrazing and degradation.

Another obvious change was related to the forest ecosystem. There appear to be far more young saplings of sal and other trees than 20 years ago. This indicates a better regeneration than in the past. A third change was finding a large number of dead sal trees, some still standing while others were lying on the forest floor. This occurred due to a population explosion of the sal borer, that struck the forest in epidemic proportions in the late 1990s.

I was seeing Kanha after the first few showers of rain, as HS Panwar had advised. The scenery was incredible, and birds were calling just about everywhere. It has left me wanting to be there again.

| 1 | 2 |
|---|---|
| 3 | 4 |

Tribal people who live at the fringes of Kanha collect all their resources from the forest.

In spite of abject poverty, one can hear laughter in the tribal village near Kanha, at the end of a hard day's work.

Tribal women on a village market day,

The number of chital in Kanha has increased substantially over the last 20 years.

# PANNA NATIONAL PARK AND TIGER RESERVE
## PANNA (GANGAU)

| State | Madhya Pradesh | Zone | Deccan Peninsula |
|---|---|---|---|
| Area | 543 sq km | Ecosystem | Moist Deciduous Sal Forest |
| Year of Notification | 1981 | Visited | Dec 2002 |

Sal forests everywhere have a special character. They remind me of the days gone by when people like Forsyth and Brander described the teeming wildlife that existed a century ago, and that we have largely destroyed. We rarely appreciate the fact that in spite of all the destruction of our forest estate there are still forests like Panna, where the habitat is reminiscent of that era. In many of these sal tracts, wildlife values had all but disappeared. Notifying such areas in the 1960s and 70s has indeed brought back the nearly depleted wildlife values. Some areas such as Kanha and Bandhavgarh have seen wild

herbivore populations becoming so hyper-abundant that they now have a negative effect on their own habitat. While many experts in wildlife have recommended that the animals should be culled in such areas, it must be realized that this will open up an uncontrollable Pandora's box. If culling can be instituted scientifically to reduce wildlife population pressures on their own habitats, then why not use this also to curtail and limit pressures due to wildlife-people conflicts over, for example, crops, or domestic animals killed by a wild predator? Where can one draw the line once culling is considered acceptable?

In a country that venerates the cow, and has millions of livestock that we wish to be fed and survive, wildlife may be culled, mainly because it does not belong to anyone! I have never been able to accept this short-term and ethically unacceptable means to an end. Wildlife preservation cannot occur if, on the one hand, we wish to protect it from poachers, but on the other, we legalize its killing by culling. People will not accept such double standards. And in the name of legal culling, illegal poaching will undoubtedly expand till the population is decimated down to dangerously low levels.

The forests of Panna provide an excellent habitat for the tiger and several of its prey species.

1    2

In the past, the forests of Panna must have
extended to the fringes of Khajurao.

The perennial water in the river at the fringe of
Panna is dependent on the forest cover.

Elephants and horses carved in the stone walls of
a temple at Khajurao.

| State | Madhya Pradesh | Zone | Deccan Peninsula |
|---|---|---|---|
| Area | 446 sq km | Ecosystem | Moist Deciduous Forest |
| Year of Notification | 1968 | Visited | Nov 1997; Jul; Dec 2002, Jun; Dec 2003, Jul 2005, Feb 2006 |

The hills of Bandhavgarh are a part of the Vindhya Ranges. A fort was built here, in the forest once part of the personal shooting reserve of the Maharaja of Rewa, for strategic reasons. In 1965 the Maharaja of Rewa was responsible for initiating a move to declare the area a National Park.

According to the 1997 tiger census, Bandhavgarh was estimated to have 52 tigers, 7473 chital and 812 sambar (Jain, 2001). The forest is primarily dominated by sal—*Shorea robusta.* The other trees are *saj—Terminalia tomentosa, Anogeissus*

In the 1990s, Charger was a well-known dominant male of Bandhavgarh for many years.

*latifolia*tendu; *Dispyros melanoxylon* and arjun—*Terminalia arjuna.* I have been driven several times through Bandhavgarh by KK Singh or his son Dhruv Singh. Both of them have known the Park for years. Both of them are highly committed to shielding this superb Protected Area. Dhruv stops the Gipsy at the grassland. We want to quietly hear the alarm calls of the chital which indicate if a tiger is on the prowl. The chital call and we move off in their direction.

The sal forest is shrouded in mist. In the golden light. the valley is covered with

dew-studded grassland. There is an alarm call from an adjacent patch of forest. The herd of chital seems to be on alert. The Gypsy slows down to a crawl. As it comes to a stop near a patch of wet earth, all eyes are on the ground, riveted to an enormous tiger pugmark. It appears very fresh. Following the track for some distance is easy but by then the tiger has turned off and wandered down to a nearby stream. He must be around somewhere. Probably he has already heard our approach. The chance of a sighting has been missed by only a few minutes!

But so much else is happening! A pair of hornbills moves from one tree to the next; a group of three sarus cranes strut through the marshy grass; an adjutant stork moves slowly through the grass along with a small herd of chital. A kilometre down the road, a jungle cat appears to be intently stalking something beyond a row of low bushes. Strangely, beyond the bushes there is only a herd of chital! No sign of any more

appropriate small prey. The cat continues to creep through the grass until it is quite close to the chital. The deer are startled and rush off. What was the cat trying to do? Such episodes never fail to make me appreciate how little we know of animal behaviour.

The night is very cold. There is a campfire near the tent in KK Singh's beautiful tourist lodge, to keep visitors warm. Close at hand—it sounds ever so close—there is a low but resonating 'Aumph!' Then complete silence. We get into the open Gipsy and spend the next 15 or 20 minutes moving around the area fruitlessly trying to spot the tiger. A cowherd comes out of the forest, rapidly herding his cattle to safety. He has seen the tiger, he says, barely 20 metres away! There is a lot of speculation. It is probably Charger, the well-known male that frequents the forest close to human habitation. He has little fear of tourist vehicles, jeeps, domestic elephants

The fort at Bandhavgarh.

The last resting place of Charger, who was the most popular tiger in Bhandavgarh for many years.

and the like. He is used to being trailed and observed by noisy tourists. He has also learnt that making a small charge frequently drives away intruders. While speculations on where he could have gone continue, the tiger has quietly vanished.

|   | 1 |   |
|---|---|---|
| 2 | 3 |   |
| 4 | 5 | 6 |

Although a scorpion uses its front appendages as a threat, the real hidden danger is in the sting in its tail.

Chital.

Barking deer.

Jackal.

Monitor lizard.

Vultures at a kill.

One of the last pictures of Charger in his old age, before he disappeared.

| 1 | 2 |
|---|---|
| 3 | |

A tigress cooling off in a stream on a hot afternoon.

A young tiger snarls at the elephant.

A tiger stares suspiciously at the elephant.

Green pigeons.

Nala courses in Bandhavgarh are favourite places for tigers.

King vultures.

Hills of Bandhavgarh on a cold, misty morning.

| | | 2 |
|---|---|---|
| | 1 | |
| | | 3 | 4 |

Tiger!

The giant spiral lianna which is used as a landmark in this sanctuary.

A climber sculpted by nature into a great twisted corkscrew.-

First rays of the morning illuminating the forest.

Two young tigers that have just learnt to make a kill on their own.

Early next morning we hear that it was indeed Charger. His distinctive pugmarks have been sighted, moving towards a nearby hilly tract. Several Gipsies full of tourists converge on the area. An elephant is brought out. Instead, two young male tigers are discovered. They are the half-grown cubs of the best-loved tigress of Bandhavgarh—Sita. Everyone from the many Gipsy loads gets to see the two tigers from elephant back. A bulky American tourist next to me on the elephant tries to take a video shot across me—nearly dislodging me in the process! I look down through the grass at two gorgeous eyes peering up at us, the face remaining partially covered by the thick undergrowth. The eyes appear not fierce but fearful. The two cubs are nervous and move from one patch of cover to the next, pursued by the two elephants. I feel uncomfortable. Is this what wildlife tourism is about, noisy people following persistently behind young tigers through the undergrowth? It does not make me feel good. It saddens me after the excitement of the magnificent sight is over. And where was Sita? She remains unseen. Lucky Sita ! At least one morning of peace. Hidden away from the eyes of dozens of eager tourists.

A mahout and his elephant are following Charger's pugmarks, which have reappeared on the track. He seems to have been walking along the road for small stretches and zigzagging off into the grass. Perhaps he is hunting. We drive further up the hill to await his arrival. Just when we feel we will not spot him after all, he crosses the road some 20 metres below us. He moves slowly, unconcerned. He sniffs at a blade of grass, crosses over a boulder-strewn embankment and disappears into the grass. He is a magnificent animal. It must be hair-raising to see him charge!

1

2

3

A sculpture of sleeping Vishnu on the edge of a sacred tank, where several animals and birds come to quench their thirst.

Lesser adjutant stork.

Lesser adjutant storks are now extremely uncommon.

| | 2 |
|---|---|
| 1 | |
| | 4 |
| 3 | |
| 5 | |

The red jungle fowl is the ancestor of all our domestic poultry.

Pilgrims walking through the Bandhavgarh Tiger Reserve.

Tourists eagerly await their turn to see a tiger from elephant back.

Langurs feeding in a tree while chital browse.

These sarus cranes have been coming to Bandhavgarh every year.

A sambar.

Tiger, in various moods—curious, bored, pensive.

A tigress intently watching a herd of chital just before making a charge.

Both Charger and Sita have since disappeared. The cause of their death can only be speculated upon. Could it be old age, illness or conflicts with other young tigers? Or could it be a result of increasing poaching?

I have had many wonderful experiences in Bandhavgarh. I have watched a young tiger threaten an elephant that began scaring it off by throwing leaves at it with its trunk. It was some sort of game and both the young animals seemed familiar with each other. I have tried to rescue a sick vulture. Bandhavgarh has one of the few breeding populations of these birds left in India. A wolf once charged at a group of vultures at a tigers' kill, nearly catching one of them by jumping into the air as it flew off. Something new has happened in every Gypsy ride, leaving the most wonderful memories of this superb Protected Area. During one memorable two-hour drive I was able to see 11 different tigers! But there were also times when I have returned without a single tiger sighting! The experience has always been memorable, especially if one goes into areas where there are no tourists.

On the way to the top of the plateau of Bandhavgarh rests a giant 10th or 11th-century stone sculpture of Lord Vishnu reclining on an enormous seven-hooded cobra. It is superbly sculpted and borders a water tank in the fort. The moist rocks are covered with lichen, moss and ferns, creating a delightful atmosphere. Even in the heat of the summer, this area is moist and cool. Numerous tiger pugmarks show that it is frequented by tigers. The view from the edge of the hills is breathtaking. The sal forest is a brilliant green, a wide expanse of wilderness. The trees nearby

1

Crested serpent eagle.

2

The once large flocks of vultures which are no longer sighted.

3

The early morning light filters through the trees.

4

Sambar in its typical alert pose.

| 1 | |
|---|---|
| 2 | 3 |
| 4 | |

Sambar in the morning mist.

A well-known rock formation in the forest.

Black-necked stork.

Pond heron.

are entwined in the large spirals of a thick woody liana. Ants crawl up its bark, taking a long circuitous route to the top of the trees. From the macro-world of the forest ecosystem, to the micro-world of the smallest forms of life, nature brings home the fact that the forest supports a wealth of unseen diversity.

Bandhavgarh is well-known, as the poet Kabir is supposed to have lived at this site. During Ram Navmi, anywhere between three to four thousand people, all followers of Kabir, have a *mela* (fair) and the pilgrims travel to the fort in large numbers, creating a serious problem for the Forest Department.

The tourist pressures have been increasing in this Protected Area which is now well beyond its carrying capacity. There is a conflict of interests between the Tourism Department which wishes to increase tourism, and the Forest Department which complains that increasing tourist traffic will damage the conservation potential of the Protected Area. As every Protected Area is primarily notified to protect its biodiversity, there can be no question of allowing tourism pressures to increase. After several meetings with officials of both departments a compromise has been reached and several strategies for sustainable tourism have been evolved.

| 1 | |
|---|---|
| 2 | |
| 3 | 4 |

Tigers are often harassed by pests.

A tiger at the waterhole.

Wolf.

A wolf jumping at a vulture to scare it off from the remains of the tiger's kill.

# PANPATHA WILDLIFE SANCTUARY
PANPATHA

| State | Madhya Pradesh | Zone | Deccan Peninsula |
|---|---|---|---|
| Area | 249 sq km | Ecosystem | Moist Deciduous Forest |
| Year of Notification | 1983 | Visited | Jul 2002, Dec 2002 |

Many catchments of water bodies are protected by National Parks and Sanctuaries.

Even today the people living in Panpatha are dependent on the forest produce for building their homes.

Sal forest.

Golden-backed woodpecker.

One of the many epiphytes in Panpatha.

The dead leaves of the sal forest in Panpatha recycle nutrients in the soil.

The local people still live poverty-stricken lives.

Driving out of Bandhavgarh, you soon hit another patch of forest. A board says you are in the Panpatha Wildlife Sanctuary. Drive into the Sanctuary and the road goes through beautiful sal forests. A fork takes you to the foot of a small dam. Birds call around you everywhere. Drive on through the rough track and you go through sal forests and tiny settlements. The constant disturbance from hordes of tourists found at the neighbouring Bandhavgarh is conspicuous by its absence. This comes as a welcome surprise because in Bandhavgarh, the noisy crowds diminish one's appreciation of the wild. Here there are no noisy tourists in brightly coloured holiday attire. No lines of Gipsys race crazily through the forests. What we pass on the dusty track is a bullock cart with a surprised driver and an equally surprised bull that veers quickly off the road. The tiny village is lifeless in the heat of the afternoon. But as soon as we stop to take a picture of a hut a group of curious children appear, followed by an old man. We talk to them about the problems they face. The children go to a nearby school. They tell us that they enjoy the Environment Education Programme that the Bharati Vidyapeeth has instituted in this area. I get a deep sense of satisfaction from this unsolicited feedback on the programme that I have initiated around Tiger Reserves for school children.

Small Protected Areas in the vicinity of the better-known National Parks are of great importance to help divert tourists from congested, well-known places where the carrying capacity for tourism has been exceeded. While there are many tourists who are happy only if they have seen a tiger before they go home, there are also more discerning tourists who want to see at close quarters all the different creatures that demonstrate the intricate workings of a forest ecosystem. Panpatha is just one neglected opportunity where an Interpretation Centre and real eco-tourism that supports local peoples' income can become a reality.

Many such satellite areas around highly touristy Protected Areas need to be created to do something about reducing the throngs of people visiting just a few of

our Protected Areas. They also need to be used as corridors for wildlife movements from one major area to another. This would permit gene flows between adjacent Protected Areas. Our policy has till recently looked at Protected Areas in isolation. At most, we have been able to develop a Protected Area system based on the needs of a particular ecosystem. What has been lacking is the creation of a network of interconnected Protected Areas through a system of corridors and a thinking that permits the evolution of holistic landscape-level planning. Such planning should be developed to turn all the major National Parks, and their satellites of smaller Wildlife Sanctuaries, into a regional wildlands development plan. This plan could establish zones where different types of development, from a totally hands-off area in the core of a National Park to increasing levels of human activity, are carefully delineated. This approach is also enshrined

in the Biosphere method of protecting biological resources. We need many more carefully managed Panpathas to conserve all our biological diversity.

Some of these smaller areas around major Protected Areas that have not been notified could be designated as Community Reserves, managed by training local people to handle the area properly. If they saw this as a source of income, they would protect the forest and establish small ecotourism facilities. Their conservation status would undoubtedly increase and these satellite areas would become an addition to our preset Protected Areas network.

| State | Madhya Pradesh | Zone | Deccan Peninsula |
|---|---|---|---|
| Area | 1471 sq km | Ecosystem | Moist Deciduous Forest |
| Year of Notification | 1983–84 | Visited | Dec 2002 |

This Protected Area, 1471 km in size, was established in 1984. It was once part of Rewa's State forests, and constituted the Maharaja's private shooting reserve. The sal forests are extensive and interspersed with riverine tracts, small openings used for agriculture, and dotted by villages. The wildlife population is at present low and the animals are shy of tourists, which makes sightings of glamour species uncommon. The beautiful river Som's sands are home to crocodiles and gharials. The isolated forest roads are wonderful locations for bird-watching. These forests became famous for their white tigers. One male, captured as a cub and named Mohan, grew up to become a celebrity and a forefather of the white tigers now in zoos, both in India and abroad. Mohan had grey eyes, an off-white coat and pale grey stripes, and was thus not an albino but a genetic colour variation.

KK Singh, my friend of several years who comes from this area, took me up to a hilltop with a vast view over the treetops. It is evident that he is deeply concerned with the health of these forests and the superb Som River, where he had hunted in his youth. He has lobbied for their protection and is equally concerned with the welfare of people who live in and around the National Park. He plans to train local people to act as guides and work in tourist facilities, so that they get an alternative livelihood from their proximity to the Protected Areas.

A shikar hide built decades ago when the area was a private shooting reserve of the Maharaja of Rewa.

Ground flora is the least understood aspect of the biodiversity of Protected Areas.

Forest along the bank of a river.

A giant dry deciduous tree.

# SIMLIPAL NATIONAL PARK AND TIGER RESERVE
SIMLIPAL

| State | Madhya Pradesh | Zone | Deccan Peninsula |
|---|---|---|---|
| Area | 845.70 sq km | Ecosystem | Semi-evergreen Forest |
| Year of Notification | 1973 | Visited | Oct 1993 |

Simlipal in Orissa is part of the Chhotanagpur plateau, and gets its name from the large number of Simul or red silk-cotton trees that are abundant here. These trees flower profusely, attracting large numbers of nectarivorous and insectivorous birds. It is also home to three of the larger mammal species, the tiger, the elephant and the gaur. It became a Tiger Reserve in 1973. In 1979, a 2,200 square kilometre Sanctuary was declared. A part of this was proposed as a National Park in 1980, which was increased to 845 square kilometre in 1986. In 1994, the Simlipal Biosphere Reserve was created and an eco-development scheme was introduced in 1995.

Simlipal has been intensively studied to document its plant, species diversity. Current records show that there are 1076 plants, of which 92 are orchids. Its major forest type is dominated by sal trees. There are 42 species of major mammals, 242 species of birds and 30 species of reptiles. According to the 1999 census data, Simlipal has 98 tigers, 115 leopards, 449 elephants, 2500 to 3500 chital, 4000 to 4500 barking deer, 1500 to 1800 mouse deer, 7000 to 9000 sambar, 850 to 950 gaurs and 10,000 wild boars (Jain, 2001).

The conflict between people who illegally fell trees and the Forest Staff has led to continual assaults on the Forest Department personnel. Human population growth over the last two decades within the Park has gone up significantly. 'Akhand shikar' is an ancient tribal custom where a large number of people get together and participate in a major organized hunting expedition. At one time this could well have been a sustainable practice as it was done only in April and the number of people involved was limited by the small population of local tribal people. This pattern has changed and is now reported

throughout the year except during the monsoon. Large groups participate in the hunt, disturbing and killing a great number of animals.

The forests of Simlipal are mostly semi-evergreen and moist deciduous forms. The tribal people living in them have evolved complex traditional technologies that support their way of life. They are closely dependent on the natural resources that surround their villages and are linked to the forest for their entire daily needs. Early in the morning a large number of people move into the forest on their bicycles, lop trees, and load them with fuelwood to sell in the growing neighbouring villages and townships. Thus as urbanization progresses at the fringes of the Protected Areas', deforestation increases.

The small village communities are still based on traditional occupations and the people are extremely poor. It is their poverty that increasingly eats into natural resources. They use the forest to collect fruits, nuts, small timber and other material to build their homes and make their superbly crafted farm implements and woven baskets. They carve the tools needed for simple farming, out of carefully selected species of trees that they know from experience to be specifically suited

for the making of household and farming implements. Though much of what they collect from the forest is now sold in local markets, they also hunt and gather for their own needs from the forests, rivers and streams. The large variety of the products they devise out of these local resources is astounding. Their dependence on the forest for food, fodder, etc. is obvious. What is less well-documented is their use of medicinal plants, and the types of wild plants and animals that they use as a source of food. They still frequently carry bows and arrows made from forest products.

I was driving up into the forest in a rather rickety Ambassador taxi. The doors would not close properly, and once closed, were extremely difficult to open. This made photography virtually impossible, especially as the driver had never been here before and was terrified of tigers. So I was delighted when we had a puncture and I could get out to take some pictures. The flat had occurred near a small culvert over a rapidly flowing stream. Down below I could see an old man rummaging around in the rocks. I climbed down the steep slope to see what he was looking

Tribal children with pot bellies and severe malnutrition seen covered with flies (1993).

for. We smiled at each other and when I signed to ask him what he had found, he showed me a handful of snails. He kept offering them to me and I kept trying to tell him I didn't want them! We gestured a pleasant goodbye to each other and I walked back up the steep slope to the bridge. To my utter surprise I was greeted with smiles from about 20 young tribal boys with bicycles who had been watching me take pictures in the *nala* below. They were extremely interested in what I was doing. One spoke fluent Hindi, explaining that he had learnt this in the Army but had now returned to his village. We discussed the local people's resource needs, economic conditions and several other topics while the driver struggled in vain to manage to remove the punctured tire. Perhaps he was just nervous about the tiger that he imagined was waiting to pounce on him from the adjacent forest! One or two more boys who spoke a little Hindi began to open up and talk. I asked how they could earn a living once all the forest was gone, as their main income came from selling wood as fuel in the adjacent town. 'We will go to another forest and cut wood there,' was the prompt reply. That there was not all that much forestland left in the country outside areas like Simlipal had not entered their minds! While tribal people have an incredibly high level of local knowledge they are, even today, singularly insulated from the more distant world outside their own ecosystem. We, who come to their land from without, frequently fail to appreciate what the rest of the world looks like in their eyes. Their worldview is often limited to what they have experienced during their own lives; so in their minds, the outside world cannot be very different from their own real world.

| | |
|---|---|
| 1 | |
| 2 | |
| 3 | |
| 4 | 5 |

Though sal dominates the forest, the large number of simul trees have resulted in the forest being named Simlipal.

A bed of ferns.

Tribal with snails collected for dinner, in Simlipal.

Flowers in the undergrowth.

Ferns near a watercourse that provides its specific habitat requirements.

# PALAMAU NATIONAL PARK AND TIGER RESERVE
## PALAMAU

| State | Jharkhand | Zone | Deccan Peninsula |
|---|---|---|---|
| Area | 1026 sq km | Ecosystem | Semi-evergreen forest |
| Year of Notification | WLS/TR 1973; NP 1989 | Visited | Nov 1993, Jun 1997 |

A chital standing on its hind legs to feed on tender leaves.

Deciduous forest in Palamau.

Bihar had five Wildlife Sanctuaries in 1948, including Baresand, in Palamau, which was established in 1946. Palamau is thus one of the Protected Areas that predates Independence. This Protected Area is mainly covered with moist and dry deciduous forests and is situated in the Chhotanagpur plateau in what is now Jharkhand. Sal, Palas (*Butea monosperma*) and Mahua (*Madhuca indica*) along with bamboo constitute its important forest trees. The Betla National Park, together with the larger Palamau Wildlife Sanctuary, forms the approximately 1000 square kilometre Palamau Tiger Reserve. The threats to the integrity of this Tiger Reserve are proposals for coal mining and a Hydel project, which would seriously affect the area.

Settlements within several National Parks and Sanctuaries face a variety of complex man-animal conflicts and Palamau is no exception. The local people have always lived with these problems but it is only recently that they have begun to appreciate that their problems must be addressed. Keeping animals away from croplands within a Protected Area is indeed a major challenge, while protecting their cattle from tigers within a Tiger Reserve is a major concern for local people. If separating wild herbivores from crops and predators from domestic stock is not feasible, the solution must be to compensate those who live in close proximity to wildlife for their losses. Palamau has been developing new management techniques that attempt to address these issues through a site-specific ecodevelopment programme, and

enlisting help from local NGOs to develop a more participatory approach towards solving local problems. Elephant-proof trenches have been dug around villages, for example, and in peripheral areas, village surrounds have been reforested for fuelwood, fodder and other non-wood products. Local school education includes information on the need for conservation and an Interpretation Centre explains the benefits of conservation to visitors.

However, even though this is one of the eight Tiger Reserves where the Forest Department has initiated the Ecodevelopment Projects, the village life in Palamau has changed little over the last several decades. People own small farms, a few cattle whose dung is an important source of fertilizer, and hutments made from local forest resources. *Butea* trees that burst into colour like a 'flame of the forest' are found around several villages and used to produce lac. The tribal people in Palamau are a part of their forest ecosystem. Palamau is their home and provides them with all their resources. Only when they begin to see some direct benefits from the Tiger Reserve can they be expected to act productively for biodiversity-conservation.

In 1993, when I visited Palamau, the ecodevelopment project had just begun. When I again visited Palamau in 1997, the programme had been operationalized.

The first ever tiger census by the pugmark method was done here in way back in 1934. The tiger census carried out in 1997 shows that Palamau had 44 tigers (Jain, 2001). The herbivores estimated during this period account for 13,000 chital, 2000 sambar and 1800 barking deer. The conflict between people and wildlife will only be solved if the ecodevelopment programme continues to develop alternative sources of income for local people—this fact cannot be repeated often enough.

During my visit I spoke to a young schoolteacher to try to find out if he could infuse environmental information through his teaching programme. While his enthusiasm was high, he had no training that equipped him to interpret nature's wonders to his students. When will we train all our schoolteachers to do this? Perhaps it will take years. But will there be anything left to preserve if we have to wait that long?

| 1 | 2 |
|---|---|
| 3 | |

A langur family feeding on the ground.

Peacock.

Bees at a waterhole in summer.

| State | Madhya Pradesh | Zone | Deccan Peninsula |
|---|---|---|---|
| Area | 646 sq km | Ecosystem | Moist Deciduous Forest |
| Year of Notification | 1975 | Visited | Dec 1999 |

As the white light of the sun begins to dim, a land of orange and red gradually appears and then disappears under the darkening sky. The blue turns into deep indigo, the sky, finally pitch-black, studded with bright stars, and a nightjar begins to call. Its persistent call is answered by another and yet another bird. Against the sky, a darker shadow glides overhead and I hear a mild thud from the trunk of a neighbouring mango tree. There is a movement in the canopy but the creature remains invisible although the full moon is now shining brightly. As I sit outside the Forest Resthouse in Bori, I keep wondering if I have really seen a flying squirrel. I search for it with a torch but cannot spot it.

An owl flies past on silent wings. The nightlife of Bori has begun to move about. Unseen and unheard, the forest is becoming an active but soundless land space. Gradually the crickets begin to call, a frog joins the chorus and it becomes obvious that life abounds in the dark forest.

At dawn there is a sambar at the end of a cleared space that acts as a viewing gallery for the Resthouse. A wild boar runs across the opening a few minutes later.

A large gaur. This animal was known for its bad temper.

From our jeep, the hills in the distance seem to come nearer, and with each twist along the narrow road, the colour of the forest changes. It is a mixed pattern of teak forest, with a large number of tamarind trees, shrubs of bright pink-violet flowers and bamboo clumps. A few hundred metres farther, over the rise of a hillock, the first patch of sal suddenly makes its appearance and the forest turns into the verdant green of new sal leaves. We have just crossed from the southern teak belt into the north-eastern sal belt. The transition is sharp and the divide is unexpectedly sudden, as if a giant knife has cut the country into two great halves. When one thinks of kilometre after kilometre that form the teak belt through the Deccan and the forests of southern India and the great tracts of sal that extend from here up to the Himalayan foothills and beyond, it seems strange that one can walk from one type into another in a matter of a few minutes in Bori.

Forsyth was the Acting Conservator of Forests, Central Provinces in the mid-1800s. He says: 'On another occasion I secured the largest sambar horns I have ever seen in a drive. It was in the Bori teak forest, a lovely little valley nesting under the northern scarp of the Mahadeo hills, and surrounded on the sides by its mural precipices. Being very inaccessible from the plains, more teak trees have here escaped the destroying timber contractor than almost anywhere else; and RD and myself were engaged in demarcating its boundaries as a Reserved Forest.'

|   | 1 |   |   |
|---|---|---|---|
|   | 2 |   |   |
| 3 | 4 | 6 |   |
|   | 5 |   |   |

Sambar.

A male barking deer looks over its back before making a dash for cover.

A kingfisher awaiting its prey.

A barred jungle owlet.

A grey jungle fowl.

Alexandrine parakeet.

# PACHMARHI WILDLIFE SANCTUARY

PACHMARAHI

| State | Madhya Pradesh | Zone | Deccan Peninsula |
|---|---|---|---|
| Area | 417 sq km | Ecosystem | Mixed Deciduous |
| Year of Notification | 1977 | Visited | Dec 1999 |

The Pachmarhi Hills, in the Satpuras are covered by one of the most beautiful forests in India, and present an interesting situation in which both the teak and sal forests are adjacent to each other. They are full of bird-life. Flycatchers of various types flit through the undergrowth; wood spiders weave their giant webs. The abundant insect life forms the prey of the spiders and the insectivorous birds. An intricate web of life is operating in the shrub lands of the hills. The three Protected Areas of Bori, Satpura and Pachmarhi form a continuous tract of forests with several unique features related to the topography and vegetation.

Forsyth went to Pachmarhi to attempt to unite Forest Department interests with those of Gonds and Korkus to preserve the 'remnants of the fine forests that clothed the slopes of their hills' (Forsyth, 1871). He describes *rab* in detail. When Forsyth worked in Pachmarhi in the 1870s, there were likely to have been some barasingha. By the time Brander wrote on the same region in 1931, he felt they were extinct locally.

RJ Graham, a botanist who was also an economist, collected ferns for the public gardens of Pachmari between 1911 and 1914 from these hills (JBNHS Vol 23). From a small area in the hills he collected 41 species. He mentions that the ravines are most abundant in fern species, as they are extremely deep and the sun reaches the depths only a few hours in a day. He describes the perennial crystal streams which, due to the half-shade of the gorge, provide the necessary light conditions and moisture levels for a "natural conservatory".

The Pachmarhi hills have five forest types. The sal-dominated forests lie mainly on the hilltops. The middle zone has mixed forests of *Mangifera indica*, *Terminalia tomentosa*, *Terminalia bellerica*, *Syzygium cumini* and *Anogeissus latifolia*. The mixed dry deciduous forests of teak are at a low elevation, which include other trees such as *Albizzia lebbeck*. There are patches of dry thorn forests of *Euphorbia*, *Manilkara hexandra* and *Lantana camara*. Flat, open plateau grasslands are a distinctive vegetation type whose biological values are now being increasingly appreciated.

The transition from sal to teak occurs so suddenly and yet subtly. As the jeep winds upwards from the sal tract, one passes through a narrow tract of mixed vegetation with a number of tamarind trees, and suddenly we have crossed over into the teak forest. The two largest forest types lie so close to each other that one can only wonder at this phenomenon. I stand in a stream that overlooks a continuous tract of sal on one side and teak on the adjacent hill. This is what the landscape must have been before the advent of agriculture changed all this from a pristine vegetation cover to the man-modified landscapes that went on gradually evolving into more and more utilitarian functions. The last run has been the most disastrous: the period when our generation have been the custodians of our mother earth. What have we done?

This is the transition area between the teak and sal forests in central India.

Flowers in the undergrowth.

# The Teak Forests of Central and Peninsular India

In the northern Deccan a large belt of teak forests stretches from the western coast of Gujarat and Maharashtra, across into Andhra Pradesh. Another belt lies along the length of the Western Ghats and terminates in another large tract, the Nilgiris, in the south. In the centre of the plateau, where the rainfall is low, teak is replaced by thorn forests and scrublands. Teak *(Tectona grandis)* thus forms two distinct belts. This may be related to past climatic changes resulting in extensive expansion and a subsequent shrinkage of its range.

Though teak and sal forests have completely separate distributions (except in a small area in Central India), they frequently share many species such as *Terminalia* and *Boswellia* trees. Bamboo is also found in both forest types.

The ecological dynamics of deciduous teak forests is more complex than that of evergreen forests, because of the enormous variations between seasons when the canopy is covered in leaves and months when the trees are leafless. The cycles of leafless and fully-covered periods, induced by changes in temperature and rainfall, produce large fluctuations in the niches that are used by the community of plants and animals in the teak-dominated forests. The result is that the populations of insects and birds change drastically from season to season.

Teak has been known for centuries as a valuable timber species. Though it is by nature less gregarious than sal, in several areas it is seen as nearly pure stands, as it has been selectively used in forestry over several decades. However, in many natural forest forms, it is distributed among other trees as one of the dominant species. It is less frequently seen in mixed miscellaneous forests.

The teak tree gives rise to masses of loose leaf-litter. A large number of small animals, rodents, ground hunting birds, insects, spiders, worms and slugs fit into their various ecological niches in this detritus. The life cycle of several of the animals of the forest floor is highly dependent on this detritus, which is also of prime importance to the larger overall ecology of the forest, as it recycles nutrients. The teak forest protects and enriches the soil of the steep slopes in hilly tracts and is also a major moisture-retaining mechanism after the monsoons.

Wherever rainfall is high, teak trees are found in moist deciduous forest formations. This forest type also forms a distinctive feature of nala courses and riverbanks in dry deciduous forests. Here teak grows in conjunction with species such as *Syzygium* (jamun), *Lagerstromia*, *Terminallia*, and several species of ficus trees. The common species along teak trees are evergreen, especially in locally moist ground, near

The deciduous forests change dramatically from their leaf-filled canopy to their dry phase. This changes the biomass within the forest, from its canopy to the forest floor, where it is broken down to nutrients for new plant growth.

waterbodies, rivers or streams, where the undergrowth is well developed and several bushes are green throughout the year.

The dry deciduous teak belt along the Eastern slopes of the Western Ghats has variable characteristics dependent upon the amount of rainfall. In the Deccan Trap, where the monsoon has fewer 'rainy days', there is a dry deciduous belt in which teak is the predominant tree, with only a small number of other common trees. Eastwards, in the centre of the Deccan, where the rainfall decreases further, the percentage of teak reduces considerably.

The dry deciduous area constitutes parts of the Dang Forests of Gujarat and extends eastwards into areas such as Melghat, Pench, Navegaon, and Andhari in Northern Maharashtra. The north-eastern corner of Maharashtra supports miscellaneous forests with a thick undergrowth of bushes and an under-story of a variety of smaller trees. The teak component drops to a negligible

5 to 10 per cent. These are the beautiful multi-layered forests that are found at Nagzira.

The animal life in the teak belt varies. The tiger and the leopard are the chief predators, though the tiger is now seen only in a few areas. The forest herbivores are similar to those of the sal belt, chital, sambar and barking deer being species common to both teak and sal forests. However, teak being a drier belt, nilgai are more frequently seen in teak than in sal forests. In the Western Ghats, several forest tracts still have herds of sambar. The absence of chital is conspicuous in the northern parts of the Western Ghats, south of the Dangs, and in the Western Ghat tracts in Karnataka and Kerala. However, the South Indian teak forests that have patches of meadows in the Nilgiris support large herds of chital.

Primate species differ from those in the sal forests. Whereas the *Rhesus macaque* is seen north of the Tapti and Godavari Rivers,

south of this line is the range of the larger bonnet macaque. The elephant is found only in the southern part of the teak belt. Gaur is found in several hilly areas. There are only a few wild buffaloes in these forests in north-eastern Maharashtra.

The birdlife is extremely diverse. The teak forests on the western and eastern slopes of the Sahyadris are the home of several hill-bird species, similar to those of the Himalayan foothills.

Fire is a great hazard in these dry deciduous forests. Species such as the exotic shrub lantana burn vigorously, as a result of which even large trees are at times destroyed. Studies have shown that in many areas the regeneration of teak is poor. In old teak plantations there are usually only a few trees of other species, resulting in poor overall regeneration of the forest. Most of the Protected Areas of this region are in dry deciduous forests, a few such as Nagzira being moist deciduous.

Deciduous forest with its canopy of leaves.

Deciduous forest in its leafless phase.

# VANSDA NATIONAL PARK
VANSDA

| State | Gujarat | Zone | Semi-arid |
|---|---|---|---|
| Area | 24 sq km | Ecosystem | Dry Deciduous Forest |
| Year of Notification | 1979 | | |
| Visited | Dec 1975, Oct 1978, May 1981, May 1982, May 1983, Mar 1984, May 1987, May 1988, Nov 1988, Jan 1992, Dec 1994 | | |

I was a small boy in the early 1950s, when the Maharaja of Vansda took me for jeep rides into what was then referred to as the 'Sadad Devi Farm.' It is now a National Park and has the best preserved, undisturbed, uncleared patches of forest, left in the Dang Forests of Gujarat. It stretches along one bank of the river Ambika, with the small village, now nearly a township, of Vaghai across the river. As a schoolboy I recall walking through the forest to take photographs with Abdul, the caretaker of the Maharaja's mango orchards. Abdul knew his wildlife intimately and was as keenly interested in looking for jungle fowl as I was. Could he have had other, more sinister intents after I left? He once clearly steered me past an obvious trap for ground birds or small mammals, insisting he did not know what it was! A delightful soul, he was ever-ready with his two-cell torch to show me some of the farm's nightlife. 'Sadad Devi'—Sadad being the Gujarati name for *Terminalia*—is evidently the home of a deity, though I have never actually seen a shrine in the Park. The Bhils and Konkanas have small shrines dedicated to the forest gods all over the Dangs. I have even seen one where the shrine is a wooden replica of a crocodile, which is now locally extinct in the Dangi rivers. They frequently refer to Waghdev or the Tiger God, which they must have feared in the past. The last tigers in the Dangs were spotted in the 1960s or early 1970s. The gods too seem to have left the tribals' homeland as development has marched into their forest home.

Only a few chital are left in the Dangs. Most of them now live only in the Vansda National Park.

The Vansda National Park, with its open glades, is a refuge for the last chital in the Dang Forests and remains the most undisturbed natural forest in the mosaic of Reserved and Protected Forest patches, in a district entirely managed by the Forest Department in the past. The Dangs form the only part of the Western Ghats that consists of gradually ascending rows of hills rather than a sharp escarpment on the western side. Its open glades, multiple rivers and the mosaic of fragmented forests due to the differences in the management of the Reserved Forests and Protected Forests gives the area a distinctive set of landscape elements that form a patchwork of clearly observable patterns. The area was used by the British to grow teak for timber and only a few areas with a more diverse vegetation pattern that formed the natural indigenous forests of this region, remain.

Tolaram Mirchandani (1956) in his article on wildlife preservation in India, suggested Dangs as a potential site for a National Park in the Bombay State, under the Union Government. Dangs, formerly a confederation of 19 Bhil States, with an area of only 1813 square kilometres, was merged to constitute a District of the Bombay State. Forests were leased to the Forest Department of the Bombay Province and the rest of the area remained under the administration of the Political Department. Mirchandani thought that Dangs once notified as a National Park would benefit the Dangis and local wildlife.

In my many fascinating trips to this forest I have watched leopard, chital, wild boar, barking deer, hare, porcupine, hyena and, on very special nights, the very rare rusty-spotted cat. As a boy, I learned to look for signs of wildlife in this forest, watched birds, learned wildlife photography and had exciting moonlit dinners at the Sadad Devi Farm. It was a wonderful period of my life when the forests were still remote, untouched and relatively wild.

| 1 | 2 |
|---|---|
|   | 3 |

A thick grove of bamboo in the Vansda National Park.

A superbly camouflaged chameleon using its sticky tongue to trap its prey.

A tree frog in the undergrowth.

# PURNA WILDLIFE SANCTUARY

MAHAL / DANGS

| State | Gujarat | Zone | Western Ghats |
|---|---|---|---|
| Area | 160.8 sq km | Ecosystem | Dry Deciduous Teak Forest |
| Year of Notification | 1990 | | |
| Visited | Dec 1975, Oct 1978, May 1981, May 1982, May 1983, Mar 1984, May 1987, May 1988, Nov. 1988, Jan 1992, Dec 1994 | | |

On a moonless starry night I was woken by an insistent 'Hu-Hooo-Hu' repeated over and over again. I was very tired but could not resist the temptation of recording this birdcall. The owl seemed at first to be just outside the forest resthouse, but when I went out with the directional microphone I found that its call was coming from the opposite bank of the Purna River. It was 3 a.m.; should I cross the river with a tiny torch whose cells were dying? Not a very good idea at this time of the night. I had seen leopard pugmarks on the side of the bridge the previous day! And the Dangs were experiencing political disturbances. Not the safest area in the world during this time of night. And what about snakes? I had taken pictures of a Russell's viper just the previous day. But I badly wanted that call for the bird call cassettes I was recording for the BNHS. So I crossed over the old bridge. The bird had by then moved up onto the forested hillslope. Impossible to climb, but I did manage a short distance through the scrub. I settled down to record. Five minutes of recording required flipping the cassette over. In the process the torch made a final flicker and went stone dead. Several bangs on its back produced a small flicker, then total darkness again. I scrambled back down to the road. Halfway across the bridge, a truckload full of drunken, happy Bhils looked down in surprise at this lone figure walking over the bridge.

But I had a beautiful set of calls—of the owl and a nightjar. My sleeping bag felt exceptionally warm during the freezing hour left before dawn. Next morning there were fresh leopard pugmarks meandering along the dusty road and across the bridge! What if the leopard had crossed the bridge, instead of the group of tribals in their truck? But leopards in the Dangs have

Dangis in ceremonial dress (1978).

learned how to avoid people for years. One sees signs of them everywhere but sightings are always few and far between.

Memories spanning over 30 years of a large number of sojourns into the Dangs bring back visions of a varied mix of exciting episodes and sheer shock as more and more of this incredible forest vanished with each visit. The extensive forests that covered the area in the 1950s and 1960s are now shrinking and thinning out at a phenomenal pace. The growing human population is increasing in the forest villages, and the changes in the lifestyle of its people induced by growing outside influences have added to the problem. The ecosystem of the forest has

now been warped beyond repair, to which misconceptions in management have added their share. The Reserved Forests have changed less dramatically than the patches of Protected Forests, where *rab* cultivation is done by local people. In this ancient method of wood-ash cultivation, based on tree branches and dry leaves which are burnt as a fertilizer, people grow rice or *nachni,* and a small local legume. Each patch is used and then left fallow for a few years. In Vansda, which lies just outside the Dang Forest, beyond the river, there is a low range of hills that were covered by teak forests four or five decades ago. Gradually, over the years, I watched blanks appear in the continuity of this

River in the Vansda National Park.

The Dangi Chieftain of Pimpri in 1978 was a great storyteller of the good old days when wildlife was plentiful around his village.

A mutilated tree-trunk and an over-lopped forest in the backdrop. This has resulted from over-utilization of local resources.

forest, converting it into something more of a woodland. In more recent times, the hill has turned completely bald, with only a few lonely trees here and there, standing all by themselves against the horizon. And it is not only in these peripheral areas that the forest has disappeared; huge scars have formed within the core of the forest itself. These were formed during the period in which felling of trees was done by the Forest Department. The plantation work carried out to compensate for this loss in the degraded areas is inadequate. A large amount of illegal felling continues and is extremely difficult to check.

It is frequently stated that tribal practices, such as shifting cultivation or shooting of wild animals for food, do not lead to ecological degradation as they have been practised for centuries. This may have been true in the past, when tribal populations were small and the needs of the people few. In the old days, the tribal lived off the forest produce and only collected food for his family and a bare minimum of clothing and basic building material for his home. This, the forest could easily support. But the tribes

legitimate needs have now grown and they feel strongly that their lifestyle should be similar to that of people who live outside the forest. They are thus forced by these new values to exploit the forest resources to their maximum, leading to a gradual deterioration of forest cover. They begin to extract more wood for sale in the villages, and also poach animals such as chital, barking deer and even leopard for its skin, which is now extremely valuable. The Konkana community continues using the traditional method of farming much more extensively, so as to extract more produce from the land by burning more and more lopped material from the forest. They have learned no other way

of making a living and, with the rising prices of commodities, they are forced into increasing their exploitation of forest products. Little attempt has been made to improve their economic conditions and they are unfortunately only marginally better off than they were 40 years ago.

*Rab* is an old custom. In the Dangs, this agricultural practice is said to have been introduced after the influx of the Kokans, who came from the South about 200 years ago. The Bhils, who were the original tribals of the area and owned the land in the Dangs, were not traditional farmers but mainly hunter-gatherers. With the influx of kanas, the Bhils employed these more industrious and technologically superior

1

2

3

4

A heavily lopped landscape typical of the Protected Forests.

A Konkana burning biomass to plant his crop.

Konkana tribal folk harvesting their crops.

The harvest.

people to begin farming the land. During this period there was naturally a steep rise in the amount of cultivation in the forest. The Konkanas, who were more oriented towards an agro-pastoral way of life, that was better adapted to conditions along the western coastal belt, gradually took over most of the land from the original Bhil owners. A totally new land-use pattern, with agricultural practices based on collection of lopped material from the trees used for wood-ash cultivation evolved for the Dangs. While this was more sustainable in the forests of the Ghats, with their more vigorous growing period, in the Dangs it is evidently less suitable. Thus a relentless process of degradation began.

The customs and rituals attached to traditional agriculture are based on a deep and intimate understanding of ecology that supports the sowing and reaping of the crops grown in the forest. The day of planting is indicated by prolonged rituals and festivals. The lives of the people of the Dangs have always been full of music and dance. Unfortunately, their spontaneous love of life is now slowly being eroded by modern notions of lifestyle. The older generations are excellent sources of information. I recall going to the little Dangi village of Pimpri in the 1960s. On a hot summer's afternoon we reached the forest village (one that has expanded considerably in the past few years). The ruler of Pimpri, a very old and obviously happily-intoxicated man, meandered out of his hut. With a large and toothless grin on his amiable, wrinkled face, he swayed towards us. He excused himself for his intoxicated condition, which he attributed to a very small one taken the previous

night! Encouraged to talk about his life, the Bhil of the forest emerged. He told stories of the forests of his youth and its tigers, leopards, sambar and chital. Of how they were tracked and shot with their bows and arrows. And of the happy place his valley once was. The theme of the great abundance of forest resources frequently recurred during this monologue. His traditional knowledge of forest ecology was astounding! He tried to express his faith in the natural world that had been destroyed by people from outside who could not

appreciate the enormous value of the forest. 'Civilization' had touched him less than it had the younger generation in his village. His life had remained a part of the forest he had lived in and loved all his life. Now his children and grandchildren cannot share his deep feelings for the forest.

The Dangs, during the period of the *rab,* leaves me with an immense sense of sadness. The branches of teak, *Terminalia* and other trees are chopped off. The undergrowth is also cut down and piled up on the hillsides everywhere. During summer, this dry wood is spread over hundreds of patches in the forest and set ablaze. The bark of the nearby trees at the edge of the rab gets severely scorched, and the standing trees often die a quiet, untimely death. At times, with this huge burn on one side, the tree struggles and lives on until the next year, when rab is performed near its opposite side, and the tree finally falls prey to the fire. The rate of destruction escalates each year. During the *rab,* the fires have to be controlled and supervised, but at times such fires turn into an uncontrollable forest fire, and a whole hillside gets burnt.

There are other subtle ways in which the forest ecology is being changed by human factors. The practice of lopping trees, apart from rab, has been encouraged by the Forest Department to increase the straight bole for better timber. When this lopping is done, the teak trees (which should have large and thick canopies during several months of the year) are converted into shadeless totem poles (like the poplars of Kashmir). Without the natural spreading habit of these trees, excessive sunlight filters down to the ground throughout the year. The strong sunlight and intense heat change the micro climatic conditions near the ground. The result is that the ecology of the under-story and shrub layer is totally altered. And without the canopy to break the rain's force, the nutrients in the topsoil are washed away.

A more surreptitious change results from the removal of the side branches for *rab.* There are fewer leaves on the trees, leading to a reduction of the detritus on the forest floor. This must lead to a change in the detritus cycle that is related to the flow of nutrients, which is an important part of

forest ecology. Unseen and unknown, these less understood food chains are disrupted and the life cycles of various insects and worms are modified or destroyed.

The Dangis have large herds of cattle whose milk output is low. These however are the tribals' only source of crop fertilizers. They are let loose in the forest to graze, hindering the regeneration of trees and causing the loss of grass-cover in heavily grazed areas. Once the cattle have overgrazed an area, the chital cannot utilize it, as there is nothing left for them to forage on. Only the wild boar manages to survive by digging for roots underground. Even the boars require cover during the day and find this increasingly hard to locate in the fragmented forest patches.

The Dangs once had a large population of tigers and leopards that lived on chital and barking deer. With the shrinkage of their habitat, loss of their natural prey, and the inevitable poacher with his crop-protection gun and the night-time jeep shikaris from neighbouring towns, the tiger has been eliminated from the forest. The leopard still survives. Its natural prey of chital and four-horned antelope being scarce, it has learnt to live closer to the villages, to catch an unguarded calf, goat or dog that strays into the forest. With its increasing dependence on village-based prey, chance encounters with unsuspecting villagers and children are increasing, leading to unfortunate accidents. Some of the leopards have become man-eaters. In the 60s, one small leopard with a deformed front paw picked up 13 children one after another. It would sit on the roof of a hut in the evening and then enter it after dark to carry off its young victim to different parts of the Dangs, every few days. After several weeks of this, it entered a hut one night, but his intended victim, a little boy, screamed loudly and managed to escape through the door. The leopard turned on the only other occupant—the child's old grandmother. In desperation she picked up a burning log from her fire and tried to ward off the animal, while backing out of the open doorway. Once outside, she had the presence of mind to shut and bolt the door and raise an alarm. The leopard meanwhile made several unsuccessful attempts to escape through the hole in the

Simplicity is part of the charm of a Dangi household.

A 'Vagh Deo'—Tiger God of the Dangis, much revered even though the tiger is now locally extinct.

roof. At each leap it would barely miss the hole and tumble down noisily inside the kitchen section of the hut, upsetting pots and pans and the small kerosene lamp. The village Patil, with a few of his pluckier friends, climbed onto the roof with an old 12-bore gun and a small torch and was able to put an end to the snarling creature. It turned out that one foot of this leopard had been damaged by a poacher's bullet, making him too slow to catch his wild prey.

The paucity of prey species has changed the feeding pattern of the predators. Cattle kills are frequent and the unhappy villager responds by trying to kill the leopard with an inadequate gun. An animal wounded in this way has to re-adapt to get easier prey. Leopards are resourceful animals. I have even seen one catching crabs and frogs in a riverbed in the Dangs. Whether it was a gourmet and ate crabmeat by choice, or whether it was because there was no other prey left in the forest, is a mystery. The former is certainly less likely!

An interesting animal still found in the Dangs, but extremely rare in the rest of India, is an exquisite small wildcat, the rusty spotted cat, which has a kittenish face even as an adult. Its body is covered by small red-brown spots on a greyish coat and it sports a ringed tail. If one gets only a fleeting glance of one of these cats in the forest after dark, it can be easily mistaken for a village tabby. I have seen this cat on four or five occasions. They may unfortunately soon become extinct.

In spite of all the human pressure on the Dangs, it still remains a delightful forest. An aimless drive through its forested roads at night is a pleasure any time of the year. The sound of the wind rustling through the dry leaves, the call of the nightjar chucking in the darkness, the pleasant smell of the forest in the cool of the night, the excitement of seeing the reflection of

Tribal women fishing in the Purna River.

A small Bhil fish-trap with its catch.

A large tribal fish-trap.

Bhil musicians using locally made instruments.

a wild creature's eyes as it runs across our path, and the sight of the pale moonlight shimmering through the dry branches of the trees, are some of the many beautiful memories of places in the Dangs that will be gone forever unless an attempt is made to prevent further ecological deterioration of this once superb dry deciduous forest.

But few people appear to be concerned about its rapid degradation. While social activists have taken up cudgels for the need to improve the lives of local tribal communities, no efforts have been made to understand their linkages with the landscape they live in. Even less value has been ascribed to the fact that it is the intact forest that sustains their needs, or that increasing fragmentation of the forest ecosystem is incompatible with their traditional lifestyle. No assessment has been made to forecast what is likely to occur if they use the forest resources unsustainably. Some awareness programmes have been tried by the Forest Department, but these have left local people indifferent and uncomprehending.

My understanding of the ecology of the Dangs comes from studying the forest from the air. The single-engine plane flies

along lines marked on a toposheet of the Dangs. Below there is a matrix of forest and agriculture. Each village is surrounded by lopped trees and burnt areas. The four people in the aircraft are busy recording a variety of parametres every 30 seconds, taking pictures, recording their comments on tape, and filling in proformas. No one has tried to do such an exercise on a shoestring budget before this. The team is trying to study the effects of changes in land-use on the diminishing forest resources of the Dangs. The data collected over a few flights was much larger than expected. When I undertook this venture there were no tools to help facilitate this type of study. Computers using GIS— Geographical Information Systems—only existed at a few hi-tech places abroad. This project ushered in the use of GIS in the field of ecological analyses in this country. When the data was analyzed, there was great skepticism in the scientific circles—at the BNHS, the WII and in the community of naturalists in general, there was a feeling that this would just not give objective results. Today it is an accepted method used for the study of natural resources in our country. This rapidly growing science

surprisingly started off in that small Beechcraft over the Dangs in 1988.

The project jeep is rattling and bumping through a rock-strewn riverbed. A bunch of tribals sit quietly in the back, hitching a lift to a remote village where 'outsiders' hardly ever go. No 'development' people, no doctors, no teachers, not even a Forest or Government Official goes there even once in a while. I have designed a project to study the ecology of the forest which I had repeatedly visited as a schoolboy with the Maharaja of Bansda. As I saw patches that had been thick forests and glades of regenerating woods in rab areas in the 1950s turn into a skeleton forest, I began a project with Sejal Worah, who was looking for a project for her doctorate from Poona University. Our project proposed to study the ecology of the fragmented forest of the Dangs. Sejal is a highly dedicated scientist and lived for two years with the Dangis.

At nightfall our jeep moves into the forest. In the hush of the night, our tribal helper with his keen eyesight asks the driver to stop. There is tremendous excitement in the jeep. In the headlamp a tiny cat's eyes glow brightly. The quarry has been located! The rare rusty spotted cat gives a single bound and disappears into the undergrowth. This is even more exciting than seeing a leopard. And the location was predicted by studying maps created by the GIS software.

At dawn the jeep is on the trail again. The study site is half an hour's drive along the bed of the Purna River. Sejal records the calls of birds in the forest to study the effect of forest fragmentation on their population. It is observed that smaller patches of forest do not support the highly specialized forest-birds. The more generalist species however somehow survive. Again, forest patch sizes have been identified by the GIS maps.

After breakfast the jeep moves to a neighbouring village. This time we count the number of trees used for rab and we weigh the bundles of wood the people collect. We need to understand how people use resources and how much wood is burnt for the rab.

It takes two years of hard work to collect all the data from this remote area and it would have taken several months to analyze it but for the GIS software. We heard about GIS by chance, when a group of foreign ecologists visited the BNHS. I got Sejal to bring the data back from the Dangs and they agreed to generate maps for us in Germany. My friend Sumant Moolgaonkar, who headed TELCO, agreed to give Sejal a grant to take the data there. When she arrived, the computers were down and so she had to go to Rome to get the maps made. The first ever, crude but useful, GIS maps were developed for an Indian site! At the end of the project there was a new tool for understanding forest ecology.

Now, 10 years later, my MSc student, Prasanna Kolte uses the old aerial pictures to find out how many trees have been lost during this period in the Protected Forest patches of the Dangs. The evidence is that the forest is much worse off than it was 10 years ago. Much of the degradation is due to politically-motivated influences from outside the region. The poor tribal is a victim of a variety of forces he cannot understand. And the forests of the Dangs continue to disappear. We calculate that around some of the villages 40 per cent of the trees present 10 years ago in the Protected Forests where farming is permitted, have now been felled. Do the forests of the Dangs have a future? Unless one finds alternatives for the forest people to survive, the degradation cannot be reversed, the Dangs will eventually be totally destroyed.

Waterfall at Purna.

A Dangi go-cart.

# YAWAL WILDLIFE SANCTUARY
YAWAL

| State | Maharashtra | Zone | Deccan Peninsula |
|---|---|---|---|
| Area | 177.52 sq km | Ecosystem | Tropical Dry Deciduous Forest |
| Year of Notification | 1969 | Visited | May 1997 |

The Forest Department jeep drives me into Yawal in the middle of the afternoon. It is a dusty track and obviously I do not expect to see much wildlife as this is an unearthly hour for wildlife to be moving about. But as the Forest Department wanted me to inspect the area, I am invited to join them. It, however, leaves memories of a most picturesque forest base. The deciduous forest is just about to burst into leaf again and there is a trelliswork of tiny pink, pinkish-green, and bright florescent green leaflets on either side of the very bad forest track. We pass through a few villages and go past patches of forest with farmlands at the edge of the Protected Area. The huts are still similar to what they used to be decades

The new leaves of the deciduous forest give the skyline a pastel green and pink lacy effect.

Orchid.

ago, beautifully made out of local forest material, a design that has lasted many centuries. It needs no change. It could have survived forever, but modern forces changed not only the material the local people now use to build their homes with, but the pattern as well. While the modern materials are indeed more permanent, the homes have lost all that was beautiful and functional—a terrible price to have to pay for development, which has distorted the way we look at our world. Is this why the more discerning are turning their backs on modern development patterns, reclaiming the need to go back to nature? Certainly for their aesthetic value, the homes I passed fit in perfectly with

their forest enviorment, matching the trelliswork of the trees and merging into their surroundings. The strange large bird that flew through the canopy, the one I first thought was a hornbill, was a sirkeer cuckoo. An Indian giant squirrel that lived in a tree near a superb flowering orchid ran through the canopy. In the evening, the forest broke suddenly into activity. Langurs jumped through the trees and an excited chital dashed through an open patch in the forest. Night was approaching. Owls were screeching. A new world was waking up. A large moth fluttered past my face, a palpable reminder of the forest's magnificence, its soft wings reminding me of  the darkness that would follow.

| 1 | 2 | | 4 |
|---|---|---|---|
| | | 5 | 6 |
| 3 | | 7 | |

Riverine forests.

Chital dashing through a forest clearing.

Indian giant squirrel.

Langur.

A *sirkeer* cuckoo.

Trelliswork of new leaves.

Tribal children near their home in the forest.

| State | Maharashtra | Zone | Deccan Peninsula |
|---|---|---|---|
| Area | 1676.93 sq km | Ecosystem | Tropical Dry Deciduous Forest |
| Year of Notification | 1974 | Visited | Nov 1983, Dec 2001 |

The forest in northern Maharashtra, near Amravati, is called Melghat, 'the meeting place of hill ranges.' The hills are spurs that arise from the Satpura Ranges, covered by thick, moist and dry deciduous teak forests. Approaching these hills through the flat, dry dusty plains, one sees that the ranges spread out across the horizon from west to east as far as the eye can see. They rise abruptly out of the treeless plains and are clothed with thick forests. While it is obvious that a large part of this Tiger Reserve consists of old teak plantations, there remain patches of natural forest, especially along the streams and rivers.

I went to see some of the 54 Korku villages in the Protected Area. The main occupations of the inhabitants are farming and fishing. Twenty years later, when I visited Melghat again, these people were still impoverished and malnutrition was still an ever-present problem, especially among children. When will these poor children's lives change for the better?

The sanctuary, which is Maharashtra's most important Tiger Reserve, has a relatively small core and a large buffer area. For several months after the monsoon, the core area is very difficult to approach; the only entry point is over the crest of the range from the hill-station of Chikaldara. These core forests are much thicker than those in the buffer zone. I was able to visit these incredible forests because the Forest Department wanted me to develop three Interpretation Centres for Melghat. I spent several days with the Forest Guards taking pictures for these centres, which were designed to help tourists appreciate the complex ecology of the area.

The composition of the forest, though variable, is predominantly teak. Other

dominant species are dhaora—*Anogeissus latifolia*, haldu—*Adina cordifolia* and saj—*Terminalia tomentosa*. Tall clumps of bamboo are found in abundance. The areas around Chikaldara Hill Station support picturesque, moist deciduous vegetation. Though the plant species are different, the structure of the forest is reminiscent of the broad-leaved evergreen vegetation of some regions of the Western Ghats. However, the rainfall is only 1784 mm and the resemblance is mainly due to the stunted and twisted boles of the trees with their closed canopy. In the drier areas teak forms nearly pure stands, probably encouraged by past forestry practices. The under-story is not well developed and the diversity of the undergrowth of shrubs and climbers is seriously affected by an influx of exotic plants such as lantana. Here this shrub has become a semi-climber on teak trunks, growing to a height of even 15 feet. In open areas it forms a dense scrub, which may be one of the

factors that prohibits the regeneration of teak and other saplings in this forest. It is highly combustible in summer and adds considerably to the already inflammable dry teak leaves that form a large part of the detritus of the forest floor. Lantana is absent wherever grasses or bamboo are in abundance. However, this weed may spread further when the next periodic bamboo flowering occurs and the bamboo clumps die. This will reduce the distribution of the beautiful bamboo that

Melghat is a meeting place of several hill ranges.

Birds of prey are a part of the apex of the forest's food pyramid.

A snake winds its way through the rocky forest floor.

A pair of forest calottes.

important component for maintaining a diversity of specialized insects, birds and other animals. They contain snags and hollows, which are nesting sites for birds and small mammals. Dead and dying trees are also important as microhabitats for fungi and other detritivorous animals.

The winters can be severe in certain valleys in Melghat. This produces frost holes, which have been known to kill off all the teak saplings in a short time. Fire is also a hazard for saplings. Large-scale fires are difficult to prevent in summer, especially as communication systems are poor in the more remote areas of Melghat.

The Kolkaz forest bungalow is situated on a precipice overlooking a picturesque bend in the Sipna River. At dawn, the hooting of a brown fish owl heralds

creates a mosaic of vegetation types. Our short-sightedness in introducing an exotic species will again prove that we stand to gain only if we preserve what nature has evolved over millions of years within each ecosystem. Once the undergrowth, with its diversity of shrubs and climbers, is totally taken over by a single species, it is bound to lead to changes in the composition of insect and bird-life that require a great variety of plants in the undergrowth to maintain a natural community. Gradually, the forest's richness of species will be seriously affected.

Over several years, the natural regeneration of teak in Melghat has been reported to be very poor. Even the saplings that were planted have a high mortality rate. Until a few decades ago, this forest

was worked intensively for its timber. On the Chikaldara slopes the teak trees take on strange shapes, developing low branches from a short, often crooked trunk and becoming a kind of miniaturized teak tree. This is a result of the shallow depth of the soil and the high velocity of the wind.

Some parts of Melghat have been denotified in the recent past, even though there have been protests from several conservation groups. It is essential that no large development projects should be done in this area. It is estimated that to achieve a substantial volume of timber, a teak tree must live for over 80 years to grow to an average girth of 124 cm. If these large trees are felled it will be a long period before the natural teak in these forests grow back into a mature forest. A proportion of over-mature trees with hollow trunks and even dead trees is an

the new day. Its silhouette can be seen against the growing redness in the east, perched on a tall dead tree. Gradually the forest comes to life. A troop of langurs crashes through the trees nearby. A little later there is a persistent distress call of a juvenile langur, perhaps indicating the presence of a predator. A troop of about 20 langurs can be seen jumping around on the trees on the steep drop that forms the riverbank. Some sit on the bank in the grass. Others play or groom each other. The sad calls come from the opposite bank. There, sitting all by himself and looking very forlorn and nervous, is a very young monkey. He jumps back and forth on the rocky bank looking for a place to cross. He repeatedly approaches the edge of the water, gets ready to jump across and then retreats, squealing nervously. One of the adult females then jumps

across the river using a few large rocks as a bridge. This demonstration is of no avail as the youngster probably fears that he will not be able to imitate this agile performance. The troop finally begins to move downstream, apparently abandoning the noisy youngster. This leads to an even greater degree of agitation. He runs up and down the bank and looks over his shoulder at the forest, as if anticipating that some predator might now emerge and pounce on him. As the group moves along the bank, the young monkey keeps pace on the opposite bank, squealing repeatedly. While moving along the narrow pathway on the bank, my attention on the langur down below, I nearly stepped on a Russel's viper basking in the sun. Its head and tail were hidden in a bush. I began to set up the tripod, changed the lens of my camera and turned to peer through the viewfinder. To my utter surprise I saw the snake moving out of the bush towards me! I had to abandon tripod and camera until it slowly turned around and began moving off into the bush, with me nearly toppling over the tripod in the process! By this time the langur troop had moved down the river and I did not get a chance to find out how the young monkey's unfortunate episode ended.

The forest is full of the calls of flocks of parakeets. Large mixed groups of rose-ringed and blossom-headed parakeets hover around a tall dry tree. Every few seconds, one of them takes off and dive-bombs a small raptor on a neighbouring tree. As each parakeet buzzes in on the raptor, it spreads its wings, only to settle down again. When eventually it flies off in disgust, the parakeets promptly disappear in the opposite direction. The forest has large feeding parties of birds, treepies, drongos, orioles, flower-peckers, fly-catchers and many others, moving in groups through the forest.

Chikaldara has an old Government Resthouse that takes one back into history. The township is placed in the centre of a plateau and the local people have their tiny farms around the settlement. What is remarkable is the immense quantity and variety of flowering herbaceous plants that grow on the open parts of the plateau on the top of the hill. The orange flowers of the lantana shrubs contrast sharply with turquoise-blue, lemon-yellow, iridescent-violet, pale-pink and dark shocking-pink flowers that dot the landscape. The lantana however has been spreading over the last 20 odd years. In 1983 I recorded that it had entered many parts of the forest. During my recent visit, I found that it was much more widespread. Eventually this will lead to a serious loss of diversity of the local ground flora.

The Chikaldara Ghat is a beautiful drive. The hillslopes support a large population of jungle fowl. A line of five hens crosses the road in front of the jeep. One actually moves towards us, clucking quietly. Suddenly it gives a startled squawk and flies into the bushes. Another flies into a tree, uttering an alarm call and clucking anxiously, while peering and craning its neck and

A large wood spider with its recently caught prey.

A tiger's old kill being broken down in the detritus by ants and beetles.

Tribal people are being employed to work in the forest.

repeatedly bobbing its head up and down to have a better look. After a short scrutiny it flies into the nearest thicket.

As one goes down the steep slopes of the hill, the forest thickens into some of the finest areas in Melghat. This is the core area of the sanctuary, thick with large trees and impenetrable shrubs. The low evening rays of the sun penetrate the thick canopy, filtering the golden light into a small open glade. It turns the tall dry grass into many shades touched with silver and gold. Peacocks move majestically through the grass, occasionally taking off to glide towards a small watercourse in the distance. Hoping to take advantage of the evening light, I follow one sporting a long tail into the waist-high grass. I move along cautiously—the morning's episode of the Russell's viper is still fresh in my mind. The peacock keeps a fixed distance between us. As I stop it freezes, if I move forward it advances slowly uphill through the grass. All I can see is the movement of the grass ahead of me as it cautiously moves deeper into the forest. In a small pool of water in a

streambed, there are fresh tiger footprints. Only a few bird sounds now interrupt the stillness of the jungle. Night is about to fall.

A group of sambar warily approaches the water as the sky darkens. A tiger roars somewhere in the distance. It is time to leave. Can this idyllic glade be destroyed by the hand of man without nature taking revenge?

Walking through the forest in Melghat 20 years later is again an exciting experience. Out of nowhere, I hear the twittering of many birds, as a large feeding party of several different species of birds moves through the forest. If we watch carefully, it is evident that they are all helping each other to search for their specific food sources. While birds that eat fruit or feed on flower nectar among the branches and leaves hunt for their food, they disturb insects, which fly out of their hiding places under the surface of leaves and from crevices in the bark of trees. These are prey for birds such as rollers, flycatchers, drongos and bee-eaters. Birds that specialize in hunting for food in the form of berries and caterpillars in the undergrowth also disturb insects, which are captured by birds like thrushes and babblers that skulk among the shrubs. Different species of birds thus form complex interrelationships, and their movements are linked to each other's behaviour patterns as they flit through the forest from one tree to another.

A woodpecker arrives and knocks on the bark of a tree to look for insects. A flock of parakeets feed on fruit and fly off, screeching loudly. A fantail flycatcher opens and closes its tail to disturb insects so that it can catch them as they fly off. Then as suddenly as they arrived, all the birds move towards another fruiting tree in the forest.

There is a noisy crash of branches and a loud whoop. A troop of langurs, which have been quietly eating young leaves, decide to move off. As they jump from tree to tree with noisy crash after crash one realizes just how quiet they have been until then. As they move away, the forest regains its silence. Far away on the hillslope a barking deer calls. Perhaps both langur and deer have sensed that a tiger is on the move!

The trees in the less disturbed areas are of a variety of colours, shapes and sizes. Where the forest was planted in the old days with teak trees, they are in straight rows. The more natural core forests have a much greater variety of trees and shurbs and the grass is tall, as there are fewer domestic animals grazing there. After walking through it, one returns with millions of pointed spikes of grass, a painful reminder of the beautiful patches of grass for weeks even after the trousers have been repeatedly washed! This is how grass spreads its seeds, from one place to another, by animals on which they stick.

The *nala* is cold and damp. It smells fresh, of damp moss and moist detritus. The trickling sound of water, with an occasional birdcall, gives the forest a wonderful feeling. It is very empty until one begins to look for all the small details that are signs of silent life in the watercourse. In the many pools of water along the stream there are thousands of living creatures. Fish of various kinds dart through the water. A crab climbs out from its hole, moving sideways in a straight line to another hiding place. On the surface of the water there are a large number of water beetles swimming rapidly in continuous tiny circles. In another part of the pool water-skaters dart from place to place on the water's surface, using their long legs and special feet to support their weight. Below the surface, several other species of beetles swim around looking for food. A kingfisher flashes past on bright blue wings to settle on a nearby rock. The *nala* is a very special microhabitat in the forest as the vegetation on its banks is highly specialized and all the birds and animals must come to it every day to drink.

A great Arjun tree grows on the edge of the stream. If one sits and watches a tree it is soon apparent that from the roots to the canopy, it is a microhabitat in itself. Arjun is a species that is specially adapted to these waterlogged areas. Its roots absorb water from the *nala* and bind the soil along the banks of the watercourse during the monsoon floods. In the water there are many varieties of small fish. While some species feed on aquatic vegetation such as algae and other weeds, other species are carnivores and feed on aquatic insects and worms. Small frogs live on the bank of the *nala* and jump into the water if disturbed. Around the roots of the tree there are webs of a number of spiders that are constructed in the form of tunnels. They catch the insects that crawl on the forest floor. The drying leaves that fall from the tree add nutrients from the terrestrial ecosystem into the aquatic ecosystem of the stream.

On the trunk of the tree there are lizards that catch insects hiding in the bark. Among the branches and the thick canopy of leaves there are a large variety of birds. They flit from branch to branch calling to each other. A giant squirrel jumps through the branches and its 'chock chock chock' call rings out through the forest. Giant wood spiders have built their great webs a metre in diameter, high up among the branches, to catch flying butterflies, grasshoppers and other insects. On the branches at the top of the tree there are several huge beehives. Thousands of bees buzz around them. They bring back nectar and pollen for their grubs, pollinating the forest plants during collection. That bears have been climbing the tree to get honey from the hives is evident from many claw marks on the trunk of the tree. The tree thus forms a microhabitat in which several different creatures spend most of their lives. It is home to a complex community of animals, all dependent on each other.

The Arjun tree has big seeds with wings that can be carried far and wide by the wind. Only a few of its widely spread seeds will land in conditions where they can germinate and become seedlings. Many of these seedlings will die. Only a few of them will grow into saplings, and only a very few saplings will eventually grow into big trees. The few that survive this long period of growth will one day grow into the tall giants of the forest. Ancient Arjun trees must eventually fall down during storms or monsoon floods that create torrents eroding the soil of the banks. Once they fall, the canopy opens up and younger trees grow into the new giants of the forest. Occasionally, a few roots of a fallen giant remain intact and the trunk may sprout new branches, one of which will grow to re-form a tree. When an uprooted tree dies, ants, fungi, and bacteria break down the large amount of material in its dead trunk, branches, and leaves. This releases nutrients on which the surrounding trees will grow. Thus even in its death a tree will support other forms of life in the forest by recycling nutrients.

Having to move through the forest with a group of Forest Guards is not always the best thing for a wildlife photographer. There is usually too much talk. If that is controlled there are coughs. Control the cough and one becomes aware of noisy footsteps. So this time my guards are requested to follow 100 odd metres behind, as I start walking up a *nala* course. While this is not usually permitted, I am given special permission as I am taking

Farming in a village in Melghat.

Tribal boy with his cow.

A tribal village in Melghat.

Several rivers have their origin in these forested hills.

pictures to develop the three Nature Interpretation Centres for Melghat.

The *nala* course still has pools of water, which I negotiate silently. I notice tiger pugmarks, and hoof marks of sambar and wild boar. Peacock feet have left their large imprints at the waters edge. I walk towards a bend in the *nala*, trying to be as silent as possible. As I cautiously negotiate it, I see a bear walking quietly towards me. He is intently peering at the ground before him as he ambles along the edge of the stream and doesn't see me. Not more than 10 metres away from him, I raise my camera. The movement makes him look up. His face in the viewfinder is one of utter bewilderment! He appears to raise himself, evidently wondering if he should rear up on his hind legs. My camera clicks. It is a long, long double-click. Something has gone wrong! Has the shutter malfunctioned? I look at my camera settings and realize it is not on auto mode, as I had been using a manual wide-angle lens just before walking down the *nala*. By now the bear is uncomfortably close. He hesitates and I sidestep towards the shrubs at the edge of the nala. Strangely, he responds by turning towards the shrubs himself. Together we enter an open grassy patch through the gaps in the bushes under the forest canopy and look at each other again. Now he moves towards me again, apparently more out of curiosity than to threaten me. I manage to get a shaky hurried picture and I begin to step slowly backwards, still facing him. Suddenly he seems to stare past me over my shoulder and I glimpse the rest of the party emerging from the forest. He begins to move off, repeatedly looking over his shoulder while climbing up the hillock.

I feel unhappy about the loss of a good picture in the bright sunlit *nala* bed. We try in vain to locate him again but he has vanished into the forest. In retrospect it was a close call. I could have been severely mauled. I had done the right things. Don't run! Don't look scared! Don't do the instinctive things one feels like doing at that moment! But this is not easy. One needs presence of mind and repeated exposure to such events before one develops the correct responses. But then, who wants to live as dangerously as that?

In 1911, CA Crump, who was one of the BNHS' collectors, made a survey of mammals in Melghat and Chikaldara (JBNHS Vol 21). He describes the 'fine heavy jungles' he found in the Semadoh and Sipna valley. He mentions that though flying squirrels were plentiful, he saw only one before dark. He collected wild dogs, rats and mice, and shot bear, muntjac and four-horned antelope. Dunbar Brander mentions having seen black leopard in Melghat in 1913. He appears to have seen it again 10 years later in 1923.

The 1997 tiger census in Melghat accounted for 73 tigers, a figure that has remained essentially stable over the last 10 years (Jain, 2001). The estimated leopard population, as reported by Project Tiger, however, appears to have grown from

57 in 1993 to 79 in 1997. The sambar population shows a decline, from 2796 in 1993 to only 1718 in 1997. A similar decline is shown for gaur and barking deer. If these estimates are accurate, these trends are in fact alarming, when coupled with the denotification of a large part of the sanctuary a few years ago.

The Forest Department has never given any clear, convincing reasons for denotifying a large part of the Protected Area. However, the vague reason given was that there were just too many villages in the area. As a member of the Wildlife Advisory Board of Maharashtra, I was the sole dissenting voice when the Chief Minister announced this step. I was told that other adjacent areas would be added to compensate for this. This could well have been done without the denotification, making the area more viable, especially to support the prey base for the tiger. In the recent past, Melghat has been consistently threatened by a proposal to set up a Pumped Storage System at Chikhaldara. While the dams would lie outside the Protected Area, they would undoubtedly create a negative impact on the area. This could well have been the reason for the earlier denotification.

Deep in the forest of Melghat there is a sacred place of the local people. It is called Chikhal Aam—which translates into, 'mud and mango trees.' The name clearly indicates what one sees around there. A pool of water is fed by a perennial stream, its muddy banks permanently moist. Its edge is surrounded by giant mango trees. It is the watering place for all wild creatures. A paradise flycatcher flutters around, displaying its white ribbon-like tail. A grey jungle fowl calls. A frog begins to croak from under a rock. The sun is about to set. A barking deer gives a sharp alarm call and rushes up the hill slope at the edge of the stream. A zillion mosquitoes emerge. It is time to leave Chikhal Aam to the nightlife of the forest.

# PENCH NATIONAL PARK AND TIGER RESERVE
PENCH

| State | Maharashtra and Madhya Pradesh | Zone | Deccan Peninsula |
|---|---|---|---|
| Area | 257.26 sq km | Ecosystem | Dry Deciduous forest |
| Year of Notification | NP 1975; TR 1993–94 | Visited | Dec 1990, Jan 1991, Nov 1997–2001 |

The twin Protected Areas on the banks of the Pench River lie on the border of Madhya Pradesh (758 square kilometres) and Maharashtra. Pench in Madhya Pradesh was the nineteenth Tiger Reserve, declared in 1992. The India Ecodevelopment Project was started here in 1996–97 (Jain, 2001). Pench, in Maharashtra was brought under the Tiger Reserves in 1999. There is a need to integrate a comprehensive and viable management strategy that covers both the Protected Areas, though they lie on either side of the Madhya Pradesh and Maharashtra borders.

The Pench River is now a large lake that has its catchment area in the Satpura-Maikal ranges. The forest was severely damaged during the construction of Pench Dam and workers who were brought in for constructing the dam have now settled within it. Overfishing has been a constant cause of serious disturbance. For years, fishermen have been entering the lake in boats from the Madhya Pradesh side and living on the banks in the part of the forest that lies in Maharashtra where they cut wood, light fires and disturb the wildlife and its habitat. A surprising sight is the enormous rows of bicycles confiscated from people undertaking these illegal activities! Fishing has been banned by a judgement of the Supreme Court but the whole issue has been a long and contentious one for the two State Forest Departments.

The forests on the banks of the Pench River are mainly moist and dry deciduous forests. The river below the dam is itself awe-inspiring. Its giant rock formations have been carved over millennia by the great force of water, which has sculpted the most fantastic shapes in a variety

A trickling stream covered with plant life forms a distinctive microhabitat.

of colours and textures. Any modern sculptor would envy these forms! The rocks have been the focus of attention for people over several generations. A small shrine among the rocks on the riverbank is an important place of pilgrimage, but the large number of pilgrims and picnickers have a serious impact on the ecology of the river. They litter the bank with plastic and pollute the water with wasted food. Uncontrolled access into the surrounding forest constitutes a persistent disturbance to wildlife. The dam site also has a large housing colony, which cuts off movement between the two sides of the river for the wildlife.

The settlements in Pench have large herds of cattle, and several families with large herds of buffaloes are relatively very well-off. They farm the surrounding land, own tractors, use motorcycles to transport milk, and live in big houses. Giant piles of cattle dung surround their houses. They send their children to a nearby village school. Even with this growing affluence, their livestock remain dependent on the forest in which they graze. Apart from buffaloes with young calves, all the others are free grazed in the forest surrounding the village. With these huge herds grazing deep in the forest, regeneration is bound to be limited.

I once walked up a tributary of the Pench River. There were fresh tiger footprints in the sand. I changed lenses and left my open camera bag on the edge of the river in my excitement to follow them. The Forest Guard with me looked nervous. After he coughed meaningfully several times and grumbled below his breath, I decided to turn back. There were crashing noises in the treetops. When I got back, there was a curious langur sitting beside my camera bag and contemplating whether the lenses were edible. I rescued my equipment in the nick of time!

In the course of several visits to Pench National Park in Maharashtra, I have found that although the habitat is good, the wildlife values are low. In contrast, just across the border in Madhya Pradesh, I have seen herds of chital, a few sambar and barking deer within a short time. It is often difficult to understand why similar looking habitats have great variations in the population density of wildlife.

Waterhole in Pench.

A brightly coloured spider that mimics a dry leaf.

Rocks in the Pench riverbed sculpted by the running water of the river over the years.

Teak forest of Pench in northern Maharashtra.

A bird of prey perched on its usual vantage point from where it can spot even a tiny movement on the ground below.

A macaque mother and infant.

The water of the Pench dam has been used illegally for fishing, mainly by people from Madhya Pradesh.

| 1 | | |
|---|---|---|
| | 2 | |
| | 3 | 4 |

A brilliantly coloured spider.

A shrine in a sacred part of the forest.

Female wood spider.

Cormorants.

| State | Maharashtra | Zone | Deccan Peninsula |
|---|---|---|---|
| Area | NP 116.54 sq km; TR 620 sq km | Ecosystem | Deciduous Mixed Forest |
| Year of Notification | NP 1955; TR 1993–94 | Visited | Nov 1983, Nov 1997 |

Nagzira at the edge of the teak zone in the north-east corner of Maharashtra has an exceptionally beautiful tract of miscellaneous moist deciduous forest. The terrain consists of small hillocks separated by meandering streams. The forest extends onto their banks, which are covered by thick undergrowth. The rainfall in the region is heavy enough for the growth of teak, which accounts for only 45 per cent of the trees in the mixed forests that grow in thick profusion. Other tree species include *bija* (*Pterocarpus marsupium*), *saj* (*Terminalia tomentosa*), *garari* (*Cleistanthus collinus*), etc. The *Lagerstroemia*, which forms a leafy under story, is mixed with small, dense clumps of bamboo. The undergrowth consists of a variety of bushes and flowering herbaceous plants intermixed with patches of grass.

The Forest Department log cabin overlooks a picturesque lake, its clear water

| 1 | |
|---|---|
| 2 | 3 |

A sambar dashes through the forest.

A termite mound.

Catterpillar on a termite mound.

Sambar after a dip in the lake on a misty morning.

A spider with its prey.

mirroring the lush thickly forested hills beyond. At dawn the mist rises over the still waters. The diffuse pink glow imparts a painting-like quality to the scene.

On the opposite bank a loud splash sends ripples across the water. A sambar fawn has decided to take a dip while its mother stands on the water's edge, watchfully peering around for signs of danger. This small sanctuary teems with wildlife—gaur, chital, sambar, nilgai, barking deer, wild boar, leopards, wild dogs, jackals and even a few tigers.

Several forest birds are twittering among the trees nearby. The call of a chital is heard close at hand. As the sun's rays creep over the crest of the forested hills, the mist begins to rise and rapidly the colours change until all the world turns a shimmering green and gold. Dewdrops clinging to the flowers in a patch of grass glitter like thousands of diamonds in the morning light. A pair of hornbills fly from tree to tree. Several chital that have spent the night nearby begin to move off into the forest for their morning session of grazing.

Moving through this forest it appears that nature seems to have outdone herself! Quiet streams of clear water meander through the forest, huge cobwebs, a metre in diameter, stretch between the branches of the trees, with large spiders poised at the centre of each web, ready to grab their prey. An old dead tree sports several holes with the nest of a hornbill and a woodpecker.

During my visit in 1997 a party of tourists watched a pair of leopards playing on the road at the entrance to the guesthouse. I missed this spectacle by a few moments. When WA Rodgers and Shri Indurkar, then the Chief Wildlife Warden, visited Nagzira, they saw a tiger kill and drag a sambar onto the road. It was just bad timing that I did not join them on this visit. Knowing my poor luck this would not have happened if I had been with them!

Viewing wildlife is much easier in summer, but even in winter I had several sightings of herds of chital, several sambar, a good sized nilgai and a small herd of gaurs. A large troop of langurs insisted on raiding the Forest Department's garden for flower buds. Not only are the monkeys driven off from the premises of the guesthouse, but barbed wire fencing has been constructed to keep the deer out of the garden! It seems strange to keep wildlife away from the guests in a Wildlife Sanctuary. Incongruously, in this superb wild place there is a well-planned garden with lawns and formally groomed bushes and manicured flowerbeds. Perhaps it is meant to keep the city dwellers from being frightened off by the total unfamiliarity of a forest outside the window! What if a tiger should come out of the forest and jump through their windows at night? That fence around the garden is indeed a terrible mistake, as herds of chital gather outside it just after dark. It would be much more exciting if they could be enticed to feed in and around the tourist complex. I was given to understand that a long time ago a Minister who was visiting the sanctuary had recommended that a garden was a must around the VIP guesthouse! His instructions have been followed to the letter by developing this 'beautiful' garden. I am sure the Minister is no more in the seat of power. So why not allow the wilderness to reclaim the garden and let wildlife into the tourist complex?

| State | Maharashtra | Zone | Deccan Peninsula |
|---|---|---|---|
| Area | 133.05 sq km | Ecosystem | Dry and Moist Deciduous Forest |
| Year of Notification | 1975 | Visited | Nov 1983, Nov 1997 |

The Navegaon Sanctuary is both a forest and a lake ecosystem. Its magnificent teak forests can be seen from a road that runs around the lake. The water attracts a large number of waterfowl in winter. Flocks of wild ducks such as poachards, pintails and garganey teals form mixed groups on the water.

Navegaon's forest ecosystem and the lake offer very different experiences to a wildlife tourist. The Forest Department used to chase fishermen by using paddleboats. I once found myself paddling furiously along with the other boats to chase poachers with the guards. Needless to say our paddleboats were just too slow and the fishermen disappeared into the forest along with most of their catch!

Naxalite activities have periodically created serious management problems in this sanctuary. During one of my visits I had to provide emergency medical help to a guard who had been assaulted by Naxalites. Terrorists and violent activist groups find a haven in several Protected Areas because they are remote, the terrain is difficult and there are hiding places in to which a group can quickly disappear. The local people in most Protected Areas are extremely poor and their voices remain unheard. Terrorist groups find them easy to deal with as they are the most gullible section of society. It is thus difficult for the Forest frontline unarmed staff to counter the influence of politically active extremist groups, poachers of timber or wildlife and even highly armed dacoits. It is frequently difficult to tell these different groups apart.

When I first went to Navegaon in 1983, there were few tourists. During my last visit in 1997, there were hoards and hoards! While we need to encourage tourism, the larger the number, the greater the disturbance to wildlife. How does one deal with this? Implementing a sustainable level of tourism in these Protected Areas needs careful site-specific strategies and must inevitably be linked with fulfilling the needs and aspirations of the local people.

Lake at Navegoan.

Ducks on the lake at Navegaon.

The grass cover in a forest is ecologically as important as large trees.

Molluscs form an important part of aquatic food chains.

A motionless lizard awaits its prey.

Chital.

# TADOBA NATIONAL PARK AND TIGER RESERVE
TADOBA

| State | Maharashtra | Zone | Deccan Peninsula |
|---|---|---|---|
| Area | NP 116.54 sq km; TR 620 sq km | Ecosystem | Dry Deciduous Forest |
| Year of Notification | NP 1955; TR 1993–94 | Visited | Dec 1990, Nov–Dec 1997 |

The twin sanctuaries of Tadoba and Andhari are covered by extensive teak forests. Other common trees are Ain and Tendu. Tadoba National Park declared in 1955, was transferred to Maharashtra the following year and became the State's first National Park. Recent census figures report 43 tigers in the 625.39 square kilometre Park between 150 to 200 bears, which is a high population for a single Protected Area, and over 2000 chital and 650 sambar (Jain, 2001).

The forests stretch in an unbroken wall along the sides of the roads in the tourist section. The bamboo forms a thick tangle of vegetation that screens most of the wildlife from the viewer. There are no villages for miles and only a few stray cattle graze on its periphery. The impact of people is significantly less here than in most of the other Protected Areas in Maharashtra.

My first visit in 1990 was to write about various issues for the conservation aspects of the World Bank's Forestry Sector Project for Maharashtra and I recommended that it should be included in the Tiger Reserves.

Tadoba Lake contains a number of crocodiles. They have now become used to being watched by noisy tourists often approaching them while they sit on the banks.

In 1997 I visited Tadoba after a gap of seven years. This second visit was to take MSc students of the BVIEER for a study tour to appreciate forest ecology. The Forest Department also wanted pictures of wildlife taken at night for their guest house. While this is not something I like to do as it does lead to unnecessary disturbance for the animals, I agreed. It had to be done by getting as close to the animals as possible as I did not have a powerful flash gun. The Forest Department driver

was excellent. He got the vehicle close to a herd of gaur with the head lights off. He was to put them on at the last moment so I could get a quick close up of a gaur and leave without disturbing them. However I had to get out of the jeep to be able to get a better angle, fully aware that this could be risky. As the lights blazed and I pressed the shutter the nearest gaur from the herd decided to make a dash for cover. Unfortunately it chose a path directly towards me! When it saw me, it veered away just in time and thundered past me into the bush. It was a close encounter. A few metres towards me and I might never have got to see the picture I'd taken. I have a special feeling for that picture. It might well have been my last!

Shrines of forest deities have traditionally led to community action that has preserved forests all over the country.

The teak forests of Tadoba are among the most beautiful deciduous forests I have ever encountered.

A brightly coloured orbweb spider.

Nightjars are becoming less common all over India. This is probably an effect of pesticides in the food chains.

A violet splash of colour attracts insect pollinators.

Langurs are dependent on the forest for a large variety of foods.

A golden cocoon of an insect appears as a bright speck in the forest undergrowth.

Owls eat small mammals, birds, reptiles, amphibia and even insects.

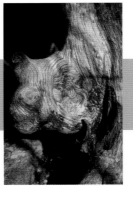

# ANDHARI WILDLIFE SANCTUARY

ANDHARI

| State | Maharashtra | Zone | Deccan Peninsula |
|---|---|---|---|
| Area | 508.85 sq km | Ecosystem | Dry Deciduous Forest |
| Year of Notification | 1986 | Visited | Dec 1990 |

This area was declared a sanctuary in 1986 along with the Tadoba National Park, and as the Tadoba-Andhari Tiger Reserve in 1993. The teak forest has very few settlements dependent on it. No landscape provides the sharp contrasts between seasonal changes as teak forests do. The large, bright green leaves turn rapidly to brown in winter and are shed, leaving the skeletons of dry trees that remain dormant for several months. The forest and all its denizens await the next flush of leaves before the monsoon. During the summer it is the bamboo that reduces the bareness of the forest. Animals such as gaur feed on it. It is also part of the cover used by a large number of forest birds.

Bamboo flowers gregariously after several years, each species having its own cycle. For the commonly seen bamboo of Andhari, this happens once in 27 years! After the bamboo flowers, the clump dies. Forest fires, under these conditions, can become uncontrollable and lead to a serious situation in which all the young regenerating trees are destroyed.

Controlling a forest fire is an incredibly difficult task, one that the forest staff has to do frequently. I have joined them at some of these disastrous events. One uses a branch of a tree to beat the flames down, while the smoke burns one's eyes and, if the wind changes its direction, breathing becomes difficult. And at the end of a session, the skin of one's palms begins to peel. It is not an enviable task. Dry lantana shrubs burn briskly, its shrubs are impenetrable and during a fire, one's orientation is disrupted. In the absence of modern fire-fighting facilities, it is often impossible to put out a fire quickly. It is however very easy to ignite one!

A snag in a tree trunk forms a microhabitat for several species.

A shady forest patch which is frequently used by a large tiger to rest in.

# The Deccan Grasslands and Scrublands

I have spent all my life in Pune on the edge of the Deccan Plateau. For me this arid flat plateau and the low hills around Pune are 'home'. To most people the Deccan presents a very uninteresting landscape, but for those like me, who have grown up in it, the plateau has a charm of its own that only long familiarity induces in people. For those of us who have wandered through these stark landscapes for several years, the change is so sudden that one hardly believes it is really happening. Areas one thought of as desolate a decade ago are transformed into gigantic industrial complexes. Fields of bajra and jowar have given way to sugarcane and sugar factories. The grassland has been converted into Social Forestry Plantations. This has not happened only around Pune. Great expanses of open wilderness of the semi-arid grasslands of the Deccan are now highly impacted by human development.

The residual, natural or less impacted semi-arid ecosystem has several different forms covering the central part of the Deccan Plateau. A fair proportion of this landscape was once the common grazing land of all our villages. As the management of such lands changed from traditional, local control to a more top-down control during the British period, these areas became one of the most rapidly affected wilderness ecosystems in the country.

Whereas the British policy of creating Reserved Forests and Protected Forests was instrumental in policing the Reserved Forest against illegal timber extraction, changes in the control over grasslands were not universally adopted. As human and cattle populations expanded, the 'common' grasslands became the targets of rapid degradation. No one realized the seriousness of this growing impact for several decades. RG Burton, an army officer posted in what is now Northern Maharashtra, hunted around the Wardha and Painganga Rivers in 1928, where he says tigers were numerous, but preyed on cattle, as wild herbivores such as chital were scarce due to shikar. During a six-week trip he shot 14 tigers, leopards, bears and other species. Today much of this area is degraded scrubland and these animals have long since disappeared.

He remarks that near the village of Argaum near Aurangabad, 'There were great herds of antelope which ravaged the wheat and other cultivation in which they wandered at will. There might be five or six hundred of these animals in sight at once.' He also records that there were thousands of quail, partridges and a few floricans.

Over the last few decades the thorn trees of these savanna-like grasslands have been gradually felled for much-needed fuel wood. There has been an escalation

The Deccan grasslands have isolated thorny trees.

| 1 | 2 |
|---|---|
| 3 | |

Storm clouds are rarely seen in this semi-arid tract.

In many parts of the Deccan there are large rocky outcrops and boulders. They constitute a microhabitat that fulfills the special requirements of flora and fauna.

Grassland ecosystem.

of cattle pressure and the resultant overgrazing of the grasslands has led to the formation of what is usually referred to as 'wasteland'. These biotic factors have produced a degraded form of thorn forest or scrubland with very scanty grass cover.

Until recently Wildlife Sanctuaries and National Parks were created in the great forest belts of India and attempts to preserve such wild, dry-grass covered, treeless tracts were few and far between. With the growing awareness of the value of preserving other landscapes of ecological uniqueness, grasslands are now being included in our Protected Area Network.

Wherever flat stretches of semi-wilderness still exist in the Deccan, they are covered by scrubland and open savanna-like woodlands. The common sparse tree cover in this region consists of Acacia and Zizyphus trees, which are scattered in small clumps in the grassland. The vegetation of some areas consists mainly of bushy xerophytic species. There are also grassy tracts in which Euphorbia is the only prominently visible plant.

The small hills that form out-crops over the flat plateau support specialized plant and animal communities. Some areas are covered by exposed and weathered boulders called rock fields, which act as a niche for several species of insects, reptiles and birds. The plateau has several river systems that flow from west to east, and is dotted with man-made tanks and lakes that have grown in number ever since the Peshwa period, changing the arid landscape.

For the major part of the year this ecosystem presents a sombre, dry landscape. The monotonous contours of surrounding farmland are coloured in various shades of brown. As the monsoon clouds appear the koel begins to call, heralding the onset of the rains. Whirlwinds wheel across the plateau carrying dust, dry grass and twigs through the sky. As the clouds gather and darken before they break, there is a sense of great anticipation. When the first drops of rain splatter over the scorched land a fresh, earthy perfume permeates the air. Brief but torrential thundershowers usher in the end of the hot season, each shower of rain followed by a brief fall in temperature.

Semi-arid grasslands in the summer.

The parched ground cracked into a crazy pavement pattern allows the water to seep into itself hungrily. Suddenly the landscape is totally altered. The functions of the ecosystem that were dormant throughout the dry period, as if in suspended animation, now spring back to life. Tiny green shoots of grass sprout everywhere, and in a short time the dull brown of the barren earth is covered by several shades of green. Life seems to reaffirm itself with

the beginning of another new cycle of growth. For most animals and birds this is the breeding season. Their lives are closely adapted to the cycle created by Nature in the Deccan Plateau of an extremely long dry period and a brief and unpredictable wet period. The dry nalas begin to trickle and then to swell and often overflow their banks. During a cloudburst brief flash floods inundate the flat land, creating large expanses of temporary muddy water. The monsoon brings about a drastic change. It is a time for Nature to regenerate herself, a time for plants to grow and for people to plant crops. The rains bring about a new world of herbs that bloom among the green grasses. Each species has a very brief flowering period. After this short period of growth the grassland dries, and the herbs and grasses form the seeds that will repeat this incredible cycle year after year. At the end of this period, the temperature begins to drop, ushering in a new phase. Thousands of migrant birds from the cold Arctic and the tundra find their way through the Himalayan passes to the Deccan looking for a wintering place that is less harsh. The grassland sky is suddenly alive with swallows and martins, and the songs of larks and pipets are heard everywhere. With the onset of summer they move north again. The annual cycle of life has turned yet another full circle.

The Indian cheetah, once the chief predator of the grassland, is now extinct. Domesticated and used for hunting by the Maharajas of old, its disappearance is related to the shrinkage of its habitat and its genetically homozygous condition.

As its population was always small and its habitat was fragmented and isolated from each other, there was a great deal of interbreeding. This led to a lowered level of successful breeding. In 1923, Brander wrote that 'The hunting leopard has now almost entirely disappeared from the Province without apparent reason. Rumours of their existence in parts of Berar, the Seoni Plateau, and Sangar still persist, and it is possible that one or two may still persist.' By the 1950s it was almost certainly extinct in India. Like the cheetah, many other animals may well disappear from our grassland ecosystems unless their residual habitat is preserved. Other predators such as wolves are rapidly becoming uncommon, and even the jackal and fox, which were once considered vermin, have disappeared from several areas where they were common up to the 1950s. The main predator of the grasslands is now the wolf. Beleaguered by shepherds, who persecute it persistently, this animal's existence is now seriousy threatened.

The leopards of the scrub jungle and thorn forests are seen wherever there are thickets for them to take cover. Due to

the reduction in their prey, they frequent places of human habitation, feeding on stray goats, dogs, and chickens. Wild cats, civets, foxes and jackals are the smaller predators of the scrubland. All these carnivores seem to be disappearing.

The most beautiful herbivore, and one that is especially adapted to the arid zone, is the blackbuck. This is the only true antelope found in India. It probably evolved on the Indian subcontinent itself several million years ago, for it is found nowhere else in the world. Related fossil forms have, however, been found in other parts of South East Asia, suggesting that it might have existed there in the past. The black-and-white coat of the male makes it a most striking animal, while the long spiral horns form a large V, adding to its overall magnificence. Once, huge herds of these agile, majestic animals were found all over the Deccan. Today they are scattered over a few small areas and the herds are small compared to those of the 1920s and 1930s. This is most certainly the result of a loss of habitat as well as poaching. The blackbuck can travel for a fairly long time at over 60 kilometres an hour, taking

Splashes of colour dot the grasslands in the flowering season.

long strides and bounding into the air. With the extinction of the cheetah, the blackbuck antelopes have few other natural predators that are large enough or fast enough to catch them. The wolf, with its ability to hunt in small family parties, can occasionally chase and corner them. In areas where there are no wolves left, humans are the only predators, and they have taken a great toll on this beautiful animal since Independence. Its population in the 1960s came crashing down. Though it has recovered in some areas, where it has now reached hyper-dense populations, the number of blackbuck today is far lower than it was a few decades ago.

The chinkara has a narrower ecological niche and is found wherever the plateau is covered by undulating hills and scrubland. Though much smaller than the blackbuck, it is lighter and even more graceful on the run. Chinkaras form smaller herds,

have always been less common than the blackbuck, and appear to be more frequently preyed upon by wolves.

Small mammals like hare, mice and rats scurry around busily in the grassland. As they have large populations, they require enormous quantities of food.

Various species of reptiles are commonly found on the plateau. The lizards vary from large monitors, two feet in length, to small creatures a few centimetres long. Some sitanas have beautifully coloured skin flaps on their throats, which they display during territorial skirmishes. Snakes find their homes in the crevices of rocks and in the cracks in the hard, dry ground.

Locusts, grasshoppers, beetles and many other insects abound in the open grassland. In terms of numbers, insects are the most abundant of all species in the grasslands.

All this terrestrial life is an attractive source of food for predator birds that were

once seen in large numbers. During the winter months one could see many of these beautiful birds sitting on the telephone poles in the grasslands. Evidently, with the persistent felling of the Acacia trees, the only other vantage place for these birds is the top of a pole to survey the area for prey. Raptors such as eagles, falcons, kestrels, sparrow hawks, merlins, harriers and kites move effortlessly through the air scanning the grasslands for prey, their individual hunting methods varying considerably. Some of them fly at a great height and stop to hover over a place where they can observe even a slight movement on the ground. Once they have spotted their prey, they swoop down rapidly, clawed feet extended to capture the prey and carry it off to a favourite vantage point. Others scan the more open country by flying close to the ground and make a rapid low dive for their prey.

Grasslands have a large number of flowering plants that form an important component of their ecosystem.

A bachelor herd of blackbuck. These males live together till one of them joins a mixed herd or becomes a breeding territorial male.

The semi-arid belt is also home to a large number of small birds. Several species of larks live here, each requiring a slight variation in the habitat often too subtle to decipher. The little brown dove and the ringdove both use this habitat. Plovers and lapwings use the grassland areas near water sources. The common and painted sandgrouse, which were once abundant species of the dry areas, are less common today. The Jerdons courser, considered extinct, was rediscovered a few years ago by Bharat Bhusan, a BNHS scientist. Its relative, the Indian courser, can still be found in small groups in the Deccan. This was also the favoured habitat of the floricans and bustards. The Deccan still has a few small breeding pockets of the great Indian bustard, but the florican is vanishing along with its threatened grassland habitat.

A few sanctuaries have now been created to preserve these arid landscapes. We know very little about how these systems should be managed to preserve their biological diversity. The present trend of irrigating these areas to develop farmland for intensive agriculture and planting trees in the grasslands that are not part of the ecosystem will, in the long term, produce a negative impact on the biodiversity of such specialized dry areas. These substituted landscapes are detrimental to the ecological balance of this ecosystem. Detailed studies are necessary before tampering with such a habitat, based on several intricate seasonal changes. If the plant species and the insects, reptiles, birds and mammals that have evolved within this ecosystem are to be preserved, new management techniques

need to be developed. Grassland sanctuaries must retain their natural structure. They should neither be planted with trees nor used as fodder development areas. Unfortunately grasslands and the sanctuaries in them are managed by the Forest Department personnel, who are primarily trained in growing timber and do not usually think in larger ecological terms. That the Forest Department is primarily a Wilderness Conservation Department is yet to be included in the thinking of most forest officials. It is only recently that they have begun to appreciate their role as major players in the preservation of biological diversity as a national asset.

A black-shouldered kite taking off from its perch in search of prey.

```
  1   2
    3
  4   5
```

A Dhangar shepherd with his daughter and flock of sheep. They migrate each year along a traditional route between the Deccan Plateau and the Ratnagiri Coast in Maharashtra.

The bright turquoise and orange-red flap of these grassland lizards, when open, acts as a warning to other lizards.

Munias are common grassland birds. They frequently clean each other's feathers.

Herd of blackbucks in the Drought Prone Area Project Plantation in which they live.

Blackbucks are known for speed and agility.

| State | Maharashtra | Zone | Deccan Peninsula |
|---|---|---|---|
| Area | 2.17 sq km | Ecosystem | Grassland |
| Year of Notification | 1980 | | |
| Visited | May, Jun, Dec 1986; Apr, Oct, Dec 1987; Jan, Mar, Nov 1989; Jun 1990; Jun–Jul 1993; Feb 1995; Aug–Sep. 1997; Oct 2003 and Nov 2003 | | |

A young research scholar walked through the thorny grasslands two decades ago. Her name was Kiran Asher and she was a student of St. Xavier's College, Mumbai. She had hardly ever been out of the city before. That was really the 'back of beyond' for her. But weekend after weekend she walked the same route in the hot, dry, drought-prone area. I had been visiting Rehekuri for a number of years and watched the blackbuck growing in number. My father had seen thousands of blackbuck in this area in the 1950s. I would be thrilled if I saw herds of 20 or 30. But as the numbers grew, so did the problems arising from crop damage. The Forest Department had asked me to look into this as I was a frequent visitor, and this led to my interest in looking at conflict issues between conservation and development in several other similar,

contentious situations. When I started studying this problem, Kiran was looking for a wildlife-related problem for her M.Sc. thesis. She had already approached several institutions. I was reluctant to make her do this as it was extremely difficult for a girl to work there in those days. Her tears at being refused made me relent.

The area she had to work in is an arid, degraded landscape that has been planted with Acacia, eucalyptus, neem and a few other tree species. The trees have not grown well ever since they were planted in the 1970s. Outside the Drought Prone Area Plantation (DPAP) the scene during this terrible drought year is pathetic. There is no grass left, cattle starve to death, the land thirsts for rain, people are desperate. In this landscape blackbuck from surrounding areas have aggregated to use the scarce resources of Rehekuri, a two

Blackbucks have adjusted to living in plantations.

A large mixed herd. They have three or four males and about 20 females. These have moved out to graze in a fallow field.

This fox occupied a tiny scooped-out depression in a rocky ledge for several years.

The only residual open grassland patch used by territorial male blackbuck.

square kilometre sanctuary in Maharashtra. There are over 250 of these agile antelopes using this tiny area as a refuge. They too find it difficult to survive, especially in the drought years. Their pelvic bones and ribs show that they are starving. They feed on the meagre grass in the sanctuary, browse on Acacia plants, and supplement their food with crops in 'good' years. Kiran is studying the way in which blackbucks use the landscape modified by human activities, their natural grassland habitat having all but vanished from the semi-arid Deccan Plateau region between Pune and Sholapur. At the end of a year we know much more about their habitat needs. We have a better understanding of how they form herds, the way in which they survive on their scant resources, and the extent of crop damage done by these animals on the agricultural holdings of the poor marginal farmers who live around the sanctuary. In 1985, the farmers frequently travelled all the way to Mumbai to agitate in front of the Mantralaya and sent letters to the Chief Minister to solve their problems. They complained bitterly about the serious crop damage by blackbuck. The work we did produced a set of management criteria and predicted that the blackbuck would retain their high density for a short period, then disperse—if aiiowed to do so—into other neighbouring DPAP plots that were being developed during this period. The Forest Department used to drive them out as soon as they went into their new plantations outside sanctuary limits. Once this was changed, the blackbuck did indeed disperse, and crop damage for individual farmers was reduced as our study had predicted. We also identified several other problems. Kiran reported that she suddenly found that the male territorial blackbuck had begun to chase females all over the sanctuary. When I went to investigate this strange occurrence, I discovered that the dung piles that form the territorial markers of the breeding males had disappeared. On making inquiries I was told that the Forest Department had begun to collect the blackbuck pellets as fertilizer for their nursery. The local Forest Official had even been complimented for this by his superiors. No one had realized what chaos this small change would induce

in the social structure of these animals. The males, without their territorial markers, were running amok all over the sanctuary. It took some time for them to re-establish their territories. Several males relocated their territories in neighbouring croplands! They were driven off again by the farmers.

Counting blackbuck was difficult in the plantation. I induced the late Dr SV Bhave to fly me in his beechcraft to see if I could get a better estimate. We flew along the Pune-Sholapur highway. For the first time I realized the spread of industry into the heartland of the Deccan Plateau. The warning signs of development were already there. Looking down, I thought of it as a good way to help poor farmers earn wages. I hardly could have imagined how rapidly this would grow to an unsustainable level of economic growth, one that would lead to drastic changes in the landscape.

We reached Bhigwan, the backwaters of the Ujani Lake, where I had a small WWF-sponsored project to look at the ecology of this incredible wetland. I 'navigated' Dr Bhave towards where I knew flamingoes fed in this vast expanse of water. He was so thrilled that he circled the area several times, photographing the flamingoes. We then turned northward towards Rehekuri and were promptly lost. I had to get him to backtrack to identify the road from Bhigwan to Rehekuri. When we reached the Sanctuary we were low on fuel and film. I realized it was difficult to make a count of the blackbucks and we returned to Pune. I could not afford to fund another sortie and gave up the idea.

Around this time I had a frantic call from Dehradun. WA Rodgers wanted to know if I knew of a 217 square kilometre sanctuary in Maharashtra for blackbuck called Deulgaon. 'Such a place does not exist,' I said. 'But the Forest Department says so...crackle, crackle....confirm.' I did: local conservation people know Deulgaon Sanctuary by the name of the neighbouring village of Rehekuri, and it has an area of only 2.17 square kilometres! Somewhere between the multiple levels of communication from

Rehekuri to Pune to Mumbai to Delhi and finally Dehradun, someone forgot to put in the decimal point. Alan's 217 square kilometre sanctuary had to be brought down to 2.17 square kilometre, changing all his wonderful statistical analysis.

Twenty years down the line, the dispersed population of blackbuck has grown substantially. A new and serious threat now looms over the blackbuck's dry horizon. Irrigation canals now traverse most of its semi-arid habitat, converting it into irrigated farmland. Sugarcane fields and sugar factories have suddenly sprung up out of nowhere. Another field scientist, Shamita Kumar, has taken on the task of trying to understand what will happen to the blackbuck. The future looks bleak. Her studies reveal that the blackbuck have had to move into the small residual hilly tracts, which are not irrigated. Their homeland has shrunk grossly. They are refugees aggregated into tiny fragments of the landscape that has as yet not been changed by modern agriculture. Can they survive? Only time can tell. But aspects that we have looked into since the mid-1980s, such as creating crop protection co-operatives and schemes, have only recently been accepted. In the Indian Board for Wildlife meeting, I was happy to hear a mention of this for the first time. Till recently people were recommending culling the blackbuck, which fortunately has never been accepted. There are alternatives. There is still hope for the blackbucks if we begin to understand their needs.

# GREAT INDIAN BUSTARD WILDLIFE SANCTUARY

NANAJ

| State | Maharashtra | Zone | Deccan Peninsula |
|---|---|---|---|
| Area | 8496.64 sq km | Ecosystem | Thorn Forest |
| Year of Notification | 1979 | Visited | 1984; May 1987; Jan 1989; Sep 1997; Jun, Sep 1998 |

Nanaj is a very small area about 40 kilometres from Sholapur. The flat land is covered with grass and is an old Drought Prone Area Project plantation. Though it is rocky and its soil poor, thanks to controlled cattle grazing over the last decade, parts of the area are now covered with a fairly thick growth of grass. Unfortunately, the tiny area cannot be expanded due to the surrounding agricultural lands and the presence of 'common' village grazing lands. These open areas are either being degraded and disappearing rapidly due to the spread of other forms of land use, or are being converted into plantations under Social Forestry programmes. A main road linking Sholapur with Baramati passes through the area. The Nanaj Sanctuary is in fact

a part of the larger Great Indian Bustard (GIB) Sanctuary, which constitutes about half of the area covered by sanctuaries and national parks in Maharashtra. The GIB Sanctuary was initially notified in 1979. Between 1981 and 1983, there was a sudden increase in bustards at Nanaj as the area was protected for the first time. This has been a Protected Area only in name as it includes enormous tracts of agricultural lands, villages and the city of Sholapur within it. BR Koppikar was Additional CCF and Director, Nature Conservation in Maharashtra in 1984 when Indira Gandhi asked for new Protected Areas to be established. The large unviable Great Indian Bustard Sanctuary, as the area has been called for the last 30

years, has led to serious people-wildlife conflicts. The issue is contentious because it is clear that adequate consideration for the real habitat needs of a bird like the bustard had not been adequately understood before its notification. In the 1970s, when Maharashtra wanted to expand its Protected Area network, I suggested to the Forest Department that a Protected Area should be made for the great Indian bustard's breeding areas. I had first seen and photographed this bird at Nanaj in 1981. In fact, very few people visited the area in those days, and the bustards would allow a car to drive up to them without fear. Today they are wary of people due to the large influx of tourists. The hoards of noisy tourists are

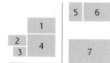

An unusually large herd of blackbuck at Nanaj.

A great Indian bustard flying low over the scrubland.

A bird of prey swoops towards its prey.

A magnificent sunset at Nanaj.

Clumps of Deccan Caralluma Gregarious (*Caralluma adscendens*), a succulent, leafless herb, are seen in drier regions. The putrid smell of the flowers attracts flies for pollination.

A large male blackbuck.

A majestic male bustard is the alpha male in the sanctuary.

now thankfully not allowed anywhere near them in the sanctuary. These are some of the unfortunate results of growing wildlife tourism. During the 1970s little was known about the range of these birds in the Sholapur District. The BNHS reported isolated great Indian bustard sightings from several talukas in Maharashtra. Thus a gigantic 7460 square kilometre Protected Area was created. While I objected to this as being unrealistic, there was no data that could be used to create a rational boundary for a Bustard Sanctuary. Over the next 30 years most areas of Maharashtra rapidly developed a colossal sugar industry and other sectors of small-scale industries that spread into most agricultural areas where canal water was available. The whole state was also electrified. Every taluka and every

Blackbucks at sunset.

small village wanted an industrial complex. While industrial growth spread through most of the rural areas of Sholapur and Pune Districts, talukas such as Shrigondha and Karjat were not allowed to develop industries as they were within the Great Indian Bustard Sanctuary. This led to local demonstrations for setting up industries around their villages. Being part of the Wildlife Advisory Board of Maharashtra, I was appointed as one of the members of a committee to look into the matter. The issues were complex, but it was obvious that this paper sanctuary could never become a reality and was totally unviable. Most of the area was primarily intensive agriculture, with no bustards, and the residual grasslands were small fragments of the extensive grasslands that had existed three decades ago. Some of the leftovers had been converted into plantations by the Forest Department. Bustards do not like plantations. We thus suggested a viable compromise by reducing the size of the Protected Area to 400 square kilometre in the Reserved Forest lands that had already been notified several decades earlier. While this would release the rest of the area for development, my fear was that local people would demand de-notification of other Protected Areas as a consequence. While the rationale used here is based on the fact that the initial notification was inadequately conceived, other lobbies may use this precedent for less justifiable reasons. During the recent past, the Supreme Court has ruled that the notification of Protected Areas must be completed all over the country. Teams of specialists have been selected to undertake a rationalization of contentious boundary issues. Much work has been done by these committees to rationalize Protected Area boundaries, so that the Forest Departments and District Administrators can finalize the notifications of our sanctuaries and national parks. As a Committee Member, I provided the information available to rationalize the Protected Areas and compensate for the loss of this area in the Protected Area Network by adding alternate grassland sites in the state. This has still not been implemented.

For several years these grassland areas around Sholapur have been known for

blackbuck, chinkara, wolf as well as the great Indian bustard. There appears to be an ecologically-related partnership between the blackbuck herds and the bustard, as some of these ponderous, stately birds are frequently seen following blackbucks. Perhaps the blackbuck, while walking through the grass, disturbs locusts and grasshoppers that the bustard can spot. It is rarely appreciated that bustards feed mainly on grassland insects. Thus the practice of planting trees in such areas has an adverse influence on their habitat.

The bustards come to Nanaj each year to nest. The dominant male struts about during the mating season, puffing out the white feathers on his neck. At Nanaj he has acquired a low hillock, which he patrols diligently, chasing away other males. His area is adjacent to the last patch of grassland that has not been planted with trees. But where can other males establish territories in this belt, now converted to extensive sugarcane fields and Forest Department plantations?

The blackbuck herds in Nanaj are dominated by the larger males and move their herds from one grassy area to another. If they feel threatened by the approach of a vehicle they quickly begin to move away. Several of them jump up and down in the same place as if their legs were made of springs. This form of jumping, called 'spronking', enables them to look around a wider area. If one animal begins to spronk, several others follow suit. It is an incredible sight to see them spronk and then take off in long leaps towards safety.

In this country, where human population pressure is incredibly high and land is used by human beings to the maximum limit, it has become extremely difficult to set aside large tracts of land for Nature without explaining the value of preserving these threatened ecosystems to local people. One cannot imagine having extensive grassland and thorn forest sanctuaries like those of East Africa here. An alternative strategy will have to be evolved, and even small patches should be set aside as semi-wilderness. These pockets of grasslands must protect a variety of rare and endemic grassland species that would at some point in time become the Noah's Arks of our grassland inhabitants.

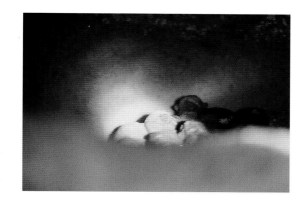

| 1 | 2 |
|---|---|
|   | 3 |
| 4 | 5 |
| 6 | |

1. A rainbow appears after the first drizzle of rain.

2. Wolf cubs in their den.

3. Blackbucks in Nanaj.

4. In the blackness of midnight a flash of quiet wings streaks through the sky as the nightjar flies across the stark landscape.

5. A female kestrel surveys the surrounding grasslands.

6. When rains arrive on the dry plains the frogs instantly begin to call.

# RANIBENNUR WILDLIFE SANCTUARY

RANIBENNUR

| State | Karnataka | Zone | Deccan Peninsula |
|---|---|---|---|
| Area | 119 sq km | Ecosystem | Grassland and Scrubland |
| Year of Notification | 1974 | Visited | May 1990 |

Never having been in Australia, I find it difficult to visualize its eucalyptus forests, but I imagine they must be quite similar to Ranibennur in Karnataka. This is a sanctuary in the Deccan Plateau that has been developed into a virtual woodland where no forests were ever located. It is a large plantation of eucalyptus and other planted species in an extensive tract of semi-arid grass and scrubland. The sanctuary has wild boar, blackbuck, leopard, barking deer and great Indian bustards. It is indeed difficult to identify the conservation objectives of such an area. Does it make sense to protect a plantation of exotic trees? Ranibennur is an example of a place preserved not for its ecosystem values but to protect its population of wild mammals that can be easily seen by visitors. It is by no means a biologically 'natural' area. It is an example of some of the unusual aspects that must be dealt with in trying to create a set of clearly defined objectives for Protected Areas in India. Ideally, a Protected Area must protect both a wilderness ecosystem and its naturally occurring species diversity. The changed patterns of land and resource use, however, in our overpopulated nation make it essential to develop strategies to save whatever is left that is conservable. Unfortunately such conditions become the root cause of people-wildlife conflict issues. These controversies have no easy solutions.

A grassland that was heavily planted with eucalyptus has now been made into a sanctuary in Karnataka.

A great Indian bustard in flight. Only a few are seen in the sanctuary.

# BANNERGHATTA NATIONAL PARK
BANNERGHATTA

| State | Karnataka | Zone | Deccan Peninsula |
|---|---|---|---|
| Area | 104.27 sq km | Ecosystem | Scrub Forest |
| Date of Notification | 1974 | Visited | Oct 1998 |

A few kilometres outside the spreading city of Bangalore, there is a small group of low hills that are still covered with patches of scrubland and tree cover. Its unique landscape is dominated by formations of giant rocks. They have been smoothed over through eons of weathering by wind and rain, and sculpted into nearly freestanding shapes. As one drives along a small track into the hills, one begins to appreciate the biological value of a scrubland. It is full of bird life flitting through the shrubs. The ground is covered with a wide range of grasses and herbaceous plants. Flowers dot the ground cover with brilliant colours.

There are several ancient stone relics made by a bygone culture in the Protected Area. These simple rock structures of various shapes and sizes remind one of the fact that this area has been used by humankind for hundreds of years. But the utilization of this area by local people, static for many generations, is now undergoing rapid changes. The city of Bangalore is spreading towards this ancient landscape. The 'sanctuary' status will save this area, but in the near future, all the surrounding land will become an urban concrete jungle. Bangalore will inevitably spread around the borders of this sanctuary, degrade the ecosystem and alter its biological diversity. Bannerghatta will become an island amidst the developing city.

It was reported in the past that Bannerghatta was plagued by leases held for quarrying even inside the Protected Area, leading to changes in elephant movements and increasing people-elephant conflicts. In 1999, there were ten instances in which local people living around the Protected Area electrocuted or shot straying elephants.

In March 2001, *The Times of India* reported that the area was threatened due to mining. This led to a controversy between the Forest Department and the Mines and Geology Departments for having provided mining lease for black granite for a period of ten years. With the new rules on Ecologically Sensitive Zones declared by the MoEF, this can be stopped by using the Environment Protection Act even outside the boundary of the Protected Area.

The rocky outcrop in the distance is the habitat of several plant species that grow only on exposed rocks.

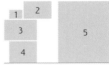

Ground flora.

A special microhabitat for plants adapted to grow on rocks with very little soil.

*Nala* courses form a habitat in semi-arid forests.

A formation of rocks shows that the area was used by man in ancient times.

The colour and structure of flowers are among nature's most fascinating features.

View from Bore Ghat, which is now called Bhore Ghat—Grindlay (1830).

# The Forests of the Western Ghats

FORESTS WESTERN GHATS

his range of ancient hills that runs parallel to the western coast of India forms several ecological regions depending upon the altitude, rainfall and soil characteristics. The vegetation varies between the western escarpment, the crest with its lateritic plateaus and the drier eastern slopes. In a few areas that are relatively undisturbed, the crest line has isolated patches of unique tropical evergreen forest with open short grassland. These forests are now severely fragmented in the northern part of the range, while in the south they still cover several larger stretches. The western slopes have a more moist vegetation pattern, whereas on the eastern side, drier vegetation merges into the scrubland of the Deccan. Offshoots, such as the Nilgiri Annamalais and the Annamalais in south India, form corridors between the Western and Eastern Ghats. The southern ranges have a higher rainfall, leading to some of the most lush evergreen forest tracts in the country. In undisturbed locations the forest has giant trees. As

A tree frog peers from its leafy hiding place.

The forests of the Western Ghats consist of evergreen, semi-evergreen and deciduous forests. There are also important specialized microhabitats such as plateau tops with a large number of endemic herbs and waterfalls which support water-tolerant species.

the soil depth is generally poor, these develop great buttress roots as support. The undergrowth, especially along the forest edges, is dense and consists of a wide diversity of shrubs, palms and ferns. Huge climbers trail from the branches of the trees. The canopy is totally closed, so that even in the afternoons, only small specks of light filter through to the ground. While the trees are covered with orchids and ferns, in extremely dense areas there is very little undergrowth, as little light penetrates to the forest floor.

Twenty years ago the forests of the Western Ghats were much thicker than they are today. Their continuity is rapidly being destroyed by development projects such as dams, tea and coffee plantations, roads and growing settlements. The residual forests have become islands of forest in a matrix of degraded bald hills, with the naturalness and species diversity of plants decreasing as the fragments become smaller and more isolated.

In several areas, the high temperature and the torrential monsoons that strike the crest of the ranges have, over millions of years, washed away the soil. This leaching process has led to the formation of a hard acidic layer of laterite that forms flat, rocky plateaus. These are covered with grasses and herbs, several of which are highly endemic to these microhabitats. These plants may occur as very small isolated patches, and are as important for conservation as the lush evergreen forests that surround them. Some of these areas, such as Mahabaleshwar, Panchgani and Ooty, have become hill resorts with thousands of visitors each year. With the increasing tourism and housing development, these hill resorts may soon become completely devoid of their natural vegetation.

The Western Ghats constitute five per cent of India's landmass. However, this small part of India is home to 33 per cent of its mammals with 12 per cent being endemic. The Ghats have 40 per cent of India's birdlife of which four per cent are endemic. It has 50 per cent of India's reptiles of which 50 per cent are endemic to the region. A phenomenal 60 per cent of the amphibians of India are found in the Ghats of which over

Duke's Nose seen from the Mumbai-Pune highway. Below it lies the valley where Father Santapau identified many rare species.

Ground flora on a plateau top in the Western Ghats.

75 per cent are endemic to the Ghats alone! About 40 per cent of freshwater fish are located in the streams and small rivers emanating from the Ghats. This enormous diversity and endemism places the Western Ghats at the global level among some of the most highly valued hotspots of diversity. Its plant life is equally diverse and forms a mosaic of habitat types with distinctive plant communities which change on the western slopes, crest line and eastern slopes. They also change from the north near the Dangs and gradually show alterations in their trees, shrubs, climbers and ground flora through Maharashtra, Karnataka and finally, Kerala. The northern sector is primarily semi-evergreen, while the southern Sholas are primarily evergreen. The ecosystem diversity is thus phenomenal.

Between 1920 and 1980 estimates have shown that the forest cover loss was around 40 per cent. This led to the formation of a number of forest patches. Over time, as each patch shrank, the isolation between patches gradually increased such that several species are now unable to cross from one isolated patch to another.

The dominant tree of the forests of the drier eastern slopes is teak, much of it planted. The sub-tropical broadleaved evergreen forests seen in the northern parts of the Ghats, such as Bhimashankar, Mahabaleshwar, Koyna, Chandoli and Radhanagari, are unique, relict forest ecosystems. In many of these forests, the trees are short, the trunks gnarled and their branches are twisted into unruly and sometimes grotesque shapes. The forest is festooned with moss and lichens, and is rich in ferns and orchids. A unique microhabitat in this part of the Ghats are treeless flat lateritic plateau tops. These form a specialized habitat of monsoonal ground flora of high diversity and endemism that needs urgent protection. The southern part of the Western Ghats has diverse and localized tree communities not found elsewhere in the world. Though less disturbed than those in the northern part, tea and coffee plantations have now spread over large sectors of this magnificent ecosystem.

These diverse vegetation patterns include a variety of types, such as Bridelia, Syzygium, Ficus and Terminalia. Another form has Memecylon-Syzygium-Actinodaphne as dominant trees. There are areas with a Persea-Holigarna-Diospyros forest type. The extremely lush green Dipterocarp forests are called 'Shola' forests and are characterized by a climate in which the wet season is very long and the monsoon extremely heavy. Out of 29 Dipterocarp species found in India, 13 are located only in the Western Ghats. These patches, which are thick with undergrowth and clothed with moss, ferns and lichen, have several

Madeo Kolis are hill folk who fish in the streams and rivers that flow out of the Western Ghats. They make bunds in the *nalas* and use complex traps made of cane to catch fish.

Katkari tribals fishing in a torrent at the onset of the monsoons in the Western Ghats.

*Smithia.*

Berries in the undergrowth.

Several plant species are endemic or rare in the Western Ghats. They have varied methods of seed dispersal.

Pods of *Sterculia guttata* burst open to release a large number of seeds.

*Phyllocephalum tenue.* Several species in the undergrowth have very small seeds.

*Abrus* seeds are used to make various artifacts

Plants that flower in the monsoon season bloom for a very brief period.

Many plant species in the Western Ghats have short flowering periods that follow each other.

*Impatiens* grows on moist rocky surfaces .

*Argyreia cuneata.*

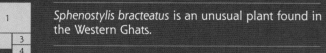

1  Sphenostylis bracteatus is an unusual plant found in the Western Ghats.

2  3
   4

Argyreia.

Exacum lawii.

Pandanus.

 1
2 3

*Smithia racemosa.*

*Viscum species.*

*Rotala floribunda.*

giant lianas. The forests lie along the hill and alternate with open grassland.

These evergreen forests are not only rich in species but highly fragile in nature. Once disturbed, they do not regain their original glory. Though there are a large number of Protected Areas, only a few have significantly large patches of undisturbed evergreen vegetation. Other Protected Areas in this sector are mainly semi-evergreen and moist deciduous. In the southern sector several Protected Areas have a complement of evergreen vegetation. The best known are in the Nilgiri, Annamalai and Agasthamalai ranges. Well preserved areas include Protected Areas such as Topslip, Silent Valley and Munnar.

In the northern part of the Western Ghats the forests are so highly fragmented that their wildlife has been greatly depleted. One now comes across only the more adaptable wild boar, a few sambar and barking deer. Animals like the tiger and the bison that once lived here have become scarce or have disappeared altogether. Only a few gaurs survive in sanctuaries of the northern sector of the Ghats such as Koyna, Chandoli and Radhanagari. Viable populations of gaurs are now found only in sanctuaries south of Goa. During the last five years species such as the tiger and the elephant that have not been seen in the northern sector of the Ghats have suddenly reappeared and are moving northwards, though in small numbers.

The tiger disappeared many years ago from most areas. The more adaptable leopards, however, are still to be found. In the southern part of the Ghats where the forests are much thicker, there is a fair population of sambar, wild boar, bison, tiger, leopard, dhole and other animals. Larger patches of forest in the south have the best populations of wild elephant.

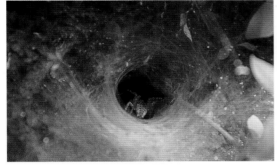

| 1 | | 3 | 4 |
|---|---|---|---|
| 2 | | 5 6 | 7 |
| | | | 8 |

Ferns on a moist tree in the Western Ghats.

The streams that originate in the forest of the Western Ghats feed the rivers of the Deccan Plateau.

There is still a ray of hope for conserving the biodiversity of the Western Ghats.

The jewel bug beetle.

A tunnel web spider.

Recently hatched young beetles.

It is observed that butterflies which migrate in large numbers aggregate at the same spot year after year.

This small tree frog can camouflage itself superbly.

A cascade of water flowing down a nala course in the Western Ghats.

Ground orchid.

The red leaves indicate new growth in the forest.

The shrub layer in the undergrowth is a key food resource for animals and birds.

Flowers opening to the morning light.

A climber with brightly coloured berries.

There are several species of squirrels in the Western Ghats. The Malabar giant squirrel, a highly arboreal species, is found only in the thicker undisturbed tracts of forest and is becoming increasingly rare. It has several colour variations from the northern part of the Ghats to the southern part of its distribution, varying from a light orange-brown in the north, to a dark maroon, and finally, to nearly black in the south. It is over two feet long and has a long bushy tail. Its presence is often better heard than seen, as it is frequently shy and elusive. In better protected patches of forest that have a continuous canopy it can be seen jumping from one high branch to another.

There are an estimated 16 species of endemic birds in the southern Western Ghats and its offshoots. The Nilgiri laughing thrush is one of the rarest birds in the country and is endemic to a small

part of the Nilgiris. SACON scientist Lalitha Vijayan estimates their population to be only around 1800 birds. There are 197 reptiles in the Western Ghats of which 50 per cent are endemic. There are no estimates about the rate of loss of these cryptic species. It is obvious that highly arboreal species will be maximally affected by habitat fragmentation. Thus species such as the lion-tailed macaque, the Nilgiri langur and the various sub-species of giant squirrel have been seriously affected.

The high species diversity of flora and fauna and variations in ecosystem diversity have given this area the status of a globally accepted hotspot of biological diversity. The Protected Areas of this region are thus of great conservation significance.

## PROTECTED AREAS OF THE NORTHERN SECTOR

These lie along the crestline and in the adjacent coastal areas of Gujarat, Maharashtra and Goa. They are of great importance as the forests of this sector are under immense pressure due to the rapid economic development of Maharashtra and the resulting urban sector that is pushing into the Ghats.

| | 1 | | 5 |
|---|---|---|---|
| | | | 6 |
| 2 | 3 | 4 | 7 |

A wild banana plant.

*Arisaema* species.

Moss on a moist tree trunk.

*Striga* grows as a root parasite.

Flowers of *Stobilanthus* also known as *karvi*. It flowers profusely only once in every seven years.

*Arisaema tortuosum*.

*Senecio* species (*hiwali-sonki*).

# BHIMASHANKAR WILDLIFE SANCTUARY

| State | Maharashtra | Zone | Western Ghats |
|---|---|---|---|
| Area | 130.78 sq km | Ecosystem | Evergreen Forest |
| Year of Notification | 1985 | Visited | Apr 1950, Oct 1981, Sep 1990 |

The forest in Bhimashankar has been preserved because it has several sacred groves.

The wind rushing through the trees is the only sound, until a cicada begins to screech in some dark corner. Soon others begin to rend the air with their loud harsh screech and the forest resounds deafeningly with the noise. Gradually the din dies down and a deep quiet prevails again. Suddenly there is a fluttering among the leafy branches of nearby trees and the calls of various birds are heard. A feeding party composed of several species of hill birds arrives. Tiny rustlings in the undergrowth announce the presence of warblers and babblers, ground hunting birds that scatter the detritus on the forest floor, looking for insects. A woodpecker knocks on the tree trunk, expelling insects. Frugivorous birds like barbets, pigeons and doves hop from branch to branch among the fruiting trees, dropping uneaten fruit and seed on the forest floor where they are picked up by ground feeders. Flower peckers and sunbirds flit from one blossom to another in rapid succession. Drongos and flycatchers hunt flying insects. The forest is alive with bird life until, as suddenly as they arrived on the scene, they depart to another part of the forest. Such gregarious feeding parties are a common occurrence, each bird fitting into its own ecological niche to find its own specialized source of food. The whole group acts like hungry people being fed in a well-organized 'community kitchen'.

The forests in the sanctuary of Bhimashankar have been preserved by local sentiments. The tribal people have ancient shrines in the hills long venerated by their forefathers. In these devrais or sacred groves survives an old growth of vegetation that has disappeared from other areas. Great trees covered with giant lianas tower over the shrines. The shrine frequently comprises a few boulders with

a low stone surround. The people who venerate it have complex rituals that permit or deny access to the resources of the grove, preventing overuse of the resources within it. Thus a form of sustainable extraction has evolved over time, using chance as a tool to limit extraction. For instance, the ritual may require a stone to be placed on the deity after a pooja and access to removal of forest produce may depend on the side on which the stone falls. The ceremony cannot be repeated for a specified length of time, thus limiting the extraction process. Unfortunately, such traditions are rapidly being wiped out. New values will eventually lead to the destruction of these forested islands, which are the haunts of the ancient gods of the tribal people of the Western Ghats.

In the 1950s Bhimashanker was a tiny village visited by a few pilgrims only on specific occasions. The road was little better

than a cart-track. On my first visit in April 1950, when I was 7, we met Dr Salim Ali walking down from the dak bungalow. We sat on the old verandah, Salim Ali making it a point to ask me, the only youngster in the group, what I had seen in the forest. An animated discussion followed. Several dead giant squirrel skins were being treated on the verandah. I cannot remember now who was working on the giant squirrels—it could have been Humayun Abdulali. I had never seen a Malabar giant squirrel and seeing dead ones saddened me immensely. My father tried to explain that this was scientific work and very important. But I was unwilling to accept that these beautiful skins taken from a living creature were of any importance to the science that I studied in school. I think I did not see a live squirrel on that trip. Perhaps all the squirrels around the bungalow were strung up in the guest house! I guess

for the wildlife and are now being seriously polluted at their sources.

In the past half century, the changes I have witnessed in this sanctuary have been unimaginable. Can we return these forests to their deities that the village folk have venerated for generations? Or will the march of progress destroy the very resources that led to their being held sacred?

they are in the BNHS collection now. But the forest experience was fabulous. The place was incredibly isolated; one rarely met anyone for hours when walking through the forest paths. There was evidence of a large number of sambar, barking deer and wild boar around every waterhole. The water was crystal clear.

The sanctuary has seen many changes since then. Soon after it was notified, a social activist claimed that leopards had increased and were killing cattle. An NGO instigated local people to pull

down the sanctuary board and a major conflict between the Forest Department and local people ensued. It was difficult to convince people that notifying a sanctuary cannot in a brief period lead to a sudden increase in leopards!

The growth of both pilgrims and tourists has led to serious problems with garbage. Water resources are stretched and the once crystal-like trickles of water in the forest, especially around the pilgrimage area, are now highly polluted. I got one of my M.Sc. students, Nitin Pawar, to look into this all-important aspect of water resources in the sanctuary. He discovered that deep in the forest illicit distilleries have been set up along the nalas. These streams are a critically important resource

| | 1 | |
| 2 | 3 | |

An approaching thundershower from the western escarpment in the early monsoon.

This variation in colour of the Malabar giant squirrel is found from Bhimashankar to Koyna in the Western Ghats.

A fairy bluebird.

# MULSHI/RAJMACHI WILDLIFE SANCTUARY

RAJMACHI AND MULSHI

| | | | |
|---|---|---|---|
| State | Maharashtra | Zone | Western Ghats |
| Area | 100 sq km each | Ecosystem | Semi-evergreen Forest |
| Year of Notification | Proposed | | |
| Visited | Sep, Nov 1993; Feb, Apr, Jul, Oct 1996; Jun 1997; 1998; 2001; Nov, Dec 2002; Jun 2003; Feb 2004; Dec 2005; Jan, Feb 2006 | | |

The cascade above and the pool below are habitats for different aquatic species.

This area has been proposed as a potential sanctuary for a long time. A large number of conservationists and botanists have felt that the area should be named after Father Santapau, a renowned botanist who worked in this area up to the 1960s. He began as a college botany teacher and retired as the Director of the Botanical Survey of India. The St. Xavier's School has a bungalow between Lonavla and Khandala on the old Bombay-Pune highway. Father Santapau was a frequent visitor and made many field trips into the adjacent valley where he first identified a large number of uncommon and threatened plants. The sanctuary would not only serve the purpose of commemorating the name of this great scientist, but also conserve a unique botanical entity in the Ghats and form an important forest corridor between Bhimashankar in the north and Koyna in the south.

Professor Gammie of the Botany and Agriculture Department, College of Science, Pune, wrote a note on the trees and shrubs of the Lonavla and Karla groves in the JBNHS, Volume 15. In it he describes five sacred groves, the largest in Lonavla at the head of the Bhor Ghat. He describes this as a broad belt of large trees with many enormous climbers. The second area was a small wood to the north near the Tower of Silence with *Annodendron* and *Gnetum*. The third was a small wood to the south of no special interest. The fourth is a larger wood on a small conical hill near the railway line halfway between Lonavla to Karla, where he describes the trees as literally festooned with large climbers. The fifth was a wood at Karla between the railway station and the cave temple. He says that in many respects this was the most interesting of all. Gammie points out that the greater proportion of trees and shrubs here belong to the Konkan flora. While the first three of the sacred groves he describes are in the Ghats, the fourth and the fifth are on isolated mounds.

Father Santapau (1950) writes that he searched Khandala for orchids such as *Aerides crispum* and *Aerides maculosum*, noting that till a few years before the date of writing there would be over 20 such orchids on practically every tree. But these had rapidly vanished. He also writes how Charles McCann had shown him a place with *Isoetes coromandeina*, which grew there in profusion. Shortly thereafter, these plants disappeared entirely. The *Platantheria susannae*, Susan's orchid, what is now referred to as nun's orchid or the Queen of Khandala, was seen by him occasionally in the 1950s, but McCann had observed these twenty-five years earlier in large numbers in Khandala, especially on Bhoma Hill and Echo Point. He ascribes its disappearance to repeated collection as it is very beautiful and has a lovely scent. He writes, 'Last year I did not see a single specimen in Khandala of the once common orchid Platantheria.'

I myself was lucky in the 1970s and saw one near the same area, just 10 metres from the edge of the Mumbai-Pune highway where the road begins to descend down the escarpment. I photographed it as I breathed in its heavenly fragrance. Alas, this tract of forest has vanished due to

the road widening for the expressway. We drive today over the graves of countless plant species of the Western Ghats.

The landscape of this area was spectacular until a few years ago. On one side of the valley the forest was broken only by a set of hydroelectric pipes; on the other, the old Railway Bridge blended into the rocks of the narrow Bombay-Pune highway. The escarpment was dominated by a towering rock pinnacle referred to as Duke's Nose. Now the Mumbai-Pune Expressway has damaged the area beyond repair. Enormous quantities of rock and road debris have been pushed over the side of the newly widened expressway during construction. Tunnels meant to

The forest is responsible for keeping some of the streams perennial.

Typical stunted evergreen vegetation seen in the northern part of the Western Ghats.

A typical forest edge forming an ecotone.

The Curcuma is used during the Gauri festival before Ganesh Chaturthi.

A translucent fragile flower in the undergrowth.

prevent the cutting of large wedges from hillside have not been executed carefully, and rock and debris that will take decades for plants to re-colonize remain on either side of them. The proposed sanctuary was to include this important valley. Though the Wildlife Advisory Board of Maharashtra accepted that it should be created, the need to widen the highway, putting in a number of relief lanes to smooth traffic and a new major six-lane expressway, has all but destroyed what is left of this superb area. While it was agreed that the two sanctuaries would be notified to mitigate the disastrous effects of this expressway, nothing has been done to protect regional biodiversity since the expressway was commissioned.

Neighbouring Ambavane and Mulshi, another important crestline forest tract, have felt the impact of the development plans of the Pune region, which include a 'tourist city' around the Mulshi Lake. The building of a large number of tourist facilities, holiday resorts and farmhouses is increasingly leading to a serious loss of the area's valuable biological diversity. Sahara built an enormous complex by bulldozing a large tract of land and deforesting the area of its natural vegetation, and planted species of trees that are not indigenous to the area around its giant residential complex. These development activities are likely to have a serious impact on the only viable corridor between existing Protected Areas of the bio-rich hotspots of the Western Ghats in this region.

In the early 1970s, the hillslopes of the catchment areas of the hydroelectric dams of the Tata Electric Company were planted with exotic trees—eucalyptus, subabul (*Leucina leucocephala*), and *Acacia auriculiformis*—in thousands each year by the Forest Department and the Tata Electric Company. In 1991 I was requested to join Tata Electric Company's Afforestation Committee. I studied the plant community and wildlife values of their catchments at Andhra Lake, Shirowata Lake, Walvan Lake and Mulshi Lake with a large number of young field scientists who helped me in

collecting field data. We looked at plant communities and the bird and insect diversity in vegetation types of varying degrees of degradation. This data was used by the Tata Electric Company to reorient its plantation strategy. A nursery of local trees, shrubs and climbers was established. SN Ogale, who is a fisheries expert and has bred the highly endangered mahseer, took a keen interest in this and a large tract of land below Walvan Dam was afforested with these species. Within ten years the trees had grown to a height of five metres and several began flowering and fruiting. The number of insects and birds increased substantially in this kilometre-long stretch. Unfortunately this excellent eco-restoration programme had to be destroyed to strengthen the 100-year-old dam! However, the catchments are in much better ecological health than most of the other areas in this part of the Western Ghats. There is also increasing support for these pro-conservation actions at the local level, fostered through a School Environment Education Programme for the local village schools funded by the Tata Electric Company and run

by the Bharati Vidyapeeth Institute of Environment Education and Research, Pune. This outreach programme has used schoolteachers and students to create a local pro-conservation action movement. Today, these school children know the plants, birds and insects of their area. They prepare maps of the resource areas of their villages and develop conservation programs with the help of trained schoolteachers and have begun to appreciate the biodiversity of the 40 sacred groves in the Mulshi region. BVIEER students and staff have collected information on the folklore of these groves and documented their biodiversity values. School students are taken to the groves to

| 1 | | 3 |
|---|---|---|
| 2 | | |
| | 4 | 5 |

Flowering plants are a very diverse group of species and add great biological richness to the proposed Protected Areas of the Western Ghats.

The varied plant life of this region gives it high priority for conservation.

This coil of a liana was in a sacred grove.

This brilliant red fungus grows only in a few locations in this proposed sanctuary.

A velvety fungus that grows under specific habitat conditions.

learn about the structure and functions of these undisturbed forests. All this has led to an increasing appreciation of the value of conserving the unique features of these forests at the local level. A conservation movement is beginning to emerge from interactions between the local people, a sensitive industry and a university environment department at the BVIEER. It has been a highly rewarding partnership.

Unfortunately the regional development plans for Pune have placed this sector as a tourism development zone. The rapid urbanization of the fringe of Pune city in the Mulshi Taluka has led to a land grab phenomenon of an unprecedented nature. In most parts around the Mulshi Lake, local people have parted with their agricultural lands to speculators who picked up the land at a pittance in the 1990s. By 2005 around several villages as much as 80 to 90 per cent of the land had been sold off by local villagers to rich urban individuals. If the impact of land use changes is to be prevented, this area must be rapidly notified as a Protected Area.

| | |
|---|---|
| | 1 |
| 2 | 3 |
| 6 | 4 |
| | 5 |

Bracket fungi.

Bracket fungi.

Amphibia include frogs and toads which are voracious insectivorous animals.

A colony of beetles in the detritus.

Species that live in colonies create the most complex homes. This ant colony is high up in a tree.

A tree frog flattens itself out so perfectly that it is difficult to spot.

A ray of sunlight illuminates the orbweb spider's web.

This little girl growing up in the forest has an inborn love for the flowers around her.

The shrine is one of the 40 sacred groves in the proposed sanctuary. Many of these *deorais* are rich in species and contain very ancient trees.

A Katkari settlement at the edge of the forest in the outskirts of the proposed sanctuary.

Duke's Nose where Father Santapau did most of his research.

# KOYNA WILDLIFE SANCTUARY

KOYNA

| State | Maharashtra | Zone | Western Ghats |
|---|---|---|---|
| Area | 423.55 sq km | Ecosystem | Evergreen Forest |
| Year of Notification | 1985 | Visited | Nov 1984, Dec 1986, 2000 |

kept the memories of this superb forest vividly alive for me over the next several days. A fitting start to an important sanctuary which was yet to be born!

Like Koyna, several other Protected Areas owe their existence to the initiatives of individual forest officials who went out of their way to help create a wildlife sanctuary or national park. Doing this involves much more work for them and creates problems that have to be solved even after the area has been notified.

Sightings wildlife in Koyna are not frequent, but even today there are reports of tiger and gaur and the area has a large bird population. We know too little about the insects, amphibia and reptiles of this forest. Documenting and studying major wildlife usually leaves out these important parts of the web of life of the forest ecosystem. Koyna is the only long north-south oriented lake created by a dam and its ability to act as a conservation area at the regional level is thus unique in the Western Ghats. This long stretch of forest that has a north-south orientation is of greater importance since, with the adverse effects of global warming, species adapted

to southern sectors of the Ghats must move northwards to be able to survive in the long term. Thus corridors of forests that have a north-south orientation could turn out to be an important aspect of protecting biodiversity as global warming and serious climate changes begin to affect ecosystems.

Along the eastern edge of the Protected Area lies a series of plateau tops, the largest being the Kas plateau. These areas, of great biological significance for their endemic plant life, are now being threatened by the proposed development of a new tourist township to lessen the tourist load in adjacent Mahabaleshwar. The plateau has also been used for giant wind farms. The disturbance caused could have a serious impact on the floral diversity of these plateaus.

Koyna, like several of our other Protected Areas in the Western Ghats, is situated around a hydel project. The forests of the western bank are fairly intact, while those of the eastern bank are patchy and degraded. Several years ago the District Forest Officer of Satara, Shri Walke, took me on a boat trip to help identify the boundaries of this sanctuary that was to lead to the official notification of this area. We walked through several patches of untouched forests infested with a large number of insects. The severe itching of bites from jungle ticks

The forests of Koyna have evergreen vegetation with a high diversity of trees, shrubs, climbers, epiphytes and ground flora.

*Ixora nigricans.*

# CHANDOLI WILDLIFE SANCTUARY
CHANDOLI

| State | Maharashtra | Zone | Western Ghats |
|---|---|---|---|
| Area | 308.97 sq km | Ecosystem | Evergreen Forest |
| Year of Notification | 1985 | Visited | Dec 1985 |

Most dam sites in the Western Ghats were built in areas where human habitation was in the form of small hamlets, and it was an easy matter, however insensitive, at that time to move people out of their homes. These were remote areas where development processes such as roads, electrification, etc. had not reached the wilderness. Developing a dam site includes providing new motorized access to such areas so that large amounts of building material can be brought in, for creating an infrastructure during its construction. Unfortunately these roads give access to illegal forest extraction, increase the size of settlements from in-migration of people and allow a host of other 'development' activities that destroy the area's species-richness and ecosystem diversity.

It is during construction itself that the surrounding forest begins to disappear, as is clearly evident at Chandoli. As one walks up from the dam site along the edge of the lake, the recently degraded forest suddenly changes to the less impacted evergreen forests that once covered these hill slopes. The contrast is striking. The forest canopy in Chandoli's less disturbed areas is close to 100 per cent. It is dark under the canopy even at midday. The forest floor is covered with thick detritus of leaf material full of a myriad of insect life. Fungi of various types grow in the detritus and on the trunks of trees. *Nala* courses and small hollows are full of ferns and the exposed rocks are covered with moss and bryophytes. The tree trunks covered with moss and ferns characterize this stunted forest that is typical of the crest line forests of this part of the bio-rich Western Ghats.

Though Chandoli has excellent forests, its population of mammals is small.

The forest is fragmented by old cultivation sites.

Fungi range from a miniscule size to large fan-like projections. Their favourite growing sites are on dead wood.

After a profuse flowering the *karvi* plants die. The great quantity of seeds produced germinate into thousands of seedlings.

| State | Maharashtra | Zone | Western Ghats |
|---|---|---|---|
| Area | 351.16 sq km | Ecosystem | Evergreen Forest |
| Year of Notification | 1958 | Visited | Nov 1981; Jan 1983; 1984; Jan, May 1991; Jun 1998 |

I have made several visits to this incredibly beautiful sanctuary since 1981. Its forest has always enchanted me. I recall moments of intense pleasure at witnessing a Malabar whistling thrush call out on a misty morning, the breeding display of a shama, the flight of an Atlas moth in the headlamp of the car, the twinkling of fireflies on a dark night, the bright red and black of a male lizard courting a female, the broken wing display of a nightjar, several fascinating encounters with gaur and an exciting experience with a leopard. While each of these memories is coupled with an event, the whole ambience of this evergreen forest leaves behind a delightful sense of the matrix in which these events have occurred. The moss-covered trees with sparkling dewdrops, the hillsides covered with the violet blue of flowering *karvi*. All these memories have a sense of timelessness.

This sanctuary was once the shooting reserve of the Maharajas of Kolhapur and was famed for its gaur. The undisturbed forests cover the very steep slopes of the Western Ghats, and overlook an old dam. Unfortunately, mining is an ever-present threat to this area. Manganese is mined on the edge of the sanctuary and the movement of people and trucks, the dust, and the removal of ground cover have all had disastrous effects on this precious area.

The evergreen tree cover has a continuous canopy and the thick undergrowth is impenetrable even in summer. This lush vegetation creates an ideal habitat for gaur. However, due to their shy nature, their numbers have not been accurately determined. They remain hidden in the thick forest and only emerge onto a large grass covered plateau top at dusk to drink water from a small tank. The little forest clearings with edges of thick *Strobilanthus*, locally known as *Karvi*, are the bison's favorite

haunts. The forest also has a small population of sambar and barking deer. The hill birds of the Sahyadris are better heard than seen. One thus has to learn to identify birdcalls. This was where I realized the need for creating a set of birdcall cassettes, which I finally made for the BNHS many years later. These bird species are difficult to watch in any evergreen forest as they reside in the interiors. Among the several spectacular species are the paradise flycatcher, the shama and the spurfowl. One of the frequently seen raptors in the hills is the crested-serpent eagle, while over the lake the osprey can be observed catching fish.

I will always recall my first visit to Radhanagari with great pleasure. Few people then visited this superb area. It was a cold November morning in 1981. We climbed up into the hills on the very rough jeep track and had hardly entered the forest when up ahead we saw a pair of jackals ambling along the road. At the approach of our jeep both disappeared into the forest on opposite sides of the

road. Suddenly one of them seemed to decide it had taken a wrong turn and scurried across the road to join its mate. Our Forest Guard said that seeing a pair of jackals was a lucky sign, which indeed it must have been, as we saw several animals and birds during the course of the day.

In those days, the road on the steep gradients was terrible. On rounding a sharp turn we had a face-to-face encounter with a huge gaur. It was standing on the road, its massive rump towards us, a string of *karvi* leaves dangling from its mouth, switching its tail to and fro to ward off the flies that are a perpetual nuisance for this animal. Unhurriedly, as if unaware of us, it moved into the forest. Further up the track there was a herd of several females with a young calf. We saw 13 gaurs as we worked our way up to the plateau, in my small Standard Herald. The forest ranger with me was terrified during the bumpy ride and constantly wanted to return.

| | 2 | 3 |
|1| 4 | |
| | 5 | 6 |

The maharajas developed this lake to supply water to Kolhapur. The surrounding forests formed their shooting reserve. It is now the Radhanagari Wildlife Sanctuary, one of the most important Protected Areas in Maharashtra.

A charging herd of gaur on the plateau top.

A gaur peering through the undergrowth.

A leopard in the forest opening at sunset.

A gaur emerges from the forest to cross the only road leading up to the plateau top in Radhanagari.

Moss in the canopy retains moisture in evergreen forests. It acts as a microhabitat for several insects.

Radhanagari has a small, flat, open grass-covered area as one approaches the plateau along the crest of the Ghats. As the road climbs upwards through the forest one can sense that another clearing lies ahead when the gradient begins to suddenly level off. These openings are always exciting.

As we drove up a steep slope and cautiously rounded a bend, I felt a sense of anticipation. The sun had just set and as we approached the pink glow ahead, I had to carefully negotiate the car around the boulder-strewn road into the clearing beyond where the cause of this unknown excitement was sitting in the middle of the dry grassy clearing.

Staring in our direction, ears cocked, was a full-grown male leopard! His coat was glistening in the vanishing light. I quietly got out of the car and took a few steps towards him. With an expression of curiosity, he began moving unhurriedly in a circle to get a closer look at me. Several times he stopped to crouch and watch, seemingly as curious about me as I was about him. Moving towards the edge of the forest, he quietly slipped into the shadows. Those few moments in the small clearing have left a silent thrill that I can never forget—a feeling of being very close to Nature herself.

In the 1980s and 1990s two factors created changes in Radhanagari that are of major concern—mining and tourism. Mining for manganese has been a constant threat that comes up repeatedly. Each time NGOs and interested conservation people

have successfully brought in the pressure required to stall this horrendous onslaught on Maharashtra's most important Western Ghats Sanctuary. The response from the mining lobby is that such activities should be permitted on the periphery of Protected Areas. The anti-mining lobby has pointed out that trucks, mines, dust, noise and a variety of settlement issues would be disastrous even on the periphery. One can only hope that this project remains in abeyance permanently. I raised this issue with the Forest Department of Maharashtra in 1999 as a serious concern of the Committee for Rationalizing Boundaries of National Parks and Wildlife Sanctuaries in Maharashtra so that it would be included in the report to the Supreme Court. During my visits in the past ten years, I have seen the road inside the sanctuary surfaced and tourism expand considerably. The gaurs that once frequented the small jungle track now remain hidden in the forest. How much more disturbance can be permitted in this idyllic setting?

Before tourism expanded one could go with the local forest guard for a walk around the sanctuary. I spent summer nights in the early 80s sleeping next to a waterhole called *waghacha pani*, which means the tiger's waterhole. I never got to photograph anything except a big

frog that jumped into the water, but the night sounds are unforgettable! Calls of nightjars, owls, jackals, and once, a leopard within a few metres of the water's edge.

A forest guard I know well is an excellent tracker and wandered around with me on my earlier visits when there was little need to prevent the rare visitor from going into the forest. We once walked all day long looking for gaur. At dusk I photographed a nightjar that did a 'broken wing' display to fool me into moving away from its nest. I knew what it was trying to do and obliged, taking several pictures of this interesting

| 1 | 2 | |
|---|---|---|
| 4 | | 3 |

| 5 | |
|---|---|

White flowers are designed by evolution to attract insect pollinators at night.

A crested serpent eagle.

The bright red and black display of the forest calottes is used to ward off other males and attract females. This male closely follows the female as she ascends the tree trunk.

Dragonfly.

Atlas moth—this large moth has become increasingly rare as a result of man's incessant onslaught on its habitat.

Evergreen and semi-evergreen patches of forest cover these hills.

A waterhole in Radhnagari called *waghacha pani* (the tiger's water hole).

*Cinnamomum.*

The single forest road on a misty morning in Radhanagari.

behaviour. But the light was fading and my guide, disappointed that he had not been able to show me a gaur all day, wanted me to move on. He stopped me on a culvert on the forest road and insisted there were gaur in the forest. I could see nothing. 'How do you know they are here?' I asked. He replied that he could smell them! I took this with a big pinch of salt. 'So what do we do?' I asked. 'Shall I get them out?' he queried. I didn't think it was a good idea, but without another word he slipped into the forest. I heard him cough and chuck a stone. There was an instant blood-curdling bellow and a herd of gaur came tearing out of the forest! I realized instantly that they were making for the road and would go over the culvert where I stood. I jumped on to the low wall—a ten or fifteen metre drop on one side, and a group of charging gaur on the other. It was a very narrow escape. Today, 20 years later, no one would or should be permitted to do this.

A patch of forest.

Salsette scene, which is now a part of Mumbai— Forbes (1813).

## WESTERN SLOPES OF THE SAHYADHRIS AND COASTAL FORESTS

The western slopes of the Ghats and the coastal plains receive great quantities of rainfall that give it typical floral characteristics. The coastal plains have been deforested for centuries and converted into paddy lands and coconut plantations. There are only a few patches left of ancient forests. Many areas were planted with teak under British rule. The few undisturbed patches now form a very important group of Protected Areas. Unfortunately, the existing corridor forests between them are now vanishing. The steep escarpment provides the most awe-inspiring vistas with torrential waterfalls during the monsoon months. The forests vary considerably in composition of trees from north to south. The regions' diversity of plants and animals places these forests among the globally important hotspots of biodiversity.

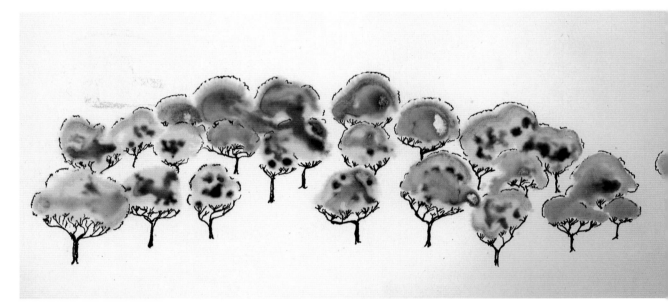

| State | Maharashtra | Zone | Western Ghats (Malabar Coast) |
|---|---|---|---|
| Area | 320 sq km | Ecosystem | Moist Deciduous Forest |
| Year of Notification | 1970 | Visited | Jan 1991, Mar 1996 |

The Tansa Lake provides water to Mumbai's huge population.

The dry deciduous forest of Tansa.

The forests of Tansa are typical of the western coastal belt. High rainfall, long humid periods and an equitable climate produce conditions in which vegetation grows rapidly. Most of the coastal forests were converted into paddy fields generations ago. The forests that are left are mostly located where spurs of the Western Ghats approach the coastline, which is not as suitable for growing paddy as the flat coastal belt. These hilly areas are, however, used to plant hill rice and *nachni* by creating small, narrow terraces. Thus the residual forests along the coast are among some of the highly threatened forest types in the country.

National parks and sanctuaries have several functions quite apart from the protection of wildlife. Several Protected Areas provide a variety of natural resources that are used by local people. Fuel,

fodder, medicinal plants, small timber for building houses, reeds, bamboo and a host of other sustenance resources are still being collected to support local livelihoods. In several sanctuaries this is permitted by the Forest Department. In national parks however, this is legally not permitted. Needless to say, this cannot be legislated very strictly and continues in many areas despite the efforts made by the Forest Department. A Protected Area has other less obvious benefits that are rarely quantified. Tansa Sanctuary, for instance, preserves the catchment area for one of the major lakes, which is a source of water for Mumbai. The forest holds the soil and prevents excessive siltation of the lake. Without this the great city of Mumbai would die of thirst. This area produces a large amount of fodder from the patches of grassland in the forest, which is harvested and bailed. Dam sites are a problem for several species. Others benefit from the constant source of water. It is a complex trade-off. The large pipes that traverse the forest form serious barriers for wildlife movements, but carry life-giving water for the people of the megacity of Mumbai.

| 1 | 2 | 3 |

| 4 |

The backwaters of the lake have many small marshy tracts.

The pipes that carry water from the lake to Mumbai pass through Protected Area.

Amplipeget is a predator of the forest floor.

Grass that grows in this region forms a fodder bank of great economic value.

# SANJAY GANDHI NATIONAL PARK
## BORIVALI

| State | Maharashtra | Zone | Western Ghats (Malabar Coast) |
|---|---|---|---|
| Area | 104 sq km | Ecosystem | Moist Deciduous Forest |
| Year of Notification | 1983 | Visited | Nov, Dec 1985; Apr 1987; Nov 1997 |

Coastal forest.

This Protected Area is one of our most unusual wilderness areas as it borders on a mega city. My earliest memories of this forest are from the 1950s when it was considered to be way out of town, a wild place that was dangerous and a refuge for antisocial elements. Much later I learnt that these were bootleggers who had a thriving business in the prohibition years. The city of Mumbai has now nearly engulfed this forest tract. On its edge there are large slums, whose inhabitants use the forest for a variety of purposes. WII's Ravi Chellum studied the leopards here in 1998 and found that they now depend mainly on rodents, domestic dogs and dead buffalos as their natural prey base has become extremely scarce.

Borivali serves a large number of tourists who visit its Zoological Park and

A beautiful spider makes its web in the forest canopy.

the Canari Caves that are situated within its boundaries. The National Park has over 150 species of butterfl ies, more than 800 species of flowering plants and over 300 species of birds. The most visible wildlife is its wide variety of birds. Hornbills, woodpeckers, flycatchers, thrushes, babblers and several species of birds of prey are common. There is also a good population of reptiles. Apart from leopards that are fairly abundant, the park probably has a few rusty spotted cats. Some juveniles of this species were unfortunately found trapped in a rat trap in the zoo a decade ago. They were very small and sadly, they died. Their skins were given to me by the Conservator of Forests, Shri Walke and have been preserved in the BNHS. The park also has a few chital and barking deer.

The park is one of Mumbai's major ecological assets and has not been given its due importance as an environment educational asset. It could be an important resource for the school children of the city learning to appreciate the values of the natural world. While the BNHS as

well as the Forest Department do have interpretation facilities for tourists, these have not been used optimally. A pity, as few major cities in the world can boast of having a large, relatively undisturbed tract of wilderness on their very doorstep!

I have had many, many memorable visits to this national park. And yet many people of Mumbai have never visited it, nor are its citizens aware of its great conservation value. My most memorable trips were with Dr Salim Ali and Humayun Abdulali during the 1970s. I recall being with Dr Salim Ali early one morning. We heard a bird call and being hard of hearing, he asked me what I thought it was. I said it was a racket-tailed drongo. He then recounted one of his many delightful true-life stories, always with a strong message. He told me that a famous foreign birdwatcher once told him that he had never seen a racket-tailed drongo and would love to see one. Salim Ali took him to Borivali and within the first 15 minutes the quarry was observed through a powerful pair of binoculars. Salimbhai described how the birdwatcher

then whisked out a little black book from his pocket, made a small notation, carefully returned the book to its pocket, and turning to him said, 'Thank you so much, we can go back to Bombay now!' Salim Ali never failed to make fun both of 'list makers' who collected bird sightings, and people like myself who, he said, had only seen birds through a camera lens! Nowadays, I find that, having collected an enormous number of pictures over the last 30 years, I seem to see and observe more wildlife than in the past. It is indeed more fun. The old man, which is what many of us called him when we knew he was out of hearing range, was right after all!

On another memorable trip with Humayun Abdul Ali, he suddenly stopped his car and laboriously got out. I thought he had seen something interesting and stepped out too. He walked slowly towards a large rock that a truck driver had placed in the middle of the steep road, picked it up and chucked it off the road. An eager disciple, I picked up many such errant

rocks, frequently of near boulder size, on many subsequent trips with him thereafter!

Perhaps no one has visited Borivali as frequently as Humayun Abdulali. He has recorded several aspects of the area, knew it like the palm of his hand and was reportedly mugged by bootleggers. In 1950 he got hold of 18 grey jungle fowl, banded and released them as very few were reported in the area. In 1957 he records that the number had subsequently increased. Evidently it is their progeny whose calls I recorded some three decades later for a cassette on birdcalls I made for the BNHS.

I have also spent many delightful hours in Borivali taking pictures of spiders. Borivali is a paradise for spider watchers. For me, watching spiders spin their webs and use such varieties of strategies to catch their prey has always been exciting. This activity is no different from watching a tiger stalk and kill a deer or a bird of prey swoop down on a rodent. Tunnel web spiders, signature web spiders and orb spiders abound in the Protected Area. Each has its own strategy. Tunnel web spiders build webs on the ground to catch insects moving on the forest floor. Signature web spiders build in the shrub layer and in the canopy among the leaves. The great hexagonal webs of the orb spiders are built among the higher tree branches where they mainly catch flying insects such as butterflies.

Borivali has always faced serious management issues. These confl icts have seen many changes over time. Early offenders were 'anti-social elements', who made illicit liquor or felled trees for timber. But what occurred during the recent past was the enormous growth of tourism with its attendant hawkers, noise, dirt, plastic strewn entertainment areas and restaurants. Managing garbage had become a major issue around the tourist facilities. This has been now been reduced to a great extent. The lion, and more recently, tiger safaris could have been developed elsewhere, keeping the national park as a place for nature watching. Zoos can be built in any accessible place. Locating them inside Protected Areas is an inappropriate venture, disturbing the area by adding visitors who are not wildlife tourists. Pilgrimages to the Caneri Caves is yet another issue that adds to biotic pressures on the park.

But the most severe pressure is from the growth of slums on the periphery of the area. Their spread has been so unbelievably rapid that within the last couple of decades they have extended along many parts of the park's boundary. This rapid transition from a low-population density forest ecosystem to a throbbing slum with a giant human population is alarming. It has led to a high frequency of attacks on humans by leopards. The constant proximity of a large number of people moving into the forest for a variety of purposes has changed the behavioural pattern of leopards in Borivali. In 1995, the Bombay Environment Action Group put in a PIL against the Government of Maharashtra for its inaction in removing encroachments from the Sanjay Gandhi National Park in Borivali. The problem of the slums at the very edge of the Protected Area is a serious concern as leopards live close to thousands of people. Several children have fallen unfortunate victims to these leopards that frequently stray into the slum.

The problem appears insurmountable. If errant leopards are caught and translocated, they will continue to misbehave in other areas after release. Besides, a vacant habitat will soon be taken over by another leopard from the existing extremely dense population of predators dependent on a rather meagre source of wild prey. This park must rank as one of the most difficult to manage in the country.

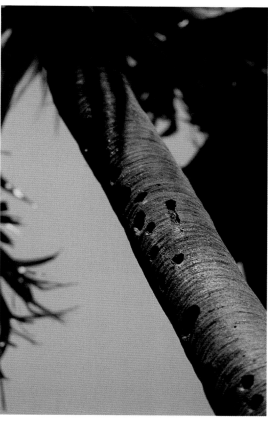

This aggressive macaque is known to threaten visitors if not fed. This has become an increasingly complex management concern.

Woodpecker holes in a palm tree.

# KARNALA BIRD SANCTUARY

KARNALA

| State | Maharashtra | Zone | Western Ghats (Malabar Coast) |
|---|---|---|---|
| Area | 4.27 sq km | Ecosystem | Moist Deciduous Forest |
| Year of Notification | 1968 | Visited | Dec 1987 |

There are some areas that grow on one as familiarity increases. Karnala on my first visit was unattractive. With repeated visits the wide diversity of its bird life began to catch my attention. The close relationship between its plants and bird life is of special interest. The large numbers of ficus trees attract several frugivorous birds such as hornbills, bulbuls and parakeets. There is also a high diversity of insect-dependent birds—paradise flycatcher, fantail flycatcher, tickles blue flycatcher are only a few prominent examples. At night the forests are full of fireflies and the call of nightjars. In the course of a brief visit one can observe most of the species of birds of the Western Ghats. I have recorded birdcalls in the forests just beyond the tourist centre on the roadside. Noise from the road was a permanent problem.

Unfortunately the large numbers of people out on picnics generate an enormous quantity of garbage that has a serious impact on this ecosystem. Environmental awareness programmes and information on the local bird life are opportunities that have yet to be explored here.

The forest undergrowth provides a haven for bird life.

# PHANSAD WILDLIFE SANCTUARY
PHANSAD

| State | Maharashtra | Zone | Western Ghats (Malabar Coast) |
|---|---|---|---|
| Area | 53 sq km | Ecosystem | Evergreen Forest |
| Year of Notification | 1986 | Visited | Dec 1987, May 1991 |

Phansad is one of the few intact forests of a significant size that has survived along the west coast of Maharashtra.

While the birth of a sanctuary happens at times by careful design, at others it is fairly ad-hoc. Occasionally it is through the actions of individuals who have been especially attracted by its glamour species of mammals or birds. Less often, it has been related to the presence of threatened plant life that botanists have identified in the area. Sheer accidents of fate have frequently influenced the selection of an important site, leading to its subsequent notification. One begins to realize how the fate of biodiversity, which is dependent on the notification and consequently the survival of natural ecosystems and threatened species of wildlife, is so frequently governed by chance occurrence. Phansad is one such sanctuary that has a strange beginning. Shri Kopikar was a Conservator of Forests in Pune during the 1970s, looking after wildlife issues. He was asked by the Central Government to identify new areas in need of notification as sanctuaries in Maharashtra. Several routine suggestions had been considered and a

number of areas in forest ecosystems were identified as potential sites. I had always believed that sanctuaries should be created in different types of ecosystems, rather than only in the teak forests that had large mammal concentrations, though most experts consulted at the time favoured areas with major mammals in the north-east of Maharashtra. I suggested that other ecosystems such as wetlands, grasslands and coastal areas should be represented. In the discussions that followed forest officials knew of no area that could fill the void in the coastal belt of Maharashtra. During the discussion, a clerk who had entered the office to get some papers signed, requested permission to speak. He said that he had seen a file, perhaps 20 years old, that mentioned that the rulers of the State of Janjira had in the past preserved a forest tract in Phansad as a shooting reserve. The file suggested that there was a possibility of creating a Protected Area at the site. It mentioned the forest type and a few details about faunal species that included the golden cat. No doubt the Forest Official had mistaken a common jungle cat for this rare species. No action had been taken for several years and the proposal was virtually forgotten. The clerk hesitatingly suggested that this area might well be the area we were looking for on the coast.

I agreed that for want of information on the existence of other intact coastline forests, this might indeed fill the gap. A tattered file was produced. None of the Forest Officials present knew where Phansad village was situated and no one present had visited this area. An RFO was dispatched to Ratnagiri to ascertain 'if any forest was left there!' Two days later this patch of reserved forest was included in the list of new proposed Protected Areas in Maharashtra.

The strange coincidence of my having insisted on looking for a viable patch of coastal forest, an interested senior forest official who was ready to accept a

Open areas and forest form a mosaic of vegetation types adding to the diversity of plant life.

The evergreen vegetation of the coastal forests in Phansad Wildlife Sanctuary was once the private shooting reserve of the rajas of Janjira.

new idea, a clerk with a good memory for old files and an enthusiastic RFO, combined to bring about a new Protected Area. Most important, a forest official had made a mention of this area many years ago as a potential sanctuary, and though unused, the file had been preserved for 20 years! A chain of accidental events thus brought about the notification of a Sanctuary in Phansad.

I did not have an opportunity to visit Phansad at the time of its notification, but had mentioned its importance to WA Rodgers when he was writing *Planning a Wildlife Protected Area Network for India*. Later Rodgers and I helped work on the conservation aspects of the World Bank's Forestry Sector Project for Maharashtra. The World Bank officials and the Forest Department wanted me to prioritize sanctuaries and national parks to which funds should be allocated. To prevent being carried away by my personal

considerations, I evolved a complex numerical grading scale to rate the 29 Protected Areas, so that funds could be allocated on some objective bases. Phansad figured high up in this list. As I had never seen the area, I made a brief visit. The vegetation looked quite different from the type seen in other areas. I consulted some botanists to establish if it was really a unique forest type. As no one had worked there, I requested Shri Indurkar, who was the Chief Wildlife Warden, and Alan Rodgers to visit the sanctuary with me. Alan found the plant community fascinating and we allocated funds for conservation and research on its biodiversity. During the recent past, several groups, NGOs and botanical researchers, have begun investigating this patch of forest and found it extremely interesting. But for a quirk of fate it might have been left to degrade into a scrub jungle and we would have lost yet another bio-rich area!

Walking through the forest I found a bird trap cleverly designed to catch jungle fowl. Even here local people are poaching whatever they could find. Sambar and barking deer tracks were present everywhere but were concentrated around a small waterhole. At the summit of the sanctuary is the old broken down rest house of the Raja of Janjira, from where one can get an incredible view of forest and sea. On several occasions I walked up into the forest to sit in the solitude of the setting sun with the sea spread out below me. The silence can be so intense that a leaf falling sounds unduly loud. The evening silence is punctured by the calls of forest birds. After sunset, I sat by the beach, one of the few clean beaches left in Maharashtra, with the sound of the waves. That was one beach that hoards of noisy tourists had not yet wrecked in 1991. Is it the same today? Rather doubtful!

Phansad still has patches of superb forests which are a delight to walk through.

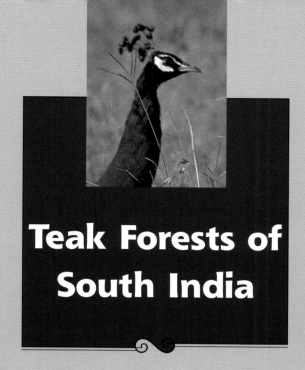

# Teak Forests of South India

𝔄 large variety of forests in the southern part of Peninsular India are dominated by teak. They include dry and moist deciduous forest to evergreen forest formations. Most of them are situated in the hill ranges of Southern India and the Deccan Plateau biogeographic zones. Several areas that are now Protected Areas were areas that were felled for timber and reforested using teak as a monoculture. Most of these forests also have bamboo patches and are all rich in plant and animal species. The most highly natural are those where there have been low levels of deforestation for timber production in the past.

A young elephant touching its mother for reassurance.

The teak forests of South India are found in two biogeographic zones—the Western Ghats and the Deccan Plateau.

# BHADRA WILDLIFE SANCTUARY

BHADRA

| State | Karnataka | Zone | Western Ghats |
|---|---|---|---|
| Area | 492.46 sq km | Ecosystem | Moist and Dry Deciduous Forest |
| Year of Notification | 1974 | Visited | May 1990 |

**B**hadra is situated in the Western Ghats and surrounded by coffee plantations. In 1951 a small area was notified as Jagara Valley Game Sanctuary and in 1972 it became the Bhadra Wildlife Sanctuary. Dominant tree species are *Tectona grandis, Dalbergia latifolia, Terminalia tomentosa, Terminalia paniculata, Lagerstromia lanceolata,* a variety of *Ficus sp.* and patches of bamboo. It has an estimated 30 to 40 tigers and 200 elephants (Jain, 2001).

Around a bend on the forest road there is a clearing. A large *makhna,* a tuskless male elephant, crosses the road and stands in the clearing. He decides to scratch his large rump against a dry tree trunk. He stands in full view for a long time, scenting the wind with raised trunk repeatedly in the direction of the jeep. He is a massive animal with a large, wide forehead. Further down the road a pack of wild dogs cross over. There are seven of them. Each crosses the opening separately and turns around suspiciously to watch the jeep while the next one crosses the road.

The small village settlements in Bhadra are picturesque hamlets surrounded by paddy fields and thick forest. It is a landscape out of the distant past of India's wilderness settlements. It is a peaceful existence but one in which the people have to undergo great hardships. These people subsist directly on the forest's resources. During the monsoon months the villages are nearly cut off from the outside world.

The periphery of Bhadra is formed by hill slopes that are covered by coffee plantations. This is another landscape type that has superb scenery. These two different landscape elements create an extremely different set of management issues. The first is related to the needs of the local people who use the forest for their day-to-day lives, coming into conflict with the habitat and food supply of animals such as the elephant, the deer, and the tiger that damage their crops and kill their livestock. The second is the conflict between the coffee planter and the wildlife that damages their plantations. Both are highly complex issues. We still do not have either clear-cut policies or implementation of measures such as compensation for crop damage and for the loss of cattle and, most importantly, of human life.

We follow fresh tiger footprints along the narrow road for several hundred metres with Kausy Sethna, a coffee planter from Aldoor who has championed the cause of conservation in the Protected Areas in the region for several decades. Willing to argue his case for wildlife at every level,

The unbroken canopy cover of a hillslope in Bhadra gives the forest a microclimate that maintains high moisture levels and low temperatures throughout the year.

| | 2 |
|---|---|
| 1 | |
| 3 | |

Post-monsoon forests with an undergrowth of herbs and shrubs.

Flowering plant in the undergrowth.

A tusker this size is now a rarity in South India, where poaching for ivory has been increasing over the years.

Kausy is an unforgettable personality. One of the old-time hunter-turned-conservationists, his emotions come out strongly in support of what he believes in.

As the sky turns black with thunderclouds, we sit in a watchtower in a downpour of rain, sipping hot coffee and eating cookies. It passes off rapidly and as the dusk approaches, the fireflies blink their meandering paths through the forests of Bhadra. In the late 1990s, there have been attempts by the Karnataka Government to permit opening up the iron ore mines at the edge of the Protected Area. This battle has raged for several years and is reopened every few years. With all these pressures will the fireflies continue to blink their zigzag wanderings through the forests of Bhadra?

| 1 | |
| 2 | 4 |
| 3 | 5 |

Langurs at play.

Farmland in Bhadra.

A pack of wild dogs is said to be able to drive even tigers out of the area.

Bandipur has large herds of chital which aggregate at dusk near the tourist centre and move into the forest at dawn.

Sambar rarely aggregate in herds of this size.

| State | Karnataka | Zone | Western Ghats |
|---|---|---|---|
| Area | 874.20 sq km | Ecosystem | Dry and Moist Deciduous forest |
| Year of Notification | 1974 | Visited | Nov 1980, May 1992, Oct–Nov 1993 |

The forests of Bandipur were the shooting reserves of the Maharajas of Mysore. In the pre-independence era, the wildlife and the forests were in fact managed by personnel appointed by the Maharaja. Madhav Gadgil (2001), in his book *Ecological Journeys*, mentions that 200 years ago this land must have been cultivated. He bases this on the presence of old irrigation tanks. He suggests that during Tipu Sultan's wars people may have fled the area, leading to the growth of forests.

In 1931 Bandipur was notified as a sanctuary. It is one of the oldest Tiger Reserves, initiated in 1973 when Project Tiger was begun. It has remained an important part of a complex of sanctuaries that includes Mudumalai and Wynad. The flora includes large stands of *Tectona grandis*—teak, *Dalbergia latifolia*, *Pterocarpus meroupium*, *Adina cardifolia* and *Grewia tilifolia*.

One of its unique features is the mosaic of dry deciduous forests with open grassy clearings, which are mainly located in the tourist zone. As the chital are primarily grazers, a fair proportion of them aggregate around the rest house and the adjacent grassy patches. There is also an old eucalyptus plantation under which there are large grassy clearings in which chital frequently graze. The large herds of chital were mentioned in EP Gee's book *The Wildlife of India* written in 1964. He claims that there were even larger herds in earlier years. During my earlier visits in the 1970s, I saw larger aggregations than in subsequent visits, an indication of changes in animal population trends that have occurred over the years. The large size of the herds of chital is one of the most remarkable features of this Protected Area. In the 1980s, if a torch was flashed

around the open ground in the tourist complex, hundreds of eyes reflected the light through the thick grass. At sunrise, the chital would move away into the forest. One of the herds contained a huge dark male, perhaps the largest stag I have ever seen. He had a very large harem of females. After sun-up the deer would slowly break up into smaller groups to feed on the grass in adjacent clearings. In the 1980s when there were very few visitors, one could slowly walk along with the animals. Groups of sambar and several peafowl could be seen frequently around the tourist zone. I had seen the uncommon stripe-necked mongoose several times in the forest clearings.

I discovered that large herds of chital gather around the tourist facility at night purely by accident. I heard the call of a fishing owl late one night and crept out of the tourist hut onto the porch. The chital were everywhere. I could not resist taking a picture with a small flash so all I have left of that memorable experience is hundreds of eyes staring at the camera. The chital were used to tourists and were not disturbed if one watched quietly from the roadside. They would come and graze around you and provide excellent opportunities for photography.

During my subsequent visit to Bandipur for an evaluation of the park for Project Tiger, I estimated chital populations in different parts of the sanctuary including the core area and the tourist zone. Interestingly, the tourism area had the highest chital density in the sanctuary. This is probably related to the fact that

a larger proportion of the open grassy areas are located in the tourism zone.

Bandipur had an estimated 75 tigers in 2001 (Jain, 2001). During my several visits I have seen only their pugmarks, but the prey base and the habitat can easily support this high a density of great cats.

Mudumalai, Bandipur and Nagarhole constitute one of the last continuous forest habitats for elephants in South India, which can still provide them with all their seasonal habitat requirements. The elephants move from the open grassy area, in which they feed on tender grasses after the monsoon, into adjacent forest tracts once the grass has matured, and there change to browsing on the leaves of favoured trees and on patches of young bamboo. The under story vegetation of the forest is thus crucial to the well-being of these magnificent animals. Unfortunately, several tracts of the undergrowth in these sanctuaries have been invaded by *Lantana* shrubs, an unpalatable species which elephants cannot use. This is probably one of the factors that reduces fodder availability for elephants in these forests. BNHS scientists have documented movements of several elephants for many years in the forests of Mudumalai and

Bandipur. These studies have demonstrated the need for vast tracts of forest that elephants require for foraging, each herd moving through a large tract of forestland during different seasons. Bandipur alone has an estimated population of about 3000 elephants. There is now evidence to show that, with this density, the debarking and uprooting of young trees by the elephants can severely alter the forest composition.

In the river, I have seen turtles basking by the riverside, otters emerging from the water and wild elephants descending to bathe in the water. The river, its tributaries, and the gorge down which it flows forms an optimal deciduous forest habitat for a large number of bird species. The undergrowth teems with a variety of butterflies.

Deep in the forests of Bandipur there is a remarkable old resthouse, which is now unfortunately dilapidated. It is situated in the most idyllic location and must have once been surrounded by a wide stretch of uninhabited wilderness teeming with wildlife. It must have been a great experience to live there. This deep isolation can never return.

Peacocks can move noiselessly through the grass.

A brown fish owl surveys the forest for its prey.

Elephants consume great quantities of food consisting of grass, bamboo, leaves and even the bark of trees. They thus act as a great controlling influence on the habitat.

Chital herd at night, near the resthouse in Bandipur.

Chital eyes dot the grassland just before dawn.

# MUDUMALAI WILDLIFE SANCTUARY
MUDUMALAI

| State | Tamil Nadu | Zone | Western Ghats |
|---|---|---|---|
| Area | 217.76 sq km | Ecosystem | Semi-evergreen Forests |
| Year of Notification | 1940 | Visited | Jan 1986, Feb 1988, Nov 1989, June 1990, Jun 1991, May 1992 |

This area once belonged to the Rumalpad, the local ruler of the Nilambur Kovilagam. He was the local ruler who leased the forest to the Government for five years in 1863 at a rent of Rs. 3500 per year. In 1914 the forests became the property of the State Government and were declared Reserved Forests in 1927. In 1940 the Government notified the 23 square mile area adjoining Mysore State as one of our earliest wildlife sanctuaries. A jungle warfare camp was set up here during World War-II, which had a serious impact on the habitat. In 1956 Mudumalai was expanded to 114 square miles. Till 1968 the entire sanctuary was exploited for forest produce; teak and eucalyptus plantations were razed while bamboo was planted for supply to the rayon mills in Kerala. Minor forest produce such as wild honey, antlers, soap nut (*Sapindus emarginata*), fruit, etc. were also collected. Characteristic tree species include *Terminalia tomentosa*, *Terminalia chebula* and *Terminalia belerica*, *Annogeissus latifolia*, *Gmelina arborea*, *Lagerstromea lanceolata*, etc.

The forest of Mudumalai supports about 200 tigers in its 310 square kilometres. It has, however, 200 local families living in six settlements—the Chetties who live here are farmers and grow paddy.

The two adjacent sanctuaries of Mudumalai and Bandipur are situated on the road from Mysore to Ooty in the Nilgiri range of hills. Mudumalai is at a higher elevation than Bandipur, and its forests are thicker and more evergreen in nature than in Bandipur. The forests are of variable composition with teak being less frequently encountered. Bandipur has larger grassy glades than Mudumalai.

Elephant herds roam widely in these forests from one sanctuary to the other, crossing large areas in search of fodder. Each herd has a large home range, which includes grassy glades on which they feed after the monsoon and trees for browsing once the grass starts to dry. They have a variety of favourite browsing trees and love bamboo shoots. Today the distribution of elephants is much smaller than it was a century ago. M Shakespear (1860) writes in his book *Wild Sports of India*, 'The great Wynand Jungle, which lies at the foot of the Western Ghats, from Mahantoddy to Coimbatore, the great range of mountains that run from

Mudumalai has deciduous and evergreen forests.

Giant squirrel in Mudumalai.

An elephant scenting the air for intruders.

Trichone almost to Trichinopoly—as well as the Coorg country—all hold elephants. The Anamullee (which translated means elephant hills) and I believe the Bruma geese are overrun by them though every year their numbers are being thinned.'

This shows that even in those 'good old days' the elephant populations, though still widespread, had begun to dwindle. What surprises me is how it has taken so long to appreciate the drastic fall in the population of so many valuable species. It seems that the decline in the population of several species was a well-known phenomenon for several decades. It was however not linked with the fact that this could end in their extinction. It is now obvious that unless species such as elephants are carefully protected and their habitat preserved, they will disappear forever. While the elephant will in all likelihood manage to survive in smaller and smaller numbers for sometime, for several other species, extinction may occur during our own generation.

In earlier years it was possible to wander through the Mudumalai forests on foot. I recall walking along one of the forest roads with a local boy who was enthusiastically acting as my guide in 1986. We planned to walk through the forest and join the main road from where I could catch a bus back to Mysore. I carried a haversack and a heavy camera bag. As we walked

along at sunset we spotted a fairly large female elephant feeding on the side of the forest road. We waited for several minutes for her to move away, but she had spotted us and decided to stay put. My guide was extremely nervous and when the elephant decided to move towards us, he ran like hell! A charge followed. I had to drop my haversack and run. I had a feeling that the chase would not last long. When an elephant begins to chase you, it appears to move fairly slowly. However, as each of its strides is very long, the speed with which it can cover the ground is indeed surprising. It is only when you look back that you realize that the elephant is moving much faster than you. That is what makes one sprint. On this occasion the elephant suddenly veered into the forest and promptly disappeared. Retrieving my bag after she had gone off was yet another problem. The last bus to Mysore had gone by the time we hit the main road and I had to hitch an uncomfortable ride in the back of a truck to reach Mysore that night. I seem to have had my fair share of having to run away from unpredictable, but eventually, well-meaning elephants! Most chases end when one runs. Accidents, however, are known to happen, especially if one does not know how to respond to these mock charges.

The newly constructed hydel dam at Mudumalai provides only a small amount of power. For this insignificant amount of electrical energy the last forest corridor between the Nilgiris and the Eastern Ghats has been permanently severed, hampering the migratory movements of elephants in their search for a sufficient supply of food. Worse, it limits their ability to interbreed successfully with adjacent populations and inbreeding is yet another route to extinction.

Over the years Mudumalai has been the focus of a large number of research projects by institutions such as the BNHS, the Centre for Ecological Studies, Bangalore, SACON and other individual researchers. One of the earliest works on the Protected Area in the 1950s was by EP Gee. He mentions that in 1955 shooting was permitted in these blocks. As visibility was poor, Gee suggested creating a few grassy areas 200 to 300 yards wide for viewing wildlife. This was evidently carried out, as there are several such patches at present. He also suggested several other measures such as stopping timber extraction or planting trees. However, he suggested eliminating 75 per cent of the wild dog population, a suggestion that may very well have been carried out as there are very few dholes at present.

Research on elephants by the scientists of the BNHS began several years ago by identifying large bulls through the shape of their tusks and ears. The Project's Principal Investigator, JC Daniel, known to conservationists as 'JC', had

| | | 4 |
|---|---|---|
| 1 | | 5 |
| 2 | 3 | 6 |

Waterfall in Mudumalai.

Mudbaths keep an elephant cool in the afternoon heat.

Male elephants without tusks are known as *makhnas*. They are spared by poachers.

The forest along the side of the tourist road is cleared to facilitate sighting animals.

The dappled coats of chital provide camouflage in the light and shade of the forest.

A clump of moist grass growing out of a snag in a tree forms a tasty morsel for this elephant.

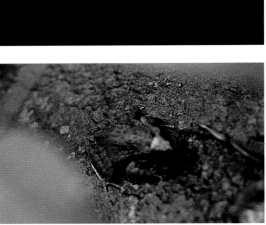

| 1 | 2 | | |
|---|---|---|---|
| 3 | | 5 | |
| 4 | | 6 | |

The eyes of a nocturnal flying squirrel reflected in the flashlight.

Three woodpeckers looking for insects in the bark of the tree.

Frog.

A juvenile jungle crow hunts for termites.

A grey tit catching termites as they emerge from the mound after a shower of rain.

Peacock flying across the river.

a group of young scientists monitoring elephant movements and studying their behavioural patterns over several years. Following elephants is risky fieldwork. It is also difficult, arduous work that calls for great patience and perseverance. We had no radio collars for the elephants in those days. Shivaganeshan looked at vegetation patterns and Ajay Desai studied the elephants' behavioural patterns and family structure. Unfortunately, within a couple of years most of the big bulls were mercilessly killed off by Veerappan, the infamous ivory poacher. Each time an elephant was killed, it came as a great shock to the young scientists who had become emotionally attached to these magnificent animals. It was like losing a family member or a close friend. The study then centered around radio-collared elephants which were tracked over a period of four or five years. This provided an enormous amount of data on habitat utilization by the elephants. To manage the habitat scientifically, it is important to appreciate how the different clans of elephants are distributed through the forest and how they share the resources present in the shrinking forests of this region. There were several stories of these elephants that the scientists never documented. I recall some of them with a sense of pleasure and others with great sorrow. Ajay and Shiva, the two scientists who worked on elephants for a long time, had several close encounters. As a consequence they became adept at rapidly climbing trees! Ajay was once 'treed' by a large bull for several hours. The elephant refused to budge. Ajay kept himself busy making notes. At dusk he dropped his plastic pencil, which fell below him close to the elephant who picked it up, broke it with his trunk, threw it away and then walked off into the forest.

Ramesh, one of our BNHS scientists, was once watching elephants in the degraded forests of Hosur close to Bangalore when he was picked up by Veerappan's gang. He was blindfolded with bandages over his eyes and was made to walk several kilometres into the forest. The next day, he was interviewed by Veerappan, told to 'lay off' the area, and not to inform the police after he was released. A harrowing incident for a young scientist!

Tragically, we lost Chenna, our most experienced tracker, who had saved our field scientists from being trampled by elephants time and again through his great knowledge of the jungles and its denizens. I have been out with Chenna several times walking with one of our researchers. How he was able to find elephants deep in the forest I could never quite understand. On one occasion, however, in trying to help me get a close-up picture, we accidentally walked into the middle of a group of elephants. There were elephants all around us. Chenna quietly indicated this to us and got us to backtrack very carefully out of the herd. For some strange reason, the elephants never got to know we had been there. Perhaps it was a windless time and they were too busy feeding to scent us. Or perhaps they recognized Chenna and the researcher who frequently visited them. They probably knew these two were harmless.

One unfortunate day, Chenna was returning with his wife from the forest when they were charged by a tigress. Chenna was instantly killed, a great loss to our team. Super trackers are an increasingly rare breed of people today. It was always a great delight to go into the forest with Chenna. During our video shooting of elephants in Mudumalai, he gave me great confidence. With him around I always felt safe. He knew his wildlife intimately, and yet he eventually bungled into the path of the tiger, one last unfortunate, fatal error.

When I was working with the Salim Ali Nature Conservation Fund (SANCF) of the BNHS, I felt that the Paul Getty Award he had received could best be used to train BNHS members and young scientists in modern methods of studying ecosystems that could lead to conservation action. Dr. Salim Ali would have surely approved of this strategy had he been alive. We thus started running training programmes, and Bharat Bhushan, who was appointed as the Conservation Officer of SANCF, organized workshops at Mudumalai and Sariska. One of the key trainers was Alan Rodgers, a faculty member at the Wildlife Institute of India (WII) who was working on *Planning a Wildlife Protected Area Network for India*. Alan is a wonderfully effective trainer and the field-training sessions he organized for the workshop were a great success. During these workshops he saw to it that they were always fun and a great learning experience. The workshop in Mudumalai gave all of us a deep understanding of the nature of the Sanctuary, its management issues and some sense of what the future held in store for the threatened wildlife of these incredible jungles. During this workshop I also got some of the most memorable pictures of Mudumalai that I have ever recorded. These include an otter on the road drying itself on the warm tarmac; a

flying squirrel as it glided across the river after sunset; and a termite mound that decided to burst into thousands of flying insects minutes before we reached the site. Parked besides the termite mound for a few minutes, I took pictures of a variety of insect predators ranging from a flycatcher, a drongo, a grey tit, a bee-eater and even a young immature jungle crow. The party fare was shared even by a garden lizard. Events such as this demonstrate how the ecosystem works and the number of food chains that are linked to even a single insect species. I described this event, and the linkages of the system that forms the food chains and the food web of this forest ecosystem, to the participants as a part of the training session. Many of them still recall this moment with nostalgia. It had just begun to rain, the light was superb and in a few idyllic moments Nature demonstrated beautifully what can never be fully appreciated by reading a book.

I recall also sitting by the roadside on a culvert, discussing our workshop strategy with Alan early one morning. Down the road a small movement caught my eye. To our mutual surprise, we saw a jungle cat cautiously walking towards us. I slowly got off the culvert, and walked through the *nala* on the side of the road, taking care to see that Alan's rather wide frame hid me

from the cat. I had managed to get my camera out of the BNHS jeep, and readied it when one of the BNHS members decided to jump up onto the road. The cat, with equal agility, jumped off the road nearly simultaneously! Everyone thought it very funny that I had taken so much trouble for a jungle cat picture that never materialized. But in wildlife photography one wins some and loses many. Wildlife pictures are like the enormous fish that always gets away!

Lalitha Vijayan of SACON studied the bird diversity of Mudumalai in 1994. The undisturbed scrub had the highest species richness while abundance of birds was highest in disturbed scrub. Dry deciduous forests had higher abundance and species richness than teak plantations. The coffee plantations had the lowest number of species as well as number of birds both in winter and monsoon months.

Recent work in 2002 by BNHS scientists in Mudumalai suggests that the tiger prey consists of 47 per cent sambar and 46 per cent chital as a major source of food. Leopards use 66 per cent of chital and only 23 per cent of sambar, 5 per cent of langurs and several other smaller animals. The wild dog's main prey is 65 per cent chital and 23 per cent sambar. Thus the three major predators kill different proportions of herbivores. They also need a different amount of biomass over a unit of time and use the area's different forest types in their own preferred way. For example the BNHS study shows that the tiger is found almost exclusively in the moist and dry deciduous tracts and avoids the thorn forest belts. The leopards on the other hand are frequently observed in thorn forests.

Masanagudi is a growing settlement on the edge of the Protected Area, which has large herds of cattle that have degraded the adjacent forest. The elephant corridor is disappearing and more crop raiding by elephants is occurring as the migratory route of elephants are cut off by human activities, the man-animal conflict will inevitably escalate, leading to the untimely deaths of both people and elephants that are being constantly reported from this part of the forest.

The misty valley in Mudumalai at dawn.

| State | Andhra Pradesh | Zone | Deccan Peninsula |
|---|---|---|---|
| Area | 3568 sq km | Ecosystem | Deciduous Forests |
| Year of Notification | TR 1978; 1982–83 | Visited | 1993; Oct 2004 |

The Deccan around Hyderabad is a unique landscape of flat plateaus dotted with outcrops of gigantic rock formations. Tons of rock, balanced on each other, with thorny vegetation in the crevices, make up the landscape for 150 kilometres until suddenly one is confronted with a range of steeply rising hills clothed with scrub forest. A few kilometres further I approach the Shrisailam Tiger Reserve only to find myself turned back at the gate. I drive 17 kilometres to the nearest District Forest Officer's Office to get an entry permit. He is out and his Ranger has gone to the entry gate. I go back the same 17 kilometres up the hills. Another restless 45 minutes pass before I finally convince the Range Forest Officer of my genuine interest in wildlife. It appears that I might be an excellent target for the active Naxalites of the area,

so I am ultimately given two frontline forest staff, unarmed of course, to protect me from highly armed extremists! We drive off and land up at a tiny poverty-stricken village of 13 tribal hutments. The local tribal Eco-development Committee Chairman accompanies us into the forests. He is optimistic that eco-development will make a difference. We wind our way down a steep slope to the single water source about two kilometres away, a tiny stream on which the village is entirely dependent. There is very little evidence of wildlife. The path is strewn with goat hoof prints and pellets. A few birds are still calling near the water. Further on we come to a steep gorge with a waterfall. The hill slopes are clothed with forests and scrub in varying stages of degradation, but the pool at the base of the waterfall is a mass of very

tall trees with canopies that spread at the crown high up into the sky to form thick, unbroken shade. The sunlight touching the top of the falls causes the drops of water to light up like brilliant sparks as they freefall down to the pool below.

I lie on a rock looking up at the crown of trees, each species forming its own structure at the top, a mosaic of exquisite shapes, each filled by a different shade of green. Sunlight trickles through in tiny freckles to the forest floor in a constantly changing pattern, and touches the giant trunk of the nearest tree. I marvel at the magnitude of living material that goes to make up one ancient forest tree. Its girth is huge and its sloping angle makes me wonder how it is able to balance itself. High up above the hill slope a crested serpent eagle circles. The silence is broken

An unimaginably beautiful waterfall in Shrisailam.

A tribal hut deep in the sanctuary.

Local people who live in the sanctuary are still economically deprived.

Flowering shrubs of the exotic *Lantana* weed have covered the undergrowth layer pushing out diverse local species.

Aggressive Bonnet macaques demand food.

A giant banyan tree with aerial roots.

only by the long, peaceful swish of water splashing into the pool. Two Bonnet macaques are watching me curiously from the treetops. Wondering why they appear so keenly interested, I decide to have lunch in the cool grove. A terrible mistake! The two forest department staff, the driver and I unpack our sandwiches. We are instantly joined by two highly aggressive monkeys. They are not very

large but their threatening postures are sufficiently alarming to force us to share our meagre meal with them. They press closer and closer after each titbit, until we are as good as chased off. This waterfall is obviously a picnic spot where they have learnt to threaten people for food.

This is a good birding area, although the afternoon sun seems to have made them somnambulant. Otherwise the forest, or at least the areas I saw, is strangely devoid of wildlife. The last tiger census showed that there are less than 20 tigers here. For an area of this size (356 square kilometres, one of the largest Tiger Reserves in the country) such a low count must be due to a severe shortage of prey. Forests like these make me wonder why protection has still not permitted wildlife populations to expand.

Perhaps it is the pressure from domestic animals, or poaching, or the movements of the Naxalite gangs. None of these reasons, when taken separately, is convincing. More research is needed to develop the right approach to managing those of our Protected Areas where wildlife populations are low.

The bark of a tree harbours a large number of insects.

A large family of bonnet macaques spread across the road.

A termite infested tree trunk.

Rock fields of the Deccan trap at the edge of the Protected Area.

A spider's web.

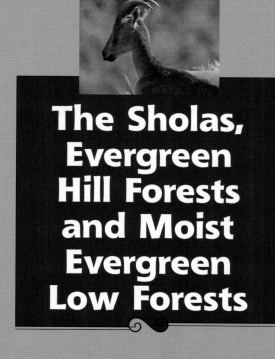

# The Sholas, Evergreen Hill Forests and Moist Evergreen Low Forests

The Sholas are forests in the southern part of the Western Ghats, and the hill ranges of the Nilgiris, Annamalais and Agasthamalais. These evergreen forests have a typical structure and are found in sharply demarcated patches surrounded by wide, open grasslands. The topography is hilly, typically a range of rolling hills and lofty crags with sheer, precipitous slopes. The tall, impenetrable forests spread along *nala* courses and river valleys. The smooth, rolling hills are maintained as grasslands by repeated fires. Within the forest the undergrowth at the edge is extremely thick with a large variety of shrubs. Lianas, cycads, ferns, fungi, moss and bryophytes form a major component of this rich diversity of plant life. A remarkably beautiful plant is the tree fern, which looks like a relic of ancient carboniferous forests. There are also a variety of herbs and medicinal plants that are used by local people. The trees are extremely tall and the canopy in undisturbed areas forms a continuous, evergreen mantle. Under it the forest floor has only a few plants, a thick humus that recycles nutrients and a large variety of fungi. The tree trunks grow straight upwards and the branches begin at a great height. They are richly covered with mosses, ferns and climbers. A few tall emergent trees break through and grow to a great height above the canopy.

Evergreen forests of the Sholas have a high diversity of plant life.

Shola forest.

The forests are home to a large number of major mammals. Elephants, gaurs, deer, tigers, leopards and wild dogs roam the forests and cross from one forest patch to another across the grasslands. The twin ecosystem is of great importance to species such as elephants and gaurs that graze on grass in the post-monsoon period, and shift to browsing on the leaves of trees and bushes for the rest of the year.

The rare Nilgiri *tahr*, an animal restricted to this part of the country, lives in a few isolated groups in the least disturbed and remote parts of the hills, frequenting the steeper slopes. The *tahr* form large herds. A few of the dominant males live separately, joining the herd only during the breeding season. These elusive large males, referred to as saddlebacks are rarely seen.

Of the large variety of different ecosystems in the country, the Sholas contain forests with some of the greatest diversity of plant life. They are equally rich in insects, amphibia and bird life.

The Sholas are structurally two clearly demarcated subsystems. There are large treeless expanses of grasslands on exposed areas, especially on hilltops. In contrast, valleys and watercourses are covered by some of the most incredible forest types found in the subcontinent including trees such as Dipterocarps, which are not found in the rest of the peninsula. Though the species of trees and shrubs differs from one area to another, these evergreen high-rainfall forests are structurally similar. The canopy is nearly without a break. The ancient forests contain gigantic trees that break through the canopy and tower above the rest of the forest. These are frequented by birds of prey that nest in them and use them as vantage points. These giants of the forest can usually be identified on the forest floor by their wide buttress roots that fan out from the tree trunk. In areas where the fall of a tree has opened up the canopy, the gaps are rapidly re-colonized by secondary species which are in turn slowly replaced by climax species over many decades. The forest thus contains a mosaic of plant communities.

Nearly all the trees in the Sholas are evergreen. The thick canopy throws deep shadows on the forest floor on which the thick humus is nearly always damp. This layer contains a large group of plants and animals that support an active and vibrant detrivore cycle. All the nutrients of the forest floor are rapidly recycled in a thin layer of top soil. Unseen fungi, soil animals and insect life form a vital part of of the forest ecosystem. Along paths and treefalls, which have some light filtering onto the forest floor, the undergrowth is rich in plant life. Flowers of various colours, several species with iridescent blues and bright yellows, attract a great diversity of pollinating insects.

The bird life is extremely rich in diversity but difficult to see, several species being found mainly at the canopy level. A few insectivores descend to the forest floor and skulk around in the detritus looking for insects.

The incredible variety of life in these forests has never been fully explored. These forests are likely to have angiosperms from which a variety of new drugs could be discovered. Local tribal people have used several plants as remedies for a variety of disease conditions; these are yet to be studied. The abundant insect life could yield a variety of eco-friendly products for industry.

The richness and complexity of these ecosystems create serious problems for those attempting to understand the linkages between their great varieties of species. Insect caterpillars require specific host plants to feed on for their survival. Rocky exposed outcrops have plants that are specially adapted to surviving only in such special locations. Watercourses are home to a group of highly specialized plants. Pollinators of the *Ficus* species, for instance, are different for each of the many *Ficus* species. The *Ficus* trees are known to play keystone functions in the forest ecosystem. However, the number of insect, bird and mammal species that are linked to them and the abundance of different interdependent animals still remain unexplored. Even less known is why some species are restricted only to a special microhabitat.

There are large gaps in our understanding of plant regeneration within gaps created in these forests by natural and man-made factors. When a tree falls, the opening allows light to enter the darkness of the forests. Seeds that have remained dormant and seedlings that have grown only a few centimetres tall now get the light they require to grow. A whole series of ecological events that can last several human generations slowly unfolds until the forest regains its original vegetation.

The importance of these evergreen patches to further man's economic development is shrouded in the mystery beneath the dark canopy. In these forests there is a great wealth of species that are yet to be discovered. Several are likely to become extinct before science discovers them. We may never be given a chance to utilize the enormous diversity of life forms within them. Time is running out for this incredible ecosystem and its species of plants and animals.

## THE SHOLAS—EVERGREEN HILL FORESTS

The Sholas of these hills have several formations. A typical hill forest lies along *nala* courses with interesting areas of grassland. The distant hills take on a bluish haze in misty days. Cloud cover in the mornings hides the valley and as it lifts, the mountains emerge beyond. Some are forested or have small forest patches and extensive grasslands. Still others have extensive rock faces of giant proportions. Each biogeographic entity is breathtaking.

| State | Tamil Nadu | Zone | Western Ghats Offshoot |
|---|---|---|---|
| Area | 841.49 sq km | Ecosystem | Shola Forest |
| Year of Notification | WLS 1976; NP 1984 | Visited | Jan 1986; May 1992; Jan, Aug 1993; Nov 1996 |

The Annamalai Sanctuary is frequently known as Top Slip. It was notified after the completion of the Perambiculam-Aliyar Hydroelectric project in the 1960s. In 1850, it was decided to extract timber from the Annamalais. The forest extended from Kollengode to Numbadi. Major FC Catton, Civil Engineer 7th division, gave sanction for the work and Michaels was appointed Superintendent of the Annamalai forests. In the past the timber felled from these great expanses of forests was pushed down the high mountain range in this area. They first made a cart road to the top of the ghat through the forest and a slipway for the timber. Another road was made to access the river from where the timber was floated to the coast. From 1854 to 1878, an enormous amount of timber was felled and Michaels started protecting teak forests against annual fires.

In 1986, on my first visit to Annamalai, the bus rattles up the steep slope into a clearing in the forest. It is already dark. A few lights glow dimly at the top of a grassy opening. Someone grabs my bag as I jump out of the bus. I am enthusiastically welcomed. This is WWF-India's training camp for trainers. I have been asked to talk to the young potential coordinators of WWF's conservation awareness programmes, the future volunteer force, which was the backbone of WWF activities in its early years. In those days, apart from the WWF and BNHS, there were no other NGOs involved in these nature education programmes. The man behind the Nature Clubs of India movement in those days was my friend Chandrakant Wakankar. Chandu had the ability to repeat these superb programmes with clockwork regularity. It required great

The Karian Shola is the most popular site for watching wildlife in Top Slip.

perseverance and a lot of hard work—planning, coordinating and activating training on a regular basis—a tough task on the small budgets that were available.

I enjoyed being with these young people, discussing programmes and talking wildlife. These young people who loved to look at my slides were capable of appreciating the problems of taking wildlife pictures in the remotest areas of India and sharing the excitement I felt of having been there. They could identify with this most closely. I made friendships there that have lasted over a quarter of a century.

On this first trip to Top Slip, I was woken well before dawn. We walked through the forest into the Karean Shola and climbed into the hide overlooking the grassy opening in the forest. Most wildlife enthusiasts have a large number

of excellent pictures taken from this hide. I have had several encounters with wildlife from here, and they bring back many memories. There are pictures of the unusual bee eaters on a neighbouring dead tree, birds of prey and a civet.

Top Slip is the most important residual habitat of the lion-tailed macaque. In the deep Shola a tribal guide imitates their call to which we hear a number of excited vocal responses. Quietly we move through the cover of the giant trees. A black shadow moves through the canopy far above us. We have found our first lion-tailed macaque. The guide points in another direction: yet another shadow. The monkeys are all around us, unheard, unseen—feeding happily on flower buds that fall onto the detritus of the forest floor. In my excitement I lie on my back on a fallen log. Forgetting the fact that this is

1 Evergreen forests in the Annamalai Hills.

2 Mist passing through the trees in the Annamalais.

3 Unlike most grasses that flower every year, bamboo has a long flowering cycle. All the bamboo clumps in an area flower at the same time once in several decades

4 Epiphytic plants are abundant in evergreen forests as the bark of trees retains moisture for long periods of time.

1

2

3

The varied and complex structure of flowers is a marvel of nature.

A newly opened leaf on the forest floor.

An elephant looking for browseable plants amidst unpalatable *Lantana* shrubs which spread prolifically through the forest.

a tick-infested forest, I am engrossed in taking pictures of these beautiful monkeys. A macaque ropes its way down a climber and jumps onto a neighbouring tree trunk. From the low branches its orange-brown eyes peer down bright with curiosity. In my excitement I load film after film, only to find out later that the film speed was wrongly adjusted on the camera! The lion-tail is a beautiful monkey. It has long black shining hair, a grey fringe around its dark face, and a lion-like tassel on the tip of its tail.

The forest is full of bird-life. Hornbills make strange sounds as they fly across the valley in undulating flight lines. A *baza* floats silently through the trees. The all-pervasive odour of a dead animal nearby makes me instantly aware of the presence of a tiger or a leopard that could well be extremely close but remains unseen.

Walking back to the camp in the evening past a small settlement, we see that the villagers are huddled outside their huts. They point down the road. We see a group of wild elephants foraging near the roadside in a large clump of *Lantana* bushes. This could hardly be palatable for the elephants. But they seem to be feeding from it nevertheless. Are they selectively looking for other plants growing in the thickets or are they forced to feed on it? What effects could this exotic weed have on their metabolism? Would this garden plant brought in by a British lady in the early part of this century eventually completely take over the diversity of shrubs on which so much of our wildlife depends? It may not be long before this exotic weed will change the ecology of these areas so drastically as to have a serious negative impact on a variety of animals, birds and insects. Can elephants adapt to such drastic changes? We have few good answers to such questions. But can we wait to get the real answers?

In the evening all the WWF camp volunteers gather around to hear what each group has seen through the day. Tourists mingle with the volunteers, asking what these young people are doing here. Two British girls, who are on a wildlife tour of India, join the motley crowd of volunteers. Karen Lewis is an artist and spends the rest of her holidays illustrating

| 1 | 5 |
|---|---|
| 2 | 6 |
| 3 | 7 |
| 4 | |
| 8 | |

Brown palm civet.

The forest in Top Slip consists of a mosaic of vegetation patterns.

An emerald dove.

A hornbill flies noisily through the canopy.

A community nest which is home to a large number of wasps.

Butterfly populations fluctuate seasonally.

Top Slip has a large diversity of butterflies.

A butterfly feeding on *Lantana* nectar.

1  2

3

Flowers in the undergrowth.

A carcass is part of the detritus cycle that shifts nutrients from animals back to the soil on which plant life depends.

A young elephant calf follows its mother in the forest. With habitat loss and increasing levels of poaching it may never reach adulthood.

a wildlife poster for WWF-I. Karen has remained a friend ever since. The close friendships that Chandu's camps could generate in a few days provided the background for developing a variety of conservation awareness programmes in the country. I have made several trips to Top Slip since then but it is that first visit which will always remain the most memorable.

During the last 15 years, there have been several changes in Top Slip. The number of tourists has risen sharply. Pressures are inevitably increasing. There are, however, some important aspects that need to be studied in great detail. For instance in 1986, seeing the Nilgiri langur in Top Slip was fairly uncommon. At present one sees them in fairly large numbers even in and around the tourist area. Does this indicate a real increase in their population, or a feeling of security arising from a decrease in hunting pressure that makes them live in the tourist area? They are still more nervous of human presence than the common langur. As soon as they realize they are being watched, they leap into the air with the most astonishing agility. No common langur jumps from branch to branch with this effortless ease and grace. I have seen them, one after another, use the very tall bamboo by climbing to the very top and allowing their weight to bend it down and using this tensile strength to plummet themselves into the air to a branch of an adjoining tree several metres away. They float through the air, legs and tail spread like sky divers, to land onto a neighbouring fragile branch, bending it down when they crash into it.

What is really unique about Top Slip is its enormous variations in habitat diversity. There are the key areas of evergreen Shola patches with high diversity such as the Karian Shola a few metres off the road, on which the tourist complex is situated. Across the road there is a mixed deciduous forest with patches of teak, *Terminalia* and bamboo. A couple of hundred metres away, there is a dry deciduous forest.

In summer, this is so different from the adjacent evergreen Shola that it comes as a shock. Parts of this must be formed by the cleared forests that had been planted with teak over 100 years ago. *Hopea arviflora*, *Mesua ferra* and *Vitex altissima* are some of the common trees. *Strobilanthus* is a common undergrowth species and the giant *Entada phaseoloicks* climber is frequently seen twining around the great tree trunks. It is only as recently as a decade or two ago that the real value of the highly diverse species rich, evergreen and moist deciduous forests that are critical as food sources for herbivores has come to light. The board near the tourist complex however still extols the fact that there have been 100 years of scientific forestry—which means destroying all the forest's glorious diversity and reducing it to yield a utilitarian short-term gain, timber! The natural forest wall of giant evergreen trees of Karian Shola as one enters it from the tourist area is what excites me most. It is still as it was 15 years ago except for the absence of a few old and dried trees that I recall from those days. The waterhole is still the same in the opening in the forest. It is a wonderful place to be in.

The Indira Gandhi National Park has 144 bird species, of which eight are endemic to the south Western Ghats and the Nilgiris. An important finding of the BNHS team studying the area is a report suggesting that there are five bird species sighted at higher elevations that were not recorded at this height during earlier surveys. One could speculate that this may be due to the effect of global warming.

I have walked around these diverse forests with Valli, a local tribal guide, who knows everything a field ecologist would wish to learn about a forest. He knows by instinct and experience where the wildlife will aggregate in each season, by day or by night. Following in his footsteps, hour after hour, one can only wonder and learn.

Threat display of a harmless grass snake.

| State | Kerala | Zone | Western Ghats |
|---|---|---|---|
| Area | 285 sq km | Ecosystem | Western Ghats (Mountains) |
| Year of Notification | 1973 | Visited | Aug 1993, Nov 1996 |

The drive through Top Slip to Perambiculam takes one through a gradual transition in the forest pattern. The main feature of Perambiculam is its multiple dams. They not only inundate large tracts of evergreen forests but also break the continuity in the habitat so essential for several species. The dam filled with water creates conditions in which many animals can no longer use their habitat optimally. Wildlife movements are seriously affected. Their fragmented populations contain lower numbers—too low for successful breeding. This results in genetic erosion, making the individuals within a population less capable of retaining the heterozygous genetic nature of each individual essential for successful breeding. Ill effects, such as changes in plant and animal populations due to 'development' projects like dams, canals, roads and pipelines, are not taken into account when Environment Impact Assessments (EIAs) are carried out for these activities. The EIAs tend to pass this off as being of very little importance. The current EIAs done in the country need to be carefully screened from a biodiversity point of view if conservation is to be implemented in the face of these growing pressures. Was this done, if at all, when these dams were built? Today's growing problems with elephants damaging crops may have their genesis in these projects undertaken decades ago. And the secret disappearance of species that have not been studied could well be due to the isolation of habitats caused by these development projects.

A forest tract in Perambiculam opens onto a small clearing. Standing in the clearing is the Giant, said to be the largest teak trees in India. The old tree towers above the other large, mature teak trees that surround the clearing.

Apart from its massive girth, the tree has a unique, highly-fluted trunk quite unlike most teak trees. Standing before it, one feels dwarfed and humbled. Its antiquity makes one highly aware of the age of the forest. The giant tree appears to be timeless. It is magnificent!

| 1 | 2 |
|---|---|
| | 3 |

This old massive tree is said to be the largest teak tree in the country. It towers above all the large teak trees in Perambiculam.

Cycas.

This famous teak tree overshadows all the other teak trees in the sanctuary.

# SILENT VALLEY NATIONAL PARK
## SILENT VALLEY

| State | Kerala | Zone | Western Ghats Offshoot |
|---|---|---|---|
| Area | 89.50 sq km | Ecosystem | Tropical Evergreen Forest |
| Year of Notification | 1980–84 | Visited | Jul 1992, Jun 2002 |

One has heard so much about Silent Valley and its great diversity of plant life. The fact that it is considered to be one of India's conservation success stories gives it additional value. Known locally as Sairandhrivanam, it is said that it is referred to as a 'silent' valley because of the absence of cicadas. My first visit in 1992 was only for a few hours. I had three films with me, which I thought would be enough for the short trip that was planned as a brief visit to the area before taking a flight out of Coimbatore. While walking towards the proposed dam site, there was so much to photograph that I had run out of three rolls of film in the first 200 metres after getting out of the car! And I nearly missed my flight that day.

There was a profusion of flowering plants. Myriads of insects scrambled through the undergrowth. An unusual-looking frog jumped through the moist grass. Numerous species of birds flitted from branch to branch among the trees and shrubs. Nature is simply astounding in its great diversity in the Silent Valley.

In a 1994–95 study on birdlife in Silent Valley, Lalitha Vijayan of SACON has shown that in undisturbed evergreen forests, there were 201 birds of 31 species encountered in the study plots. In contrast, in disturbed evergreen forests there were only 94 birds of 30 species. As against this, in adjacent coffee plantations there were only 41 birds of 13 species! This pertains to counts done in the winter and monsoon months and shows the dramatic difference in bird species abundance and richness once an evergreen forest is altered by human activity.

The primates in the valley were studied by K Ramachandran and GK Joseph from 1993 to 1996. Silent Valley has 14 troops of lion-tailed macaques, mostly in the southern part. The specific trees it uses are *Cullenia—palaquium, Palaquium mesua* and

The proposed site of a dam at Silent Valley that led to a great controversy.

| | 3 |
|---|---|
| 1 | 4 |
| 2 | 5 |
| | 6 |

Evergreen forests of the Silent Valley shelter a great biological diversity.

This river with its incredible forests would have been submerged under a hydel project in the 1970s but for timely public protest and support from Prime Minister Indira Gandhi.

We know very little about the diversity of plants in the undergrowth.

Flowering plants growing in a small amount of soil in a crack in the rock.

More research is needed to study the medicinal properties of plants.

Exciting events in the life of a forest are constantly happening on the forest floor. Seeds fall, germinate, grow into seedlings and eventually create the giants of the forests.

1

2

3

No description of an ecosystem is complete without documenting its fungal diversity.

A settlement at the fringe of Silent Valley National Park.

The fronds of a fern.

*Mesua calophyllum*. There are 275 of these endangered animals and their average troop size is 19 individuals. Troops vary from 9 to 30 animals, with an average of one male and five females. They also counted 501 Nilgiri langurs in 85 troops, which, unlike the lion-tailed macaque, used a much wider variety of food.

Some years ago there was a plan to construct a hydel dam which, had it gone through, would have submerged Silent Valley. This led to a great environmental battle to save this incredible Shola forest. The story begins in the late 1960s and early part of the 70s when, the Government of Kerala proposed to build a hydroelectric dam in Silent Valley. It was not a well-known area, as it was neither a Wildlife Sanctuary, nor a tourist destination. There was, in fact, very little scientific documentation of its flora and fauna. Fortunately it came to the attention of a large number of environmentalists and scientists who supported each other to create a public awareness campaign that came to be known as the Save Silent Valley Movement. How did it happen? Today many people claim to have been the prime movers of saving the valley. Perhaps some of these are true stories; others are exaggerations out of proportion to what really happened. But the important milestones are clearly documented facts. The movement lasted well over a decade, beginning in the early 1970s and gathering momentum through the early 80s. Between 1977 and 1980, it became not only a national battle but grew into a major international conservation concern. In many ways, it was an agitation by the elite, scientists, press reporters, and even artists who joined hands to fight for this little-known valley that most of them had not even seen.

In 1979, the pressure to save the valley had grown to such proportions that MS Swaminathan, Secretary to the Ministry of Agriculture, Gvernment of India, was asked to visit Silent Valley with a team of scientists and Senior Government Officials. Among the people who fought for the valley were Madhav Gadgil and Zafar Futehally. They even declined to be included in an 'Environment Monitoring Committee' set up to 'safeguard' the valley after the dam was built! Scientists and NGOs who approached the Government of Kerala and India were not given a hearing. Morarji Desai, the Prime Minister at that time, is said to have endorsed the building of the dam.

After Indira Gandhi became Prime Minister for the second time, a number of people requested her to get the proposal reviewed. She asked MGK Menon, Secretary to Government of India in the Department of Science and Technology, to constitute another committee. The

Dam site at Silent Valley.

Prime Minister herself appears to have been convinced that there should be no dam. In 1981, she declared at the Science Congress in Varanasi that Silent Valley would be protected. However, when the notification was issued, it excluded the submergence area of the dam. This led to another set of protests, letters to the Prime Minister, meetings and agitation. The KSSP and individuals like MKL Prasad influenced the findings of the MGK Menon review. Indira Gandhi got the final report in 1982. In 1983 she firmly vetoed the project. It is said that it was Salim Ali's request that greatly influenced her thinking. The State and Central Governments abandoned the project. By November 1984 it was decided to create a Protected Area and on 7th September 1985 a National Park was created at Silent Valley. Unfortunately, Indira Gandhi was no more and it was Rajiv Gandhi who attended the function to inaugurate Silent Valley. The long battle for survival had lasted over 15 years! It had too many heroes to mention here. All of them played a variety of key roles in making it happen.

But environmental battles based on individual sporadic efforts are neither sustainable nor consistent. They are won only when there is a combination of environmentally conscious individuals with access to sensitive policy makers. One cannot expect this to happen at every site where conservation and development enter into a confrontation. As of now, the environmental lobby appears to be losing many more environmental battles than they are winning. If this trend is to be reversed it can only grow out of a mass conservation awareness movement. This cannot be initiated unless it is generated through formal environment education in schools and informal conservation awareness activities among people everywhere.

In July 2001, *The Hindu* reported that the Kerala Government once again planned to develop a hydel project in Silent Valley. This was of great concern as this battle had been waged in the 1970s and won after a long and protracted public protest. Thus after 30 years the spectre has been raised again.

Silent Valley was a lucky victory. We need, however, to win many more battles for other silent valleys, remote mountains, great lakes and rushing rivers. What intrigues me most is the large number of people from different walks of life—conservation NGOs, administrators and scientists—all of whom wish to take credit for saving Silent Valley.

Southern Indian Shola forests have a remarkable diversity of amphibian life.

Silent Valley is very rich in angiosperms.

# ERAVIKULUM NATIONAL PARK

ERAVIKULUM / MUNNAR

| State | Kerala | Zone | Western Ghats Offshoot |
|---|---|---|---|
| Area | 97 sq km | Ecosystem | Shola Forest |
| Year of Notification | 1978 | Visited | May 1995, Jan 2001 |

The Rajamalai region was declared a Wildlife Sanctuary long ago in 1936, but the present Sanctuary, established by the Kerala Government, was only notified in 1975 and upgraded to a National Park three years later. In 1933 Salim Ali visited several areas of Travancore and Cochin for a bird survey (JBNHS, Vol, 37, 1937). He writes that the forests of Munnar had been extensively cleared over the preceding 60 years making way for tea plantations, eucalyptus trees for fuel for tea factories, and shade trees for coffee plantations. Over the years, animal and bird life here depleted and concentrated mainly in the scrubby areas.

Great stretches of the Sholas have been converted into tea and coffee plantations. Surrounded by tea gardens, the Munnar grassland is one of the last refuges of a viable population of Nilgiri *tahr*, the only wild goat found in India south of the

Himalayas. It is an extremely shy animal, extensively hunted in the past as it was considered a much sought after prize of adventurous shikaris. The large males, referred to as saddlebacks, were especially targeted as they had large horns and were difficult to bag, as they lived solitary lives high up on the steep hill slopes. In 1999, the estimated population of *tahr* in Eraviculum National Park was 700 animals. The Sanctuary is also the home of elephants, gaurs and other animals.

Tata Tea has taken an interest in protecting the area and its *tahr* populations for the last several decades. A small NGO, the Nilgiri Wildlife (formerly Game) Association, was established in 1877 and now interacts with the Forest Department to protect the *tahr*. In the vicinity of the Forest Department's tourist zone the *tahr* have become extremely trusting and will approach human beings to within a few

A typical patch of Shola forest in a long *nala* course with surrounding dry grass.

Grazing herd of *tahr*.

A Nilgiri *tahr* with her kid surveys the hill slope.

A large alert flock of *tahr* on the hill.

| 1 | 2 |
|---|---|
| 3 | 4 |
|   | 5 |
| 6 |   |

A lake in Eravikulum at sunset.

Bank of a water course covered with ferns.

Plants growing in very little soil on a rock.

A rock surface covered by plant life harbours several insects.

Flowers in the undergrowth.

Though tree frogs are heard all over the forest they are difficult to spot.

metres if they are not disturbed. This creature, once very wild, has now become semi-tame as a result of the protection it has had over the last few decades. Some of the excitement of getting close to a *tahr* has disappeared as a result of the high level of protection. The growing number of tourists is a serious menace.

From the grassy hillslope at Eravikulum, one can see several ranges across the deep valley covered by tea plantations. The view of the Sholas on one side and of the tea plantations on the other is spectacular. The distant hills look blue and fleecy white clouds stretch across the horizon. Rolling clouds frequently sweep up from the valley to engulf one in a cold, moist whiteness. Suddenly the far away hills are gone and one feels totally isolated by a few metres of visibility. The clouds pass by as suddenly as they come. A brilliant sunlight now bathes the dew-covered grass. The world is still there. At the edge of the slope a group of *tahr* graze in unison. A kid jumps from rock to rock. One feels far removed from any human disturbance. An incredible experience! At night I decide to go looking for tree frogs. Their call, 'pit pit pit', rings out all over the forest. I worry about snakes but forget this risk after a few minutes as I scramble through the undergrowth. A tree frog must be photographed. Every time I approach a 'pit pit pit' sound, the frog stops calling. This goes on for a long time until I am too cold to continue. I walk back in disappointment, to find that I have been locked out of the guest house! Then, just when the door is about to be opened, I notice it. It is bright green and has settled on the white wall next to the door under the tube light. The frog lets itself be photographed but it is out of its usual habitat and to me the pictures are of little interest. Wildlife photography is always full of surprises.

My second visit to Munnar was with my friend Changappa who worked in Tata Tea. Saving this area has been his lifelong battle. A saddleback! The word itself conjures up an image of an extremely shy creature. It appears in the grassy clearing, gazes at us fixedly, then turns around and disappears. Some of the herd settles down in the grass, while others graze unconcerned. Changappa

*Tahrs* resting on the grasslands covering the crest of a hill.

Sunrise.

knows the sanctuary intimately and has many stories of these superb animals.

A highly endangered species, (big males are indeed a rare sight), the *tahr* herds are now small in size and isolated from each other. Its ability to climb high up on a rocky overhang, peer fearlessly over a cliff and jump gracefully backward off the edge is astounding. Its sure-footed gait as it clambers up the steepest slopes can rarely be matched by any of the other hill species. Its only obvious predator is man.

During my last visit, as I gazed at the astounding view from the hilltop of Munnar, which the *tahr* frequents, it suddenly turned white. Blanket after blanket of clouds passed slowly over the hillside, blanking out the distant valley and the herd of *tahr* in the foreground. When the sun emerged again the emerald-green grass sparkling with water drops contrasted sharply with the deep blue of the distant hills. The scene could well have inspired Beethoven to write yet another *Pastoral Symphony*! As one comes down from this idyllic scene, plastic bags and bottles litter the side of the road. The hill is a picnic spot that is misused in all possible ways. There is a story that people have even fed smashed glass pieces of a bottle to the *tahr* for fun! Glass pieces are mistaken by the *tahr* for salt that the forest department has been giving to *tahr* to lure the herd to the tourist zone. What is urgently needed is to introduce strong messages in the Interpretation Centre telling tourists more about the uniqueness of this threatened animal. On the one hand, wildlife tourism must be increased to develop a larger interest in biodiversity conservation. On the other hand, widespread tourism can lead to grave disturbances to habitats and wildlife unless there is a parallel effort at converting the average tourist into one who is sensitive to the needs of wild creatures and their habitat. The tourists at Eravikulum, however, blare horns at the *tahr* and even chase them to make them run. This isolated wild goat of the Nilgiris may perhaps hold the key for future genetic management of the domestic goat. And one can never forget the fact that it is the only wild goat found in India south of the Himalayas.

| State | Kerala | Zone | Western Ghats Offshoot |
|---|---|---|---|
| Area | 90.44 sq km | Ecosystem | Shola Forest |
| Year of Notification | 1984 | Visited | May 1995 |

Down by the river in the Chinnar Sanctuary there is a grove of ancient tamarind trees. If one waits long enough, a curious squirrel will make an appearance and quietly watch you from behind a branch. During my single visit in 1995, the squirrels were extremely cooperative. Two of them decided to chase each other through the canopy, completely ignoring the presence of three or four people for a full 10 minutes of bedlam. Rapid chases occurred from one tree to another and back again, until the noisy rustling of the branches attracted the attention of a large bird of prey. It swooped down from the sky and sailed through the branches along the course of the river. Though there were alarm calls from several small birds, the squirrels were just too busy chasing each other, until the raptor moved across the river to settle on a branch to watch the excited chase. Once he was noticed, there were multiple alarm calls and a hurried retreat by both the warring animals. The eagle quietly made its exit chased by a pair of drongos.

The Chinnar Sanctuary is probably the only location in the country that now has a viable population of the grizzled giant squirrels. This Sanctuary is the home of one of the last few pockets of this very rare squirrel. It lives only along the narrow riverine tracts of specialized forests where it frequents large old tamarind trees.

The grizzled giant squirrel is one of the rarest squirrels in India. It is mainly found in Chinnar.

# GRASS HILLS WILDLIFE SANCTUARY
## GRASS HILLS

| State | Kerala | Zone | Western Ghats Offshoot |
|---|---|---|---|
| Area | 89.50 sq km | Ecosystem | Shola Forest |
| Year of Notification | — | Visited | May 1992 |

The approach to Grass Hills in the Annamalai Western Ghats hill complex is on the road to Valparai from Pollachi. The Forest Department jeep labours up the steep track to Grass Hills. Dr MK Ranjeetsingh, who was the Additional Secretary, Ministry of Environment and Forests, and I have decided we should get away from it all for two days. We stop midway up the slope, as he wants to take a picture of a pair of quails on the roadside. He takes a series with his large tele-lens from the car. I can't take pictures from the backseat. So once he has got his pictures, I carefully get out from the back, expecting the birds to fly away in fright. To my surprise they continue to walk towards me till they are ten centimetres from my shoes!

As we ascend, the jeep track becomes extremely narrow, steep and full of loose

Shola singed by a large forest fire.

rocks. Down in the valley the slopes are covered with tea plantations. The distant hills are a deep turquoise blue. Suddenly it becomes misty and cold. The track leads up into a flat area surrounded by smooth spherical hills. Each depression contains an island of forest. The lower slopes remain engulfed in mist. The grass is a bright green. Through the grassy clearing a crystal clear stream winds its way down to the edge of the plateau. In the distance there is a single hut. The landscape is like an impressionist painting—apart from the swirling mist everything else is completely motionless.

The hut was built decades ago for the tea planters who stayed here on holidays to fish in the stream. It is now dilapidated though its surroundings are perfect, situated as it is in the most magnificent landscape left in the Shola forests in the country. Though there is supposed to be a lot of wildlife, except for a gaur in the distance and a few small herds of Nilgiri *tahr*, nothing appears in the clearing for two days. The vegetation is superb: lilies, ferns, fungi of many different species cover the grassland. There is a constant twittering of birds from the nearby patch of forest. Feeding parties of many different species flit across from one forest patch to another. Down by the brook there is a large lily in flower. Fish dart through the crystal-clear rushing water. A kingfisher sits on a nearby rock. In the sky two large raptors are circling over a patch of Shola forest. Looking for *tahr*, I walk towards a distant patch of forest behind which Dr Ranjitsingh says they have vanished. The isolation is complete; there is not a single person in sight. The *tahr* have vanished over the hill before I get there.

J Williams studied bird life in the Annamalai Hills and the Grass hills area in 1938 (JBNHS Vol 39). He mentions that Grass Hills, which was originally dense evergreen forest, was planted with tea, coffee, cardamom and cinchona as far back as 1898 and the change in land use expanded significantly between 1917 and 1930. Loss of biodiversity in terms of a natural unique ecosystem was thus

This stream was used for angling before this sanctuary was notified.

jeopardized at least a 100 years ago. The rate of loss however, has increased manifold during the last few years.

As I walk through the grassland I realize that a part of the Shola has recently been through a large fire. The fire has singed the leaves of the peripheral trees. Within the tree cover the damage is minimal. The mechanism by which the two vegetation patterns remain sharply delineated is obvious. The nearest Shola patch has an impenetrable edge of thick shrubs and climbers. Along the *nala* that emerges from the Shola forest, there are several tree ferns. The multiple shades of green create another impressionist painting in real life. This is God's own world.

Quail searching for food, oblivious of anything happening around it.

Flowering plants bloom for a very short period.

| State | Kerala | Zone | Western Ghats (Coastal Forest) |
|---|---|---|---|
| Area | 128 sq km | Ecosystem | Evergreen Forest |
| Year of Notification | 1958 | Visited | Dec 2003 |

A constantly twisting road from Thiruvananthapuram goes to the Neyyar Sanctuary on the Kerala-Tamil Nadu border. The evergreen forest skirts the multi-pronged catchments of a dam site. The hills are picturesque. On the edges are rubber plantations and tiny hamlets. I will remember this Sanctuary for several reasons. Where was the wildlife in this superb forest? But for birds and lizards and a solitary sambar, I saw no mammals throughout the day. Sadly, I found an *Acacia auriculiformis* sapling deep in the forest. It was a full three feet tall and I got the guard to yank it out. I don't know if he really appreciated why. And the driver was equally surprised when I told him

he couldn't leave the plastic water bottle behind in the forest. To top it all the Tourist Department has made nearly life-size plaster statues in the tourist centre of chital, tiger and a man shooting the tiger! What a message for a Protected Area's tourists.

The peak is the Agastha, a massive outcrop reflected in the water of the lake. There are hills which the guide claims are those of the Kalakad-Mundanthurai Tiger Reserve. So it is here that the Agasthamalai range must be connected to the Western Ghats. This would make it one of the most important linkages between the two ranges. Corridors such as these must now be clearly documented and carefully protected if the biodiversity of the hills is to be preserved in the long-term.

The Keralites have names for many plants and animals. Birds too—the drongo is referred to as a bird with a forked tail. A bright green climber that has fleshy leaves is called Sita's Necklace. Malayalam is probably richer in taxonomic names than other Indian languages. It would be interesting to find out if this is so and why. Are they closer to nature owing to the way they live with patches of vegetation around every home? Even patches they preserve in their backyard are sacred.

|   | 1 |   |
|---|---|---|
| 2 | 3 |   |

A model of a shikari pointing his gun at a deer put up at the door

A climber.

A dry tree trunk with an interesting structure.

A forestscape in the Sanctuary.

Tribal people who live in this forest have depended on its resources for generations.

This river has been fed by streams from the Neyyar forest.

# KALAKAD MUNDANTHARAI WILDLIFE SANCTUARY
## KALAKAD MUNDANTHARAI TIGER RESERVE

| | | | |
|---|---|---|---|
| State | Tamil Nadu | Zone | Western Ghats Offshoot |
| Area | Kalakad: 223.58 sq km | | |
| | Mundantharai: 582.07 sq km | Ecosystem | Evergreen/Semi-evergreen Forest |
| Year of Notification | 1962; 1972 | Visited | Feb 2003 |

The Agasthamalai Ranges form a group of hills separated from the Western Ghats near the tip of peninsular India. They are surrounded by the highly populated belts of Kerala and Tamil Nadu, but once in the range, the area is completely isolated from development. They are fortunately not high-profile tourist locations, and still provide a sense of isolation from the rest of the world. One finds oneself in the cool of the forest less than a kilometre after leaving the rice fields. The vehicle climbs through the forest and comes to a makeshift bridge. The remains of the old bridge washed down in a flood lie strewn across the riverbed. Across the bridge is a forest guest house built in the 1890s.

Mundanthurai is an incredible experience. The single road through the forest reaches an old hydel lake where the road terminates. The semi-evergreen forest has very few chital but a fair population of sambar. Many researchers from different organizations have worked in these forests on various species, especially the Nilgiri langur and the lion-tailed macaque. The most fascinating species is the tiny slender loris, which at present is of interest to Kauveri Kath whom I have known since the early days of WII when she was an M.Sc. student. She lives here with her delightful two-year-old daughter, who is growing up surrounded by a rather arrogant group of over-tame, overbearing rhesus macaques that demand that they should be fed. Kauveri has radio collared several slender loris, and as they are highly nocturnal, we are able to track two of them in the dark and see them gaze down at us with their enormous red lantern-like glowing eyes. One cannot imagine that a tiny creature can have such enormous eyes. As they are insectivores of the night, super night vision is crucial to their existence.

A blue mormon's flashing wings attract attention in the forest by their size and brilliance.

A boat ride across the hydel lake gets one to the western part of the Tiger Reserve, and as one walks through the forest for an hour, the riverine vegetation gives place to evergreen forests with gigantic trees. There is a profusion of plant life. Birds call in the forest. Deep in the forest the Nilgiri langurs call. It is an idyllic location. One has to come out from Mundantharai to reach the foothills at Kalakad to see the southern most part of the Sanctuary as Kalakad-Mundantharai Tiger Reserve is a long strip along the Tamil Nadu–Kerala border. The road to the forest guest house is steep and rough with a series of hairpin curves. It is a single track and when one encounters another vehicle coming from the opposite direction, a lot of dangerous reversing and manoeuvering at the edge of the road is necessary. Vehicles have

A cascade of crystal-clear water in the Kalakad-Mundanthurai Tiger Reserve.

The aggregation of butterflies settles on a moist sloping rock.

*Following page*
An estimated 5000 butterflies form a great swarm that aggregates on the rocks around this water course. When disturbed, the forest turns a bright lemon yellow of fluttering wings.

to be helped upslope with a push if this happens on an exceptionally steep slope.

At the end of the road is the resthouse overlooking a deep valley with surrounding semi-evergreen forests and craggy rocky exposures of immense size. The landscape in the Agasthamalai is more awesome than that of the Nilgiris or Annamalais due to the very rugged nature of the mountains.

Scientists of the Salim Ali School of Ecology, Pondicherry, are working on a research project on the forest types and the Nilgiri langur. They find this tough, as the Nilgiri langurs here are exceptionally

shy. They give you one brief stare and bolt. Why would someone want to look at the behavioural ecology of a species in an area where they are definitely more afraid of people? It is a challenge. This species has been extensively poached and several of them could have been massacred here before the area was declared a Sanctuary.

One walks out of the guest house and into an incredible forest. The forest was a cardamom plantation two or three decades ago and it is heartening to see the undergrowth and natural climbers returning. A few patches of old cardamom

still remain but most of the forest appears to be returning to its natural state. One has to walk up a steep slope for two or three hours however before reaching the undisturbed natural forests that are near evergreen formations.

Elephant dung, much of it quite fresh, is strewn around. The path through the thick undergrowth is extremely narrow and there is virtually nowhere to run if a herd is headed your way. There is a fresh tiger scat in the middle of the path adding to the spice of life in this thick impenetrable vegetation—not to mention the ticks.

A Nilgiri langur leaps from tree to tree in the canopy.

Members of a bonnet macaque family groom each other.

New leaves create a patch of contrast in the evergreen forest.

The darkest colour variation of the sub-species of the Malabar giant squirrel lives in the Agasthamalai Hills.

Beetles mating.

Evergreen forests near the tip of the Indian peninsula in the Agasthamalai Ranges gets both monsoons.

First light over the Agasthamalai Ranges of Kalakad-Mundanthurai Tiger Reserve.

Chital crossing the road in the Tiger Reserve.

Amphibia link aquatic and terrestrial ecosystems.

A forest calotes displaying its brilliant colours.

The Agasthamalai floral diversity is extremely rich and warrants a large amount of botanical research.

1
2
3   4
5

A climber that is a necessary part of the structure of the ecosystem. In formal forestry, climbers are frequently removed. This reduces the naturalness of the forest.

Brightly coloured fungi. Some fungi are edible, while others are poisonous.

Snow white fungi in a moist depression growing on dead leaves and twigs.

Nightfall at Kalakad's Mundanthurai Tiger Reserve.

Flowers in the undergrowth form an important component of the ecosystem.

Near the crest of the massive hill the vegetation turns into thick short bamboo clumps. The climbers include cane, which at times spreads across the path as it has been scattered by a recent elephant herd. The hill forests are a long arduous climb, but the reward is the incredible diversity of plant life of the Agasthamalais, the southern most forested hills in India and our last Protected Area before we touch the tip of India at Kanyakumari, which is only an hour's drive from the Sanctuary.

Just outside the Tiger Reserve Guest house are two *Bombax* trees, which are just about to flower. A Malabar giant squirrel has found its storehouse of food certainly for the next couple of months or weeks if it manages to strip the two trees before its buds flower. Like most other animals in Kalakad it is exceptionally shy and looks nervously at me before it vanishes into the adjacent canopy of evergreen trees through which one can see nothing.

The waterfalls of Kalakad are its most appealing feature. They cascade down hundreds of metres in multiple broken noisy cascades. One of the falls offers an incredible sight. It has an enormous number of butterflies that roost on the watercourse in hundreds. They settle shoulder to shoulder so close that the next one trying to land has to squeeze itself into an ever-narrowing gap. As they settle, their flashing white wings close and magically turn it into a yellow triangle with a thin line and a dot at its wingtip. Together they paint the slope a luminous yellow. The roosting site has a thin layer of trickling water. Both the rocks they use have this thin film of water and are covered by algae. If they are disturbed by a movement they turn the sky white with their fluttering wings, only to resettle themselves on the same place within minutes.

On the hill slopes a profusion of flowering plants of every description covers the open grassy scrub-covered windy areas. Within the forests there is an incredible diversity of ferns from the large tree ferns with fronds well over a metre in length, to the tiniest ones that are less than a centimetre in size and cover the rocks with a fuzzy fur-like covering. The rock feels moist and cool. At the base of a rock, there is a strange plant that has emerged from the thick humus-filled soil. Before opening it forms a hard round ball. When open it has a bright red colour with small white projections. It contrasts so strongly with the green of the rest of the undergrowth that one cannot miss it.

At the forest rest house, the talkative cook with a very loud voice says to anyone who wishes to listen how he has cooked for VIPs and well known people like Rauf Ali. When he is told I know him, my image grows instantly. I am then told that he has been asking why an old man like me wants to trudge up mountainsides with a heavy camera and with a long lens. Young researchers need to do this but why should an old doctor go through all this trouble? It does get harder trudging through forests up and down steep hills. Not to speak of ticks and leeches that add to the discomfort for weeks because I am allergic to tick bites which give me 3-centimetre wheels that itch like mad for six weeks to remind me continuously of the beauty of the forest I have visited.

Rauf Ali and his colleagues have been undertaking a variety of research projects at Mundanthurai-Kalakad since the 1970s. This has included detailed studies on the Nilgiri langur and various aspects of the unique vegetation patterns of this superb area. The young research scholars live in a small house nestled in an opening in the forest. It is a perfect setting where the Nilgiri langurs cross over everyday. Birds flit through the shady glade and hardly anyone else ever visits the secluded spot. They offer me a hot cup of tea and we sit together to talk about the forest and its wildlife. It is these young scientists who will help make it possible to use hard scientific facts for far better management of this Tiger Reserve.

A religious procession to a temple on the border of Kalakad-Mundantharai Tiger Reserve.

## MOIST EVERGREEN LOW FORESTS

The coastal and riverine vegetation in Kerala form great forests of immense biological diversity. They have several local endemic species of plants and animals.

# THATTEKAD WILDLIFE SANCTUARY

THATTEKAD

| State | Kerala | Zone | Western Ghats (Riverine System) |
|---|---|---|---|
| Area | 25.16 sq km | Ecosystem | Evergreen/ Riverine forest |
| Year of Notification | 1983 | Visited | Feb 1995 |

There are two river valley stretches in Kerala not far from each other. One is a Proteced Area on the Periyar River, which is notified as the Periyar Wildlife Sanctuary, while the other is the Thattekad Bird Sanctuary. The latter is a valley that Dr Salim Ali visited repeatedly during the 1930s and 1940s. JC Daniel describes this region as having been nearly inaccessible. 'Hardly anyone went there!' It must have been a pristine valley full of the twittering of birds, the haunt of great elephants and herds of gaurs. A number of tigers and leopards must have lived there, as there was plenty of prey. The distinctive riverine vegetation, which includes a dwarfed variety of bamboo, must have made access into the forest extremely difficult. Under the thick canopy of these bamboo clumps the shaded area was so complete that nothing grew below it. During the recent past these bamboo clumps have been extensively exploited. As the bamboo disappears a variety of weeds and shrubs take their place. The bamboo is made into large rafts and floated down the river to the settlements where it is processed and loaded onto trucks.

Salim Ali (1985) in his autobiography says that 'Thattekad…lingers in my memory as the richest bird habitat in peninsular India….' He deplores the development projects and deforestation in subsequent years and writes that, 'Thattekad has become a travesty of its former self, with most of the superb natural forest replaced a by monoculture of commercial species to pander to industrial development, or drowned in the huge reservoir created by damming of the Periyar river.' He visited Thattekad in 1933 and described the river and its forest types (JBNHS Vol 37). The right bank of the river already had plantations of teak, rubber and *bombax* created by the Forest Department, which were about 25 years old. The *bombax* plantation had been recently planted. He records that there were hundreds of lorikeets all day. Salim Ali mentions the gigantic trees with straight boles of 70 to 80 feet to their first branch in the evergreen forest.

JC Daniel and I go upriver in a Forest Department boat. I am looking for flying lizards. Elusive little creatures when you look for them. But overtly present when you are walking down a jungle path looking for larger animals to photograph. During the previous night a large tusker had invaded the nearby village and destroyed their banana crops. We were told he was dangerous and frequently attacked unsuspecting people. He could either have gone up into the hills or down into the valley close to the river. We decide to take a boat to avoid the area where the elephant is likely to be feeding. We leave JC and the boatman on the riverbank so that I can go on my search for the flying lizard that I have never photographed. Though the forest staff with me are obviously apprehensive, we walk quietly down a jungle track looking for lizards on the tree trunks at the side of the path…. or none. I take a few forest pictures. It is a peaceful setting. One begins to forget the possibility of elephants or gaurs or tigers after a while. One can get so carried away that one soon feels confident that nothing can happen. Suddenly an earsplitting, angry trumpet rends the silent forest. There is a crashing of branches. The canopy just

the boat, all in one continuous motion. I only wish the elephant had descended to the water so I could take his picture, but he never showed up. I have no flying lizards and no angry elephant pictures from the great forests of Thattekad.

We return to a small Interpretation Centre and I take one more walk before leaving. While I don't find a flying lizard, I come across the rare forest tortoise, a species that is highly endemic to the region and perhaps the only tortoise to inhabit evergreen forests in India. My day is made.

|   |   | 3 | 4 | 5 |
|---|---|---|---|---|
|   |   |   | 6 |   |
| 1 | 2 |   | 7 |   |

The river in the Thattekad Sanctuary where Salim Ali did his bird surveys many decades ago.

Bamboo being floated down the river.

The variety of plant life is a delight for botanists.

The racket-tailed drongo is distinctive in flight as it looks like a bird followed by two bumble bees.

Darter or snake bird.

Storks live on the fish, amphibia, crustaceans and molluscs on the river.

The Travancore forest tortoise is a unique species with a very restricted distribution in South India.

below the road seems to be alive with movement. We run! The Forest Guards with me are definitely faster than I, but then they don't have a heavy camera bag and a camera with a big 400 mm lens! The elephant is crashing through the forest parallel to the road. We look back. He has not climbed onto the road but is moving rapidly along the embankment beside it. A few more trumpets reverberate through the forest and echo back from the hills. All you can do is to keep running if you cannot scramble up a large tree. Should I drop my camera bag with my equipment? But it was bought with my life's savings. No, that's out! We make it round to the bay where we had moored the boat. It is not there! Then we see it in the water several metres away, with the boatman in it. JC is sitting on the bank looking apprehensively in the direction of the forest. After we are all safe in the boat, JC described how the sleeping boatman, as if electrified by the first trumpet, shot up from his horizontal sleeping position and turned into a vertical, wide-awake, running person who could take a flying leap into

| State | Kerala | Zone | Coasts (West Coast) |
|---|---|---|---|
| Area | — | Ecosystem | Riverine |
| Year of Notification | 1983 | Visited | Feb 1995 |

Pooyamkutty, a tributary of the Periyar in the Idukki district in Kerala, is a river that may die. Its gorge is deep, the water is crystal clear, and the banks covered by a near-continuous tract of evergreen rain forest. The trees are towering giants. The jeep track winds through these ancient forests providing only glimpses of the river down below in the deep gorge. Very few of the giant lowland evergreen forests in Kerala still have a large proportion of gigantic trees with huge girths and broad, sculptured buttress roots. Pooyamkutty is a very special forest type, one that has nearly disappeared. Droves of forest birds move through the canopy. Pooyamkutty has an incredibly variegated vegatation. The great evergreen forests have gigantic buttress roots and lofty canopies. It also has semi-evergreen and moist deciduous forests. The unique riverine vegetation is seen all along the banks of the river. This is a rare vegetation type, with bamboo breaks and

Pooyamkutty has many gigantic trees.

The tranquil river is surrounded by ancient forests. It would be an ecological disaster to dam this incredible site for generating power.

grassland patches. The area surveyed by SACON has documented 526 plant species. The riverbanks are covered mostly by a species of bamboo that has an extremely thick canopy through which no light filters to the ground. Deer tracks abound in the *nala* courses. The remoteness of this region, with only a few isolated scattered hamlets, makes it a great conservation asset for the preservation of biological diversity.

This riverine forest that should be a Sanctuary may turn into a lake if the proposed dam downstream is cleared for construction. Several efforts at clearing this project have been rejected. But the pressure persists. Dam sites can be shifted, but ancient forest systems are rooted to the wilderness in which they have grown and are immovable, in fact, irreplaceable. If the dam is cleared, thousands of old trees along the riverbed as well as one of the last tracts of evergreen rain forest of the lowlands of Kerala will disappear. The tribal hamlets will be submerged. One of South India's most spectacular forest landscapes will be gone forever. And the home of elephants, gaurs, sambar and many other species will be inundated for a few kilowatts of electrical energy.

One of the characteristic features of this forest is its unbroken canopy and the huge individual trees that emerge through the forest. No other forest in this region has so many tall trees with massive girths. Can we thoughtlessly lose the germ plasm of these ancient trees for a small gain in hydropower? The power could well come from any other less ecologically valuable region or from alternate energy sources. Does it have to be generated at the cost of losing this incredible forest? Or is the financial gain from this ancient timber the additional short-term motive for selection of this site for a hydroelectric project?

A few years ago, SACON did a formal Environmental Impact Analysis (EIA) for this project, demonstrating its enormous ecological and biodiversity values. The Report firmly rejects the proposal for the dam. Government has given this scant attention. Another organization is asked to review the project in the hope that the next Environmental Impact Analysis will return a positive verdict for the dam! Eventually will this superb habitat become a hydel project or a Sanctuary for conserving biological diversity? Only time will tell.

Bamboo is a resource that is of great value.

Ferns are indicators of high moisture levels.

# P E R I Y A R

PERIYAR

| State | Kerala | Zone | Western Ghats (Riverine System) |
|---|---|---|---|
| Area | 777 sq km | Ecosystem | Dry and Moist Deciduous Forest |
| Year of Notification | Closed to hunting, 1950; NP 1982 | Visited | Feb 1995, Jan 2001, Mar 2004 |

Situated in the hills of the Western Ghats in Kerala, this is a well-known wildlife tourist spot, known for its elephants. The dam across the Periyar River was built in 1895 and the forests were declared as Reserve Forests in 1899. In 1934 the area was given a Sanctuary status and was extended and given its present name in 1950. In 1978 it was made a Tiger Reserve, and given National Park status in 1982. The tiger census in Periyar in 1997 accounts for some 30 tigers (Jain, 2001). However, tiger sightings are uncommon in the tourism area. The Kerala Forest Research Institute has done floral studies in the area, and documented about 2000 plant species from the area.

The Sabarimala Ayyappam Temple is a focus of religious tourism and an estimated five million pilgrims visit the shrine annually over a brief period of two months. This causes a great deal of disturbance,

fire, garbage, movement of large numbers of people, all leading to serious impacts on wildlife populations. The amount of garbage created is enormous. Pilgrims also need fuelwood, which comes from the Protected Area. Modern pilgrims have little real respect for nature though it is possible that sites such as this are linked to the presence of the remote forests, which must have been a deterrent to the less fervent. Perhaps the wilderness itself gave the place sanctity. Sabrimala must have once been difficult for people to reach due to its remoteness and wild animals. One important pressure is the deforestation done by ganja cultivators who clear patches of forest and settle near their crops deep inside the forest for several months.

If one wants easy wildlife sighting from the safe comfort of a boat, Periyar is a good choice. The boat is however frequently full of noisy tourists who move around and jostle to get a better view of elephants, gaur, chital and sambar at the side of the lake. The boat wobbles and photography with a large tele-lens becomes fairly difficult if the light is poor.

The lake has old trees sticking out of it, which act as roosts for cormorants, kingfishers, ibis and other water birds. I have had a lucky sighting of an otter catching fish and a herd of over 50 sambar at the water's edge. But it is the scenic beauty of the place that remains an indelible feature in my mind.

In bygone years, Periyar was a popular site for wildlife photographers. Wildlife lovers such as EP Gee and M Krishnan did much of their photography here. Wildlife photographers have contributed largely to the conservation awareness that has taken place in our country over the last few decades. Their dedication to the cause is no less than their commitment to taking pictures. The Periyar River and its wildlife

The Periyar River has been dammed to create a lake.

An elephant suspiciously scents the approaching boat.

Elephants on the bank of Periyar.

A warbler in the undergrowth.

Dead trees of the forest still emerge from the waters of Periyar Lake.

Grazing sambar at the water's edge.

Cormorants find safe roosting and nesting sites on dry old stumps.

A cormorant drying its wet wings in the breeze at sunset.

A deciduous tree in its leafless phase.

Exoskeletons of cicadas.

An unusual frog sits at the edge of the river.

| 1 | 2 |
|---|---|
| 3 | 4 |
| | 5 |

Turtles emerge from the water to bask in the sunlight.

A large sounder of wild boar.

White-bellied treepie.

Moss on a tree trunk.

The landscape of Periyar.

have been more intensively photographed by the hoards of tourists it gets annually than most other Sanctuaries in the country.

Periyar Tiger Reserve has a unique eco-development programme for the local people who live around the Protected Area. There are several initiatives that have been unique. I would rate these initiatives as some of the best efforts at reducing people-wildlife conflict in the country. A group of poachers have been given respectability by being allowed to work as frontline forest department staff. They now wear uniforms and apprehend poachers. I asked them if they earned more from their wages or from their past practice of illegal hunting and trapping activities. They admitted that they now earned much less but could live in peace with their families without being constantly chased by the police and forest officials. One of them said that now he could go to his children's school for parents-teachers meetings which he could not do in the past as his children would have had to hide his true illegal occupation. A group of village women have also been doing duty as forest watchers and helping as informants of illegal tree felling. Several villages have elected committees that debate how to use funds from the India Ecodevelopment Project equitably and have formed Forest Protection Committees to preserve their forest resources. They also market products made by the village communities and have set up an Interpretation Centre in a village hut surrounded by a spice garden. All this goes to show how a sensitive forest official can make things happen.

A large male gaur.

Nilgiri langur.

Heron.

# KUKERBELLUR WILDLIFE SANCTUARY
KUKERBELLUR

| State | Karnataka | Zone | Deccan Peninsula |
|---|---|---|---|
| Area | — | Ecosystem | Rural Village Settlement |
| Year of Notification | — | Visited | May 1992 |

This Sanctuary for birds is in several ways unique. Its bird life, comprising open-billed storks, ibis and pelicans, has been protected by local people for several generations. The birds used to nest at the edge of the village of Kukerbellur, which means 'bird village'. The original nesting colony was restricted to a few old large trees around the village temple, and villagers traditionally collected bird droppings from under this colony. The birds are mostly fish eaters that feed their fledglings on large amounts of fish. The droppings are rich in nutrients, and are used as a valuable source of fertilizers for crops. Gradually, local people began to collect the guano and sell it to nearby villages. As people began to appreciate the economic value of this as a saleable product, they began to plant trees around their huts to encourage more birds to nest as the old trees were overloaded with scores of nests. On these low young trees birds now nest in hundreds all around the village. Shallow pits are dug under the trees to collect the droppings. This is a good example of a sustainable form of economic development based on the local wildlife of the area.

A tree planted near the house in the village to attract birds so that the owner of the hut can collect guano for his farm.

Young stork on a roof top.

Young storks still unable to fly need large quantities of food. The parents have to fly long distances to bring fish and other prey to the nest.

There are several nesting colonies of various fish-dependent birds in the village.

A young pelican trying its wings.

A homestead in Kukerbellur village with a nesting colony in the background.

*Following pages*
Every breeding colony of birds in Kukerbellur is associated with a hut.

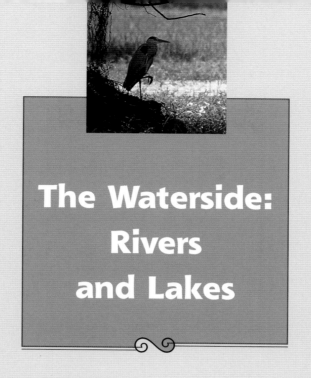

# The Waterside: Rivers and Lakes

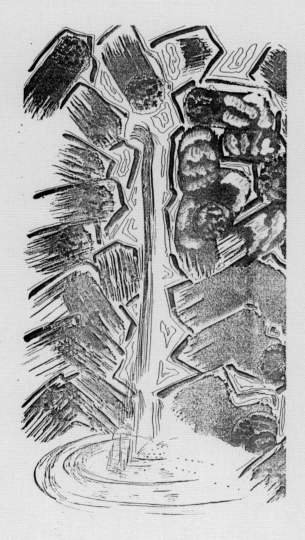

Rocks of Colgong—Forest (1824).

Waterfall.

I sit alone in a reed bed of emergent typha on the squelchy mud of the wetland. It is very cold; I am chilled to the bone. The dawn is breaking. From the sky, a never to be forgotten sharp whistling sound attracts attention. Two ducks, wings swept backwards, are descending sharply, extremely fast, twisting and turning in unison during their rapid descent to the only patch of water where there are no reeds. Their webbed feet are outstretched as they reach their landing strip on the open water. Splash-splash! They settle only to rise again as the double barrel gun goes off. My father has missed them. The ducks, along with other unseen birds that were in the marsh, rise out of the water with a whirring of hundreds of wings. Secretly I am gleeful. Poor ducks. Good for them they got away. And for years I hide my secret pleasure at the ones that got away. It would sound unsportsman-like in the presence of my father's friends. I didn't want to be singled out, for I loved going out on these trips. So the secret remained with me for years thereafter. How values change with time and circumstances! My father stopped his shikar when he found that game was becoming scarce and started quietly campaigning for conservation. Though in the early years I went along to the shoots of which I disapproved, I was nevertheless deeply affected by these early exposures to Nature and learned a lot about the behaviour of wild creatures that the shikaris went after.

My earliest visits to the wetlands around Pune were in the 1950s. These were memorable Sunday duck shoots where I was a silent observer as my father and his group of friends sat patiently around a lake. The shikar was in fact an excuse for him to get out into the wilderness. And these expanses of wilderness were everywhere. A few kilometres from the edge of the town in any direction, and the wildness of the landscape took you into Nature's heartland. The large numbers of small percolation tanks around Poona had few human inhabitants. A few village folk and their cattle did not detract from the experience. There was tranquility everywhere, especially around the more isolated percolation tanks.

They were marvellous trips. Each time I would see something new. My father's shikar friend, Meherwanjee Kotwal, was in his late 60s. Meherwanjee, 'uncle' to everyone, was an intrepid small game shikari. I was told that in the 1940s he would get onto his sports cycle in the morning, ride to the Aga Khan Palace at the edge of town, bag a blackbuck and return in two hours or so with the animal on its carrier. Today, this is a bustling part of Pune City. The nearest blackbuck is 150 kilometres away! The ducks that Meherwanjee loved to bag, however, still come to the rivers and lakes although it is evident that their numbers have fallen. Sojourns with him into the wetlands were as educational as they were fun. His English was rather poor. We would all joke about his unique use of the English language. As his knee joints pained, we would find him a place near the car at the water's edge. The ducks, once disturbed, would rarely fall to his gun as they distrusted the large 1951 Chevrolet that doubled as a jeep and luxury car of the period. But Meherwanjee's patience was unmatched. He could sit motionless with ants crawling over him. His displeasure at a quiet cough would be demonstrated by a silent, disapproving look that could make you feel incredibly ashamed at the age of ten, making you want to slide into the marsh if you could. All of us joked about his duck shooting prowess. He would invariably miss. His eyesight at 65 plus had begun to dim with cataracts. He claimed however that he had '6 by 6' vision and said he distrusted ophthalmologists. On one of these memorable shikar mornings, he bitterly complained that a village kid who acted as a duck retriever had robbed him of his shikar. When we met after the shoot, he loudly proclaimed that he had hit two birds in one shot. 'But,' he said, 'that rascal village boy who went into the reeds to collect them has hidden my two buttucks!' The Parsi-Gujarati word for 'ducks' can be highly misleading! The joke lasted for years, much to Meherwanji's own quiet amusement. He loved people laughing at him and made sure that everyone laughed.

Driving out to the wilderness invigorated one. Lungs filled with clean air, and the closeness to Nature provided a feeling of wellbeing that no other experience can ever match. That part of Nature so close to town has vanished entirely. Good for Meherwanjee, he did not live to see his beloved wild places disappear completely. Shikaris like Meherwanjee were a breed apart from the rest of mankind. They were in their own way as close to Nature as the tribal people who live in the forest. Meherwanjee knew where and when an animal that had run into a forest thicket would re-emerge into view. He knew where and how to sit it out for an animal. And he knew how everything tasted! This band of shikaris

knew their favourite areas by day or night as well as they knew the palms of their own hands. They shot wild creatures but they also loved wild animals. Most of all, they soon became extremely sensitive to the gradual loss of the habitat of their beloved wildlife. Many turned into the country's greatest conservationists as the wilderness and its creatures began to disappear. Meherwanjee died in disillusionment. He realized way back then, that his treasured wild places and their denizens had begun to vanish. But I am sure he could not have ever imagined what has happened to the wilderness just 30 years after his death. I feel happy that he and so many others like him are not here to bemoan the death of India's many wild areas.

The presence of water is an element in an ecologically distinct landscape that considerably modifies the terrestrial ecosystem around it. The water changes both the pattern of the surrounding vegetation and its animal life. These ecosystems that form a special microhabitat are found in and around the lakes, jheels, tanks and ponds. They are also associated with the banks of the flowing waters of hill streams, waterfalls, rivulets, rivers and deltas. The characteristics of each of these ecosystems are linked to the nature of the surrounding terrestrial systems. And the aquatic ecosystem has a different role to play in each of the terrestrial ecosystems. This creates an enormous number of microhabitat types.

In the last few decades several dams, large and small, have been built all over the country, changing the landscape patterns of these areas. In several instances these artificial impoundments have done immense harm by inundating large tracts of forest and by opening up the wilderness to human activities. However, in some instances, these modified ecosystems have resulted in ecological benefits by creating a new habitat for water birds, or a year-round provision of drinking water for wildlife, which reduces the stress of the dry summer months.

Energy moves through every ecosystem, controlling its plant and animal life. In the vicinity of water there is a change in the pattern of energy transfers that occur in Nature. Here the presence of life forms

within the water itself is frequently the basis of the food chain. Algae, unicellular animals, molluscs, crustaceans, fish and amphibians that live in water form the basic food material for several reptiles, birds and mammals living in the terrestrial ecosystem around it. Some mammals such as the fishing cats and otters live on fish, and are hence usually found close to the water. Several raptors such as fishing eagles, ospreys and marsh harriers also hunt for prey that lives in the water. A large number of animal species frequent water not only to quench their thirst, but also to wash or cool themselves. Elephants are highly dependent on water holes to cool their large surface areas. Swamp deer and sambar often enter water and even browse on aquatic vegetation. Tigers habitually take a dip, especially in summer.

The torrents that flow out of the Himalayan snows have plenty of fish, and the Kashmir streams are good trout fishing areas. Birds such as the little dipper and several species of kingfishers frequent these rocky streams.

Most waterfalls in the Western Ghats flow only during the monsoon. The streams form the life support systems of fish, amphibians, and crabs. The crabs settle under the rocks in the rapidly flowing

Rocks in river.

water and catch their food material as it flows past them. Several herbaceous plants grow on the edge of the nalas, and die off once the cascade becomes dry. Ferns, moss and bryophytes are all ecologically sensitive species that live close to water. These constitute an important component of the biodiversity of a water-dominated microhabitat.

Wherever a large river has a shallow bed, water birds abound. Waterfowl like ducks and teals upend themselves to feed underwater on aquatic vegetation, worms and crustaceans. Several birds feed only on snails and crustaceans, others are dependent only on fish, which are in turn dependent on underwater crustaceans or smaller fish. These are in turn dependent on aquatic plant-life. Birds such as the waders, which have long legs, feed on aquatic insects that move on or near the surface of the water. Some birds only feed in the shallows or on the shoreline. Waders such as sandpipers and stilts enter the very shallow water on the bank to snatch at their food flowing by. Others feed on the molluscs, crustaceans and worms that live in the moist mud on the bank. Birds also frequent areas such as steep, rocky riverbanks. Several owls for instance live in the holes of the Marble Rocks at Bedaghat on the Tapti River near Jabalpur.

The migrants that settle on our rivers show a constantly changing pattern, which is difficult to account for. In the Mula Mutha Bird Sanctuary, a one kilometre stretch of river at Pune, the commonest duck in the early 1970s was the common teal, accompanied by a few gargany teals. Gradually the gargany teals increased in number and the common teal became much less common. After 1982 a major change in bird communities was observed. Instead of the usual teals, there was an influx of a large number of pintails. The teals seemed to have been displaced as their numbers dropped by at least 75 per cent. The niche occupied by the two birds is marginally different,

inasmuch as the pintail, being larger, upends in deeper water. Both however are basically vegetarian and, once the larger duck occupied the area, the smaller evidently changed their wintering area. Surprisingly, the very next winter the pintails became less common and the river was occupied again by a nearly equal proportion of gargary and common teals. From 1975 onwards the gull-billed terns increased in number, perhaps as a result of an increase in floating garbage on which they live. These however were replaced in subsequent years by the more

common river tern. In the course of the last five years the waders have all but disappeared, probably due to increasing industrial effluents. Strangely, the ducks that feed mainly on aquatic vegetation are more resilient. The waders have been drastically reduced in number, perhaps an indication that the small aquatic animals they feed on cannot survive in polluted water. Such changes in local bird populations around our water bodies and rivers frequently remain unexplained.

Flamingoes behave in a most curious way. Sudden unexplainable changes in

Marble rocks on the banks of River Narmada at Jabalpur.

*Following page*
Sunset on the Mula Mutha River.

A leaf in a stream.

their migratory patterns are well known. These archaic birds move between Kachchh in Gujarat, which is their breeding station, to their wintering grounds at wetlands such as Chilka in Orissa and Point Calimere in Tamil Nadu. Several years ago they began to stop over at several lakes in Maharashtra, shortening their migration by almost 50 per cent. They now also stop over on the highly polluted coast near Mumbai.

In the 1980s large groups of flamingoes began to settle on the backwaters of a relatively new dam called Ujani on the Pune-Sholapur road. The spectacle of a thousand bright scarlet, black and white birds winging their way over the deep blue water made a magnificent sight. They used the newly created mud banks that emerged in summer to feed in. As the water receded, these mud banks formed temporary islands that were used as nesting sites for birds such as terns, pratincoles and plovers. The hydrobiological pattern of this lake however then began to change.

In a newly formed lake several events succeed each other underwater before a stable ecological condition is reached. Ujani, in an early stage of aquatic plant succession was highly suitable for the flamingo. As the ecosystem gradually changed from mud banks into a marshy pattern, the commoner marsh birds increased in number while the food for the flamingo, which is found in open mud banks, decreased. Over the years, several changes have been documented in this lake creating changes in the population of a large number of aquatic birds. Similar changes are obviously occurring in several water bodies at the same time, creating a need for waterfowl to continually shift their movement patterns in response to man-made changes.

During the early 1980s, wetland conservation became my passion. The backwaters of Bhigwan at Ujani dam had begun to attract flocks of flamingoes. I was delighted by this discovery. I would go back time and again to photograph these majestic white and scarlet birds. A

few years later I thought that there was a need to understand more about the local ecology of this wetland. Pradumna Gogate—'Praddy' —was a WWF volunteer, and I, a a Member of the recently established Pune Branch Committee of the WWF-I, was offered a miniscule grant to study the birds. This got me a salary for Praddy and petrol for his bike. We began documenting the areas selected by the flamingo for feeding. Within two years we realized that their microhabitat was shrinking. As we were making a video film for a UGC Open University Programme with the Educational Media Research Center on flamingoes, the final output, which took four years to complete, had unwittingly documented a series of changes in the ecosystem. The edited film had less to do with flamingoes and more with the wetland ecosystem. It became a film on The Changing Nature of a Wetland. It showed how habitat loss in the wetland was due to the heavy inputs of fertilizers used by sugarcane farmers at the periphery of the lake, leading to its eutrophication. The video demonstrated how large areas of the open mud banks, in which hundreds of flamingoes and thousands of waders that had been feeding in the shallows of this newly formed lake, rapidly lost their microhabitat in the course of three or four years. These rapid changes due to the extreme sensitivity of wetlands to human induced activities have to be seen to be believed. At Bhigwan, it happened so suddenly and so dramatically that we were able to put this together in three or four years on a fascinating film. For a few hectares of sugarcane we had lost a wetland habitat of incredible value. Another 20 years later, the landscape has again changed. Sinnar Mass, a giant paper factory, has been built at Bhigwan—a new threat has been added to this sensitive ecosystem.

Several small bunds that were built in the country over a century ago, are now silted up and extremely shallow. These are home to a large number of water birds. Storks are especially fond of such silted lakes. A small bund called Mayeni in Maharashtra attracts a large number of spoonbills, painted storks, white-necked storks, flamingoes and other water birds. The density is incredibly high for a small area. Local villagers do not disturb the bird life and the area is well known to bird-watchers who have made it their own personal habitat! On weekends I have seen hordes of visitors in the place.

Bird movements are indeed unfathomable. An increasing number of seashore birds sporadically work their way inland. The seagulls and terns are found in increasing numbers to the east of the Western Ghats. Is this a response to increasing levels of disturbances, or pollution, or lack of food due to over fishing in adjacent coastal ecosystems? The crab plover is traditionally a coastal estuarine bird and restricted to the northern part of the Western coast. In the winter of 1982 I found a large flock of these estuarine birds at a lake close to the city of Kolhapur, a great distance from their usual coastal haunts. I took their pictures to Dr Salim Ali and told

Lake at sunset.

him where I had seen them. He said, 'Let's consult a good book.' I wondered which book he could be referring to until he picked his own book from off the shelf! Salim Ali was always able to make highly appropriate lighthearted quips. Finding birds away from their usual haunts could well imply that a variety of environmental changes are occurring in their natural seacoast habitat, forcing them to locate new types of habitats inland.

One of the peculiar man-made ecological changes in our rivers has been the introduction of several plants and fish that have modified aquatic ecology. One of the most damaging examples is the spread of water hyacinth, a weed from South America, introduced into aquatic ecosystems, just as *Lantana* was introduced into the country as a garden plant which spread into several of our forests. The *Echornia* or water hyacinth has covered many of our rivers. Once these slowly flowing waters are covered with hyacinth, birds such as ducks, terns, waders, kingfishers and others, which require an open expanse of water to feed on, are unable to use these areas. Their microhabitat, which is open water, is covered by several feet of tall and impenetrable floating vegetation. The birds must thus move elsewhere, into over-populated areas where the high density of herds must compete heavily for food in places not infested by the weed. However, birds such as jacanas, purple moorhens and white-breasted waterhens adapt to such weed-infested areas. Mosquitoes find this an extremely good place to breed. Another weed that has substituted the all-important typha reed beds is *Ipomea*, locally known as *besharam*, which translated means 'shameless'. This indicates its ability to grow just about anywhere. I have observed these habitat changes caused by the spread of exotic weeds alter wetlands over the last 20 years and take over large parts of natural habitats reducing the natural biodiversity at both the ecosystem and species level.

Aquatic landscapes can thus be easily influenced by human beings in a variety of subtle ways. Just as deforestation can change a forest ecosystem and totally destroy it, dams, bunds, water pollution, canals and the introduction of imported

Mountains of Rajemahal—Forest (1824).

Near Currah on the River Ganges—Daniel (1797).

forms of life can destroy the sensitive ecological balance of a natural waterbody. Wetlands, which are included in a variety of aquatic ecosystems as well as highly man-modified systems such as paddy fields, could account for as much as 18 per cent of the country. 12.8 per cent of this is paddy land. Only 5.5 per cent are wetlands. Of these only a small fraction are real natural wetlands while the rest are man-made habitats such as irrigation tanks, dams and hydel lakes. These aquatic systems, however, support 20 per cent of species found in India. Man-made aquatic ecosystems created by dams however have been increasing during the past few decades and providing a suboptimal substitute for the rich natural wetlands that are vanishing from our country.

Hindoo pagodas below Barrakpore on the Ganges—Forest (1824).

The Rock of Trichinapoly taken on the River Cauvery—Daniel (1796).

# KEOLADEO GHANA NATIONAL PARK

BHARATPUR

| State | Rajasthan | Zone | Semi-arid |
|---|---|---|---|
| Area | 28.73 sq km | Ecosystem | Wetlands |
| Year of Notification | BS 1956, NP 1981 | Visited | Dec 1976, Oct 1986 |

Interventions through human activities have not always been a total disaster. There are places where the ecosystem has benefited from a judicious management of the habitat. Bharatpur is one such area that has seen the habitat improve as well as deteriorate due to man-made changes over the past several decades.

This natural depression must have once been a seasonal rain-fed wetland. About 250 years ago the rulers of the State of Bharatpur built a dam, the Ajanbund, about a kilometre from the depression. This was used to flood the area periodically and create a marsh for supporting waterfowl. Earthen bunds with sluice gates were later constructed in the 1920s to regulate water levels and maintain the required depth for aquatic birds. The rulers of Bharatpur carefully developed this area as a personal duck shooting reserve back in 1899! It was well planned and purposeful wetland management. The natural depression became a living 8 square kilometre swamp. The river water of the Gambhir and Banganga Rivers was diverted so as to empty into the Ajanbund. Sluice gates not only brought in water but also fish fry and other fauna on which the aquatic birds live. It was thus a fairly complex habitat management programme. An early reference to the need to notify Bharatpur as a Protected Area is to be found in the Proceedings of the BNHS in 1953, which states that Salim Ali had ranked the area as one of the best in the world. The Indian Bird Preservation Committee had recommended to the Central Government that it should be protected. KS Dharmakumarsinhji mentions the fact that

The sky gets clouded with birdlife in winter.

Open water at Bharatpur.

the Keoladeo Ghana was severely neglected until a special directive was received from Prime Minister Nehru in 1953 (JBNHS Vol 51). In 1953 Salim Ali had recorded in the BNHS Journal Vol 51 that, 'One of the first Acts of the newly constituted National Committee for India for Bird Preservation was a recommendation to the Central Government to notify Keoladeo Ghana as a National Bird Sanctuary.'

In 1956, the Forest Department took over its management and created the Keoladeo Ghana Bird Sanctuary, at the request of Dr Salim Ali. However, the Maharaja retained rights for shooting waterfowl up to 1972. Several appeals were made by Salim Ali and others requesting him to stop the annual shikar. Finally, Salim Ali wrote to Indira Gandhi requesting her to intervene. The large scale shikar parties in which thousands of birds were massacred in a single day was stopped.

Bharatpur was notified at the instance of Salim Ali who had heard that the wetland was to be converted into agricultural land for local people. It was being used by the Maharaja for shooting parties where as many as 4000 waterfowl were massacred by gun men who were placed strategically around the water body. As the area was covered with ducks, one could never

miss, and as in each season three or four such killing sprees were organized, the number of birds killed in a season must have been enormous. Salim Ali who was a regular visitor, used his influence with Jawaharlal Nehru to get this prevented.

Salim Ali (1953) estimated that there were 4000 breeding pairs of storks among other aquatic birds, many of which are dependent on fish. Salim Ali's estimate of the amount of fish required to feed the large number of young birds in the nests showed that the painted stork alone required 8000–12,000 pounds of fish per day to sustain the colony, which amounts to 90 tons of fish for the season.

Julian Donahue (1962) raised the issue of overgrazing in Keoladeo Ghana Sanctuary in Rajasthan and felt that this had serious negative influences on the Park. This appears to have triggered off moves to curtail domestic cattle grazing. In 1966, an IUCN delegation visited Bharatpur. One of the delegates was Sir Peter Scott of Slimbridge Waterfowl Trust, who made a note of his visit in the JBNHS, Vol 63 (1966). He estimated that there were 3000–4000 Greylag geese and 150 barheaded geese and giant flocks of 15 species of ducks. He however bemoaned the fact that it was

not yet a proper Sanctuary and there was a considerable amount of shooting. He considered zoning the area and limiting the amount of shikar. He also suggested that grazing domestic animals in the Sanctuary be strictly controlled, and that boats should not be allowed to ply near breeding colonies. He suggested providing facilities for school parties to visit the area. Stanley and Belinda Breeden (1982) described the drought of 1979–80 in great detail in JBNHS Vol. 79, when large numbers of turtles wandered around in the drought and died.

Bharatpur is severely drought prone and in bad years dries up completely unless water is pumped into it before the monsoon. It is possible that such fluctuations may benefit some aspects of the ecosystem as it kills off excessive weeds, allowing a larger mosaic of habitats containing open water in subsequent years. Large numbers of migrant waterfowl have continued to winter in these waters and local water birds such as storks, ibis, spoonbills, and cormorants still aggregate here to form large highly successful breeding colonies.

In 1976, when I first visited Bharatpur, the spectacle of watching the thousands of water birds rise thunderously from the water was an unbelievable experience. Ducks, teals, geese, cormorants, storks and cranes are only some of the long list of birds that I photographed during those two idyllic days. How does one describe a row of nearly leafless thorny trees silhouetted against a red-gold dawn covered by hundreds of black cormorants, as if the trees are festooned with great blossoms, or the whirring sound of thousands of pairs of wings as ducks rise out of the water, or the mosaic-like wings of painted storks flapping around their nests? The morning sun of Bharatpur heralds each new day with a spectacular beauty unmatched in this country. In those days one could take a small boat into the water. There were few visitors and the disturbance levels were thus not high. Today, with the great influx of visitors, this would be impossible.

Bharatpur's status was upgraded to National Park in 1981. It was this move that led to the banning of buffalo grazing in the wetland, seriously affecting the aquatic ecosystem.

Ecological systems created by humans always have complicated problems. For a long time it was thought that domestic buffaloes should not be allowed to graze in these marshes. However, when the livestock were driven out of the area, the grasses and weeds spread over the water, preventing the water birds from having enough clear water to settle and feed on. For some inexplicable reason, probably related to the non-accessibility of fish, even birds such as storks could not breed successfully once the open water was converted to a dense marshland of emergent vegetation. Any change contemplated in an ecological system must thus be looked at very closely. Otherwise, Nature can frequently spring an unpleasant surprise, with an unexpected change in species diversity.

The growth, as a matter of succession, of terrestrial grasses, especially the highly invasive *Paspalum distichum*, is checked by rapidly filling water in the bunded area from the Anjan Dam before the onset of the regular monsoon. If it is filled before the rains, *Pseudoraphis spinenscens* replaces the *Paspalum*, making it an aquatic habitat as the biomass per unit area is reduced. Ducks and geese feed on these new grass shoots. Thus, the rate at which the wetland is replenished by water is critical to the pattern of the mosaic that forms a patchwork of habitat types in the wetland for the next year.

By May or June the water is insufficient to maintain an aquatic ecosystem and the area usually dries up almost entirely. During this period, the fish are concentrated in smaller pools, which then form a major source of food for fish-eating birds. Aquatic flora and fauna then remain dormant till the next monsoon. As Ajanbund is filled, the water is released along with fish fry and other aquatic fauna, bringing the wetland back to its active phase. Life seems to throb in this incredible man-made wetland as nowhere else in our country. Most local water birds feed in the marshes throughout the year. But the full complement of bird life expands dramatically in species and abundance after September, when wave upon wave of migrant waterfowl arrive from the north over the Himalayas. The influx continues till December and remains at this level till the middle of March when the return migration begins. As summer approaches, the dry phase brings one more magnificent cycle to a close and the wetland awaits the life-giving water so critical to the cyclical nature of this incredible ecosystem.

One of the features that affect the Park is the irregular supply of water from the bund, which can vary from negligible, in drought years, to over 15 million cubic metres. While these variations are advantageous to certain elements of the ecosystem, it has adverse effects on other components. If there are several dry years in succession, most of the aquatic vegetation dies. Seasonal variations create a mosaic of open-water aquatic habitats with patches of marshy emergent vegetation, and underwater weeds good for supporting a variety of waterfowl such as waders, ducks and marsh-dependent birds, each group using its own specific niche. In other years, the emergent reeds and invading *Ipomea* shrubs spread to cover the whole area, creating a more uniform habitat that only some species can use. In the dry years, the habitat of birds that need open water such as diving ducks and fish eating birds is reduced in extent, and molluscs and larvae of insects also decrease in abundance.

Plankton and zooplankton, which form an important aspect of the food chain, vary with the amount of water. In years when water levels are low the *Paspalum distichum grass, the emergent* weeds and Ipomea shrubs expand and phytoplankton and zooplankton diminish in abundance. Open water is an essential component for the growth of algal forms and the zooplankton that survive on it. As aquatic vegetation spreads, the plankton diminishes in abundance.

The BNHS team at Bharatpur documented that the vegetation consists of 96 wetland plants and that the plants increase in abundance in the drier years. During the course of the study, the vegetation began to increase soon after grazing by domestic buffaloes was prohibited in 1982. Thus an apparently rational management measure—removing domestic buffaloes—led to disastrous consequences for this sensitive ecosystem, destroying its ability to sustain habitat requirements of a great abundance of a variety of wild fowl. Several attempts to control the weeds such as bulldozing, burning and harvesting were all ineffective and had their own negative impacts.

---

Bharatpur before it was overgrown by *Paspalum* grass.

---

Marshland with sarus cranes.

Black-necked stork awaiting a fish.

Multiple drought years after 1986, however, again reduced the extent of weed cover. Each of the elements of the ecosystem such as open water, emergent reeds, muddy areas and their combinations form a specific microhabitat for a group of fauna. Fish, crustaceans and water birds have several species that are adapted to using each of these components in their environment in different seasons. Diving ducks need open water to feed in. The microhabitat of the cranes, such as the sarus and the very rare Siberian crane, consists of submerged vegetation of a specific depth. Unfortunately the Siberian cranes have disappeared during the last few years.

Less light penetrates areas covered by grass, with the result that algae do not multiply and oxygen levels are lowered. Lowered oxygen levels due to pollution can seriously affect the sensitive ecosystem, especially as it has an inflow of water but no constant outflow, and the concentration of salts dissolved in the water is high.

In the wetland there are about 40 species of fish. Non-air breathing fish require open water. For several species of migratory waterfowl the habitat is optimal when there is 70 per cent open water and 30 per cent grass, with a water depth not exceeding 130 centimetres.

Siberian cranes used to feed on tubers or rhizomes of *Scirpus tuberosus*, *Cyperus rotundus*, *Eleocharis dulcis* and *Nymphae sp*. After the area was overrun by *Paspalum distichum* and frequent droughts occurred, the food sources of the cranes shrank considerably.

The short, the dry period is an essential part of the seasonal dynamics that maintains optimal conditions for a variety of fauna. Siberian cranes that once lived in ideal conditions where the tubers were abundant took six seconds to find a tuber as reported by Spitzer in the late 1970s. BNHS scientists working in the 1980s after the domestic buffalo were eliminated found that it took 25 seconds for a bird to locate a tuber. This indicated that they could have suffered from a shortage of available food.

Active heronries, which were initially surrounded by water, were abandoned once grass grew below them. BNHS scientists felt that the birds need to see water, which could well act as a visual stimulus for breeding. Storks need open water to fish. Darters, cormorants, painted storks and ibises also need to catch fish in open water. They thus may not breed if feeding conditions are not conducive for bringing up their young. Nature probably has primed them not to expend energy on an essentially useless task, and they may then wait for a better year.

The forest ecosystem that surrounds the wetland is of great importance. Vegetation patterns, if looked at from the point of view of a habitat for different species, may appear similar, but be very different when one views them from the point of the animals that utilize them. For example the savanna-like thorny trees and grassy openings of the Sanctuary are dominated by babul or *ber*. The *ber* attracts a specific group of birds and animals when in fruit, which differ from those attracted to the babul that does not form a diet source for the *ber*-dependent species. The forest type of Bharatpur is essentially a dry deciduous and thorn forest of *Acacia catechu–Anageissus pendula* series. The few patches of thicker vegetation are of *Mitragyna parvifolia* or *kadam* groves. The woodlands have only a few trees and a luxuriant growth of grasses and herbs covering the open areas. The most common grass is *Cynodon dactylon*. *Mitragyna*, *Acacia nilotica* and *Zyziphus* trees grow in patches in this grassland. Scrubland with shrubs of similar species to those found in the woodland spread over a fair proportion of the National Park, while in the wetlands, *Paspalum distichum* is the dominant grass. Other species include *Erianthus procerus*, *Scirpus sp.*, *Cyperus sp.*, *Typa angustata* and the exotic weed *Ipomea aquatica* and *Vitiveria zizanioides* grass which frequently spreads into the wetland. All these ecological entities ensure that the National Park can support a great diversity of both aquatic and terrestrial fauna.

Several studies have been made on the fauna of Bharatpur. The population and breeding of the sarus cranes has been monitored by the BNHS and SACON. It has suffered significantly. Aldrin, an insecticide which was sprayed on crops between 1987 and 1990, resulted in the death of 18 cranes.

Pythons have been studied in the National Park by Dr S Bhupati of the BNHS in 1986–87 and again in 2000 by SACON. Of the 38 burrows observed in 1986–87, only 13 were relocated. There were, however, nine new burrows in the same area. The python population thus appears to be stable.

The forests around the wetland and on the artificial bunds consist of thorny arid species, mainly babul. There are also a large number of *Butea* and *Cassia* trees, and a few open patches of dry grasslands with small herds of blackbuck. This animal requires the grassland patches for its habitat.

The spectacular phenomenon of thousands of birds that aggregate in this relatively small area in Bharatpur comes as an unbelievable surprise to most nature lovers who see this great wetland phenomenon for the first time. The incredible number of water birds is a breath-taking experience.

Bharatpur is now a Ramsar Site, which is known for its enormous population of waterfowl. It still has great concentrations of roosting birds and colonies where storks and herons nest in large numbers, but it must be noted that there has been a serious drop in the population and breeding success of sarus cranes and other colony nesters in Bharatpur.

Lead, cadmium, zinc, chromium and copper concentrations are present in high levels due to industrial pollution in the aquatic ecosystems around the Park. Birds move out of the Park to satellite wetlands, canals and lakes to feed. The effects of these high levels on aquatic fauna are not clearly defined, but if the levels continue to rise, they could well affect birds unless the pollution is controlled.

The most threatened species that lived at Bharatpur was the celebrated Siberian crane. Over the years, the 30 or 40 birds that used to come here dwindled to only two or three each winter. The location of their breeding site in Siberia has remained a mystery. The Siberian cranes fed on an underwater plant. After the removal of domestic buffaloes, this aquatic vegetation has been smothered

Storks breed in large numbers in Bharatpur only if there is an abundant supply of water and fish.

by *Paspalum* grass. The cranes found it difficult to search for their food material in the thick mat of grasses. It is sad that there are no more Siberian cranes at Bharatpur. The only other known flock of Siberian cranes migrates from the cold Siberian marshes to China. Now that the last couple of Siberian cranes that used to come to India are gone, we have witnessed the extinction of yet another beautiful species that once graced our country.

Cormorants' roost.

Darter of Snake-bird

Bird populations fluctuate depending on the amount of water released into a wetland.

Thorn-forest ecosystem.

Early mornings and late evenings are delightful moments in the Sanctuary.

The last of the Siberian cranes that were seen at Bharatpur.

| 1 | | |
| 2 | 3 | |
| 4 | | |

Vultures at their nests.

Eagles at Bharatpur are highly fish-dependent.

A nilgai at dawn.

Painted storks at their nests.

*Following pages*
We can see Siberian cranes only in photographs.
India will never see these superb birds again.

# BHINDAWAS WILDLIFE SANCTUARY
BHINDAWAS

| State | Haryana | Zone | Gangetic Plains |
|---|---|---|---|
| Area | 4.06 sq km | Ecosystem | Wetlands |
| Year of Notification | 1986 | Visited | Aug 1995 |

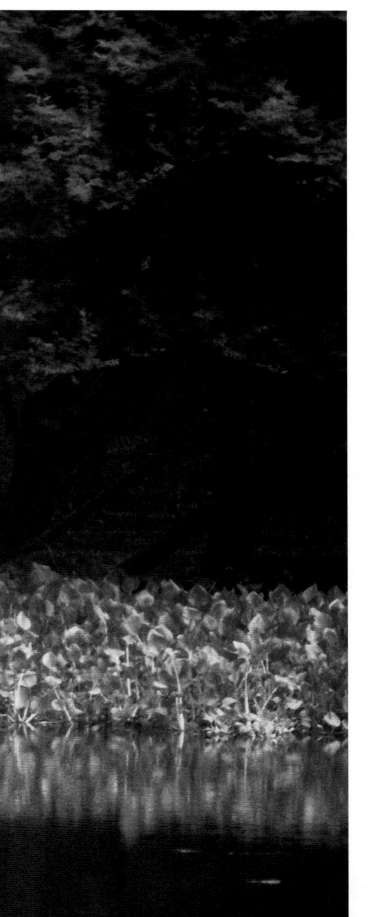

This wetland, situated in the Rohtak District of Haryana, 80 kilometres from Delhi, was declared a Bird Sanctuary in 1985. In winter it is a major waterfowl refuge capable, according to some estimates, of supporting as many as 30 thousand ducks. The bund was built as a flood control mechanism after a disastrous flood in 1978 in the Sahibi River. It is surrounded by eucalyptus plantations and agricultural land, which supports a large diversity of aquatic life, and its resources are used by local people who live around it. With land for farming becoming increasingly scarce in the region, these semi-aquatic ecosystems began to disappear.

The wide expanse of water forms a unique landscape that is now an increasingly uncommon sight. Shekhar Singh, who took me to see this wetland in 1995, has a deep interest in conservation and wrote the first book on *the Management of National Parks and Sanctuaries in India* with Ashish Kothari, Dilnavaz Variava and Pratibha Pande in 1989. He also has a deep interest in people-related issues, eco-development

and dams, all of which led to the *Biodiversity Conservation Prioritization Project (BCPP) Report* published in 2000. Our innumerable discussions have stimulated thought processes that have helped me in implementing a variety of conservation, research and educational activities. It is a pleasure being out with Shekhar in the field, and at Bhindawas we discussed a variety of issues related to aquatic ecology: the spread of *Echornia*; how such residual wetlands can be used to balance the needs of conservation; and economic development. Bhindawas suffers if water is not let into the marsh. There have been reports that local people block the canals and that this may be a cause for it drying up in drought years (Protected Area Update 34–35).

Ecosystems such as Bhindawas have greater threats from developments around them than the more well-documented ecosystems such as forests. Impacts of tree-felling, fishing, poaching, and the spread of water hyacinth are major conservation concerns. Only public concern can save them from complete destruction.

*Following page*
Bhindawas is a wetland that supplies water to the Delhi region.

Hyacinths have invaded several wetlands causing a loss of biodiversity.

The lake provides a habitat for a great number of birds.

# VEDANTHANGAL WILDLIFE SANCTUARY
## VEDANTHANGAL

| State | Tamil Nadu | Zone | Deccan Peninsula |
|---|---|---|---|
| Area | 0.30 sq km | Ecosystem | Wetlands |
| Year of Notification | 1936 | Visited | Dec 1979 |

The area around Chennai has several water bodies that have been used as nesting sites by aquatic birds. Vendanthangal, one of India's smallest reserves and the oldest Water Bird Sanctuary, has been preserved by local sentiment as far back as 1798, though it was officially notified as a Sanctuary in 1936 (Spillet, 1968). EP Gee claims this lake was 'rediscovered' by RSP Bates, a famous bird photographer in the 1920s. Local people had realized the value of the nesting birds, whose droppings fertilized the water they used for irrigation. The rain-fed tank is dry throughout most of the summer.

The lake is created by an earthen bund from which water is used for farming. Trees include *Baringtonia acutangula*, a species capable of withstanding water logging and forming a grove inside the tank. It has large nesting colonies of storks, ibises and cormorants that are dependent on the water for fish. Nesting

Spotbills in Vedanthangal. This area was traditionally protected for generations.

The large nesting colony of aquatic birds at Vedanthangal is an important conservation site.

Vedanthangal is one of the earliest sanctuaries to have been officially notified in India.

colonies require very special protection. Any disturbance can lead to the birds abandoning a key breeding area, and it may take years before they find alternate sites once a traditional colony is disturbed. The number of large heronries has not been well documented, perhaps because their management requires very specific inputs, which can only emerge from detailed, long-term studies.

The bird population of Vedanthangal is dependent on the success of the monsoon. In good years bird counts have totaled a staggering 35,000 birds. In the drought of 2001 there was only a small fraction of the usual population.

Aquatic bird life can be disturbed by both changes in abiotic features such as water quality, and alterations in the micro- and macroscopic plants and animals that are part of the aquatic food chains. As terrestrial ecosystems that surround wetlands are intensively developed, aquatic ecology is seriously affected. Managing these important ecosystems needs much greater attention and forms an important aspect of conservation.

My single visit to Vedanthangal first brought home to me that local protective measures for a habitat are highly effective and frequently can sustain themselves, even though changing values affect the society in different ways. During my brief exposure to Vedanthangal, I was struck by the sheer number of birds and the size of the nesting colony that had been supported by generations of local people, long before it was declared a Protected Area.

# NALSAROVAR AND THOL WILDLIFE SANCTUARIES
## NALSAROVAR AND THOL

| State | Gujarat | Zone | Semi-arid Deccan Plateau |
|---|---|---|---|
| Area | Nalsarovar: 120.82 sq km; Thol: 6.99 sq km | Ecosystem | Wetland |
| Year of Notification | Nalsarovar: 1969; Thol: 1988 | Visited | Oct 2004 |

Nalsarovar, near Ahmedabad in Gujarat, is a 100-square kilometre wetland. Its waterfowl population fluctuates enormously, depending on the monsoon. Taking the boat ride is an experience in itself; one gets a feeling of incredible stillness except for the flutterings of flocks of birds. Far on the horizon is a string of white dots—a flock of feeding flamingoes; *nakta* ducks fly past in formation and settle down to feed; the stillness is broken by the call of a brahminy duck. One begins to appreciate the great value of wetlands like this, with their underwater vegetation, reeds, fish, molluscs and crustaceans, as a resource for people. Once, such wetlands extended over a much larger proportion of India. The few residual ones like Nalsarovar have to be strictly protected as they can no longer sustain both the needs of an expanded local population and their wild biodiversity.

At Thol, from a large tract of fields, one climbs onto a dam. The landscape beyond throngs with a variety of waterfowl. Thol is a small Sanctuary outside Ahmedabad and takes one back to what it was like in the days of great duck shoots during the British times. In most of Gujarat however, pro-wildlife sentiments were generally present and much of the waterfowl have been given protection for several decades by local people.

Thol has small islands on which *nakta*s, brahminys, teals and waders aggregate in winter. It is a jewel of an aquatic sanctuary.

Nalsarovar is a large wetland in Gujarat.

1
2
3

The wetland attracts huge flocks of waterfowl.

Purple moorhen.

The islands in Thol provide a roosting area for a large number of waterfowl.

White ibis.

| State | Maharashtra | Zone | Deccan Peninsula |
|---|---|---|---|
| Area | 3.83 sq km | Ecosystem | Saline Lake with Scrub Forest |
| Year of Notification | 2000 (Proposed) | Visited | Nov to Dec 1997 |

The grandeur of this magnificent meteorite crater is breathtaking. Widely-acclaimed as one of the largest such sites in the world, the crater evokes a feeling of awe. The impact must have been immense to create a hole of this enormous size in the ground. It must have crashed as a ball of flame, creating a great quantity of rocky debris and dust that spread widely over the region for several square kilometres. The release of energy would inevitably have shaken the whole region with its astounding force. What if it were to happen today on an earth that is full of human beings? It would locally be worse than an earthquake or a large storm or even a volcanic eruption. It would instantly annihilate life in the region. Watching the crater and just thinking of such a repeat performance by Nature is frightening. The incredible power of Nature's episodic upheavals throughout geological time could, if repeated, have serious consequences for human beings on earth!

But now, thousands of years later, the crater is only a reminder of a long-forgotten prehistoric period. The landscape is incredible. The near-circular crater has a deep blue saline lake in it, surrounded by scrubland. The ancients, realizing how unusual such a landscape is, made a temple at the site giving it sanctity and protection through religious sentiment that still lives today. The flowers of a variety of herbs bloom at the edge of the crater and form a part of the surrounding semi-arid landscape.

Grassland birds such as larks, lapwings and sand grouse abound and the grasses attract a large number of insects. As the area has not been notified as a Sanctuary, it is being developed for intensive tourism, and there are plans to develop a tourist complex at the edge of this grand vista. This would distort the incredible landscape beyond repair! What has to be preserved is the whole grand vista of the crater, its great expanse of bleakness and the still water in the saline lake below, surrounded by trees and shrubs. The only break in its wild and prehistoric nature is the temple on the shore reminding one of God and man.

---

This unique geological formation and the lake within it has been recognized and venerated from ancient times.

---

This is one of the largest basaltic landforms resulting from the impact of a pulverized giant meteor that dropped out of the sky in the distant past.

# MAYANI WILDLIFE SANCTUARY

MAYANI

| State | Maharashtra | Zone | Deccan Plateau |
|---|---|---|---|
| Area | 4 sq km | Ecosystem | Wetland |
| Year of Notification | Proposed | Visited | Feb 1983 |

Mayani is an old percolation tank. Flamingoes frequent this tiny waterbody year after year.

Pratincoles on the shore.

Painted storks rest in a shallow silted part of the old tank

The Mayani Tank is an old silted-up bund, which favours long-legged waders and mud-bank feeders. Stilts, plovers, godwits and flocks of pratincoles are frequently seen. Its bird density and diversity is high, giving it a substantial conservation value even though it is very small in size.

A group of bird-watchers from Kolhapur—all amateur naturalists—visited this small tank near Satara in Maharashtra in the early 1980s. Though local villagers had long known that the area attracted a large number of aquatic birds, this was unknown to bird-watchers. On their first visit they saw large numbers of flamingoes, spoonbills, and storks, and were fired with a new enthusiasm to protect this superb small habitat. During their subsequent visit they bumped into a shikar party. They photographed the proud shikaris with their trophies. Most of their game was not even edible! The bird-watchers, a doctor, a zoologist and their friends began a campaign against this useless killing. They complained to forest officials and

made a press release, but found that they could do little to book the culprits. They were threatened by the shikaris and were told that they would be harassed if they continue to raise a stink. They persisted however, in their efforts to get the birds protected. This new group of conservation-conscious people of Kolhapur decided to hold a *Pakshi Mitra Samela*, 'Friends of Birds Meeting'. I was requested to talk on aquatic avifauna in Maharashtra. Someone mentioned the need to protect Mayani, and I was hijacked and taken there the next day by a passionate group of bird-watchers. Several months of lobbying later, and after several unofficial meetings with Forest Officials and other Government Officials in Mantralaya, enough pressure had been mounted on the Government to make them agree to protect the birds of

the Mayani Tank. It also found a place in Rodgers and Panwar's *Planning a Wildlife Protected Area Network for India* (1988). The little Peshwa Tank, forgotten for so many decades, was now known to most conservation groups in the State. The bird-watchers have been responsible for keeping the shikaris at bay. And the area has been preserved for posterity.

Painted storks at Mayani.

A variety of bird life frequents the lake.

# JAIKWAD WILDLIFE SANCTUARY
JAIKWAD

| State | Maharashtra | Zone | Deccan Plateau |
|---|---|---|---|
| Area | 341.05 sq km | Ecosystem | Wetland |
| Year of Notification | 1986 | Visited | Jan 1984 |

Aquatic ecosystems are as threatened as evergreen forests. As they have a much smaller geographical spread, they are highly threatened ecosystems.

The backwaters of lakes created by irrigation dams have substituted the wetlands that man has drained away in the Deccan Plateau.

A large flock of waders flies past the banks of the large lake formed by the irrigation dam at Jaikwadi.

The star attraction of the bird-watchers' meeting at Aurangabad in 1984 on the banks of the Jaikwadi Lake is not an exciting bird species. The interest of all the amateur bird-watchers is centered around the presence of the doyen of Indian Ornithology who, in his 90s, is still active enough to join a bird-watching session. Dr Salim Ali's presence is electrifying. He is frail and old but refuses help while walking along the rocky banks of Jaikwadi Lake. He has binoculars and a rose in his hands. I quietly take pictures while he is looking through the binoculars at a few storks nearby. Unfortunately, these slides have since been 'borrowed' and never returned! He fascinates the group with his jovial quips. Talking to a small child, he asks if the rock she has collected has gold in it! He acknowledges everyone—forest guards, the driver, and the dignitaries who flock around him as soon as he gets out of the car at the shore of the lake. Jaikwadi becomes a Sanctuary endorsed by the guru himself.

Jaikwadi is an irrigation dam on the Godavari River. Bird counts done here by BVIEER field staff showed that the commonest species were pintail ducks, coats and spotbilled ducks. There are more ducks than waders. Jaikwadi has a large number of fishing cooperatives and the extensive fishing has begun to lead to a fall in the catch in recent years.

About a quarter of the lake consists of a large shallow peripheral area which is exposed during the summer when water is released for agriculture. The water is used by surrounding villages and about 50% of the periphery is used for farming. Essentially the lake is unprotected even though it is a notified Protected Area.

# NANDUR MADHMESHWAR WILDLIFE SANCTUARY
## NANDUR MADHMESHWAR

| State | Maharashtra | Zone | Deccan Plateau |
|---|---|---|---|
| Area | 19.62 sq km | Ecosystem | Wetland |
| Year of Notification | 1986 | Visited | Aug 1999 |

Not far from Nasik there is a well-known wetland area. The dam on the Godavari River creates a fairly shallow water spread in most parts of the lake. A large part is unfortunately covered by water hyacinth. The water spread and aquatic vegetation form a habitat for wintering waterfowl that migrate from the north. The ducks fly overhead in great 'V' formations. Pied kingfishers in small family parties hover over the water. Occasionally an osprey flies past. From the top of a rather inappropriate tower, tourists watch fishing boats ply over the water and use binoculars to sight birds beyond the hyacinth. The dawn is beautiful, as ducks with sharply-angled, steady wings dive steeply towards the water with a whistling sound of wind over stiff feathers.

During bird counts an unusual species was the curlew sandpiper. The wetland has large populations of ducks and glossy ibises. About half the species are migrants. Local people use the wetland for fishing and watering their buffaloes. It is one of the three important wetlands in Maharashtra.

A wetland mosaic of aquatic vegetation and open water spreads over Nandur Madhmeshwar which is a shallow irrigation dam.

A tern looking for fish.

# BHIGWAN UJANI WILDLIFE SANCTUARY
BHIGWAN

| State | Maharashtra | Zone | Deccan Peninsula |
|---|---|---|---|
| Area | 100 sq km | Ecosystem | Wetland |
| Year of Notification | Proposed | Visited | Frequent visits every year. Last visit: Feb 2005 |

Greater flamingoes flash their scarlet wings as they fly past from one feeding area to another.

Flamingoes at Bhigwan in the backwaters of the Ujani Dam in Maharashtra.

The whiring of hundreds of wing beats is an unforgettable sound.

Greater flamingoes lift off from the water.

In 1982 the newly created Ujani Dam was filled with water. This new ecosystem which was converted from a river to a wetland had extensive mudbanks along its periphery. As no aquatic weeds had been developed, from seemingly nowhere, a small group of flamingoes found this was a superb habitat. Flamingoes had not been seen in this part of Maharashtra ever since I had been in school and had seen a small flock in Pashan Lake, which was then well outside Pune limits. Each year the flamingoes at Bhigwan kept increasing in number. This amazing bird that could inject the most incredible colours into the lake's almost monochrome blue, had me completely fascinated. I began to visit the backwaters at Bhigwan nearly once every fortnight. One afternoon Vijay Paranjape and Pradumna Gogate, who was studying the ecology of the wetland, went with my wife, my five year old daughter and me on a trip to show my daughter flamingoes. There were a few fairly heavy clouds in the sky but the sun was shining. I didn't like the look of the clouds so I asked a village youngster if he thought it would rain. There was a prompt response. 'It never rains in Bhigwan especially in drought years like this one,' he said, firmly shaking his head. We went down to the edge of the lake about a kilometre from the road. I took cover in a jowar field and stalked the flamingoes so I could get as close as possible. After the first few pictures there was a clap of thunder and a bolt of lightning—the sky turned black—and big drops of rain began to descend from the sky. The earth smelt wonderful. Then suddenly the clouds seemed to break asunder and the rain came down in torrents. We were all wet to the skin. We couldn't agree more with the villager who had said it didn't rain in Bhigwan—he was right—because when it rained, it only poured! The torrential rain continued for half an hour in that drought year. The field between the road and us seemed to vanish before our eyes. It was a great flash flood and all around us was a sheet of bubbling brown water. It was impossible to see any familiar landmarks. After a brief discussion we headed for what we thought was the direction from which we had entered the

Greater flamingoes.

A river tern alights at its nest to feed hungry chicks.

field for cover. We heard someone call out to us out of the rain. Our 'rain man' and trusted predictor of dry weather came running to us, splashing through knee-deep water to tell us that we were headed in the wrong direction! Another few metres and the current in the nala, which had assumed the proportions of a major flash flood, would have swept us into the lake! Rambhau took us back to the road to the safety of his hut and gave us blankets of local sheep's wool to remove the chill from our bones. His mother gave us sweet hot tea. We have kept in touch ever since. Many years have passed. I used a bit of influence to get him a job in the Forest Department. Ever grateful, for many years he sent me postcards about the current status of the local flamingo population.

One afternoon in summer I saw an incredible sight for the first time. The flamingoes were grouping together, croaking loudly extending their scarlet wings and raising the feathers on their backs like white powder puffs. This superb breeding display went on for half an hour. I reported this to Dr Salim Ali. He said that he had not observed this outside their breeding grounds in Kachchh and that perhaps we could induce them to breed. He recalled that in the south of France, in the Camargue, when flamingoes stopped breeding, the ornithologists made artificial nests which induced them to start breeding again. The local forest official and I then made about 50 nests by filling black cotton soil in buckets and turning them over. The local villagers looked at us strangely and their stares clearly said what they thought of us: The good doctor from Pune and his friend the forest official had obviously gone cuckoo! We kept round-the-clock front line Forest Department watchers on the job for two weeks. Nothing happened. I then got another idea. Why not lay artificial eggs in some of them! So we got a local potter to make us flamingo eggs from clay. We put them in the back of the jeep and drove off to Bhigwan. The egg-laying nearly led to a stampede—all the villagers stood around as we put one egg after another into the nests. The result was that they were now quite sure that we were utterly crazy. The flamingoes however completely ignored the nests and the clay eggs. Praddy reported that once he actually saw one bird attempting to sit on a nest. The rest however walked past the only bird who had taken to our weird idea in a single file. The rain then washed off the mud nests. What became of the clay eggs we never knew.

A voracious chick incessantly calls for food.

Greater flamingoes in an unusual breeding display.

|   | 1 |   |
|---|---|---|
| 2 | 3 |   |
| 4 | 5 |   |

A large flock of spoonbills.

Waders are good indicators of the health of a wetland.

River terns at Bhigwan.

Seagulls at the lake are an indicator of the amount of fish.

Seagulls are known to move to fresh water lakes at great distances from the sea.

| 1 | | 3 | | 5 | |
|---|---|---|---|---|---|
| 2 | | | | | |
| | 4 | | | 6 | |

Egret.

Brahminy ducks.

This osprey lived for several years at the same location.

A flock of seagulls.

Painted storks.

This fisherman from Andhra Pradesh has settled at Bhigwan and makes fish traps.

One of the special features of the lake that needs attention is its nesting colonies of terms, pratincoles and plovers that form on the flat mudbanks that emerge as islands after January each year. This is the largest colony known in Maharashtra and remains essentially unprotected even today.

Bhigwan was for several years a well-managed fishing area that provided local people with large fish at a high market value. In the last few years the cooperatives have been formed mainly by fishermen from outside the state. They have begun to use nets with a very small mesh size. This over-harvesting of even the small fish has led to a fall in the size of the fish. They also build traps that catch not only fish but birds as well. These conflicting issues must be solved by getting the different government agencies together on a common platform.

|   | 1 |
|---|---|
| 2 | 3 |

A common green bee-eater on a wire at the water's edge.

Painted stork.

Bar-headed geese.

# MULA MUTHA BIRD SANCTUARY
MULA MUTHA

| State | Maharashtra | Zone | Deccan Plateau |
|---|---|---|---|
| Area | 1 sq km | Ecosystem | Wetland |
| Year of Notification | — | Visited | Frequent visits every year since 1974. The author lives on the river banks at this site. |

Not all the wildlife of the country is located in remote Sanctuaries and National Parks. There are several species that can be protected around urban settlements and even within cities. Birds such as egrets usually nest in large trees frequently found in urban areas. The large flying foxes or fruit bats also have colonies in large trees in urban areas. There are several well-known examples of waterfowl areas in or around cities. Both Kolkata Zoo and Delhi Zoo have water bodies that attract aquatic birds.

An important example of how a river can attract waterfowl is the Mula Mutha within Pune City. The river has a stretch of about a kilometre which was once a traditional fishing site. The fishermen had built a series of stone bunds on which they could tie their nets. The outlets create eddy currents, which deposit silt on either side, providing a mudbank on which waders and ducks find their food material. Worms, larvae, snails, etc. live in these muddy areas in large numbers, barely 10 to 15 centimetres below the surface of the water.

A small stretch of the Mula Mutha River in the city of Pune attracts large numbers of aquatic birds.

The great advantage of such a site is its proximity to an urban area where nature education can be easily undertaken. The WWF-Pune realized this during the 1970s. Dr Salim Ali formally inaugurated a Bird Sanctuary in the area. Dr and Mrs Wadia, who were WWF members, gave over a stretch of land to develop a Nature trail on the bank of the river. The WWF had plans to develop the area into a formal education centre. The river became a popular site for bird-watchers in the 1970s and 80s. Over the last few years, however, the number of visitors have begun to dwindle as the WWF began taking visitors outside Pune. The Mula Mutha birds were forgotten, except by a few enthusiastic bird-watchers. The Forest Department's fencing deteriorated around its plantations of trees on the bank of the river. The bank was increasingly used for washing clothes as other parts of the bank became built up. The growing level of organic pollution from untreated sewage led to increasing eutrophication, favouring the growth of hyacinth on the surface of the water. Industries that release untreated effluents from Pune's mega industrial zones is leading to a rise in chemical pollution. This, however, is the only stretch of river on which the birds can still survive. On a cold winter morning, 5000 ducks and waders can be seen here from the banks of the river.

Ten years ago the BVIEER re-started nature education programmes for school children focused around the Mula Mutha. Every week groups of children came to the river. They become familiar with the functions of the river, its complex ecology, and the large diversity of life even in the presence of increasing levels of pollution. The value of preserving this stretch of river is far greater than its use for other purposes if one considers its enormous educational potential. It acts as a sensitizer of Pune's future citizens to the enormous diversity of life on their own river. However during the last decade the river has become a drainage for industrial effluents and an open sewer for its urban sewage. Its banks are covered with plastic. The waders have become less abundant and the fish have all but disappeared. As in many other rivers in the country, the people must begin putting pressures on both Government and industrial houses and housing societies to prevent pollution. This would be better than to try to clean up rivers after they have been converted into sewers.

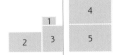

Pintails.

Ducks taking off.

A black-winged stilt.

A large flock of pintail ducks on the rocks in the river.

Black-winged stilts.

Waterfowl aggregate on the bank of the river in large numbers if they are left undisturbed.

Pintails and shovellers.

The increased amount of sewage in the river and stagnant pond leads to the breeding of mosquitoes that provide food for the frogs.

Froth from industrial pollution on the Mula Mutha River is highly damaging to its biodiversity. The number of waterfowl is gradually decreasing.

# RANGANTHITTOO WILDLIFE SANCTUARY
RANGANTHITTOO

| State | Karnataka | Zone | Deccan Peninsula |
|---|---|---|---|
| Area | 0.67 sq km | Ecosystem | Riverine Forest |
| Year of Notification | 1940 | Visited | Jan 1986, Jun 1990 |

Ranganthittoo is a traditionally known site where aquatic birds breed.

White ibises take off from their roost.

Our boat moves slowly towards a rock in the still waters. Astride the rock there is a colossal crocodile, completely motionless, apparently oblivious of the approaching boat. Suddenly, the animal seems to have been electrified! It springs straight up into the air off the rock and splashes into the water with a huge crash and dives into the narrow space left between the rock and the boat. The boat rocks precariously while the croc vanishes.

Above the boat circle thousands of birds, storks, ibises, spoonbills, cormorants, egrets, all in constant motion. Their calls are deafening. This is Ranganthittoo, a Bird Sanctuary that has been developed on the Cauvery River, not far from Mysore. Several species of water birds breed here in large numbers. They are now used by

tourists who visit the Sanctuary in hordes to view the nesting colonies at close quarters from a number of small boats.

There are several species other than the more spectacular large birds that breed here. River terns, stone plovers, lapwings and others mill about over the water. A noisy river tern chases a bird of prey, until it disappears high up into the sky. From an overhang under a rock a metre above the water surface, a large number of martins emerge as the boat approaches. They have a large nesting colony made of muddy material.

To control the flow which is responsible for its high biodiversity values, a weir and aqueduct were constructed on the river in the 1650s by Kanthirava Narasaraj, the ruler of Mysore. This river and its bird life were studied by Dr Salim Ali several decades ago, and he suggested that it should be notified by the Forest Department as a Sanctuary. In 1940 the river was declared as a Santuary comprising many islands and named after the Ranganthittoo Island with its large concentration of nesting birds (Neginhal, 1982). It has since become a major site for introducing people to bird-watching. The Sanctuary however requires a large Interpretation Centre to impart information regarding the importance of nesting colonies so that a lobby is formed to notify and protect several other 'important bird areas' in our country.

| 1 |
|---|
| 2 |
| 3 |

An egret displaying feathers that were once used for adorning ladies' hats.

Cormorants perched precariously on bamboo clumps squabble with each other.

Stone plovers line up on a rock.

| 1 | 2 |
|---|---|
| 3 | |

Night heron.

A crocodile basking on an exposed rock.

Open-billed storks.

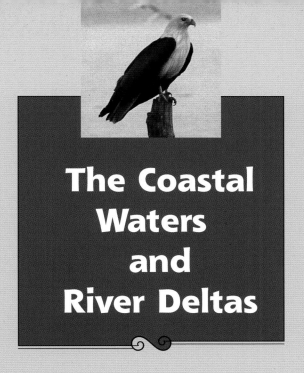

# The Coastal Waters and River Deltas

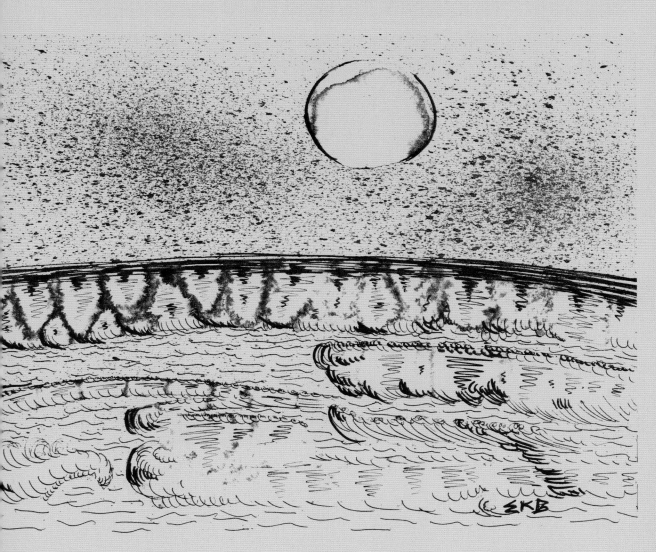

Fishing boats during the monsoon in the northern part of Bombay Harbour—Grindley (1830).

Marine ecosystem.

For millions of years, the seas crashing upon the coastline of peninsular India have created an intricate system of both marine and terrestrial life. Much of the coastline has also seen the growth of human settlements for several thousand years. Agriculture and fishing have slowly made much of the natural vegetation disappear and replaced it with rice fields and coconut groves, from the edge of the sands to the foot of the ghats. The palm stretches we see today could not have existed in this unbroken fashion before the advent of farming, and are a substitute for the mangrove and mixed forests that must once have existed along the coast.

## THE WESTERN COASTS

The long coastline on our western seaboard has only a few beautiful beaches, coves and peninsulas that are still relatively undisturbed. Most of the rivers that run out of the Sahyadris into the Arabian Sea are not large and have small deltas. On the eastern coast of India, however, the shoreline is broken by the deltas of several large rivers. These have evolved very special ecological systems due to the daily ebb and flow of the tide and seasonal fluctuations in the quantity of water brought down by the rivers.

Mangroves are very special ecosystems. Their diversity of life-forms is especially adapted to the brackish waters. Even more important, there are regions of high productivity in which the turnover of life itself is enormous. The region is in constant flux owing to the tide and marked seasonal variations. Fish, reptiles and crustacea breed here before they return to the deep seas. Fish spawn in colossal numbers, the young ones falling prey to a variety of predators. These complex biological processes make mangroves some of the Earth's most productive ecosystems.

## THE EASTERN COASTS

The eastern ecosystems of the coastal belt have several features not found in the western coastal belt. The coastal belt itself is wider and has a larger component of delta systems, brackish lakes and extensive beaches. The vegetation is fairly specific and certain coastal forest types, such as those at Point Calimere, have very localized distinctive and unique vegetation patterns. An important group of species now increasingly threatened are the sea turtles that nest on these beaches. These are being decimated by destruction of their breeding beaches and the collection of their eggs.

The beaches are a major source of economic support for local communities, specially fisher folk, who clean, dry and market their produce all along these sandy shores. This ecosystem is also repeatedly damaged by periodic cyclones. Arresting the spread of sand into agricultural areas has been achieved by using a variety of exotic trees such as *Casurina*. While this protects inland areas, it reduces local biodiversity, thus changing the characteristics of the beaches. Good management must identify local species to be included in these programmes with a view to preserving local biological values. Reintroduction of mangroves into river deltas should form an important part of coastal restorative efforts.

The few Protected Areas need to be zoned so that the utilization of their bio-productivity does not clash with species that need urgent protection in these areas.

Mangrove at Sunderbans.

A view of the opposite or Sulkhea side from the Respondentia Walk with a northwester coming on—Fraser (1826).

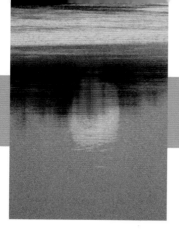

# SUNDERBANS NATIONAL PARK

| State | West Bengal | Zone | Coasts (East Coast) |
|---|---|---|---|
| Area | 1330.10 sq km | Ecosystem | Riverine Delta, Mangroves, Mudflats, Sandy Beaches, Islands |
| Year of Notification | 1984 | Visited | Dec 1978 |

The Ganga and the Brahmaputra, India's two greatest rivers, form a gigantic mangrove swamp before flowing into the Bay of Bengal. This creates the largest single mangrove tract in South Asia, and covers a large part of West Bengal and Bangladesh. While in most cases Reserved Forests became National Parks or Wildlife Sanctuaries and were much later included in Tiger Reserves, Sunderbans was first made a Tiger Reserve in 1973 and only became a Reserved Forest in 1978, and a National Park in 1984 (Jain, 2001). In view of its size and its ecological uniqueness, this delta has been on the list of World Heritage Sites since 1985 and was declared a Biosphere Reserve in 1989.

The forest types of Sunderbans have been classified as tidal swamp forest, saline water mixed forest, brackish water mixed forest and palm swamp type. The important fauna includes the tiger and the spotted deer and wild boar, which are the main terrestrial mammals. The reptiles that use both the aquatic and terrestrial system include water monitor lizards, river terrapins, Olive Ridleis and Hawksbill turtles. A variety of crabs and fish constitute the marine fauna of the delta. Gangetic dolphins, water monitors and estuarine crocodiles are few of the more important species. Chital, wild boar and rhesus monkeys are the tiger's most frequent prey, but the big cats are also known to catch crabs and fish.

The mangrove swamps of the Sunderbans cover the largest river delta

Mangrove forest at Sunderbans, in the Ganges Delta.

in India. The region is crisscrossed by hundreds of small divisions of the river, that split and again meet each other to form the myriad islands of the delta of the sacred Ganga. It is an eerie land of mudbanks thick with mangrove trees, their multiple, often grotesquely exposed roots curving into the water. The flat skyline of the canopy moves past one in a monotonous sequence as the boat wades through the shallow water. It appears

the Sunderbans was teeming with life of every sort: birds of prey, waders and several species of herons. He sighted many crocodiles, some of them 10-feet long. He found otter tracks almost everywhere and observed eight in a row, following each other. He also described the monitor lizard. Near one of the islands, local people refused to let him shoot jungle fowl as a local deity called Banadeo did not allow it and bad luck would come upon anyone

felt that there could be only three or four rhinos in the Sunderbans at that time.

Sunderbans is the home of the tiger. The tigers here are not larger than others, as traditionally believed. The so-called 'Royal Bengal Tiger' is a myth created by early British shikaris. They do have the unfortunate distinction, however, of making more frequent human kills. Most of these tragedies are accidental kills, when people are hunting for forest produce such as honey. Sunderbans is a fabulous fishing zone and this adds to close encounters with tigers, while the fishermen sleep in their boats anchored to the bank at night.

Recent census figures show that there were 251 tigers in 1992, as against 270 in 1997 (Jain, 2001). This accounts for a large proportion of tigers in India, with the mangrove having more tigers than any other single Tiger Reserve in the

like a movie shot in slow motion on monochrome film, being projected on an ultra-wide screen. The water's still surface is suddenly broken by shoals of flying fish jumping out of the water, creating a series of splashes. The abundance of crustacea and fish attracts hundreds of water birds. Terns and gulls fly past, hunting for sea life.

In the forest, the quiet is all pervading. Occasionally chital are seen standing motionless at the water's edge, their legs covered in mud; a sound of wild boar suddenly animates the motionless scene as they rush for cover.

In 1892, Vicomte Edmond de Poncins describes a hunting trip in the Sunderbans on a houseboat in JBNHS Volume 37. His main quest was for the rhinos that were thought to live somewhere in the region. He records that the whole of

not taking his wishes into account. The cutting of wood was, however, allowed on the island. He describes that in 1892, rhinos were found at only one place in Sunderbans, at a location where there was fresh water. He describes this area as being 15 miles south of Issuripore. He mentions the possibility of having seen a lesser rhino which, he says, was rare. He

A fishing boat at Sunderbans.

Fishermen fish in the Protected Area despite their fear of the tiger.

Fishing in the delta is a major occupation of a large number of people.

country. The next largest is Corbett with 138 tigers, followed by Manas, Kanha and Dudhwa, with over 100 tigers in each of these Tiger Reserves. The chital population recorded during the tiger census has remained stable between 1989 and 1993, with figures stabilizing around 30,900. The same census shows that there are 10,272 uncommon water monitor lizards. At three locations on the Mechua Island, there is recent evidence of breeding sites of the river terrapin, *Batagur baska,* a highly endangered species. There are also breeding sites of crocodiles and other reptiles, such as the water monitor lizard.

The number of people killed by tigers, which was around 40 per year a few years ago, is now down to 10 per year (Jain, 2001). This has been achieved by a variety of innovative projects such as the use of human masks worn on the back of the head, as tigers mainly attack people from the rear. The mask thus makes the tiger feel that he is confronted by a human and it tends to move away. Electrified human mannequins, which give an electric shock to the tiger, have also been tried. In 1978 I went down the river in a small boat that the Forest Department provided for me, called *The Rescue.* My visit transported me several decades back in time, the boat having been built in the 1930s! The forest officer accompanying me repeatedly assured me that her ripe old age was actually a certificate of her sea worthiness! The engine, however, broke down several times during the next two days. And much bailing of water had to be carried out. The river delta is constantly forming new sandbanks and islands. On several occasions, the boat had to reverse off a submerged bank, the old engine

Water monitor lizard.

The roots of the mangroves prevent the soil of the delta of the Ganges from being washed into the sea.

straining to get the heavy boat away. Dusk turned the waters into a glorious red-gold, the shimmering light reflecting off the shining leaves of the mangroves. Night, with the slow lap of water on the hull and the swaying motion, created a feeling of being near the heart of nature, a feeling of being cradled and secure. But one knows that outside the boat, the tigers of Sunderbans have to hunt for prey. Crocodiles also dive into the waters. And storms can devastate the landscape. At dawn, the anchor was dropped in a small clearing. Seagulls hovered around in spirals. The mangrove forest around the jetty was thick and impenetrable, down to the brown waterline. Squelching over the muddy path, we reached an observation tower where two long tracts of forest have been cleared for viewing wildlife. There is also a little bund with fresh

water, a rare commodity in Sunderbans, for animals to drink from. There are several wild boars and chital, but no tiger appears on the scene for several hours.

Chugging back up the delta, the Forest Department Ranger continues to look for the crocodiles that are found here, but which have been evasive throughout the trip. Around a bend in the river there is a movement at the water's edge. As *The Rescue* turns in its direction, a brown creature emerges from the water and crawls up the mud bank. 'Ah,' says the guide, 'Sir, I wish you had been a Minister or at least a senior Government Secretary! Then I could have told you that this animal was a crocodile and got away with it! That's what we do when the Ministers insist on being shown a crocodile in the Sunderbans.'The reptile was in fact, a large water monitor, which for me is more interesting than a crocodile.

At sundown the Sunderbans seems timeless. The very 'featurelessness' of the forests—kilometre after kilometre of mudbanks covered with mangrove,

gives the land and waterscape a near prehistoric appearance. A large group of egrets slowly fly towards the setting sun, their wings nearly touching the water at each beat. The mud banks reflect the deep red glow of the end of another day. Another giant lizard emerges from the slowly moving waters to bask in the last rays of the setting sun. This is indeed what it must have looked like in ancient times.

The area is a major resource for fishing both by small vessels and large trawlers. A proposed National Waterway through the Sunderbans may have serious implications for the mangroves, as it will pass through the Tiger Reserve. It will require dredging and the subsequent plying of large vessels, and the inevitable oil spills and floating garbage will destroy the sensitive aquatic ecosystem beyond repair. This would also affect the breeding of fish and crustacea. Birdnesting colonies and feeding areas could also be disturbed by increasing levels of human activity in this most valued of the mangrove systems in South Asia.

Sunderbans is reportedly threatened from a proposal to develop a giant Sahara Tourism Project. Even if it is outside the Protected Area, the impact of a large number of tourists in and around the site could grow to a point beyond the carrying capacity of this sensitive area. The proposed project was frequently mentioned in several news articles in 2002. There are also reports suggesting that some channels may be deepened for the movement of boats. In contrast, it is also said that the Sundarbans should be made a Ramsar Site and that the mangroves should be included as a Tiger Reserve.

These contradictory aspects, one that increases impacts and the other that attempts to enhance protection, are still being debated, though they will cancel the possible positive effects of a pro-conservation strategy for the Sunderbans.

Sunset at Sunderbans.

# PULICAT WILDLIFE SANCTUARY
PULICAT

| State | Andhra Pradesh and Tamil Nadu | Zone | Coasts (East Coast) |
|---|---|---|---|
| Area | 500 sq km; 153.67 sq km | Ecosystem | Tropical Lagoon and Coastal Lake |
| Year of Notification | 1976, 1980 | Visited | Mar 1996 |

At first sight, this could be any fishing village on the eastern coast of India. A large number of small boats with bright blue sails are plying on a large expanse of unusually calm water. The calmness is an important part of this unusual ecosystem, a brackish water lake, separated from the adjacent sea by an island. The lake's uniqueness is shared by only a few other large coastal ecosystems such as Chilka. Different from the seashore or the delta areas, these brackish water ecosystems attract great populations of fish, crustacea, mollusks and marine bird-life.

Pulicat is one of the largest lagoons in India. The southern part of the Pulicat Lake is in Tamil Nadu while the larger, northern portion is in Andhra Pradesh. Its unique feature is its large population of greater flamingoes. The flamingo population of the lagoon varies significantly depending on the rainfall. In dry years, the population drops significantly. In good years it has been estimated to reach 10,000. The flamingoes keep away from major settlements, aggregating on distant mudbanks where they feed. The water is shallow in most parts and is not more

Fishing area in the quiet waters of Pulicat Sanctuary.

Flamingoes over Pulicat Lake.

than knee-deep. The shallowness produces ideal conditions for aquatic vegetation, clams, mussels and large shoals of fish. The lake forms not only an important feeding area for the greater flamingo but is one of India's wetlands still frequented by the spot-billed pelican. Flocks have been sighted that range from about 100 to 500 birds. They feed in the shallow open water and roost on the mudflats.

The local people have serious problems resulting from a severe shortage of drinking water. The water along the coast is brackish. Strangely, the water on some of the islands is more drinkable and people move across the lake in small boats, transferring plastic pots of drinking water. Even the local crows aggregate on these pots to get a drink of non-brackish water once the containers are transported onto the shore.

The distant horizon seen from the boat is marked by several linear streaks of white. As the boat nears, they turn out to be a row of flamingoes that gradually become visible as a milling flock seen through the rising, mirage-like, wavering air.

The capricious nature of this ancient bird that has had a long evolutionary history is difficult to interpret. Local fishermen claim that their population at Pulicat fluctuates considerably. To get a close view, one has to be either very lucky or extremely persistent. As luck rarely helps me with photography, the latter becomes the only alternative! This involves getting out of the boat and wading through the knee-deep water. The mud is squishy, thick with weeds and algae. Strangely, the temperature varies locally even within a few hundred metres. The flamingoes are exceptionally shy and take off with loud croaking calls, circling around in smooth arcs and settling down on an adjacent bank. We painfully trudge through the sandy bottom, changing direction each time the flock moves. We never seem to get much closer! Terns and gulls follow the fishing boats as they come to the shore. The fishermen throw the smaller fish from their catch back into the sea. Damaged ones fall an easy prey to the hungry, fish-eating birds. The farmland around the lake has an exceptionally large

number of white-breasted kingfishers. That fish form a major keystone species in this ecosystem becomes clearly apparent as one begins to understand the pattern of life's complex food web. The terrestrial and marine ecosystems share many species, linking the two very different ecosystems with each other.

Several developmental projects such as a thermal power plant and a petrochemical plant were proposed to be set up near Pulicat in 1999, and if carried out, they are likely to severely damage this sensitive ecosystem.

The rise in biotic pressures due to a growing human population and increasing fishing are leading to several changes in this sensitive ecosystem. Greater impacts are likely to occur once growing industrialization begins to increase the amount of effluents flowing into the lake. The brackish lake will lose not only its unique bird-life, but its ability to support the local fishermen whose livelihood depends on keeping its ecology intact.

| State | Tamil Nadu | Zone | Coasts (East Coast) |
|---|---|---|---|
| Area | 17.26 sq km | Ecosystem | Wet Temperate Forest |
| Year of Notification | 1967 | Visited | Dec 1979, Oct–Nov 1988, Jun 1999 |

On our long and wild seacoast there are several areas that still attract large concentrations of sea birds. These coastal areas have been the end-points of migration routes of various birds over eons of time. There were many more of these places before man began to overexploit the resources of the seashore. One such residual area is the Point Calimere Sanctuary, south of Chennai, an area that on the map is seen to stick out into the sea. The Delta of the Cauvery forms a complex ecosystem of mudflats and sandy beaches. These have been modified to develop saltpans. It is here that the flocks of flamingoes that breed in Kachchh— hundreds of kilometres away—spend their winter. And it is here that the pelicans that breed in faraway Kaziranga, in Assam, come to spend the cold months each year. Ducks, teals, waders, terns, seagulls and other estuary birds that migrate over the Himalayas from the wetlands of distant Siberia and Tibet also find their way here.

Point Calimere appears to have been proposed as a Wildlife Sanctuary in 1968. The Point Calimere Sanctuary includes the Vedaranyam swamp, which attracts thousands of waterfowl. Until 1963, this was a relatively undisturbed swampy land, but two chemical industries were set up in Point Calimere in 1963, for manufacturing industrial salt. In 1979, the Tamil Nadu Industrial Development Corporation was planning to convert a large tract covering 60,000 acres into an industrial salt-manufacturing complex. BNHS did an EIA, which led to only 4000 acres being permitted for salt works.

Point Calimere, once a deserted sea-coast, is now extensively used for fishing activities.

At Point Calimere the birds aggregate in thousands each year for the immense quantities of food that the sea, the beaches and the mudflats provide. The sea, with its constant tidal movement, throws up large numbers of crustacea and other marine life that the birds eat on the shore. The oozy mudflats teem with microscopic forms of life, which are the favourite feeding areas of the many waders, such as sandpipers and plovers that probe for food in the mud with their long bills.

The long-legged storks and spoonbills wade into deeper waters and hunt for clams and crustacea. The spoonbills form large, close-foraging flocks, while the storks form loose parties. The flamingoes feed on algal forms and tiny marine worms that live in the mud. By inverting their highly specialized sieve-like bills, they de-silt their food, and may be seen in hundreds every winter, wading around on the shore and into deeper waters where other waders find themselves out of their depth. Some flamingoes remain at Point Calimere throughout the year, and do not migrate to their nesting grounds in Kachchh. Flamingoes that had rings from Iran and Russia were also found! Salim Ali and Hussain recorded a population of 40,000 flamingoes at Point Calimere in December 1980. By the time the BNHS

Brahminy kite.

Ibisbill—an unusual wader.

studies were completed in the late 80s, the number had significantly dwindled. However, flamingo populations are known to fluctuate enormously from year to year.

Flocks of pelicans move in fishing parties, scooping up fish into their pouched beaks. They swim in a line and drive fish into the shallows where the flock of hungry birds gobble up the trapped shoal of fish. The migrant ducks—pintails, teals, pochards, pigeons, and shovelers—fill the skies during the winter months. The flocks are most abundant soon after they arrive from their distant homes and then aggregate again before leaving for their northern summer breeding grounds in Siberia. On the sandy seashore, hundreds of plovers, seagulls, and terns gather

Blackbuck, normally an animal of the grasslands, lives here along the coastline.

Seagulls feeding.

during the night. At sunrise, the long rays reaching out to the sands signal yet another new day. The morning is full of the birds' mewing as they begin to circle the skies. The flocks gradually spread out over the beaches for their morning meal.

BNHS had bird-ringing camps here every year from 1980 to 1990, during which 1379 land birds and 1964 water birds were ringed. There were also

ringing sessions done earlier from 1969 to 1972. Eleven species of waders were trapped 10 years after their initial capture, showing that waders tend to retain the same wintering site year after year. One lesser sand plover was trapped in 1990, 20 years after it was first captured!

The feral horses have been part of Point Calimere's landscape for several decades. In 2002, a controversy seems to have arisen about their ownership. Do they 'belong' to local traders or to the Forest Department? As feral, should they be considered wild rather than domesticated species, as they have not been used for many decades? They are a pleasant sight on the open plains near the sea, their wariness a sign of their wild nature.

A remarkable feature of Point Calimere is an area covered by dry evergreen forests and thorny scrubland on the coast. The blackbuck, specialized for life in arid and semi-desert regions, has adapted itself to live on this scrubland and thorn forest along the seashore. JC Daniel (1967) did the first census of blackbuck in Point Calimere in the 1960s.

The blackbucks' beautiful dark coats gleam in the sun and their horns form wide Vs, as they stand motionless, with the rolling sea behind them. They gaze fixedly at the approaching jeep before dashing through the shallow water into the shelter of nearby bushy trees. The ground they live on here is a flat muddy and marshy area, barely traversable by jeep, often requiring the use of four-wheel drive and low gear. In this landscape the bucks run at up to 80 km per hour from one patch of scrub cover to another, often traversing adjacent patches of salt water on the edge of the sea. They are always on the run when the jeep is within picture-taking range. Hoping to get a quick picture, I try to use an organized strategy. I had been watching in dismay the blackbuck crashing into a bush so thick that one could not imagine how they could find a way into it. Now, getting out quietly, I had the driver circle the copse of thorny trees. A group of blackbucks broke cover in such a way that I could only hear their thundering hooves. But one unsuspecting buck erupted out of the bush about 10 metres away. It was high up in the air and hurtling towards me over the top of the bush. I watched its startled eyes as it landed a mere three metres from

me and bounded upwards again at right angles to its landing trajectory. Its turn off was smooth and effortless; bits of earth struck me, as it appeared to soar up and away, as if on unseen wings. It was only by quick reflex that I could raise my camera to get a picture of this agile animal as it hurtled through the air. It was fascinating to observe the abrupt change in direction, coupled with the incredible fluidity of movement and the split-second precision of its graceful leap. The timing was perfect. It is this image that Point Calimere has left deeply etched in my mind: the memory of a blackbuck floating through the air.

### THE WESTERN COASTLANDS
This belt forms one of the least protected regions of India as it has few National Parks or Wildlife Sanctuaries, all the way from Gujarat down to the

tip of peninsular India. A few forested patches in the coastal areas, such as Tansa, Borivali and Phansad, represent the forest forms north of Goa. Goa itself has only a very small part of its Protected Areas in lowland coastal areas. This is highly inadequate to conserve either the local vegetation or the important animals of the region. Several species of plants have wild relatives in this type of forest that are left unprotected and may well disappear.

Gujarat has a large Marine National Park and Maharashtra a small Marine Park at Malwan.

The eastern coast of India is rich in biodiversity. The sea food is a great but limited resource. Today it is being over-harvested.

Blackbuck in a superb display of agility and speed.

Coastal birds in flight.

Feral ponies at Point Calimere.

| State | Gujarat | Zone | Coasts (West Coast) |
|---|---|---|---|
| Area | 295.03 sq km | Ecosystem | Marine Aquatic |
| Year of Notification | Sanctuary 1980; NP 1982 | Visited | Jun 1999 |

The country's first marine reserve, it covers nearly 170 km of coastline and with its 42 islands, sprawls over 163 square kilometre of inter-tidal zone. The Marine National Park consists of a coastal ecosystem of mudbanks, salt works and mangroves. The marine ecosystem includes one of our most important coral reefs. The sanctuary attracts a large variety of bird-life. Most waders flock together, looking for their food in the shallows. Each species keeps together, moving from one feeding area to another. There are more than 200 species of molluscs, innumerable species of fish and nearly 60 species of coral.

Both marine plant- and animal-life is threatened in Gujarat's Marine National Park by increasing pressures in this ultra-sensitive ecosystem. There are a large

number of grazers in the marine world, just as there are large numbers of terrestrial herbivores on land. These feed on algae, kelp and seaweed, the producers which are the first step in the food chains of the sea. The sea cucumbers live on the bed of the sea. Their numbers are being depleted in most parts of the Park. The sand dollar is a strange creature that looks like a coin. There is a great diversity of molluscs and other marine forms on the beach.

The shrimps associate themselves with anemones, which protect them from predators. A variety of molluscs and bivalves also live among the coral reefs. The coral reef forms a habitat and breeding

Seaweed forms the food material for a large number of marine herbivores.

Sponges and corals cover a very small part of the sea-bed.

1
2
3

A multicoloured vista under the shallow sea covers the rocks.

Coral.

Every marine animal is linked to several others in the food chains of the ecosystem.

ground for a wide range of fish species. The puffer is insignificant till it decides to turn itself into a large ball. The tentacles of the octopus are used for locomotion, to catch its prey as well as to defend itself.

There is a wide variety of crab species that live among the coral islands and along the coast. They range from perfectly camouflaged species to highly coloured ones. There are several types of anemones that live among the coral reef and the sandy seashore. The anemone waits for the tide to bring food material to it. Much of the coral off the coast of Gujarat has already been destroyed. Those atolls that are still relatively intact need urgent protection. While the area has been declared a National Park, in reality there is very little protection for its incredible resources.

The coral and sponges are damaged by pollution as well as by the movement

of boats and ships in the area. The beautiful star fish and brittle star of the shallow waters are now under great threat as their habitat is increasingly polluted. The large number and great diversity of small creatures, molluscs, sea shells, mussels and microscopic animals found among coral reefs makes this ecosystem the second highest amongst the species-rich ecosystems in the world.

Several species of birds are now forced to live in highly polluted waters. Very few of their traditional feeding grounds have been left unaffected by development during the last few decades. These birds are now under great threat.

The pinker shade and smaller size of the lesser flamingo differentiates it from the much larger white-and-scarlet winged greater flamingo. While both use similar feeding techniques, they eat different types of food. This water bird frequents shallow coastal waters and different types of shoreline habitats.

A strange sight of a jackal walking around a group of flamingoes feeding in the shallows makes them move away suspiciously! These interactions between species always make one wonder at the

| 1 | | |
|---|---|---|
| 2 | 3 | |

Crab.

A crab takes a threatening posture by displaying its pincers.

Brittle star.

Sea anemone.

The puffer fish blows itself into a ball to escape predators.

millions of such behavioural mysteries in nature.

The Marine National Park has a shallow marine ecosystem. It includes islands, coral reefs and coastal mudflats. As it covers a large region that is already highly threatened by industry, shipping operations, oil installations and salt works, the National Park is highly impacted. These activities are done in the name of economic development for the region. The projects and industrial establishments are based on a development strategy that is highly unsustainable here. Satellite data collected for 1975–85 indicates that sand mining for cement has reduced the mangrove forests to half their extent in a decade.

With this, there are ship-breaking yards, oil installations and several industrial establishments that need careful monitoring so that this valuable ecosystem is not further degraded.

A brahminy kite.

Lesser flamingoes feeding in a creek.

|   | 2 |   |
|---|---|---|
| 1 | 3 |   |

A reef heron.

A stone plover.

Salt pans at a specific pH attract waders.

People of Car Nicobar—Luard.

# EMERALD ISLANDS

## THE ISLAND ECOSYSTEM

Islands are among the most fragile ecosystems on Earth, but they are rich in fascinating species not found elsewhere. Ecologists have documented that larger islands not only have a greater abundance of plants and animals but are richer in species than smaller ones. As several islands are separated from others and from the mainland by great expanses of ocean, their unique plant and animal ensembles need to be protected rigorously from many forms of human interference. While human activities to a sustainable level are possible on the mainland where several ecosystems are relatively more robust, on the islands the fragility of the ecosystems need much better protection.

Two groups of islands—the Andaman and Nicobar in the Bay of Bengal and the Lakshadweep in the Arabian Sea—are the main island ecosystems of India. Islands are the world's most sensitive and unique

A forest path in the Andamans.

Mangroves at the edge of the forest.

A large epiphyte on a tree trunk.

The tiny islands have no freshwater and consequently very few large mammals.

The bright turquoise-blue of the water indicates the presence of underwater coral. The forest is full of birds and insects.

Clouds float over the islands bringing rain nearly all through the year.

ecosystems. Their large share of endemic species of plants and animals have had a long period of time in which to evolve and form their own subspecies and new island-endemic species. These islands frequently include multiple ecosystems with forests, coastal belts and marine ecosystems, all within a small geographic area.

The Andaman and Nicobar Islands are India's most vulnerable ecosystems. The forests constitute tropical evergreen forests of various types and support great biological diversity. The producers in this ecosystem are among India's most unique and varied plant communities. The first-order consumers of the islands are mainly insects and birds, but they also include a number of endemic mammals. The forests have a unique complement of birds of prey and several reptiles, which form its major predators.

The Andaman and Nicobar Islands have 300 islands and over 260 unnamed rocky exposed areas. The terrestrial ecosystems of the islands cover about 8249 square kilometre. Only 21 islands are inhabited in the Andamans and 12 in the Nicobar group. The indigenous people have unique cultures and have only recently begun to meet with settlers who have lived there over the last one or two centuries.

While the Andaman group primarily has *Dipterocarpus*- and *Pterocarpus*-dominated forests, the Nicobar group of islands does not include these species. Genera such as *Cyathea, Otanthera, Astronia* are found in the Nicobar group, but not in the Andamans. Of the 58 species of mammals, 60 per cent are endemic. Among the 1454 angiosperms, 221 are endemic. Of the 5357 species of fauna, 487 (nine per cent) are endemic. There are 270 species of birds and their subspecies recorded on the islands, of which 39 per cent are endemic. The rare birds include the Andaman crake, narcondum hornbill, Andaman hawk-owl and Andaman scops-owl.

An interesting species in the Nicobars is the megapod. Ravi Shankaran of SACON has studied these birds in great detail over the last decade. He has colour-marked 23 birds that used 26 mounds in which they nest and use the warmth of the mound to incubate their eggs. Each of the mounds was used by one to seven pairs. Some pairs used only one mound while others used several. The heat generated as a result of microbial activity in the mounds varies from 31°C to 35°C. Mounds with higher

A typical island in the Andamans.

National Parks and Wildlife Sanctuaries of India

A mosaic of vegetation types characterizes the Andamans. Each of the many forest types forms distinctive belts of vegetation that wrap around the islands.

temperatures appear to be more popular and a maximum number of eggs are observed in these mounds. By the mid-1990s, SACON had established that there were between 4500 and 8000 Nicobar megapods on the islands. The threats to the species were identified as habitat loss of the coastal forests, hunting and egg collection.

An important threatened species is the edible nest swiftlet, which is found nesting mainly in caves or on cliffs, on some of the islands. Their nests, built exclusively out of saliva, are a much sought-after table delicacy in the Far East and perhaps one of the most expensive food products in the world. The species is rare and its over-exploitation is likely to rapidly bring it to the verge of extinction. Ravi Shankaran of SACON has initiated a project to induce the birds to form nesting colonies in local rooftops, for sustainable harvesting of nests after the young have left. An estimate of the present population of these swiftlets ranges from only about 2500 to 3500 birds in the remote caves of the islands.

Exploring the flora and fauna of these islands can draw you into one of the most fascinating excursions of your life. The diversity is incredible and few ecosystems have fascinated me as much. After my first trip here, in 2000, I could not resist going back in 2002, when Shekhar Singh asked me to attend a seminar in Port Blair. My last visit to the Andamans was after the dreadful tsunami, which hit the islands leaving hundreds dead and devastating the island's ecology.

In the Andamans, every minute one spends out in the open is an experience in itself. The forest, the seashore and the undersea coral are all equally enthralling. Nature has outdone herself.

The vegetation comprises forests on the slopes and mangroves along the sea coast.

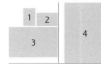

1. Mangrove and evergreen forests cover the edges of the islands.

2. The diversity of trees is apparent all over the islands.

3. Chital released on the islands have now begun to degrade the vegetation.

4. Mangrove leaves that fall into the sea constitute a mechanism to recycle energy in the ecosystem.

| 1 | | |
|---|---|---|
| 2 | 3 | |
| 4 | | |

An example of the high floral diversity of the islands.

Forest calotes.

The forests contain a large number of lizards.

The abundance of lizards is an indicator of the large number of insects in the forest.

| 1 | |
|---|---|
| 2 | |
| | 3 |

Butterfly.

The tide creates great shifts in the faunal diversity.

Pandanus palms are mainly found in the intertidal zone.

# MOUNT HARRIET NATIONAL PARK

ANDAMANS

| State | Andaman Islands | Zone | Islands |
|-------|-----------------|------|---------|
| Area | 42.62 sq km | Ecosystem | Evergreen Forest |
| Year of Notification | 1987 | Visited | Mar 2000, Jul 2001, Apr 2005 |

| 1 | 2 |
|---|---|

Many trees have tall straight trunks with a canopy on the top in which a large number of insects, reptiles and birds are found.

Palms create a magical landscape everywhere in the islands.

From the top of the hill, the calm sea stretches towards a pale horizon to the east. It is an incredible pastel orange-pink, where a pale sun appears out of nowhere. The western horizon is a dark indigo-blue sea. It is dawn. At dusk from the same point, the horizon to the west is a deep red and gold while the eastern sky is a deep ultramarine blue. Throughout the rest of the day there is a fantastic calm on both sides; a great sheet of slow-moving blue-green water. From this height one cannot hear the sea, but the white waves can be seen silently moving to and fro along the sandy shore below. White bands of froth extend across the water in great rhythmic curves.

From the hilltop, a single narrow footpath disappears into the thick evergreen forest. Ten metres into the forest

Emerald Islands

831

| 1 | 2 | | |
|---|---|---|---|
| 3 | 4 | 5 | |
| | | 6 | |

A wealth of climbers and epiphytes characterizes the forests of the Andamans.

The leech-infested path from the top of Mount Harriet leads one through a variety of forest types, till it reaches the mangroves at the edge of the sea.

The winged seed of a giant dipterocarp is an evolutionary adaptation, allowing it to waft away to distant places where it can then germinate.

A beautiful orchid beginning to bloom.

The undergrowth is full of flowering plants.

A clump of snow-white flowering orchids hangs from a branch.

there are three flowering orchids, two dazzlingly white ones, and an incredible yellow one, with yet another pastel pink one still to open fully. A few metres beyond, the path begins to descend. There are several ups and downs, which convert the short walk into a time-consuming excursion. Within a few steps, the forest seems to completely engulf me. Nothing seems to move except for the bees and mosquitoes, until I look up into the lofty canopy of the evergreen trees. There, the forest is full of life. Everything is happening at a great height above me. Life throbs among the thick green covering that produces deep shades on the forest floor. As I walk along, hoping to take pictures of the birds of the Andamans, it soon becomes obvious that this is unlikely to happen in a short time! What does present itself to a photographer however, is the sight of the scurrying lizards on the tree trunks and among the fallen leaves. The flashes of butterfly wings flit through the light and shade of the forest, hovering over flowers and settling on the dry leaves. The lianas have beautiful curves, spirals and broad 'U' shapes that link the trees into a complex web of plant life. As I descend the path through the vegetation, the pattern begins to change. The forest is full of palms, ferns and a rich diversity of shrubs.

The structure of the forest changes several times from the crest of Mount Harriet to the coastal forest at the foot of the hill. It is these structural variations that indicate is a great diversity of plant species forming different habitats.

Further down the pathway, there is an opening in the forest with a large rocky outcrop that overlooks the sea. The water is much closer from here. A bit of clear sandy shore can be seen through the foliage. A few fishing boats ply along the shallow coast.

A giant dipterocarp has fallen over. Its large root plate is exposed and it is clear that the roots must have nurtured

Some trees are completely covered by large bunches of orchids.

Mushrooms grow in the thick detritus of the forest.

National Parks and Wildlife Sanctuaries of India

The diversity of lizards is a unique
feature of the Andaman Islands

A large variety of butterflies and moths are attracted by the rich floral diversity

The amount of research on molluscs is insufficient.

the tree for decades. Close by, there are beautiful red-winged dipterocarp seeds strewn in the forest gap created by the fall of the old giant. Which of these many seeds will become seedlings? And of the many seedlings, which will, perchance, have the right conditions to grow into a sapling? Only a few will ever grow to become forest giants. The old tree trunk will decay and form the detritus which will recycle nutrients for the surrounding trees to grow on. And so life in the forests of the Andamans will go on. But

this will only happen if man does not change the web of life of these incredible emerald islands. The present trend to expand the tourist trade will undoubtedly add enormous pressures on this fragile ecosystem, perhaps killing it in the process.

The most accessible of all the Protected Areas of the Andamans, and one of the tallest peaks on the main island, Harriet is easily approached from Port Blair by a 20-minute boat ride and a half an hour drive. This accessibility itself forms a threat, as the growing tourism in the islands will adversely affect this relatively undisturbed mountainous evergreen forest. The incredible nature of the forest is heightened by seeing the sun, rising from the sea in the east, and setting again in the sea to the west, from the same vantage point at the top of the hill. Mount Harriet is a memorable experience. One suddenly realizes how small the islands are and thus how vulnerable.

| 1 | 2 |
|---|---|
| 3 | 4 |
| 5 | |

Andaman crow pheasant.

Beetle.

Seedling in the forest floor where germination is a constant struggle.

A snake in the undergrowth.

Snail.

# JOLLY BOY NATIONAL PARK

JOLLY BOY

| State | Andaman Islands | Zone | Islands |
|---|---|---|---|
| Area | — | Ecosystem | Marine |
| Year of Notification | — | Visited | Mar 2000, Apr 2005 |

The boat chugs through a tranquil and incredible blue and turquoise-green sea. Several islands of varying sizes dot the seascape. On a single tiny island there are a few trees surrounded by a strip of mangrove. On one aspect there is a rocky cliff, on the other side a clear, white, sandy beach. Such a small island, and yet it has a variety of microhabitats on its tiny surface. It has no fresh water, which limits its fauna to birds and insects that can move to the other larger islands that have fresh water. The island becomes slowly smaller as the boat moves away, turning into a tiny speck on the horizon. A fishing boat moves between the islands. It is the only human activity to be seen. Our boat moves into a strip of sea between two islands. The water is like glass. The multiple layers of vegetation of different types are clearly visible from the coast to the top of the flat islands. The tree-cover is undisturbed.

At Jolly Boy Island there are masses of tourists. They swim or sit in glass-bottomed boats to gaze at the coral just off the beach. Much of the coral is damaged, dead or dying, but a few splashes of colour still remain, indicating that patches of coral are still alive. A multitude of fish swim in and out of these incredible shapes through the blue-green water. In areas where tourists are not allowed, the coral is reported to be fantastic.

The mangrove that surrounds each island is of great importance to the marine ecosystem, as its roots hold the loose soil together. This prevents silt and soil from being washed into the sea during the heavy rains. Once the mangrove is removed, the silt is washed by the tide onto the coral, killing off its myriad forms of life.

The boat stops in a small cove. The sunlight reaches the bottom of the shallow sea and is reflected back, giving the cove a brilliant, shimmering

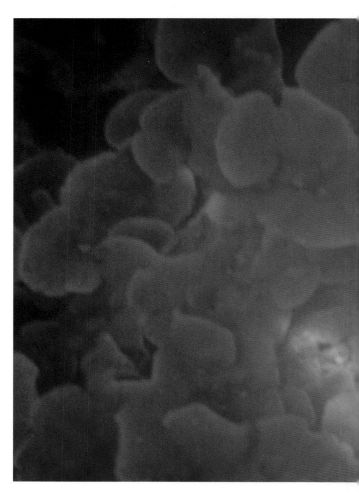

appearance. On a rock near the water's edge, several crabs emerge from the water to scuttle about chasing each other. The nearby forest is full of palms of various types. The Andamans are known to be exceptionally rich in palm species.

The mangrove leaves that fall into the sea add nutrients to the marine ecosystem. This becomes food for fish, molluscs and other marine species. This coastal belt of mangroves is thus a vital habitat that is essential for the survival of a great diversity of life.

The vast expanse of the sea is dotted with islands covered by a variety of vegetation forms, and the crystal-clear water is a living aquatic paradise. The sculpted coral have superb, intricate shapes

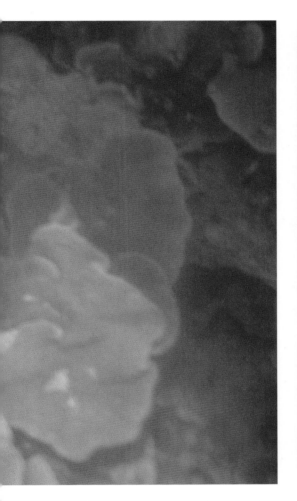

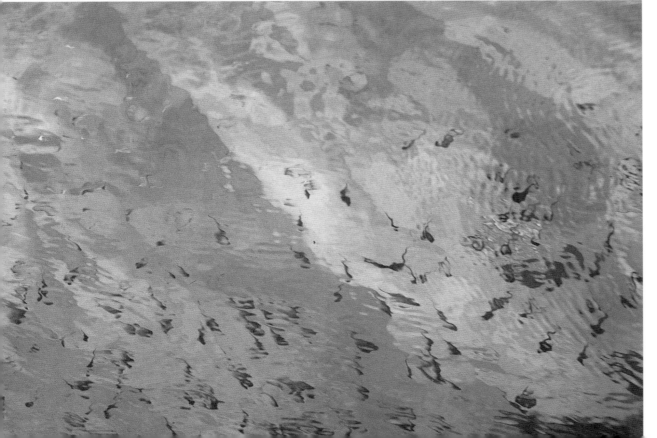

| 1 | 2 |
|---|---|
| | 3 |

Jolly Boy, which once had an incredibly rich ecosystem, is being destroyed by tourism.

Fish and coral seen through a glass-bottomed boat.

Millions of fish are found in the coastal waters of the islands.

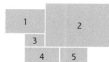

Sea cucumbers fall a prey to the exotic food market.

Coral.

Death of the coral in recent times has been attributed to global warming.

A hermit crab lives in a shell for protection.

Crabs.

Cockles, mussels and clams clothe rocky surfaces underwater.

Boats in the tourist area at Jolly Boy.

and brilliant colours, which create the backdrop for the slowly moving tentacles of anemones and the rapid, darting movements of a fascinating diversity of fish. If one rates a group of National Parks and Wildlife Sanctuaries from a single bio-geographic zone in terms of their ecosystem diversity, uniqueness, species diversity, number of endemic species and levels of threat, perhaps the Andamans, with the marine, coastal and evergreen forest systems, would get the highest rating. This high conservation value thus demands the highest level of protection and conservation action. The emerald green islands and the deep blue seas form India's foremost biodiversity conservation areas.

The overall experience of the Andamans is superb, virtually indescribable. But can it support the ever-growing number of tourists? The islands are so fragile and their ecology is so easily disturbed. Limiting tourism is a key to sustaining the integrity of the fragile ecosystems that the islands support.

Seascape.

National Parks and Wildlife Sanctuaries of India

|   |   |
|---|---|
| 1 | 2 |
|   | 4 |
| 3 | 5 |

Driftwood.

Seaweed.

Sea shell.

Seaweed.

Sea urchin.

# THE LAST REFUGE

The Protected Areas of India are some of the last refuges that our species can survive in. Man's hand has been responsible for a global disaster that threatens the lives and the very survival of millions of species of plants and animals. On the one hand species can only exist if their gene pools are left intact. On the other hand, this is not possible without an intact habitat in which they can live, interact with each other, both within their species and with other species in the community in which they are located. In this sense, the Protected Areas are at the heart of life itself and our Earth, the Mother of all living forms—microbes, plants and animals that are present on our living, throbbing planet.

We thus have a responsibility towards Mother Earth to protect her species and the diverse ecosystems they live in. It is also a responsibility towards our future generations that will inhabit Mother Earth for an indefinite amount of time. Certainly there are many, many generations. We cannot afford to lose species. This is a grave responsibility for which our future generations will hold us accountable. The Protected Areas of India need public support from a wide rage of community groups—those who live in their vicinity, those who visit them as tourists and just about every individual of the society.

We have seen the dwindling population of our wildlife in most of our country. But there have also been success stories of how Protected Areas have retained their wild creatures against all odds. The 600 Protected Areas of India form the last refuge of our biological diversity. They need your support as advocates of the philosophy behind the conservation of biodiversity.

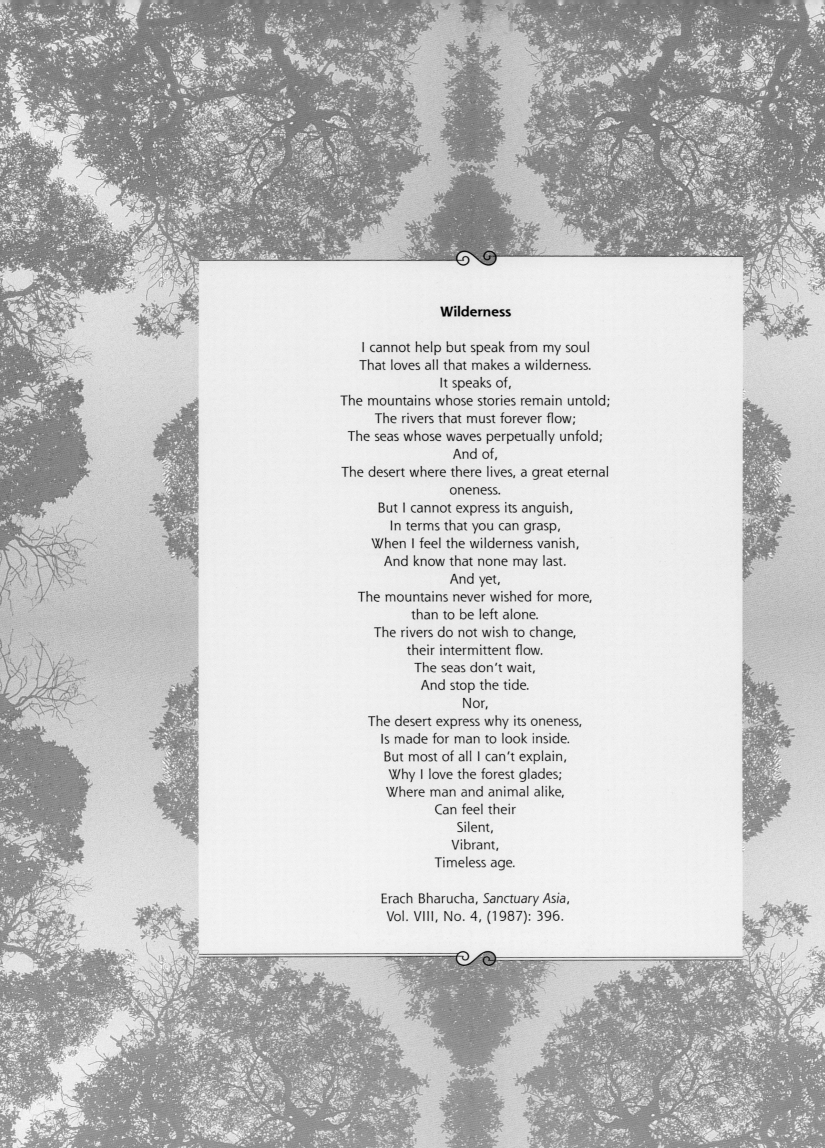

### Wilderness

I cannot help but speak from my soul
That loves all that makes a wilderness.
It speaks of,
The mountains whose stories remain untold;
The rivers that must forever flow;
The seas whose waves perpetually unfold;
And of,
The desert where there lives, a great eternal
oneness.
But I cannot express its anguish,
In terms that you can grasp,
When I feel the wilderness vanish,
And know that none may last.
And yet,
The mountains never wished for more,
than to be left alone.
The rivers do not wish to change,
their intermittent flow.
The seas don't wait,
And stop the tide.
Nor,
The desert express why its oneness,
Is made for man to look inside.
But most of all I can't explain,
Why I love the forest glades;
Where man and animal alike,
Can feel their
Silent,
Vibrant,
Timeless age.

Erach Bharucha, *Sanctuary Asia*,
Vol. VIII, No. 4, (1987): 396.

**Tiger! Tiger!**

The fiery light from your eyes has waned.

As your numbers decline
From persecution by snares and guns,
Your majestic striped form that once commanded the wilderness
Is now but a mere fleeting shadow.

As your habitats shrink
Your chance of survival is pushed to the brink.
If man's thoughtless unkindness extends yet another decade
Your stripes will be seen only in the confines of a cage.

Can the human race not see the huge magnitude of this tragedy,
Which with forethought and care could well be averted?
Let better council prevail—and perhaps—
Your eyes will burn brightly once more

To thrill us yet again.

# BIBLIOGRAPHY

### BOOKS


Agarwal, A, et al (eds). *The First Citizen's Report on the State of the Environment in India*. New Delhi: Centre for Science and Environment, 1982.

Ahmed, S. *Charger, the Long Living Tiger*. Allahabad: PrintWorld, 2001.

——. *A Naturalist on the Prowl or in the Jungle*. Bombay: W Thacker and Co Ltd, 1917.

——. *Common Birds of Bombay*. Bombay: W Thacker and Co Ltd, 1947.

Ali, S and D Ripley. *A Pictorial Guide to the Birds of the Indian Subcontinent*. Third impression. Bombay: Oxford University Press and Bombay Natural History Society, 1994.

——. *Handbook of the Birds of India and Pakistan*. Second edition. Delhi: Oxford University Press, 1996.

Ali, S and L Fatehally. *Common Indian Birds: A Picture Album*. New Delhi: National Book Trust, 1968.

——. *Indian Hill Birds*. Bombay: Oxford University Press, 1949.

——. *The Birds of Kutch*. London: Oxford University Press, 1945.

——. *The Book of Indian Birds*. Delhi: Oxford University Press, 1941.

——. *The Fall of a Sparrow*. Delhi: Oxford University Press, 1985.

Anderson, K. *Nine Man-eaters and One Rogue*. New Delhi: Indus/HarperCollins, 1991.

Andrews, HV and V Sankaran (eds). *Sustainable Management of Protected Areas in the Andaman and Nicobar Islands*. New Delhi: Andaman and Nicobar Environment Trust, Indian Institute of Public Administration and Flora and Fauna International, 2002.

Archer, Mildred. *Natural History Drawings in the India Office Library*. London: Her Majesty's Stationery Office, 1962.

Arnold, D and R Guha. *Nature, Culture, Imperialism: Essays on the Environmental History of South Asia*. New Delhi: Oxford University Press, 1998.

Arora, U. *The Wildlife Protection Act, 1972* (as amended up to 1993). Dehra Dun: Natraj Publishers, 1997.

Baker, ECS. *Cuckoo Problems*. London: HF&G Witherby Ltd, 1942.

——. *Fauna of British India, including Ceylon and Burma, Birds*. Volume I. London: Taylor & Francis, 1922.*

——. *Indian Ducks and Their Allies*. Bombay: Bombay Natural History Society, 1913.

——. *Indian Game Birds*. Volume 1, 2, 3—*Pheasants Bustards and Quails*. Reprinted from the BNHS Journal with corrections and additions. 1930.*

Bates, RSP. *Birdlife in India*. Bombay: BNHS, 1931.

Benedict, A. *The Faber Book of Exploration. An Anthology of Worlds Revealed by Explorers through the Ages*. London: Faber and Faber, 2002.

Bharucha, EK. *Textbook for Environmental Studies for Undergraduate Courses*. Hyderabad: University Press, 2005.

——. *The Biodiversity of India*. Ahmedabad: Mapin Publishing, 2002.

——. 'Cultural and Spiritual Values Related to the Conservation of Biodiversity in the Sacred Groves of the Western Ghats in Maharashtra' in *Cultural and Spiritual Values of Biodiversity*. DA Posey (ed). Kenya: UNEP, 1999.

Bharucha, FR. *A Textbook of Plant Geography of India*. Bombay: Oxford University Press, 1983.

Birdwood, GM. *Catalogue of Economic Products of the Presidency of Bombay*. Bombay: Bombay Education Society Press, 1862.

Blandford, WT. *Fauna of British India*. London: Routledge, 1891.

Blatter, E and WS Millard. *Some Beautiful Indian Trees*. Second reprint. Second edition. Bombay: Bombay Natural History Society and Oxford University Press, 1993.

Bole, PV and Y Vaghani. *Field Guide to the Common Trees of India*. Oxford: World Wide Fund for Nature India and Oxford University Press, 1986.

Booth, M. *Carpet Sahib: A Life of Jim Corbett*. New Delhi: Oxford University Press, 1986.

Bose, DM, SN Sen and BV Subbarayappa (eds). *A Concise History of Science in India*. New Delhi: Indian National Science Academy, 1971.

Brown, P. *Indian Architecture; Buddhist and Hindu Periods*. Seventh Reprint. Bombay: DB Taraporewala and Sons, 1976.

Buch, MN. *The Forests of Madhya Pradesh*. Bhopal: Madhya Pradesh Madhyam, 1991.

Burkill, IH. *Chapters on the History of Botany in India*. Calcutta: Botanical Survey of India, 1965.

Burton, RG. *The Book of the Tiger*. London: Hutchinson and Co, 1933.

Bussagli, M. *Indian Minatures*. New Delhi: MacMillan, 1976.

Carey and Wallich. *Flora Indica*. Volume 1, 1820; Volume 2, 1824.*

Carpenter, P. *Hog Hunting in Lower Bengal*. London: Day & Son, 1861.**

Centre for Environment Education. *Nature Scope India: Endangered Elephants*. Ahmedabad: Centre for Environment Education, 2001.

Champion, FW. *The Jungle in Sunlight and Shadow*. London: Chatto and Windus, 1934. ***

——. *With a Camera in Tigerland*. London: Chatto and Windus, 1928. ***

Champion, HG and SK Seth. *A Revised Survey of the Forest Types of India*. New Delhi: Government of India Press, 1968.

Chapman, G, K Kumar, C Fraser, and I Gaber. *Environmentalism and the Mass Media: The North-South Divide*. London: Routledge, 1997.

Chapman, HH and WH Meyer. *Forest Mensuration*. New York: MacGraw Hill, 1949.

Chavda, D. *The End of a Trail: The Cheetah in India*. New Delhi: Banyan Books, 1996.

Cleghorn, H. *Forests and Gardens of South India*. London: WH Allen and Co, 1861.

Cooke, TC. *The Flora of the Presidency of Bombay*. London: Taylor and Francis, 1901–8.

Corbett, J. *Jungle Lore*. London: Oxford University Press, 1953.

——. *Man-eaters of Kumaon*. Oxford: Oxford University Press, 1944.

——. *My India*. London: Oxford University Press, 1952.

——. *The Man-eating Leopard of Rudraprayag*. Oxford: Oxford University Press, 1948.

——. *The Temple Tiger and More Man-Eaters of Kumaon*. Mumbai: Oxford University Press, 1954.

——. *Tree Tops*. London: Oxford University Press, 1955.

Cornish, CJ, FC Selous, H Johnston, CH Lane, L Wain, WP Pycraft, HA Brydan, FG Aflalo and W Saville-Kent. *The Living Animals of the World: A Popular Natural History*. Volume I and II. London: The Standard Art Book Company Ltd, nd.

Council for Scientific and Industrial Research. *The Wealth of India: A Dictionary of Indian Raw Materials and Industrial Products*. Volumes 1–11. New Delhi: Publications and Information Directorate, Council of Scientific and Industrial Research, 1976.

Cubitt, G and G Mountfort. *Wild India*. London: Collins, nd.

da Orta, G. *Colloques on the Simples and Drugs of India*. Translated, Introduction & Index by Sir Clements Markham. London: Henry Sotheran & Co.*

Daniel, JC and JS Serrao (eds). *Conservation in Developing Countries: Problems and Prospects*. Bombay: Bombay Natural History Society and Oxford University Press, 1990.

——. *A Century of Natural History*. Bombay: Bombay Natural History Society, 1983.

——. *The Book of Indian Reptiles*. Bombay: Bombay Natural History Society and Oxford University Press, 1983.

——. *The Leopard in India—A Natural History*. Dehra Dun: Natraj Publishers, 1996.

Dawkins, R. *The Ancestor's Tale: A Pilgrimage to the Dawn of the Life*. London: Weidenfeld and Nicolson, 2006.

Department of Environment. *Indira Gandhi on Environment*. New Delhi: Government of India, 1984.

Desmond, R. *The European Discovery of the Indian Flora*. Edinburgh: Royal Botanic Gardens and Oxford University Press, 1992.

Dharmakumarsinh, RS and KS Lavkumar. *Sixty Indian Birds*. New Delhi: Ministry of Information and Broadcasting, Government of India, 1972.

——. *Birds of Saurashtra*. Bombay: RS Dharmakumarsinh, 1954.

Diwan, S, and A Rosencranz. *Environmental Law and Policy in India*. Second edition. New Delhi: Oxford University Press, 2001.

Dobzhansky, T, F Ayala, GL Stebbins and JW Valentine. *Evolution*. San Francisco: WH Freeman, 1997.

Dompka, V (ed). *Human Population, Biodiversity and Protected Areas: Science and Policy Issues*. Washington, DC: American Association for the Advancement of Science, 1996.

Donovan, E. *Natural History of Insects of India and the Islands of the Indian Seas*. 1800.*

Doughty, M. *Afoot through the Kashmir Valleys*. London: Sands and Company, 1902.

Douglas, J. *Bombay & Western India*. London: Samson Low, Marston's Co, 1893.**

Drayton, R. *Nature's Government. Science, Imperial Britain, and the 'Improvement' of the World*. New Delhi: Orient Longman, 2000.

Drury, H. *The Useful Plants of India*. Second edition. London: WH Allen and Co, 1873.

Dunbar, BAA. *Wild Animals of Central India*. London: Edward Arnold, 1923.

Dwivedi, AP. *Protected Areas of Madhya Pradesh*. Bhopal: Principal Chief Conservator of Forests (Wild Life), Madhya Pradesh Forest Department, Government of Madhya Pradesh, 2003.

Dwivedi, S. and Barwani MS. *The Automobiles of the Maharajas*. Mumbai: Eminence Designs, 2003.†

Eden. *Portraits of the Princes and People of India*. London: Dickinson & Son, 1844.**

Elvin, V. *Leaves from the Jungle*. Second edition. London: Oxford University Press, 1958.

Engelman, R, RP Cincotta, B Dye, T Gardner-Outlaw and J Wisnewski. *People in the Balance: Population and Natural Resources at the Turn of the Millennium*. Washington, DC: Population Action International, 2000.

Finn, F. 1915. *Indian Sporting Birds*. London: Francis Edwards, 1815.***

Forbes, J. *Oriental Memoirs*. Four volumes. London: White, Cockrane and Co. London, 1813.**

Forest and R Ackermann. *A Picturesque Journey along the Rivers Ganges and Jumna in India*. London: 1824.**

Forest Research Institute. *One Hundred Years of Indian Forestry 1861 to 1961*. Volume II, *Forests*. DehraDun: Forest Research Institute, 1961.

Forsyth, J. *The Highlands of Central India*. London: Chapman and Hall, 1871.

Fraser, JB. *Views of Calcutta and its Environs*. London: Smith, Elder & Co., 1826.**

Fryer, J. *A New Account of East India and Persia*. 1698.**

Gadgil, M. *Ecological Journeys: The Science and Politics of Conservation in India*. New Delhi: Permanent Black, 2001.

Gee, EP. *The Wild Life of India*. London: Collins, 1964.

Ghorpade, MY. *Sunlight and Shadows*. Bombay: BI Publications, 1983.

Gibson, A. *A Handbook to the Forests of the Bombay Presidency*. Nos 1 and 2. Bombay: Bombay Education Society Press, 1857.

Gosler, A. *The Hamlyn Photographic Guide to the Birds of the World*. London: Hamlyn, 1991.

Gould, J. *The Birds of Asia*. Vol. 1–7. London: John Gould, 1850–77.

——. *Birds of Asia*. Volume I.*

Government of Gujarat. *The Gir Lion Sanctuary Project*. Gujarat: Directorate of Information and Tourism, Government of Gujarat, 1972.

Government of India. *The Report of the Tiger Task Force: Joining the Dots*. New Delhi: Union Ministry of Environment and Forests, 2005.

Gray, JE. *Illustrations of Indian Zoology*. Volume 1 and 2. 1830–1832.*

Grewal, B. *Birds of India, Bangladesh, Nepal, Pakistan and Sri Lanka*. Hong Kong/ New Delhi: Guide Book Co Ltd, and Gulmohor Press, 1993.

Grimitt, R, C Inskipp, and T Inskipp. *Pocket Guide to the Birds of the Indian Subcontinent*. New Delhi: Oxford University Press, 2006.

Grindlay, RM. *Scenery, Costumes and Architecture Chiefly on the Western Side of India*. London: Smith, Elder & Co., 1830.**

Groombridge, B and MD Jenkins. *World Atlas of Biodiversity*. Prepared by the United Nations Environment Programme—World Conservation Monitoring Centre. Berkeley: University of California Press, 2002.

Guha, R (ed). *Nature's Spokesman: M Krishnan and Indian Wildlife*. New Delhi: Oxford University Press, 2000.

Hardinges, CS. Recollections of India. London: Thomas McLean, 1847.**

Hawkins, RE (ed). *Encyclopaedia of Indian Natural History*. New Delhi: Bombay Natural History Society and Oxford University Press, 1986.

Hawks, E. *Pioneers of Plant Study*. London: The Shelden Press, 1928.*

Herring, RJ and EK Bharucha. 'India: Embedded Capacities' in *Engaging Countries: Strengthening Compliance with International Environmental Accords*. E Brown Weiss and HK Jacobson (eds). London: MIT Press, 1998.

Hooker, JD. *Himalayan Journals or Notes of a Naturalist*. Volume 1. London: John Murray.*

——. *Illustrations of Himalayan Plants Chiefly Selected from Drawings Made for the Late SF Cathcart*. Plates by Fitch. 1855.*

——. *The Flora of British India*. 7 volumes. London: L Reeve and Co, 1872–97.

——. *The Rhododendrons of Sikkim Himalayas*. Edited by WS Hooker. London: Reeve & Co, 1849.*

Hooker, WJ. *Exotic Flora*. Volume 1–3. 1823, 1825.*

——. *Himalayan Journal*. Volume 1, 1854. Volume 2, 1954.

Hume, AO and CHT Marshall. *Game Birds of India, Burmah and Ceylon*. Vol 1, 2 and 3. London: John Bale, 1880–1881.*

——. *Stray Feathers: A Journal of Ornithology for India and its Dependencies*. Calcutta: Calcutta Central Press, 1873.

Huxley. *Life and Letters of JD Hooker*. Volume 1, 2.*

*Indian Drawings: Thirty Mogul Paintings of School of Jehangir and Four Panels of Calligraphy in the Wantage Bequest*. London: Stanley Clarke, 1922.**

International Union for the Conservation of Nature. *International Union for the Conservation of Nature Red List of Threatened Animals*. Cambridge, UK: World Conservation Monitoring Centre, International Union for the Conservation of Nature, 1990.

Islam, Zafar-ul, M Rahamani, R Asad (eds). *Important Bird Areas in India: Priority Sites for Conservation*. Mumbai: Oxford University Press for Bombay Natural History Society, IBCN and Birdlife International, 2004.

Jain, P. *Project Tiger Status Report*. New Delhi: Project Tiger, Ministry of Environment and Forests, Government of India, 2001.

Jerdon, TC. *Illustrations of Indian Ornithology*. Madras: American Mission Press, 1847.*

——. *The Mammals of India*. London: John Wheldon, 1867.

Johnsingh, AJT. *Field Days. A Naturalist's Journey through South and Southeast Asia*. Hyderabad: University Press, 2006.

——. *On Jim Corbett's Trail and Other Tales from Tree Tops*. New Delhi: Permanent Black, 2005.

Keay, J. *The Great Arc*. London: Harper Collins, 2000.

Kehimkar, I. *Common Indian Wild Flowers*. Bombay: Oxford University Press, 2000.

King, G and R Pantling. *Annals of the Royal Botanic Gardens, Calcutta*. Volume IX, 1901.*

Kirtikar, BD and KR Kirtikar. *Indian Medicinal Plants*. Dehra Dun: Bishen Singh Mahendra Pal Singh, 1984.

Kothari, A et al. *Management of National Parks and Sanctuaries in India: A Status Report*. New Delhi: Indian Institute of Public Administration, sponsored by the Ministry of Environment and Forests, Government of India, 1989.

Krishnan, M. *Nights and Days: My Book of India's Wildlife*. New Delhi: Vikas Publishing House, 1985.

Kunte, K. *Butterflies of Peninsular India*. Hyderabad: University Press, 2000.

Lal, R, A Kothari, P Pandey and S Singh (eds). *Directory of National Parks and Sanctuaries in Karnataka: Management Status and Profiles*. New Delhi: Indian Institute of Public Administration, 1994.

Lancum, FH. *Wild Animals and The Land*. London: Crosby Lockwood and Son, 1950.

Le Messuirier, A. *Game, Shore and Water Birds of India*. Calcutta: Thacker, Spink & Co, 1888.

*Lindenia Iconography des Orchides*. Series 2, Volume 6, March 1901. Part XXXIII, October 1893.*

Lowther, EHN and RSP Bates. *Breeding Birds of Kashmir*. London: Oxford University Press, 1952.

——. *A Bird Photographer in India*. London: Oxford University Press, 1949.

Luard, John. *Views in India*.**

Lydekkar, R. *The Deer of All Lands*. London: Roland Ward, 1898.***

MacNeely, JA, KR Miller, WV Reid, RA Mittermeier, and TB Werner. *Conserving the World's Biological Diversity*. International Union for the Conservation of Nature, World Resources Institute, Conservation International, World Wide Fund for Nature-US and the World Bank, 1990.

Malhotra, I. *Dynasties of India and Beyond*. New Delhi: Harper Collins and The India Today Group, 2003.

——. *Dynasties of India and Beyond: Pakistan, Sri Lanka, Bangladesh*. New Delhi: Harper Collins, 2003.

Marshall, J. *Mohenje Daro and the Indus Civilization*. Volume III. London: Arthur Probsthain, 1931.**

McCully, P. *Silenced Rivers: The Ecology and Politics of Large Dams*. New Delhi: Orient Longman, 1998.

McNeely, JA, et al. *Conserving the World's Biological Diversity*. International Union for the Conservation of Nature, Gland, Switzerland; World Resources Institute; Conservation International; World Wide Fund for Nature-US and the World Bank, Washington DC, 1990.

Menon, V and A Kumar. *Wildlife Crime: An Enforcement Guide*. Dehra Dun: Natraj Publishing and Wildlife Protection Society of India, 1999.

——, and M Sakamoto. *Heaven, Earth and I*. New Delhi: Penguin Books, 2002.

——. *Tusker! The Story of the Asian Elephant*. India: Penguin Books, 2002.

Ministry of Environment and Forests. *Biosphere Reserves*. New Delhi:

Ministry of Environment and Forests, Government of India, 1987.
———. *India's Wildlife.* New Delhi: Publications Division, Ministry of Environment and Forests, Government of India, 1963.
———. Securing India's Future: Final Technical Report of the NBSAP. *National Biodiversity Strategy and Action Plan—India.* Draft Technical Report of UNDP-GEF. Pune/Delhi: Kalpavriksh, 2005.
Moulton, C and EJ Hulsey. *Kanha Tiger Reserve: Portrait of an Indian National Park.* Mumbai: Vakil's, Feffer and Simons, 1999.
Moynihan, EB. *The Moonlight Garden: New Discoveries at the Taj Mahal.* Washington, DC: Smithsonian Institute and University of Washington Press, 2000.
Naipaul, VS. *India: A Million Mutinies Now.* London: Minerva, 1997.
National Biodiversity Strategy and Action Plan. *Final Technical Report of UNDP-GEF Sponsored Project.* Summary Version. Ministry of Environment and Forests and Kalpavriksh, nd.
Nebel, BJ, and RT Wright. *Environmental Science: Towards a Sustainable Future.* New Jersey: Prentice-Hall, 2002.
Niceville, Lionel de and GFL Marshall. *The Butterflies of India, Burma and Ceylon.* Calcutta: The Calcutta Central Press, 1889.
Nicols, A. *Zoologican Notes.* London: L Upcott Gill, 1883.
Noltie, HJ. *Indian Botanical Drawings 1793–1868 from the Royal Botanic Garden Edinburgh.* Edinburgh: Royal Botanic Garden, 1999.
———. *The Dapuri Drawings: Alexander Gibson and the Bombay Botanic Gardens.* Ahmedabad: Mapin Publishing, in association with the Royal Botanic Garden, Edinburgh, 2002.
Oates, E. *Handbook of the Birds of British Burma, including those Found in the Adjoining State of Karennee.* Volumes 1 and 2. London: RH Porter, 1883.
Odum, EP. *Fundamentals of Ecology.* Third edition. Philadelphia: WB Saunders, 1971.
Office of Technical Assessment. *Wetlands, Their Use and Regulations.* Washington, DC: Office of Technical Assessment, Congress of the United States, 1984.
*Oriental Ornithology.* No 1, 2. 1828–1829.**
Pant, R. *Customs and Conservation: Cases of Traditional and Modern Law in India and Nepal.* Community Based Conservation in South Asia: Theme Paper No 7. New Delhi/London: Kalpavriksh and International Institute for Environment and Development, 2000.
Pocock, RI. *The Fauna of British India.* Volume 1, *Mammalia.* Second edition. London: Taylor and Francis, 1939.
Posey, DA (ed). *Cultural and Spiritual Values of Biodiversity.* Nairobi/London: United Nations Environment Programme and Intermediate Technology Publications, 1999.
Prater, SH. *The Book of Indian Animals.* Bombay: Bombay Natural History Society in collaboration with Oxford University Press, New Delhi, 1971.
Puri GS, VM Meher-Homji, RK Gupta, S Puri. *Forest Ecology.* Volume 1, *Phytogeography and Forest Conservation.* Second edition. New Delhi: Oxford and IBH Publishing Co, 1983.
Rangarajan, M. *India's Wildlife History: An Introduction.* New Delhi: Permanent Black in association with the Ranthambhore Foundation, 2001.
Ranjitsingh, MK. *Beyond the Tiger: Portraits of Asian Wildlife.* New Delhi: Brijwasi Printers Pvt Ltd, 1997.
Rashid, MA and R David. *The Asiatic Lion.* Department of Environment, Government of India, 1992.
Rathore FS, T Singh and V Thapar. *With Tigers in the Wild.* New Delhi: Vikas Publishing House Pvt Ltd, 1983.
Reader's Digest. *The Last Two Million Years.* London: Reader's Digest, 1974.
Reaka-Kudla, ML, DE Wilson, EO Wilson (eds). *Biodiversity II: Understanding and Protecting Our Biological Resources.* Washington, DC: Joseph Henry Press, 1997.
Richard, D. *Nature's Government. Science, Imperial Britain, and the 'Improvement' of the World.* New Delhi: Orient Longman, 2000.
Ripley, SD. *A Synopsis of the Birds of India and Pakistan.* Bombay: Bombay Natural History Society, 1961.
Rodgers WA, HS Panwar and VB Mathur. *Wildlife Protected Area Network in India: A Review.* Dehra Dun: Wildlife Institute of India, 2000.
Rogers, A and HS Panwar. *Planning a Protected Area Network in India.* Volume I. Dehra Dun: Wildlife Institute of India, 1988.
Roxburgh, W. *Plants of the Coast of Coromandel.* Volume 1. East India Company, under direction of Joseph Banks, 1795.*
———. *Flora Indica.* Second edition. W Carey (ed). Serampore: Thacker and Co, 1832.
Royle, JF. *Illustrations of the Botany and Other Branches of the Natural History of the Himalayan Mountains and the Flora of Cashmere.* Volume 1, 2, 1839. London: H Allen and Co.*
Saberwal, V and M Rangarajan (eds). *Battles over Nature: Science and the Politics of Conservation.* New Delhi: Permanent Black, 2003.
Sahni, KC. *The Book of Indian Trees.* Mumbai: Bombay Natural History Society and Oxford University Press, 1998.
Saigal, S. *Does Community-based Conservation Make Economic Sense?* Community Based Conservation in South Asia: Theme Paper No 8. New Delhi/London: Kalpavriksh and International Institute for Environment and Development, 2000.
Sanctuary Magazine. *Saving India's Forest's and Wildlife. The Pioneering Role of the Supreme Court of India.* Mumbai: Sanctuary Magazine, 2003.
Sankhala, K. *Tiger! The Story of the Indian Tiger.* India: Rupa and Co and Collins, London, 1978.
———. *Tigerland.* London: Collins, 1975.
Savarkar, VB. *A Guide for Planning Wildlife Management in Protected Areas and Managed Landscapes.* Dehra Dun: Wildlife Institute of Indian and Natraj Publishers, 2005.
Schaller, GB. *The Deer and the Tiger; A Study of Wildlife in India.* Chicago: University of Chicago Press, 1967.
Seidensticker, J, and S Christie, and P Jackson. *Riding the Tiger.* Cambridge, UK: Cambridge University Press, 1999.
*Sertum Orchidaceum.* 1836.*
Seshadri, B. *Twilight of India's Wildlife.* Presented in Mysore by Mr Van Ingen. London: John Baker Publishers, 1969.
Shah, KT. 1930. *The Splendour That Was Ind'.* Bombay: VB Taraporvalla Sons & Co.
Shahi, SP. *Backs to the Wall: Saga of Wildlife in Bihar, India.* India: Affiliated East-West Press, 1977.
Shakespear, H. *The Wild Sports of India.* London: Smith, Elder and Co, 1860.
Shankar, K, and BC Choudhary (eds). *Marine Turtles of the Indian Subcontinent.* Hyderabad: Orient Longman, 2006.
Shiva, V. *Biodiveristy Conservation.* New Delhi: Indian National Trust for Art and Cultural Heritage, 1994.
Singh, A. *Tiger! Tiger!* London: Jonathan Cape Ltd, 1984.
Singh, S, et al (eds). *Setting Biodiversity Conservation Priorities for India.* New Delhi: World Wife Fund for Nature India, 2000.
———, V Sankaran, H Mandar and S Worah. *Strenghtening Conservation Cultures: Local Community and Biodiversity Conservation.* Paris: Man and the Biosphere Programme and UNESCO, 2000.
———. *Conserving India's Natural Heritage.* Dehra Dun: Natraj Publishers, 1986.
Sivaganeshan, N and Ajith Kumar. *Status of Feral Elephants in the Andaman Islands, India.* Salim Ali Centre for Ornithology and Natural History—Technical Report 1. Coimbatore: Salim Ali Centre for Ornithology and Natural History, 1994.
Smith, CW. *The Feathered Game of Hindustan.* 1828.**
Spear, Percival. *A History of India. Volume Two: From the Sixteenth Century to the Twentieth Century.* New York: Penguin Books, 2003.
Stanek, VJ. *The Pictorial Encyclopaedia of the Animal Kingdom.* Seventh edition. London: Hamlyn, 1971.
Stebbing, EP. *The Diary of a Sportsman Naturalist in India.* London: John Lane Co, 1920.
———. *The Forests of India.* London: Bodley Head, 1922.
Sterndale, RA. *Natural History of Mammals of India and Ceylon.* Calcutta: Thacker, Spink and Co, 1884.
Stracey, PD. *Wildlife in India: Its Conservation and Control.* New Delhi: Ministry of Food and Agriculture, 1963.
Teeple, JB. *Timelines of World's History.* London: DK Publishing, 2002.
Thapar, V. *Battling for Survival: India's Wilderness over Two Centuries.* New Delhi: Oxford University Press, 2003.
———. *Tiger: Portrait of a Predator.* London: Collins, 1986.
———. *Tigers, the Secret Life.* London: Hamish Hamilton, 1989.
Troupe. *Siliviculture of Indian Trees.* Volume 1–2, 1921.*
Tuncliffe, CF. *The Wonders of Nature.* London: Odhams Press, 1993.
Van Rheede, HA. *Hortus Malabaricus.* Amsterdam: Aa Balkema, 1678–93.
Vasavi, AR. *Harbingers of Rain: Land and life in South India.* New Delhi: Oxford University Press, 1999.
Verma, DD, S Arora and RK Rai (eds). *Perspectives on Biodiversity: A Vision for Mega-diverse Countries.* Ministry of Envionment and Forests, Government of India, 2006.
Wallich, N. *Plantae Asiatica Rariores.* Volume I, 1830; Volume II, 1831; Volume III, 1832.*
Watt, G. *A Dictionary of the Economic Products of India.* Volumes 1–6. Calcutta: Government of India, 1889–93.
Weiss, EB and HK Jacobson. *Engaging Countries: Strengthening Compliance with International Environmental Accords.* Cambridge, Mass: The MIT Press, 1998.
Whistler, H. *Popular Handbook of Indian Birds.* Fourth edition. London: Gurney and Jackson, 1949.
Whitaker, R and A Captain. *Snakes of India: The Field Guide.* Chennai: Draco Books, 2004.
Wight, R and GAW Arnott. *Prodromus Flora Peninsulae Indiae Orientalis.* Volume 1. London: Parbury, Allen & Co, 1834.*
Wight, R. *Illustrations of Indian Botany.* Volume 1, 1838.*
Williamson, T. *Oriental Field Sports.* Volume I and II. London: Edward Orma, 1807.**
———. *Mainstreaming the Environment.* Washington, DC: World Bank, 1995.
———. *Making Development Sustainable.* Washington, DC: World Bank, 1994.
World Health Organization. *Our Planet, Our Health.* New Delhi: Oxford University Press, 1993.
Zoological Survey of India. *Zoological Survey of India 1916–1990: History and Progress.* New Delhi: Director, Zoological Survey of India, Government of India, 1990.


**JOURNALS, PERIODICALS AND REPORTS**


Abdulali, H. 'Nightjars on Roads'. JBNHS 47, no 1 (1947): 162.
———. 'Northern Limits of the Rusty Spotted Cat (*Prionailurus R. Rubiginosus* Geoff)'. JBNHS 45, no 4 (1945): 600–1.
———. 'On the Export of Frog Legs from India'. JBNHS 82, no 2 (1985): 347–375.
ADB. 'A Flight over the Andamans'. *Indian Forester* 58 (September 1932): 469–471.
Aitken, EH and E Comber. 'A List of the Butterflies of the Konkan'. JBNHS 15, no 1 (1903): 42–55.
Akhtar, SA. *Babar the Great on Flamingoes.* JBNHS 46, no 3 (1946): 545–547.
Ali, S. 'Mughal Emperors of India as Naturalists and Sportsmen'. JBNHS 31, no 4 (1927): 833–861.
———. 'The Keoladeo Ghana of Bharatpur (Rajasthan)'. JBNHS 51, no 3 (1953): 531–536.
———. 'The Ornithology of Travancore and Cochin (with notes by H Whistler)'. Part 1. JBNHS 37, no 4 (1935): 814–843.
Ansell, WFH. 'A Note on the Position of Rhinoceros in Burma'. JBNHS 47, no 2 (1947): 249–276.
Anvery, SAA. 'All Over a Few Logs'. *Indian Forester* (May 1938): 282–286.
Bahrgava, MP. 'The Utilization of Bagasse for the Paper and Board Industries'. *Indian Forester* (1933): 714–719.
Baker, ECS. 'A Review of the Indian Swans'. JBNHS 23, no 3 (1915): 454–459.
———. 'Indian Ducks and Their Allies'. JBNHS 11, nos 1 to 4 (1897–98).
Balasubramanyan, MS. 'The Land of Hanumans; Its Forests and People'. *Indian Forester* (January 1938): 32–43.
Bates, RSP and EHN Lowther. 'The History of Bird Photography in India'. JBNHS 50, no 4 (1952): 779–84.
Bell, TR. 'The Common Butterflies of the Plains of India'. JBNHS 19, nos 1, 2 and 3 (1909): 16–58, 438–574 and 635–682.
Bhadran. 'The Manas Game Sanctuary, Assam'. *Indian Forester* (December 1934): 802–811.
Biswas, K. 'A General Review of the Marine Algae of the Western Coast of India'. JBNHS 45, no 4 (1945): 515–530.
Blanford, WT. 'The Large Indian Squirrel (*Sciurus Indicus*, Erx) and Its Local Races or Sub-Species'. JBNHS 11, no 2 (1897): 298–305.
Boulenger, GA. 'A New Tortoise from Travancore'. JBNHS 17, no 3 (1906): 560–561.
Brandis, D. 'Progress of Forestry'. *Indian Forester* 10 (1884).
Breeden, S and B Breeden. 'The Drought of 1979–1980 at the Keoladeo Ghana Sanctuary, Bharatpur, Rajasthan'. JBNHS 79, no 1 (1982): 1–37.
Burton, RW. 'The Protection of World Resources: Wildlife and the Soil'. JBNHS 50, no 2 (1951): 371–379.
———. 'Wild Life Preservation—India's Vanishing Asset'. JBNHS 47, no 4 (1948): 602–621.
———. 'Wildlife Preservation in India'. JBNHS 51, no 3 (1952): 561–78.
Cadell, P. 'The Preservation of Wildlife in India. The Indian Lion'. JBNHS 37, no 4 (1935): 162–166.
Chakraborty, S. 'The Rusty-Spotted Cat, *Felis rubiginosa* I Geoffroy, in Jammu and Kashmir'. JBNHS 75, no 2 (1978): 478.
Champion, FW. 'Air Survey of Forests'. *Indian Forester* 59 (January 1933): 12–21.
———. 'Indian Wildlife'. *Indian Forester* 1, no 1 (1936).
———. 'Preservation of Wildlife in India'. *Indian Forester* (November 1934): 774–789.
Champion, HG. 'Forestry Interests Forty Years Ago and Today'. *Indian Forester* (October 1955): 602–603.
Chavda, D. 'Note on the Sighting of a Caracal (*Felis caracal*) at the Sariska National Park'. JBNHS 84, no 1 (1987): 201.
Comber, E. 'Protective Legislation for Indian Fisheries'. JBNHS 17, no 3 (1906–7): 637–644.
Crump, CA. 'Bombay Natural History Society's Mammal Survey of India'. JBNHS 21, no 3 (1912): 820–851.
Curtis, W. *Botanical Magazine.* Volume III–IV. London: Couchman & Fry, 1790.*
———. *Botanical Magazine.* Volume XI–XII. London: Couchman & Fry, 1797.*
Daver, SR and Khan Sahib. 1938. 'Elephants'. *Indian Forester* (May 1938): 286–292.
Davidar, ERC. 'The Nilgiri Wild Life Association and Status of Wild Life in the Nilgiris'. JBNHS 65, no 2 (1968): 431–443.
Deshmukh, P. 'Role of Forests in the Second Five Year Plan'. *Indian Forester* (September 1956): 485–487.
Dharmakumarsinh, KS. 'Wildlife Preservation in India—Annual Report for 1953 on the Western Region'. JBNHS 52, no 4 (1955): 865–873.
Dodsworth, PTL. 'Protection of Wild Birds in India and Traffic in Plumage'. JBNHS 20, no 4 (1910–11): 103.
Editors, *Indian Forester.* 'The Viceroy's Speech at the Opening of the Forest Conference in New Delhi in December 1937'. *Indian Forester* (January 1938): 70–79.
Editors, JBNHS. 'Game Preservation in India'. JBNHS 32, no 2 (1927): 359–365.
———. 'The Golden Jubilee 1883–1933: Proceedings of the Fiftieth Anniversary Jubilee Meeting'. *Hornbill Centenary Issue,* JBNHS, 1983.
———. 'The Wild Animals of the Indian Empire Part III—*Carnivora* or Beasts of Prey'. JBNHS 37, no 4 (1935): supplement.
Ellison, BC. 'Game Preservation and Game Experiments in India'. JBNHS 33, no 1 (1928): 120–135.
Fenton, LL. 'The Kathiawar Lion'. JBNHS 19, no1 (1909): 4–15.
Gammie, GA. 'The Trees and Shrubs of the Lonavla and Karla Groves'. JBNHS 15, no 2 (1903): 279–293.
Gee, EP. 'The Management of India's Wildlife Sanctuaries and National Parks'. Part III. JBNHS 54, no 1 (1956): 1–21.
———. 'The Management of India's Wildlife Sanctuaries and National Parks'. JBNHS 51, no 1 (1952): 1–18.
———. 'The Management of India's Wildlife Sanctuaries and National Parks'. Part II. JBNHS 52, no 4 (1955): 717–734.
———. 'Wildlife Preservation in India: Annual Report for 1953 on the Eastern Region'. JBNHS 52, no 2 and 3 (1954): 233–240.
———. 'Wildlife Preservation; the Creation of National Parks in India'. *Indian Forester* (October 1955): 658–660.
Ghorpade, YR. 'Wildlife Preservation in India—Annual Report for 1953 on the Southern Region'. JBNHS 53, 1953: 103–109.
Gilbert, R. 'Notes on the Indian Bear (*Melursus ursinus*)'. JBNHS 10, no 4 (1897): 688–90.
Graham, RJD. 'Note on Ferns Collected at Pachmarhi, CP'. JBNHS 23, no 3 (1915): 498–501.
Grubh, R. 1978. 'Field Identification of Some Indian Vultures (*Gyps benghalensis, G indicus, G fulvus & Torgos calvus*)'. JBNHS 75, no 2 (1978), 444–449.
Guman Singh, K. 'Game Preservation in Jammu and Kashmir State'. JBNHS 53, no 4 (1956): 646–650.
Heugh, SS. 'Sarus Crane (*Grus antigone*) in Salsette'. JBNHS 19, no 1 (1909): 261.
Hole, RS. 'Forest History: Ancient and Modern'. *Indian Forester* (September 1934): 590–592.
Howard, H. 'What is Forestry?' *Indian Forester* 49, no 13 (November 1943), 421–426.
Hubback, T. 'Principles of Wildlife Conservation'. JBNHS 40, no 1 (1938): 100–111.
Indian Board for Wild Life. *Eliciting Public Support for Wildlife Conservation.* Report of the Task Force Indian Board for Wildlife, Government of India, 1983.

Inverarity, JD. 'Sambar Horns'. JBNHS 17, no 1 (1906): 23–26.
———. 'The Indian Wild Dog'. JBNHS 10, no 3 (1895): 449–452.
———. 'Unscientific Notes on the Tiger'. JBNHS 3, no 3 (1888): 143–154.
Jain, P. *Project Tiger Status Report*. Project Tiger. New Delhi: Ministry of Environment and Forests, Government of India, 2001.
Johnsingh, AJT. 'Some Aspects of the Ecology and Behaviour of the Indian Fox (*Vulpes bengalensis*—SHAW)'. JBNHS 75, no 2 (1978): 397–405.
Joshi, KD. 'Village Uplift and its Connection with Forestry'. *Indian Forester* (January 1937): 34–37.
Kinnear, N. 'The History of Indian Mammalogy and Ornithology, Part 1—Mammals'. JBNHS 50, no 4 (1952): 766–776.
———. 'The History of Indian Mammalogy and Ornithology. Part 2—Mammals'. JBNHS 51, no 1 (1952): 104–110.
———. 'The Past and Present Distribution of the Lion in South East Asia'. JBNHS 27, no 1 (1920): 33–39.
Kirkpatrick, KM. 'A Record of the Cheetah (*Acinonyx jubatus erxleben*) in Chitoor District, Madras State'. JBNHS 50, no 4 (1952): 931.
Kurup, GU. 'Distribution, Habitat and Status Survey of the Liontailed Macaque (*Macaca silensus*—LINN)'. JBNHS 75, no 2 (1978), 321–340.
Laurie, MV. 'The Beginning of Teak Plantations in India'. *Indian Forester* (March 1937): 152–154.
Lester, CD. 'The Flamingo Breeding in India'. JBNHS 8, no 4 (1893): 553.
MacLagan, Gorrie. 'Holy Groves'. *Indian Forester* (1936): 150–151.
Maitland, VK. 'Some Requirements of Post War Forest Policy in the CP'. *Indian Forester* (October 1944): 327–338.
Marshall, AH. 'Occurrence of the Pink-Headed Duck (*Rhodonessa caryophyllacea*) in the Punjab'. JBNHS 25, no 3 (1917): 502.
Mathew, DN. 'A Review of the Recovery Data Obtained by the Bombay Natural History Society's Bird Migration Study Project'. JBNHS 68, no 1 (1971): 65–85.
McCann, C. 'Additions to the Description of *Frerea indica* Dalz (*Asclepiadaceae*) and Some Observations on the Species'. JBNHS 41, no 1 (1939): 143–145.
———. 'Observations on Some of the Indian Langurs'. JBNHS 36, no 3 (1933): 618–628.
Millard, WS. 'Correspondence on "The Protection and Preservation of Game in India" '. JBNHS 19, no 1 (1909): 223–224.
———. 'Proposed Investigation and Protection of the Fisheries of Western India—Correspondence'. JBNHS 18, no 3 (1908): 667–669.
Milroy, AJW. 'Elephant Catching in Assam'. JBNHS 29, no 3 (1923): 803–811.
Mirchandani, TK. 'Wildlife Preservation in India'. JBNHS 54, no 1 (1956): 226–228.
Mishra, P. 'Problems of Private Forest Management'. *Indian Forester* (July 1947): 374–377.
Money, WT. 'Observations from the Expediency of Shipbuilding at Bombay for the service of His Majesty, and of the East India Company'. *Indian Foresters* (1931): 29–34.
Morris, RC and S Ali. 'Game Preservation in Kashmir—Report and Recommendations of the Bombay Natural History Society's Delegation October 1952'. JBNHS 53, no 2 (1955): 229–233.
———. 'Shikar Notes from South India: Destruction of Games in South India'. *Indian Forester* (1932): 555–558.
Nair, KK. 'The Cochin State Forest Tramway'. *Indian Forester* (February 1956): 91–92.
Nath, V. 'A Method to Indicate the Percentage of Land Which Should Be Under Forest: Some Comments'. *Indian Forester* (1953): 192–194.
*National Biodiversity Strategy and Action Plan—India*. Ministry of Environment and Forests, Government of India, in coordination with United Nations Development Programme/Global Environment Facility and Biotech Consortium of India, 2002.
Neginhal, SG. 'The Birds of Ranganathittu'. JBNHS 79, no 3 (1982): 581–593.
Nicholson, JW. 'A Census in Tigerland'. *Indian Forester* (September 1934): 599–601.
Osmaston, AE. 'Panchayat Forests in Kumaon'. *Indian Forester*, November 1932: 603–608.
Parker, RN. 'The Mesquite in the Punjab'. *Indian Forester* (April 1935): 238–242.
Phipson, HM. 'Proceedings'. JBNHS 14, no 2 (1902): 402–408.
———. 'Proceedings'. JBNHS 4, no 1 (1889): 71–82.
Pillai, PEV. 'Waste Land'. *Indian Forester* (February 1956): 74–78.
Pocock, RI. 'Descriptions of Some New Species of Scorpions from India. JBNHS 11, no 1 (1897): 102–117.
———. 'Descriptions of Some New Species of Spiders from British India'. JBNHS 13, no 3 (1901), 478–498.
———. 'The Civet-Cats of Asia'. JBNHS 36, no 2 (1933): 423–449.
———. 'The Lions of Asia'. JBNHS 34, no 3 (1930): 638–665.
———. 1899. 'A Monograph of the Pill-Millipedes (*Zephroniidae*) Inhabiting India, Burma and Ceylon'. JBNHS 12 (1899): 269–285, 465–474.
Prasad, NLNS. 'Seasonal Changes in the Herd Structure of Blackbuck'. JBNHS 80, no 3 (1983): 549–554.
Prater, SH. 'The Wild Animals of the Indian Empire'. Part 1. JBNHS 36, no 4 (1933).
Publications and Information Directorate, Council for Scientific and Industrial Research. *The Wealth of India*. Volumes 1–11. Ministry of Environment and Forests, Annual Report 1997–98. New Delhi: Ministry of Environment and Forest, Government of India, 1948.
RMG. 'The Need for Game Reserves'. *Indian Forester* (August 1932).
Rodgers WA and HS Panwar. *Planning a Wildlife Protected Area Network in India*. Report for the Department of Environment, Forests and Wildlife, Government of India. Dehra Dun: Wildlife Institute of India, 1988.
Rogers, A and HS Panwar. *Planning a Protected Area Network in India*. State Summary Report. Dehra Dun: Wildlife Institute of India, 1988.
Ryley, KV. 'The Bombay Natural History Society's Mammal Survey of India, Report no 10 (Kathiawar) and Report no 11 (Coorg)'. JBNHS 22, no 3 (1913): 464–513.
Sagreiya, KP. 'Forests and Rural Welfare: Central Provinces at Berar'. *Indian Forester* (December 1939): 738–742.
———. 'Revision of the National Forest Policy'. *Indian Forester* (1976).
Schaller, GB. 'Observations on the Hangul or Kashmir Stag (*Cervus elaphus hanglu*—VAGNER). JBNHS 66, no 1 (1969).
Scott, P. 'Visit by IUCN Delegation to the Keoladeo Ghana Sanctuary, Bharatpur, Rajasthan, India'. JBNHS 63, no 1 (1966): 206–209.
Shahi, SP. 'Status of the Grey Wolf (*Canis lupus pallipes* SYKES) in India—A Preliminary Survey'. JBNHS 79, no 3 (1982): 493–502.
Singh, JA. 'National Forest Policy of India, Ways and Means to Implement It'. *Indian Forester* (February 1958) no 2: 65–69.
Singh, T. 'Game Preservation in the Central Provinces and Berar'. *Indian Forester* (January 1933): 28–30.
Singh, VB. 'The Elephant (*Elephas maximus*—LINN.) in Uttar Pradesh—India'. JBNHS 66, no 2 (1969): 239–50.
———. 'The Elephant in UP (India)—A Resurvey of Its Status After 10 Years'. JBNHS 75, no 1 (1978), 71–82.
Spillett, JJ. 'A Report on Wildlife Surveys in North India and Southern Nepal, January–June 1966'. JBNHS 63, no 3 (1966): 492–628.
———. 'A Report on Wildlife Surveys in South and West India'. JBNHS 65, no 3 (1968): 633–663.
Steel, JH. 'Parasites in the Wild Ass of Cutch'. JBNHS 2, no 1 (1887): 30–32.
Sterndale, RA. 1886. 'Note on a Probable New Species of Ibex'. JBNHS 1, no 1 (1886): 26–28.
Suter, MF. 'Plaintive Cuckoo Parasitising Purple Sunbird'. JBNHS 45, no 2 (1945): 235.
Trench, CCG. 'Egret Farming in India'. JBNHS 28, no 3 (1922): 751–752.
Tyabji, FHB. 'The Great Indian Bustard'. JBNHS 51, no 1 (1952): 276–277.
Wall, F. 'Remarks on Some Recently Acquired Snakes'. JBNHS 18, no 4 (1908): 778–784.
———. 'Two New Snakes from Assam'. JBNHS 18, no 1 (1908): 272–274.
Ward, AE. 'Game Animals of Kashmir and Adjacent Hill Provinces'. Part III. JBNHS 28 (1922).
———. 'The Mammals and Birds of Kashmir and the Adjacent Hill Provinces'. Part III. JBNHS 30, no 2 (1925): 253–259.
Warty, SG. 'The Reyots and the Forests (Reply to Government Propaganda)'. *Indian Forester* (November 1932): 282–295.
Whitaker, R and D Basu. 'The Gharial (*Gavialis gangeticus*): A Review'. JBNHS 79, no 3 (1982): 531–548.
——— and Z Whitaker. 'A Preliminary Survey of the Saltwater Crocodile (*Crocodylus porosus*) in the Andaman Islands'. JBNHS 75, no 1 (1982): 43–49.
Whitaker, Z. 'Snakeman, Story of an Indian Naturalist'. In *India Magazine Book*. Bombay: India Magazine Book, 1989.
Williams, J. 'Game Birds in the Anaimalai Hills and the South Coimbatore District'. JBNHS 39, no 4 (1937): 732–739.
Wroughton, RC. 'Summary of the Results from the Indian Mammal Survey of the Bombay Natural History Society'. JBNHS 25, no 4 (1918): 547–598.
Yuvraj of Jasdan, Shree. 'The Status of the Pied Crested Cuckoo and the Great Indian Bustard in Jasdan State'. JBNHS 46, no 4 (1946): 722.

**WEBSITES**

http://collections.ic.gc.ca/gardens/Horticulture/Time%20Line.htm
http://en.wikipedia.org/wiki/Evolutionary_timeline
http://www.acad.carleton.edu/curricular/BIOL/classes/bio302/Pages/TimelineBack.html
http://www.adonline.id.au/plantevol/ptgeotimes.htm
http://www.anselm.edu/homepage/jpitocch/evolution/evoltimeline.html
http://www.anselm.edu/homepage/jpitocch/genbios/vertevol.html
http://www.nature.nps.gov/grd/usgsnps/pltec/scplseqai.html
http://www.npr.org/programs/atc/features/2002/apr/mammals/timeline.html
http://www.physics.usu.edu
http://www.redlist.org
http://www.sir-ray.com/Geologic%20Timeline.htm
http://www.strangescience.net/timeline.htm
http://www.talkorigins.org/origins/geo_timeline.html
http://www.ucmp.berkeley.edu/history/evotmline.html

**ABBREVIATIONS**

ANET—Andaman Nicobar Environment Trust
ATREE—Ashoka Trust for Research in Ecology and the Environment
BCPP—Biodiversity Conservation Prioritization Project
BNHS—Bombay Natural History Society
BSI—Botanical Survey of India
BVIEER—Bharati Vidyapeeth Institute of Environment Education and Research
CBD—Convention on Biological Diversity
CBR—Community Biodiversity Registers
CEE—Centre for Environment Education
CES—Centre for Ecological Sciences
CITES—Convention on International Trade in Endangered Species
CPR-EEC—CPR Environment Education Centre
DFO—District Forest Officer
DoEN—Department of Environment
DPAP—Drought Prone Area Project
EIA—Environment Impact Assessment
ENVIS—Environmental Information System
ESA—Ecologically Sensitive Areas
FAO—Food and Agriculture Organization
FPC—Forest Protection Committee
FRI—Forest Research Institute
FRLHT—Foundation for Revitalisation of Local Health Traditions
GIS—Geographical Information Systems
GSI—Geological Survey of India
IBWL—Indian Board for Wild Life
IGNP—Indira Gandhi National Park
IIFM—Indian Institute of Forest Management
IIPA—Indian Institute of Public Administration
IPAS—Integrated Protected Areas System
IUCN—International Union for the Conservation of Nature and Natural Resources
JBNHS—*Journal of the Bombay Natural History Society*
JFM—Joint Forestry Management
MFA—Ministry of Food and Agriculture
MoEF—Ministry of Environment and Forests
NBA—National Biodiversity Authority
NBSAP—National Biodiversity Strategy and Action Plan
NCA—National Commission on Agriculture
NCEPC—National Committee for Environmental Planning and Coordination
NCEP—National Committee on Environmental Planning
NCERT—National Council for Education Research and Training
NEAC—National Environment Awareness Campaign
NEFA—North East Frontier Agency
NWAP—National Wildlife Action Plan
PBR—People's Biodiversity Register
PIL—Public Interest Litigation
RFO—Range Forest Officer
SACON—Salim Ali Centre for Ornithology and Natural History
SANCF—Salim Ali Nature Conservation Fund
SFP—Social Forestry Programme
TELCO—TATA Engineering and Locomotive Company
TFAP—Tropical Forestry Action Plan
TPCG—Technical and Policy Core Group, Kalpavriksh, Pune/Delhi
TTF—Tiger Task Force
UGC—University Grants Commission
UKSN—Uttarakhand Seva Nidhi
UNCED—United National Conference on Environment and Development
UNDP—United Nations Development Program
UNEP—United Nations Environment Program
WII—Wildlife Institute of India
WWF-I—World Wide Fund for Nature India
ZSI—Zoological Survey of India

The illustrations in this book have been sourced from rare books belonging to:
* Aloo and Burjor Reporter's Private Collection
** Pilloo Kumarmangalam's Private Collection
*** Erach Bharucha's Private Collection
† Sharda Dwivedi and Manvendra Singh Barwani have kindly consented to the use of the pictures of the cars used by the Maharajas for shikar in the 1920s and 30s from their book *The Automobiles of the Maharajas*.
Note: For more information see Illustration Credits at the end of the book.

**Illustration Credits**

29, 152, 161, 176, 177, 181 (2), 183 (2), 187,
213, 217 (2), 222, 241, 242 (7), 257 (2, 7, 9),
252 (2), 259 (8), 281 (6), 299 (5), 302 (4), 313,
319, 323, 329, 332, 333 (4), 350, 353, 354,
355, 365
Erach Bharucha, Private Collection

---

8, 16–17, 84, 85, 88, 89, 95, 108, 112, 117,
136, 139, 140, 141, 147, 148, 154, 159, 160,
163, 169, 170, 172, 173, 178, 180, 181 (4),
182, 183 (4), 184, 186, 188, 217 (6, 4), 234,
240, 242 (4), 244, 253, 257 (1, 5, 6, 8), 258
(1, 3, 9), 259 (1, 4, 6, 7), 260 (1, 3), 261, 262,
263, 264, 267, 269, 270, 272, 273, 274, 275,
276, 277, 278, 279, 280, 281 (2), 284, 285,
287, 288, 289, 290, 293, 297, 298, 299 (3),
301, 302 (2, 3), 303, 304, 305, 306, 307, 308,
309, 311, 322, 327, 333 (5), 358, 398, 406,
407,410, 416, 472–473, 524–525, 626–627,
740, 748 (above and below), 749 (above and
below), 796, 798 (below), 816–817
Courtesy: Aloo and Burjor Reporter, Private
Collection

---

378, 379,656
Courtesy: Piloo Kumarmangalam, Private
Collection

---

36, 24–27, 45, 46, 55, 68–69, 113,
376–377, 395
Graphic design and data compilation for maps
and graphs by Prasanna Kolte